SOLDIER'S HEART

THE CAMPAIGN TO UNDERSTAND
MY WWII VETERAN FATHER

A Daughter's Memoir
By Carol Tyler

SOLDIER'S HEART

THE CAMPAIGN TO UNDERSTAND MY WWII VETERAN FATHER

A Daughter's Memoir
by Carol Tyler

FANTAGRAPHICS BOOKS

FANTAGRAPHICS BOOKS

7563 LAKE CITY WAY NE

SEATTLE, WA 98115

EDITED BY GARY GROTH

DESIGNED BY CAROL TYLER

PRODUCTION ASSISTANTS: PAUL BARESH AND KEELI MCCARTHY

ASSOCIATE PUBLISHER: ERIC REYNOLDS

PUBLISHER: GARY GROTH

TO RECEIVE A FREE FULL-COLOR CATALOG OF COMICS, GRAPHIC NOVELS, AND
PROSE NOVELS, CALL 1-800-657-1100, OR VISIT WWW.FANTAGRAPHICS.COM.

ISBN: 978-1-60699-896-0
LIBRARY OF CONGRESS CONTROL NUMBER: 2015945662

FIRST FANTAGRAPHICS PRINTING: OCTOBER 2015

PRINTED IN SINGAPORE

OTHER BOOKS BY CAROL TYLER:
YOU'LL NEVER KNOW, BOOKS I, II, & III
LATE BLOOMER
THE JOB THING

THANKS TO EVERYONE WHO HELPED MAKE THIS BOOK HAPPEN, WHETHER BY
INSPIRATION OR LENDING A HAND. JULIA & JUSTIN MOSTLY. TUE & JUNIOR, TOO.
THANKS ALSO TO MY EXTENDED FAMILY, TO FRIENDS, STUDENTS AND COLLEAGUES.
ELLEN WANG, MY PRODUCTION ASSISTANT, GETS A GIGANTIC THANK YOU FOR
HER EXCELLENT WORK ON THE DIGITAL FILES. UNIVERSITY OF CINCINNATI
DAAP SCHOOL OF ART AND THE OHIO ARTS COUNCIL ALSO GET BIG THANKS.
SPECIAL GRATITUDE TO MY FRIEND KIM THOMPSON OF FANTAGRAPHICS. HE
MADE IT EASY. AND THANKS TO GARY GROTH AND EVERYONE ELSE IN SEATTLE.
BUT THE BIGGEST THANK YOU OF ALL GOES TO THREE PEOPLE WHO WERE MY
CORE SUPPORTERS OVER THE DECADE IT TOOK TO DO THIS BOOK. MOM, GINIA,
AND DAD — YOU ARE FOREVER LOVED AND MISSED.

Dedication:

TO THOSE WHO SERVED.

TO THE LOVED ONES OF THOSE
WHO SERVED.

TO THE SEEKERS.

TABLE of Contents

1.

BUT I KNEW

WORLD WAR II

A catastrophic 6 year long global wave of aggression instigated by delusional, charismatic criminal leaders intent on incurring death, destruction and domination over nations, cultures and individuals through the use of bombs, guns, tanks, explosives and poison.

1939 - 1945

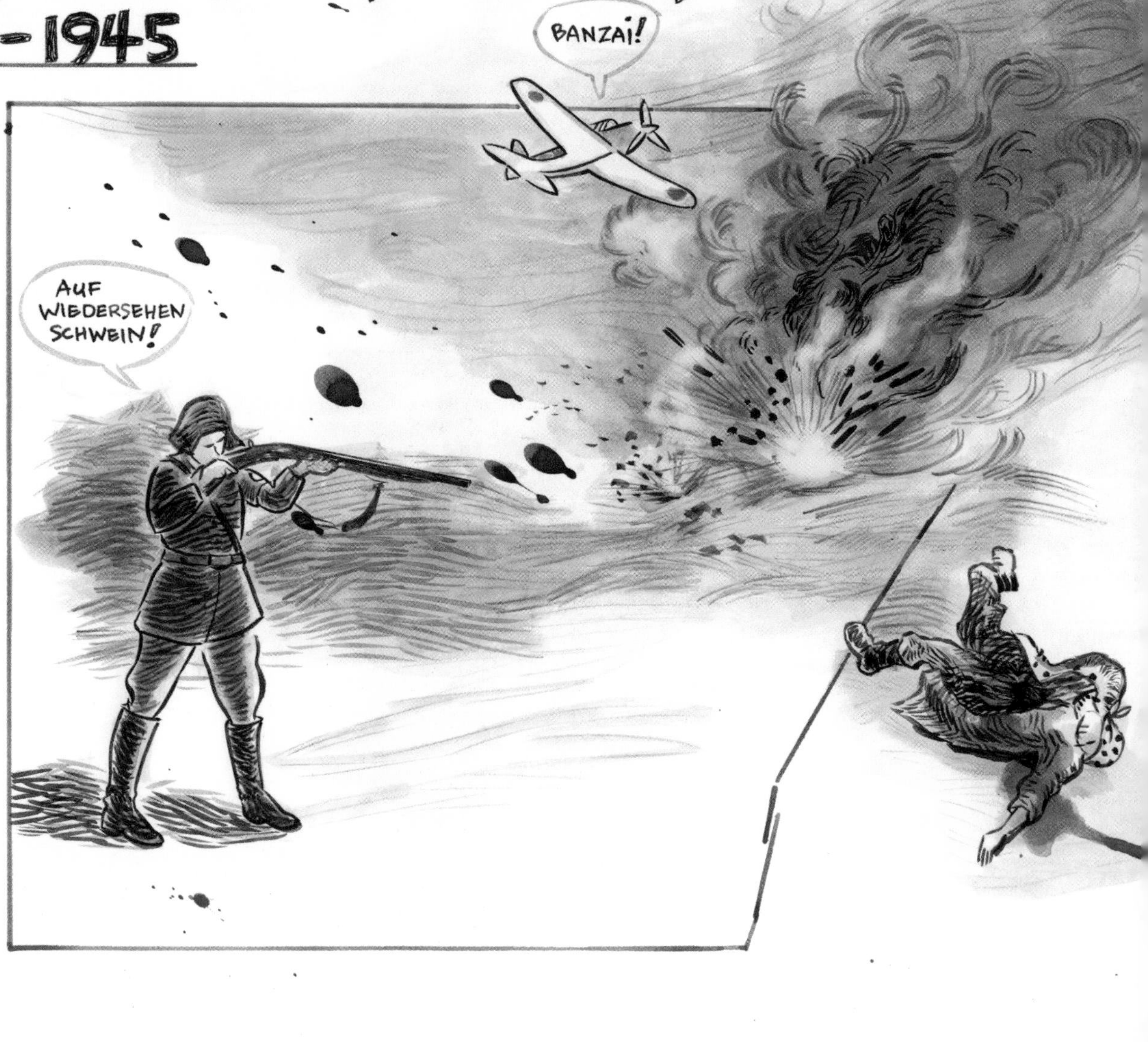
BANZAI!
AUF WIEDERSEHEN SCHWEIN!

YOU WOULD NEVER KNOW

that he had participated in it.

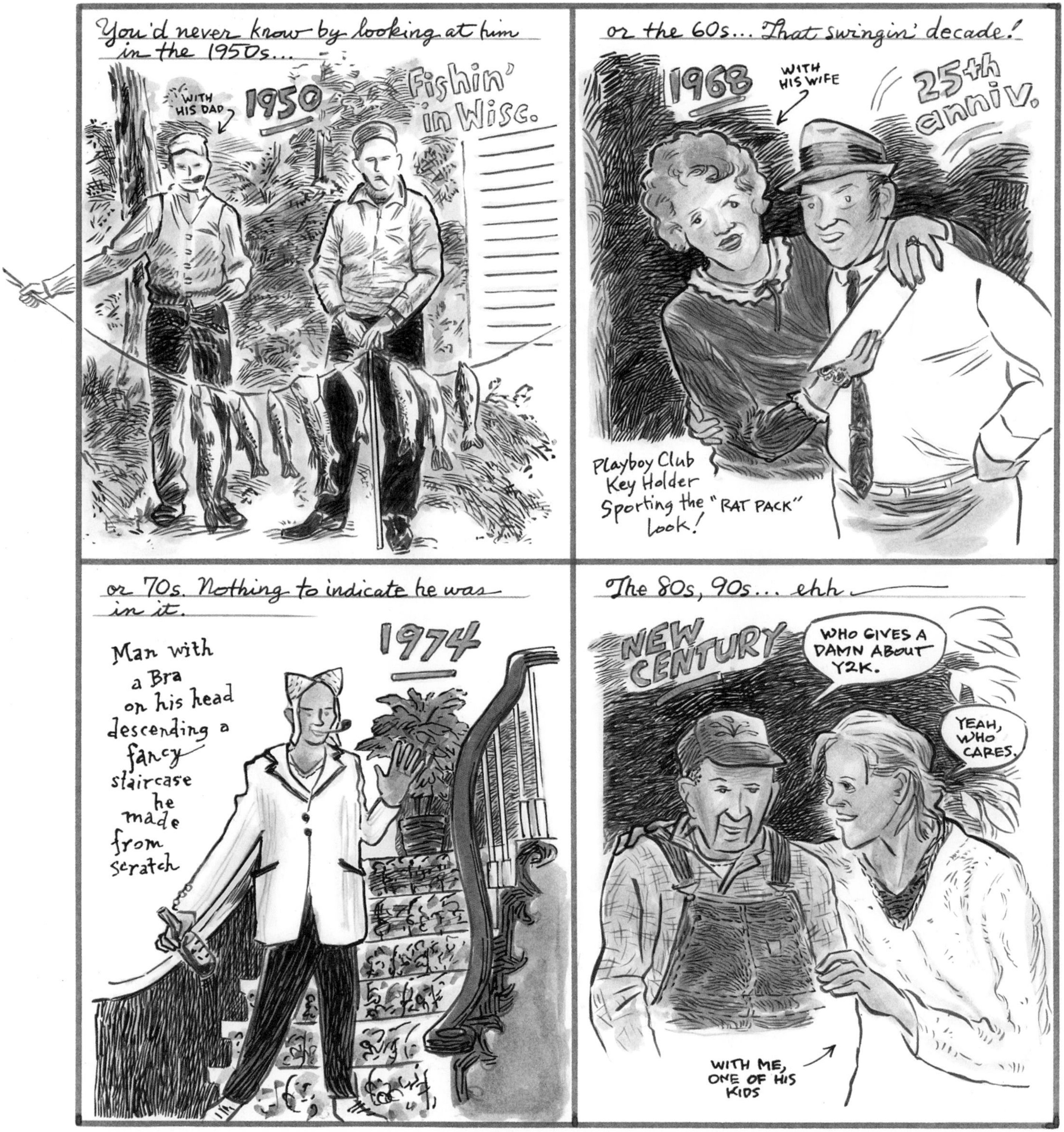
You'd never know by looking at him in the 1950s...
WITH HIS DAD
1950
Fishin' in Wisc.
or the 60s... That swingin' decade!
1968
WITH HIS WIFE
25th anniv.
Playboy Club Key Holder Sporting the "RAT PACK" look!
or 70s. Nothing to indicate he was in it.
1974
Man with a Bra on his head descending a fancy staircase he made from scratch
The 80s, 90s... ehh
NEW CENTURY
WHO GIVES A DAMN ABOUT Y2K.
YEAH, WHO CARES.
WITH ME, ONE OF HIS KIDS

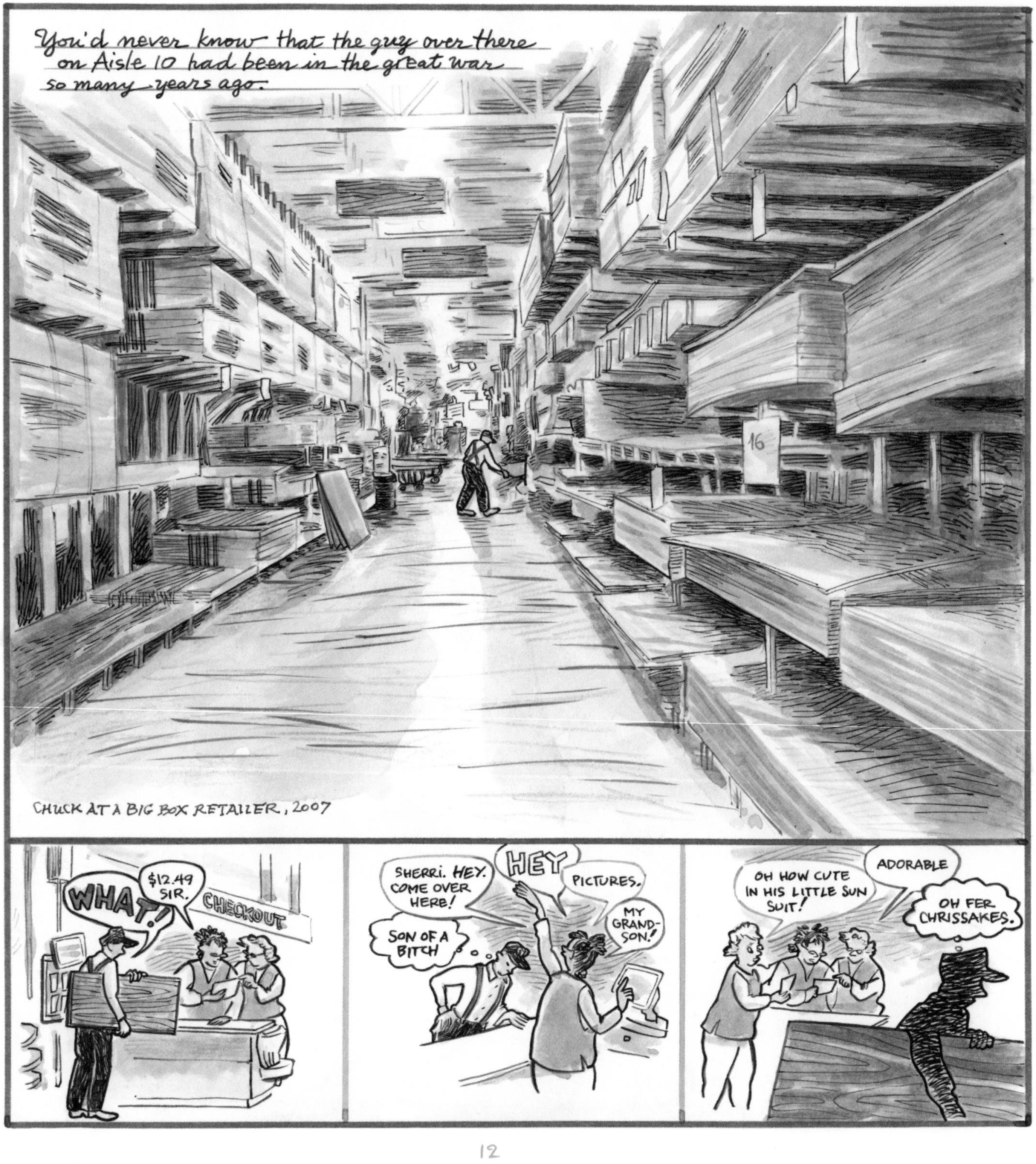
You'd never know that the guy over there on Aisle 10 had been in the great war so many years ago.
16
CHUCK AT A BIG BOX RETAILER, 2007
WHAT!
$12.49 SIR.
CHECKOUT
SHERRI. HEY. COME OVER HERE!
HEY
PICTURES.
MY GRAND-SON!
SON OF A BITCH
OH HOW CUTE IN HIS LITTLE SUN SUIT!
ADORABLE
OH FER CHRISSAKES.

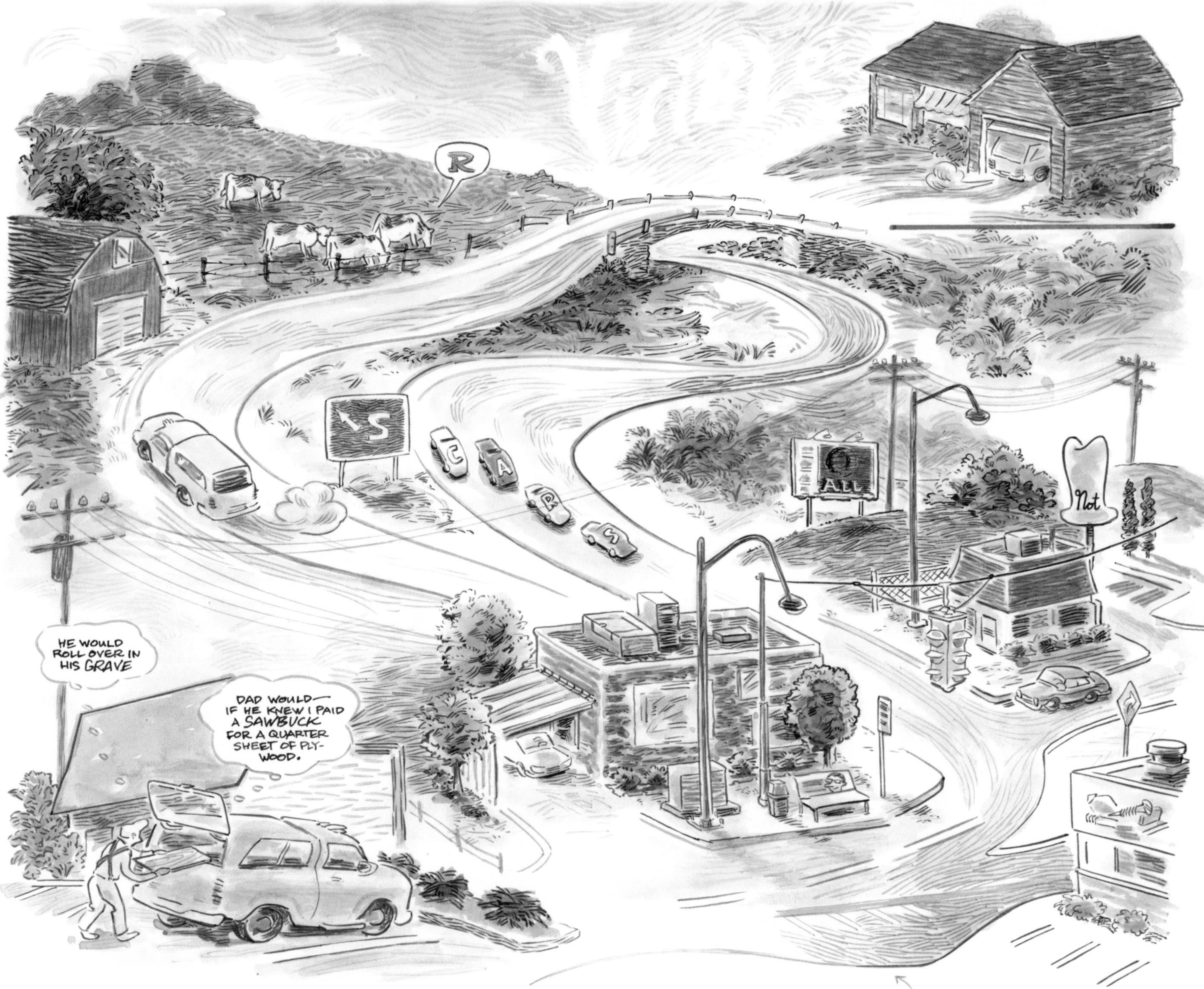
R
S
C
A
R
S
ALL
Not
HE WOULD ROLL OVER IN HIS GRAVE
DAD WOULD— IF HE KNEW I PAID A SAWBUCK FOR A QUARTER SHEET OF PLY-WOOD.

Not-all-scars R....

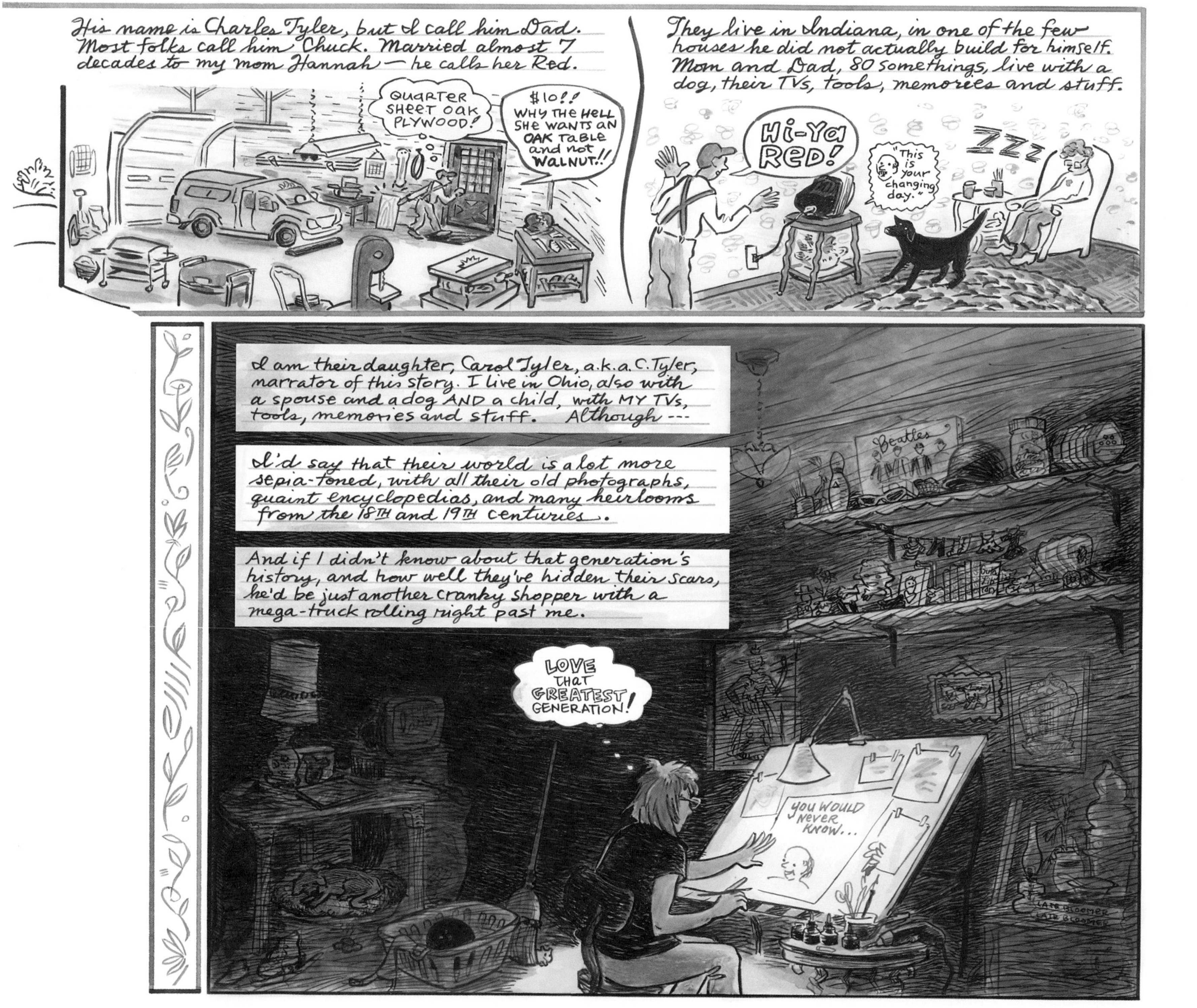
His name is Charles Tyler, but I call him Dad. Most folks call him Chuck. Married almost 7 decades to my mom Hannah — he calls her Red.
QUARTER SHEET OAK PLYWOOD!
$10!! WHY THE HELL SHE WANTS AN OAK TABLE and not WALNUT!!
They live in Indiana, in one of the few houses he did not actually build for himself. Mom and Dad, 80 somethings, live with a dog, their TVs, tools, memorees and stuff.
Hi-Ya RED!
"This is your changing day."
ZZZ
I am their daughter, Carol Tyler, a.k.a. C. Tyler, narrator of this story. I live in Ohio, also with a spouse and a dog AND a child, with MY TVs, tools, memories and stuff. Although ---
I'd say that their world is a lot more sepia-toned, with all their old photographs, quaint encyclopedias, and many heirlooms from the 18TH and 19TH centuries.
And if I didn't know about that generation's history, and how well they've hidden their scars, he'd be just another cranky shopper with a mega-truck rolling right past me.
Beatles
LOVE THAT GREATEST GENERATION!
YOU WOULD NEVER KNOW...

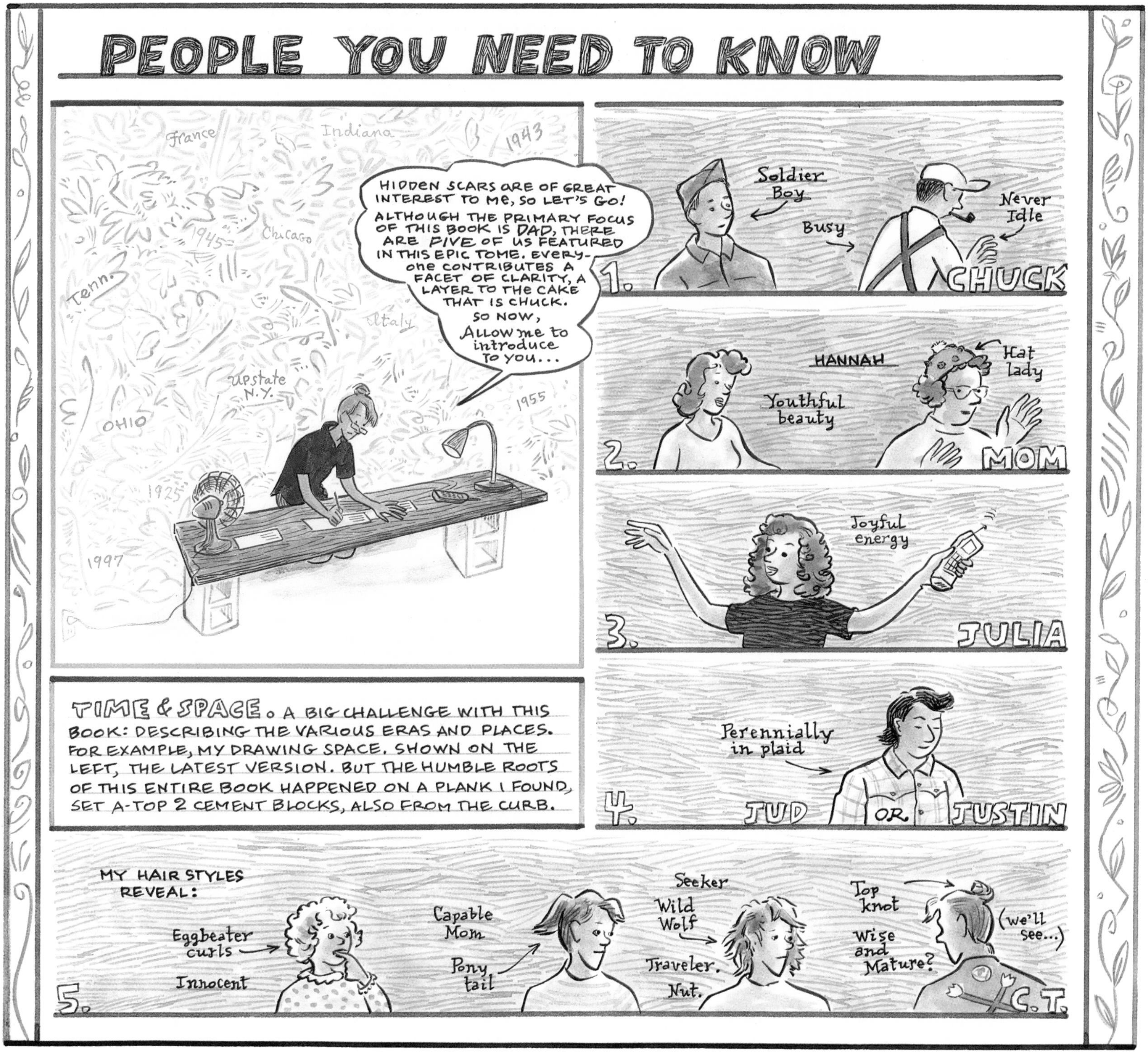
PEOPLE YOU NEED TO KNOW
France
Indiana
1943
1945
Chicago
Tenn.
Italy
upstate N.Y.
OHIO
1955
1925
1997
HIDDEN SCARS ARE OF GREAT INTEREST TO ME, SO LET'S GO! ALTHOUGH THE PRIMARY FOCUS OF THIS BOOK IS DAD, THERE ARE FIVE OF US FEATURED IN THIS EPIC TOME. EVERY-ONE CONTRIBUTES A FACET OF CLARITY, A LAYER TO THE CAKE THAT IS CHUCK. SO NOW, ALLOW ME TO INTRODUCE TO YOU...
1.
Soldier Boy
Busy
Never Idle
CHUCK
2.
HANNAH
Youthful beauty
Hat lady
MOM
3.
Joyful energy
JULIA
TIME & SPACE. A BIG CHALLENGE WITH THIS BOOK: DESCRIBING THE VARIOUS ERAS AND PLACES. FOR EXAMPLE, MY DRAWING SPACE. SHOWN ON THE LEFT, THE LATEST VERSION. BUT THE HUMBLE ROOTS OF THIS ENTIRE BOOK HAPPENED ON A PLANK I FOUND, SET A-TOP 2 CEMENT BLOCKS, ALSO FROM THE CURB.
4.
Perennially in plaid
JUD OR JUSTIN
5.
MY HAIR STYLES REVEAL:
Eggbeater curls
Innocent
Capable Mom
Pony tail
Seeker
Wild Wolf
Traveler.
Nut.
Top knot
Wise and Mature?
(we'll see...)
C.T.

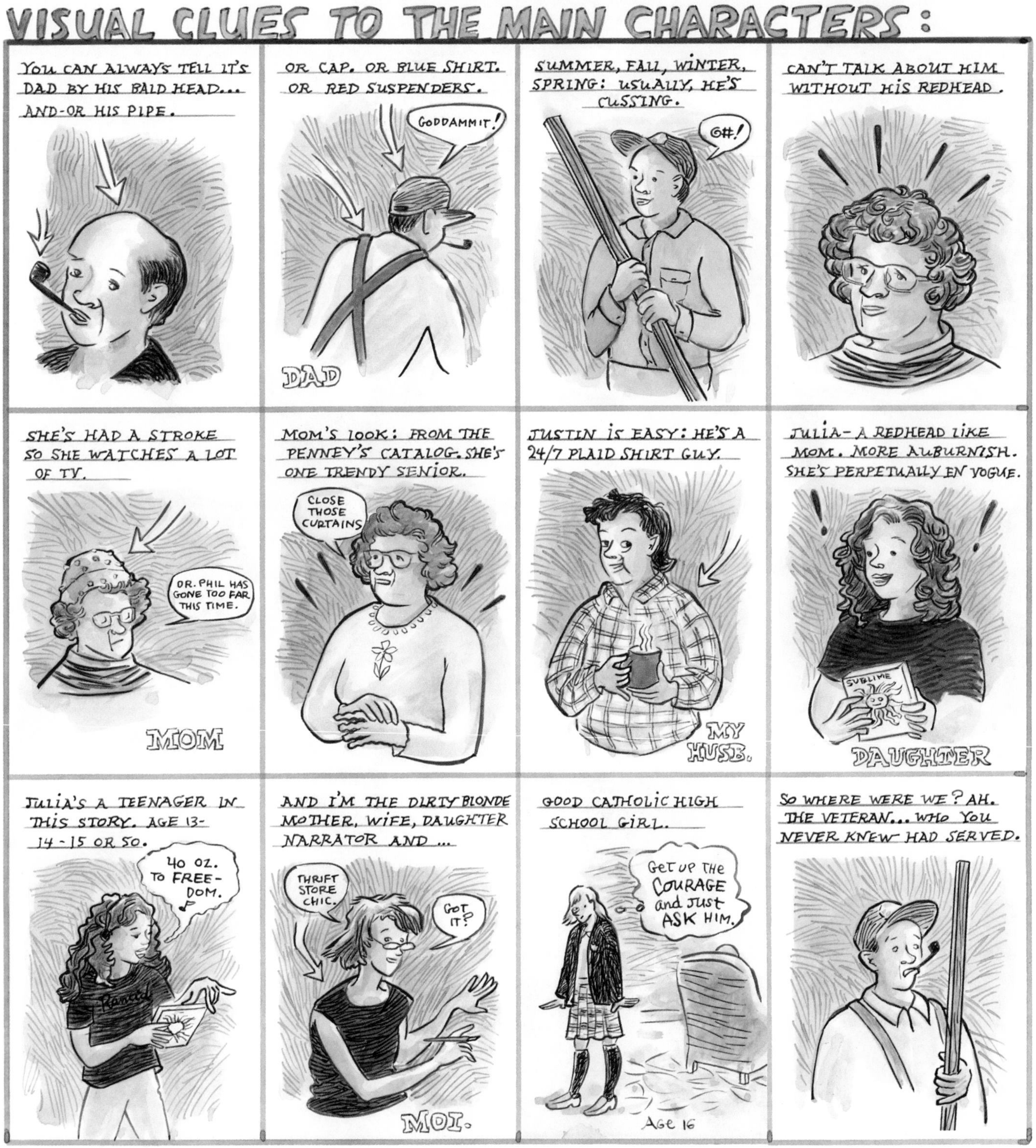
VISUAL CLUES TO THE MAIN CHARACTERS:
YOU CAN ALWAYS TELL IT'S DAD BY HIS BALD HEAD... AND-OR HIS PIPE.
OR CAP. OR BLUE SHIRT. OR RED SUSPENDERS.
GODDAMMIT!
DAD
SUMMER, FALL, WINTER, SPRING: USUALLY, HE'S CUSSING.
G#!
CAN'T TALK ABOUT HIM WITHOUT HIS REDHEAD.
SHE'S HAD A STROKE SO SHE WATCHES A LOT OF TV.
DR. PHIL HAS GONE TOO FAR THIS TIME.
MOM
MOM'S LOOK: FROM THE PENNEY'S CATALOG. SHE'S ONE TRENDY SENIOR.
CLOSE THOSE CURTAINS
JUSTIN IS EASY: HE'S A 24/7 PLAID SHIRT GUY.
MY HUSB.
JULIA- A REDHEAD LIKE MOM. MORE AUBURNISH. SHE'S PERPETUALLY EN VOGUE.
SUBLIME
DAUGHTER
JULIA'S A TEENAGER IN THIS STORY. AGE 13-14-15 OR SO.
40 OZ. TO FREE-DOM.
Rancid
AND I'M THE DIRTY BLONDE MOTHER, WIFE, DAUGHTER NARRATOR AND...
THRIFT STORE CHIC.
GOT IT?
MOI.
GOOD CATHOLIC HIGH SCHOOL GIRL.
Get up the COURAGE and just ASK HIM.
AGE 16
SO WHERE WERE WE? AH. THE VETERAN... WHO YOU NEVER KNEW HAD SERVED.

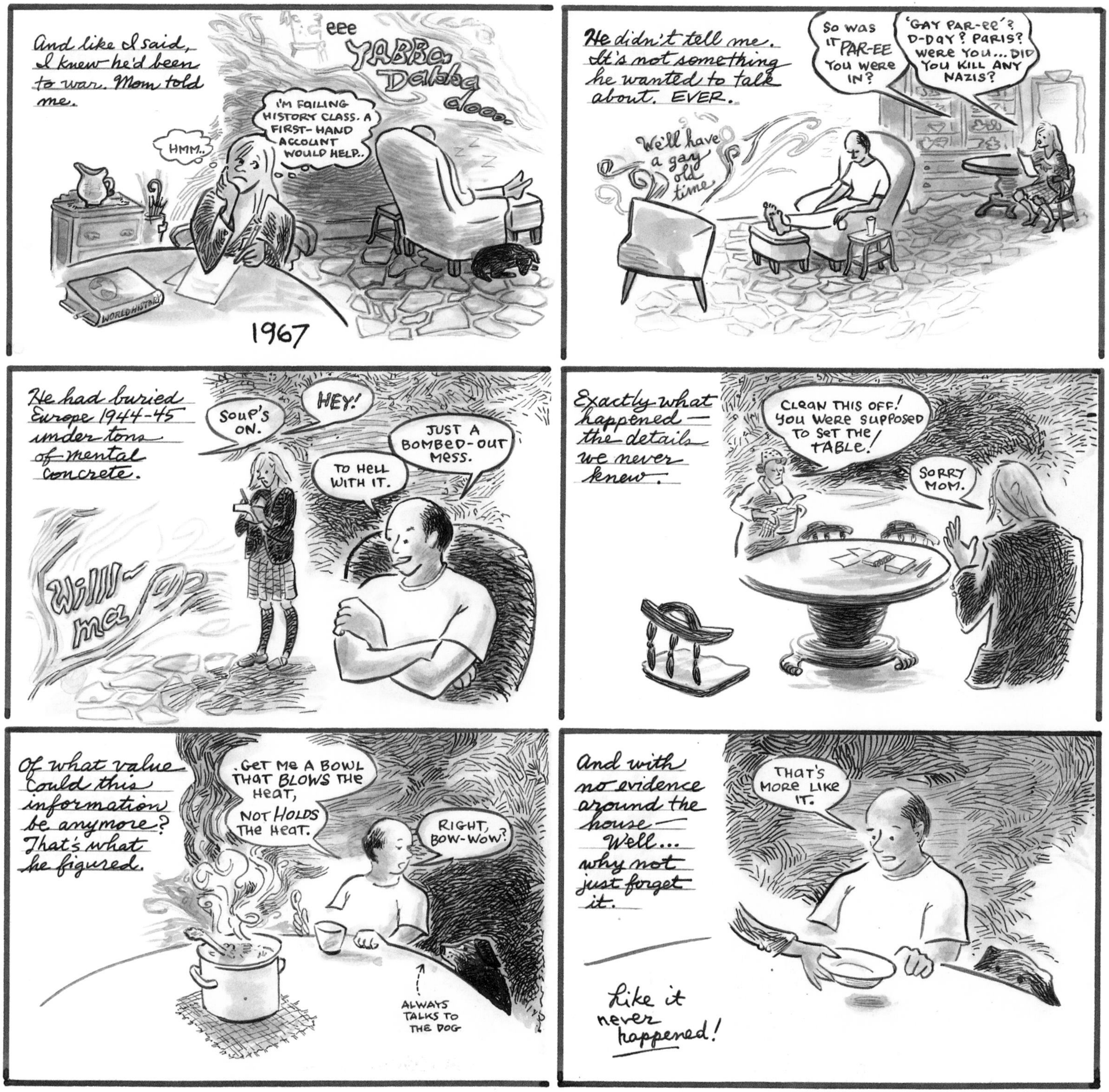
And like I said, I knew he'd been to war. Mom told me.
eee YABBa Dabba dooo..
HMM..
I'M FAILING HISTORY CLASS. A FIRST-HAND ACCOUNT WOULD HELP..
WORLD HISTORY
1967
He didn't tell me. It's not something he wanted to talk about. EVER.
SO WAS IT PAR-EE YOU WERE IN?
'GAY PAR-EE'? D-DAY? PARIS? WERE YOU... DID YOU KILL ANY NAZIS?
We'll have a gay old time
He had buried Europe 1944-45 under tons of mental concrete.
SOUP'S ON.
HEY!
JUST A BOMBED-OUT MESS.
TO HELL WITH IT.
Will-ma
Exactly what happened — the details we never knew.
CLEAN THIS OFF! YOU WERE SUPPOSED TO SET THE TABLE!
SORRY MOM.
Of what value could this information be anymore? That's what he figured.
GET ME A BOWL THAT BLOWS THE HEAT, NOT HOLDS THE HEAT.
RIGHT, BOW-WOW?
ALWAYS TALKS TO THE DOG
And with no evidence around the house— Well... why not just forget it.
THAT'S MORE LIKE IT.
Like it never happened!

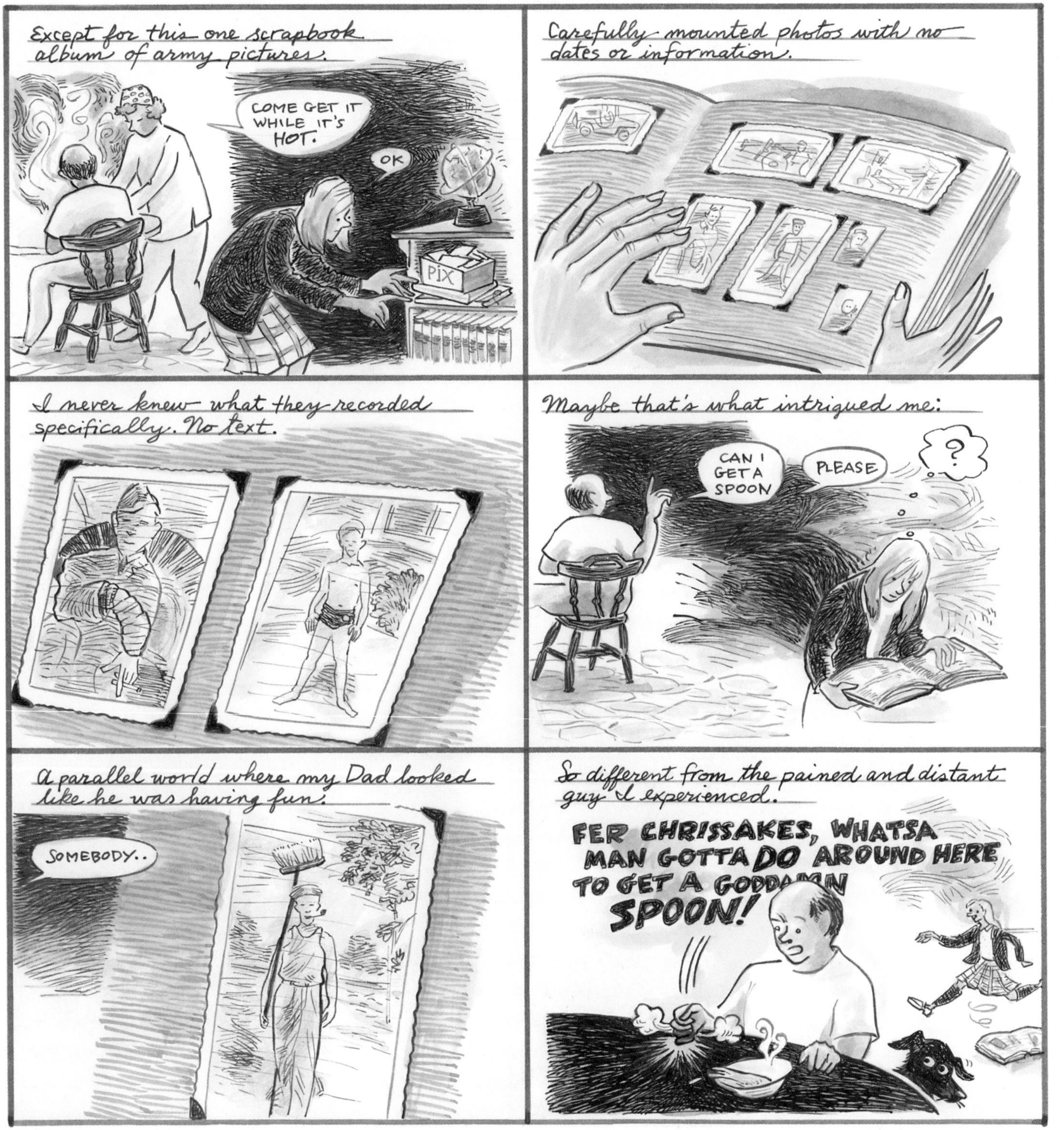
Except for this one scrapbook album of army pictures.
COME GET IT WHILE IT'S HOT.
OK
PIX
Carefully mounted photos with no dates or information.
I never knew what they recorded specifically. No text.
Maybe that's what intrigued me:
CAN I GET A SPOON
PLEASE
?
A parallel world where my Dad looked like he was having fun.
SOMEBODY..
So different from the pained and distant guy I experienced.
FER CHRISSAKES, WHATSA MAN GOTTA DO AROUND HERE TO GET A GODDAMN SPOON!

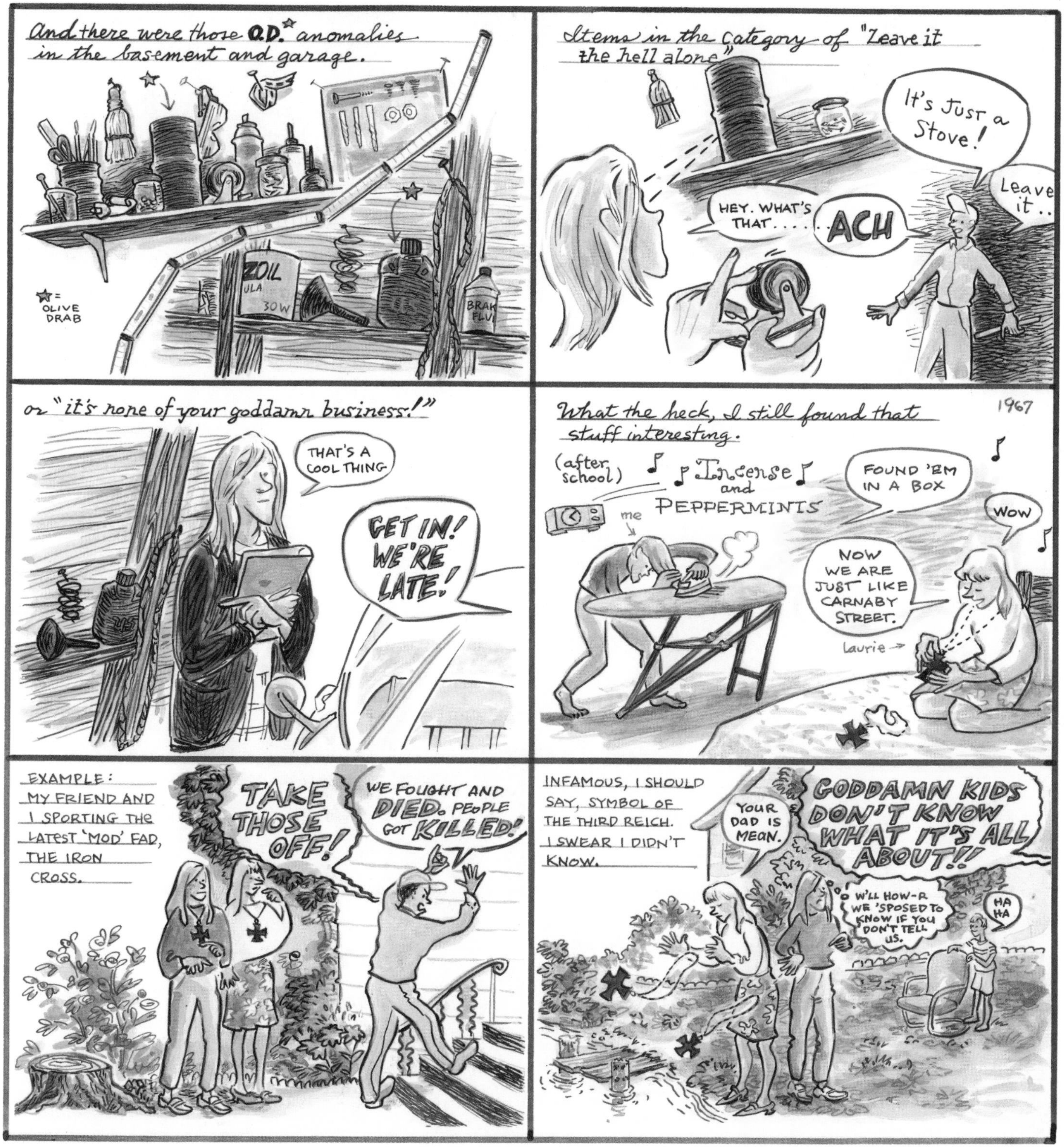
And there were those O.D.☆ anomalies in the basement and garage.
☆= OLIVE DRAB
ZOIL
30W
BRAK FLU
Items in the category of "Leave it the hell alone"
It's Just a Stove!
Leave it..
HEY. WHAT'S THAT.....
ACH
or "it's none of your goddamn business!"
THAT'S A COOL THING
GET IN! WE'RE LATE!
What the heck, I still found that stuff interesting.
1967
(after school)
Incense and PEPPERMINTS
me
FOUND 'EM IN A BOX
WOW
NOW WE ARE JUST LIKE CARNABY STREET.
Laurie
EXAMPLE: MY FRIEND AND I SPORTING THE LATEST 'MOD' FAD, THE IRON CROSS.
TAKE THOSE OFF!
WE FOUGHT AND DIED. PEOPLE GOT KILLED!
INFAMOUS, I SHOULD SAY, SYMBOL OF THE THIRD REICH. I SWEAR I DIDN'T KNOW.
YOUR DAD IS MEAN.
GODDAMN KIDS DON'T KNOW WHAT IT'S ALL ABOUT!!
W'LL HOW-R WE 'SPOSED TO KNOW IF YOU DON'T TELL US.
HA HA

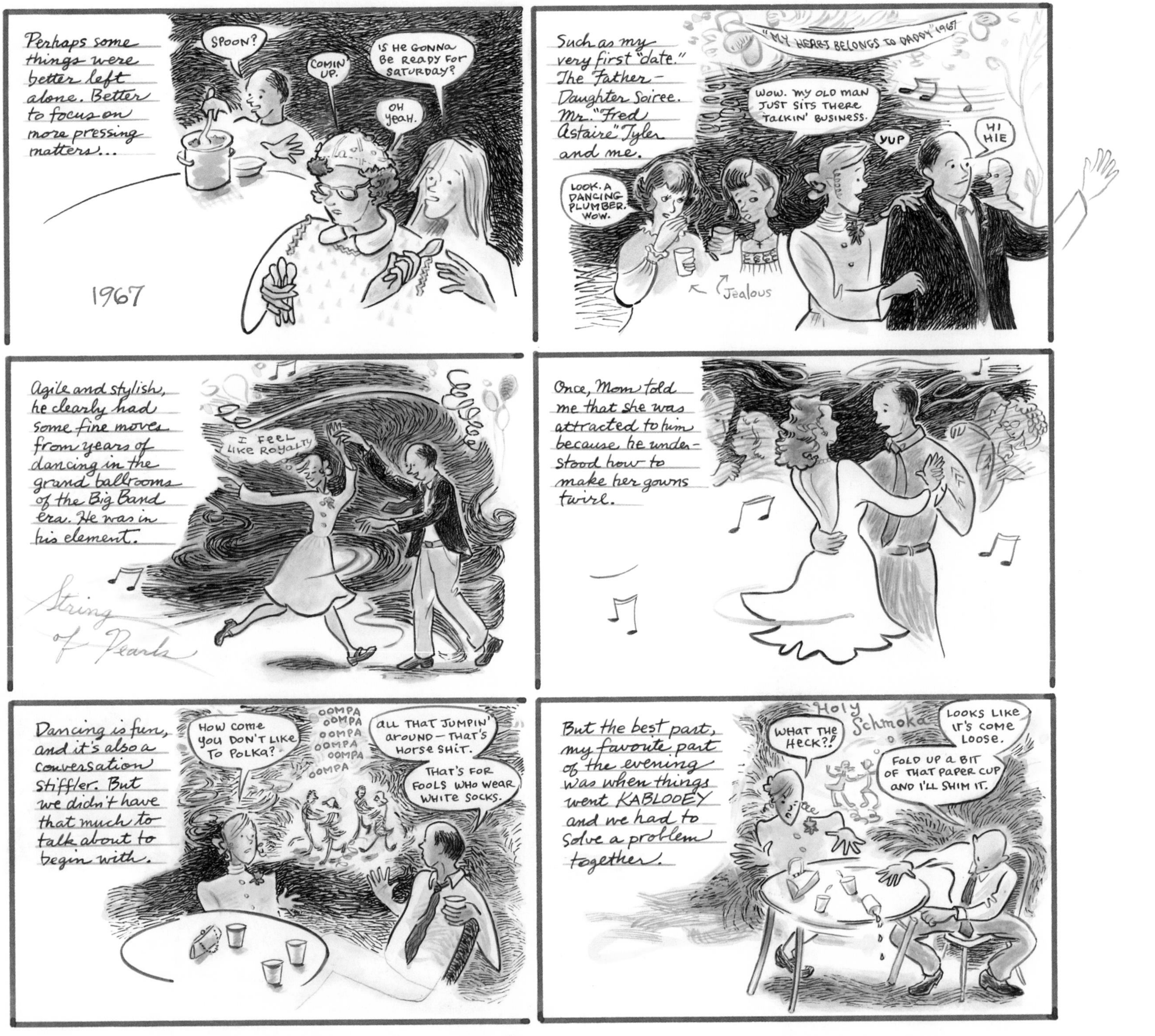
Perhaps some things were better left alone. Better to focus on more pressing matters...
SPOON?
COMIN' UP.
IS HE GONNA BE READY FOR SATURDAY?
OH YEAH.
1967
Such as my very first "date." The Father-Daughter Soiree. Mr. "Fred Astaire" Tyler and me.
"MY HEART BELONGS TO DADDY" 1967
WOW. MY OLD MAN JUST SITS THERE TALKIN' BUSINESS.
YUP
HI HIE
LOOK. A DANCING PLUMBER. WOW.
Jealous
Agile and stylish, he clearly had some fine moves from years of dancing in the grand ballrooms of the Big Band era. He was in his element.
I FEEL LIKE ROYALTY
String of Pearls
Once, Mom told me that she was attracted to him because he understood how to make her gowns twirl.
Dancing is fun, and it's also a conversation stiffler. But we didn't have that much to talk about to begin with.
HOW COME YOU DON'T LIKE TO POLKA?
OOMPA OOMPA OOMPA OOMPA OOMPA OOMPA
ALL THAT JUMPIN' AROUND—THAT'S HORSE SHIT.
THAT'S FOR FOOLS WHO WEAR WHITE SOCKS.
But the best part, my favorite part of the evening was when things went KABLOOEY and we had to solve a problem together.
Holy Schmoka
WHAT THE HECK?!
LOOKS LIKE IT'S COME LOOSE.
FOLD UP A BIT OF THAT PAPER CUP AND I'LL SHIM IT.

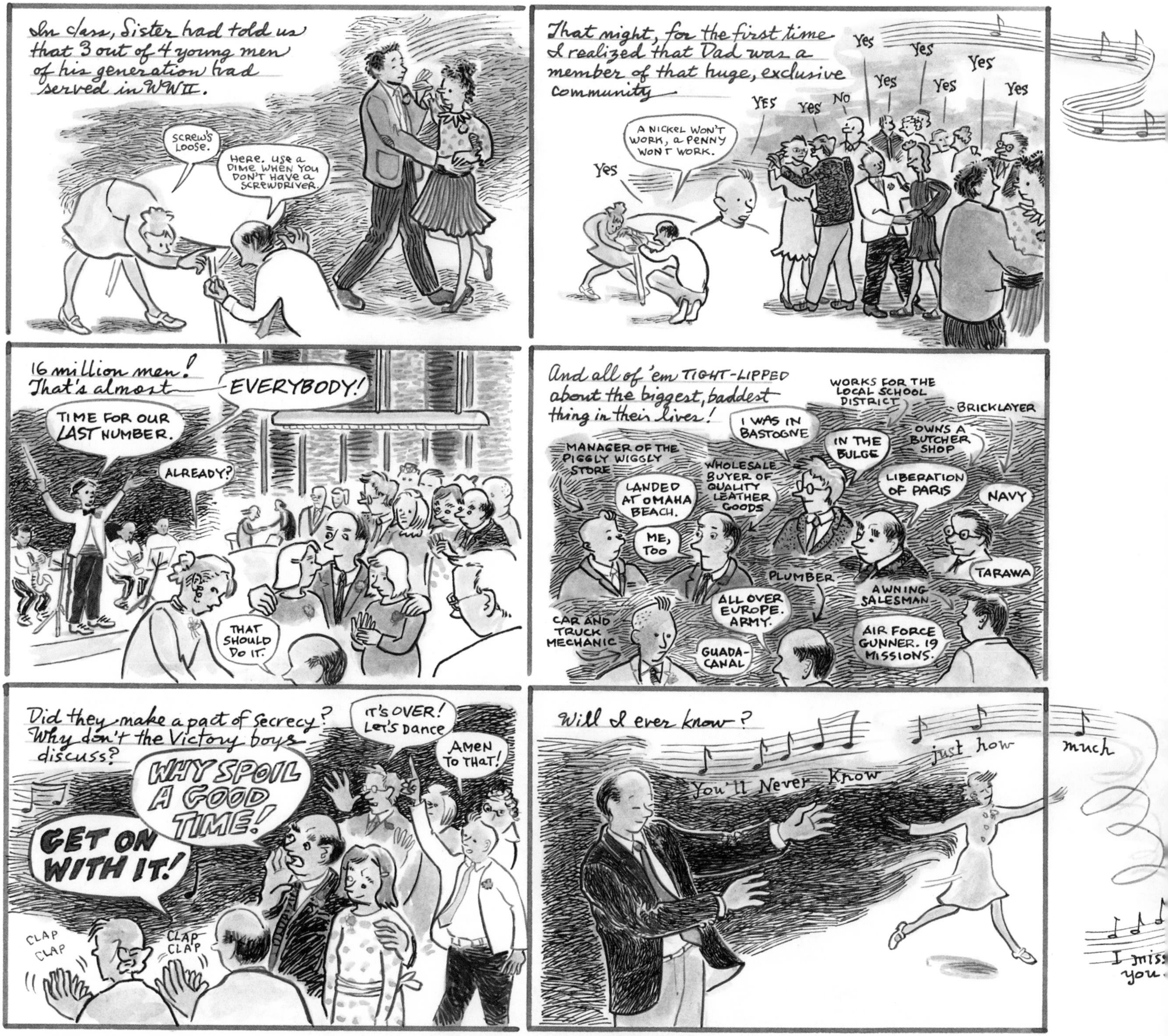
In class, Sister had told us that 3 out of 4 young men of his generation had served in WWII.
SCREW'S LOOSE.
HERE. USE A DIME WHEN YOU DON'T HAVE A SCREWDRIVER.
That night, for the first time I realized that Dad was a member of that huge, exclusive community
A NICKEL WON'T WORK, A PENNY WON'T WORK.
Yes
YES
Yes
No
Yes
Yes
Yes
Yes
Yes
Yes
16 million men! That's almost
EVERYBODY!
TIME FOR OUR LAST NUMBER.
ALREADY?
THAT SHOULD DO IT.
And all of 'em TIGHT-LIPPED about the biggest, baddest thing in their lives!
MANAGER OF THE PIGGLY WIGGLY STORE
LANDED AT OMAHA BEACH.
ME, TOO
WHOLESALE BUYER OF QUALITY LEATHER GOODS
I WAS IN BASTOGNE
WORKS FOR THE LOCAL SCHOOL DISTRICT
IN THE BULGE
OWNS A BUTCHER SHOP
BRICKLAYER
LIBERATION OF PARIS
NAVY
TARAWA
PLUMBER
AWNING SALESMAN
CAR AND TRUCK MECHANIC
ALL OVER EUROPE. ARMY.
GUADA-CANAL
AIR FORCE GUNNER. 19 MISSIONS.
Did they make a pact of secrecy? Why don't the Victory boys discuss?
IT'S OVER! LET'S DANCE
AMEN TO THAT!
WHY SPOIL A GOOD TIME!
GET ON WITH IT!
CLAP CLAP
CLAP CLAP
Will I ever know?
You'll Never Know
just how
much
I miss you.

2.

MAYBE THIS TIME 'ROUND

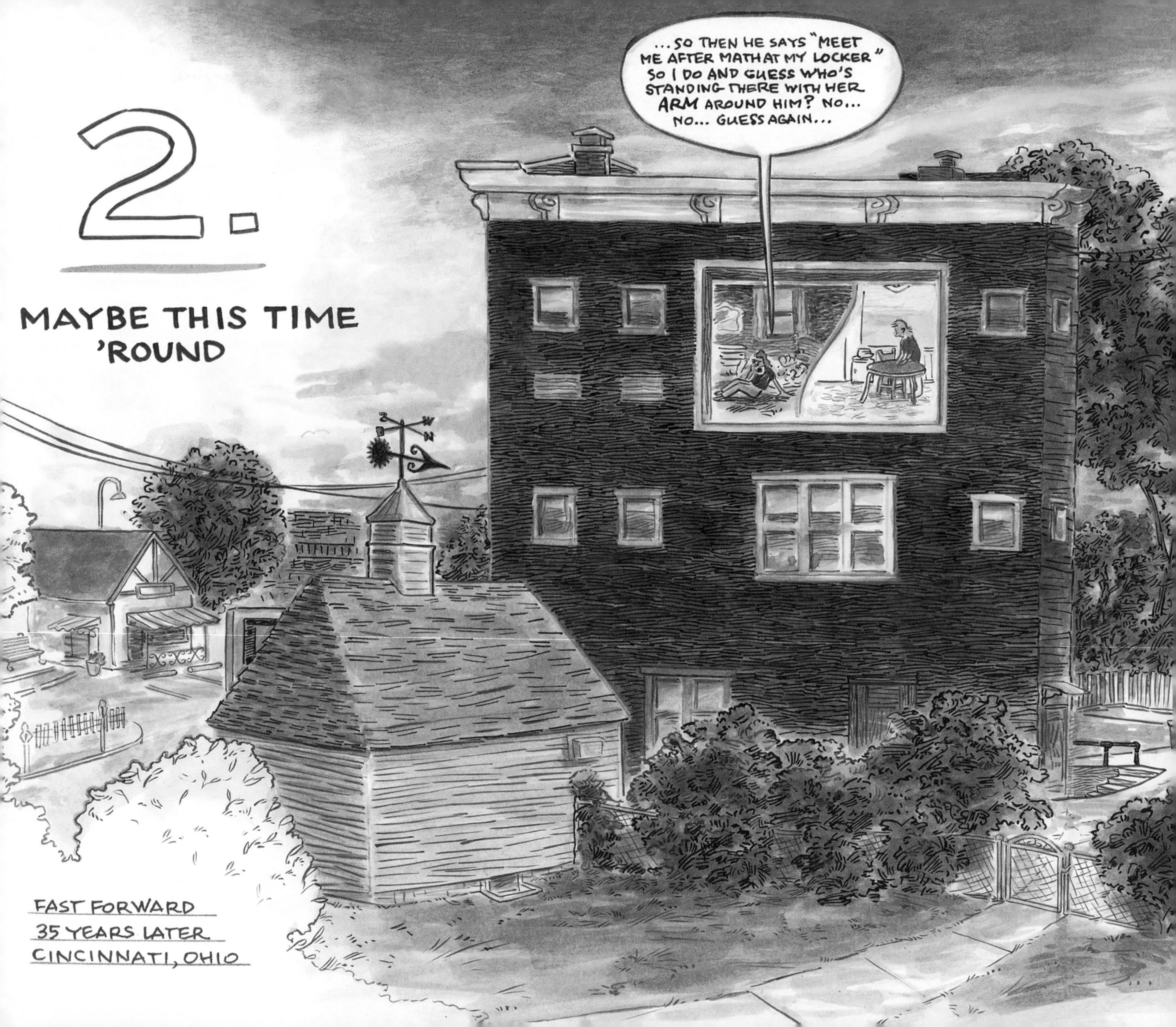
...SO THEN HE SAYS "MEET ME AFTER MATH AT MY LOCKER" SO I DO AND GUESS WHO'S STANDING THERE WITH HER ARM AROUND HIM? NO... NO... GUESS AGAIN...
FAST FORWARD
35 YEARS LATER
CINCINNATI, OHIO

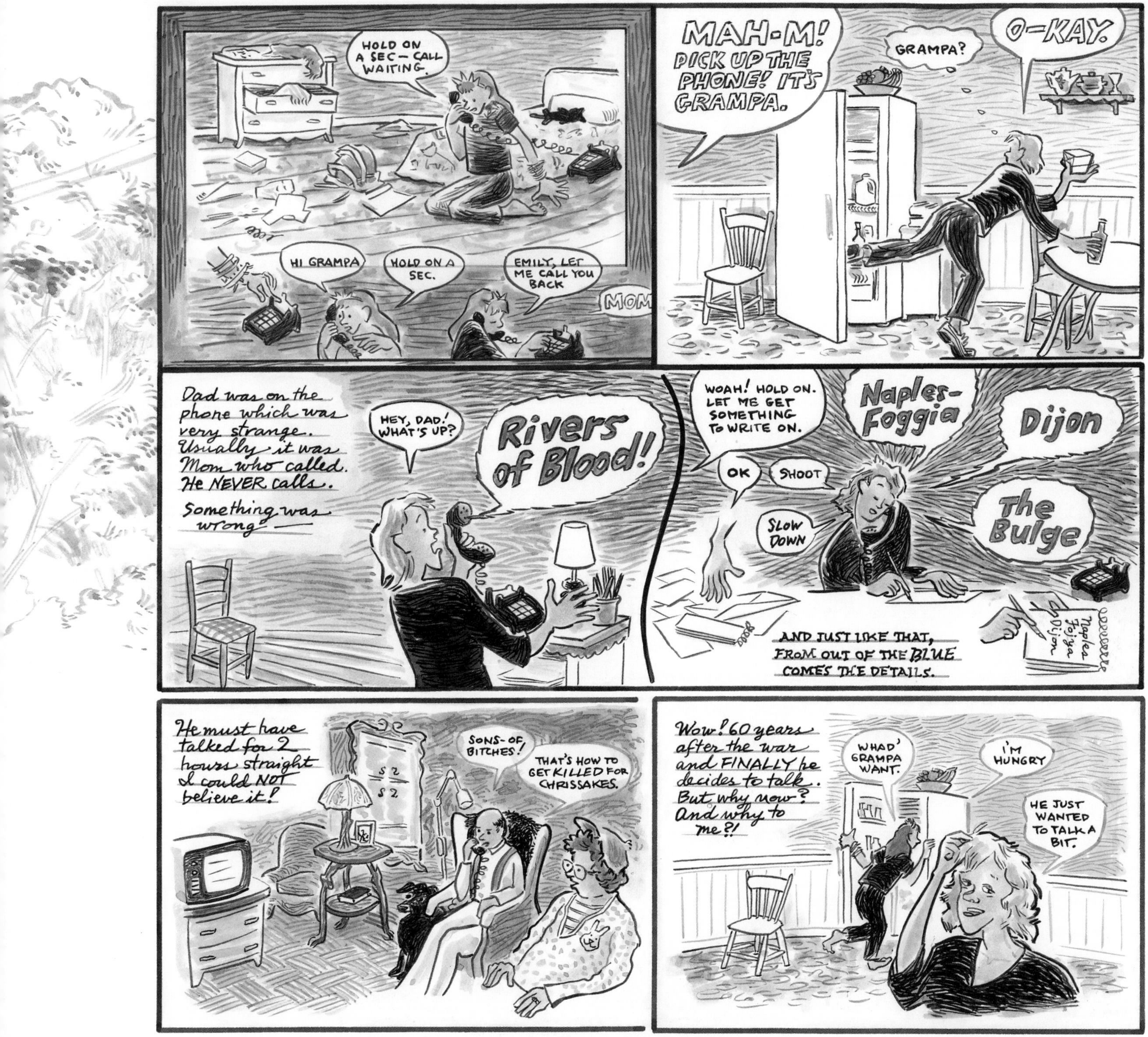
HOLD ON A SEC— CALL WAITING.
HI GRAMPA
HOLD ON A SEC.
EMILY, LET ME CALL YOU BACK
MOM
MAH-M! PICK UP THE PHONE! IT'S GRAMPA.
GRAMPA?
O-KAY.
Dad was on the phone which was very strange. Usually it was Mom who called. He NEVER calls.
Something was wrong
HEY, DAD! WHAT'S UP?
Rivers of Blood!
WOAH! HOLD ON. LET ME GET SOMETHING TO WRITE ON.
OK
SHOOT
SLOW DOWN
Naples-Foggia
Dijon
The Bulge
Naples Fojga Dijon
AND JUST LIKE THAT, FROM OUT OF THE BLUE COMES THE DETAILS.
He must have talked for 2 hours straight I could NOT believe it!
SONS-OF-BITCHES!
THAT'S HOW TO GET KILLED FOR CHRISSAKES.
Wow! 60 years after the war and FINALLY he decides to talk. But why now? And why to me?!
WHAD' GRAMPA WANT.
I'M HUNGRY
HE JUST WANTED TO TALK A BIT.

Rivers of Blood! Can you imagine?

In Italy he said.

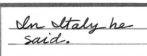

"THE BOOT"

I wonder where in Italy that was?

SOMEWHERE I'VE GOT THAT BIG OLD WORLD MAP FROM THE THRIFT STORE —

So that means a battle of some sort.

Wonder if he killed people? He must have.

I'm surprised at how much he remembered,

OH.. NAPLES. I SEE.

and how much he didn't.

So let's see, a river with a steep slope beyond.

BOLOGNA
GENOA
ADRIATIC SEA
PISA ARNO R. FLORENCE
ROMA
TYRRHENIAN SEA
NAPOLI
LEGH
ROME

"Krauts shooting the shit out of us..."

"The River turnt red with blood."

How could he ever look at water ever again

and not see blood swirling through it?

GOOD GOD ALMIGHTY!

24

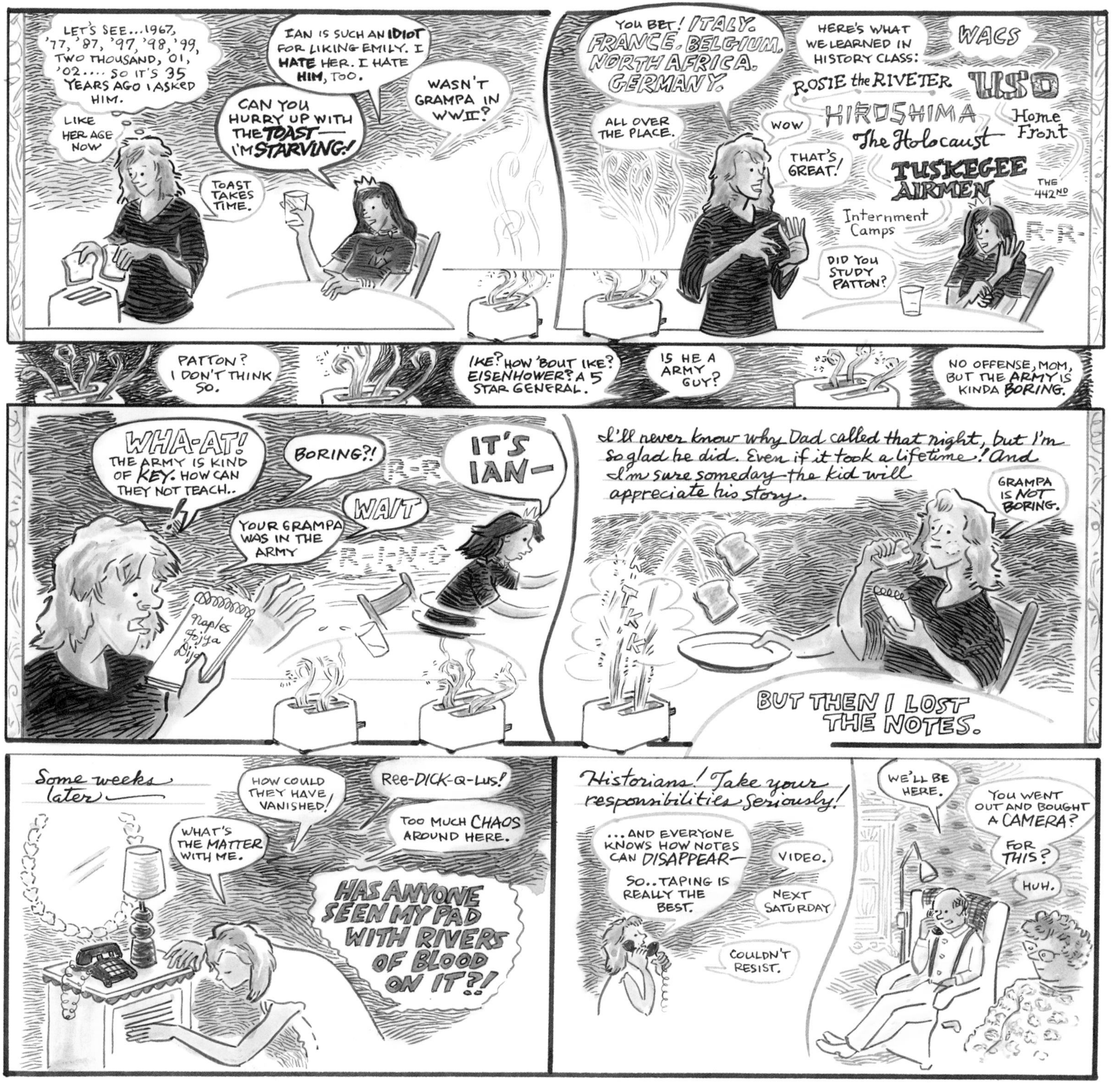
LET'S SEE...1967, '77, '87, '97, '98, '99, TWO THOUSAND, '01, '02.... SO IT'S 35 YEARS AGO I ASKED HIM.
LIKE HER AGE NOW
IAN IS SUCH AN IDIOT FOR LIKING EMILY. I HATE HER. I HATE HIM, TOO.
CAN YOU HURRY UP WITH THE TOAST— I'M STARVING!
TOAST TAKES TIME.
WASN'T GRAMPA IN WWII?
YOU BET! ITALY. FRANCE. BELGIUM. NORTH AFRICA. GERMANY.
ALL OVER THE PLACE.
WOW
THAT'S GREAT!
HERE'S WHAT WE LEARNED IN HISTORY CLASS:
WACS
ROSIE the RIVETER
USO
HIROSHIMA
Home Front
The Holocaust
TUSKEGEE AIRMEN
THE 442ND
Internment Camps
R-R-
DID YOU STUDY PATTON?
PATTON? I DON'T THINK SO.
IKE? HOW 'BOUT IKE? EISENHOWER? A 5 STAR GENERAL.
IS HE A ARMY GUY?
NO OFFENSE, MOM, BUT THE ARMY IS KINDA BORING.
WHA-AT! THE ARMY IS KIND OF KEY. HOW CAN THEY NOT TEACH..
BORING?!
R-R
IT'S IAN—
WAIT
YOUR GRAMPA WAS IN THE ARMY
R-ING
Naples
I'll never know why Dad called that night, but I'm so glad he did. Even if it took a lifetime! And I'm sure someday the kid will appreciate his story.
GRAMPA IS NOT BORING.
BUT THEN I LOST THE NOTES.
Some weeks later
WHAT'S THE MATTER WITH ME.
HOW COULD THEY HAVE VANISHED!
Ree-DICK-Q-LUS!
TOO MUCH CHAOS AROUND HERE.
HAS ANYONE SEEN MY PAD WITH RIVERS OF BLOOD ON IT?!
Historians! Take your responsibilities seriously!
...AND EVERYONE KNOWS HOW NOTES CAN DISAPPEAR—
SO..TAPING IS REALLY THE BEST.
VIDEO.
NEXT SATURDAY
COULDN'T RESIST.
WE'LL BE HERE.
YOU WENT OUT AND BOUGHT A CAMERA?
FOR THIS?
HUH.

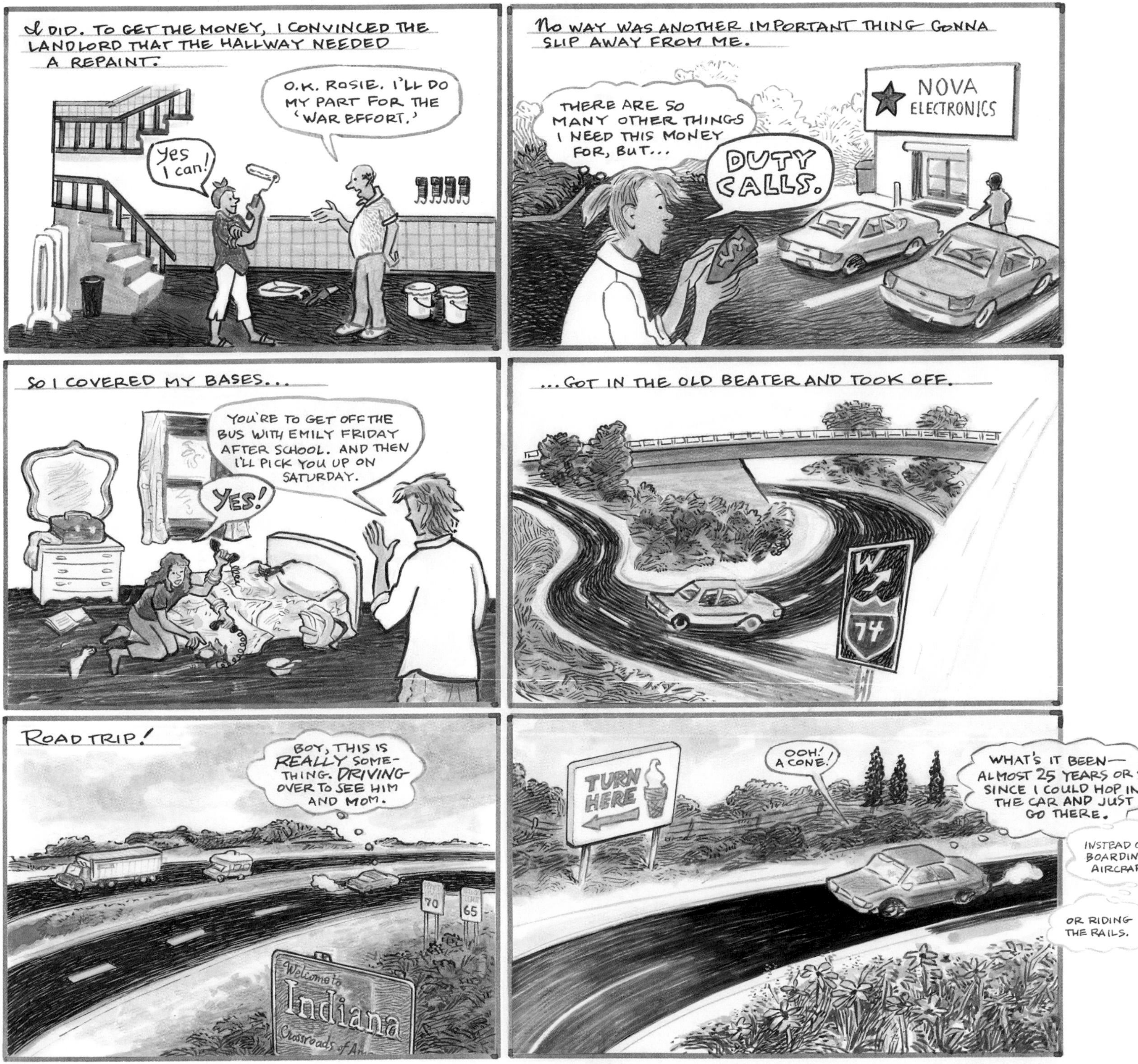
I DID. TO GET THE MONEY, I CONVINCED THE LANDLORD THAT THE HALLWAY NEEDED A REPAINT.
O.K. ROSIE. I'LL DO MY PART FOR THE 'WAR EFFORT.'
Yes I can!
NO WAY WAS ANOTHER IMPORTANT THING GONNA SLIP AWAY FROM ME.
NOVA ELECTRONICS
THERE ARE SO MANY OTHER THINGS I NEED THIS MONEY FOR, BUT...
DUTY CALLS.
SO I COVERED MY BASES...
YOU'RE TO GET OFF THE BUS WITH EMILY FRIDAY AFTER SCHOOL. AND THEN I'LL PICK YOU UP ON SATURDAY.
YES!
...GOT IN THE OLD BEATER AND TOOK OFF.
W
74
ROAD TRIP!
BOY, THIS IS REALLY SOMETHING. DRIVING OVER TO SEE HIM AND MOM.
70
65
Welcome to Indiana Crossroads of Am
TURN HERE
OOH! A CONE!
WHAT'S IT BEEN— ALMOST 25 YEARS OR SO SINCE I COULD HOP IN THE CAR AND JUST GO THERE.
INSTEAD OF BOARDING AN AIRCRAFT...
OR RIDING THE RAILS.

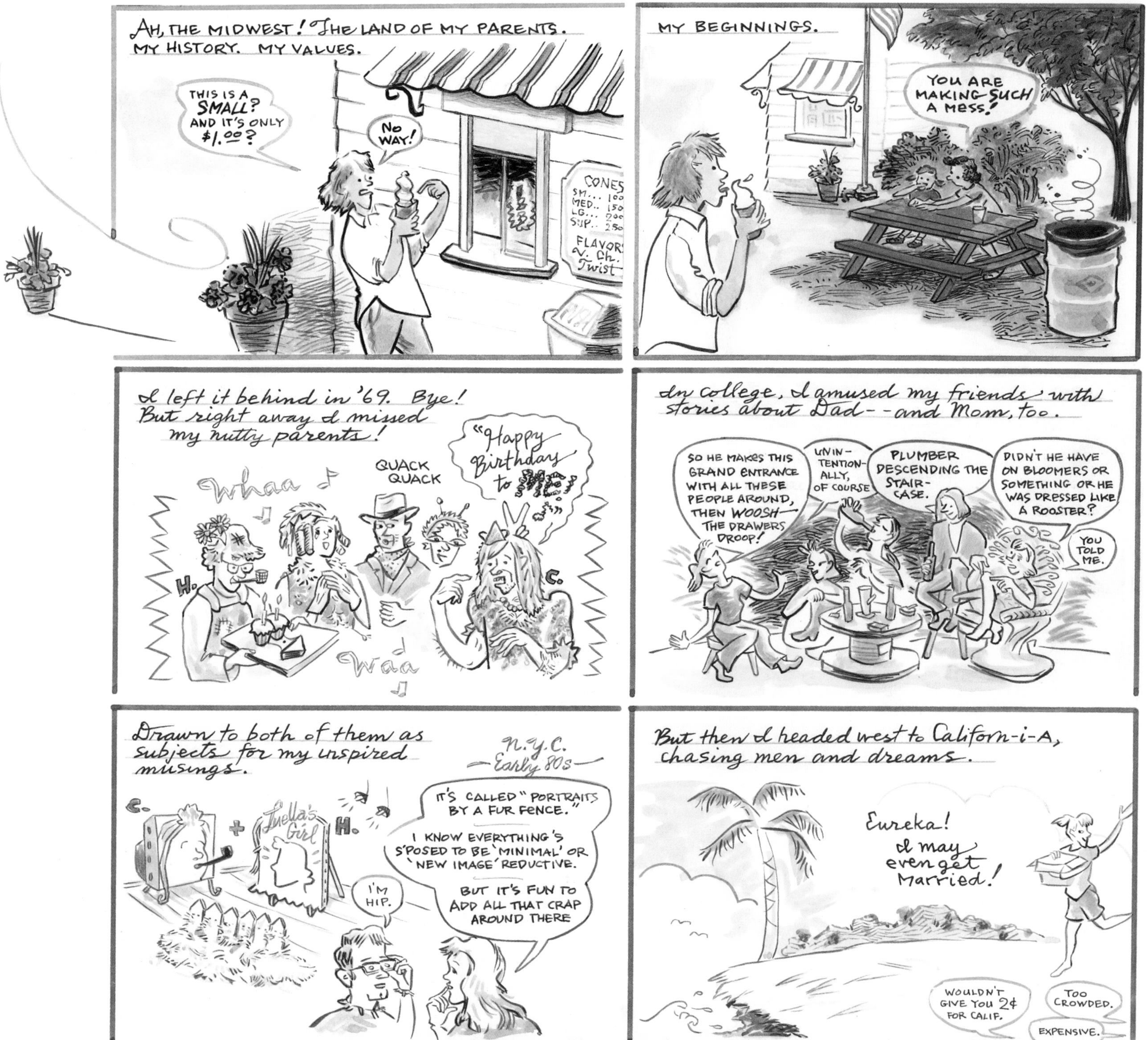
AH, THE MIDWEST! THE LAND OF MY PARENTS. MY HISTORY. MY VALUES.
THIS IS A SMALL? AND IT'S ONLY $1.00?
NO WAY!
CONES
FLAVORS
Twist
MY BEGINNINGS.
YOU ARE MAKING SUCH A MESS!
I left it behind in '69. Bye! But right away I missed my nutty parents!
Whaa
QUACK QUACK
"Happy Birthday to ME!"
H.
C.
Waa
In college, I amused my friends with stories about Dad--and Mom, too.
SO HE MAKES THIS GRAND ENTRANCE WITH ALL THESE PEOPLE AROUND, THEN WOOSH THE DRAWERS DROOP!
UNIN-TENTION-ALLY, OF COURSE
PLUMBER DESCENDING THE STAIR-CASE.
DIDN'T HE HAVE ON BLOOMERS OR SOMETHING OR HE WAS DRESSED LIKE A ROOSTER?
YOU TOLD ME.
Drawn to both of them as subjects for my inspired musings.
N.Y.C. Early 80s
C.
H.
Luella's Girl
IT'S CALLED "PORTRAITS BY A FUR FENCE."
I KNOW EVERYTHING'S S'POSED TO BE 'MINIMAL' OR 'NEW IMAGE' REDUCTIVE.
BUT IT'S FUN TO ADD ALL THAT CRAP AROUND THERE
I'M HIP.
But then I headed west to Californ-i-A, chasing men and dreams.
Eureka! I may even get Married!
WOULDN'T GIVE YOU 2¢ FOR CALIF.
TOO CROWDED.
EXPENSIVE.

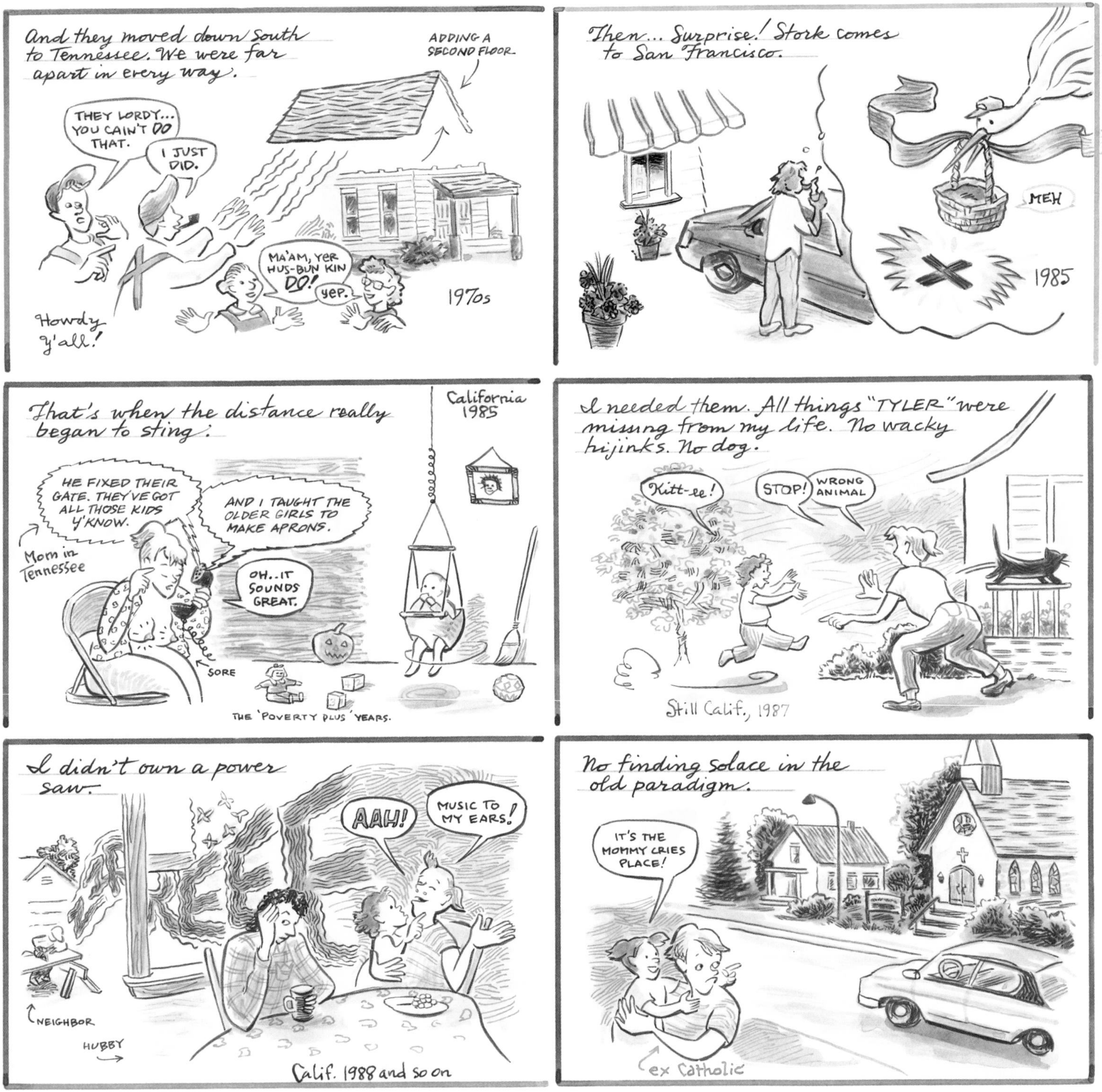
And they moved down South to Tennessee. We were far apart in every way.
ADDING A SECOND FLOOR
THEY LORDY... YOU CAIN'T DO THAT.
I JUST DID.
MA'AM, YER HUS-BUN KIN DO!
YEP.
1970s
Howdy y'all!
Then... Surprise! Stork comes to San Francisco.
MEH
1985
That's when the distance really began to sting.
California 1985
HE FIXED THEIR GATE. THEY'VE GOT ALL THOSE KIDS Y'KNOW.
AND I TAUGHT THE OLDER GIRLS TO MAKE APRONS.
Mom in Tennessee
OH.. IT SOUNDS GREAT.
SORE
THE 'POVERTY PLUS' YEARS.
I needed them. All things "TYLER" were missing from my life. No wacky hijinks. No dog.
Kitt-ee!
STOP!
WRONG ANIMAL
Still Calif., 1987
I didn't own a power saw.
AAH!
MUSIC TO MY EARS!
NEIGHBOR
HUBBY
Calif. 1988 and so on
No finding solace in the old paradigm.
IT'S THE MOMMY CRIES PLACE!
ex Catholic

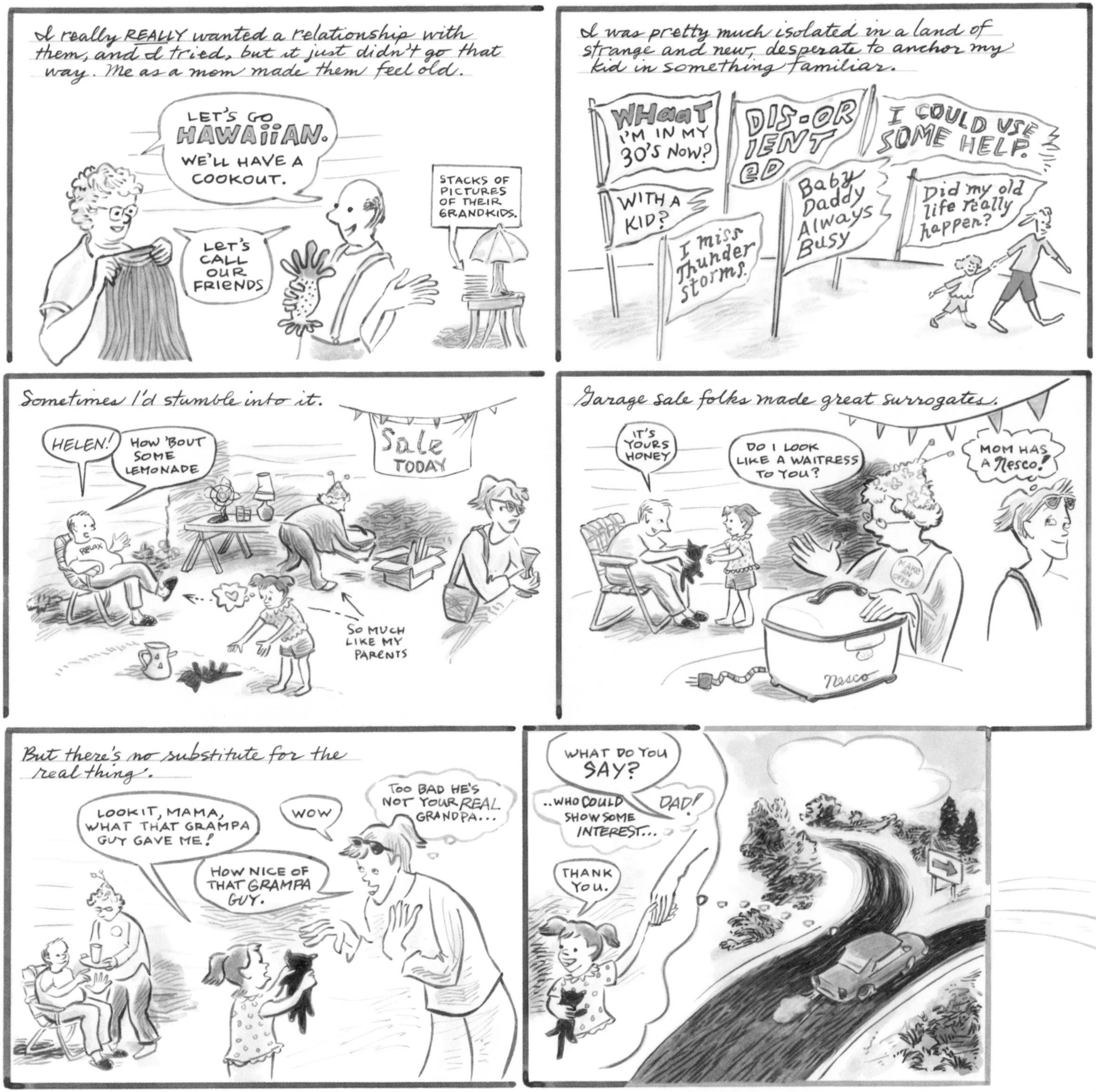
I really REALLY wanted a relationship with them, and I tried, but it just didn't go that way. Me as a mom made them feel old.
LET'S GO HAWAIIAN. WE'LL HAVE A COOKOUT.
LET'S CALL OUR FRIENDS
STACKS OF PICTURES OF THEIR GRANDKIDS.
I was pretty much isolated in a land of strange and new, desperate to anchor my kid in something familiar.
WHaaT I'M IN MY 30'S NOW?
DIS-ORIENT@D
I COULD USE SOME HELP.
WITH A KID?
I miss Thunder storms.
Baby Daddy Always Busy
Did my old life really happen?
Sometimes I'd stumble into it.
Sale TODAY
HELEN!
HOW 'BOUT SOME LEMONADE
RELAX
SO MUCH LIKE MY PARENTS
Garage sale folks made great surrogates.
IT'S YOURS HONEY
DO I LOOK LIKE A WAITRESS TO YOU?
MOM HAS A Nesco!
MAKE AN OFFER
Nesco
But there's no substitute for the real thing.
LOOKIT, MAMA, WHAT THAT GRAMPA GUY GAVE ME!
WOW
TOO BAD HE'S NOT YOUR REAL GRANDPA...
HOW NICE OF THAT GRAMPA GUY.
WHAT DO YOU SAY?
..WHO COULD SHOW SOME INTEREST...
DAD!
THANK YOU.

EVENTUALLY, I LANDED IN OHIO, THE CIRCUM-STANCES OF WHICH I WILL DESCRIBE LATER.

AFTER TENN., IT WAS A FEW TOUGH YEARS UP IN N.Y. STATE FOR THE 'RENTS—DETAILS LATER ON THAT, TOO. BUT NOW, INDIANA IS THEIR SONG.

CLINTON SPEED LIMIT 29

EVEN THOUGH THEY MOVED INTO THIS HOUSE 5 YEARS AGO...

IT STILL FEELS LIKE HOME.

HEL-LO-OH!

MAYBE THIS TIME 'ROUND, THINGS'LL BE DIFFERENT.

HOW YOU DOIN' MOMMY? I MISSED YOU. MWAH!

HELLO SWEETIE. GIVE ME SOME SUGAR.

HOW'S MR. DAD?

READY FOR YOUR HOLLYWOOD CLOSE-UP?

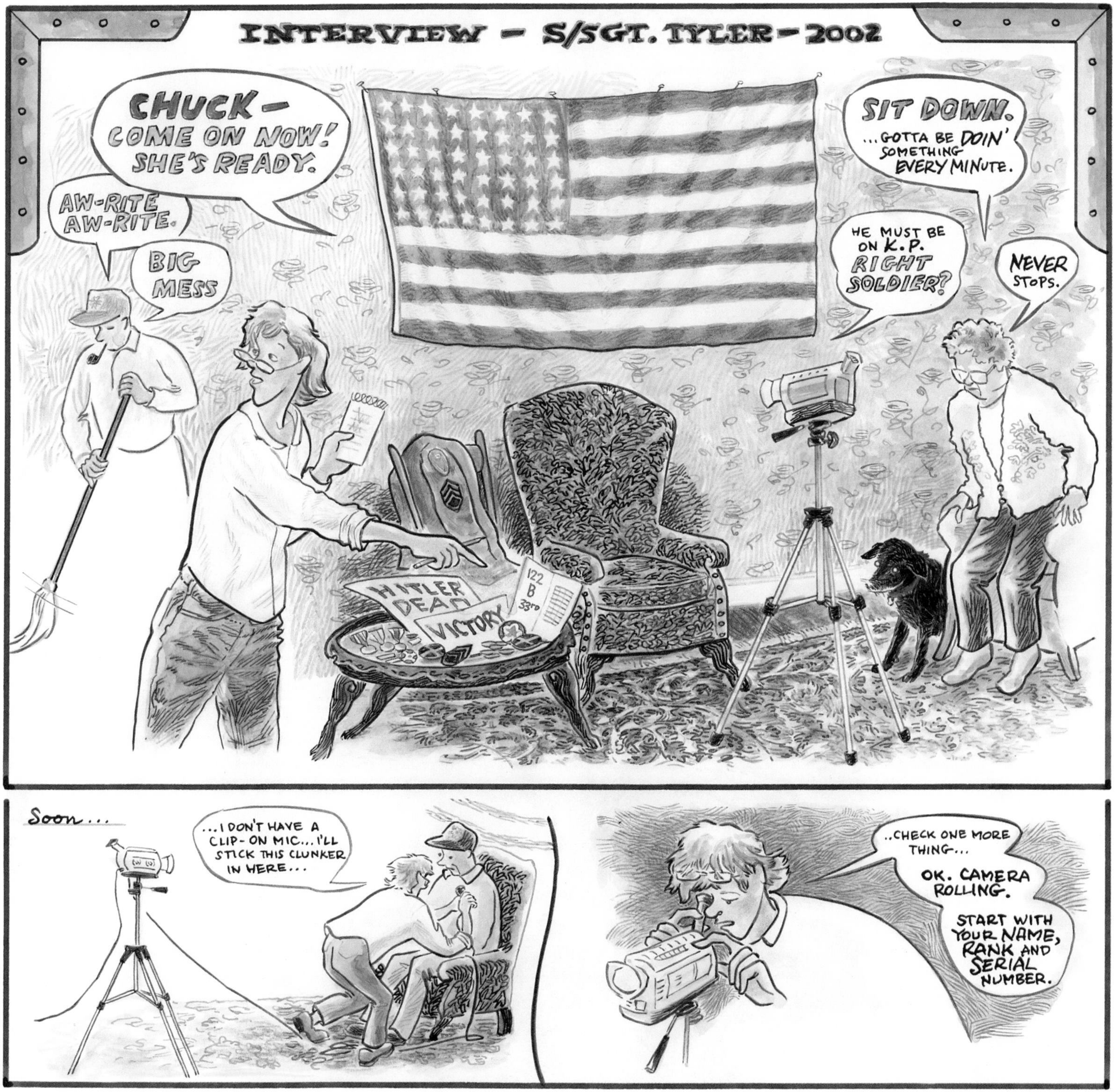
INTERVIEW - S/SGT. TYLER - 2002
CHUCK - COME ON NOW! SHE'S READY.
AW-RITE AW-RITE.
BIG MESS
SIT DOWN. ...GOTTA BE DOIN' SOMETHING EVERY MINUTE.
HE MUST BE ON K.P. RIGHT SOLDIER?
NEVER STOPS.
HITLER DEAD
VICTORY
122 B 33RD
Soon...
...I DON'T HAVE A CLIP-ON MIC... I'LL STICK THIS CLUNKER IN HERE...
..CHECK ONE MORE THING...
OK. CAMERA ROLLING.
START WITH YOUR NAME, RANK AND SERIAL NUMBER.

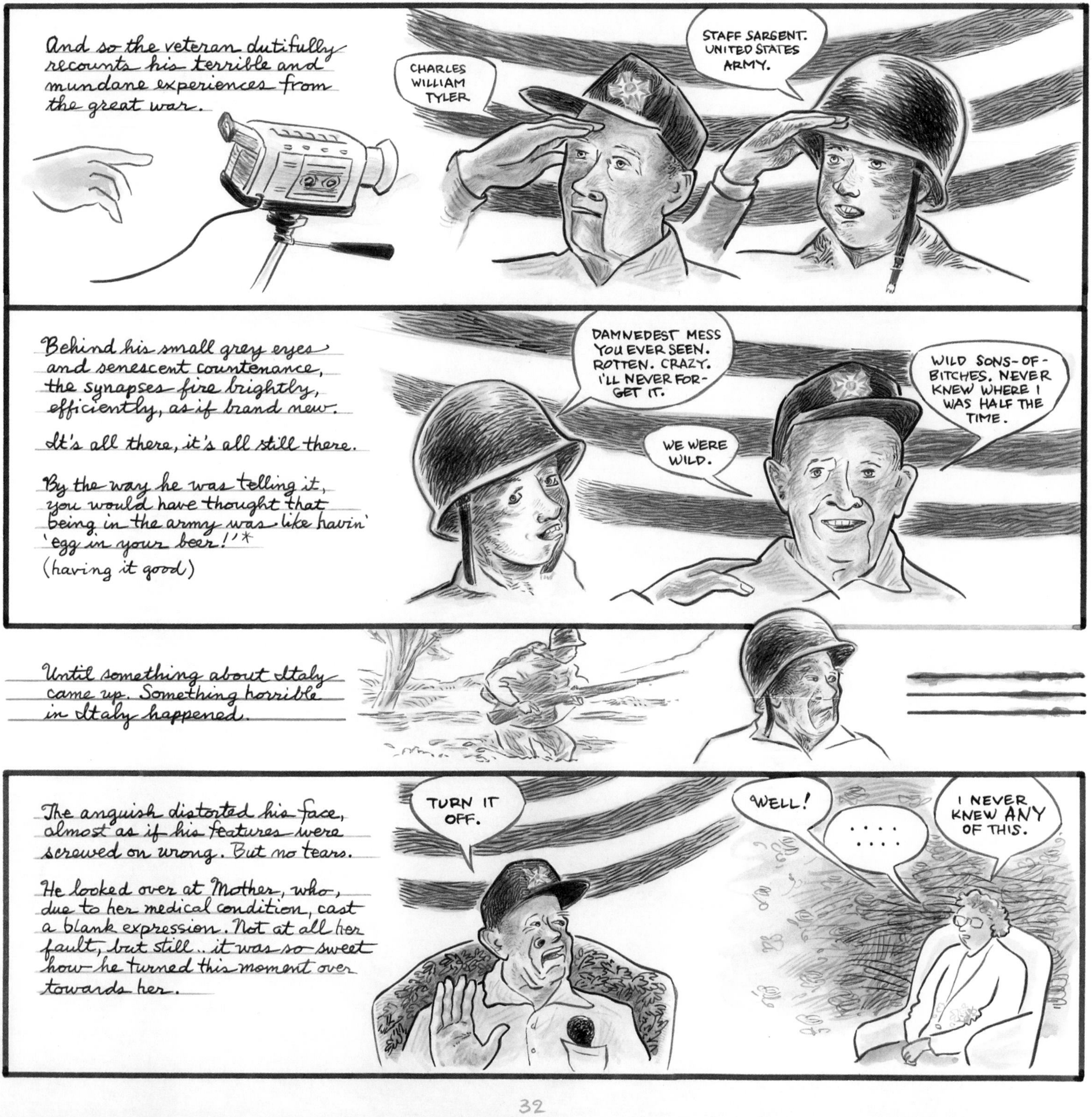
And so the veteran dutifully recounts his terrible and mundane experiences from the great war.
CHARLES WILLIAM TYLER
STAFF SARGENT. UNITED STATES ARMY.
Behind his small grey eyes and senescent countenance, the synapses fire brightly, efficiently, as if brand new.
It's all there, it's all still there.
By the way he was telling it, you would have thought that being in the army was like havin' 'egg in your beer!'* (having it good)
DAMNEDEST MESS YOU EVER SEEN. ROTTEN. CRAZY. I'LL NEVER FORGET IT.
WE WERE WILD.
WILD SONS-OF-BITCHES. NEVER KNEW WHERE I WAS HALF THE TIME.
Until something about Italy came up. Something horrible in Italy happened.
The anguish distorted his face, almost as if his features were screwed on wrong. But no tears.
He looked over at Mother, who, due to her medical condition, cast a blank expression. Not at all her fault, but still.. it was so sweet how he turned this moment over towards her.
TURN IT OFF.
WELL!
. . . .
I NEVER KNEW ANY OF THIS.

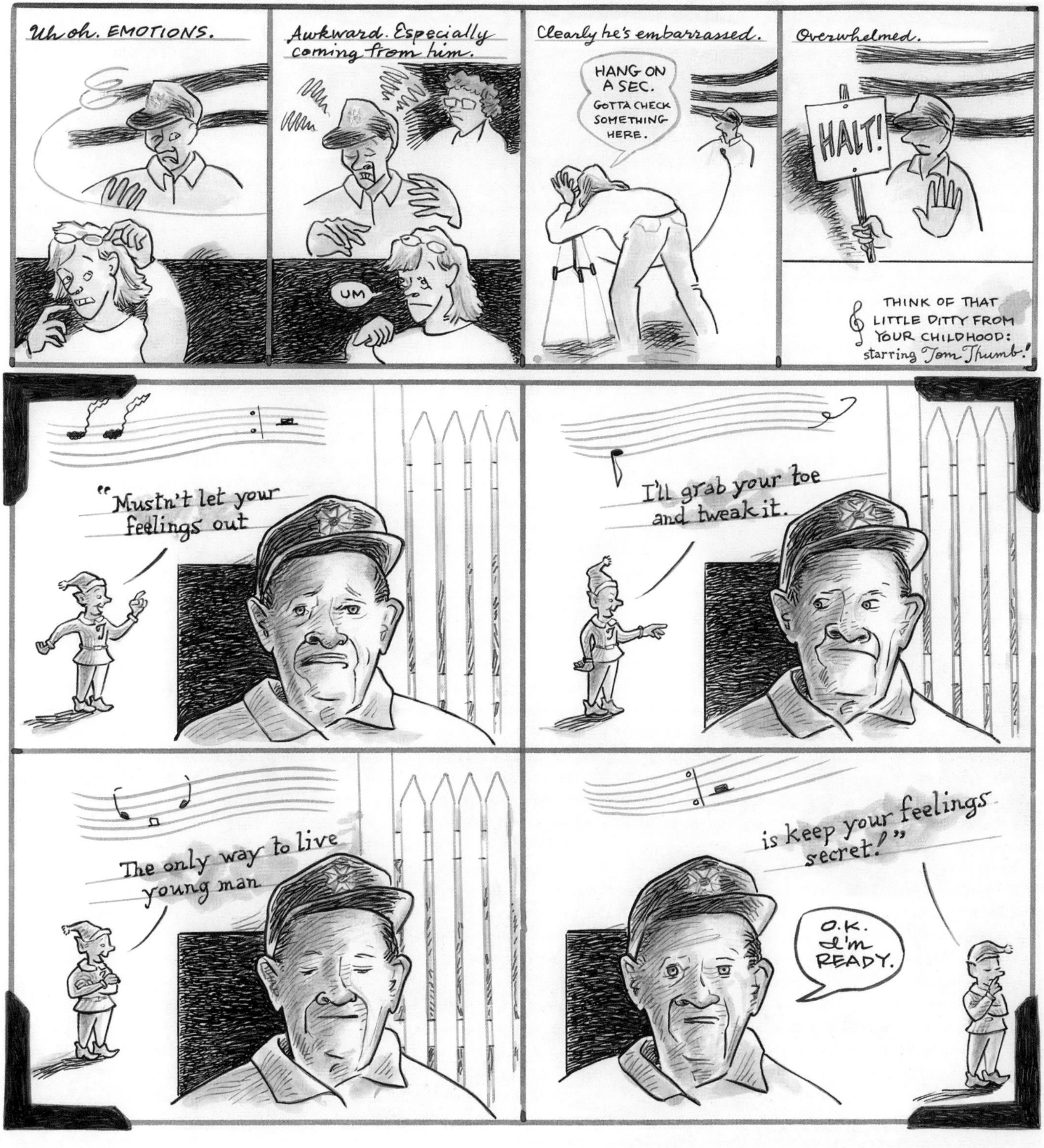
Uh oh. EMOTIONS.
Awkward. Especially coming from him.
UM
Clearly he's embarrassed.
HANG ON A SEC. GOTTA CHECK SOMETHING HERE.
Overwhelmed.
HALT!
THINK OF THAT LITTLE DITTY FROM YOUR CHILDHOOD: starring Tom Thumb!
"Mustn't let your feelings out
I'll grab your toe and tweak it.
The only way to live young man
is keep your feelings secret!"
O.K. I'm READY.

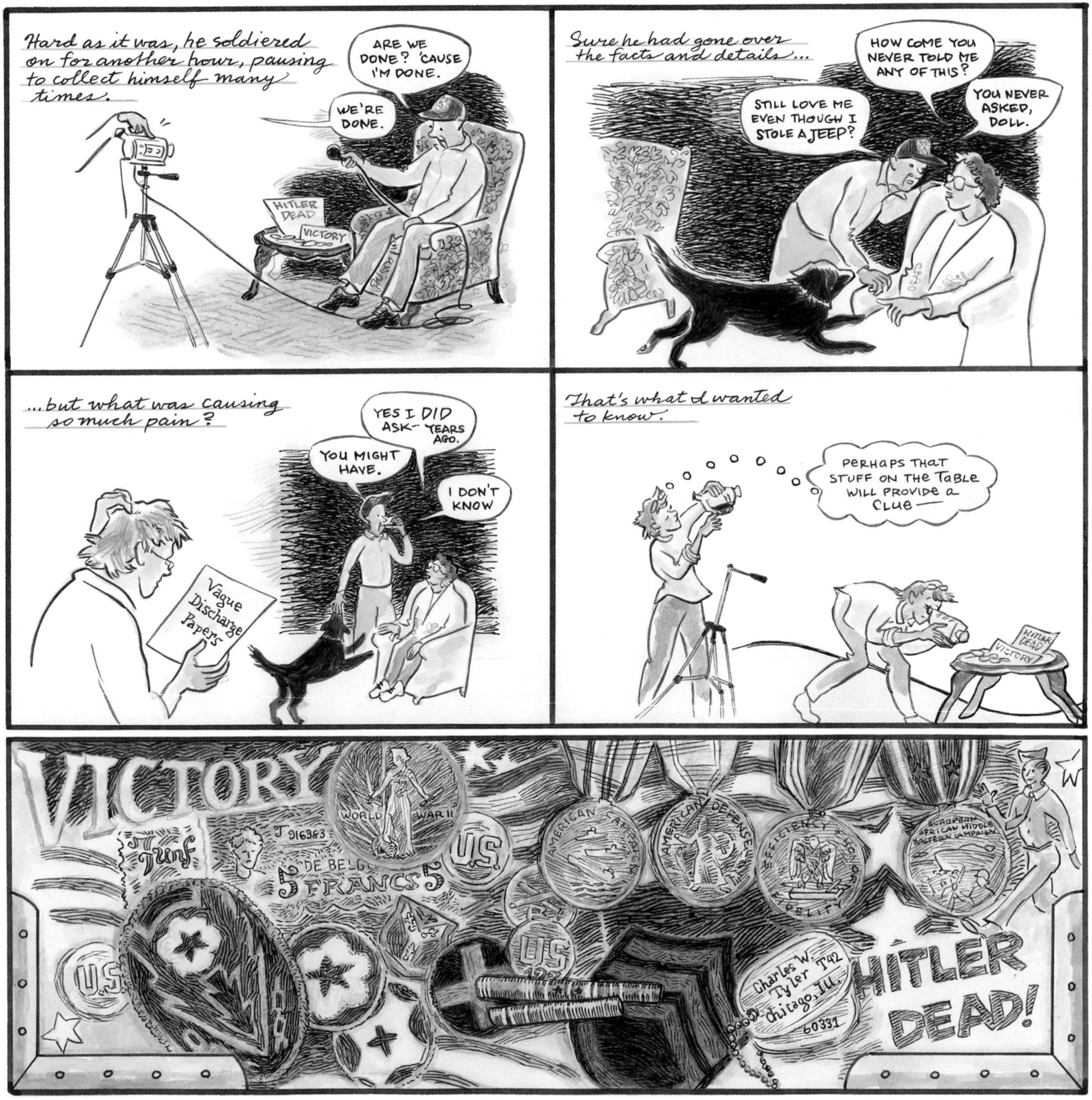
Hard as it was, he soldiered on for another hour, pausing to collect himself many times.
ARE WE DONE? 'CAUSE I'M DONE.
WE'RE DONE.
HITLER DEAD
VICTORY
Sure he had gone over the facts and details...
HOW COME YOU NEVER TOLD ME ANY OF THIS?
STILL LOVE ME EVEN THOUGH I STOLE A JEEP?
YOU NEVER ASKED, DOLL.
...but what was causing so much pain?
YES I DID ASK- YEARS AGO.
YOU MIGHT HAVE.
I DON'T KNOW
Vague Discharge Papers
That's what I wanted to know.
PERHAPS THAT STUFF ON THE TABLE WILL PROVIDE A CLUE—
HITLER DEAD
VICTORY
VICTORY
WORLD WAR II
T 916383
DE BELG
5 FRANCS 5
U.S.
AMERICAN CAMPAIGN
AMERICAN DEFENSE
EFFICIENCY HONOR FIDELITY
EUROPEAN AFRICAN MIDDLE EASTERN CAMPAIGN
Charles W. Tyler T42 Chicago, Ill. 60331
HITLER DEAD!

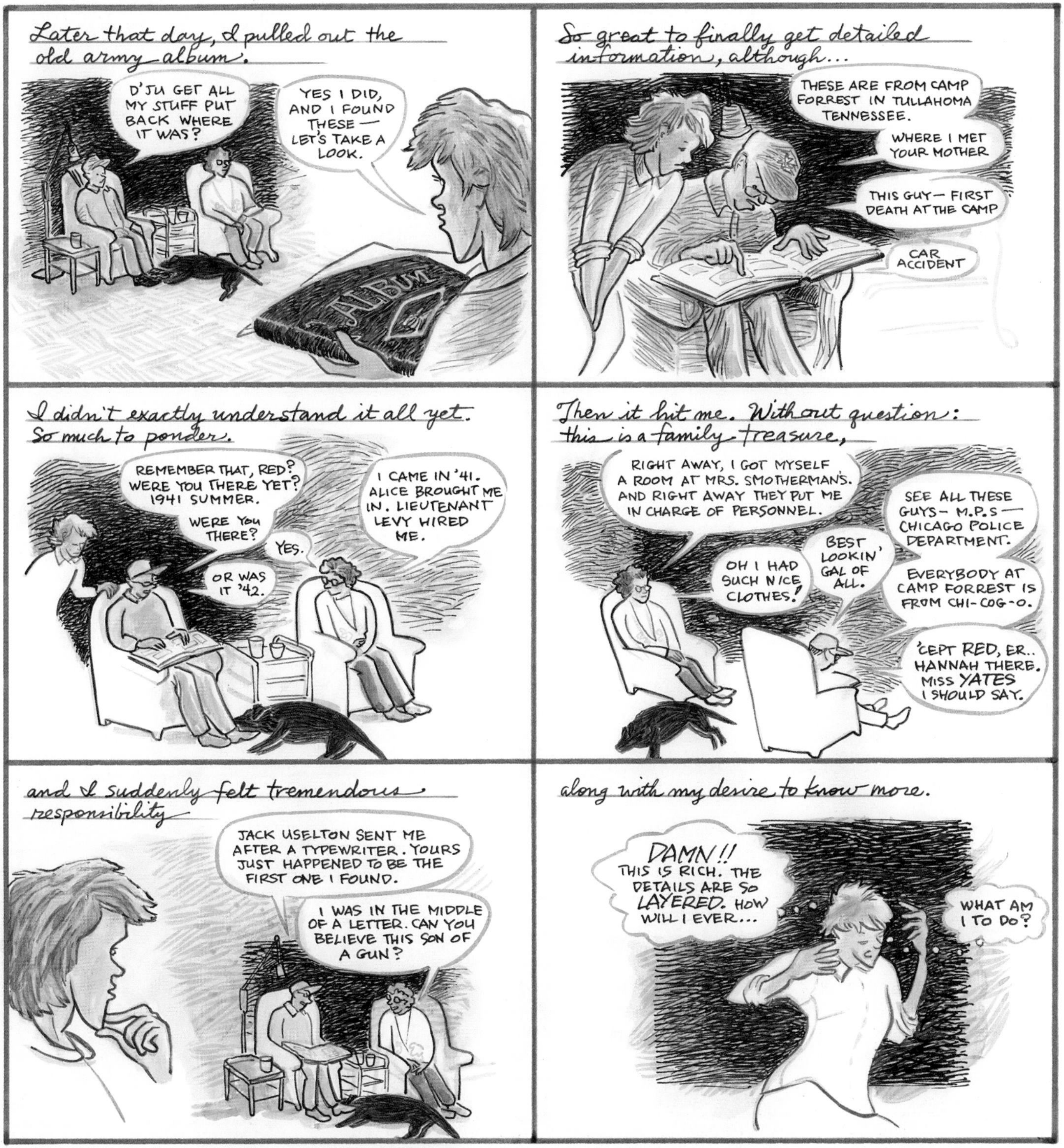
Later that day, I pulled out the old army album.
D'JU GET ALL MY STUFF PUT BACK WHERE IT WAS?
YES I DID, AND I FOUND THESE — LET'S TAKE A LOOK.
ALBUM
So great to finally get detailed information, although...
THESE ARE FROM CAMP FORREST IN TULLAHOMA TENNESSEE.
WHERE I MET YOUR MOTHER
THIS GUY — FIRST DEATH AT THE CAMP
CAR ACCIDENT
I didn't exactly understand it all yet. So much to ponder.
REMEMBER THAT, RED? WERE YOU THERE YET? 1941 SUMMER.
WERE YOU THERE?
YES.
OR WAS IT '42.
I CAME IN '41. ALICE BROUGHT ME IN. LIEUTENANT LEVY HIRED ME.
Then it hit me. Without question: this is a family treasure,
RIGHT AWAY, I GOT MYSELF A ROOM AT MRS. SMOTHERMAN'S. AND RIGHT AWAY THEY PUT ME IN CHARGE OF PERSONNEL.
OH I HAD SUCH NICE CLOTHES!
BEST LOOKIN' GAL OF ALL.
SEE ALL THESE GUYS — M.P.S — CHICAGO POLICE DEPARTMENT.
EVERYBODY AT CAMP FORREST IS FROM CHI-COG-O.
'CEPT RED, ER.. HANNAH THERE. MISS YATES I SHOULD SAY.
and I suddenly felt tremendous responsibility
JACK USELTON SENT ME AFTER A TYPEWRITER. YOURS JUST HAPPENED TO BE THE FIRST ONE I FOUND.
I WAS IN THE MIDDLE OF A LETTER. CAN YOU BELIEVE THIS SON OF A GUN?
along with my desire to know more.
DAMN!! THIS IS RICH. THE DETAILS ARE SO LAYERED. HOW WILL I EVER...
WHAT AM I TO DO?

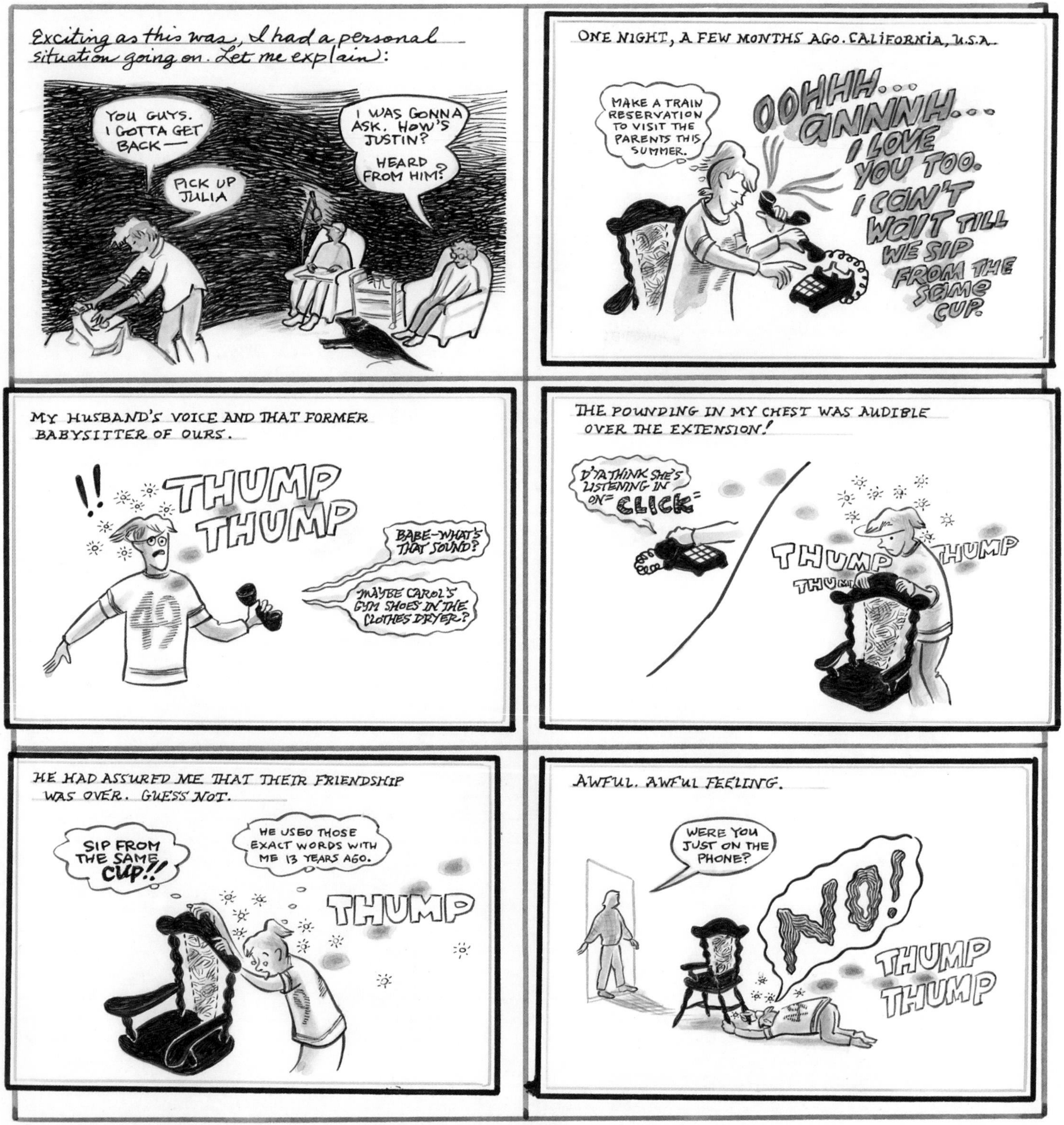

Exciting as this was, I had a personal situation going on. Let me explain:
YOU GUYS. I GOTTA GET BACK—
PICK UP JULIA
I WAS GONNA ASK. HOW'S JUSTIN?
HEARD FROM HIM?
ONE NIGHT, A FEW MONTHS AGO. CALIFORNIA, U.S.A.
MAKE A TRAIN RESERVATION TO VISIT THE PARENTS THIS SUMMER.
OOHHH... ANNNH... I LOVE YOU TOO. I CAN'T WAIT TILL WE SIP FROM THE SAME CUP.
MY HUSBAND'S VOICE AND THAT FORMER BABYSITTER OF OURS.
!!
THUMP THUMP
BABE—WHAT'S THAT SOUND?
MAYBE CAROL'S GYM SHOES IN THE CLOTHES DRYER?
THE POUNDING IN MY CHEST WAS AUDIBLE OVER THE EXTENSION!
D'YA THINK SHE'S LISTENING IN ON— CLICK
THUMP THUMP THUMP
HE HAD ASSURED ME THAT THEIR FRIENDSHIP WAS OVER. GUESS NOT.
SIP FROM THE SAME CUP!!
HE USED THOSE EXACT WORDS WITH ME 13 YEARS AGO.
THUMP
AWFUL. AWFUL FEELING.
WERE YOU JUST ON THE PHONE?
NO!
THUMP THUMP

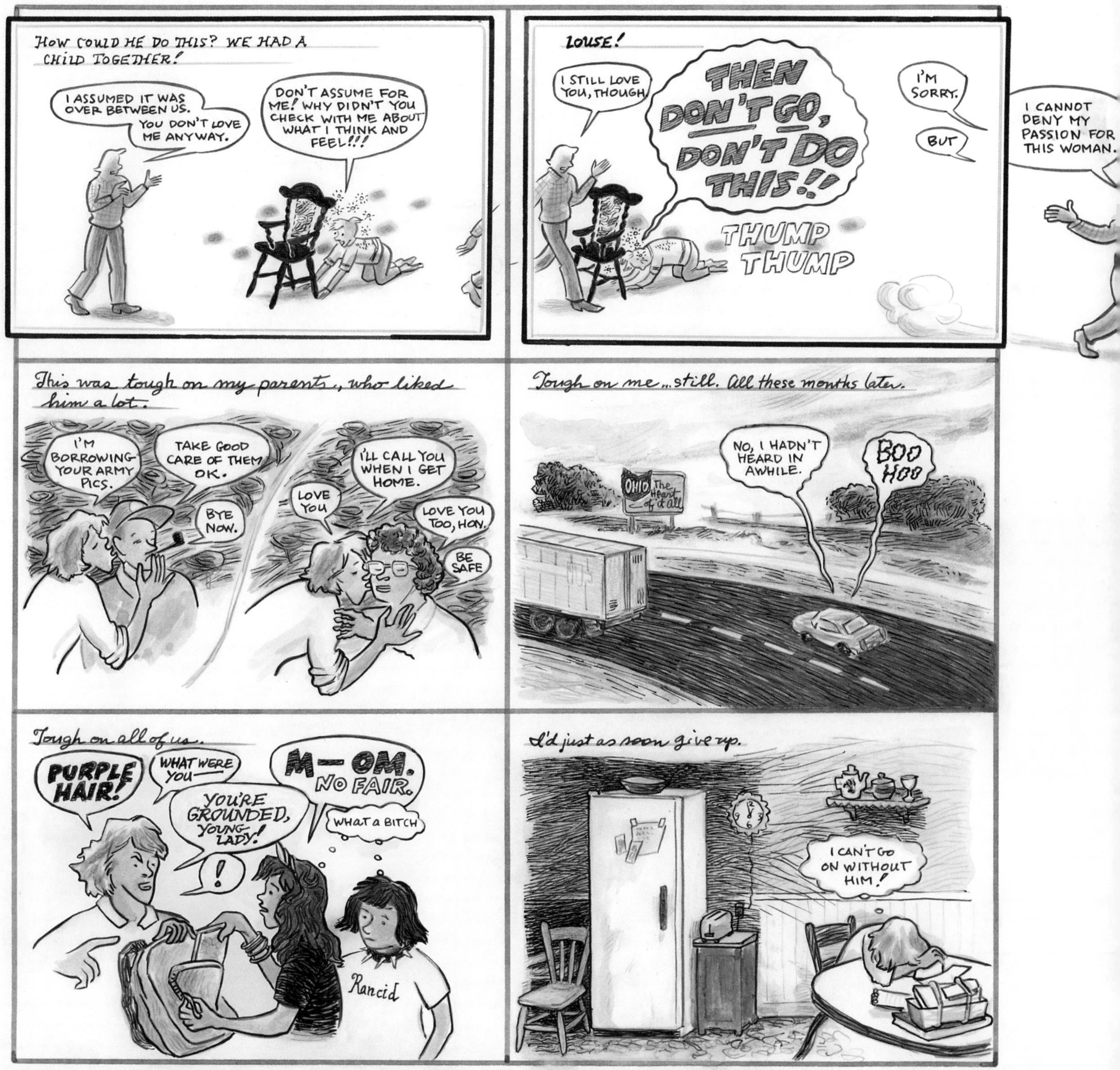

HOW COULD HE DO THIS? WE HAD A CHILD TOGETHER!
I ASSUMED IT WAS OVER BETWEEN US.
YOU DON'T LOVE ME ANYWAY.
DON'T ASSUME FOR ME! WHY DIDN'T YOU CHECK WITH ME ABOUT WHAT I THINK AND FEEL!!!
LOUSE!
I STILL LOVE YOU, THOUGH.
THEN DON'T GO, DON'T DO THIS!!
THUMP THUMP
I'M SORRY.
BUT
I CANNOT DENY MY PASSION FOR THIS WOMAN.
This was tough on my parents, who liked him a lot.
I'M BORROWING YOUR ARMY PICS.
TAKE GOOD CARE OF THEM OK.
BYE NOW.
I'LL CALL YOU WHEN I GET HOME.
LOVE YOU
LOVE YOU TOO, HON.
BE SAFE
Tough on me... still. All these months later.
OHIO The Heart of it all
NO, I HADN'T HEARD IN AWHILE.
BOO HOO
Tough on all of us.
PURPLE HAIR!
WHAT WERE YOU—
YOU'RE GROUNDED, YOUNG LADY!
!
M—OM. NO FAIR.
WHAT A BITCH
Rancid
I'd just as soon give up.
I CAN'T GO ON WITHOUT HIM!

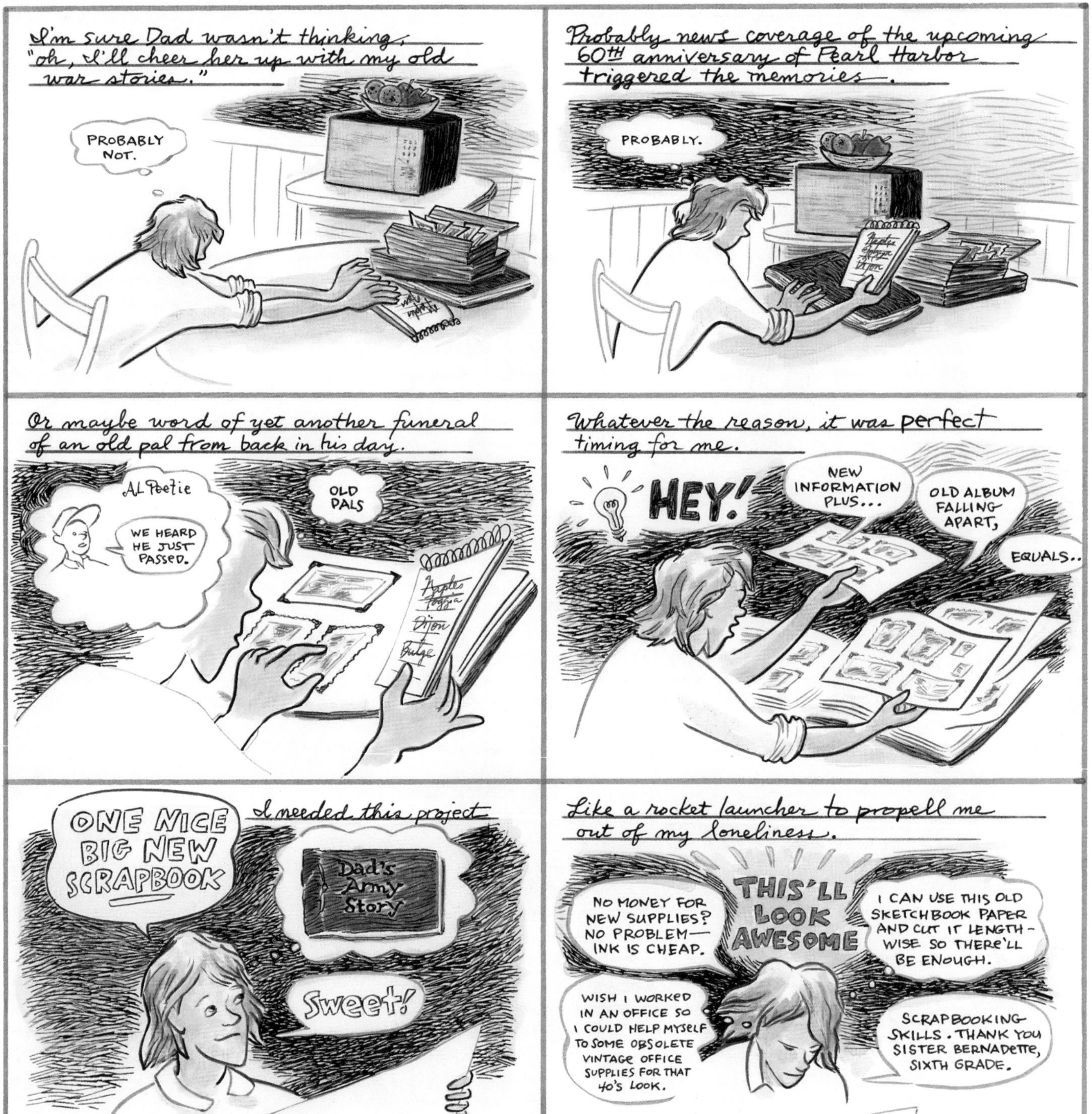
I'm sure Dad wasn't thinking, "oh, I'll cheer her up with my old war stories."
PROBABLY NOT.
Probably news coverage of the upcoming 60TH anniversary of Pearl Harbor triggered the memories.
PROBABLY.
Or maybe word of yet another funeral of an old pal from back in his day.
AL Peetie
WE HEARD HE JUST PASSED.
OLD PALS
Whatever the reason, it was perfect timing for me.
HEY!
NEW INFORMATION PLUS...
OLD ALBUM FALLING APART,
EQUALS...
ONE NICE BIG NEW SCRAPBOOK
I needed this project
Dad's Army Story
Sweet!
Like a rocket launcher to propell me out of my loneliness.
NO MONEY FOR NEW SUPPLIES? NO PROBLEM— INK IS CHEAP.
THIS'LL LOOK AWESOME
I CAN USE THIS OLD SKETCHBOOK PAPER AND CUT IT LENGTH-WISE SO THERE'LL BE ENOUGH.
WISH I WORKED IN AN OFFICE SO I COULD HELP MYSELF TO SOME OBSOLETE VINTAGE OFFICE SUPPLIES FOR THAT 40's LOOK.
SCRAPBOOKING SKILLS. THANK YOU SISTER BERNADETTE, SIXTH GRADE.

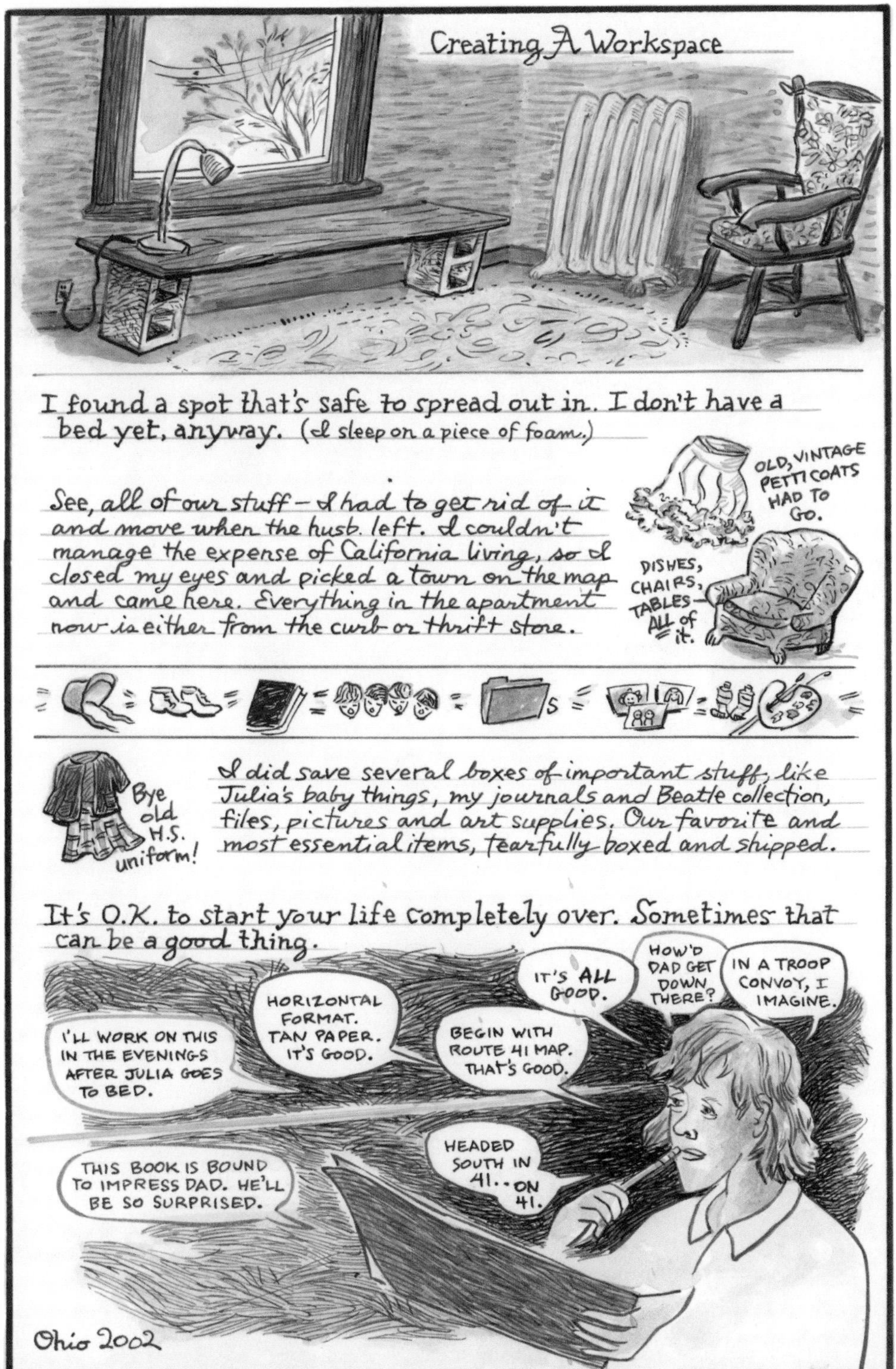
Creating A Workspace
I found a spot that's safe to spread out in. I don't have a bed yet, anyway. (I sleep on a piece of foam.)
See, all of our stuff – I had to get rid of it and move when the husb. left. I couldn't manage the expense of California living, so I closed my eyes and picked a town on the map and came here. Everything in the apartment now is either from the curb or thrift store.
OLD, VINTAGE PETTICOATS HAD TO GO.
DISHES, CHAIRS, TABLES – ALL of it.
Bye old H.S. uniform!
I did save several boxes of important stuff, like Julia's baby things, my journals and Beatle collection, files, pictures and art supplies. Our favorite and most essential items, tearfully boxed and shipped.
It's O.K. to start your life completely over. Sometimes that can be a good thing.
I'LL WORK ON THIS IN THE EVENINGS AFTER JULIA GOES TO BED.
HORIZONTAL FORMAT. TAN PAPER. IT'S GOOD.
BEGIN WITH ROUTE 41 MAP. THAT'S GOOD.
IT'S ALL GOOD.
HOW'D DAD GET DOWN THERE?
IN A TROOP CONVOY, I IMAGINE.
THIS BOOK IS BOUND TO IMPRESS DAD. HE'LL BE SO SURPRISED.
HEADED SOUTH IN 41.. ON 41.
Ohio 2002

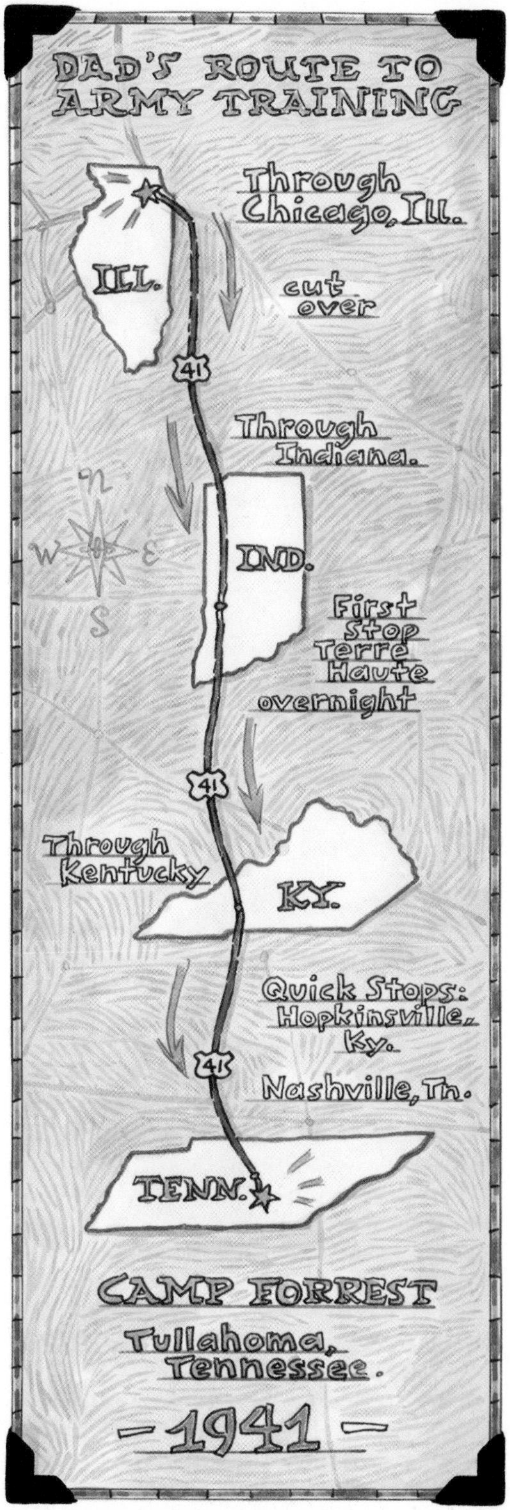
DAD'S ROUTE TO ARMY TRAINING
Through Chicago, Ill.
ILL.
cut over
41
Through Indiana.
N
W
E
S
IND.
First Stop Terre Haute overnight
41
Through Kentucky
KY.
Quick Stops: Hopkinsville, Ky.
41
Nashville, Tn.
TENN.
CAMP FORREST
Tullahoma, Tennessee.
– 1941 –

DAD'S ARMY SCRAPBOOK
AND
TOUR OF DUTY HIGHLIGHTS

PART I

CAMP FORREST
&
POST ENGINEER SERVICE

MARCH 1941 — JUNE 1944

★

Dumb Luck!

In February 1941, Chuck decided to join the Illinois National Guard "because all my buddies from the neighborhood joined." Battery B, First Battalion, 122 Field Artillery, 33RD Division. A Chicago unit with the motto: Ready and Prepared. About a month later, the Division was put on ACTIVE status.

You're in the Army *now*, pal!

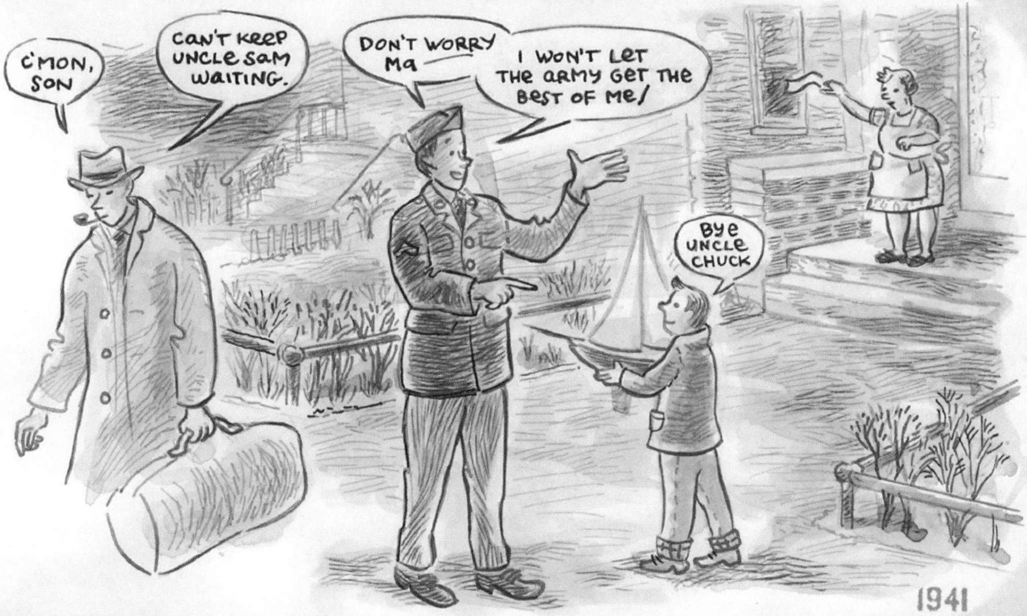
C'MON, SON
CAN'T KEEP UNCLE SAM WAITING.
DON'T WORRY MA
I WON'T LET THE ARMY GET THE BEST OF ME!
BYE UNCLE CHUCK
1941

2

So the Division, along with many other units, descended upon quaint Tullahoma, Tennessee for training at the newly being built Camp Forrest. Overnight, the little town is overrun by thousands and thousands of young men, arriving in big truck convoys, coming in by train.

Lots of opportunity for civilians, too. Especially attractive redheads with excellent secretarial skills.

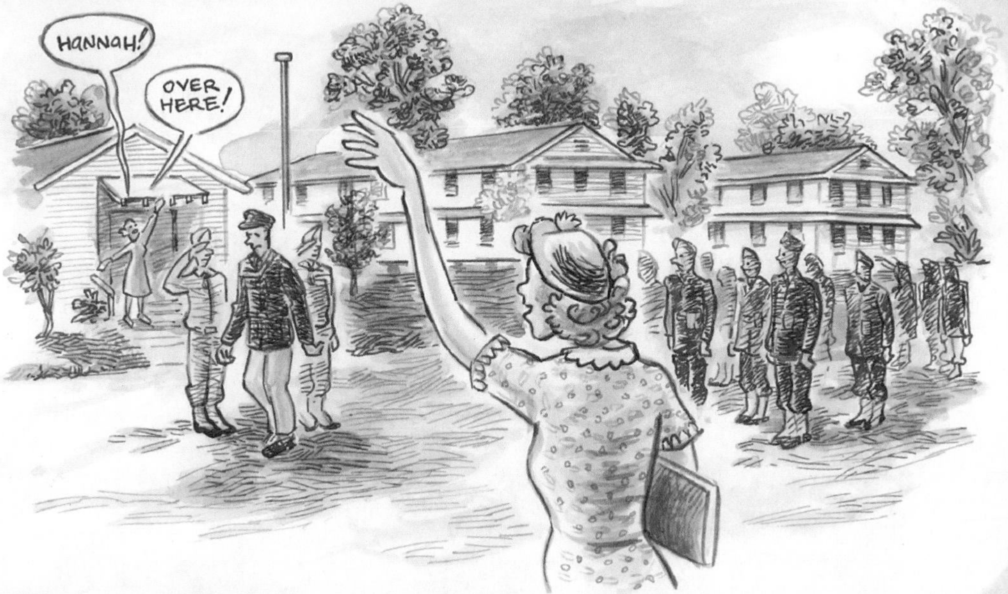
HANNAH!
OVER HERE!
1941

3

Camp Forrest was bursting at the seams! They couldn't build facilities fast enough, let alone maintain them. One night, so many pipes froze and then burst, the whole camp flooded. Chuck spoke up. He had worked as a plumber before enlisting, with his dad who was also a plumber. He knew what had to be done. Soon the Colonel had papers drawn up for his transfer out of artillery into the Post Engineers.

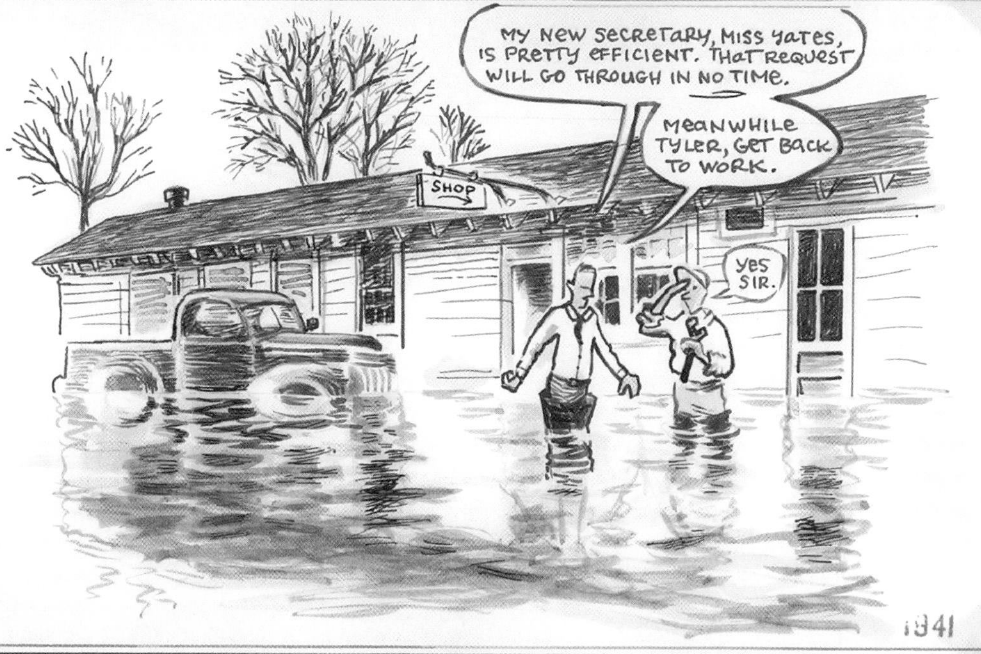
MY NEW SECRETARY, MISS YATES, IS PRETTY EFFICIENT. THAT REQUEST WILL GO THROUGH IN NO TIME.
MEANWHILE TYLER, GET BACK TO WORK.
YES SIR.
SHOP
1941

4

A critical component of military training is this male bonding thing, the 'band of brothers' and all that. Strong group identity insures better outcomes on the battlefield.

'Horseshit' thought Chuck. He was so glad when that transfer went through. It meant no more reveille, nicer sleeping quarters, a civilian boss. He could have his <u>car</u>. He had autonomy, like back at home.

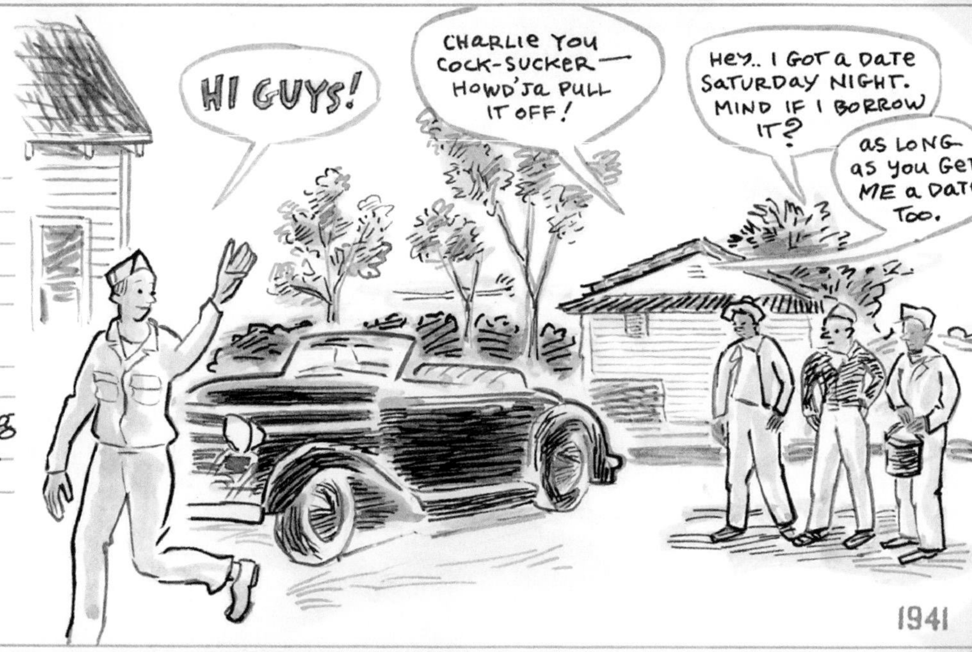
HI GUYS!
CHARLIE YOU COCK-SUCKER — HOWD'JA PULL IT OFF!
HEY.. I GOT A DATE SATURDAY NIGHT. MIND IF I BORROW IT?
AS LONG AS YOU GET ME A DATE TOO.
1941

5

But not before basic training and a trip with the 2ND Army down to Louisiana for maneuvers - aka dress rehearsal for war. The guys had to lug around Howitzers and learn how to shoot them, too, while living in bivouac conditions.

"One guy, a coral snake bit him on the ankle and SNAP, just like that he was dead. That's why I never slept in a tent while I was in the Army. I slept on gun turrets."

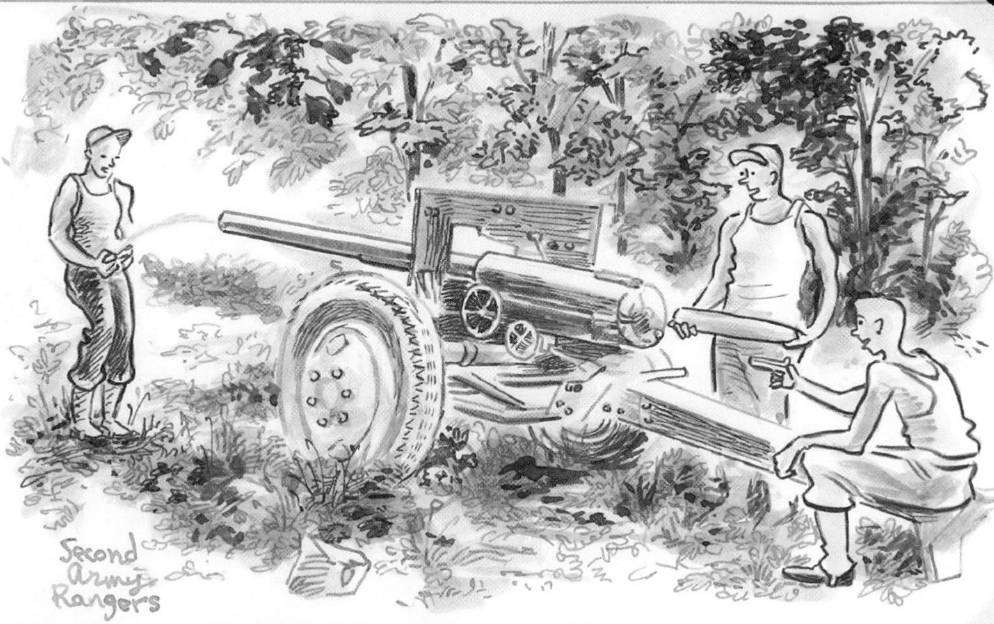
Second Army Rangers

6

"On the way back from maneuvers, while crossing the Mississippi, I tried to take a picture of a paddle wheeler. My foot got hung up, and I was hanging out of the truck, just missing the girders and cross pieces by inches. Turned my ankle pretty bad. They took me to the Marine Hospital in Memphis. Nice nurse from Alton, Ill. Not enough eats there, so she brought me rationed fruit in her blouse each day."

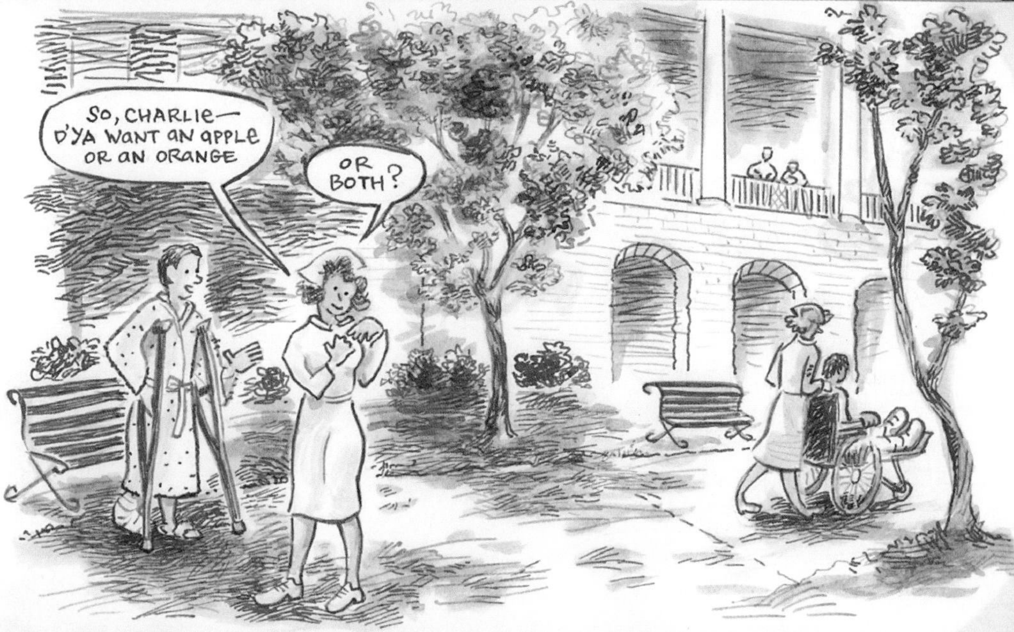
SO, CHARLIE— D'YA WANT AN APPLE OR AN ORANGE
OR BOTH?

7

"I don't even care that much about paddlewheelers but I hated being on crutches, so as soon as I could, I climbed up a smokestack, cast and all, so I could see better to snap a picture. Next thing I know, there's a bunch of nurses hollerin' up at me 'Dont jump! There's too much to live for!' Ha ha, those crazy broads thought I was tryin' to commit suicide.

"Wasn't long till they got rid of me."

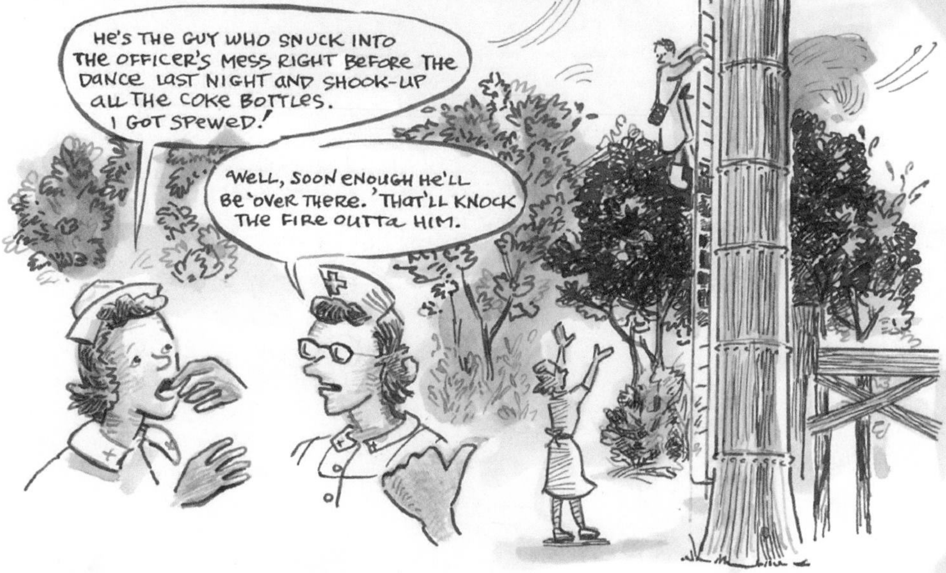
HE'S THE GUY WHO SNUCK INTO THE OFFICER'S MESS RIGHT BEFORE THE DANCE LAST NIGHT AND SHOOK-UP ALL THE COKE BOTTLES. I GOT SPEWED!
WELL, SOON ENOUGH HE'LL BE 'OVER THERE.' THAT'LL KNOCK THE FIRE OUTTA HIM.

8

"Every now and then, we'd go to Chattanooga dancin.' A rough bunch of characters we were. We decided to beat up the dress blues with the gold buttons because the girls went for them. (Marines).

"Same thing when we saw all those paratroopers with their nice boots. We had a little confrontation. At reveille, we had those boots on. Boy we got hell for that!"

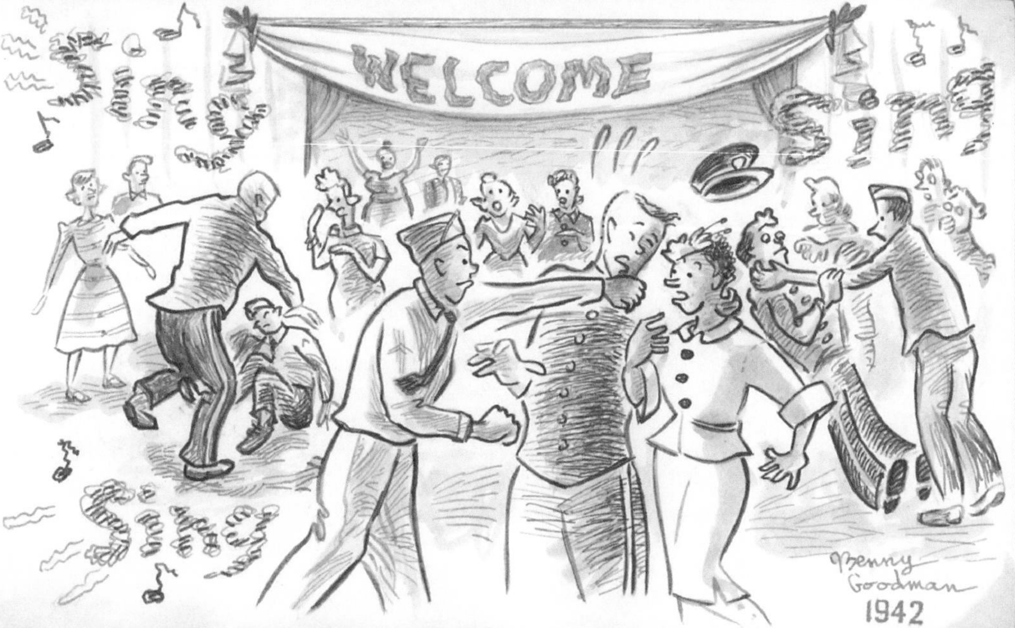
WELCOME
Benny Goodman
1942

9

"Yeah, I banged myself up pretty good in the Army. I skidded bare chested down a tree while trimming wires. My spurs gummed up and I had nothing to grip with. Then that steam burn on my hand from the Chapel boiler. Some son-of-a-bitch didn't read the sign I posted and made a fire anyway.

"I waded knee-deep through gas to shut off a leaky valve and got skin burns. Also, I twisted my knee. Lucky, or I would have been hangin' from a tree in Normandy."

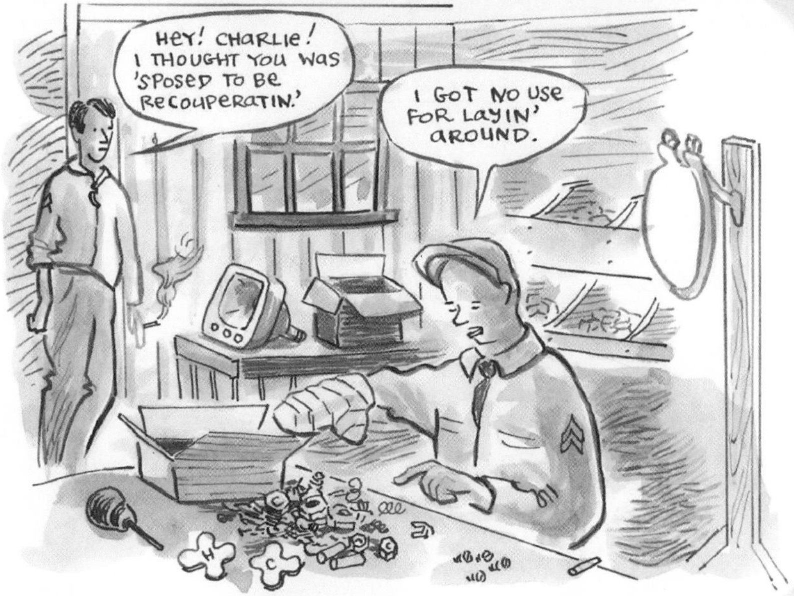
HEY! CHARLIE! I THOUGHT YOU WAS 'SPOSED TO BE RECOUPERATIN.'
I GOT NO USE FOR LAYIN' AROUND.

10

Hannah, in the meantime moved in with an established family in town. Rented a room there with her saucy friend Alice, who was also her boss. With such a desperate need for clerical personnel, Alice had Hannah call in all of her old pals from the McKenzie Business School in Chattanooga.

Hannah became the top dog when Alice resigned to get married. Such a dreadful outcome. The guy was killed at Anzio. She cried and cried. It broke her spirit.

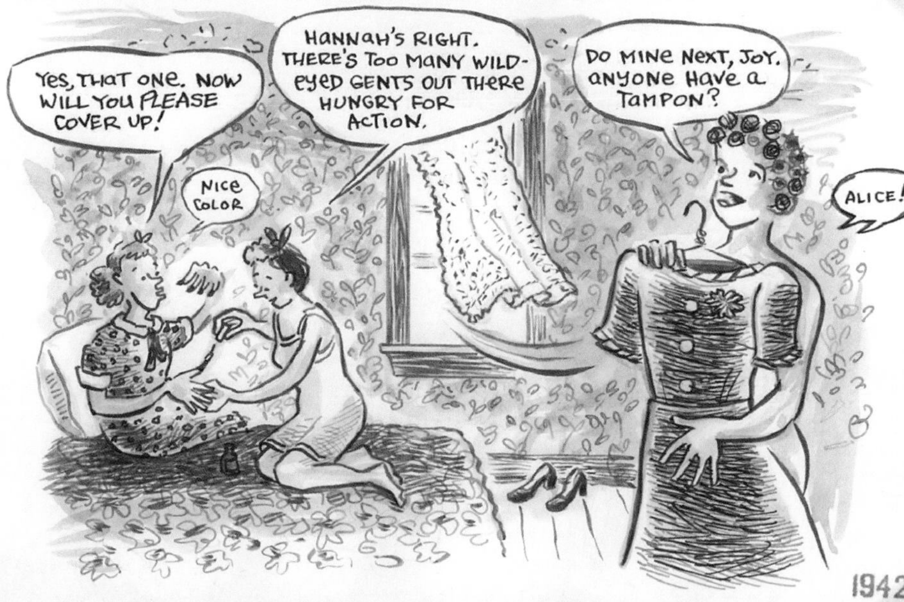
YES, THAT ONE. NOW WILL YOU PLEASE COVER UP!
NICE COLOR
HANNAH'S RIGHT. THERE'S TOO MANY WILD-EYED GENTS OUT THERE HUNGRY FOR ACTION.
DO MINE NEXT, JOY. ANYONE HAVE A TAMPON?
ALICE!

1942

11

Come and go, life in wartime. People come into your life and can be there maybe only for a minute and then be gone in an instant. It can have a wildly big impact. With so much at stake and everything so tenuous, relationships intensified. Everything: urgent.

There's a grand scale operation, and then there's this tenderness target for that expert marksman, Cupid.

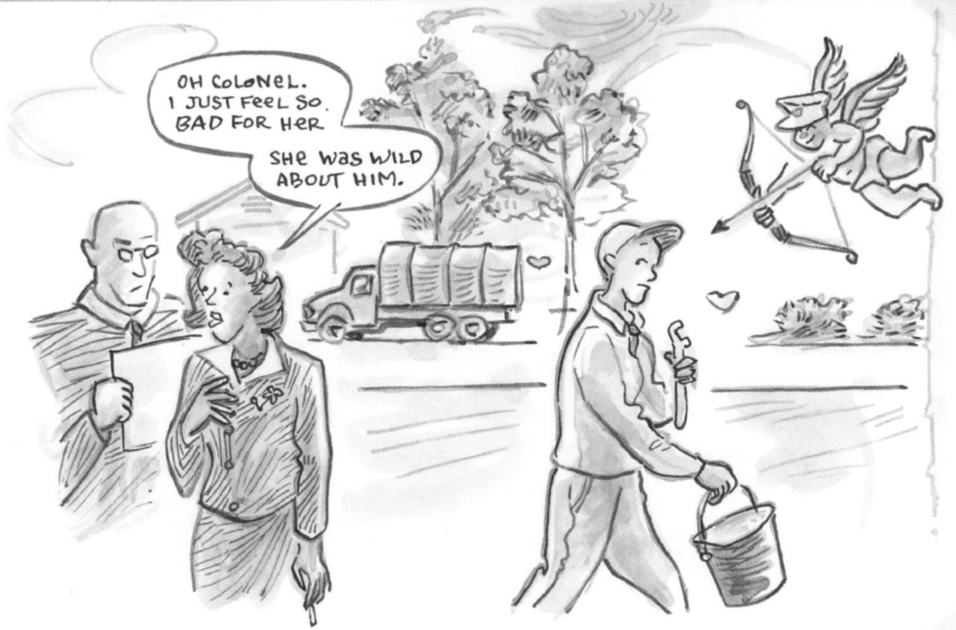
OH COLONEL. I JUST FEEL SO BAD FOR HER
SHE WAS WILD ABOUT HIM.

12

Chuck Tyler, dude, sharp dresser, clown.
Hannah Yates, clothes horse, wit, knockout.

She, using her paychecks to buy the latest in everything, suits, purses, shoes, ball gowns, furs... Putting the feed-sack calicos of childhood poverty behind her.

He, beneficiary of a comfortable middle class life, earned by the tradesmen before him. Great role models—clean, snappy, nothing but the humble best.

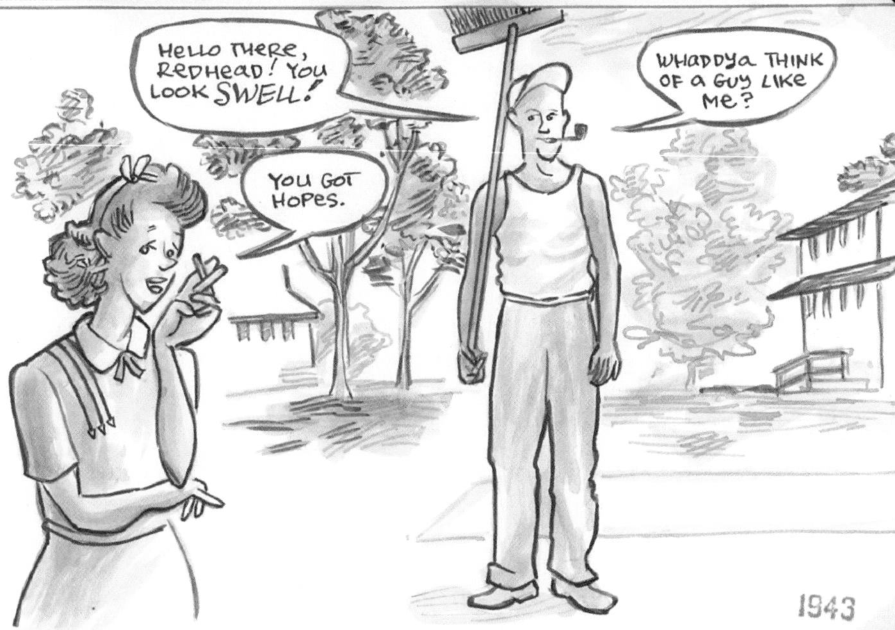
HELLO THERE, REDHEAD! YOU LOOK SWELL!
YOU GOT HOPES.
WHADDYA THINK OF A GUY LIKE ME?
1943

13

"One day my boss Jack said, 'Go get me a typewriter.' I guess he knew I had my eye on a certain redhead from over in personnel. I'd seen her around and at U.S.O. dances. The best lookin' one of the bunch. So, I walked in and took the typewriter while she was typing a letter! She was not too happy with me."

Flying fingers, flawless, furious... Miss Yates was the next target.

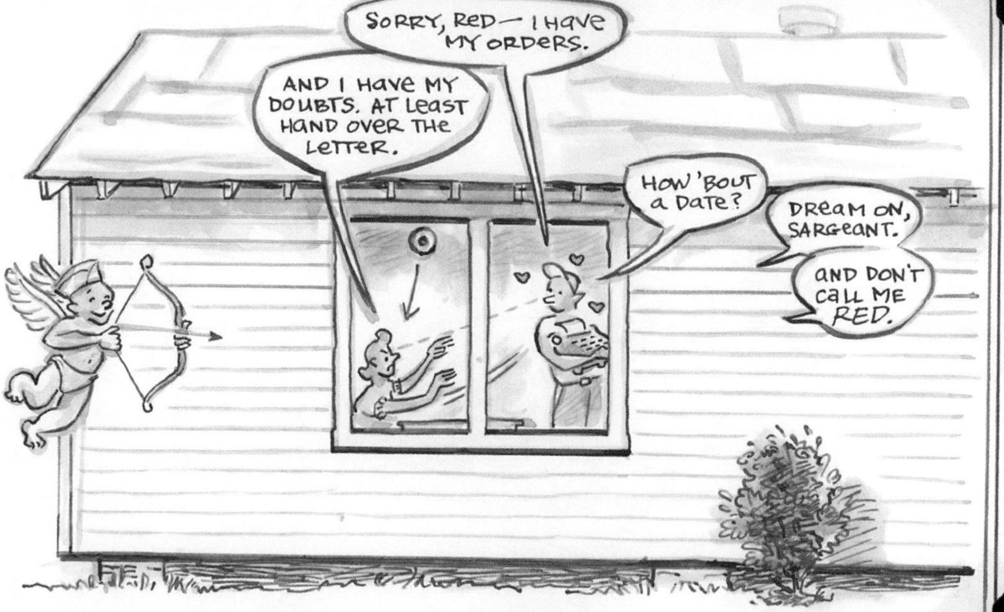
SORRY, RED— I HAVE MY ORDERS.
AND I HAVE MY DOUBTS. AT LEAST HAND OVER THE LETTER.
HOW 'BOUT A DATE?
DREAM ON, SARGEANT.
AND DON'T CALL ME RED.

14

Nonpariel, ditto.
Back in Chicago, he dated a different girl every night of the week. "..but this Red, she... wow. She..." (starts tearing up.)

She had been dating this lieutenant. Maybe things were getting serious. Walking away to his car one night, she noticed something about him that just seemed wrong — unlike that Chuck, who really had something to him. Eyes ready to see.

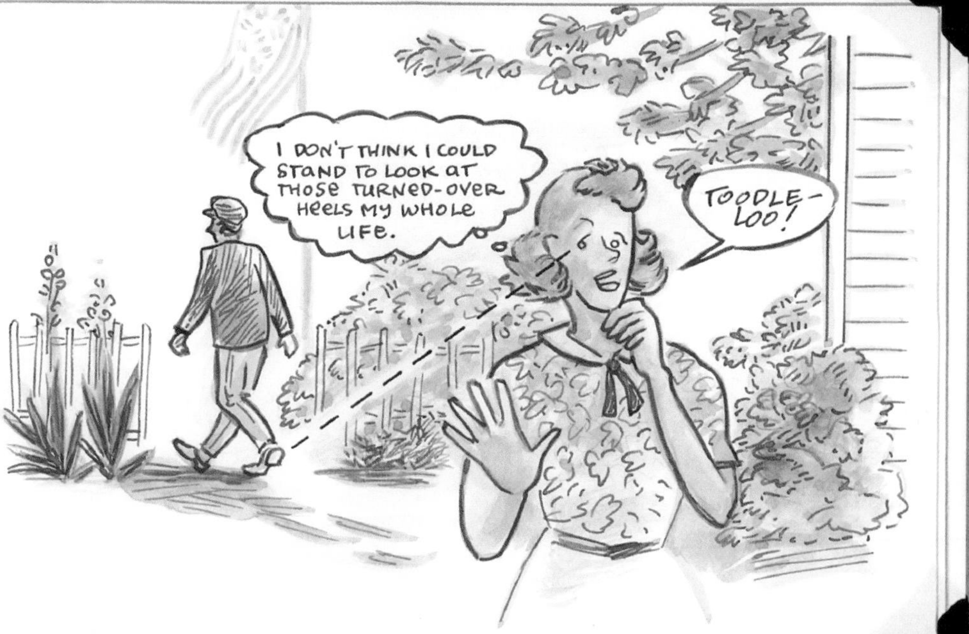
I DON'T THINK I COULD STAND TO LOOK AT THOSE TURNED-OVER HEELS MY WHOLE LIFE.
TOODLE-LOO!

15

"I knew the guys from the motor pool. They worked on the car and kept it in tip-top shape so we could all use it. M.P.'s and all that gang. We were an elite class of hell-raisers. We'd siphon off gas from the tank units, claiming it was for maintenance, but it was for the car. Quart here, gallon there. But I would need a whole lot more to get home to Chicago. Wouldn't you know who was in charge of ration tickets? This Miss Yates."

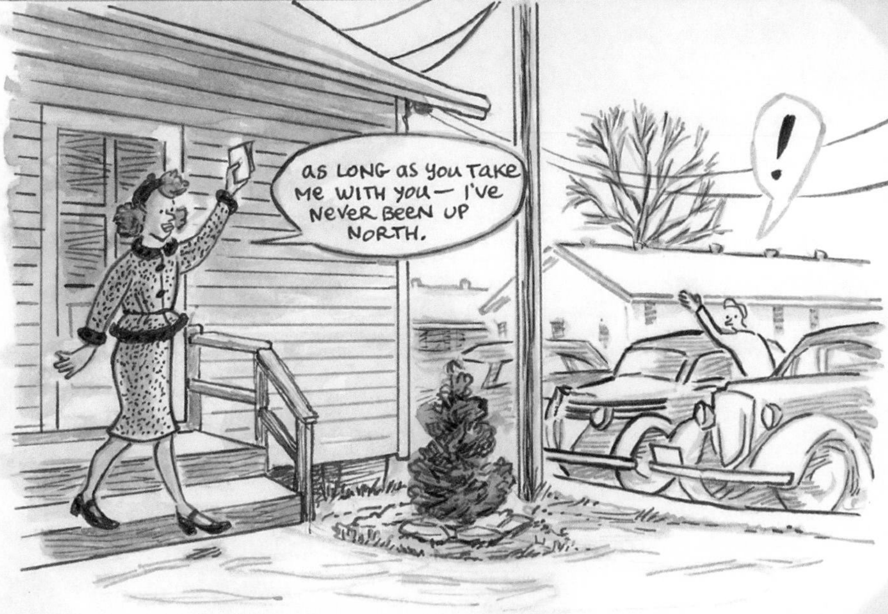
AS LONG AS YOU TAKE ME WITH YOU— I'VE NEVER BEEN UP NORTH.
!

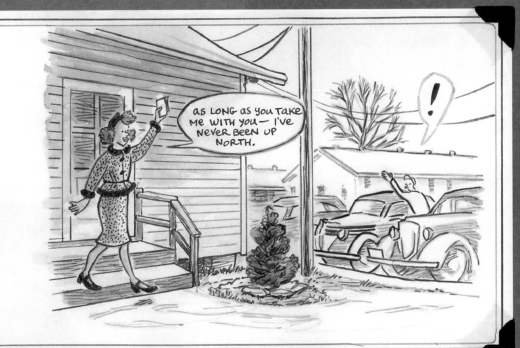

16

"We took off up Highway 41 with all these jerry cans in the back. Every so often, I'd pull onto a farm road to fuel-up. I'd say to Red, 'keep a lookout.' 'For what?!' she'd say, 'farmers? Rabbits?' 'You never know,' I said.

Before even going to the house, it was an evening of enchantment at Chicago's Aragon Ballroom (known for elegance and its springs, cork and felt-backed dance floor.) 'Magic' struck while the orchestra played their favorite song.

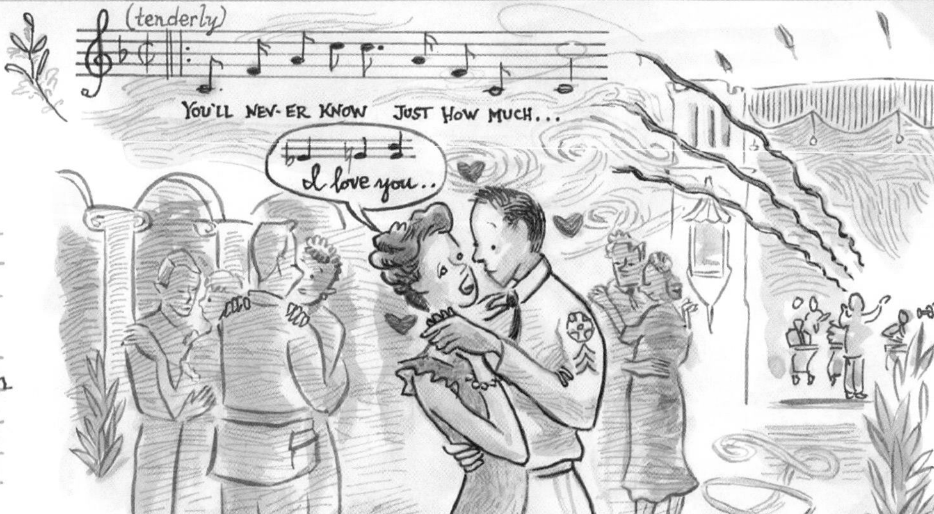
(tenderly)
YOU'LL NEV-ER KNOW JUST HOW MUCH...
I love you..
1943

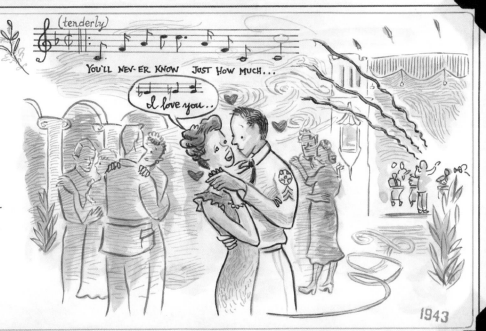

17

"We got in late and the folks had already gone to bed. Ma had fixed up the guest room for Red and I went up to my old room.

"Red froze up in Chicago — not used to it. Even in her fur coat, the one she bought from Burshays in Chattanooga. So she figured 'I'll just sit on the sofa here until I warm up a bit.' Well, lo and behold, she fell asleep. Ma found her there the next morning and had a fit. First impressions, you know, they last."

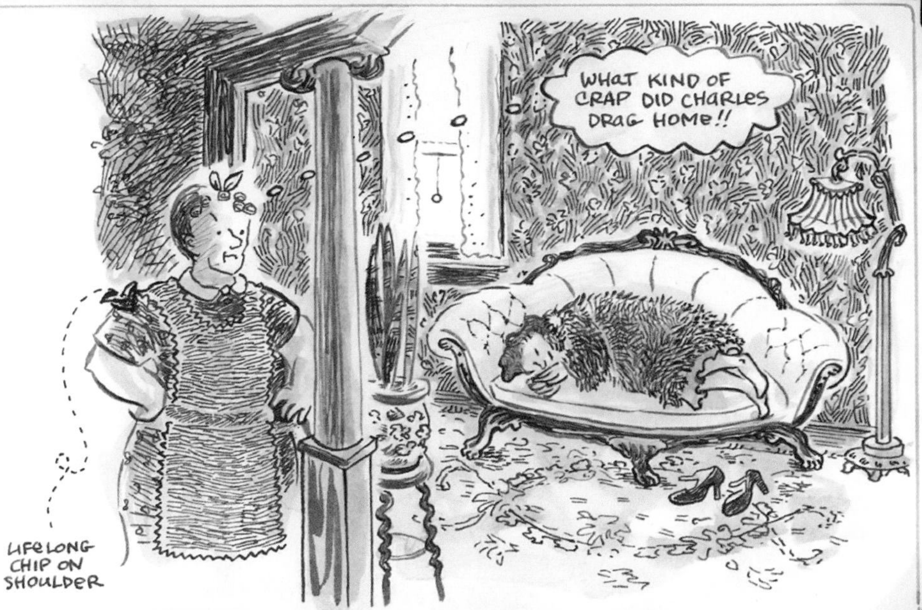
WHAT KIND OF CRAP DID CHARLES DRAG HOME!!
LIFELONG CHIP ON SHOULDER

18

"When we got back to Tennessee, I knew it was time to propose. So I went to see a jeweler in Nashville. He handed me the ring and a box of matches. 'What's this for,' I says. 'She'll want to see it in the dark.'

"Since it looked like I'd be headed overseas, Ma insisted we marry up there at St. Andrews on Thanksgiving. No such thing as going away on a honeymoon during a war, so we 'maneuvered' over to the Edgewater Beach Hotel on Lake Michigan for a few days."

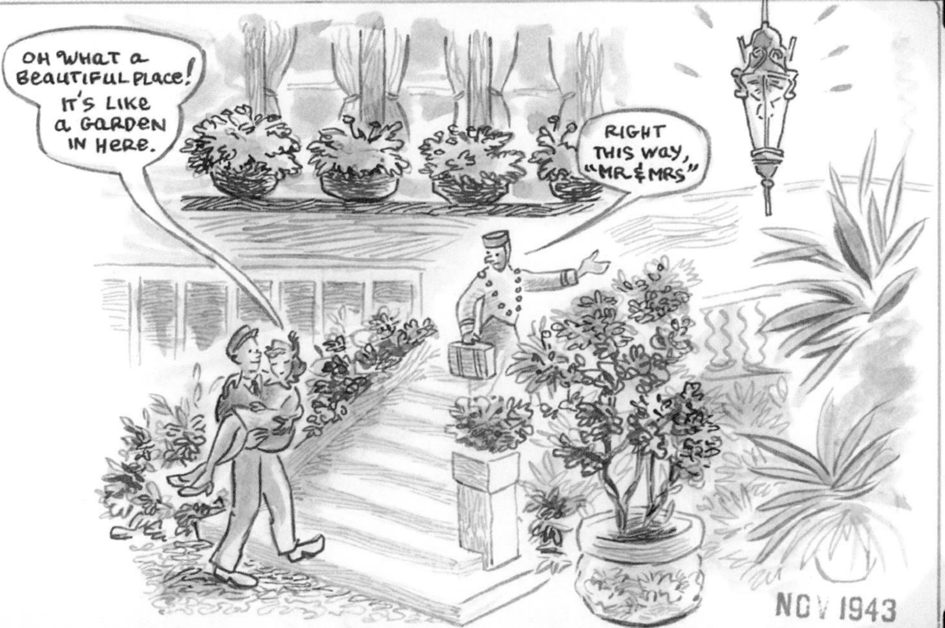
OH WHAT A BEAUTIFUL PLACE! IT'S LIKE A GARDEN IN HERE.
RIGHT THIS WAY, "MR. & MRS"
NOV 1943

19

First meal: The bride decides on a romantic chicken-'n'-rice dinner – with no cooking experience. Bride dumps an entire bag of rice into a pot with a little water, and then sets the chicken into a 550° oven. Before long, the rice is boiling over, so she gets another pot, and another, and a big bowl and so on. Meanwhile, the groom decides to "toast-up" the place by firing-up the old stove there in the front, not knowing it has flue problems. Soon, their cute little cottage is full of smoke with pots and bowls of rice everywhere.

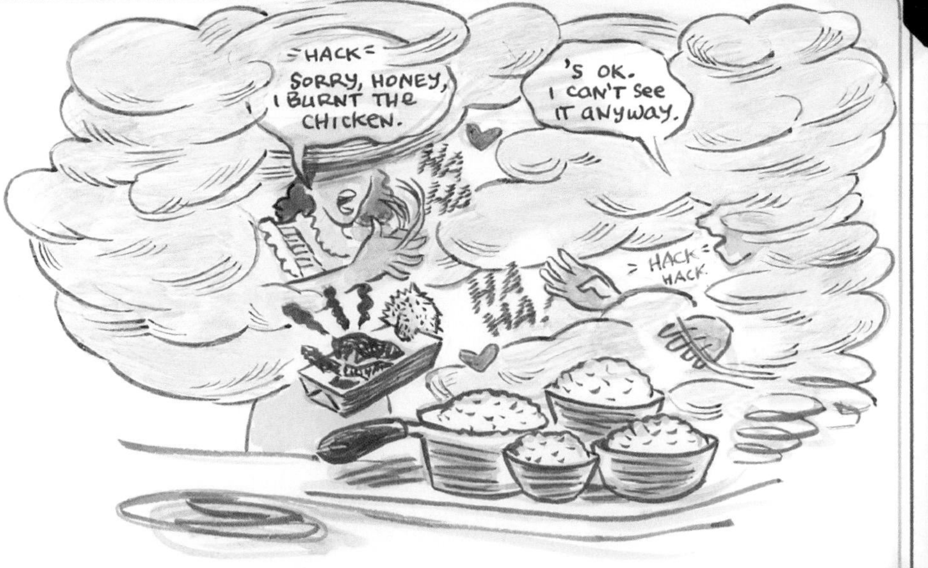

=HACK=
SORRY, HONEY, I BURNT THE CHICKEN.
'S OK. I CAN'T SEE IT ANYWAY.
HA HA
HA HA!
= HACK = HACK

20

"On to Ft. Bragg. They had me sorting scrap at a dump, I don't know why... I loved when Dad would come visit and we'd go fishin'. I guess what was to come was hard on my mind. And I hated to say bye to Red, but it was time to go.

"If I had stayed with the 122ND, I would have ended up in the Pacific. So many of those Chicago boys lost. If it wasn't for that transfer... Dumb luck, huh? I join the Army to be with my buddies, but instead I find the girl of my dreams."

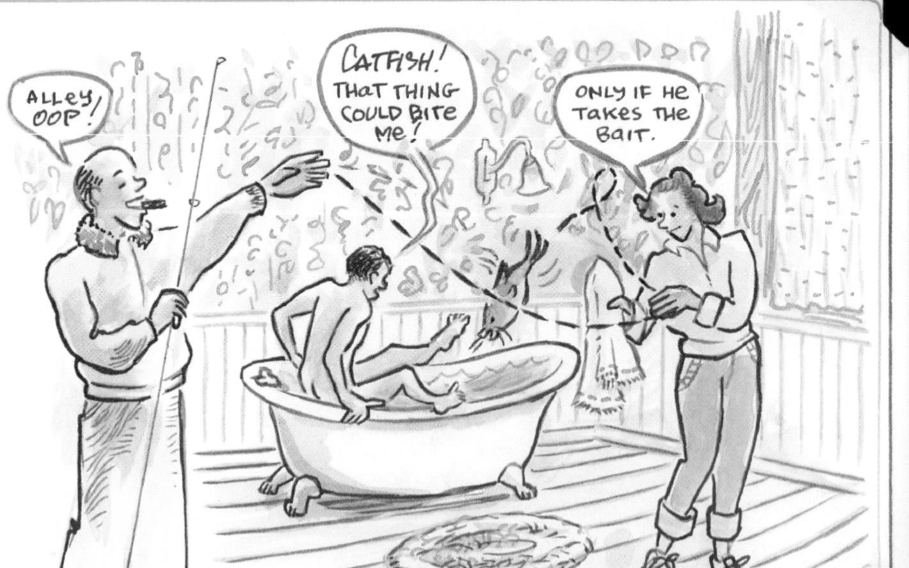

ALLEY OOP!
CATFISH! THAT THING COULD BITE ME!
ONLY IF HE TAKES THE BAIT.
MAR 1944

3.

REMARKABLE FOX

SEVERAL WEEKS LATER

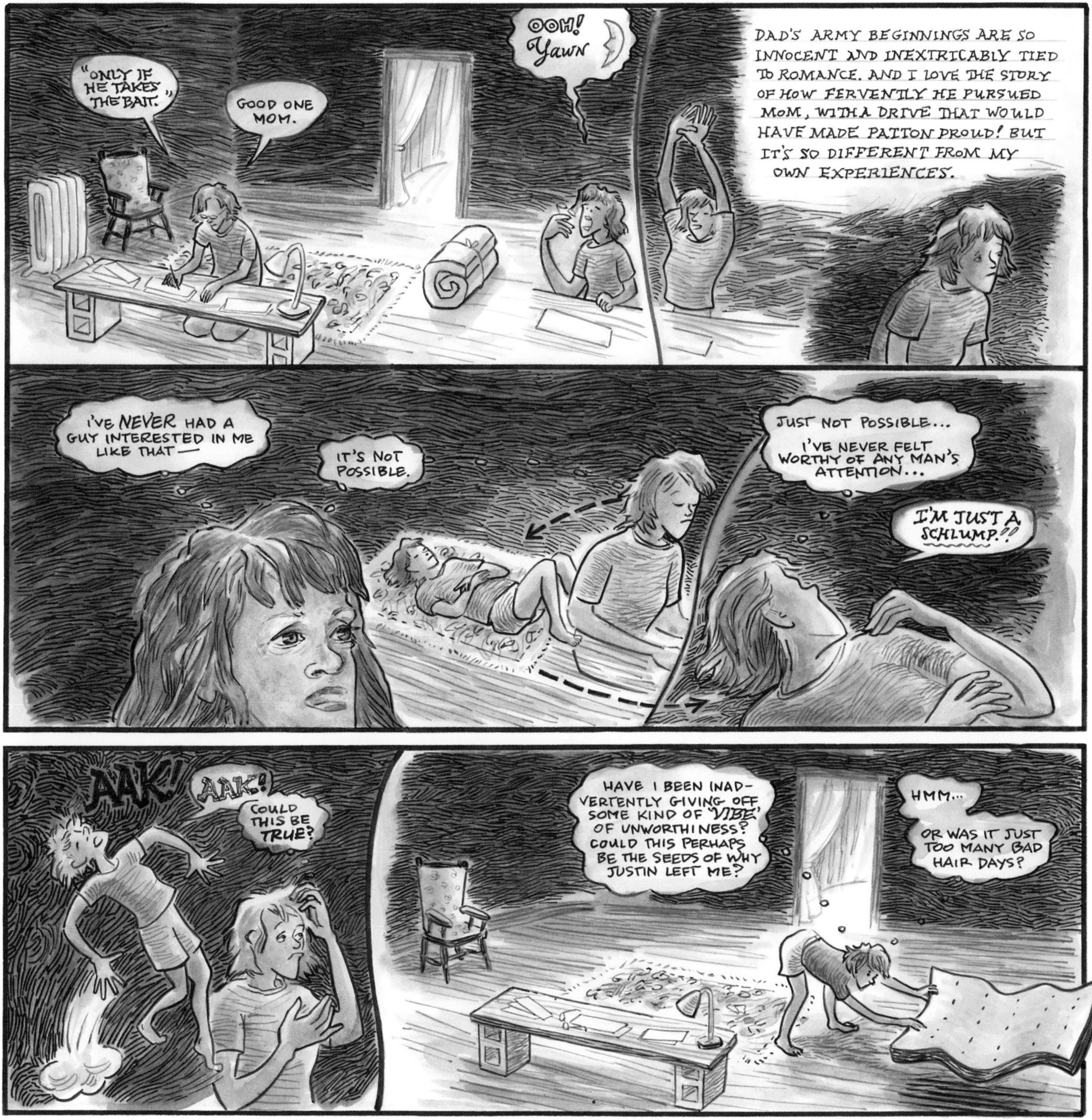
"ONLY IF HE TAKES THE BAIT."
GOOD ONE MOM.
OOH! Yawn
DAD'S ARMY BEGINNINGS ARE SO INNOCENT AND INEXTRICABLY TIED TO ROMANCE. AND I LOVE THE STORY OF HOW FERVENTLY HE PURSUED MOM, WITH A DRIVE THAT WOULD HAVE MADE PATTON PROUD! BUT IT'S SO DIFFERENT FROM MY OWN EXPERIENCES.
I'VE NEVER HAD A GUY INTERESTED IN ME LIKE THAT—
IT'S NOT POSSIBLE.
JUST NOT POSSIBLE...
I'VE NEVER FELT WORTHY OF ANY MAN'S ATTENTION...
I'M JUST A SCHLUMP!!
AAK!
AAK!
COULD THIS BE TRUE?
HAVE I BEEN INADVERTENTLY GIVING OFF SOME KIND OF 'VIBE' OF UNWORTHINESS? COULD THIS PERHAPS BE THE SEEDS OF WHY JUSTIN LEFT ME?
HMM...
OR WAS IT JUST TOO MANY BAD HAIR DAYS?

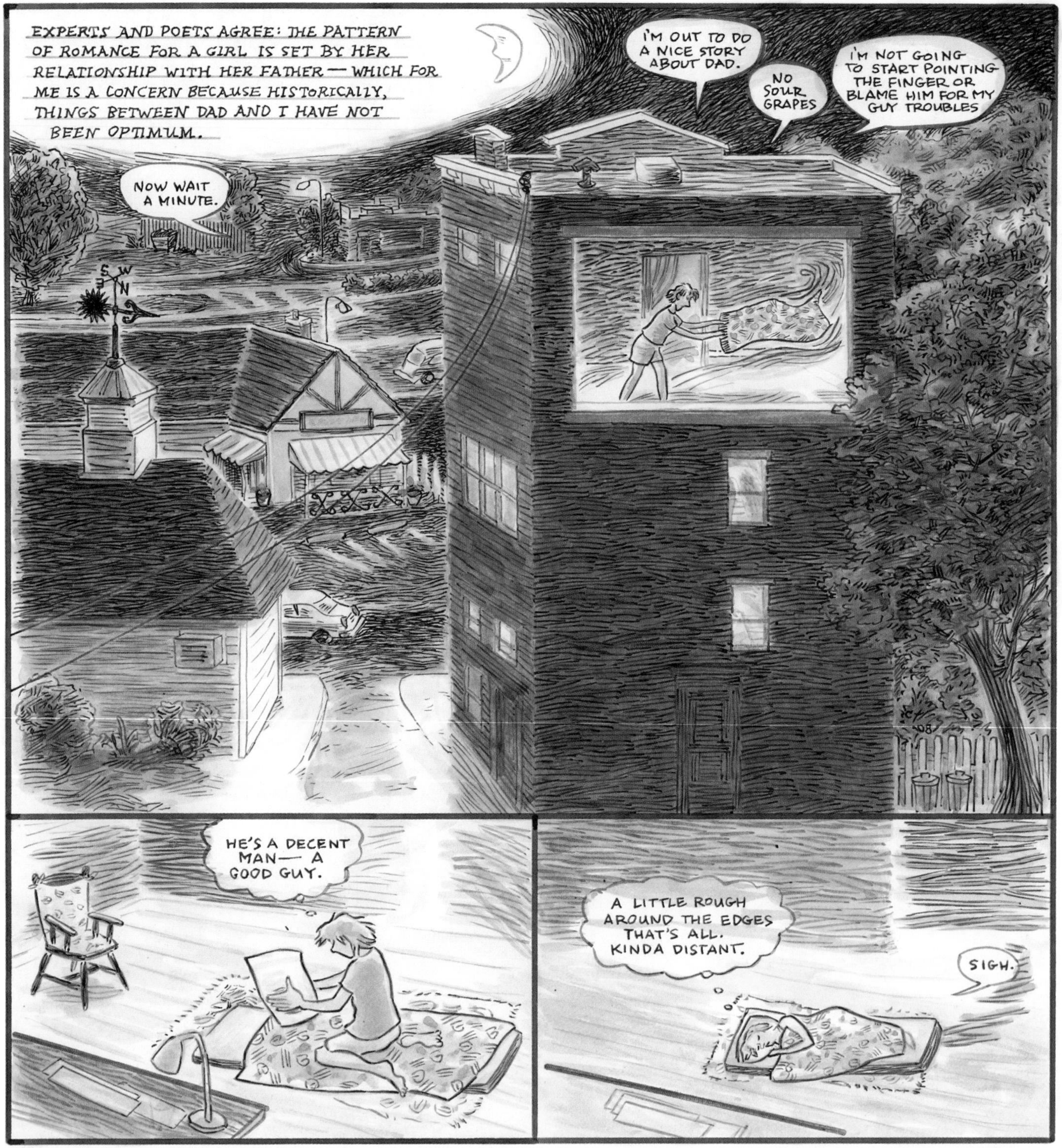
EXPERTS AND POETS AGREE: THE PATTERN OF ROMANCE FOR A GIRL IS SET BY HER RELATIONSHIP WITH HER FATHER— WHICH FOR ME IS A CONCERN BECAUSE HISTORICALLY, THINGS BETWEEN DAD AND I HAVE NOT BEEN OPTIMUM.
I'M OUT TO DO A NICE STORY ABOUT DAD.
NO SOUR GRAPES
I'M NOT GOING TO START POINTING THE FINGER OR BLAME HIM FOR MY GUY TROUBLES
NOW WAIT A MINUTE.
HE'S A DECENT MAN— A GOOD GUY.
A LITTLE ROUGH AROUND THE EDGES THAT'S ALL. KINDA DISTANT.
SIGH.

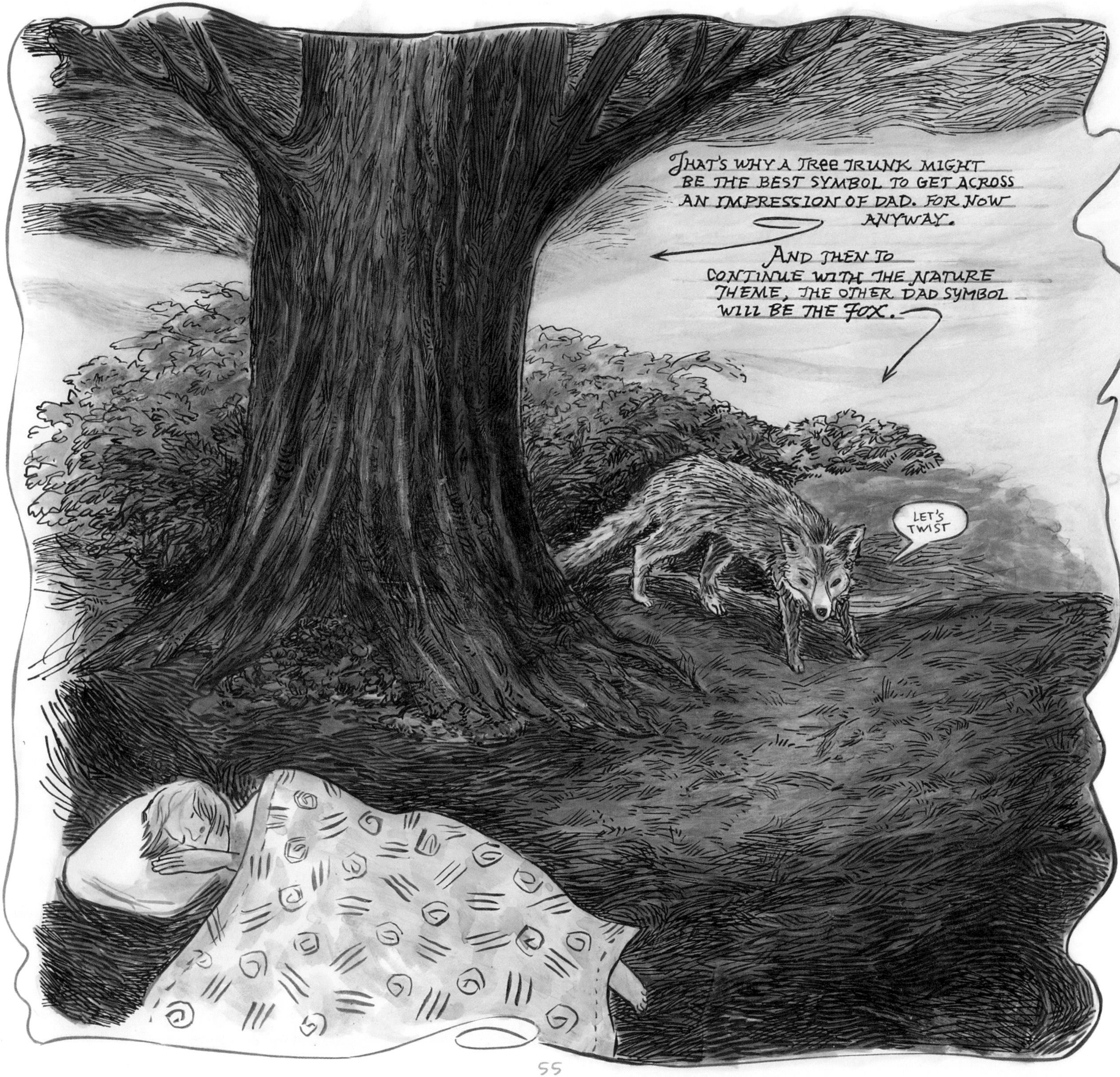
THAT'S WHY A TREE TRUNK MIGHT BE THE BEST SYMBOL TO GET ACROSS AN IMPRESSION OF DAD. FOR NOW ANYWAY.
AND THEN TO CONTINUE WITH THE NATURE THEME, THE OTHER DAD SYMBOL WILL BE THE FOX.
LET'S TWIST

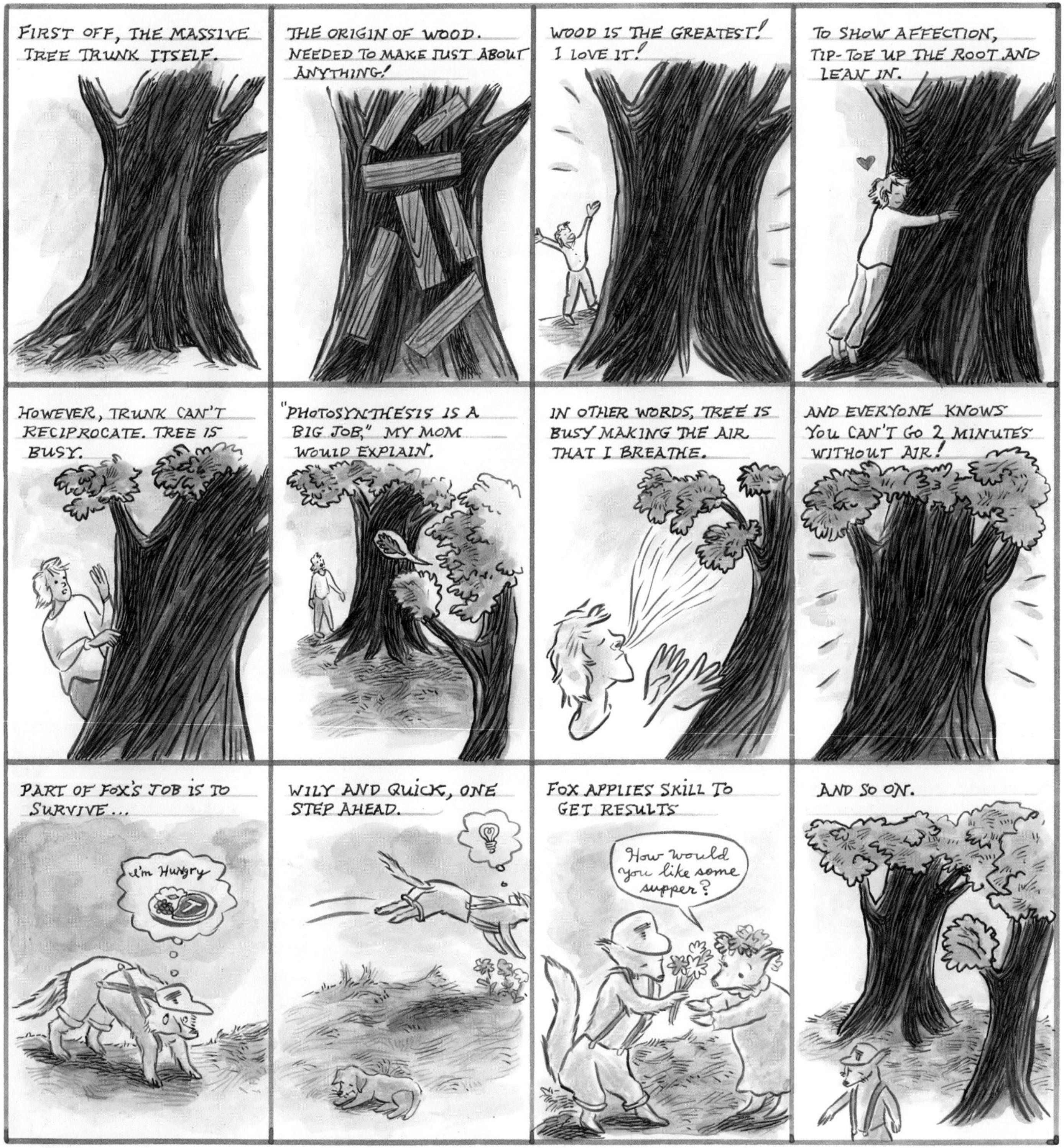
FIRST OFF, THE MASSIVE TREE TRUNK ITSELF.
THE ORIGIN OF WOOD. NEEDED TO MAKE JUST ABOUT ANYTHING!
WOOD IS THE GREATEST! I LOVE IT!
TO SHOW AFFECTION, TIP-TOE UP THE ROOT AND LEAN IN.
HOWEVER, TRUNK CAN'T RECIPROCATE. TREE IS BUSY.
"PHOTOSYNTHESIS IS A BIG JOB," MY MOM WOULD EXPLAIN.
IN OTHER WORDS, TREE IS BUSY MAKING THE AIR THAT I BREATHE.
AND EVERYONE KNOWS YOU CAN'T GO 2 MINUTES WITHOUT AIR!
PART OF FOX'S JOB IS TO SURVIVE...
I'm Hungry
WILY AND QUICK, ONE STEP AHEAD.
FOX APPLIES SKILL TO GET RESULTS
How would you like some supper?
AND SO ON.

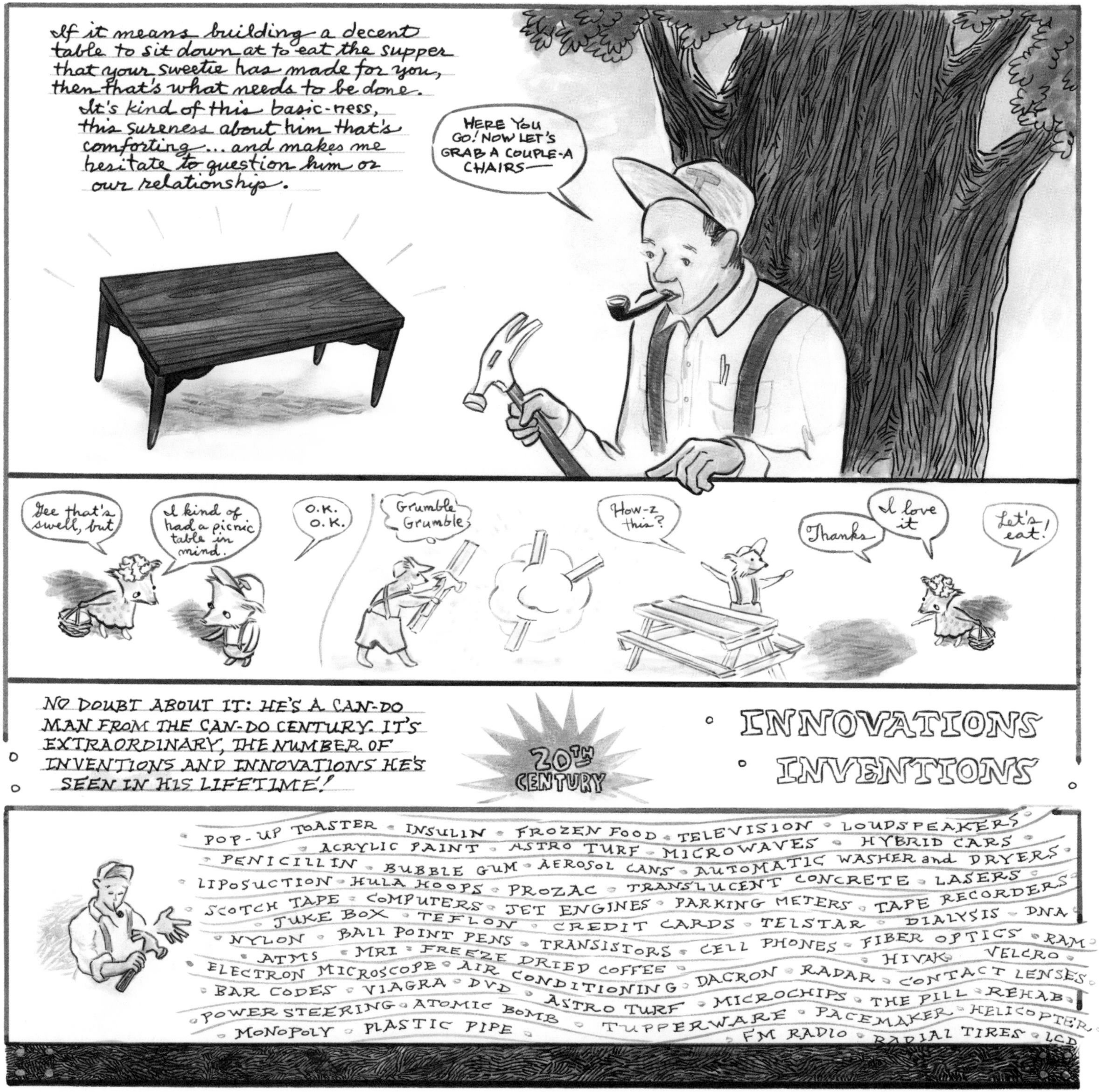
If it means building a decent table to sit down at to eat the supper that your sweetie has made for you, then that's what needs to be done.
It's kind of this basic-ness, this sureness about him that's comforting... and makes me hesitate to question him or our relationship.
HERE YOU GO! NOW LET'S GRAB A COUPLE-A CHAIRS—
Gee that's swell, but
I kind of had a picnic table in mind.
O.K. O.K.
Grumble Grumble
How-z this?
Thanks.
I love it
Let's eat!
NO DOUBT ABOUT IT: HE'S A CAN-DO MAN FROM THE CAN-DO CENTURY. IT'S EXTRAORDINARY, THE NUMBER OF INVENTIONS AND INNOVATIONS HE'S SEEN IN HIS LIFETIME!
20TH CENTURY
INNOVATIONS
INVENTIONS
POP-UP TOASTER • INSULIN • FROZEN FOOD • TELEVISION • LOUDSPEAKERS
ACRYLIC PAINT • ASTRO TURF • MICROWAVES • HYBRID CARS
PENICILLIN • BUBBLE GUM • AEROSOL CANS • AUTOMATIC WASHER and DRYERS
LIPOSUCTION • HULA HOOPS • PROZAC • TRANSLUCENT CONCRETE • LASERS
SCOTCH TAPE • COMPUTERS • JET ENGINES • PARKING METERS • TAPE RECORDERS
JUKE BOX • TEFLON • CREDIT CARDS • TELSTAR • DIALYSIS • DNA
NYLON • BALL POINT PENS • TRANSISTORS • CELL PHONES • FIBER OPTICS • RAM
ATMS • MRI • FREEZE DRIED COFFEE • HIVAK • VELCRO
ELECTRON MICROSCOPE • AIR CONDITIONING • DACRON • RADAR • CONTACT LENSES
BAR CODES • VIAGRA • DVD • ASTRO TURF • MICROCHIPS • THE PILL • REHAB
POWER STEERING • ATOMIC BOMB • TUPPERWARE • PACEMAKER • HELICOPTER
MONOPOLY • PLASTIC PIPE • FM RADIO • RADIAL TIRES • LCD

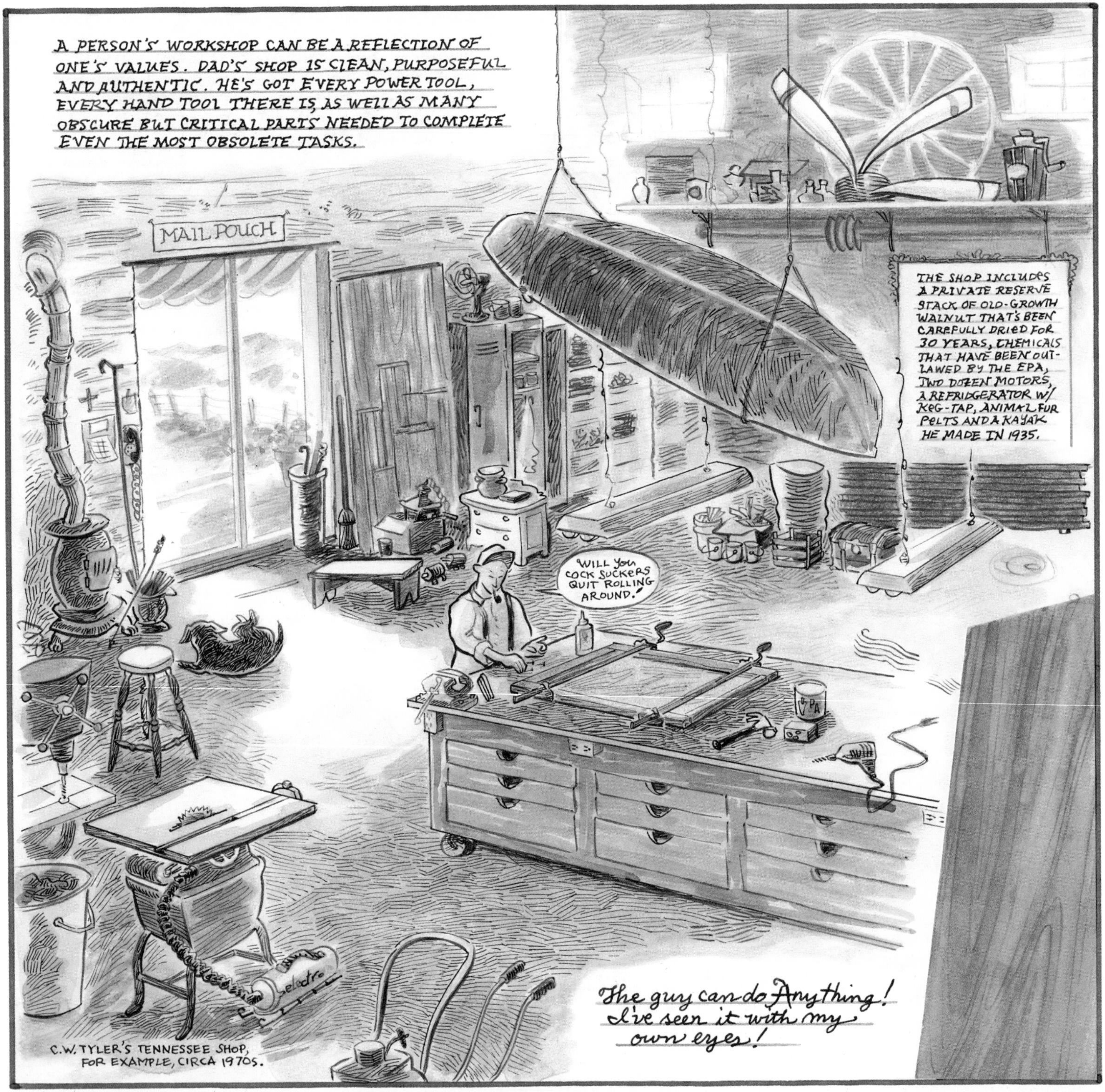
A PERSON'S WORKSHOP CAN BE A REFLECTION OF ONE'S VALUES. DAD'S SHOP IS CLEAN, PURPOSEFUL AND AUTHENTIC. HE'S GOT EVERY POWER TOOL, EVERY HAND TOOL THERE IS, AS WELL AS MANY OBSCURE BUT CRITICAL PARTS NEEDED TO COMPLETE EVEN THE MOST OBSOLETE TASKS.
MAIL POUCH
THE SHOP INCLUDES A PRIVATE RESERVE STACK OF OLD-GROWTH WALNUT THAT'S BEEN CAREFULLY DRIED FOR 30 YEARS, CHEMICALS THAT HAVE BEEN OUT-LAWED BY THE EPA, TWO DOZEN MOTORS, A REFRIDGERATOR W/ KEG-TAP, ANIMAL FUR PELTS AND A KAYAK HE MADE IN 1935.
WILL YOU COCK SUCKERS QUIT ROLLING AROUND!
EPA
The guy can do Anything! I've seen it with my own eyes!
C.W. TYLER'S TENNESSEE SHOP, FOR EXAMPLE, CIRCA 1970S.

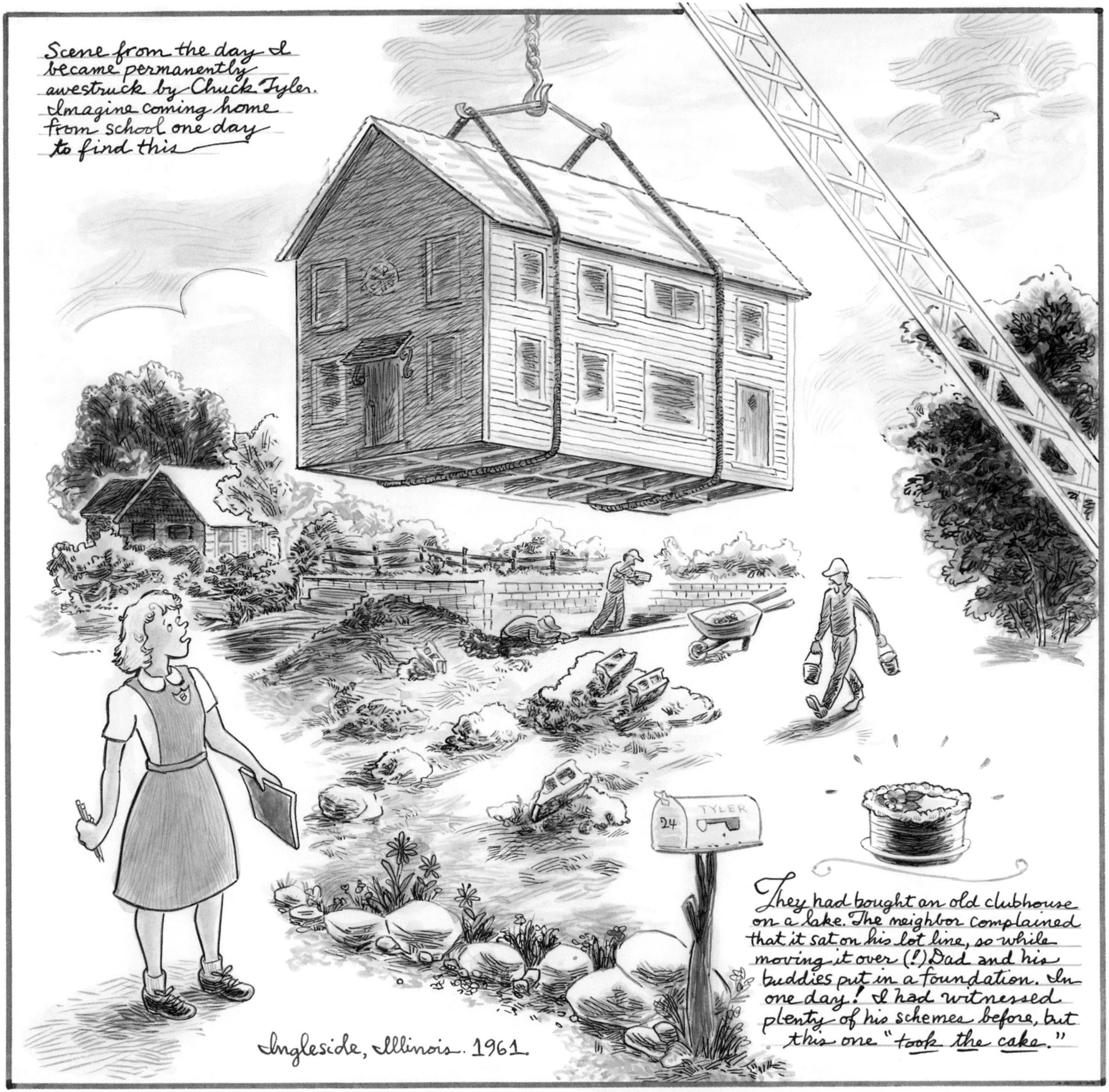
Scene from the day I became permanently awestruck by Chuck Tyler. Imagine coming home from school one day to find this
TYLER
24
They had bought an old clubhouse on a lake. The neighbor complained that it sat on his lot line, so while moving it over (!) Dad and his buddies put in a foundation. In one day! I had witnessed plenty of his schemes before, but this one "took the cake."
Ingleside, Illinois. 1961

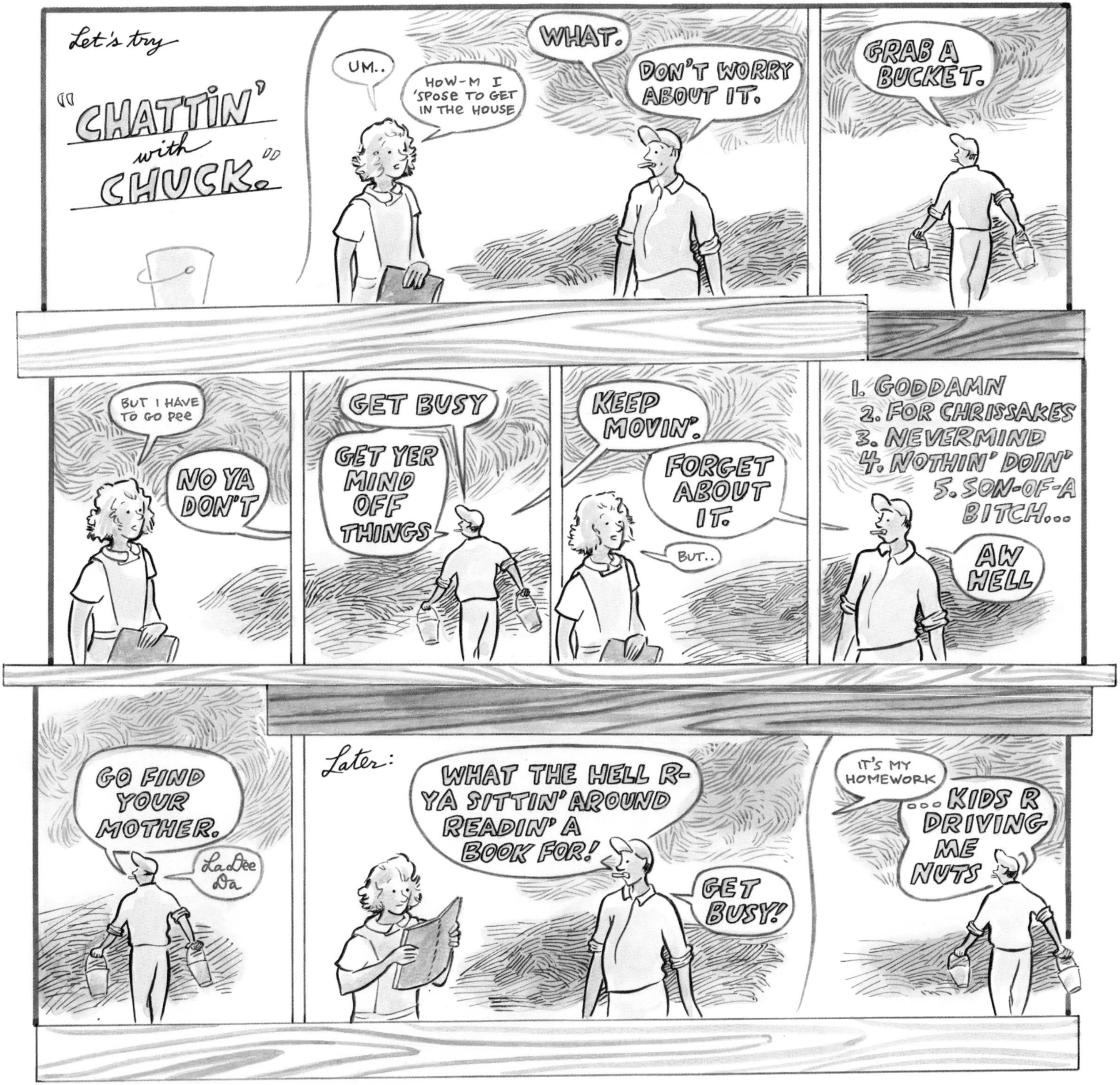
Let's try
"CHATTIN' with CHUCK."
UM..
HOW-M I 'SPOSE TO GET IN THE HOUSE
WHAT.
DON'T WORRY ABOUT IT.
GRAB A BUCKET.
BUT I HAVE TO GO PEE
NO YA DON'T
GET BUSY
GET YER MIND OFF THINGS
KEEP MOVIN'.
FORGET ABOUT IT.
BUT..
1. GODDAMN
2. FOR CHRISSAKES
3. NEVERMIND
4. NOTHIN' DOIN'
5. SON-OF-A BITCH...
AW HELL
GO FIND YOUR MOTHER.
LaDee Da
Later:
WHAT THE HELL R-YA SITTIN' AROUND READIN' A BOOK FOR!
GET BUSY!
IT'S MY HOMEWORK
...KIDS R DRIVING ME NUTS

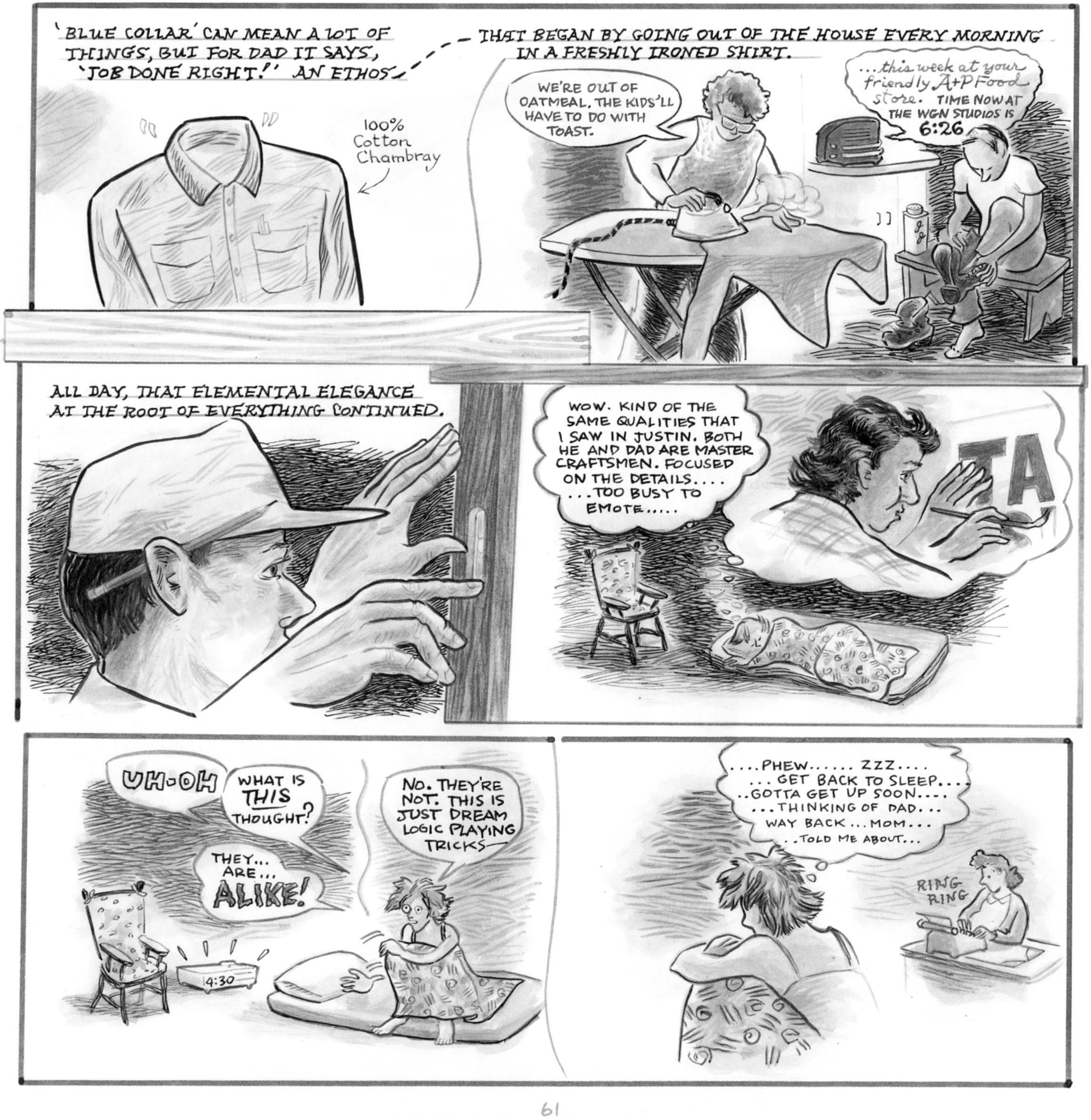
'BLUE COLLAR' CAN MEAN A LOT OF THINGS, BUT FOR DAD IT SAYS, 'JOB DONE RIGHT!' AN ETHOS
THAT BEGAN BY GOING OUT OF THE HOUSE EVERY MORNING IN A FRESHLY IRONED SHIRT.
100% Cotton Chambray
WE'RE OUT OF OATMEAL. THE KIDS'LL HAVE TO DO WITH TOAST.
...this week at your friendly A+P Food store. TIME NOW AT THE WGN STUDIOS IS 6:26
ALL DAY, THAT ELEMENTAL ELEGANCE AT THE ROOT OF EVERYTHING CONTINUED.
WOW. KIND OF THE SAME QUALITIES THAT I SAW IN JUSTIN. BOTH HE AND DAD ARE MASTER CRAFTSMEN. FOCUSED ON THE DETAILS.... ...TOO BUSY TO EMOTE.....
TA
UH-OH
WHAT IS THIS THOUGHT?
THEY... ARE... ALIKE!
NO. THEY'RE NOT. THIS IS JUST DREAM LOGIC PLAYING TRICKS—
4:30
....PHEW...... ZZZ.... ... GET BACK TO SLEEP... ..GOTTA GET UP SOON.... ...THINKING OF DAD... WAY BACK...MOM... ...TOLD ME ABOUT...
RING RING

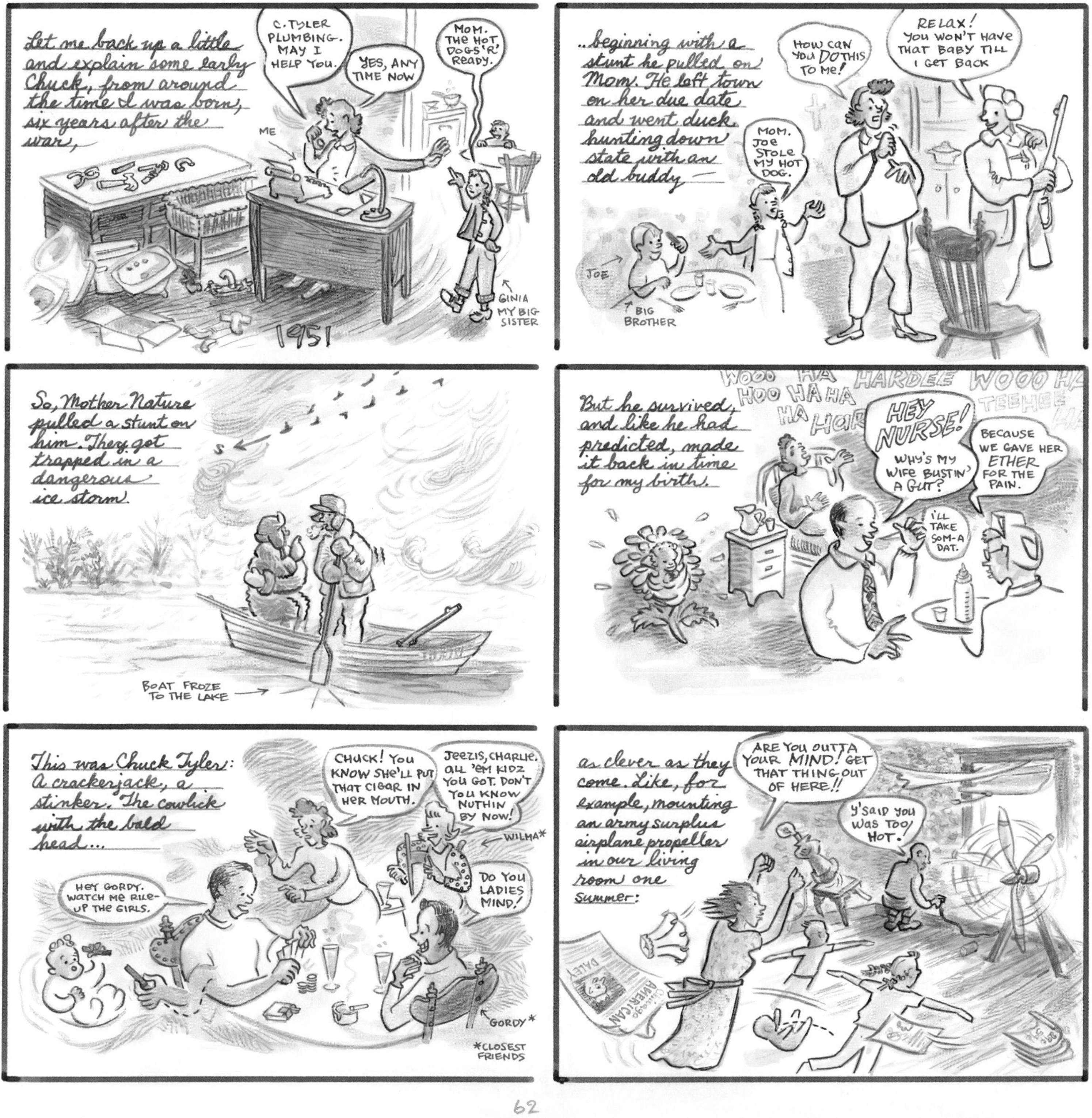
Let me back up a little and explain some early Chuck, from around the time I was born; six years after the war,
C. TYLER PLUMBING. MAY I HELP YOU.
YES, ANY TIME NOW
MOM. THE HOT DOGS'R' READY.
ME
GINIA MY BIG SISTER
1951
...beginning with a stunt he pulled on Mom. He left town on her due date and went duck hunting down state with an old buddy —
HOW CAN YOU DO THIS TO ME!
RELAX! YOU WON'T HAVE THAT BABY TILL I GET BACK
MOM. JOE STOLE MY HOT DOG.
JOE
BIG BROTHER
So, Mother Nature pulled a stunt on him. They got trapped in a dangerous ice storm.
BOAT FROZE TO THE LAKE
But he survived, and like he had predicted, made it back in time for my birth.
WOOO HA HOO HA HA HA HA HAR HARDEE WOOO HA TEEHEE
HEY NURSE! WHY'S MY WIFE BUSTIN' A GUT?
BECAUSE WE GAVE HER ETHER FOR THE PAIN.
I'LL TAKE SOM-A DAT.
This was Chuck Tyler: A crackerjack, a stinker. The cowlick with the bald head...
CHUCK! YOU KNOW SHE'LL PUT THAT CIGAR IN HER MOUTH.
JEEZIS, CHARLIE. ALL 'EM KIDZ YOU GOT. DON'T YOU KNOW NUTHIN BY NOW!
WILMA*
HEY GORDY. WATCH ME RILE-UP THE GIRLS.
DO YOU LADIES MIND!
GORDY*
*CLOSEST FRIENDS
as clever as they come. Like, for example, mounting an army surplus airplane propeller in our living room one summer:
ARE YOU OUTTA YOUR MIND! GET THAT THING OUT OF HERE!!
Y'SAID YOU WAS TOO HOT.
DAILY
CHICAGO AMERICAN

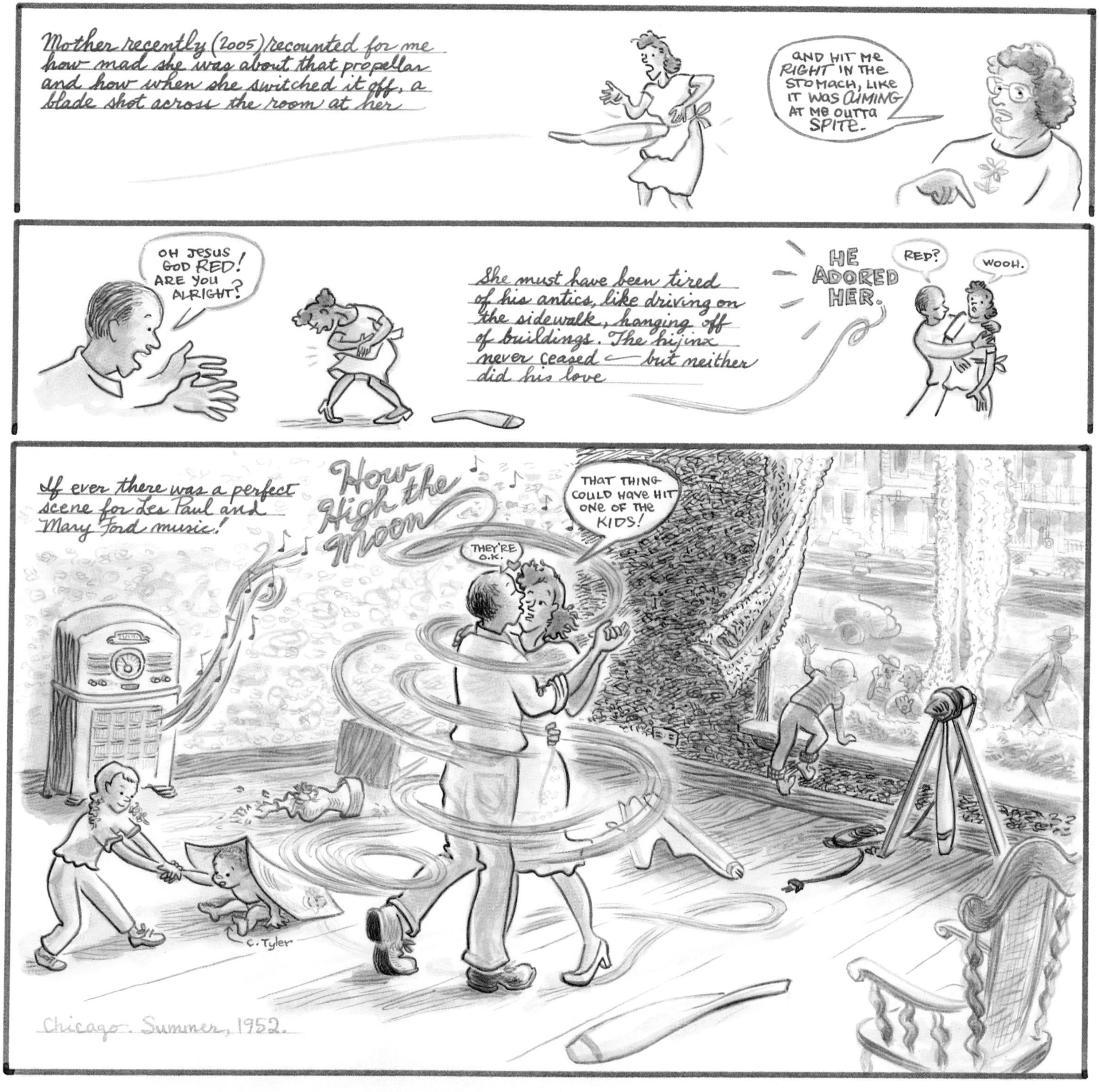
Mother recently (2005) recounted for me how mad she was about that propellar and how when she switched it off, a blade shot across the room at her
AND HIT ME RIGHT IN THE STOMACH, LIKE IT WAS AIMING AT ME OUTTA SPITE.
OH JESUS GOD RED! ARE YOU ALRIGHT?
She must have been tired of his antics, like driving on the sidewalk, hanging off of buildings. The hijinx never ceased — but neither did his love
HE ADORED HER.
RED?
WOOH.
If ever there was a perfect scene for Les Paul and Mary Ford music!
How High the Moon
THAT THING COULD HAVE HIT ONE OF THE KIDS!
THEY'RE O.K.
C. Tyler
Chicago. Summer, 1952.

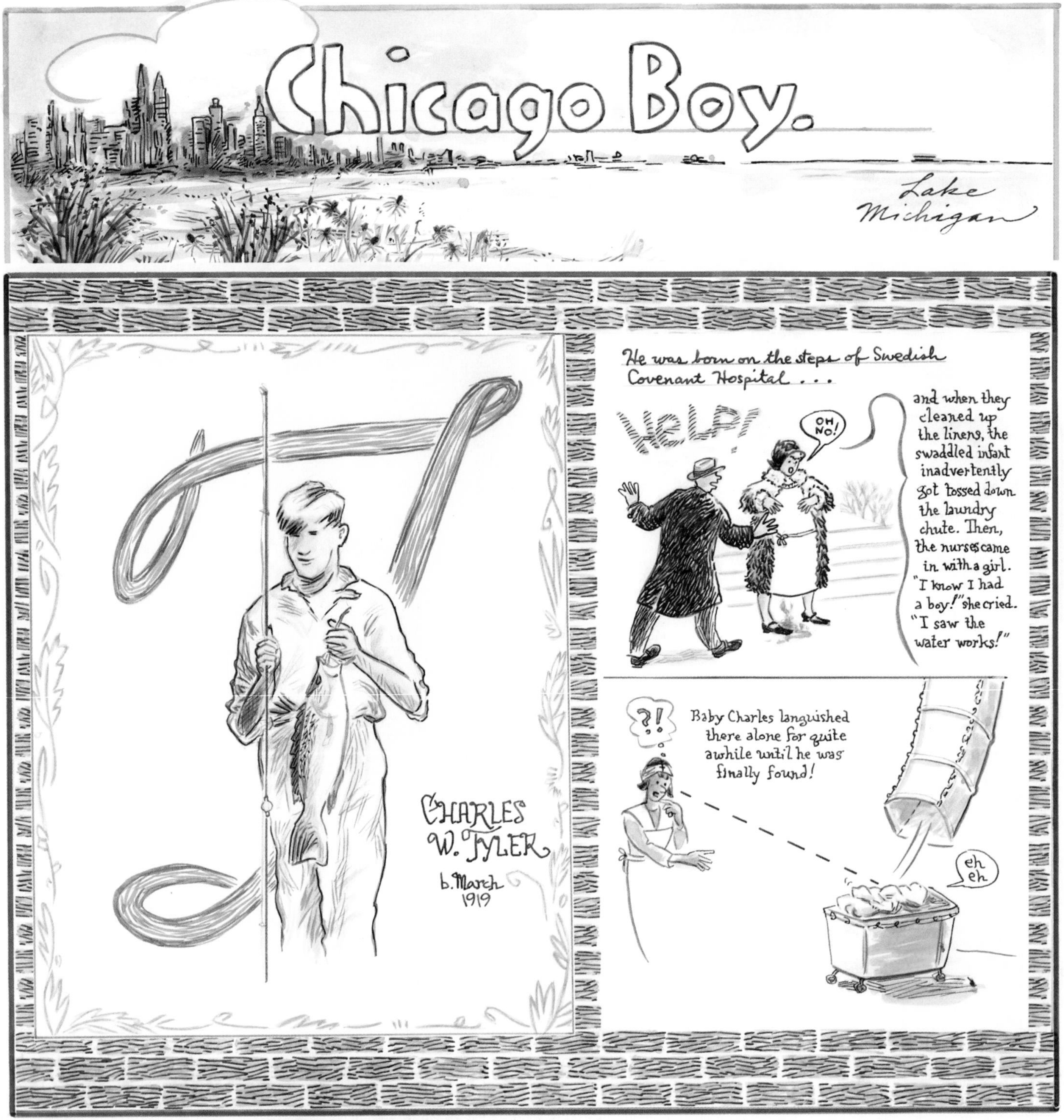
Chicago Boy.
Lake Michigan
T
CHARLES W. TYLER
b. March 1919
He was born on the steps of Swedish Covenant Hospital . . .
HELP!
OH NO!
and when they cleaned up the linens, the swaddled infant inadvertently got tossed down the laundry chute. Then, the nurses came in with a girl. "I know I had a boy!" she cried. "I saw the water works!"
?!
Baby Charles languished there alone for quite awhile until he was finally found!
eh eh

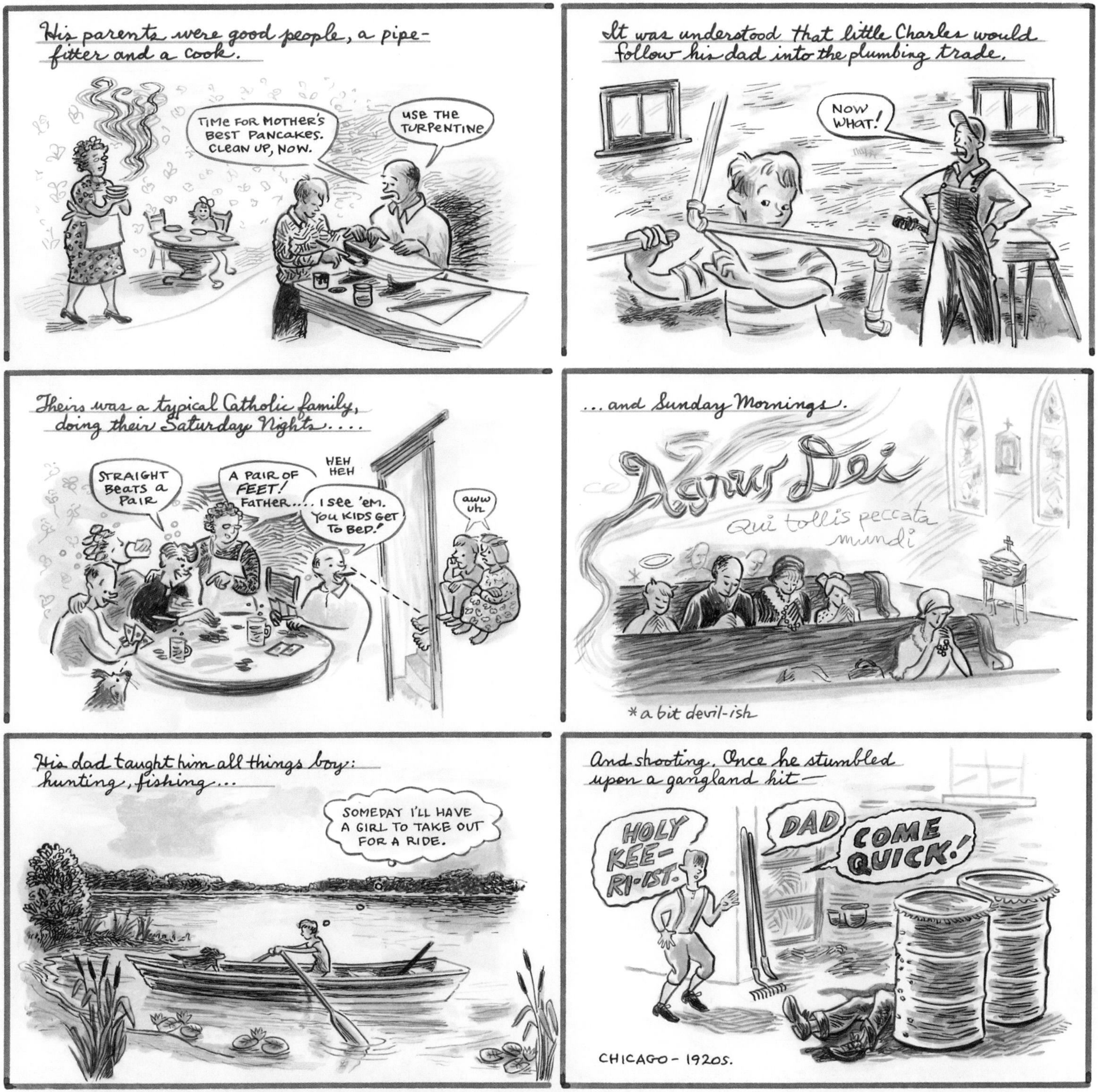
His parents were good people, a pipe-fitter and a cook.
TIME FOR MOTHER'S BEST PANCAKES. CLEAN UP, NOW.
USE THE TURPENTINE.
It was understood that little Charles would follow his dad into the plumbing trade.
NOW WHAT!
Theirs was a typical Catholic family, doing their Saturday Nights....
STRAIGHT BEATS A PAIR
A PAIR OF FEET! FATHER....
HEH HEH
I SEE 'EM. YOU KIDS GET TO BED!
AWW UH.
...and Sunday Mornings.
Agnus Dei
Qui tollis peccata mundi
*a bit devil-ish
His dad taught him all things boy: hunting, fishing...
SOMEDAY I'LL HAVE A GIRL TO TAKE OUT FOR A RIDE.
And shooting. Once he stumbled upon a gangland hit—
HOLY KEE-RI-IST.
DAD
COME QUICK!
CHICAGO - 1920S.

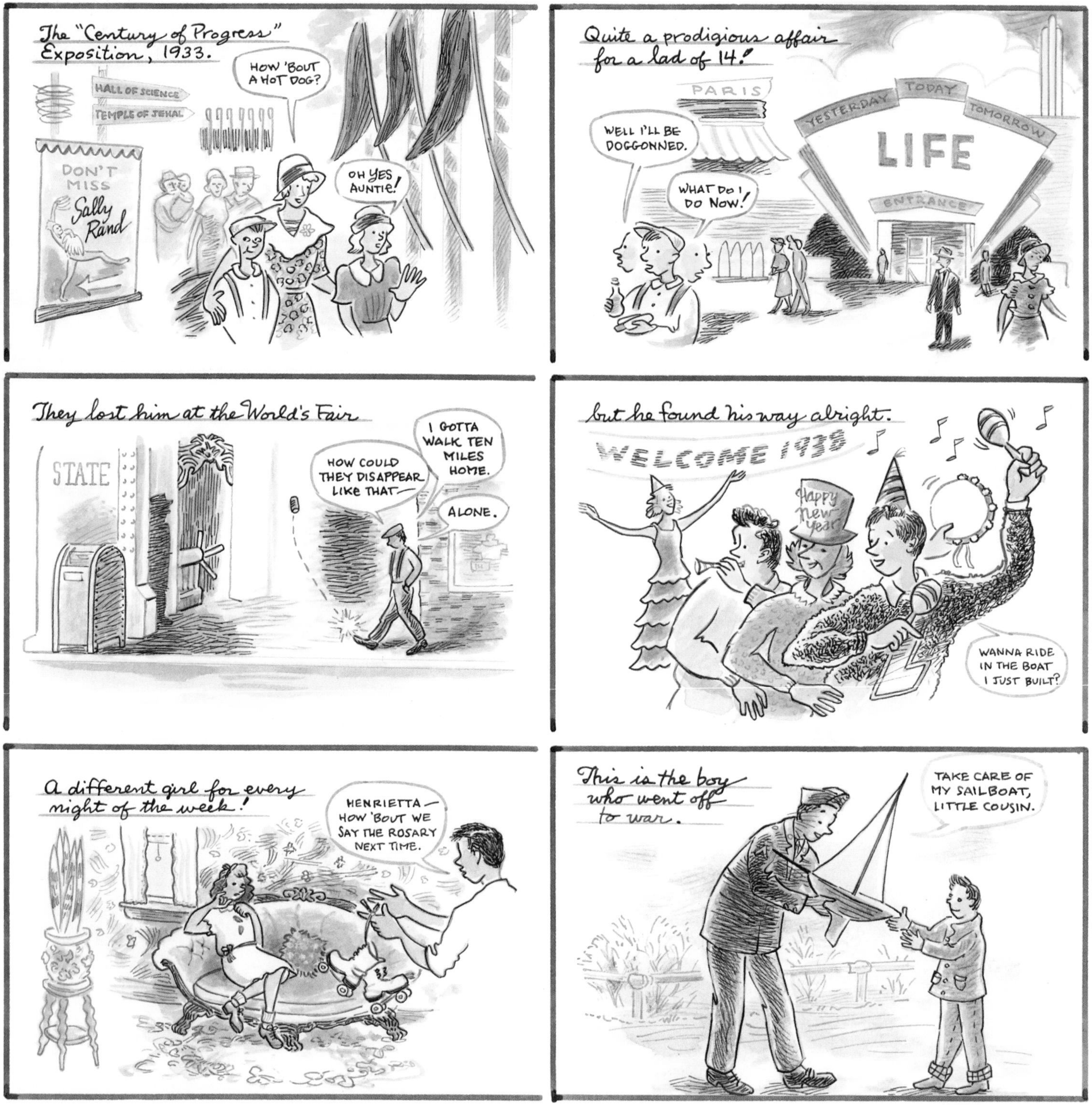
The "Century of Progress" Exposition, 1933.
HALL OF SCIENCE
TEMPLE OF JEHAL
DON'T MISS Sally Rand
HOW 'BOUT A HOT DOG?
OH YES AUNTIE!
Quite a prodigious affair for a lad of 14!
PARIS
YESTERDAY TODAY TOMORROW
LIFE
ENTRANCE
WELL I'LL BE DOGGONNED.
WHAT DO I DO NOW!
They lost him at the World's Fair
STATE
HOW COULD THEY DISAPPEAR LIKE THAT—
I GOTTA WALK TEN MILES HOME.
ALONE.
but he found his way alright.
WELCOME 1938
Happy New Year
WANNA RIDE IN THE BOAT I JUST BUILT?
A different girl for every night of the week!
HENRIETTA— HOW 'BOUT WE SAY THE ROSARY NEXT TIME.
This is the boy who went off to war.
TAKE CARE OF MY SAILBOAT, LITTLE COUSIN.

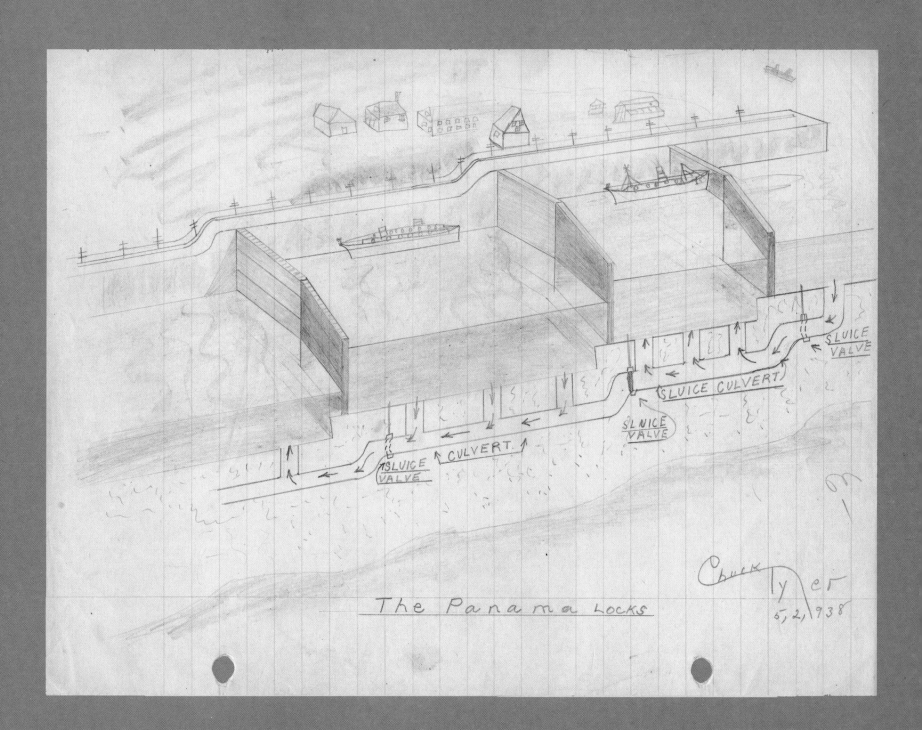

SLUICE VALVE

SLUICE CULVERT

SLUICE VALVE

↑ CULVERT. ↑

SLUICE VALVE

The Panama LOCKS

Chuck Tyler
5, 2, 1938

(1)

LANE TECH HIGH SCHOOL

4/18/38 Chuck Tyler

"Me, Myself and I"

~~On March 13, 1918 there was born a son to the family~~ wife of Alfred M. Tyler

On March the 13, 1918 there was a son born to Mrs Stella Tyler, whose ~~name~~ was later decited on to be Charles William. With him came joy and happiness to the family, it has remained here ever since. As he grew he changed in shape, size, looks, and his will power ~~became~~ became stronger for which he was sorry many times. At the age of three being able to get around by myself I enherited a ~~rather large~~ scar on my forehead from the bottom end of a milk bottle which was thrown at me by ~~my~~ loveing sister.

this is the first of my expirences
that I remember of this life.
Since then I have received
many cuts and scars, too

In Grammar school I was
not a very good
~~much of~~ a student specially
for studies which required a lot of
memoriezing. It was here in
grammar school where ~~I first~~
started on the mechanic side
of the field of choice. ~~In high school~~
For my high school education
I picked Lane Tech because it
gave me a fair opportunity to
try out my field mechanics. in
my first year I decided that
I would not like a mechanical
occupation where I would be
always working under some body
else and besides getting all dirty
so I thought of Engineering, it
had mechanics and also it was
not ~~a~~ dirty work at all after I
made up my mind to that I set
out to find a field best suited
for my thoughts which

69

WORTH FIGHTING FOR

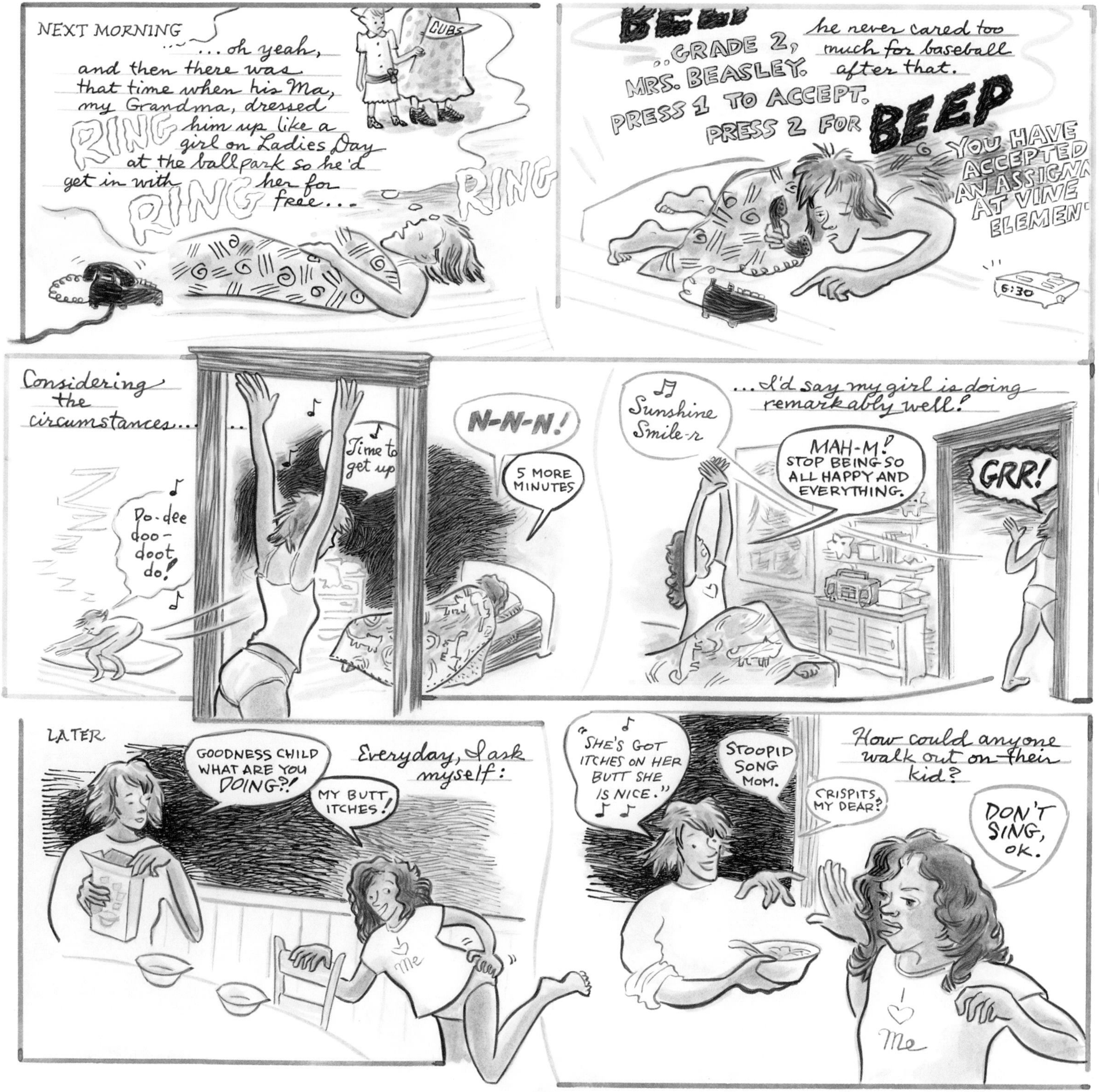
NEXT MORNING
...oh yeah, and then there was that time when his Ma, my Grandma, dressed him up like a girl on Ladies Day at the ballpark so he'd get in with her for free...
CUBS
RING
RING
RING
..GRADE 2, MRS. BEASLEY.
he never cared too much for baseball after that.
PRESS 1 TO ACCEPT. PRESS 2 FOR
BEEP
YOU HAVE ACCEPTED AN ASSIGN AT VINE ELEMEN
6:30
Considering the circumstances...
Do-dee doo-doot do!
Time to get up
N-N-N!
5 MORE MINUTES
...I'd say my girl is doing remarkably well!
Sunshine Smile-r
MAH-M! STOP BEING SO ALL HAPPY AND EVERYTHING.
GRR!
HOW'S THAT.
LATER
GOODNESS CHILD WHAT ARE YOU DOING?!
MY BUTT ITCHES!
Everyday, I ask myself:
"SHE'S GOT ITCHES ON HER BUTT SHE IS NICE."
STOOPID SONG MOM.
How could anyone walk out on their kid?
CRISPITS, MY DEAR?
DON'T SING, OK.

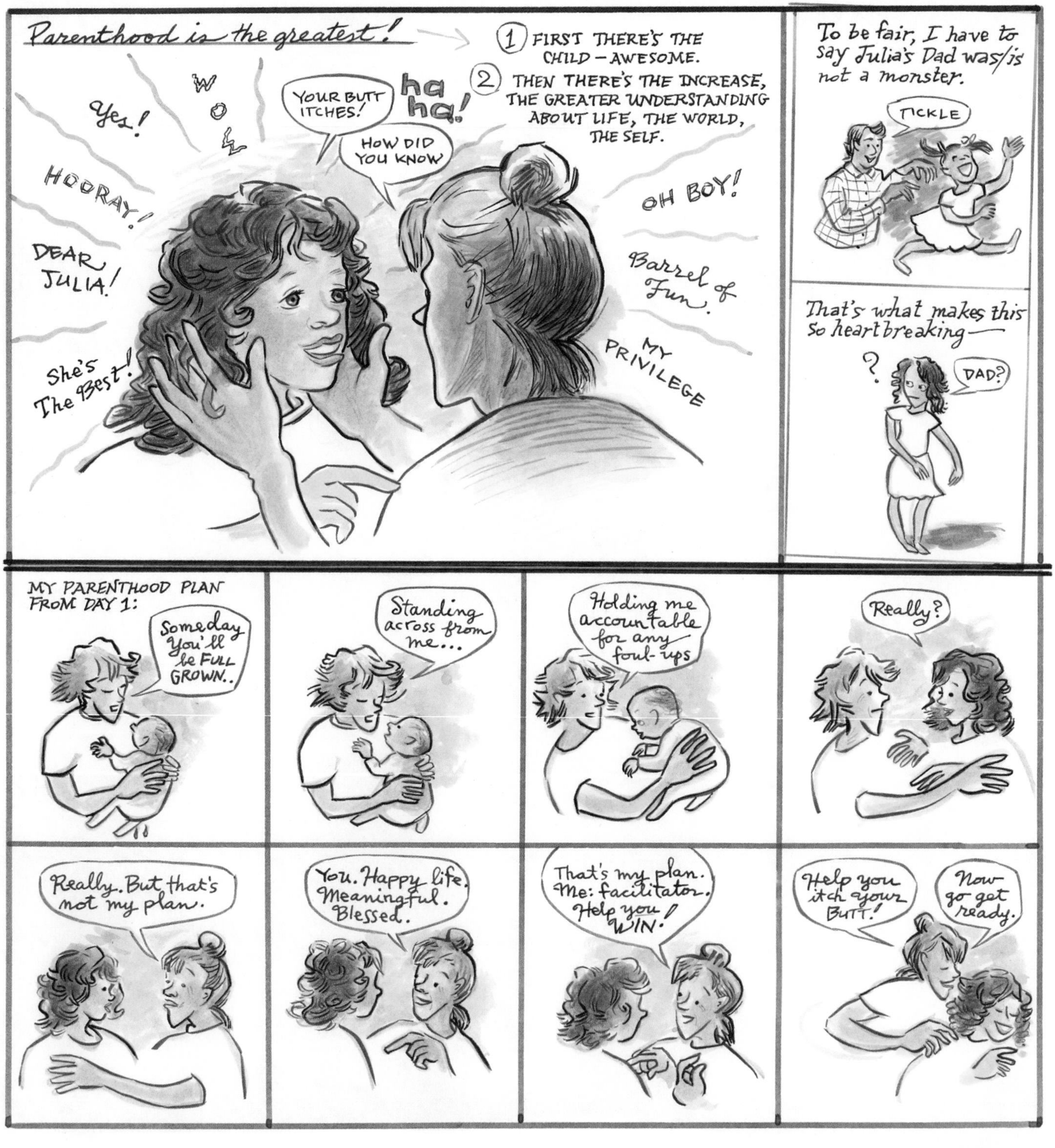
Parenthood is the greatest!
1 FIRST THERE'S THE CHILD — AWESOME.
2 THEN THERE'S THE INCREASE, THE GREATER UNDERSTANDING ABOUT LIFE, THE WORLD, THE SELF.
Yes!
WOW
YOUR BUTT ITCHES!
ha ha!
HOW DID YOU KNOW
HOORAY!
OH BOY!
DEAR JULIA!
Barrel of Fun.
MY PRIVILEGE
She's The Best!
To be fair, I have to say Julia's Dad was/is not a monster.
TICKLE
That's what makes this so heartbreaking—
?
DAD?
MY PARENTHOOD PLAN FROM DAY 1:
Someday you'll be FULL GROWN..
Standing across from me...
Holding me accountable for any foul-ups
Really?
Really. But that's not my plan.
You. Happy life. Meaningful. Blessed.
That's my plan. Me: facilitator. Help you WIN!
Help you itch your BUTT!
Now go get ready.

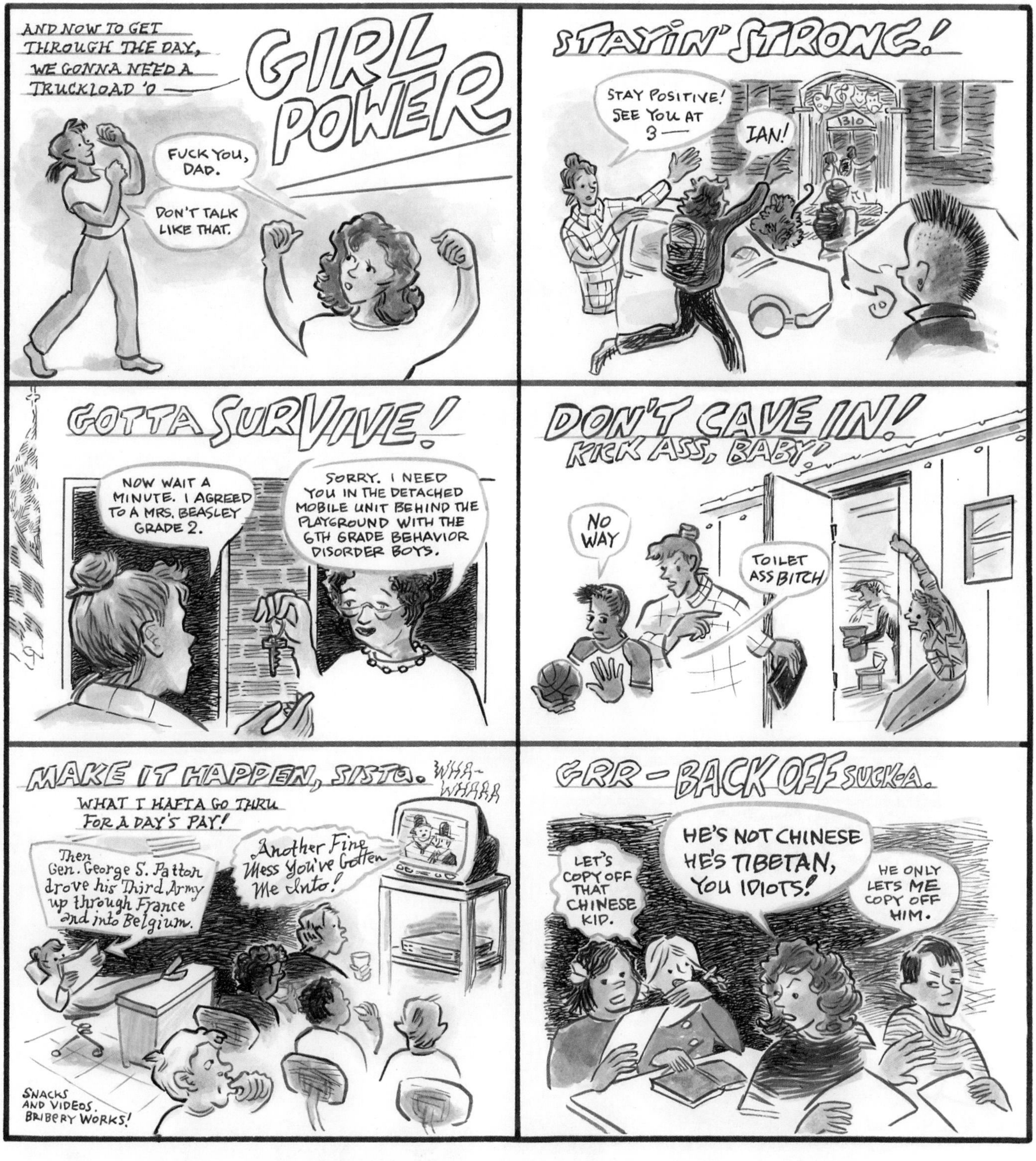
AND NOW TO GET THROUGH THE DAY, WE GONNA NEED A TRUCKLOAD 'O
GIRL POWER
FUCK YOU, DAD.
DON'T TALK LIKE THAT.
STAYIN' STRONG!
STAY POSITIVE! SEE YOU AT 3—
IAN!
1310
GOTTA SURVIVE!
NOW WAIT A MINUTE. I AGREED TO A MRS. BEASLEY GRADE 2.
SORRY. I NEED YOU IN THE DETACHED MOBILE UNIT BEHIND THE PLAYGROUND WITH THE 6TH GRADE BEHAVIOR DISORDER BOYS.
DON'T CAVE IN! KICK ASS, BABY!
NO WAY
TOILET ASS BITCH
MAKE IT HAPPEN, SISTa.
WHA-WHAAA
WHAT I HAFTA GO THRU FOR A DAY'S PAY!
Then Gen. George S. Patton drove his Third Army up through France and into Belgium.
Another Fine Mess You've Gotten Me Into!
SNACKS AND VIDEOS. BRIBERY WORKS!
GRR - BACK OFF SUCK-A.
LET'S COPY OFF THAT CHINESE KID.
HE'S NOT CHINESE HE'S TIBETAN, YOU IDIOTS!
HE ONLY LETS ME COPY OFF HIM.

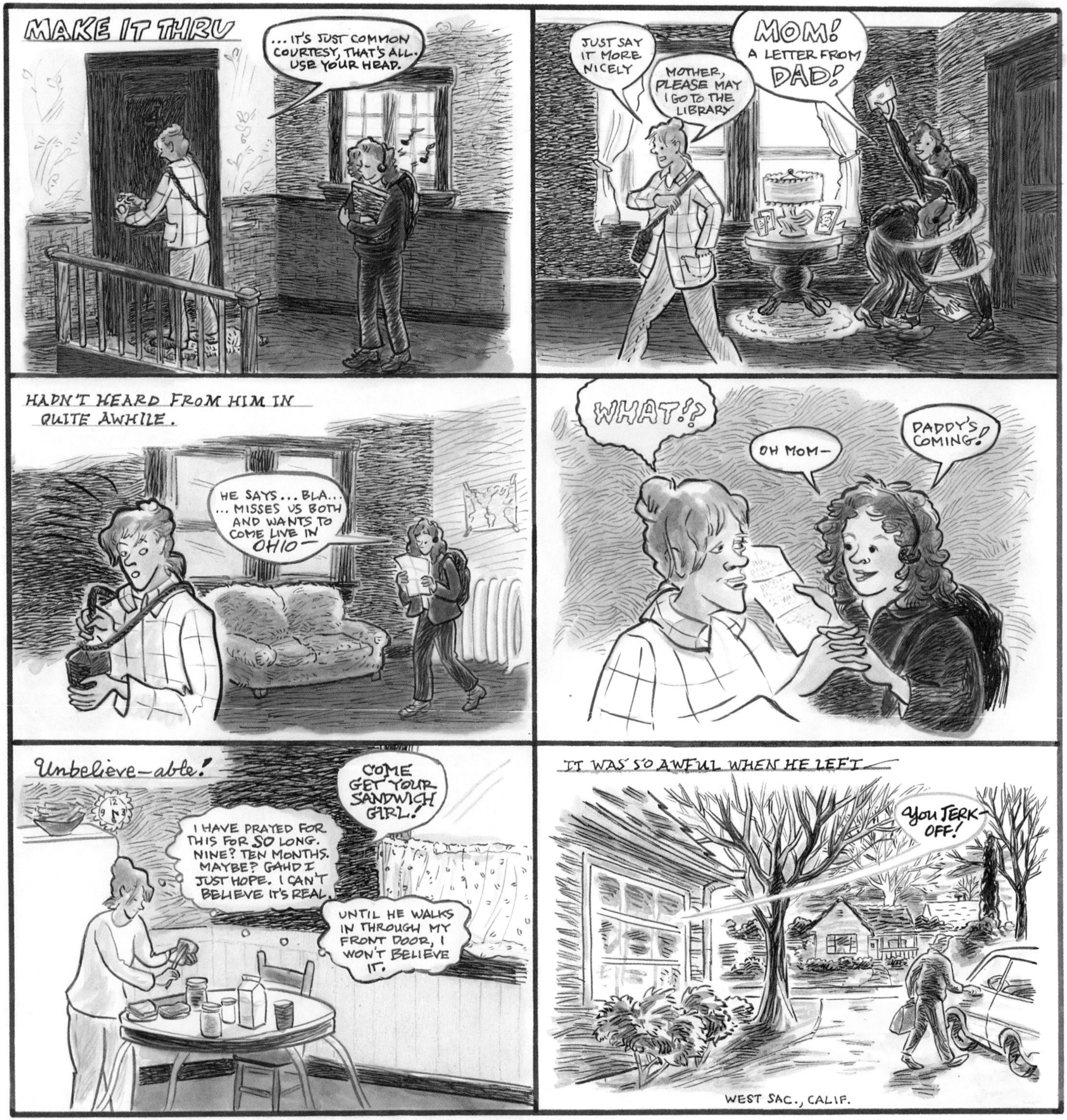
MAKE IT THRU
... IT'S JUST COMMON COURTESY, THAT'S ALL. USE YOUR HEAD.
JUST SAY IT MORE NICELY
MOTHER, PLEASE MAY I GO TO THE LIBRARY
MOM! A LETTER FROM DAD!
HADN'T HEARD FROM HIM IN QUITE AWHILE.
HE SAYS... BLA... ... MISSES US BOTH AND WANTS TO COME LIVE IN OHIO—
WHAT!?
OH MOM—
DADDY'S COMING!
Unbelieve-able!
COME GET YOUR SANDWICH GIRL!
I HAVE PRAYED FOR THIS FOR SO LONG. NINE? TEN MONTHS. MAYBE? GAHD I JUST HOPE. I CAN'T BELIEVE IT'S REAL.
UNTIL HE WALKS IN THROUGH MY FRONT DOOR, I WON'T BELIEVE IT.
IT WAS SO AWFUL WHEN HE LEFT
You JERK-OFF!
WEST SAC., CALIF.

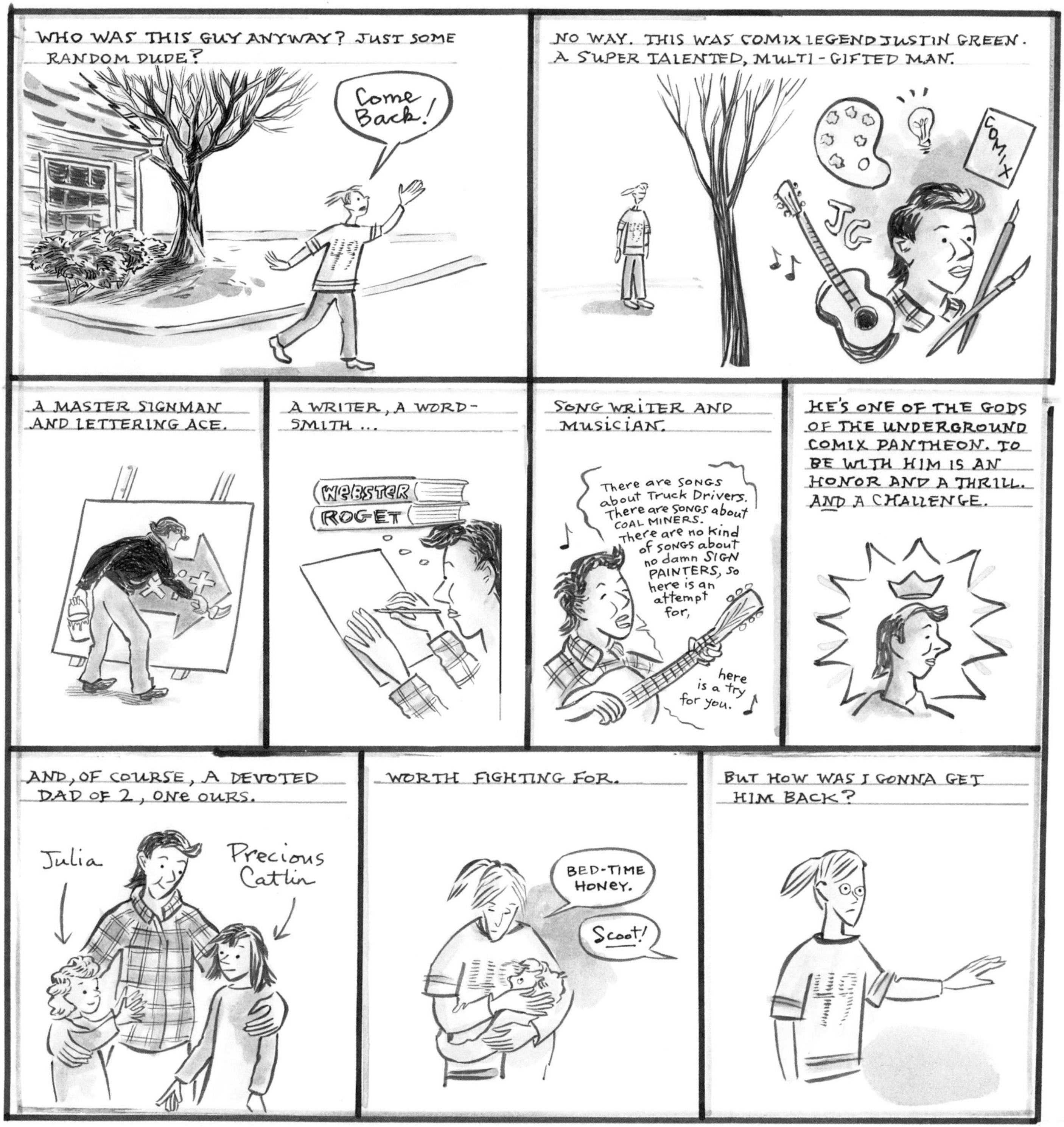

WHO WAS THIS GUY ANYWAY? JUST SOME RANDOM DUDE?
Come Back!
NO WAY. THIS WAS COMIX LEGEND JUSTIN GREEN. A SUPER TALENTED, MULTI-GIFTED MAN.
COMIX
JG
A MASTER SIGNMAN AND LETTERING ACE.
A WRITER, A WORD-SMITH...
WEBSTER
ROGET
SONG WRITER AND MUSICIAN.
There are songs about Truck Drivers. There are songs about COAL MINERS. There are no kind of songs about no damn SIGN PAINTERS, so here is an attempt for,
here is a try for you.
HE'S ONE OF THE GODS OF THE UNDERGROUND COMIX PANTHEON. TO BE WITH HIM IS AN HONOR AND A THRILL. AND A CHALLENGE.
AND, OF COURSE, A DEVOTED DAD OF 2, ONE OURS.
Julia
Precious Catlin
WORTH FIGHTING FOR.
BED-TIME HONEY.
Scoot!
BUT HOW WAS I GONNA GET HIM BACK?

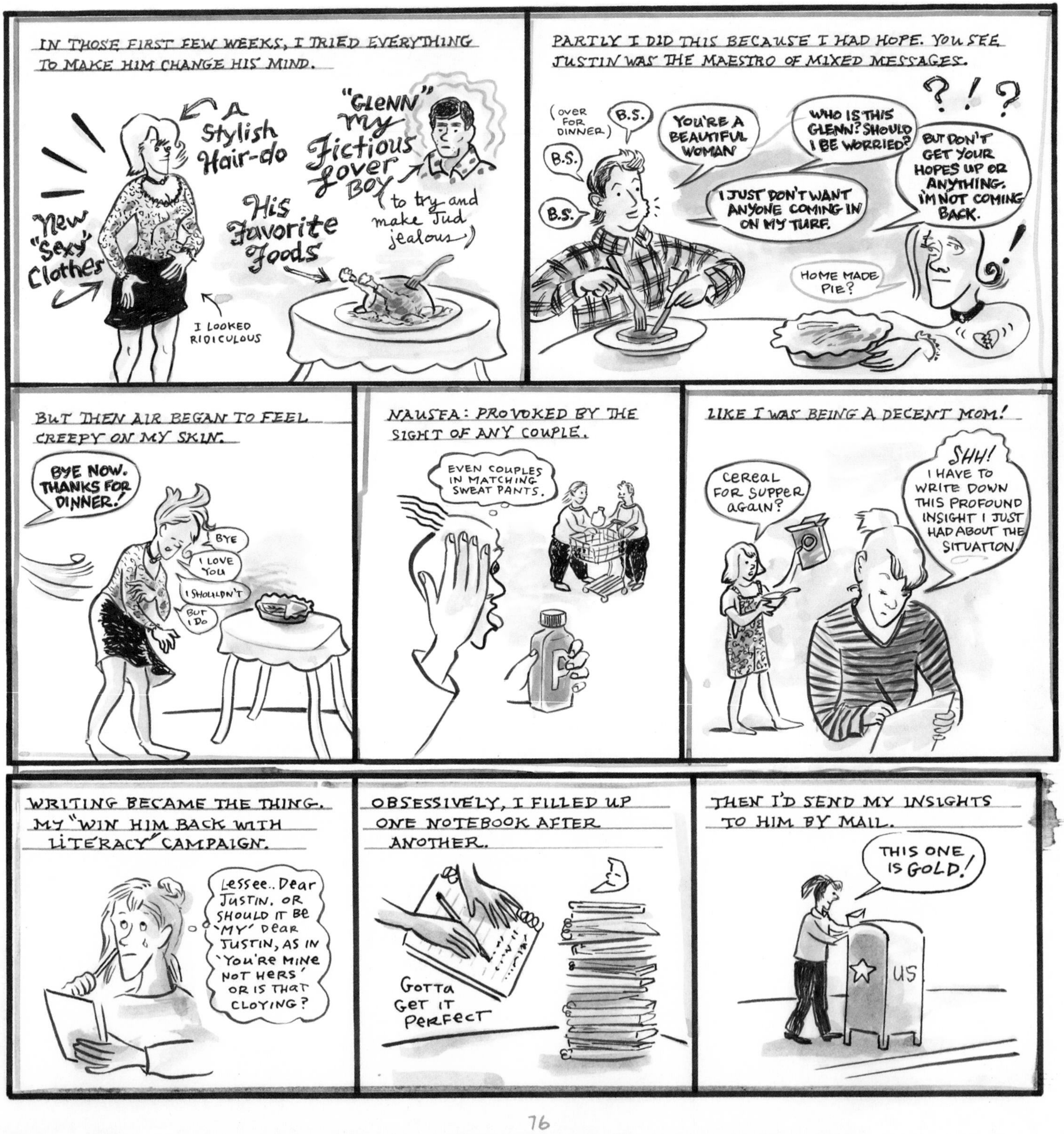
IN THOSE FIRST FEW WEEKS, I TRIED EVERYTHING TO MAKE HIM CHANGE HIS MIND.
A Stylish Hair-do
"GLENN" my Fictious Lover Boy
(to try and make Jud jealous)
New "Sexy" Clothes
His Favorite Foods
I LOOKED RIDICULOUS
PARTLY I DID THIS BECAUSE I HAD HOPE. YOU SEE JUSTIN WAS THE MAESTRO OF MIXED MESSAGES.
(OVER FOR DINNER)
B.S.
B.S.
B.S.
YOU'RE A BEAUTIFUL WOMAN
WHO IS THIS GLENN? SHOULD I BE WORRIED?
? ! ?
BUT DON'T GET YOUR HOPES UP OR ANYTHING. I'M NOT COMING BACK.
I JUST DON'T WANT ANYONE COMING IN ON MY TURF.
HOME MADE PIE?
!
BUT THEN AIR BEGAN TO FEEL CREEPY ON MY SKIN.
BYE NOW. THANKS FOR DINNER!
BYE
I LOVE YOU
I SHOULDN'T
BUT I DO
NAUSEA: PROVOKED BY THE SIGHT OF ANY COUPLE.
EVEN COUPLES IN MATCHING SWEAT PANTS.
LIKE I WAS BEING A DECENT MOM!
Cereal for supper again?
SHH! I HAVE TO WRITE DOWN THIS PROFOUND INSIGHT I JUST HAD ABOUT THE SITUATION.
WRITING BECAME THE THING. MY "WIN HIM BACK WITH LITERACY" CAMPAIGN.
Lessee.. Dear Justin. or should it be 'My' Dear Justin, as in 'You're mine not hers' or is that cloying?
OBSESSIVELY, I FILLED UP ONE NOTEBOOK AFTER ANOTHER.
Gotta get it perfect
THEN I'D SEND MY INSIGHTS TO HIM BY MAIL.
THIS ONE IS GOLD!
US

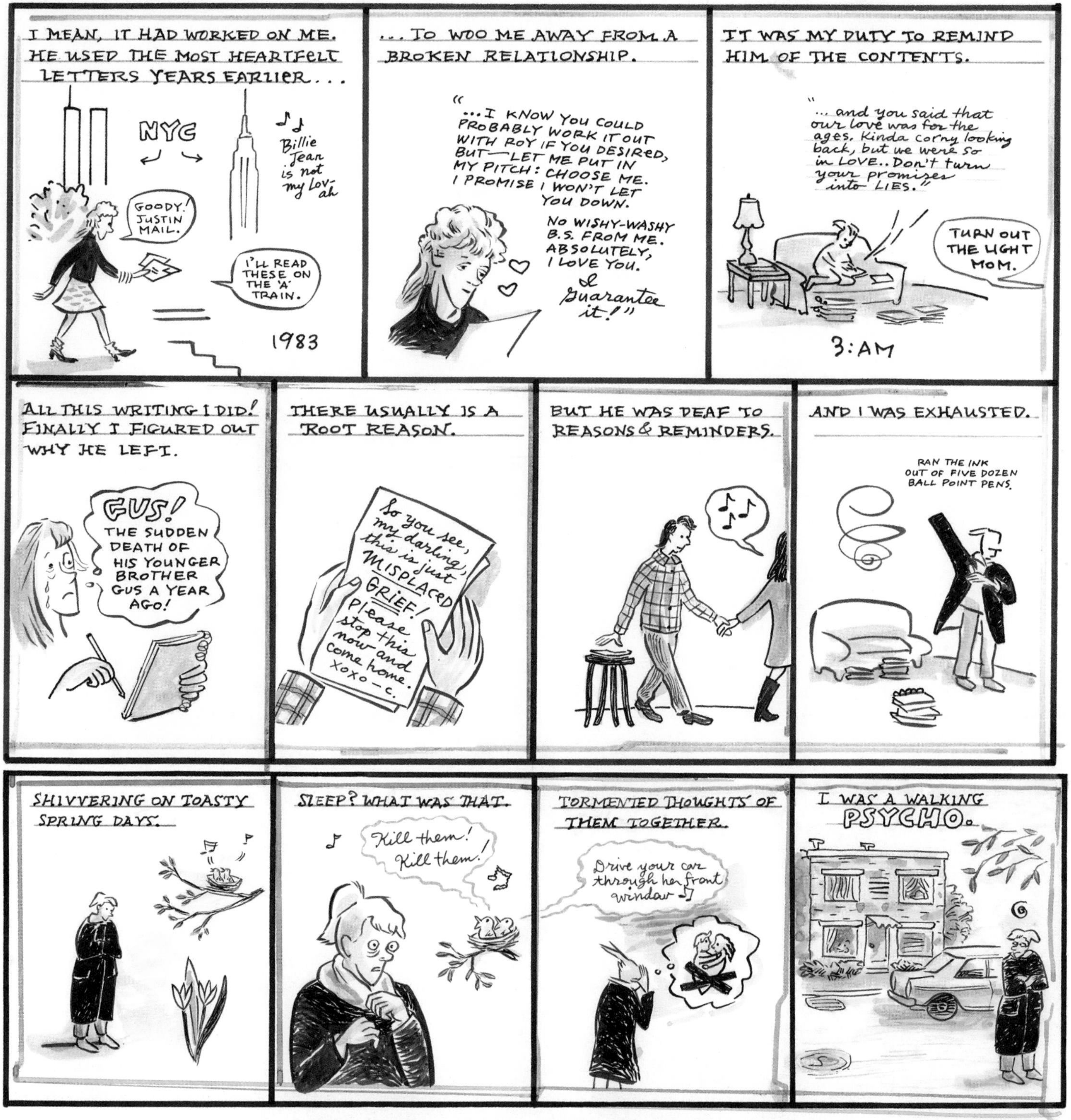
I MEAN, IT HAD WORKED ON ME. HE USED THE MOST HEARTFELT LETTERS YEARS EARLIER...
NYC
Billie Jean is not my Lov-ah
GOODY! JUSTIN MAIL.
I'LL READ THESE ON THE 'A' TRAIN.
1983
...TO WOO ME AWAY FROM A BROKEN RELATIONSHIP.
"...I KNOW YOU COULD PROBABLY WORK IT OUT WITH ROY IF YOU DESIRED, BUT—LET ME PUT IN MY PITCH: CHOOSE ME. I PROMISE I WON'T LET YOU DOWN.
NO WISHY-WASHY B.S. FROM ME. ABSOLUTELY, I LOVE YOU.
I Guarantee it!"
IT WAS MY DUTY TO REMIND HIM OF THE CONTENTS.
"... and you said that our love was for the ages. Kinda corny looking back, but we were so in LOVE.. Don't turn your promises into LIES."
TURN OUT THE LIGHT MOM.
3:AM
ALL THIS WRITING I DID! FINALLY I FIGURED OUT WHY HE LEFT.
GUS! THE SUDDEN DEATH OF HIS YOUNGER BROTHER GUS A YEAR AGO!
THERE USUALLY IS A ROOT REASON.
So you see, my darling, this is just MISPLACED GRIEF! Please stop this now and come home. XOXO—C.
BUT HE WAS DEAF TO REASONS & REMINDERS.
AND I WAS EXHAUSTED.
RAN THE INK OUT OF FIVE DOZEN BALL POINT PENS.
SHIVVERING ON TOASTY SPRING DAYS.
SLEEP? WHAT WAS THAT.
Kill them! Kill them!
TORMENTED THOUGHTS OF THEM TOGETHER.
Drive your car through her front window
I WAS A WALKING PSYCHO.

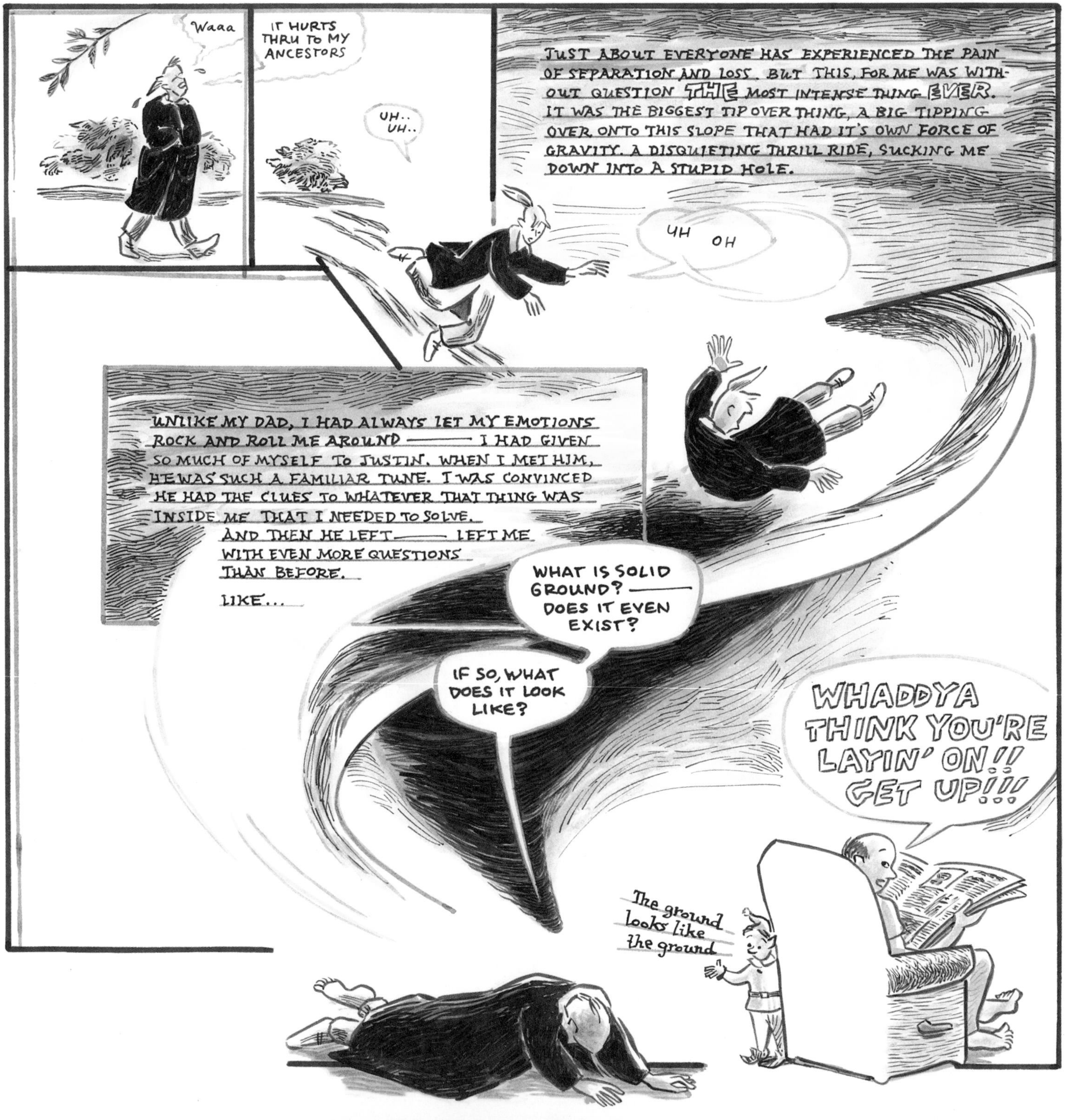

Waaa
IT HURTS THRU TO MY ANCESTORS
UH.. UH..
JUST ABOUT EVERYONE HAS EXPERIENCED THE PAIN OF SEPARATION AND LOSS. BUT THIS, FOR ME WAS WITHOUT QUESTION THE MOST INTENSE THING EVER. IT WAS THE BIGGEST TIP OVER THING, A BIG TIPPING OVER ONTO THIS SLOPE THAT HAD IT'S OWN FORCE OF GRAVITY. A DISQUIETING THRILL RIDE, SUCKING ME DOWN INTO A STUPID HOLE.
UH OH
UNLIKE MY DAD, I HAD ALWAYS LET MY EMOTIONS ROCK AND ROLL ME AROUND —— I HAD GIVEN SO MUCH OF MYSELF TO JUSTIN. WHEN I MET HIM, HE WAS SUCH A FAMILIAR TUNE. I WAS CONVINCED HE HAD THE CLUES TO WHATEVER THAT THING WAS INSIDE ME THAT I NEEDED TO SOLVE.
AND THEN HE LEFT—— LEFT ME WITH EVEN MORE QUESTIONS THAN BEFORE.
LIKE...
WHAT IS SOLID GROUND? —— DOES IT EVEN EXIST?
IF SO, WHAT DOES IT LOOK LIKE?
WHADDYA THINK YOU'RE LAYIN' ON!! GET UP!!!
The ground looks like the ground

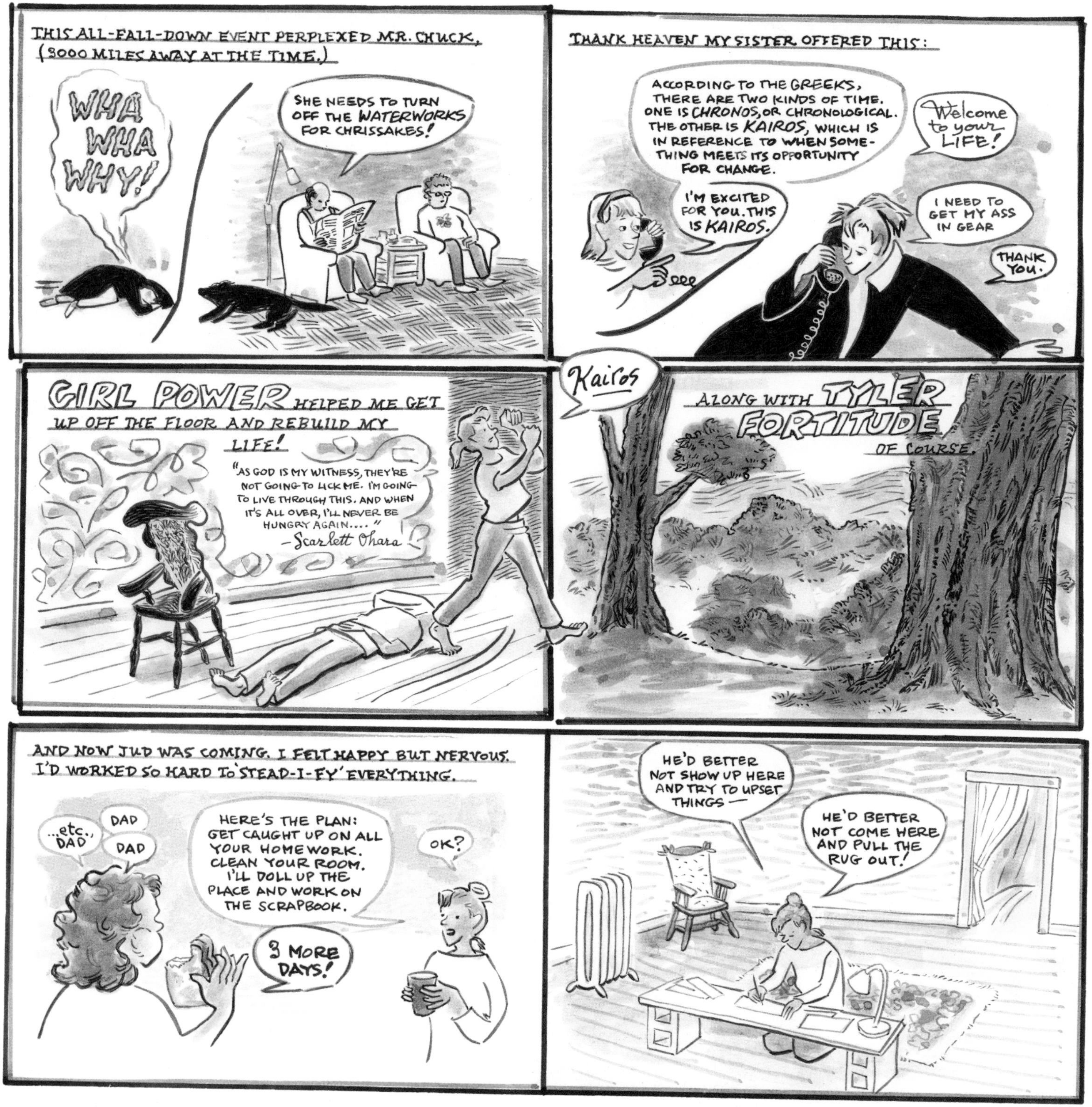
THIS ALL-FALL-DOWN EVENT PERPLEXED MR. CHUCK, (3000 MILES AWAY AT THE TIME.)
WHA WHA WHY!
SHE NEEDS TO TURN OFF THE WATERWORKS FOR CHRISSAKES!
THANK HEAVEN MY SISTER OFFERED THIS:
ACCORDING TO THE GREEKS, THERE ARE TWO KINDS OF TIME. ONE IS CHRONOS, OR CHRONOLOGICAL. THE OTHER IS KAIROS, WHICH IS IN REFERENCE TO WHEN SOME-THING MEETS ITS OPPORTUNITY FOR CHANGE.
Welcome to your LIFE!
I'M EXCITED FOR YOU. THIS IS KAIROS.
I NEED TO GET MY ASS IN GEAR
THANK YOU.
GIRL POWER HELPED ME GET UP OFF THE FLOOR AND REBUILD MY LIFE!
"AS GOD IS MY WITNESS, THEY'RE NOT GOING TO LICK ME. I'M GOING TO LIVE THROUGH THIS. AND WHEN IT'S ALL OVER, I'LL NEVER BE HUNGRY AGAIN...." —Scarlett Ohara
Kairos
ALONG WITH TYLER FORTITUDE OF COURSE.
AND NOW JUD WAS COMING. I FELT HAPPY BUT NERVOUS. I'D WORKED SO HARD TO 'STEAD-I-FY' EVERYTHING.
...etc., DAD
DAD
DAD
HERE'S THE PLAN: GET CAUGHT UP ON ALL YOUR HOMEWORK. CLEAN YOUR ROOM. I'LL DOLL UP THE PLACE AND WORK ON THE SCRAPBOOK.
OK?
3 MORE DAYS!
HE'D BETTER NOT SHOW UP HERE AND TRY TO UPSET THINGS—
HE'D BETTER NOT COME HERE AND PULL THE RUG OUT!

DAD'S ARMY SCRAPBOOK
AND
TOUR OF DUTY HIGHLIGHTS

PART II

~ NORTH AFRICA ~

JUNE 1944 — JULY 1944

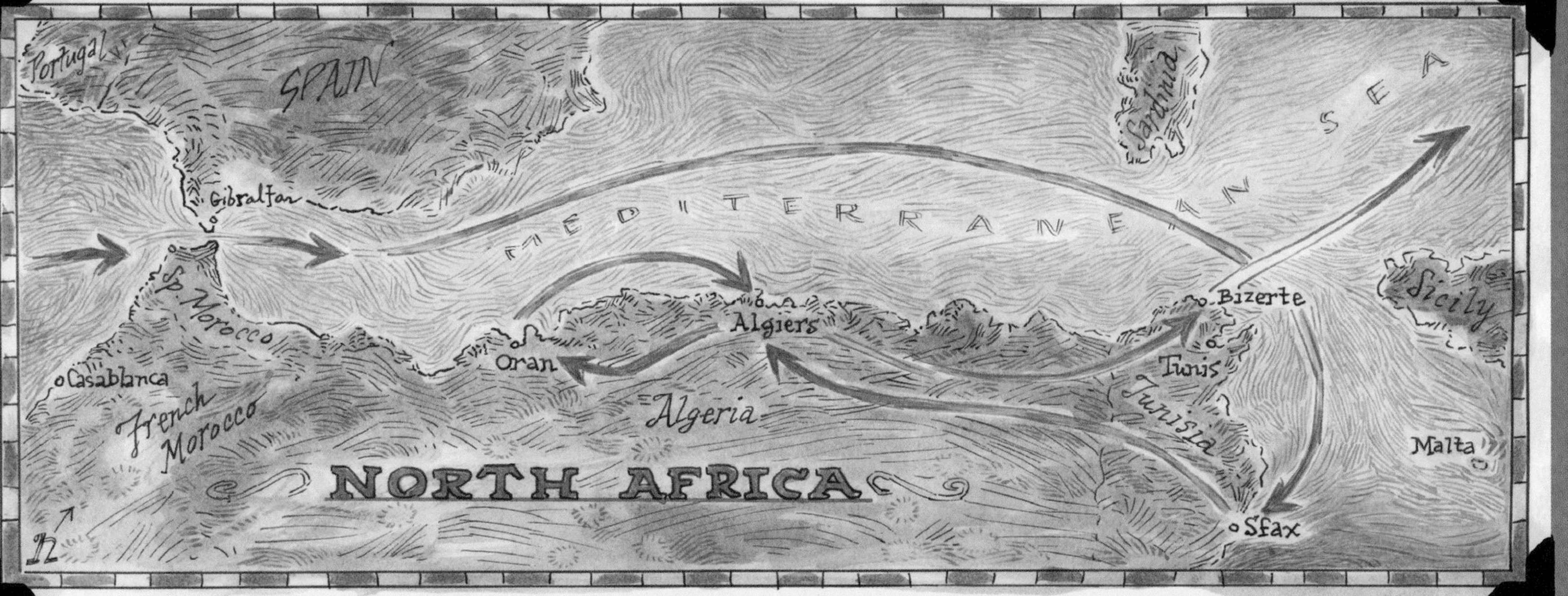
Portugal
SPAIN
Gibraltar
MEDITERRANEAN SEA
Sardinia
Sicily
Sp. Morocco
Casablanca
French Morocco
Oran
Algiers
Algeria
Bizerte
Tunis
Tunisia
Malta
Sfax
NORTH AFRICA

The Sandbox
22

"Disembarkment from Shenango, Pennsylvania. 'Par-tee and never return' we used to say. I shipped out with the 8TH Air Force. Anyone who volunteered to be a 'ships fitter' got special eats. So I said 'yeah' and they gave me a mop, 'cause everyone was seasick. Not me.

"When we hit Africa, the captain didn't want to run a-ground... ordered guys to start jumping off. An airman swapped me his pistol for my rifle and he gave me his sunglasses, too. That first bunch never came back up. Him included."

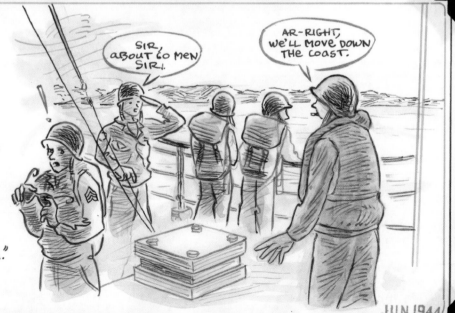

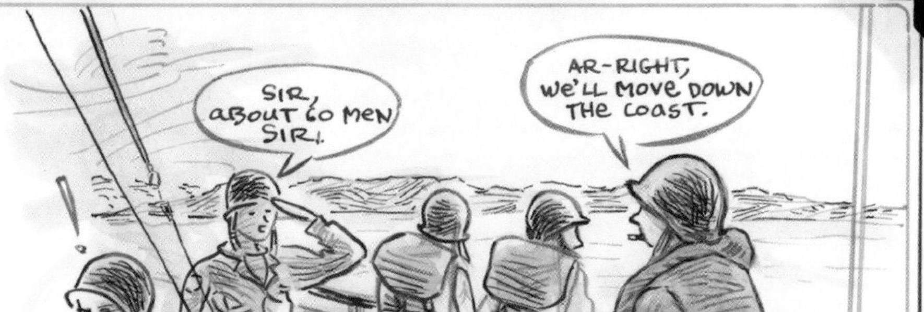
!
SIR, ABOUT 60 MEN SIR!
AR-RIGHT, WE'LL MOVE DOWN THE COAST.
JUN 1944

23

"So they decided to go through Gibraltar, where we seen all kinds of stuff floating. We're thinking, 'Boy, we must-a sunk a German ship bigger than hell,' but I didn't find out till we were in France, much later, that it was our records floating."

"My records — what a mess! I'd get with an outfit, then someone else would need my skills and I'd go with them. They'd post a list each morning. I got transferred so many times, I felt like I was AWOL!"

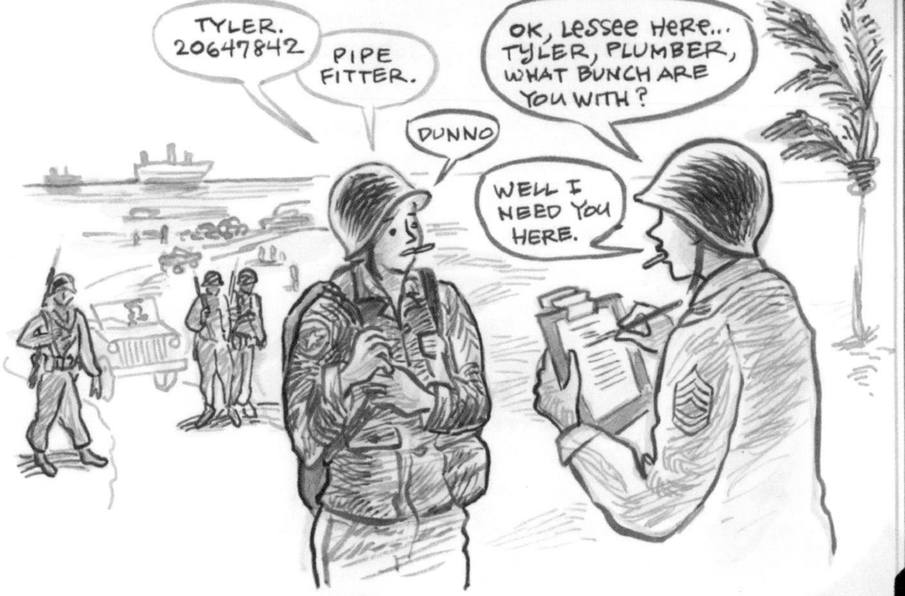
TYLER. 20647842
PIPE FITTER.
OK, LESSEE HERE... TYLER, PLUMBER, WHAT BUNCH ARE YOU WITH?
DUNNO
WELL I NEED YOU HERE.

24

"I think Sfax was the first stop. Right away they sez, 'you engineers and plumbers, go to the tents area.' The Navy ship had a de-salter and they needed us to run a fresh water line to the hospital. 'Here, put these pipes together.' I couldn't. No wonder: they were metric! I'd never seen metric before. Our group, trying to screw on American SAE threads — we're welding it. I made a lead pot with wipe joints, I even used candles — I tried everything and got the job done."

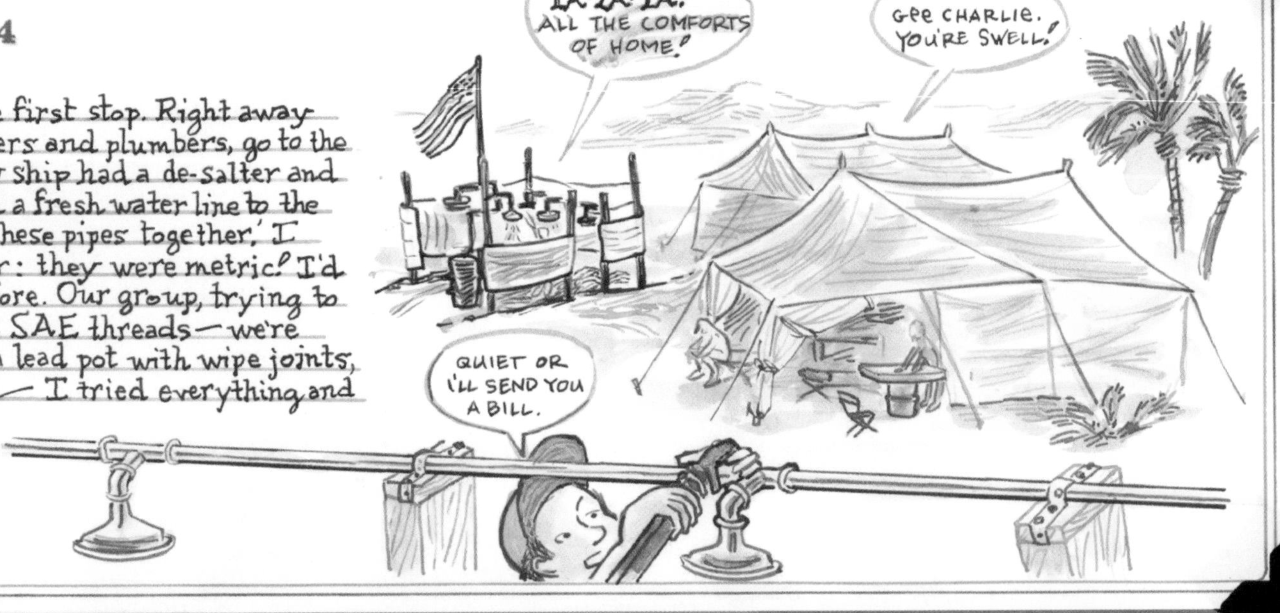
LA-LA-LA! ALL THE COMFORTS OF HOME!
GEE CHARLIE. YOU'RE SWELL!
QUIET OR I'LL SEND YOU A BILL.

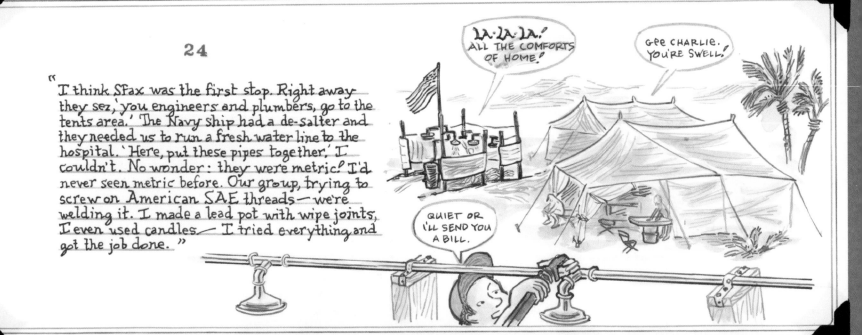

25

"I had a little run-in with the FBI over this— Fort Benning Idiot. This bossy lieutenant was telling me how to join pipes. I told him 'you're full of shit, it don't go like that,' and he said 'Do as I say or I'll have your stripes!' He wanted a court martial. So I told the Judge Advocate, 'My dad's a plumber, my grandpa's a plumber... I've been involved in construction my whole life!" And then the judge points to the lieutenant and says 'Let the professional do his job, fer Chrissakes!' I built a nice shower."

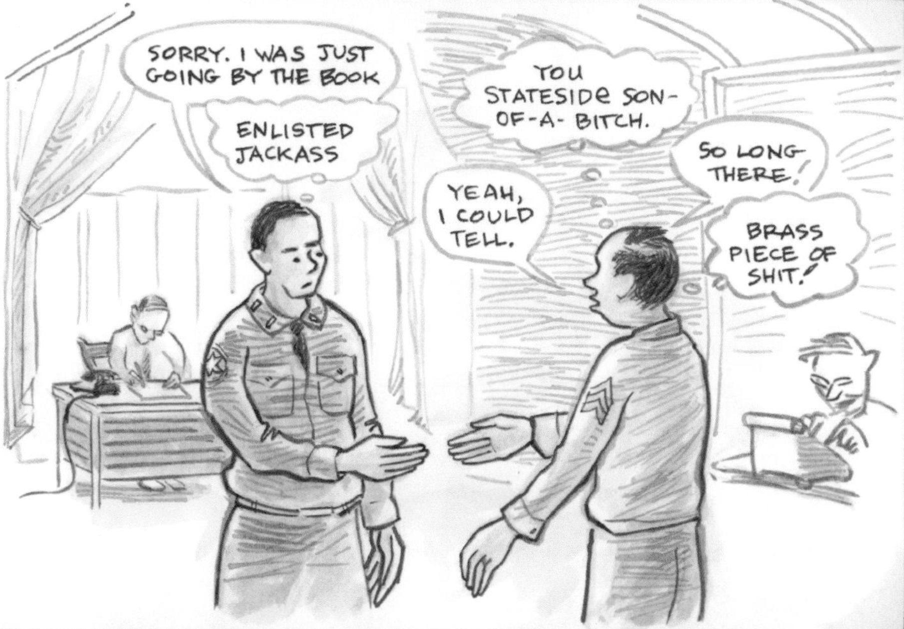
SORRY. I WAS JUST GOING BY THE BOOK
ENLISTED JACKASS
YOU STATESIDE SON-OF-A-BITCH.
YEAH, I COULD TELL.
SO LONG THERE!
BRASS PIECE OF SHIT!

26

"After that, we had so much water, they decided to wash planes, wash trucks— everything. We didn't know the unwritten rules of the desert: that to have water spilt all over like that was a no-no. low and behold, everyday our water line would get a new hole in it. And we were losing a soldier, two soldiers a night. When I had night duty, I saw men sneak down to try and shoot or stab our soldiers. They'd tear their clothes off and then cut holes in the lines. Next morning, through special intelligence, we got hold of a Sheik."

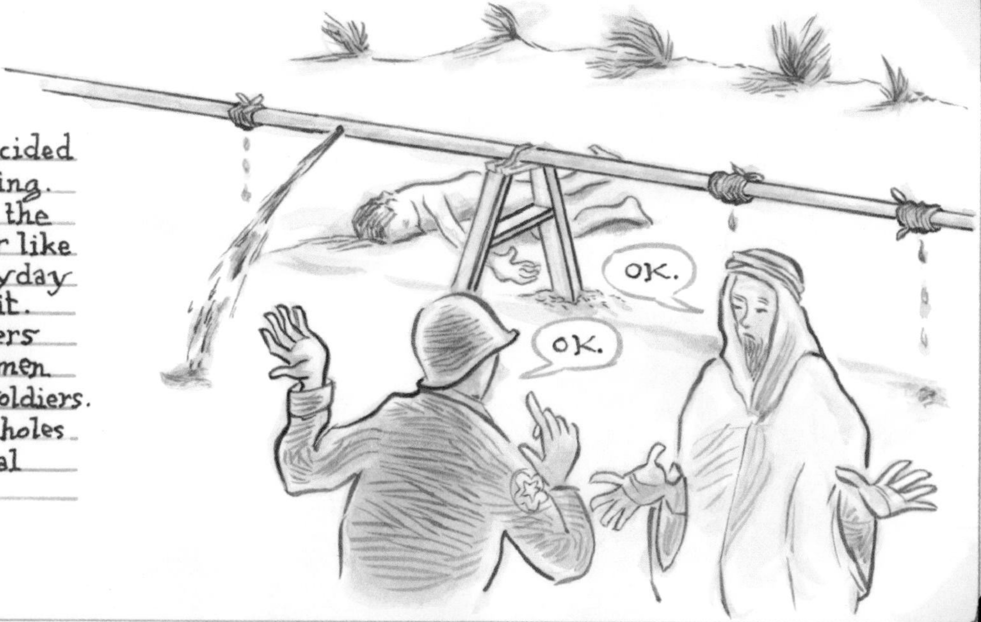
OK.
OK.

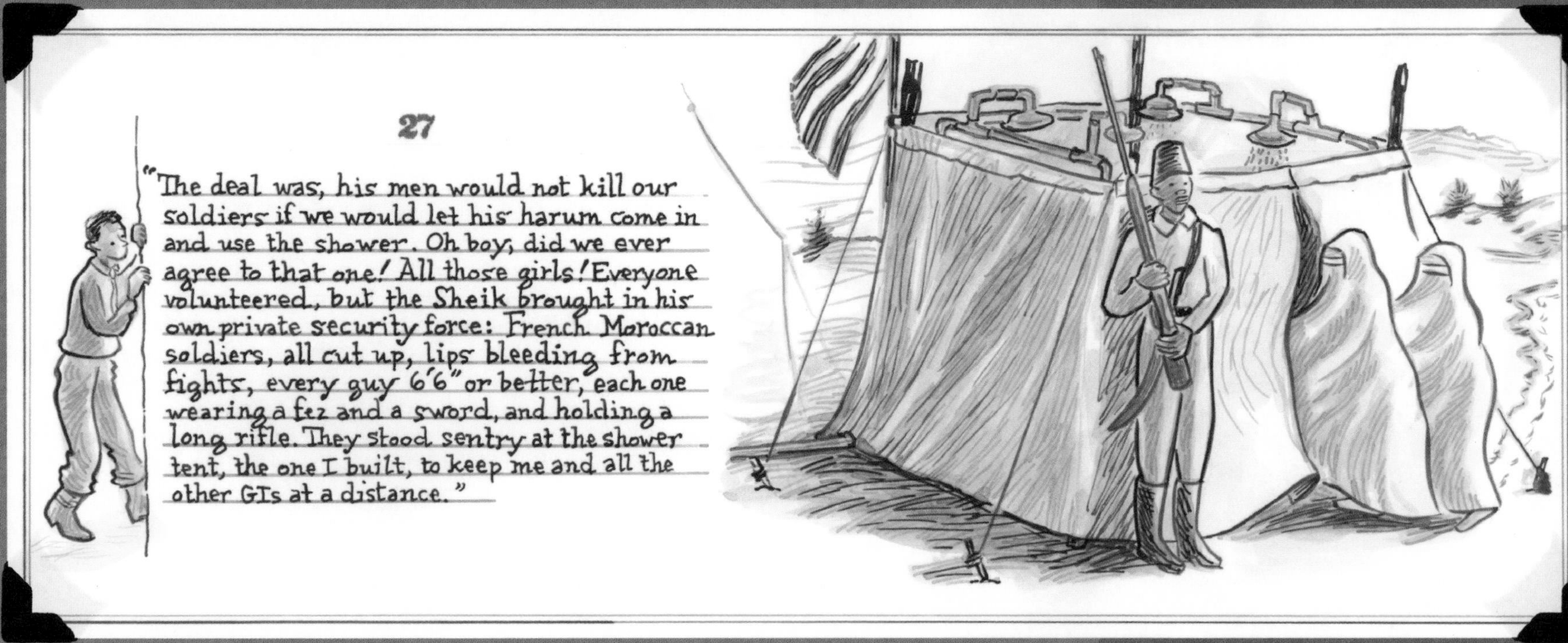
27
"The deal was, his men would not kill our soldiers if we would let his harum come in and use the shower. Oh boy, did we ever agree to that one! All those girls! Everyone volunteered, but the Sheik brought in his own private security force: French Moroccan soldiers, all cut up, lips bleeding from fights, every guy 6'6" or better, each one wearing a fez and a sword, and holding a long rifle. They stood sentry at the shower tent, the one I built, to keep me and all the other GIs at a distance."

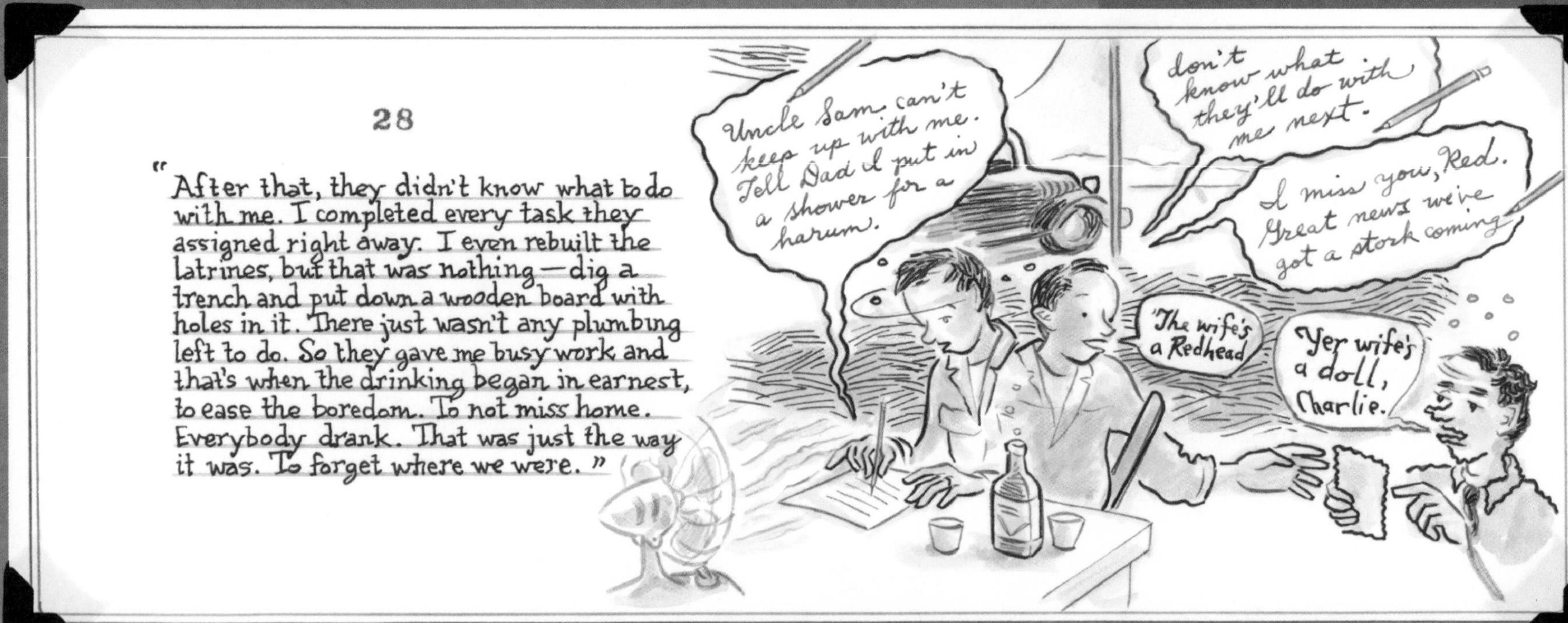
28
"After that, they didn't know what to do with me. I completed every task they assigned right away. I even rebuilt the latrines, but that was nothing—dig a trench and put down a wooden board with holes in it. There just wasn't any plumbing left to do. So they gave me busy work and that's when the drinking began in earnest, to ease the boredom. To not miss home. Everybody drank. That was just the way it was. To forget where we were."
Uncle Sam can't keep up with me. Tell Dad I put in a shower for a harum.
don't know what they'll do with me next.
I miss you, Red. Great news we've got a stork coming
"The wife's a Redhead"
"Yer wife's a doll, Charlie."

29

"Enlisted had beer, but the officers had booze. The Navy always had booze on the ships. And since I had to work with the Navy on water projects, I had access. Once, I was working out in the heat and this guy hands me a little bottle of Anisette. I drank it down. 'This is nothing,' I thought. So I went over to the Navy ship and got 3-4 more bottles. Swilled it all down, clean like water. Boy, the next morning, I couldn't scratch my head with both hands. Oh, that was awful!"

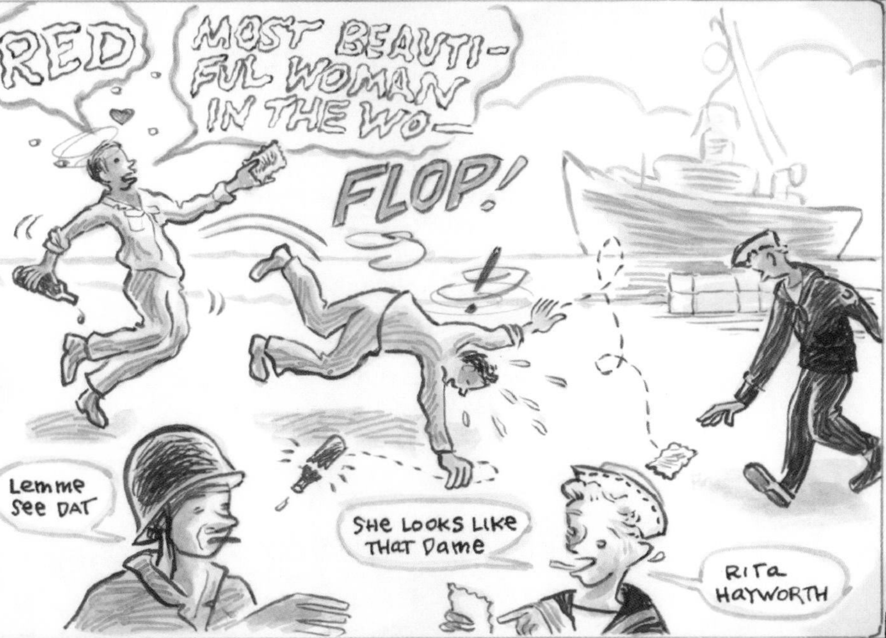
RED
MOST BEAUTI-FUL WOMAN IN THE WO—
FLOP!
Lemme see DAT
SHE LOOKS LIKE THAT Dame
RITa HAYWORTH

30

"Bad times the next morning, too. My head was pounding and I was never so thirsty. So I stumbled over to the middle of the base to get me a drink of water. They had this triangular bag hanging there with these nipple spouts below. I drew myself a long, cool drink of water, but AWGH!—Quinine water for malaria. On top of my Anisette hang-over. P.U.! But was the only water available. And then when I realized that I had lost my picture of Red... this was worst of all. After this incident, I quit foolin' around with shit I didn't know."

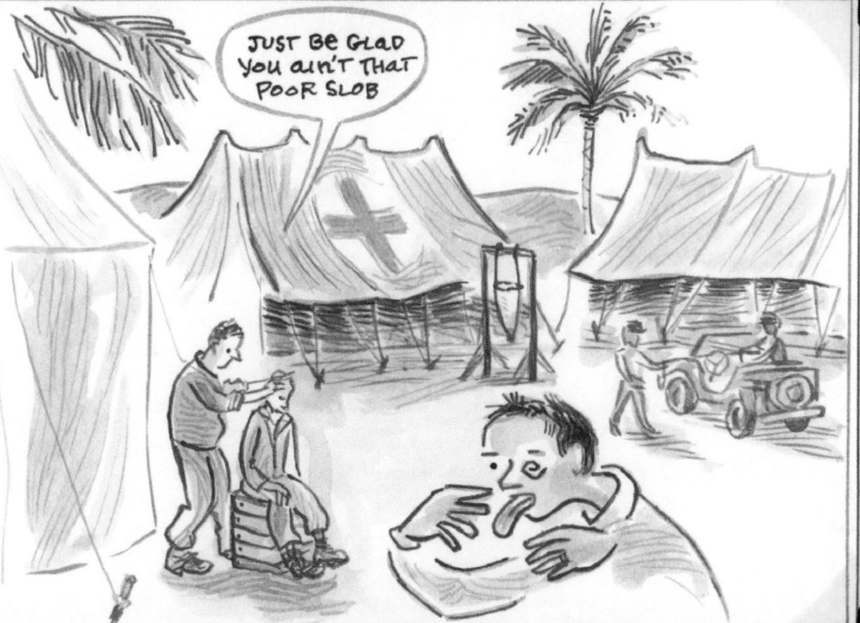
JUST BE GLAD YOU AIN'T THAT POOR SLOB

31

"As a boy, I had a darkroom. Photography was one of my hobbies and I took plenty of pictures of Red before I left. The one I lost that night was my favorite. —— Before I came over here, we decided she'd be better off in Chicago with my parents. Wartime, you know. We wrote letters back and forth and every month I'd send her my pay; $60 dollars, (but Ma took $50 for expenses!). Army censors worked over my letters pretty good — they cut out almost everything I wrote!"

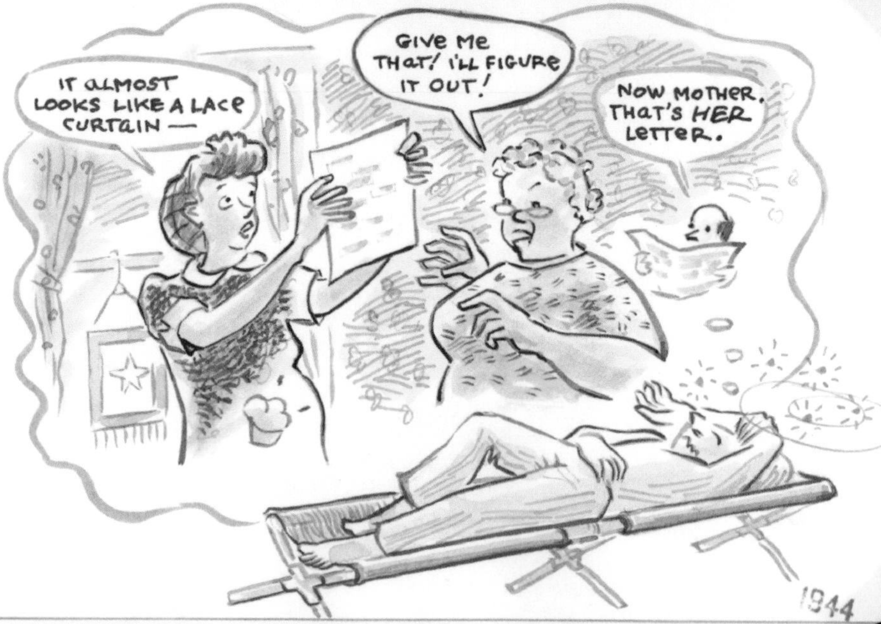

IT ALMOST LOOKS LIKE A LACE CURTAIN —
GIVE ME THAT! I'LL FIGURE IT OUT!
NOW MOTHER. THAT'S HER LETTER.
1944

32.

"Goddamn, it was as hot as hell in the daytime. So we made ice cream with gasoline. We got sugar, eggs and cream from the cook, stirred it up nice and put it in a big jar, set the jar in a washtub full of 3/4 hi-octane, then stirred the jar. Ice formed on the sides and bottom and froze the cream inside. —— At night it could get pretty cold in the desert. One of my duties was to crawl up under the tanks with my little camp stove at 3 a.m. to warm up the oil so that the pistons would move first thing in the morning. Huge 8 cylinder engines."

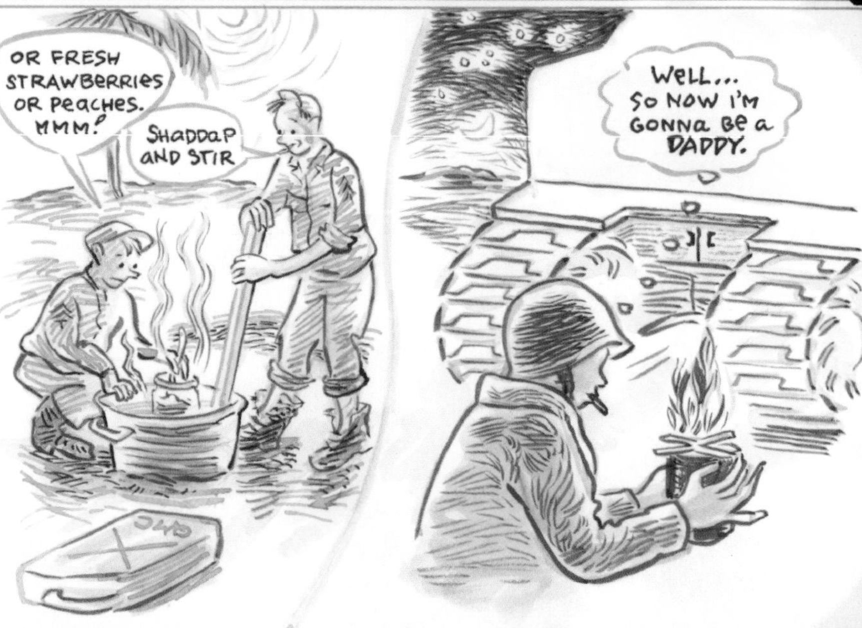

OR FRESH STRAWBERRIES OR PEACHES. MMM!
SHADDAP AND STIR
WELL... SO NOW I'M GONNA BE A DADDY.

33

"Binoculars. Nice souvenir. I was with some squad and we went after some tanks with a bottle of gasoline and a rag in it. We got a hold of one tank and burned it up good, burned the two guys out of there and it was the first Germans I helped capture. Some place in North Africa. I don't know where the hell it was.

"That's where I picked up my first souvenir. Spoils of war, I guess you could say. But now I had to be vigilant with my stuff."

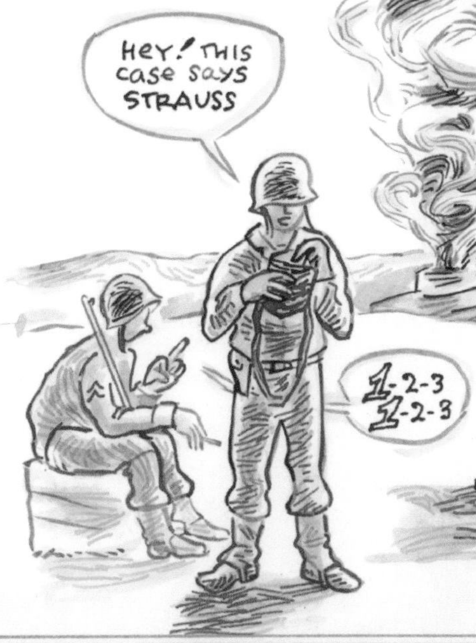
HEY! THIS case says STRAUSS
1-2-3 1-2-3
YOU MEAN LIKE THE "WALTZ KING?"

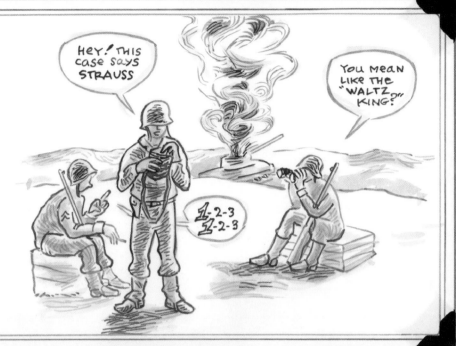

34

"Sons-of-bitches stole things, our own guys! The brass would say, 'Put your dufflebags in a pile..' for somebody to rifle through later on, when we weren't around. I seen this happen, so I always put my bag in the middle, under the others. Maybe some guys didn't get back, they got killed or something. S-O-Bs would take their souvenirs — guys who hadn't seen any action, hadn't earnt the stuff. Once I seen this guy who got caught stealing — the others drug him into the shower, beat the hell out of him then pissed all over him. Taught him a lesson."

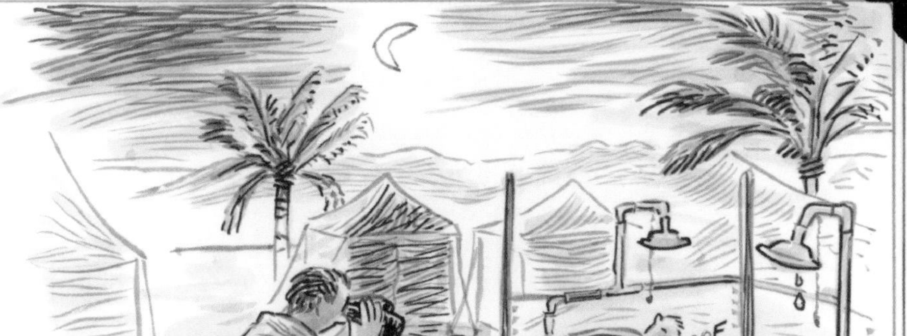
OOOF
OOOF OOOF

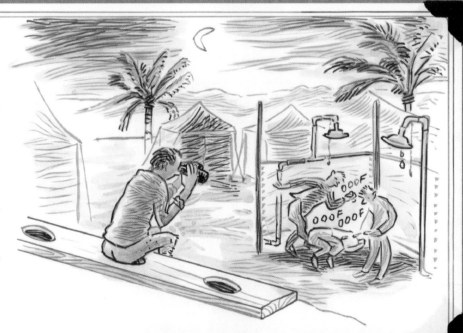

35

"Oran to Algiers by train. Stopping every mile or so. These guys would come up to the side of the boxcar interested in our 'mattress covers.' (Body bags. We each had one.) 'Sure, we'll sell 'em to ya.' So we'd tie the cord to the inside of the car door while they inspected the merchandise. They kept their money in a bag that hung between their legs. So then *toot toot* the train started to go. We'd give them the bag and take their money and then the train would *yank* the bag back in. They'd chase us with their pouches flappin'! Woo, every few miles or so we'd play this trick, our gang."

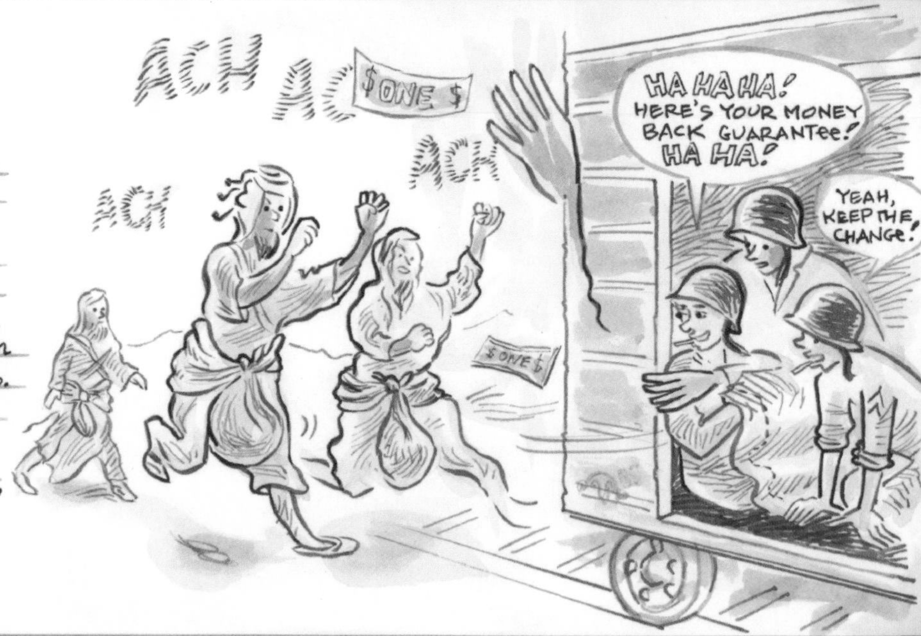
ACH
AC
$ONE $
ACH
ACH
HA HA HA!
HERE'S YOUR MONEY
BACK GUARANTee!
HA HA!
YEAH,
KEEP THE
CHANGe!
ONE

36

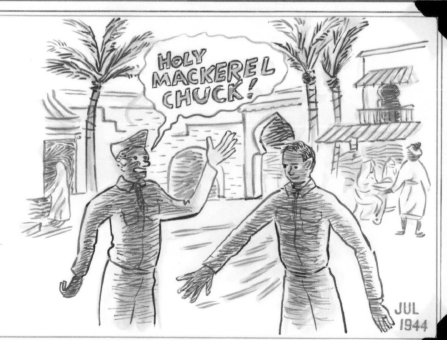

"I walked into the Casbah, but found out later I could've had my throat slit. Off limits. — On the train again to Bizerte, a 40 and 8 boxcar (40 men, 8 horses). So I says, 'This 48 is stinky. I'm going to ride on top of the gondola. It had a canvas top, soft as a hammock. I figured I'd get fresh air and nobody would bother my stuff. Me and this other guy in our spanking clean cottons. Next morning, when we got up, we were black top to toe, covered in coal soot. Leaving Africa, headed for Italy on a ship, as black as those French Moroccans.'"

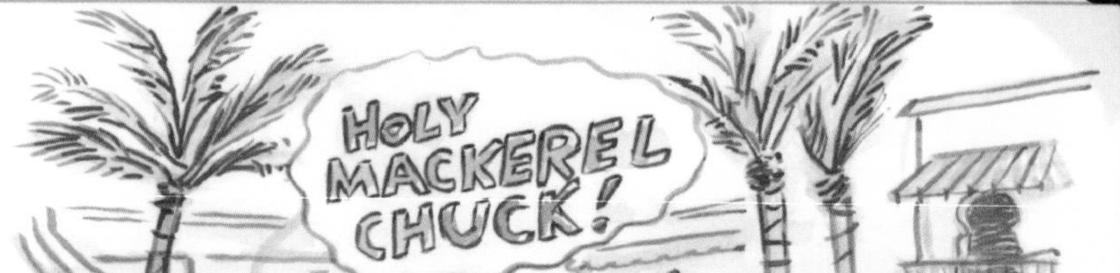
HOLY
MACKEREL
CHUCK!
JUL
1944

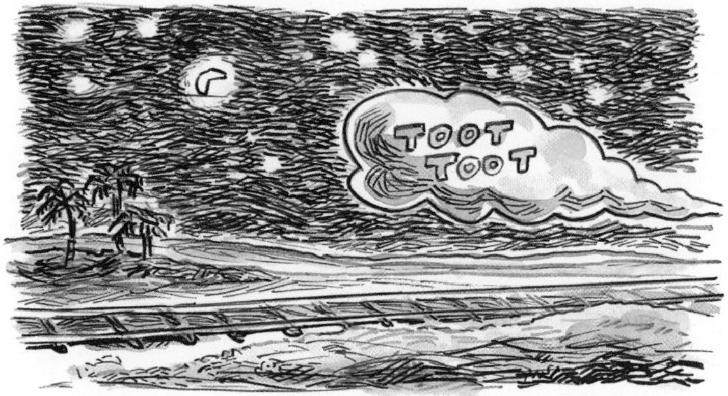
TOOT
TOOT

5.

DADDY SO DEAR

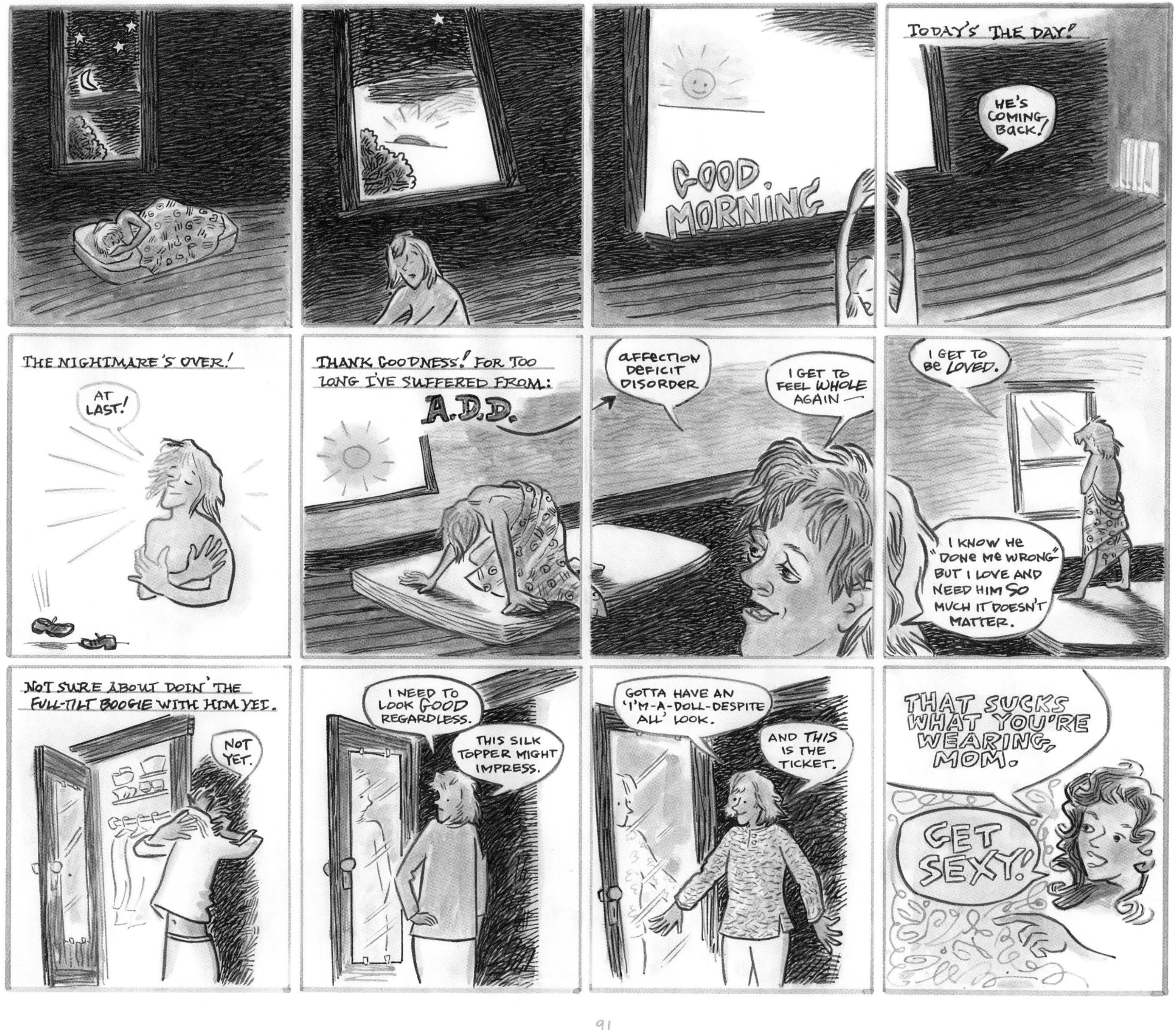
GOOD MORNING
TODAY'S THE DAY!
HE'S COMING BACK!
THE NIGHTMARE'S OVER!
AT LAST!
THANK GOODNESS! FOR TOO LONG I'VE SUFFERED FROM:
A.D.D.
AFFECTION DEFICIT DISORDER
I GET TO FEEL WHOLE AGAIN —
I GET TO BE LOVED.
I KNOW HE "DONE ME WRONG" BUT I LOVE AND NEED HIM SO MUCH IT DOESN'T MATTER.
NOT SURE ABOUT DOIN' THE FULL-TILT BOOGIE WITH HIM YET.
NOT YET.
I NEED TO LOOK GOOD REGARDLESS.
THIS SILK TOPPER MIGHT IMPRESS.
GOTTA HAVE AN 'I'M-A-DOLL-DESPITE ALL' LOOK.
AND THIS IS THE TICKET.
THAT SUCKS WHAT YOU'RE WEARING, MOM.
GET SEXY!

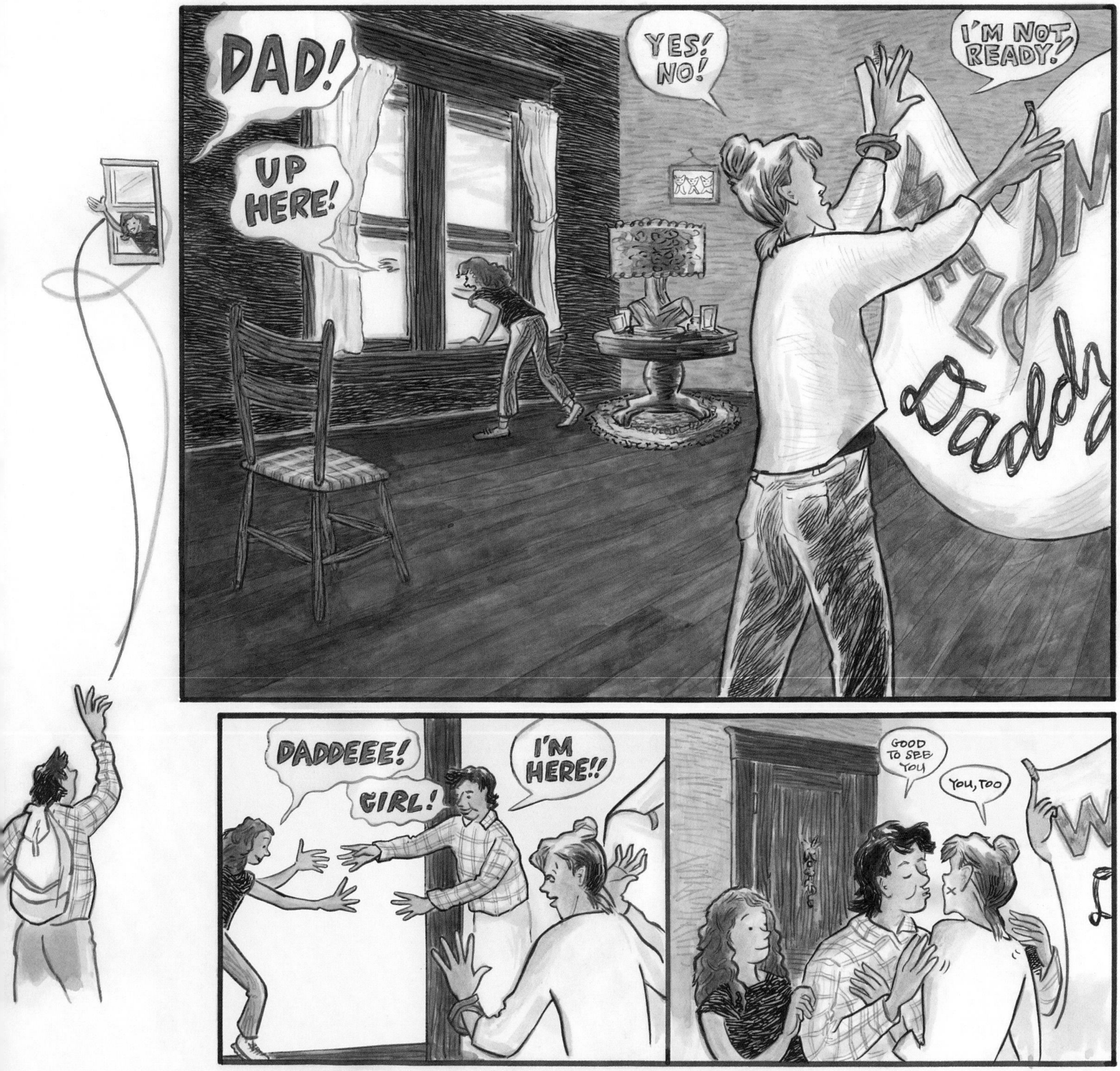
DAD!
UP HERE!
YES! NO!
I'M NOT READY!
Daddy
DADDEEE!
GIRL!
I'M HERE!!
GOOD TO SEE YOU
YOU, TOO

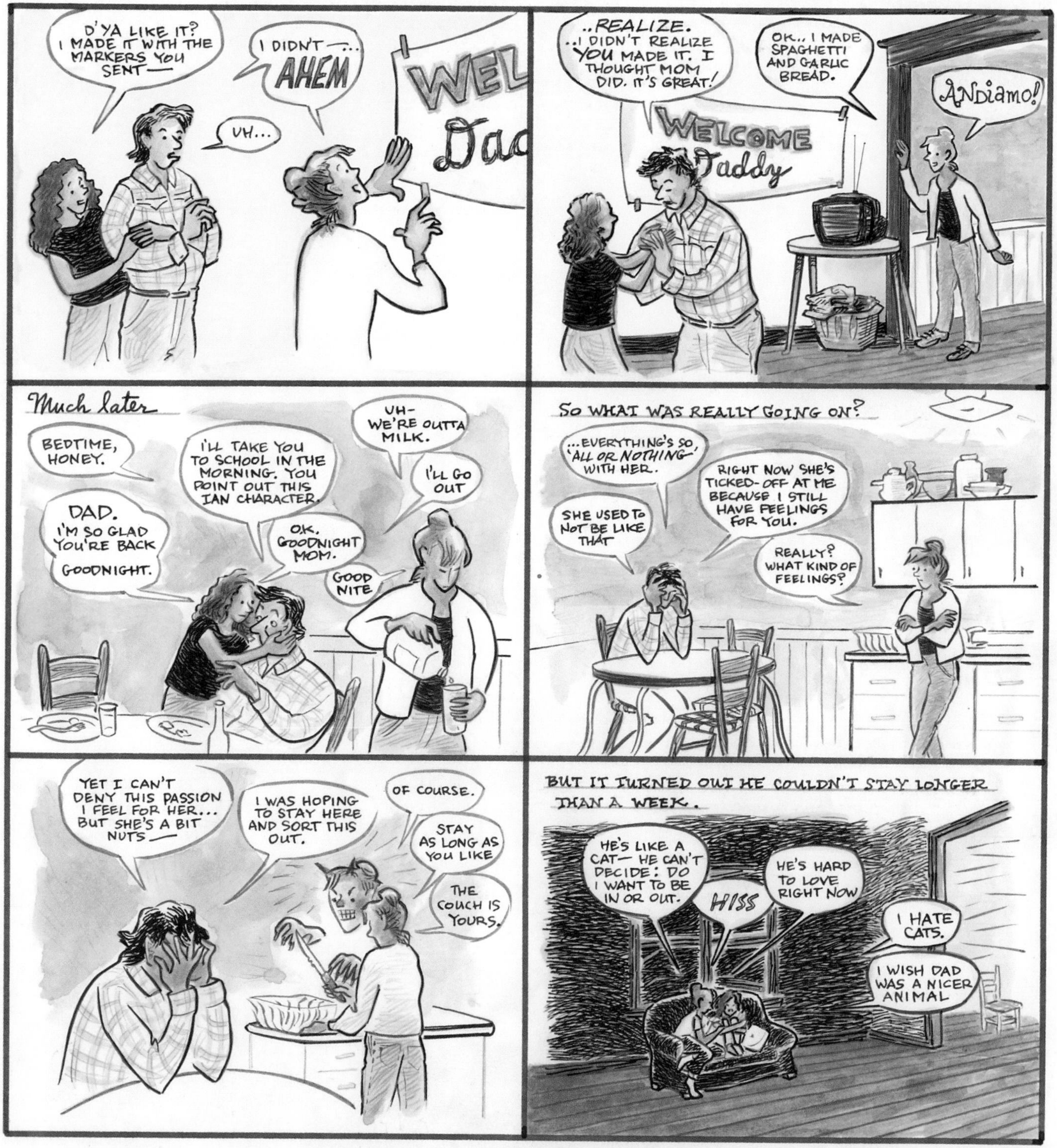
D'YA LIKE IT? I MADE IT WITH THE MARKERS YOU SENT—
I DIDN'T—...
AHEM
UH...
WEL
Dad
..REALIZE. ..I DIDN'T REALIZE YOU MADE IT. I THOUGHT MOM DID. IT'S GREAT!
OK.. I MADE SPAGHETTI AND GARLIC BREAD.
WELCOME Daddy
ANDIAMO!
Much later
BEDTIME, HONEY.
I'LL TAKE YOU TO SCHOOL IN THE MORNING. YOU POINT OUT THIS IAN CHARACTER.
UH- WE'RE OUTTA MILK.
I'LL GO OUT
DAD. I'M SO GLAD YOU'RE BACK
GOODNIGHT.
OK. GOODNIGHT MOM.
GOOD NITE
SO WHAT WAS REALLY GOING ON?
...EVERYTHING'S SO 'ALL OR NOTHING' WITH HER.
SHE USED TO NOT BE LIKE THAT
RIGHT NOW SHE'S TICKED-OFF AT ME BECAUSE I STILL HAVE FEELINGS FOR YOU.
REALLY? WHAT KIND OF FEELINGS?
YET I CAN'T DENY THIS PASSION I FEEL FOR HER... BUT SHE'S A BIT NUTS—
I WAS HOPING TO STAY HERE AND SORT THIS OUT.
OF COURSE.
STAY AS LONG AS YOU LIKE
THE COUCH IS YOURS.
BUT IT TURNED OUT HE COULDN'T STAY LONGER THAN A WEEK.
HE'S LIKE A CAT— HE CAN'T DECIDE: DO I WANT TO BE IN OR OUT.
HISS
HE'S HARD TO LOVE RIGHT NOW
I HATE CATS.
I WISH DAD WAS A NICER ANIMAL

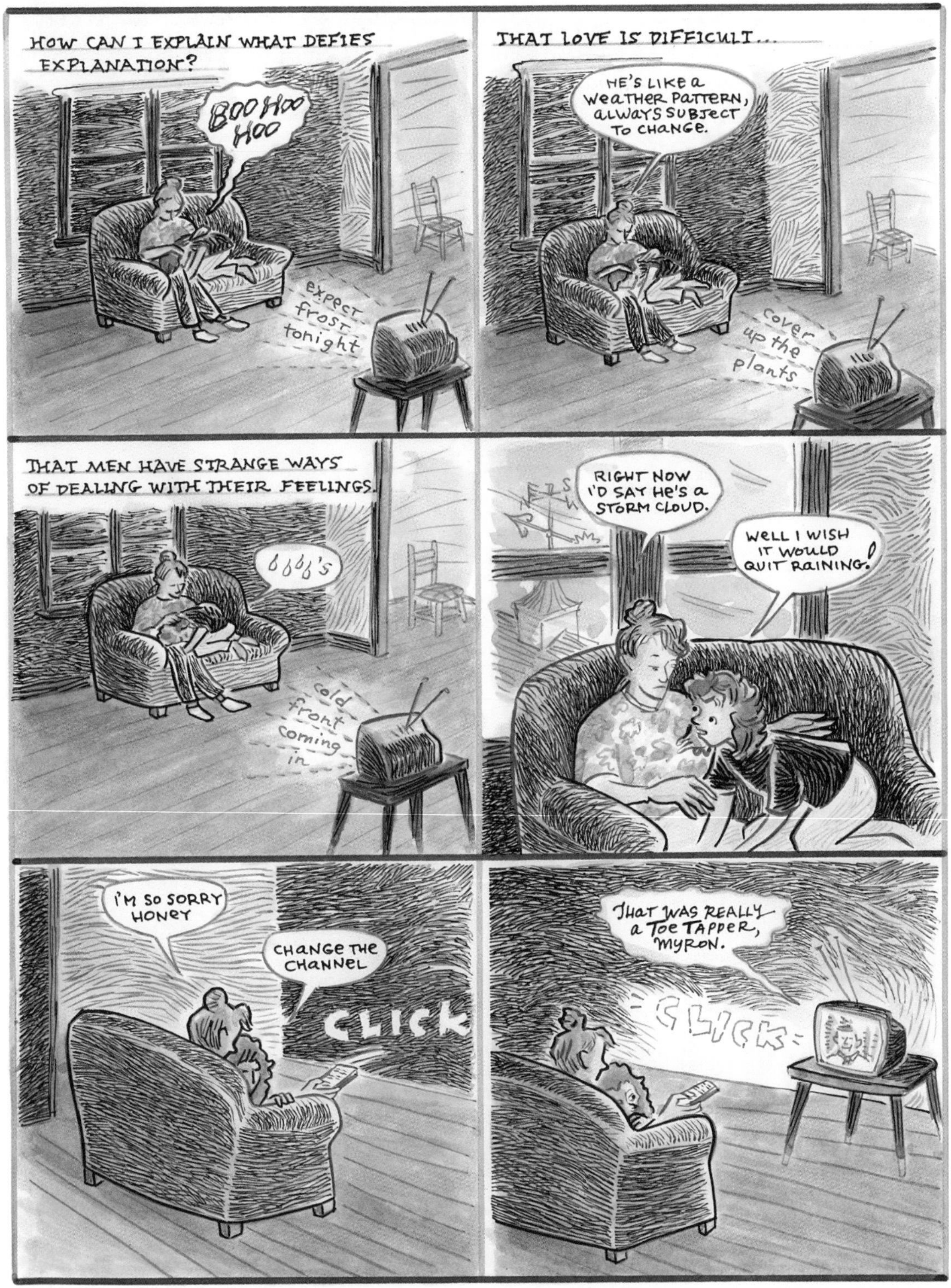
HOW CAN I EXPLAIN WHAT DEFIES EXPLANATION?
BOO HOO HOO
expect frost tonight
THAT LOVE IS DIFFICULT...
HE'S LIKE A WEATHER PATTERN, ALWAYS SUBJECT TO CHANGE.
cover up the plants
THAT MEN HAVE STRANGE WAYS OF DEALING WITH THEIR FEELINGS.
cold front coming in
RIGHT NOW I'D SAY HE'S A STORM CLOUD.
WELL I WISH IT WOULD QUIT RAINING!
I'M SO SORRY HONEY
CHANGE THE CHANNEL
CLICK
THAT WAS REALLY A TOE TAPPER, MYRON.
CLICK

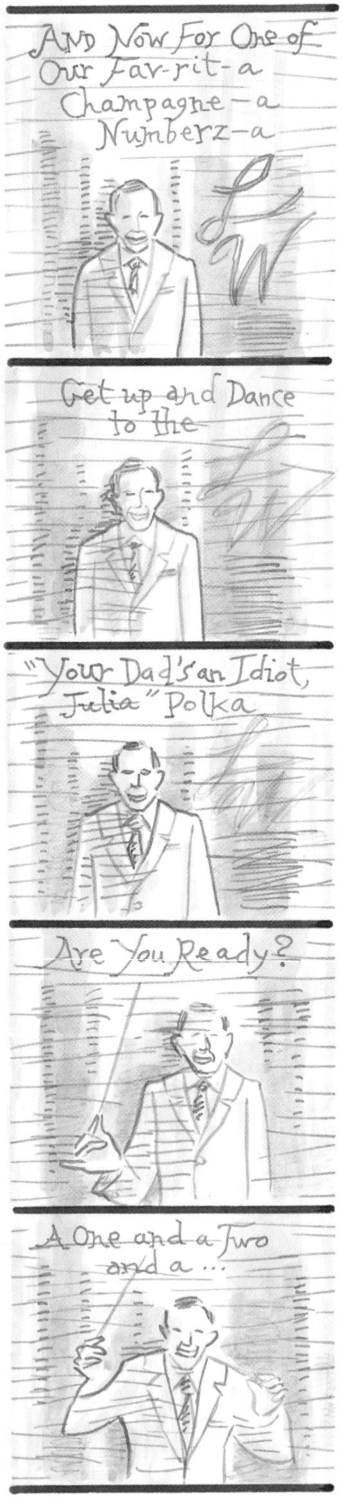
And Now For One of Our Far-rit-a Champagne-a Numberz-a
Get up and Dance to the
"Your Dad's an Idiot, Julia" Polka
Are You Ready?
A One and a Two and a...

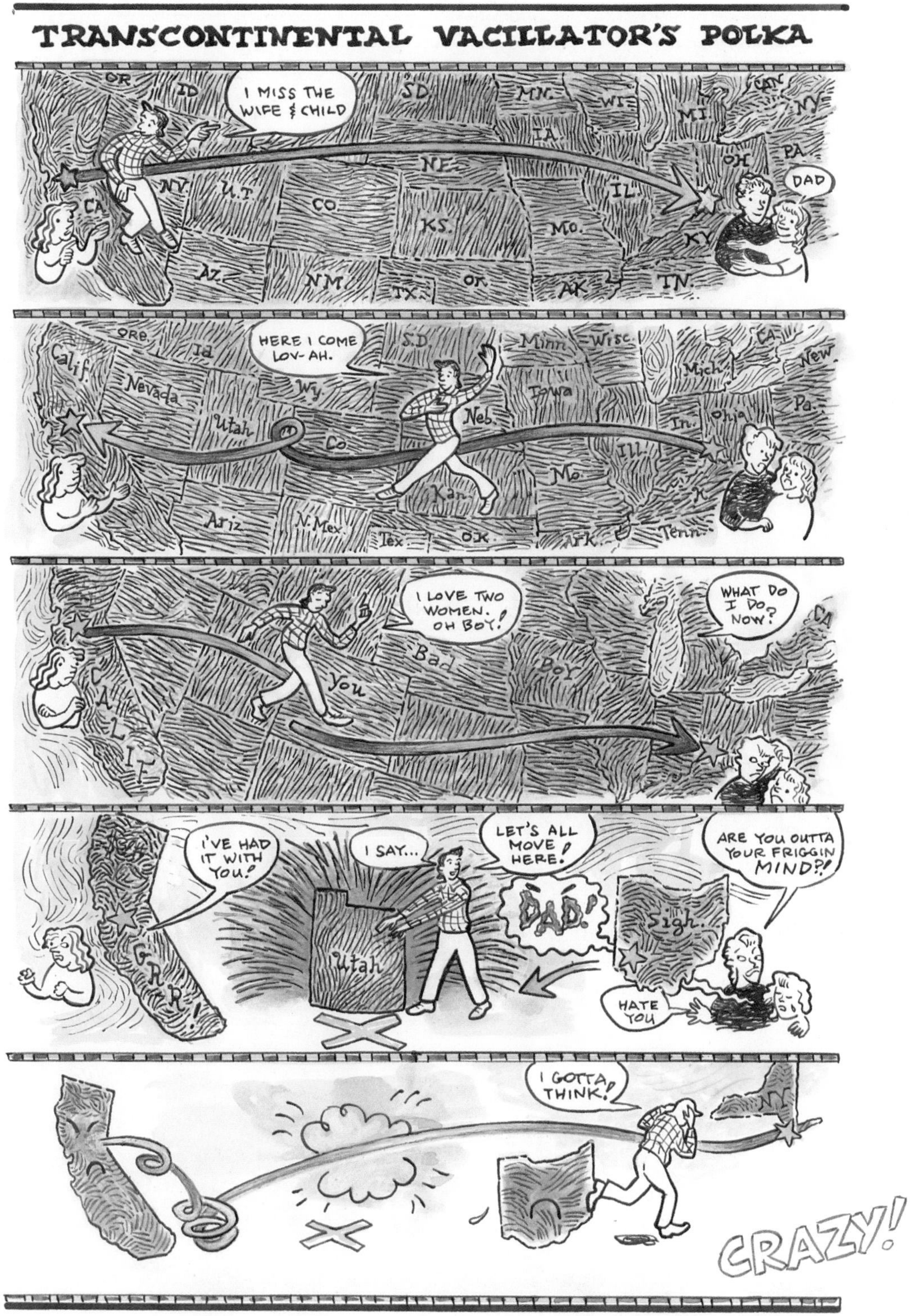
TRANSCONTINENTAL VACILLATOR'S POLKA
I MISS THE WIFE & CHILD
DAD
HERE I COME LOV-AH.
I LOVE TWO WOMEN. OH BOY!
WHAT DO I DO NOW?
Bad Boy You
I'VE HAD IT WITH YOU!
I SAY...
LET'S ALL MOVE HERE!
ARE YOU OUTTA YOUR FRIGGIN MIND?!
DAD!
Sigh.
Utah
GRRR!
HATE YOU
I GOTTA THINK!
CRAZY!

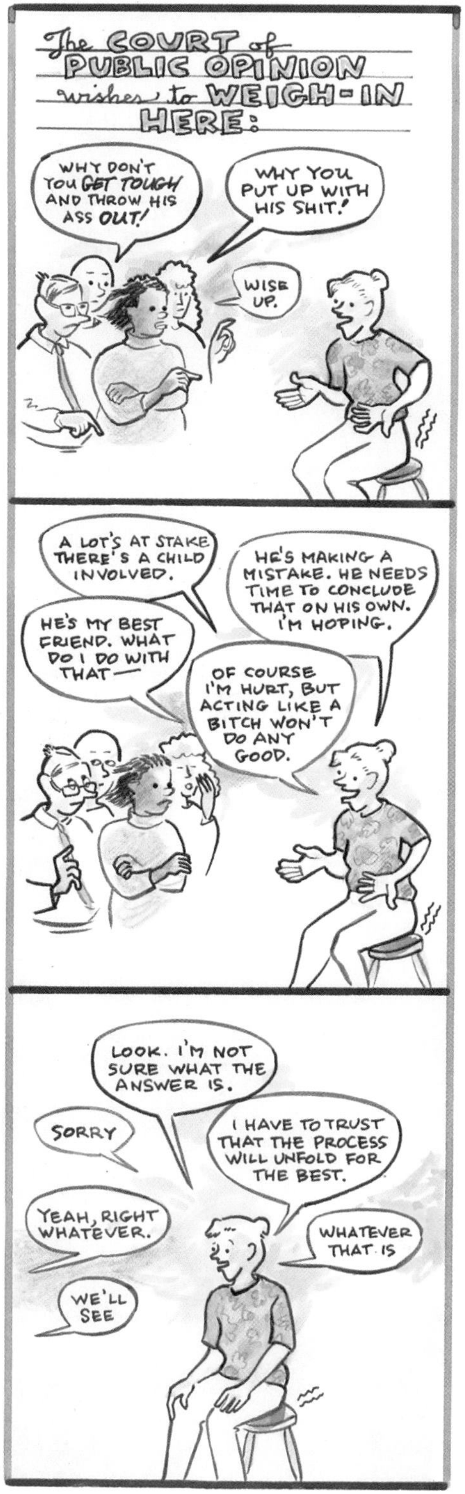
The COURT of PUBLIC OPINION wishes to WEIGH-IN HERE:
WHY DON'T YOU GET TOUGH AND THROW HIS ASS OUT!
WHY YOU PUT UP WITH HIS SHIT!
WISE UP.
A LOT'S AT STAKE THERE'S A CHILD INVOLVED.
HE'S MAKING A MISTAKE. HE NEEDS TIME TO CONCLUDE THAT ON HIS OWN. I'M HOPING.
HE'S MY BEST FRIEND. WHAT DO I DO WITH THAT—
OF COURSE I'M HURT, BUT ACTING LIKE A BITCH WON'T DO ANY GOOD.
LOOK. I'M NOT SURE WHAT THE ANSWER IS.
SORRY
I HAVE TO TRUST THAT THE PROCESS WILL UNFOLD FOR THE BEST.
YEAH, RIGHT WHATEVER.
WHATEVER THAT IS
WE'LL SEE

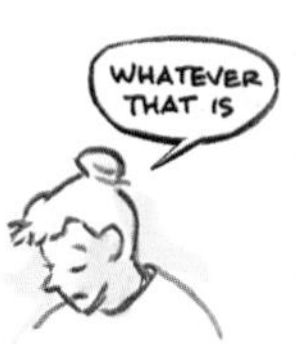
WHATEVER THAT IS

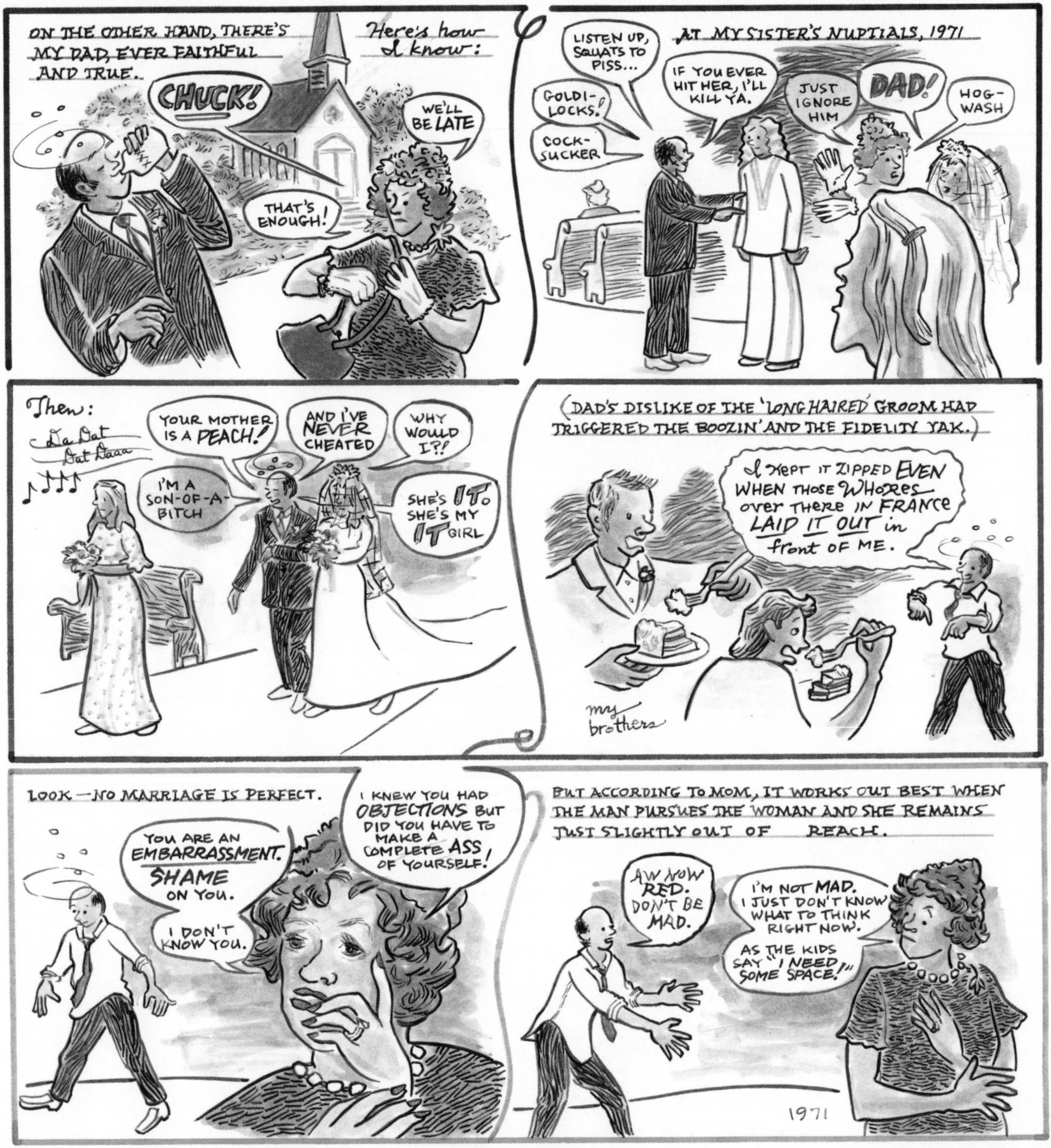
ON THE OTHER HAND, THERE'S MY DAD, EVER FAITHFUL AND TRUE.
Here's how I know:
CHUCK!
WE'LL BE LATE
THAT'S ENOUGH!
AT MY SISTER'S NUPTIALS, 1971
LISTEN UP, SQUATS TO PISS...
GOLDI-LOCKS!
COCK-SUCKER
IF YOU EVER HIT HER, I'LL KILL YA.
JUST IGNORE HIM
DAD!
HOG-WASH
Then:
Da Dat Dat Daaa
YOUR MOTHER IS A PEACH!
AND I'VE NEVER CHEATED
WHY WOULD I?!
I'M A SON-OF-A-BITCH
SHE'S IT. SHE'S MY IT GIRL
(DAD'S DISLIKE OF THE 'LONG HAIRED' GROOM HAD TRIGGERED THE BOOZIN' AND THE FIDELITY YAK.)
I kept it zipped EVEN WHEN THOSE WHORES over there in FRANCE LAID IT OUT in front of ME.
my brothers
LOOK—NO MARRIAGE IS PERFECT.
YOU ARE AN EMBARRASSMENT. SHAME ON YOU.
I DON'T KNOW YOU.
I KNEW YOU HAD OBJECTIONS BUT DID YOU HAVE TO MAKE A COMPLETE ASS OF YOURSELF!
BUT ACCORDING TO MOM, IT WORKS OUT BEST WHEN THE MAN PURSUES THE WOMAN AND SHE REMAINS JUST SLIGHTLY OUT OF REACH.
AW NOW RED. DON'T BE MAD.
I'M NOT MAD. I JUST DON'T KNOW WHAT TO THINK RIGHT NOW.
AS THE KIDS SAY "I NEED SOME SPACE!"
1971

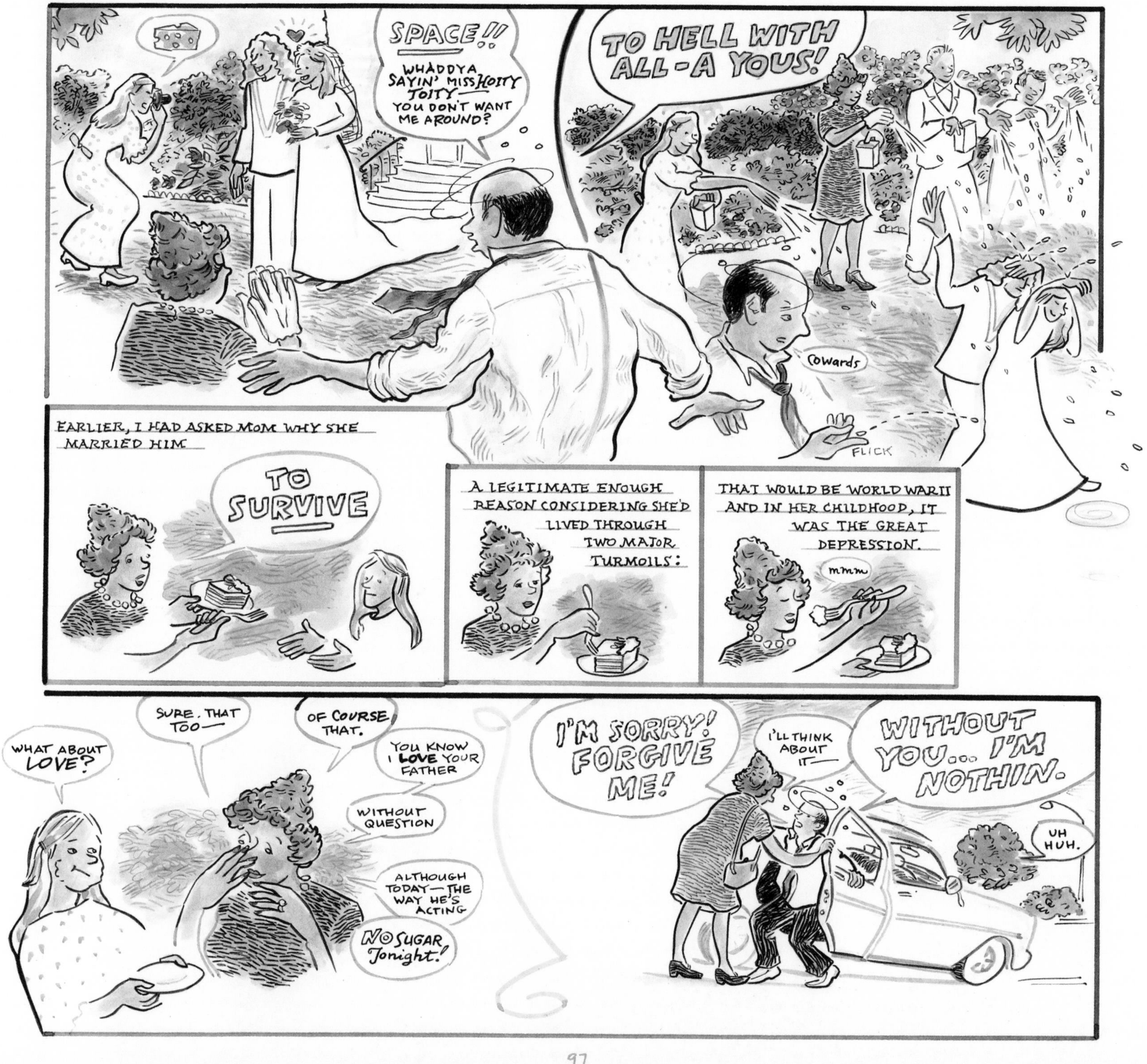
SPACE!!
WHADDYA SAYIN' MISS HOITY TOITY— YOU DON'T WANT ME AROUND?
TO HELL WITH ALL-A YOUS!
COWARDS
FLICK
EARLIER, I HAD ASKED MOM WHY SHE MARRIED HIM
TO SURVIVE
A LEGITIMATE ENOUGH REASON CONSIDERING SHE'D LIVED THROUGH TWO MAJOR TURMOILS:
THAT WOULD BE WORLD WAR II AND IN HER CHILDHOOD, IT WAS THE GREAT DEPRESSION.
MMM
WHAT ABOUT LOVE?
SURE. THAT TOO—
OF COURSE THAT.
YOU KNOW I LOVE YOUR FATHER
WITHOUT QUESTION
ALTHOUGH TODAY— THE WAY HE'S ACTING
NO SUGAR Tonight!
I'M SORRY! FORGIVE ME!
I'LL THINK ABOUT IT—
WITHOUT YOU... I'M NOTHIN.
UH HUH.

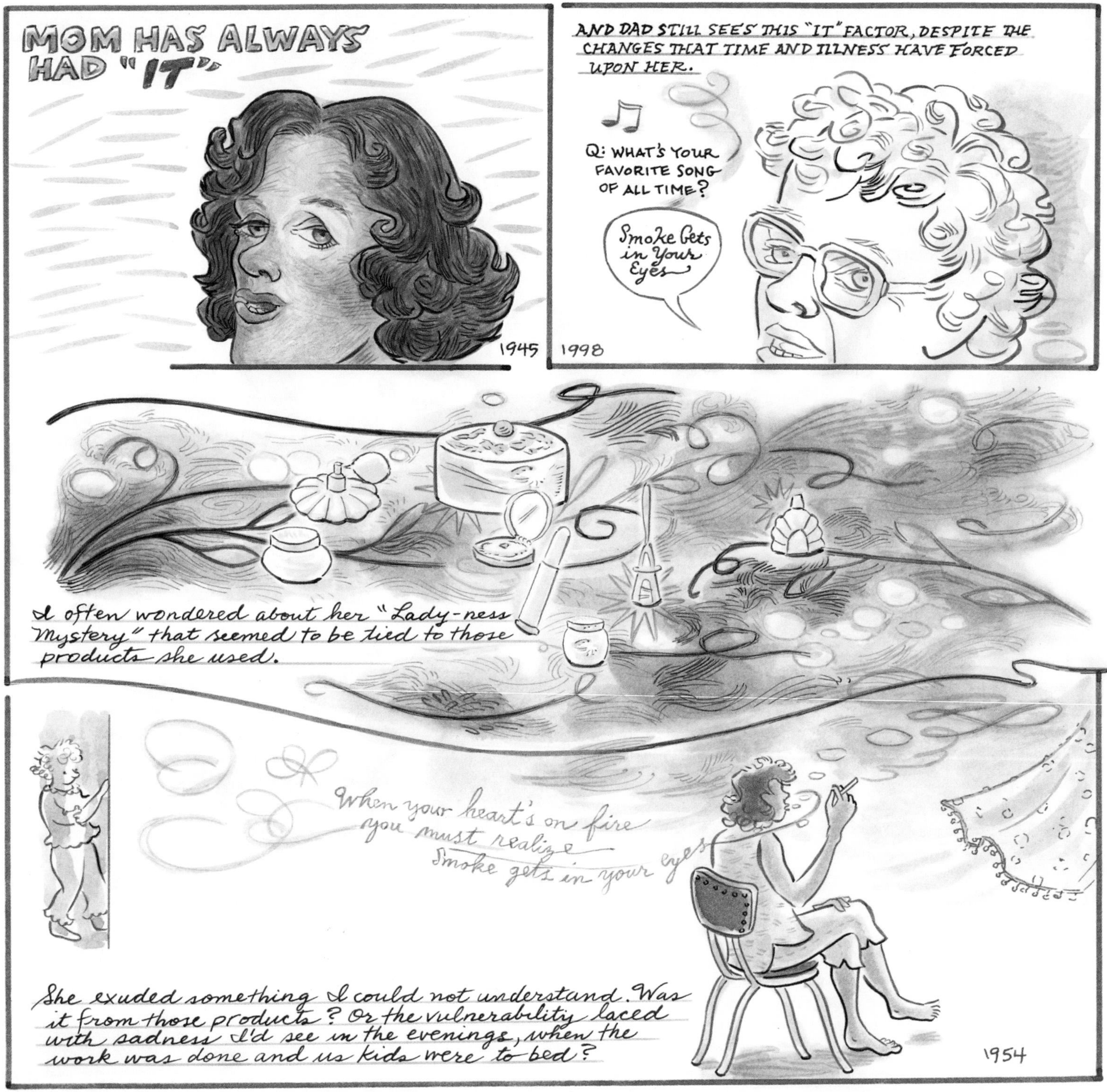
MOM HAS ALWAYS HAD "IT"
1945
AND DAD STILL SEES THIS "IT" FACTOR, DESPITE THE CHANGES THAT TIME AND ILLNESS HAVE FORCED UPON HER.
Q: WHAT'S YOUR FAVORITE SONG OF ALL TIME?
Smoke Gets in Your Eyes
1998
I often wondered about her "Lady-ness Mystery" that seemed to be tied to those products she used.
When your heart's on fire
you must realize
Smoke gets in your eyes
She exuded something I could not understand. Was it from those products? Or the vulnerability laced with sadness I'd see in the evenings, when the work was done and us kids were to bed?
1954

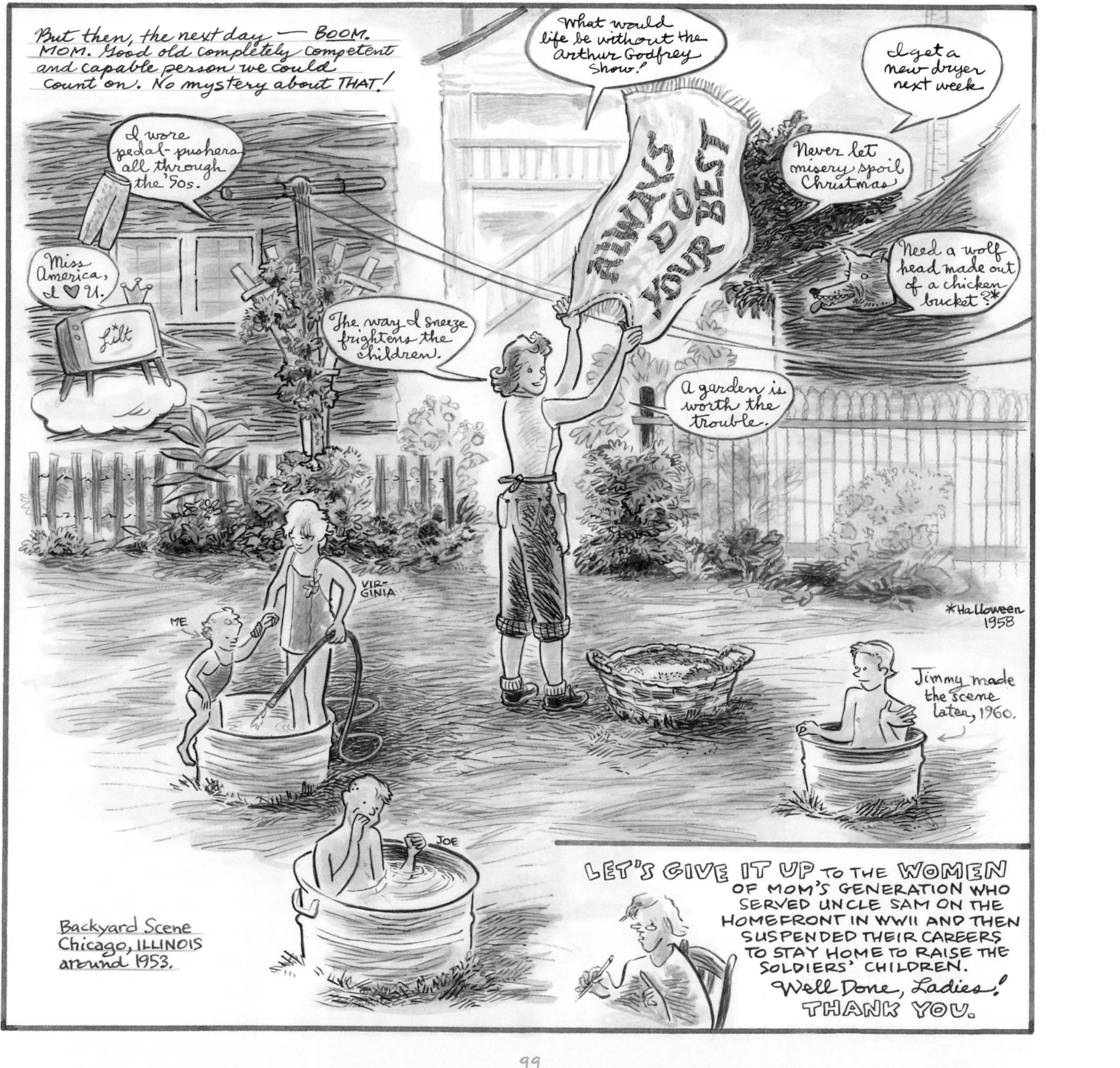

But then, the next day — BOOM. MOM. Good old completely competent and capable person we could count on. No mystery about THAT!
I wore pedal-pushers all through the '50s.
What would life be without the Arthur Godfrey Show!
I get a new dryer next week
Miss America, I ♥ U.
Lilt*
ALWAYS DO YOUR BEST
Never let misery spoil Christmas
Need a wolf head made out of a chicken bucket?*
The way I sneeze frightens the children.
A garden is worth the trouble.
VIR-GINIA
ME
*Halloween 1958
Jimmy made the scene later, 1960.
JOE
Backyard Scene Chicago, ILLINOIS around 1953.
LET'S GIVE IT UP TO THE WOMEN OF MOM'S GENERATION WHO SERVED UNCLE SAM ON THE HOMEFRONT IN WWII AND THEN SUSPENDED THEIR CAREERS TO STAY HOME TO RAISE THE SOLDIERS' CHILDREN.
Well Done, Ladies!
THANK YOU.

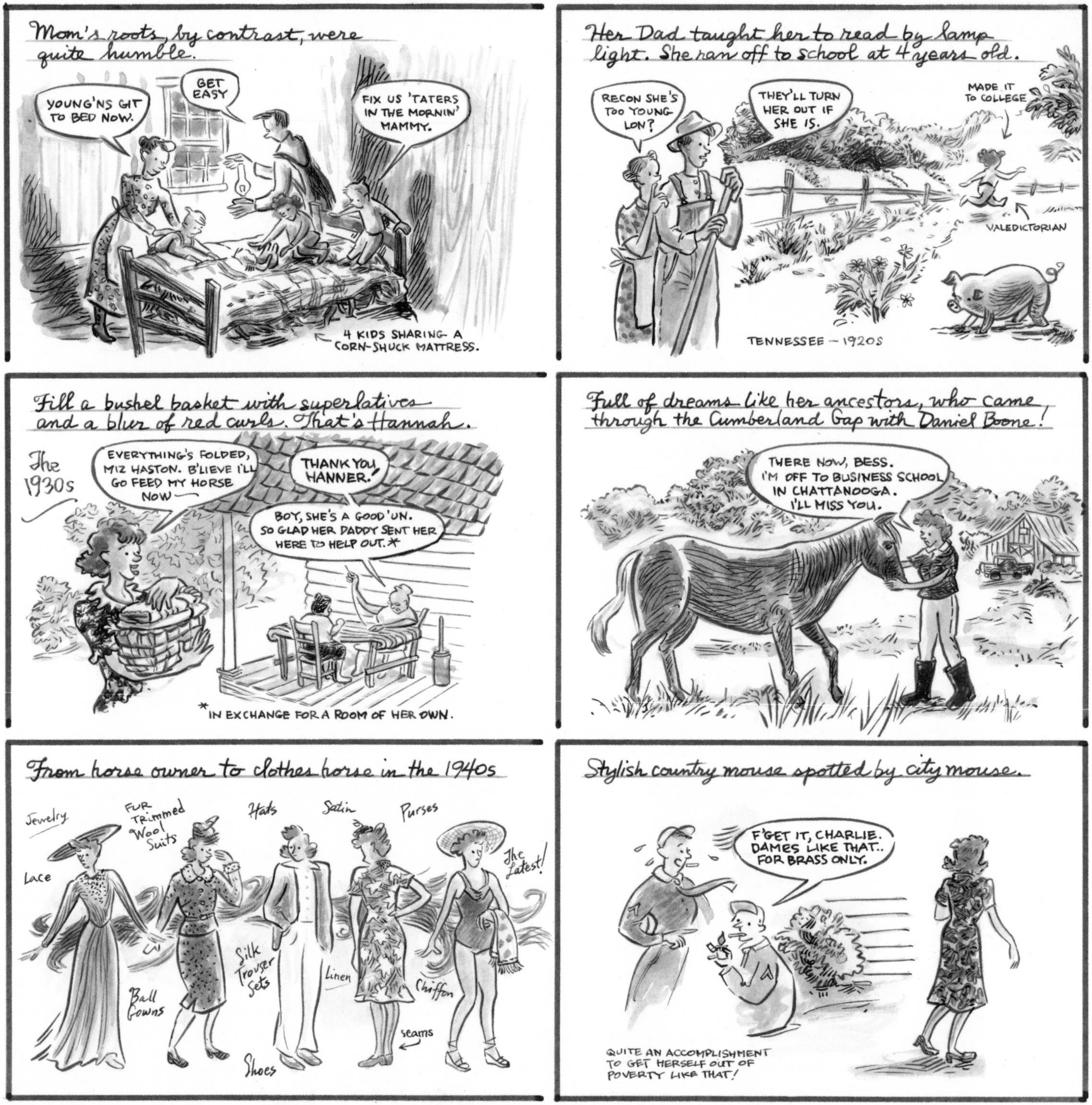
Mom's roots, by contrast, were quite humble.
YOUNG'NS GIT TO BED NOW.
GET EASY
FIX US 'TATERS IN THE MORNIN' MAMMY.
4 KIDS SHARING A CORN-SHUCK MATTRESS.
Her Dad taught her to read by lamp light. She ran off to school at 4 years old.
RECON SHE'S TOO YOUNG LON?
THEY'LL TURN HER OUT IF SHE IS.
MADE IT TO COLLEGE
VALEDICTORIAN
TENNESSEE — 1920S
Fill a bushel basket with superlatives and a blur of red curls. That's Hannah.
The 1930s
EVERYTHING'S FOLDED, MIZ HASTON. B'LIEVE I'LL GO FEED MY HORSE NOW—
THANK YOU, HANNER.
BOY, SHE'S A GOOD 'UN. SO GLAD HER DADDY SENT HER HERE TO HELP OUT.*
*IN EXCHANGE FOR A ROOM OF HER OWN.
Full of dreams like her ancestors, who came through the Cumberland Gap with Daniel Boone!
THERE NOW, BESS. I'M OFF TO BUSINESS SCHOOL IN CHATTANOOGA. I'LL MISS YOU.
From horse owner to clothes horse in the 1940s
Jewelry
FUR Trimmed Wool Suits
Hats
Satin
Purses
The Latest!
Lace
Silk Trouser Sets
Linen
Chiffon
Ball Gowns
seams
Shoes
Stylish country mouse spotted by city mouse.
F'GET IT, CHARLIE. DAMES LIKE THAT.. FOR BRASS ONLY.
QUITE AN ACCOMPLISHMENT TO GET HERSELF OUT OF POVERTY LIKE THAT!

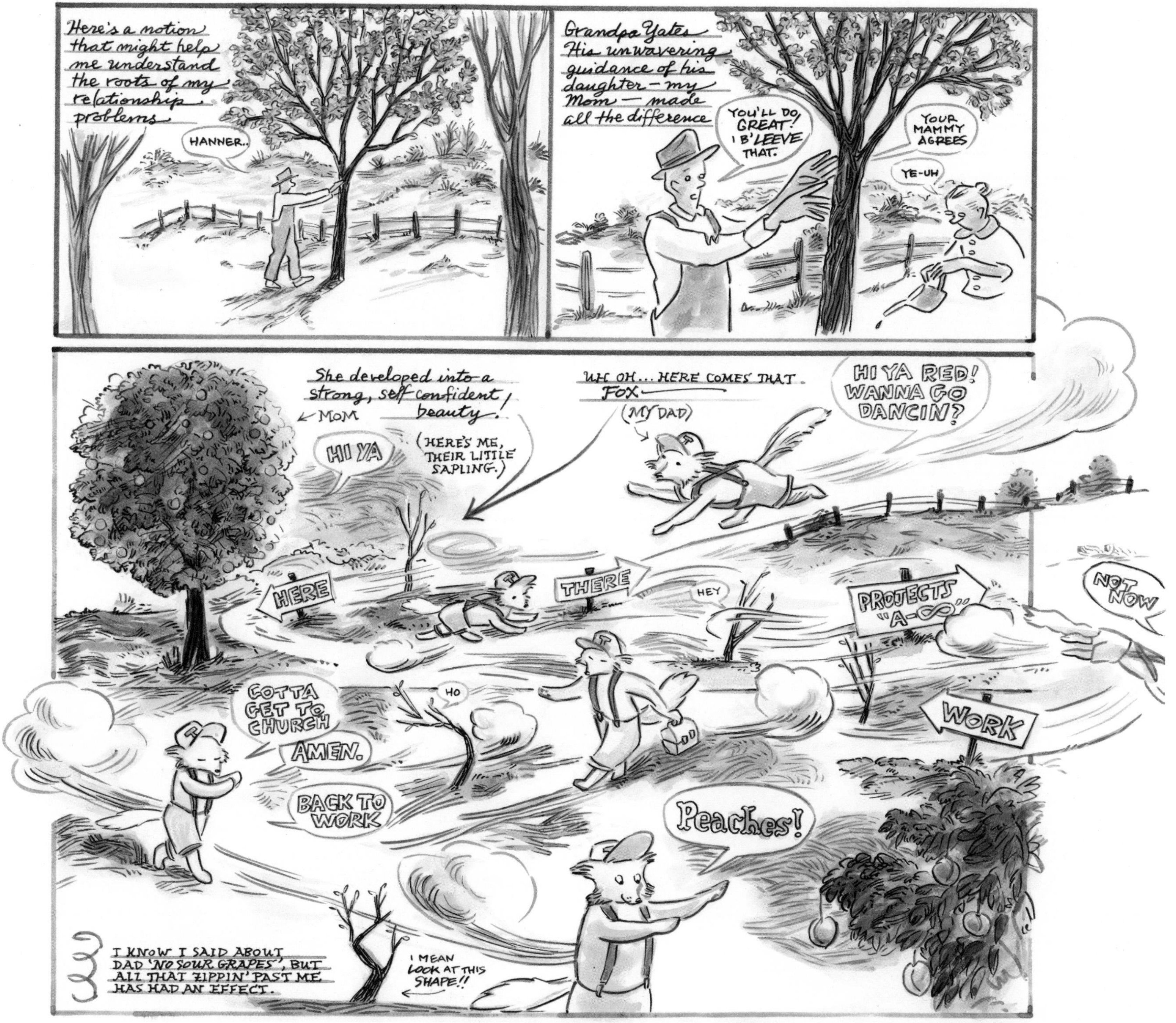
Here's a notion that might help me understand the roots of my relationship problems
HANNER..
Grandpa Yates His unwavering guidance of his daughter — my Mom — made all the difference
YOU'LL DO GREAT! I B'LEEVE THAT.
YOUR MAMMY AGREES
YE-UH
She developed into a strong, self confident beauty!
← MOM
HI YA
(HERE'S ME, THEIR LITTLE SAPLING.)
UH OH... HERE COMES THAT FOX
(MY DAD)
HI YA RED! WANNA GO DANCIN?
HERE
THERE
HEY
PROJECTS "A-∞"
NOT NOW
GOTTA GET TO CHURCH
HO
AMEN.
WORK
BACK TO WORK
Peaches!
I KNOW I SAID ABOUT DAD 'NO SOUR GRAPES', BUT ALL THAT ZIPPIN' PAST ME HAS HAD AN EFFECT.
I MEAN LOOK AT THIS SHAPE!!

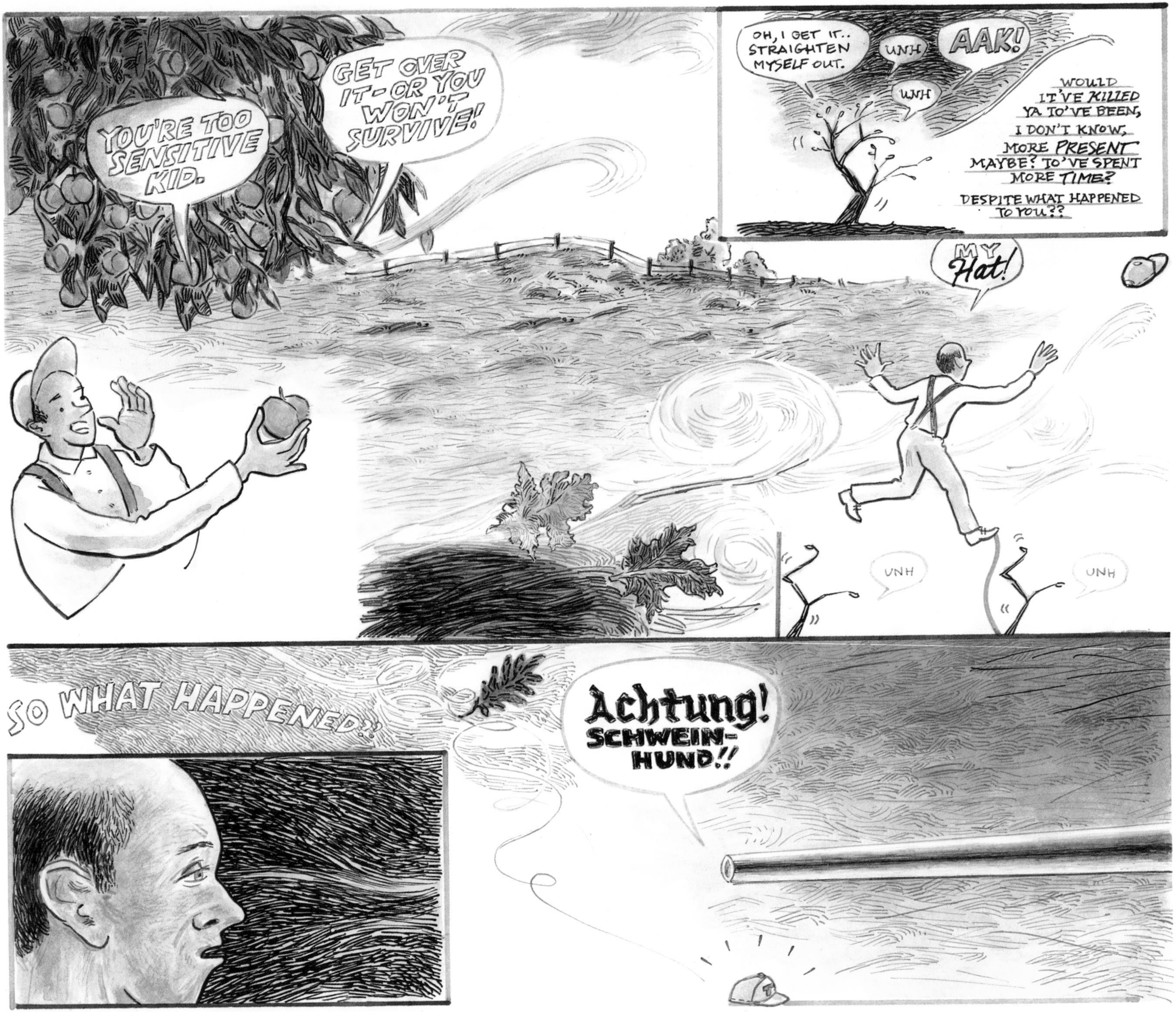
YOU'RE TOO SENSITIVE KID.
GET OVER IT - OR YOU WON'T SURVIVE!
OH, I GET IT.. STRAIGHTEN MYSELF OUT.
UNH
UNH
AAK!
WOULD IT'VE KILLED YA TO'VE BEEN, I DON'T KNOW, MORE PRESENT MAYBE? TO'VE SPENT MORE TIME?
DESPITE WHAT HAPPENED TO YOU??
MY Hat!
UNH
UNH
SO WHAT HAPPENED?!
Achtung! SCHWEIN-HUND!!

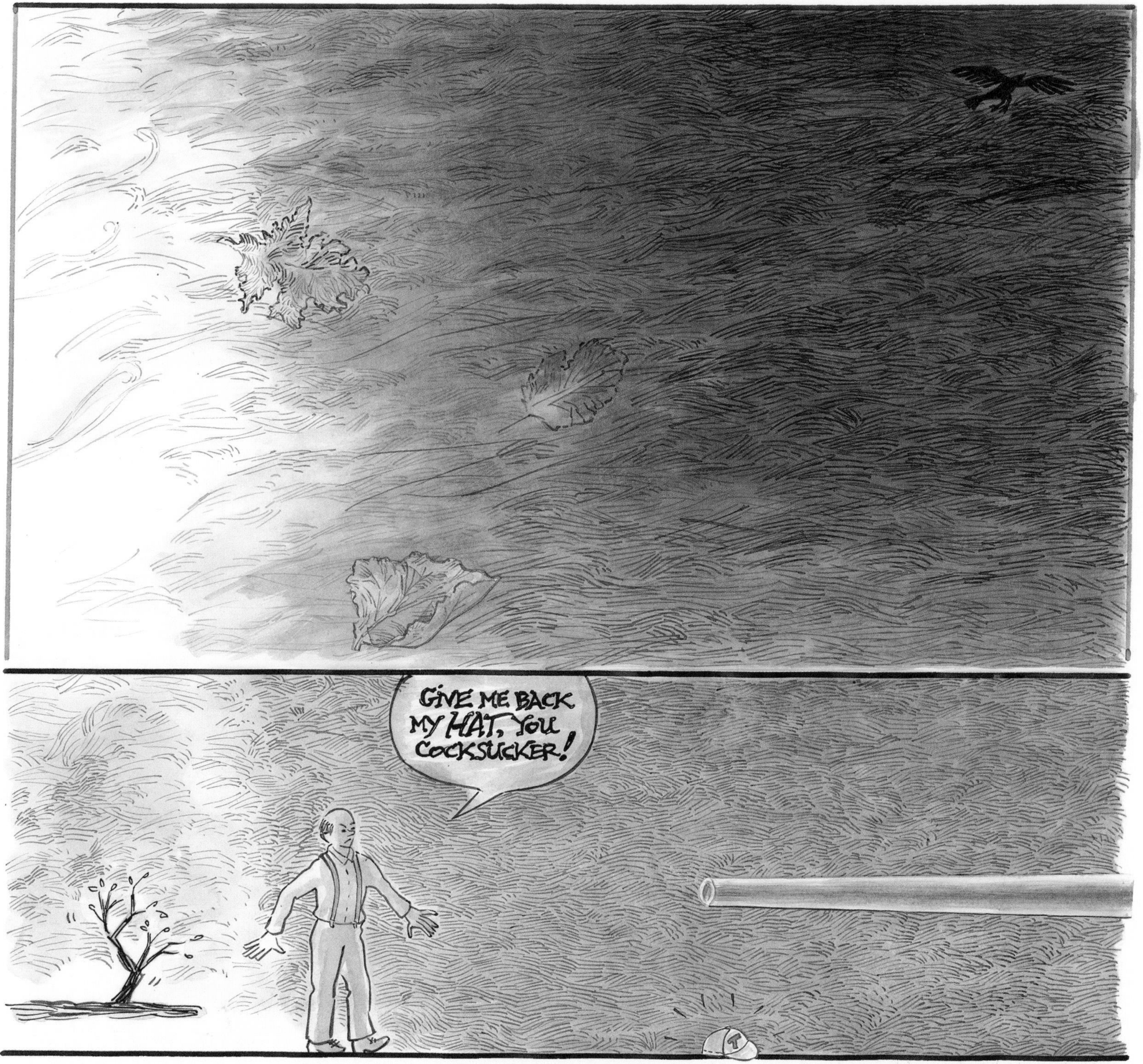
GIVE ME BACK MY HAT, YOU COCKSUCKER!

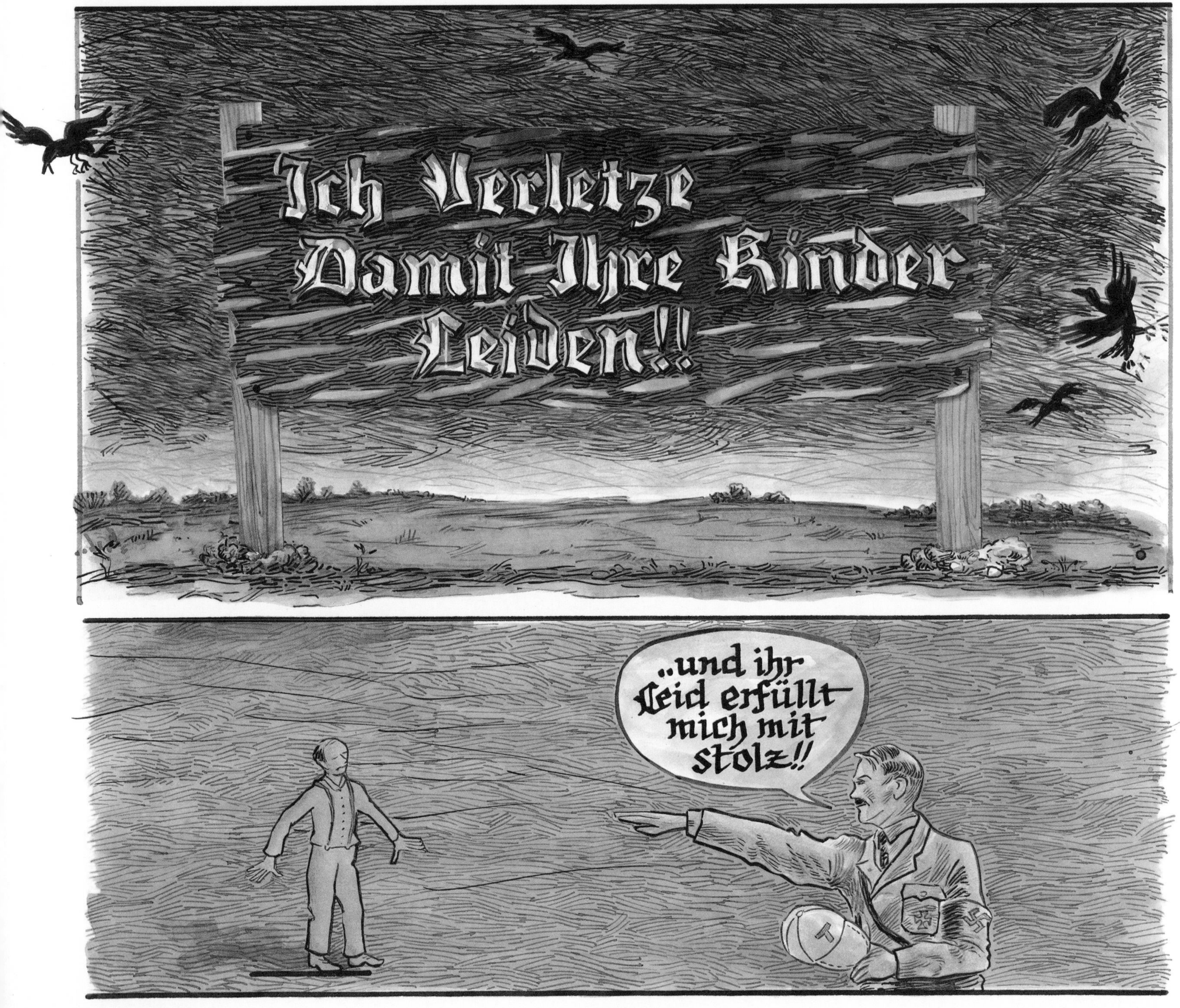
Ich Verletze
Damit Ihre Kinder
Leiden!!
..und ihr
Leid erfüllt
mich mit
stolz!!

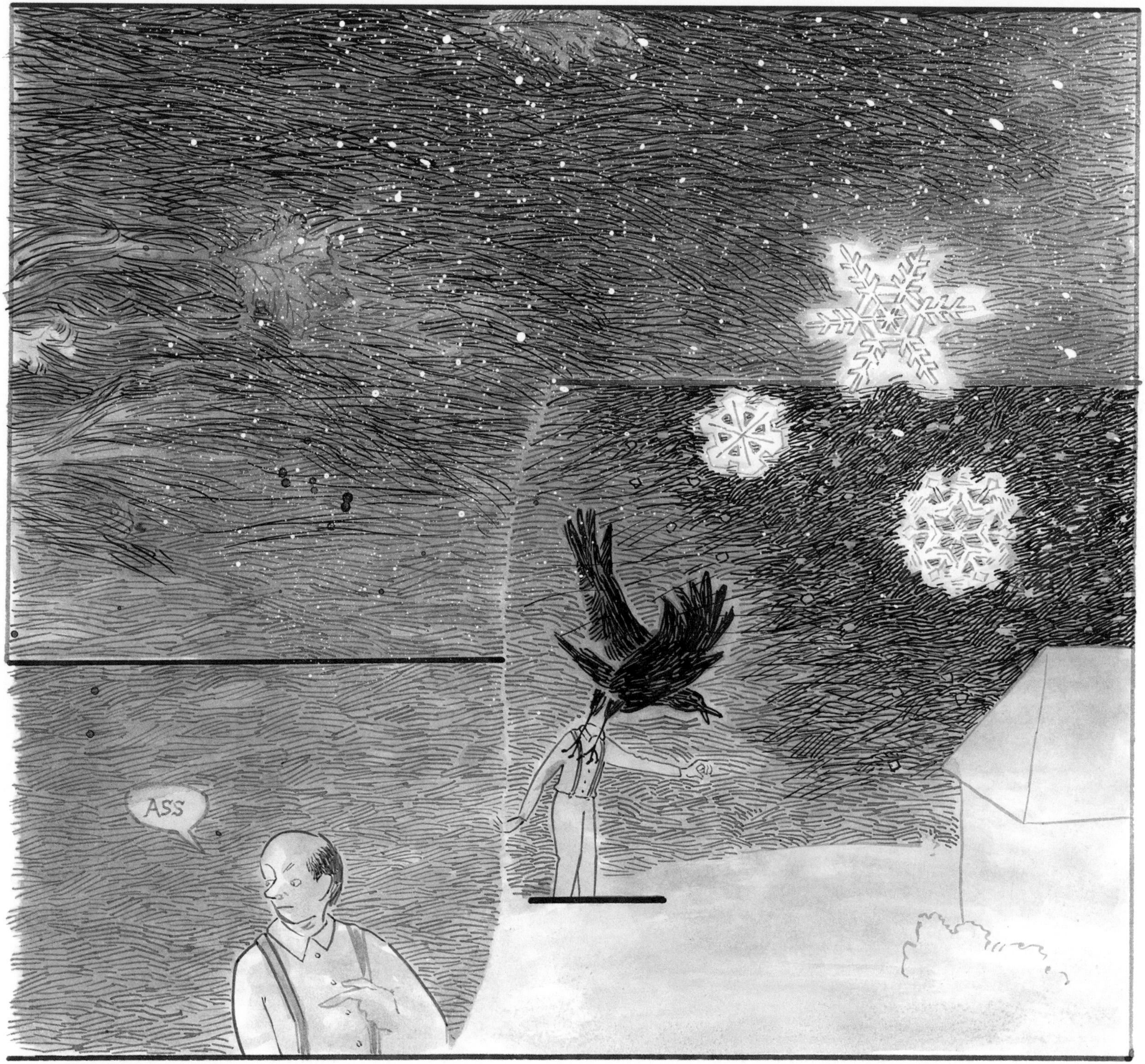
ASS

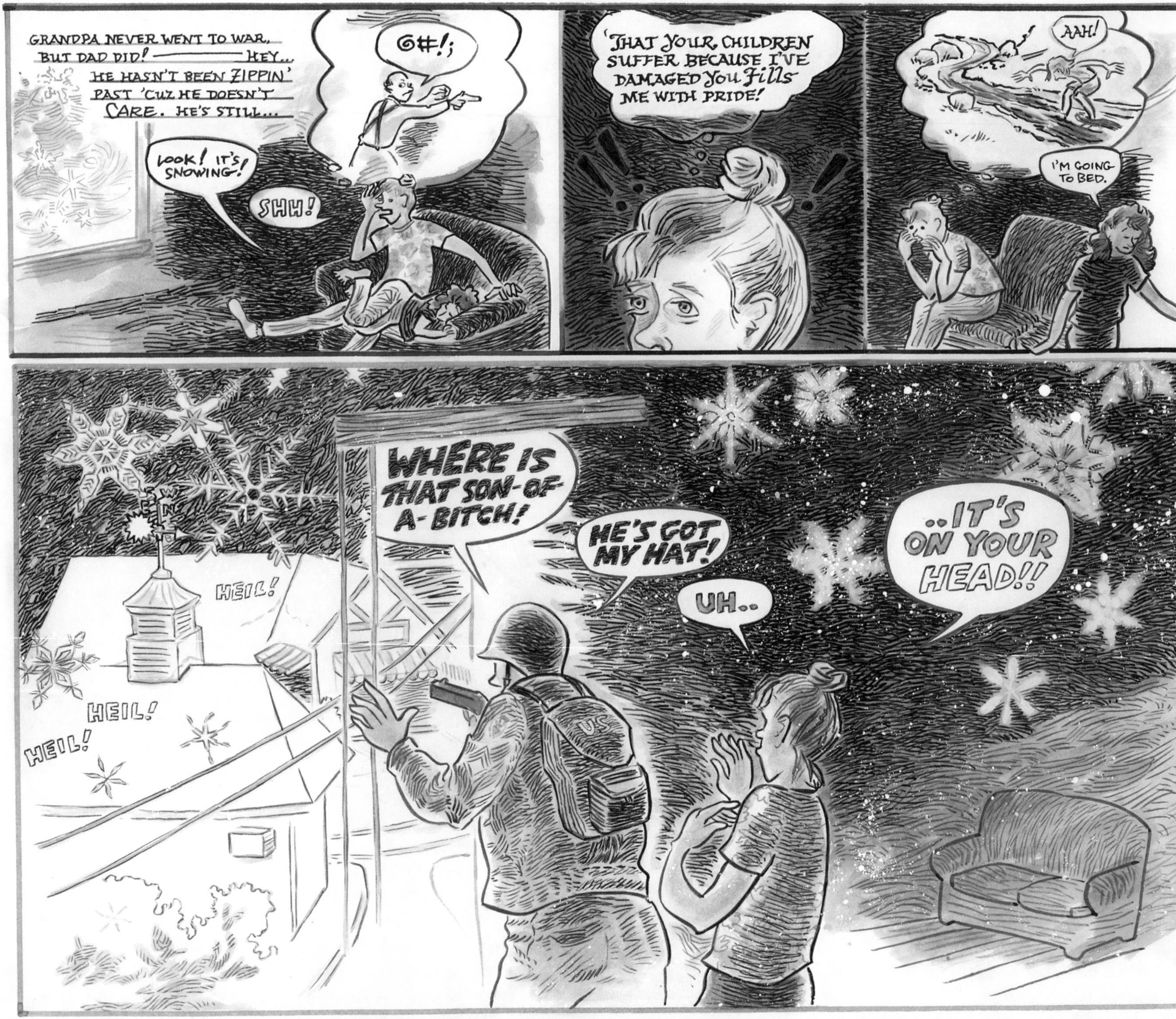
GRANDPA NEVER WENT TO WAR, BUT DAD DID! ——— HEY... HE HASN'T BEEN ZIPPIN' PAST 'CUZ HE DOESN'T CARE. HE'S STILL...
@#!;
LOOK! IT'S SNOWING!
SHH!
THAT YOUR CHILDREN SUFFER BECAUSE I'VE DAMAGED YOU FILLS ME WITH PRIDE!
AAH!
I'M GOING TO BED.
WHERE IS THAT SON-OF-A-BITCH!
HE'S GOT MY HAT!
UH..
..IT'S ON YOUR HEAD!!
HEIL!
HEIL!
HEIL!
US

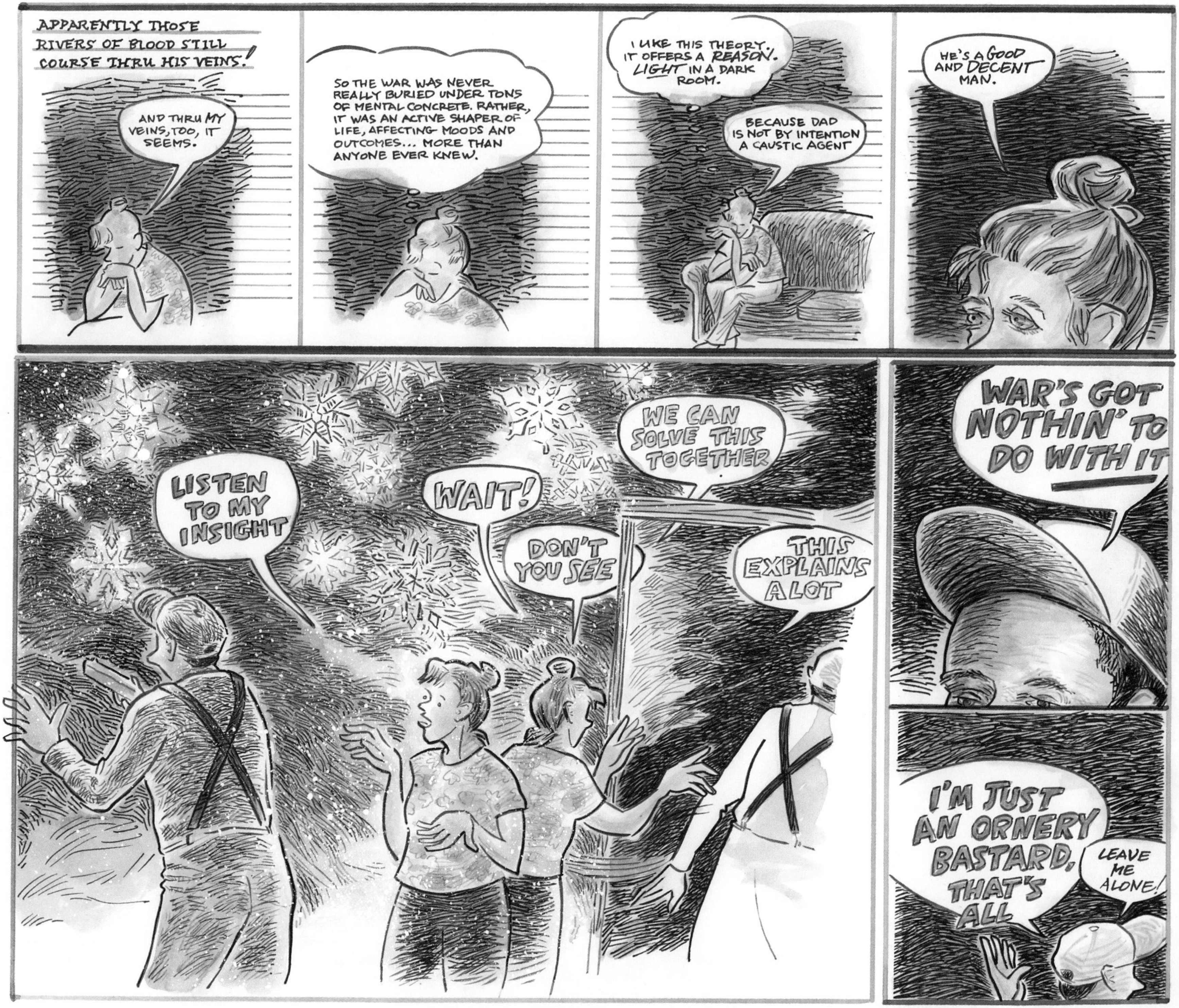
APPARENTLY THOSE RIVERS OF BLOOD STILL COURSE THRU HIS VEINS!
AND THRU MY VEINS, TOO, IT SEEMS.
SO THE WAR WAS NEVER REALLY BURIED UNDER TONS OF MENTAL CONCRETE. RATHER, IT WAS AN ACTIVE SHAPER OF LIFE, AFFECTING MOODS AND OUTCOMES... MORE THAN ANYONE EVER KNEW.
I LIKE THIS THEORY. IT OFFERS A REASON. LIGHT IN A DARK ROOM.
BECAUSE DAD IS NOT BY INTENTION A CAUSTIC AGENT
HE'S A GOOD AND DECENT MAN.
LISTEN TO MY INSIGHT
WAIT!
DON'T YOU SEE
WE CAN SOLVE THIS TOGETHER
THIS EXPLAINS ALOT
WAR'S GOT NOTHIN' TO DO WITH IT
I'M JUST AN ORNERY BASTARD, THAT'S ALL
LEAVE ME ALONE!

WHO IS HE KIDDING? NO-BODY CAN GO TO WAR AND *NOT* BE AFFECTED.

AND YET NOTHING HE'S TOLD ME OR THAT'S ON HIS PAPERS IS ALARMING.

EXCEPT FOR THAT REACTION RESPONSE OVER "IT'LY."

CONVINCED THAT SOLVING THE ARMY RIDDLE COULD HELP US BOTH...

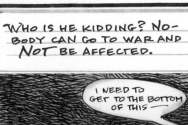

I NEED TO GET TO THE BOTTOM OF THIS—

HONORABLE DISCHARGE

4 YEARS 8 MONTHS 26 DAYS

ARMY, USA

"UNITED STATES ARMY IN WORLD WAR II" D769. US ser 2 v.1

& APPLIED MYSELF IN EARNEST TO THE TASK OF FINDING THE TRUTH.

& BECAME A SLEUTH, A SCHOLAR, THE ULTIMATE CRAFTSMAN...

...STITCHING TOGETHER THE STRAIGHT-CUT FACTS..

....WITH THE TIME-WORN MEMORIES OF A VERY OLD SOLDIER.

"THE ORGANIZATION AND ROLE OF THE ARMY SERVICE FORCES" by JOHN DAVID MILLETT 1954

DUST

"THE ROLE OF THE S-O-S IN THE DEFEAT OF GERMANY" Lt. Col. LEIGH ETOUSA Paris, 1945

"THEY CALLED IT PURPLE HEART VALLEY" —Margaret Bourke-White, 1944

"HERE IS YOUR WAR" —Ernie Pyle, 1943

"CASSINO TO THE ALPS" —Ernest F. Fisher, Jr.

Other WAR DEPT. DECLASSIFIED MAPS, ORDER OF BATTLE, etc.

I'M GONNA ASK HIM IF HE EVER HEARD OF THIS...

1 7 6 3 5 5 5 e-t-c

HU-LO

"R-R-R"

MOM? WHAT'S WRONG!

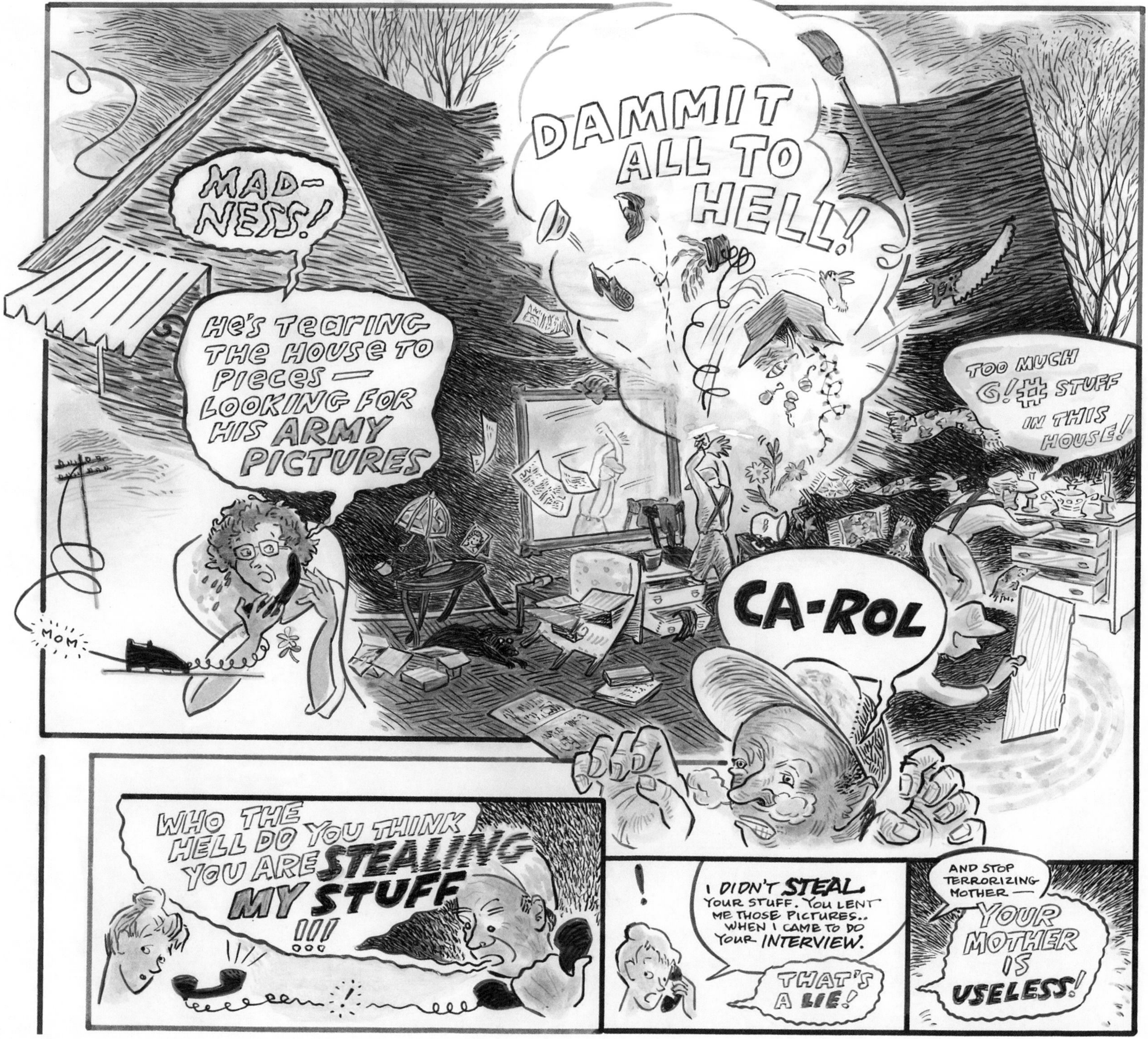
MAD-NESS!
He's tearing the house to pieces — looking for his ARMY PICTURES
MOM
DAMMIT ALL TO HELL!
TOO MUCH G!# STUFF IN THIS HOUSE!
CA-ROL
WHO THE HELL DO YOU THINK YOU ARE STEALING MY STUFF !!!
!
I DIDN'T STEAL YOUR STUFF. YOU LENT ME THOSE PICTURES.. WHEN I CAME TO DO YOUR INTERVIEW.
THAT'S A LIE!
AND STOP TERRORIZING MOTHER —
YOUR MOTHER IS USELESS!

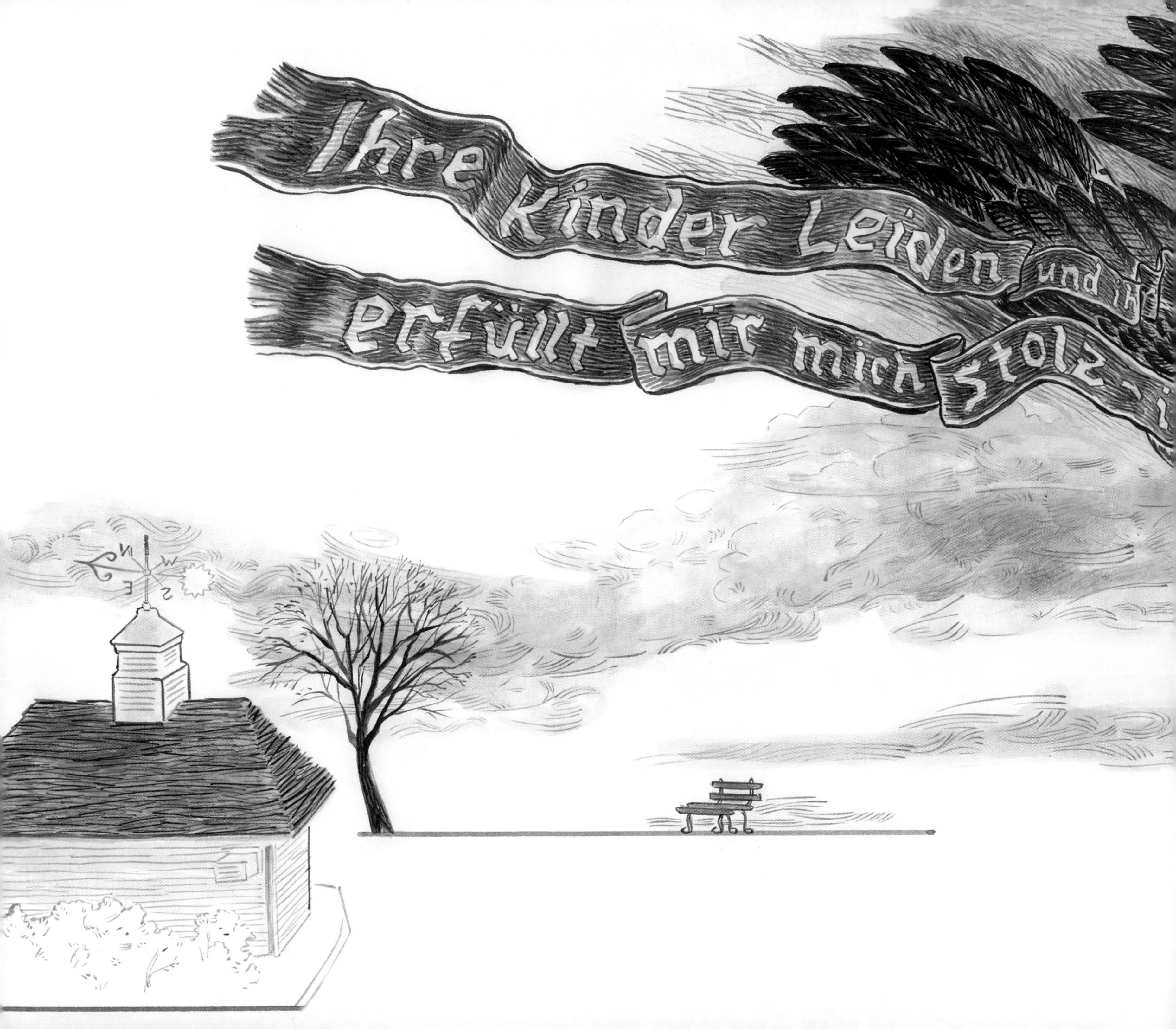
Ihre Kinder Leiden und ih
erfüllt mir mich stolz - i

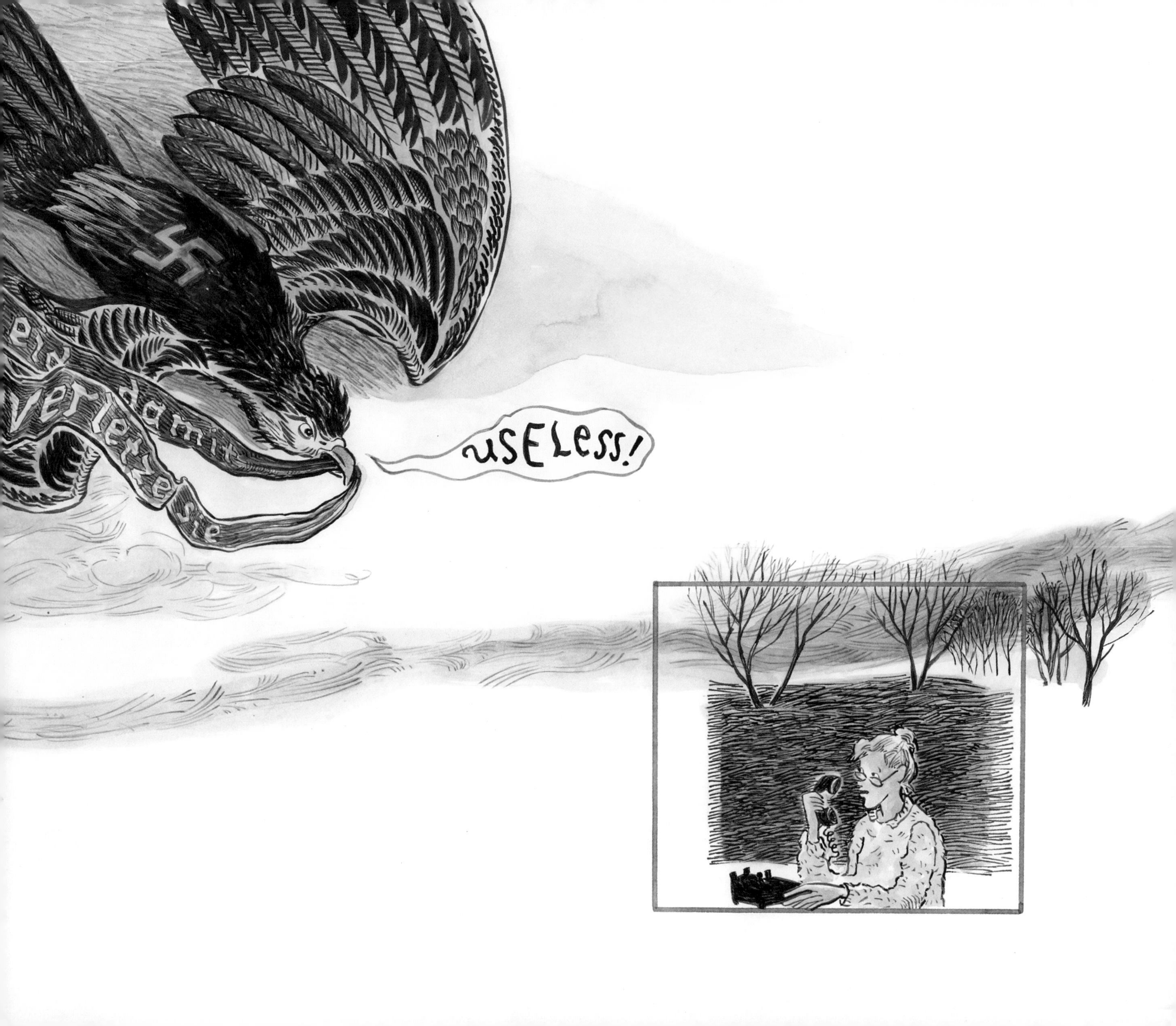
damit
verletze sie
USELESS!

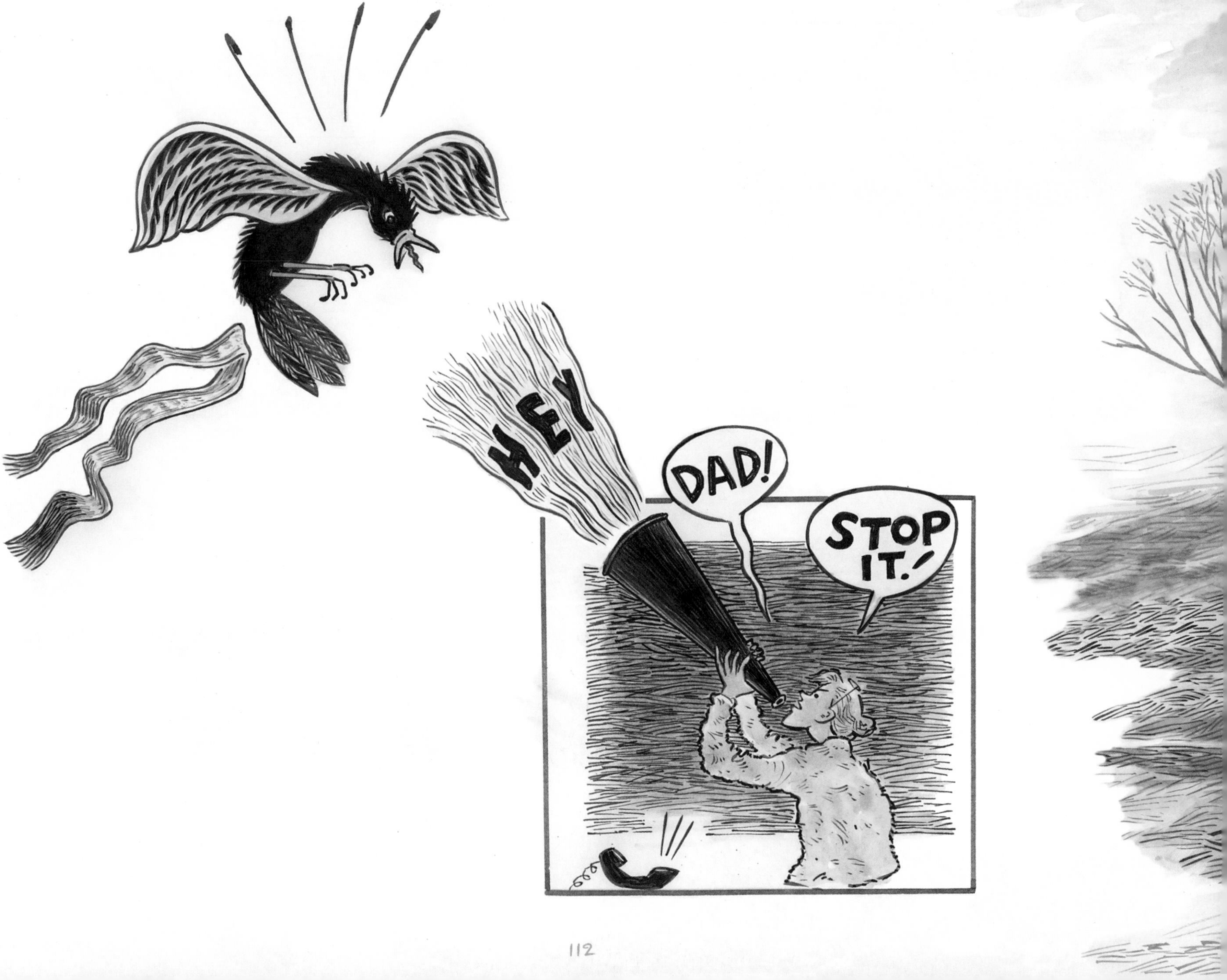
HEY
DAD!
STOP IT.!

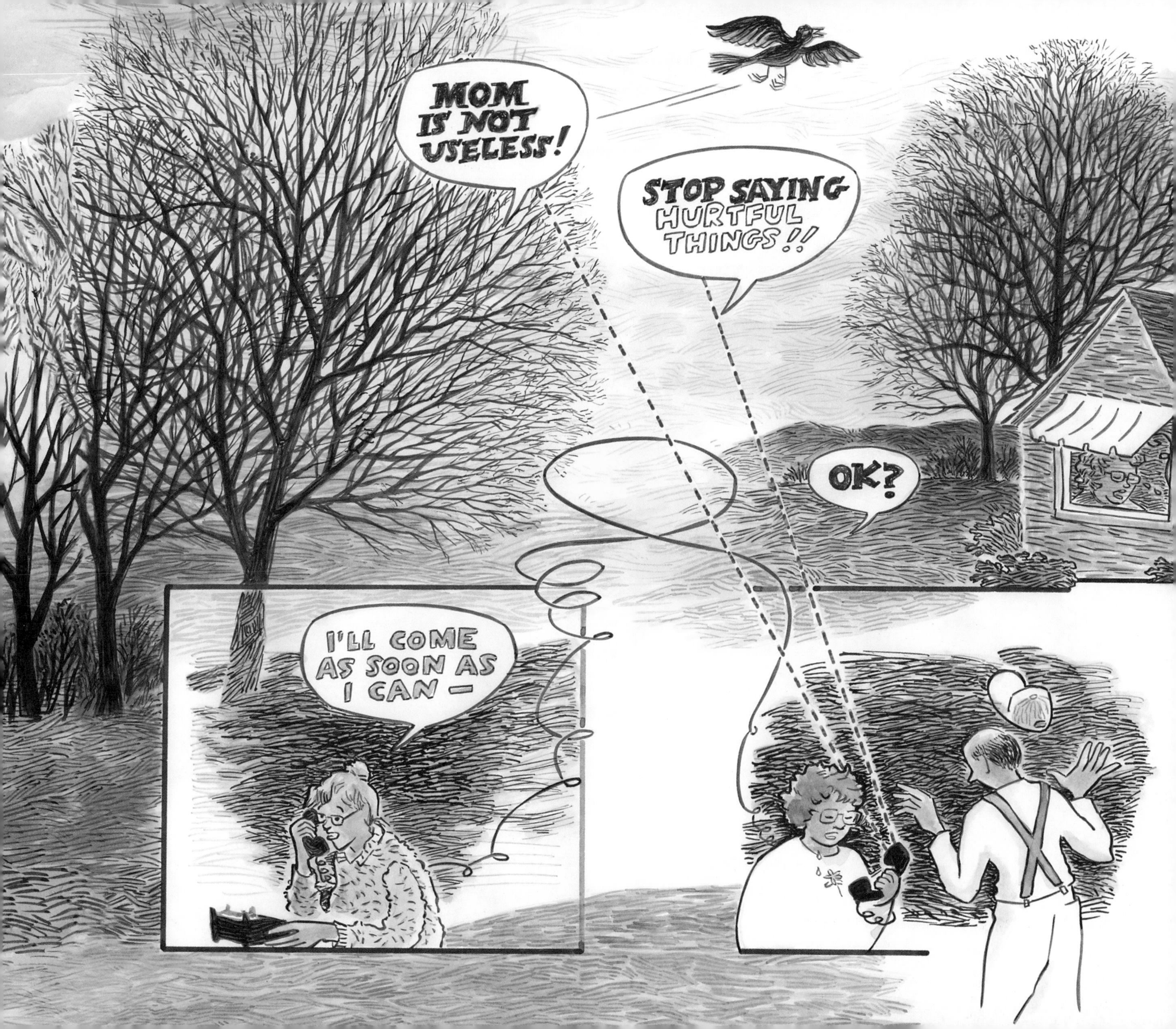
MOM IS NOT USELESS!
STOP SAYING HURTFUL THINGS!!
OK?
I'LL COME AS SOON AS I CAN –

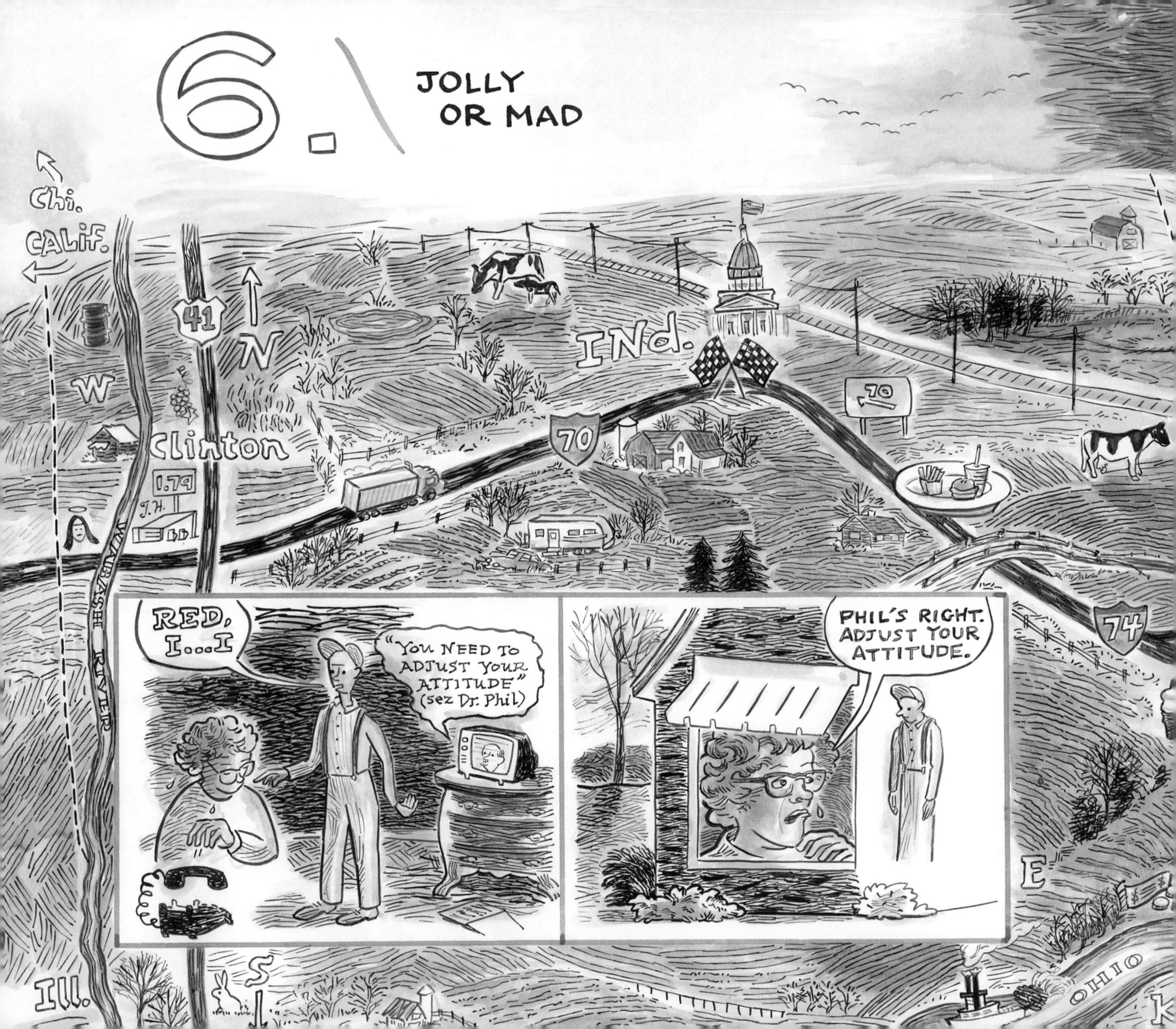
6.
JOLLY OR MAD
Chi.
CALIF.
41
N
IND.
W
Clinton
1.79
J.H.
70
74
WABASH RIVER
RED, I...I
"YOU NEED TO ADJUST YOUR ATTITUDE" (sez Dr. Phil)
PHIL'S RIGHT. ADJUST YOUR ATTITUDE.
E
S
Ill.
OHIO

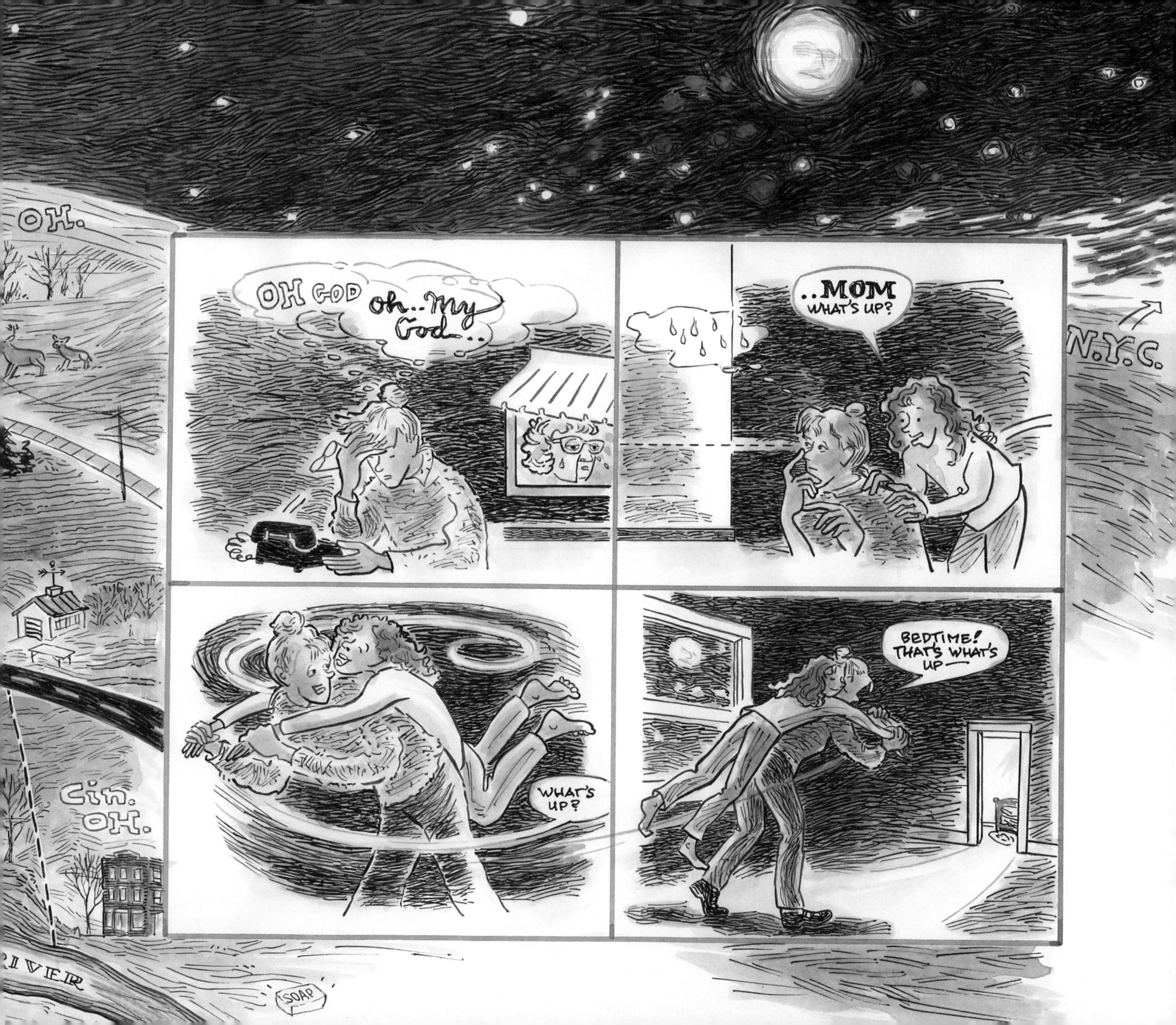
OH.
N.Y.C.
OH GOD oh.. My God...
..MOM WHAT'S UP?
WHAT'S UP?
BEDTIME! THAT'S WHAT'S UP—
Cin. OH.
RIVER
SOAP

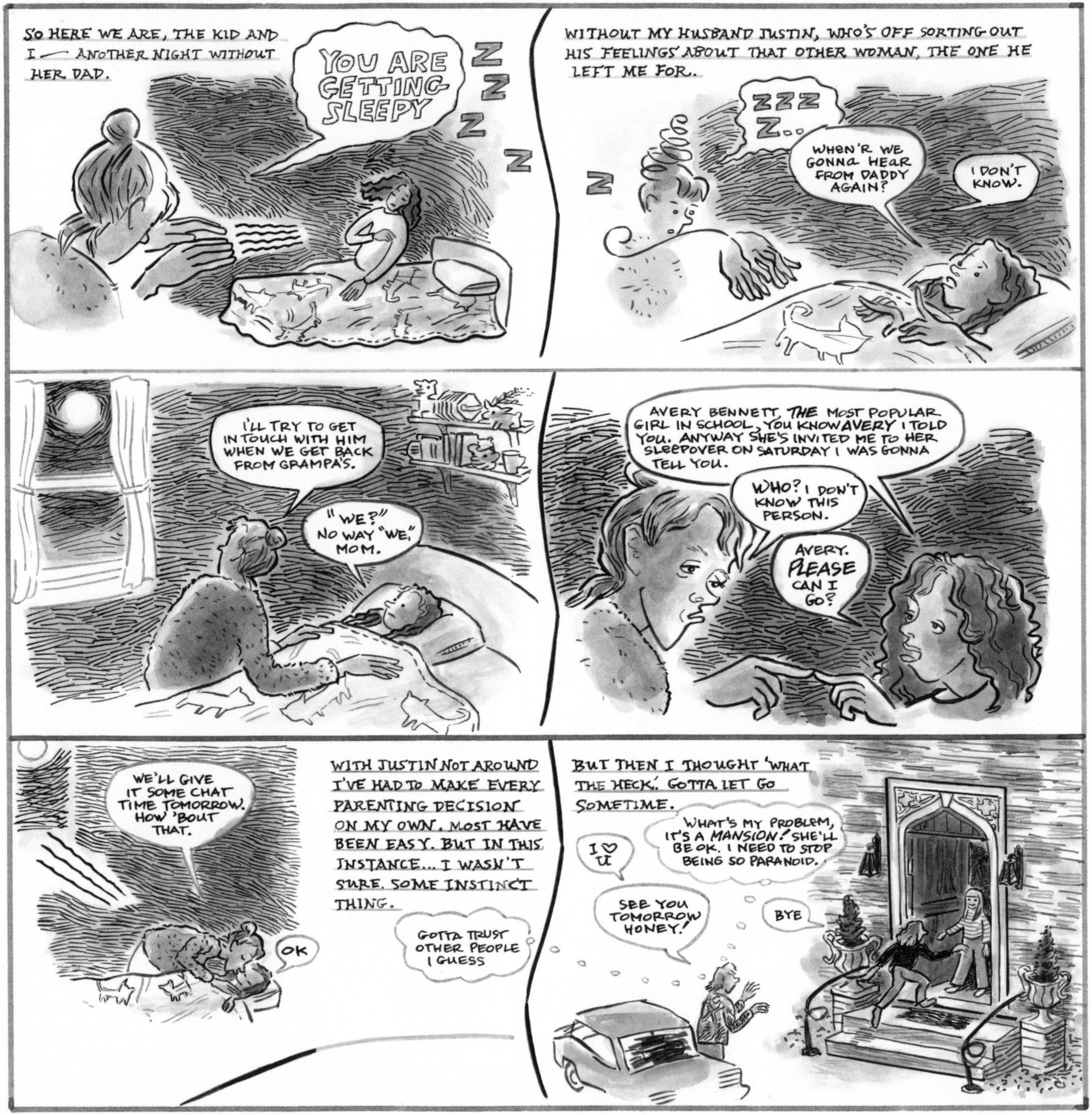
SO HERE WE ARE, THE KID AND I — ANOTHER NIGHT WITHOUT HER DAD.
YOU ARE GETTING SLEEPY
Z Z Z Z
WITHOUT MY HUSBAND JUSTIN, WHO'S OFF SORTING OUT HIS FEELINGS ABOUT THAT OTHER WOMAN, THE ONE HE LEFT ME FOR.
ZZZ Z..
Z
WHEN'R WE GONNA HEAR FROM DADDY AGAIN?
I DON'T KNOW.
I'LL TRY TO GET IN TOUCH WITH HIM WHEN WE GET BACK FROM GRAMPA'S.
"WE?" NO WAY "WE," MOM.
AVERY BENNETT, THE MOST POPULAR GIRL IN SCHOOL, YOU KNOW AVERY I TOLD YOU. ANYWAY SHE'S INVITED ME TO HER SLEEPOVER ON SATURDAY I WAS GONNA TELL YOU.
WHO? I DON'T KNOW THIS PERSON.
AVERY. PLEASE CAN I GO?
WE'LL GIVE IT SOME CHAT TIME TOMORROW. HOW 'BOUT THAT.
OK
WITH JUSTIN NOT AROUND I'VE HAD TO MAKE EVERY PARENTING DECISION ON MY OWN. MOST HAVE BEEN EASY. BUT IN THIS INSTANCE... I WASN'T SURE. SOME INSTINCT THING.
GOTTA TRUST OTHER PEOPLE I GUESS
BUT THEN I THOUGHT 'WHAT THE HECK.' GOTTA LET GO SOMETIME.
WHAT'S MY PROBLEM, IT'S A MANSION! SHE'LL BE OK. I NEED TO STOP BEING SO PARANOID.
I ♡ U
SEE YOU TOMORROW HONEY!
BYE

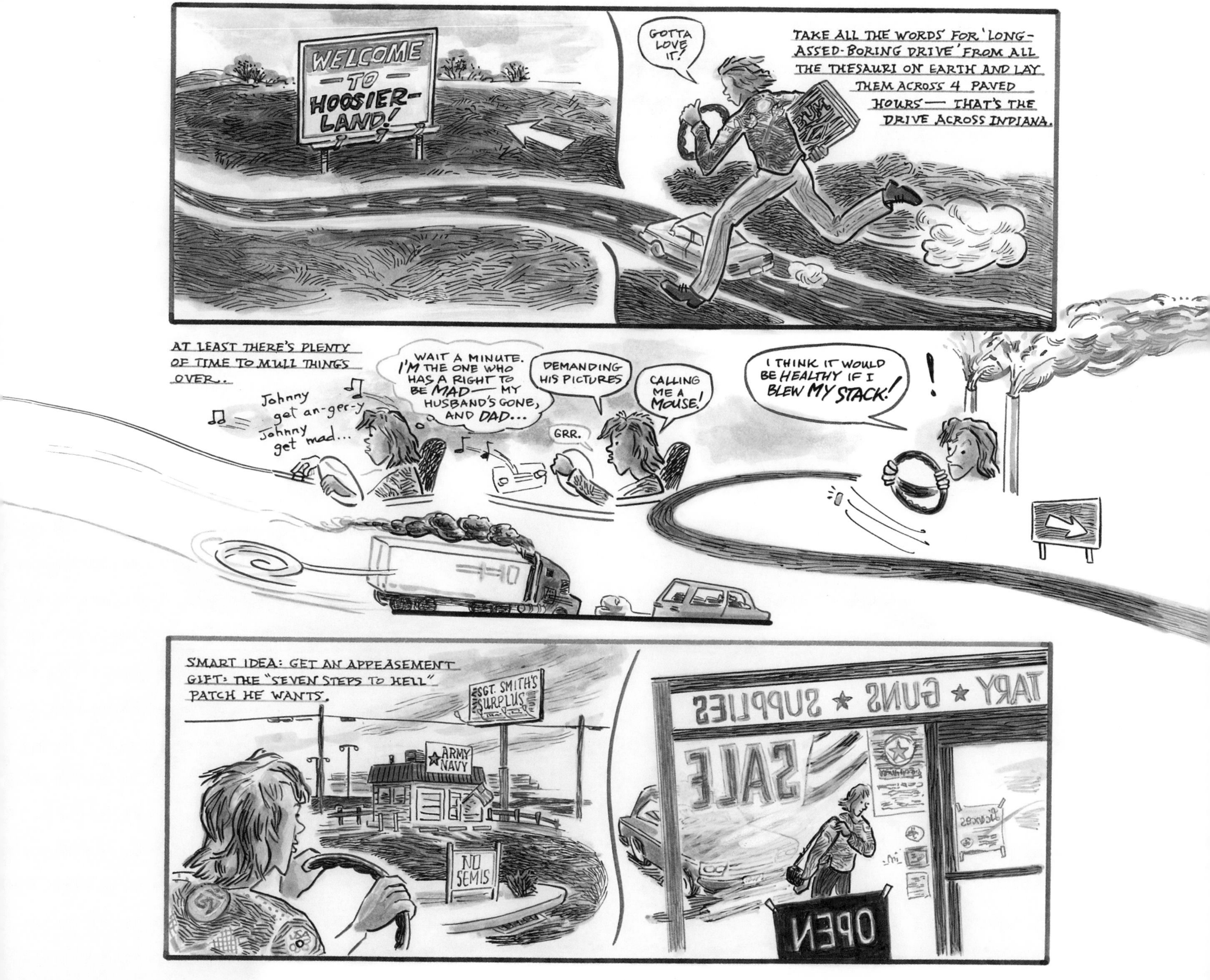
WELCOME TO HOOSIER-LAND!
GOTTA LOVE IT!
TAKE ALL THE WORDS FOR 'LONG-ASSED-BORING DRIVE' FROM ALL THE THESAURI ON EARTH AND LAY THEM ACROSS 4 PAVED HOURS — THAT'S THE DRIVE ACROSS INDIANA.
AT LEAST THERE'S PLENTY OF TIME TO MULL THINGS OVER..
Johnny get an-ger-y Johnny get mad...
WAIT A MINUTE. I'M THE ONE WHO HAS A RIGHT TO BE MAD— MY HUSBAND'S GONE, AND DAD...
DEMANDING HIS PICTURES
CALLING ME A MOUSE!
GRR.
I THINK IT WOULD BE HEALTHY IF I BLEW MY STACK!
!
SMART IDEA: GET AN APPEASEMENT GIFT: THE "SEVEN STEPS TO HELL" PATCH HE WANTS.
SGT. SMITH'S SURPLUS
ARMY NAVY
NO SEMIS
TARY ★ GUNS ★ SUPPLIES
SALE
OPEN

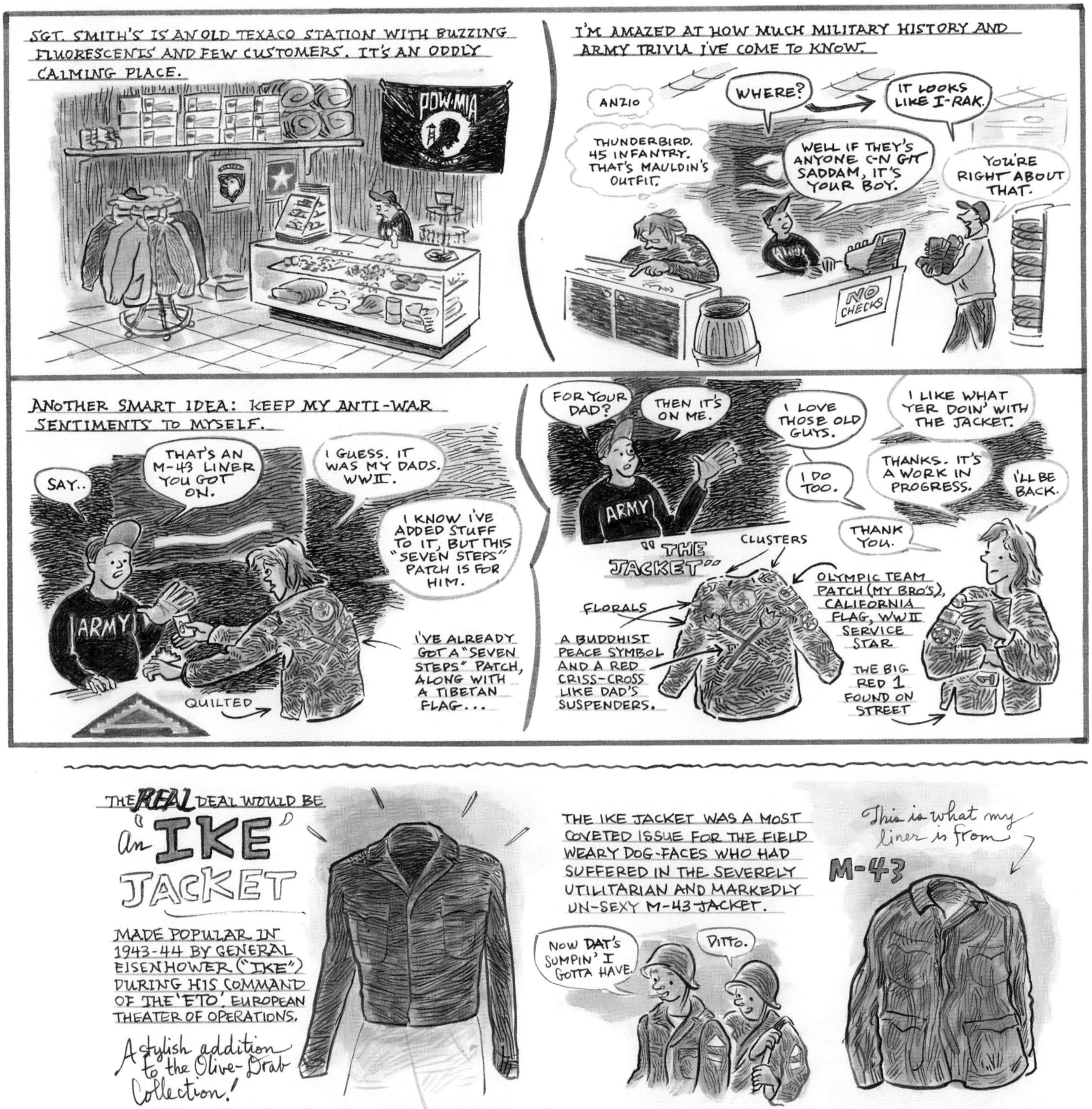

SGT. SMITH'S IS AN OLD TEXACO STATION WITH BUZZING FLUORESCENTS AND FEW CUSTOMERS. IT'S AN ODDLY CALMING PLACE.
POW·MIA
I'M AMAZED AT HOW MUCH MILITARY HISTORY AND ARMY TRIVIA I'VE COME TO KNOW.
ANZIO
THUNDERBIRD. 45 INFANTRY. THAT'S MAULDIN'S OUTFIT.
WHERE?
IT LOOKS LIKE I-RAK.
WELL IF THEY'S ANYONE C-N GIT SADDAM, IT'S YOUR BOY.
YOU'RE RIGHT ABOUT THAT.
NO CHECKS
ANOTHER SMART IDEA: KEEP MY ANTI-WAR SENTIMENTS TO MYSELF.
SAY..
THAT'S AN M-43 LINER YOU GOT ON.
I GUESS. IT WAS MY DADS. WWII.
I KNOW I'VE ADDED STUFF TO IT, BUT THIS "SEVEN STEPS" PATCH IS FOR HIM.
ARMY
I'VE ALREADY GOT A "SEVEN STEPS" PATCH, ALONG WITH A TIBETAN FLAG...
QUILTED
FOR YOUR DAD?
THEN IT'S ON ME.
I LOVE THOSE OLD GUYS.
I LIKE WHAT YER DOIN' WITH THE JACKET.
I DO TOO.
THANKS. IT'S A WORK IN PROGRESS.
I'LL BE BACK.
THANK YOU.
ARMY
"THE JACKET"
CLUSTERS
FLORALS
OLYMPIC TEAM PATCH (MY BRO'S), CALIFORNIA FLAG, WWII SERVICE STAR
A BUDDHIST PEACE SYMBOL AND A RED CRISS-CROSS LIKE DAD'S SUSPENDERS.
THE BIG RED 1 FOUND ON STREET
THE REAL DEAL WOULD BE AN "IKE" JACKET
MADE POPULAR IN 1943-44 BY GENERAL EISENHOWER ("IKE") DURING HIS COMMAND OF THE 'ETO', EUROPEAN THEATER OF OPERATIONS.
A stylish addition to the Olive-Drab Collection!
THE IKE JACKET WAS A MOST COVETED ISSUE FOR THE FIELD WEARY DOG-FACES WHO HAD SUFFERED IN THE SEVERELY UTILITARIAN AND MARKEDLY UN-SEXY M-43 JACKET.
NOW DAT'S SUMPIN' I GOTTA HAVE.
DITTO.
This is what my liner is from
M-43

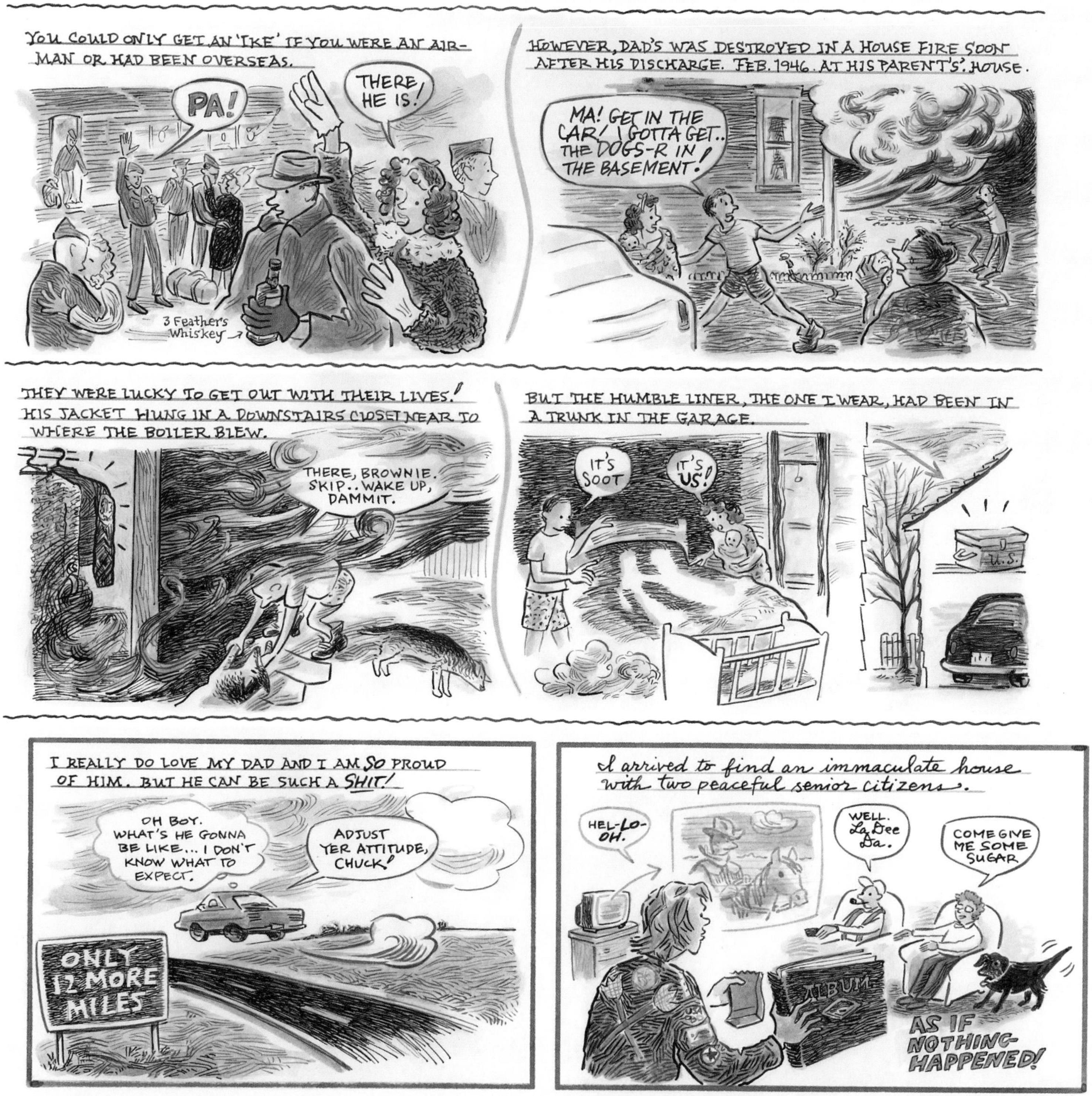
YOU COULD ONLY GET AN 'IKE' IF YOU WERE AN AIR-MAN OR HAD BEEN OVERSEAS.
PA!
THERE HE IS!
3 Feather's Whiskey
HOWEVER, DAD'S WAS DESTROYED IN A HOUSE FIRE SOON AFTER HIS DISCHARGE. FEB. 1946. AT HIS PARENT'S'. HOUSE.
MA! GET IN THE CAR! I GOTTA GET.. THE DOGS-R IN THE BASEMENT!
THEY WERE LUCKY TO GET OUT WITH THEIR LIVES.! HIS JACKET HUNG IN A DOWNSTAIRS CLOSET NEAR TO WHERE THE BOILER BLEW.
THERE, BROWNIE. SKIP.. WAKE UP, DAMMIT.
BUT THE HUMBLE LINER, THE ONE I WEAR, HAD BEEN IN A TRUNK IN THE GARAGE.
IT'S SOOT
IT'S US!
U.S.
I REALLY DO LOVE MY DAD AND I AM SO PROUD OF HIM. BUT HE CAN BE SUCH A SHIT!
OH BOY. WHAT'S HE GONNA BE LIKE... I DON'T KNOW WHAT TO EXPECT.
ADJUST YER ATTITUDE, CHUCK!
ONLY 12 MORE MILES
I arrived to find an immaculate house with two peaceful senior citizens.
HEL-LO-OH.
WELL. La Dee Da.
COME GIVE ME SOME SUGAR
ALBUM
AS IF NOTHING HAPPENED!

Everything was as it should be.

 MOM
 MWAH DAD
 Hello THE DOG
 P-K EW THE T.V.

HERE'S YOUR PICTURES BACK

WHAT. I DON'T NEED 'EM

So calm ———
YOU WOULD NEVER KNOW THAT THERE HAD BEEN YELLING, THAT THERE HAD BEEN AN UNSETTLING CYCLONE BLOW THROUGH HERE.

WHAT!

HERE'S YER SEVENTH PATCH —

WHADDYA MEAN YOU DON'T NEED 'EM. I DROVE ALL THE WAY OVER HERE —

— IT'S MY STUFF, THAT'S ALL.

YOU GOT MOM ALL UPSET. AND ME...

DAMN IF I DIDN'T TAKE THE BAIT. AGAIN!!

SHE'S FINE, ARENCHA, RED.

UM

CONFUSIONS SHIFTS

JUST LIKE WHEN I WAS

A KID.

Pencil feels good on flat paint

In our home, there were two distinct tones:

AS IN CRABBY AND EXHAUSTED

JOLLY AND Mad.

the 1950s

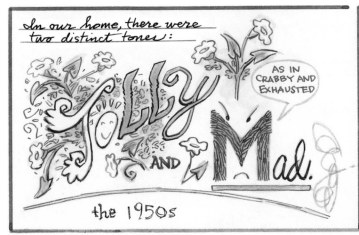

Much of the time, both of them seemed like they were mad.

MOM

WHO DID THIS.

SCRIBBLING ON THE WALL!

HaHa YOU'RE IN TRUB-BL

I guess I'm gonna have to go out in the yard and get me a pepper stick!

GIVE 'EM ALL A SPANKIN'

DAD

NOT ME.

I DUNNO

GUILTY

120

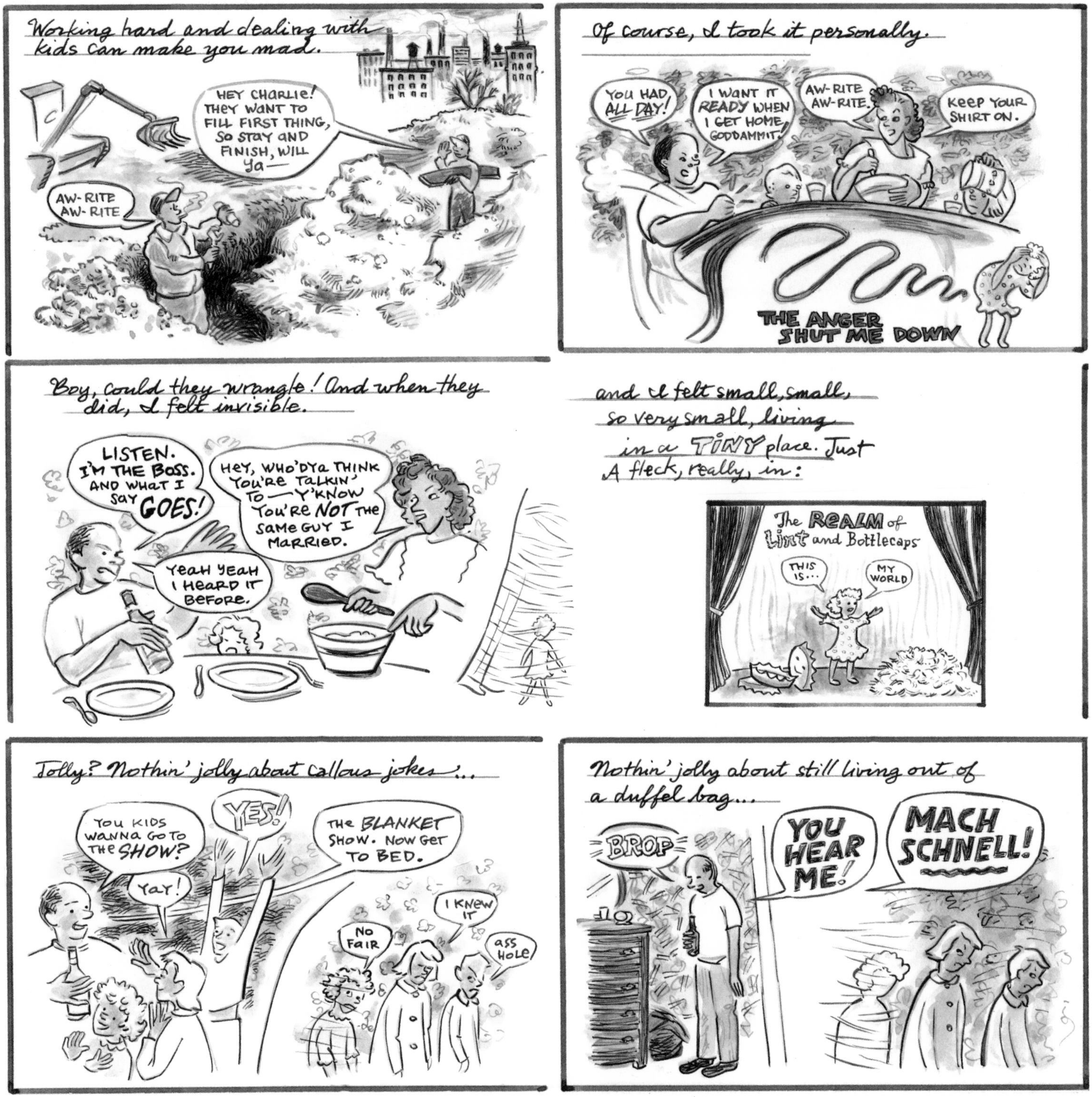
Working hard and dealing with kids can make you mad.
HEY CHARLIE! THEY WANT TO FILL FIRST THING, SO STAY AND FINISH, WILL YA—
AW-RITE AW-RITE
Of course, I took it personally.
YOU HAD ALL DAY!
I WANT IT READY WHEN I GET HOME, GODDAMMIT!
AW-RITE AW-RITE.
KEEP YOUR SHIRT ON.
THE ANGER SHUT ME DOWN
Boy, could they wrangle! And when they did, I felt invisible.
LISTEN. I'M THE BOSS. AND WHAT I SAY GOES!
HEY, WHO'D'YA THINK YOU'RE TALKIN' TO — Y'KNOW YOU'RE NOT THE SAME GUY I MARRIED.
YEAH YEAH I HEARD IT BEFORE.
and I felt small, small, so very small, living in a TINY place. Just A fleck, really, in:
The REALM of Lint and Bottlecaps
THIS IS...
MY WORLD
Jolly? Nothin' jolly about callous jokes...
YOU KIDS WANNA GO TO THE SHOW?
YES!
YAY!
THE BLANKET SHOW. NOW GET TO BED.
NO FAIR
I KNEW IT
ass hole
Nothin' jolly about still living out of a duffel bag...
BROP
YOU HEAR ME!
MACH SCHNELL!

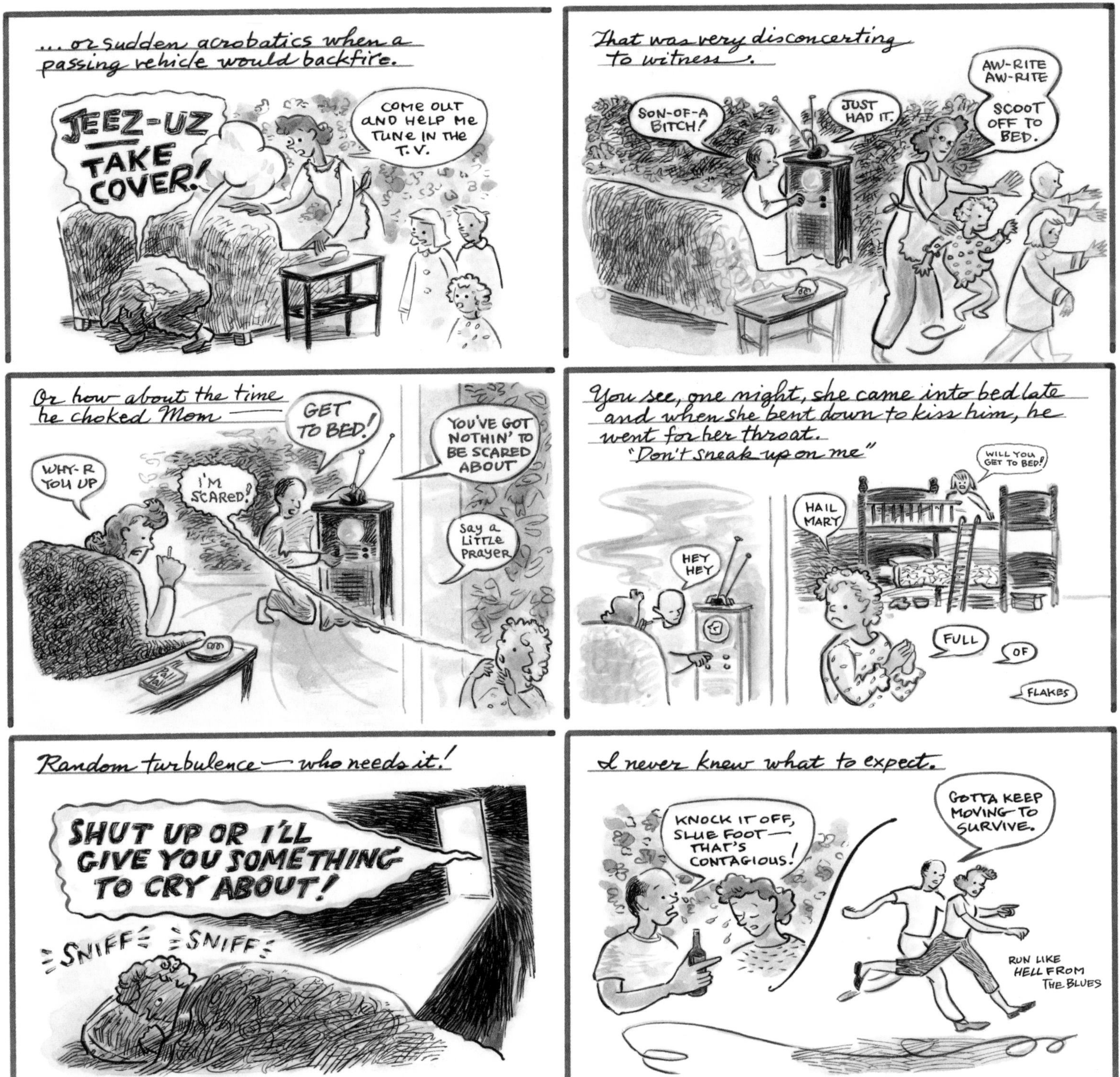
...or sudden acrobatics when a passing vehicle would backfire.
JEEZ-UZ TAKE COVER!
COME OUT AND HELP ME TUNE IN THE T.V.
That was very disconcerting to witness.
SON-OF-A BITCH!
JUST HAD IT.
AW-RITE AW-RITE
SCOOT OFF TO BED.
Or how about the time he choked Mom
WHY-R YOU UP
I'M SCARED!
GET TO BED!
YOU'VE GOT NOTHIN' TO BE SCARED ABOUT
Say a Little Prayer
You see, one night, she came into bed late and when she bent down to kiss him, he went for her throat.
"Don't sneak up on me"
HEY HEY
HAIL MARY
WILL YOU GET TO BED!
FULL
OF
FLAKES
Random turbulence—who needs it!
SHUT UP OR I'LL GIVE YOU SOMETHING TO CRY ABOUT!
SNIFF SNIFF
I never knew what to expect.
KNOCK IT OFF, SLUE FOOT— THAT'S CONTAGIOUS!
GOTTA KEEP MOVING TO SURVIVE.
RUN LIKE HELL FROM THE BLUES

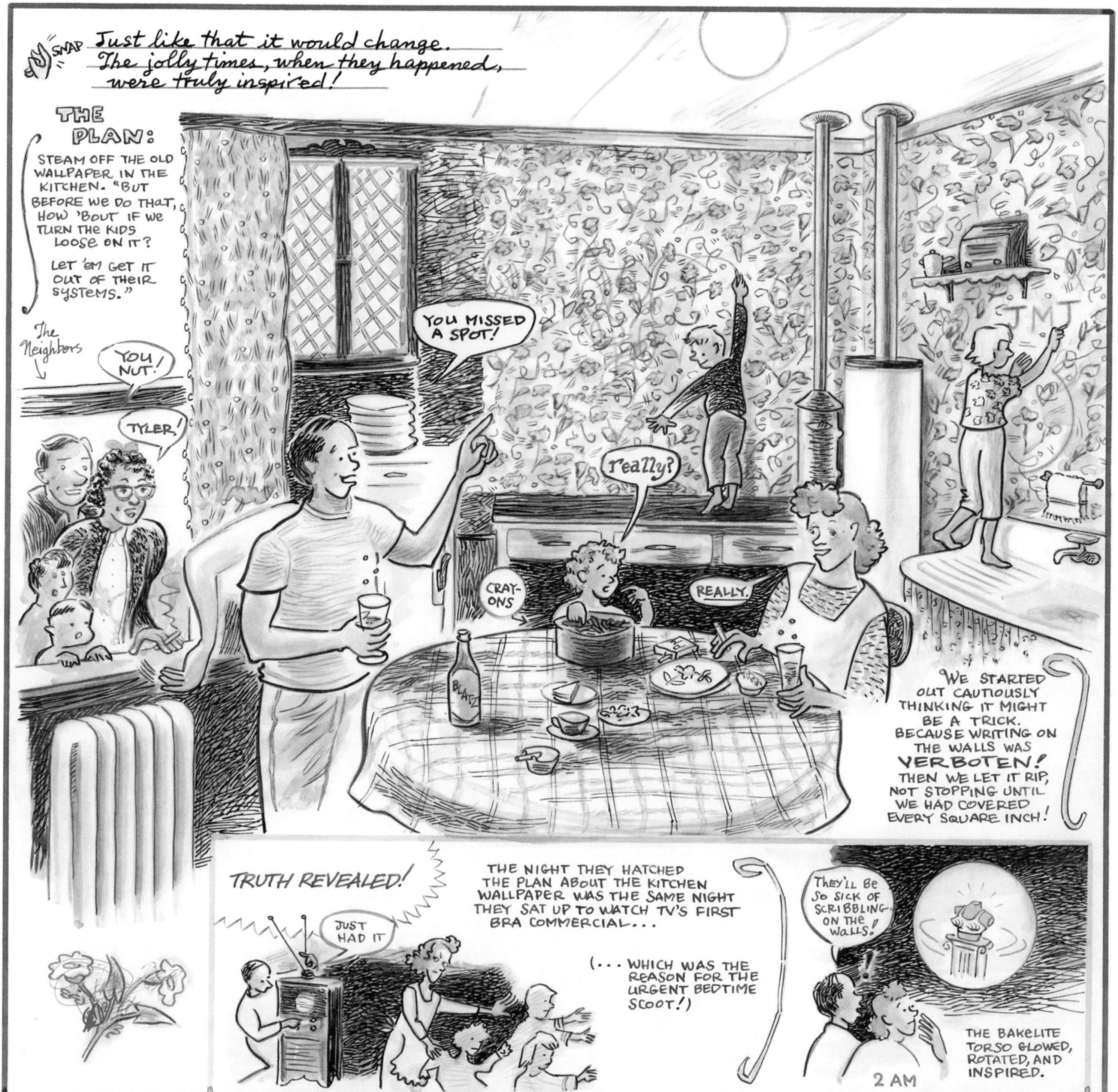

SNAP
Just like that it would change. The jolly times, when they happened, were truly inspired!
THE PLAN:
STEAM OFF THE OLD WALLPAPER IN THE KITCHEN. "BUT BEFORE WE DO THAT, HOW 'BOUT IF WE TURN THE KIDS LOOSE ON IT?
LET 'EM GET IT OUT OF THEIR SYSTEMS."
The Neighbors
YOU NUT!
TYLER!
YOU MISSED A SPOT!
really?
REALLY.
CRAY-ONS
BLATZ
JMT
WE STARTED OUT CAUTIOUSLY THINKING IT MIGHT BE A TRICK. BECAUSE WRITING ON THE WALLS WAS VERBOTEN! THEN WE LET IT RIP, NOT STOPPING UNTIL WE HAD COVERED EVERY SQUARE INCH!
TRUTH REVEALED!
JUST HAD IT
THE NIGHT THEY HATCHED THE PLAN ABOUT THE KITCHEN WALLPAPER WAS THE SAME NIGHT THEY SAT UP TO WATCH TV'S FIRST BRA COMMERCIAL...
(... WHICH WAS THE REASON FOR THE URGENT BEDTIME SCOOT!)
They'll Be So SICK OF SCRIBBLING ON THE WALLS!
THE BAKELITE TORSO GLOWED, ROTATED, AND INSPIRED.
2 AM

The next day, I thought I would work on the wall again — but as all things go in the realm of Jolly and Mad...

MISSED A SPOT.

WHAT THE **HELL** ARE YOU DOING!

What's o.k. one time isn't automatically the next.

How is a person ever to know?

STOP THAT!

So I skulked off to start on a new project: An autograph book.

GREAT

one-sided used memo sheets

from Mom's old office supplies.

Everyone signed, except Dad. To ask required a summoning of courage.

SURE THING. GIVE IT HERE.

The king's entry said it all.

When you're up you're up
When you're down you're down
When you're with Chuck Tyler you're upside.

And then there was my lifetime label: "La-Dee-Da." Bestowed upon me by Dad's best friend Gordy (seen on previous page. Our neighbors.)

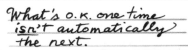

One day, he and Dad had this little job to do but first...

doo dee doo dee doo ♪

slacked lime

cement

...they left to go get beer. What's a kid to do?

la la la

Will ya look at "LA-DEE-DA."

And so the label stuck. Set in cement. Thanks a lot, Gordy!

"La Dee Da."

Silly Bean.

It's how my Dad saw me for the next 50 years!

!

HA!

7.

UNDER IT

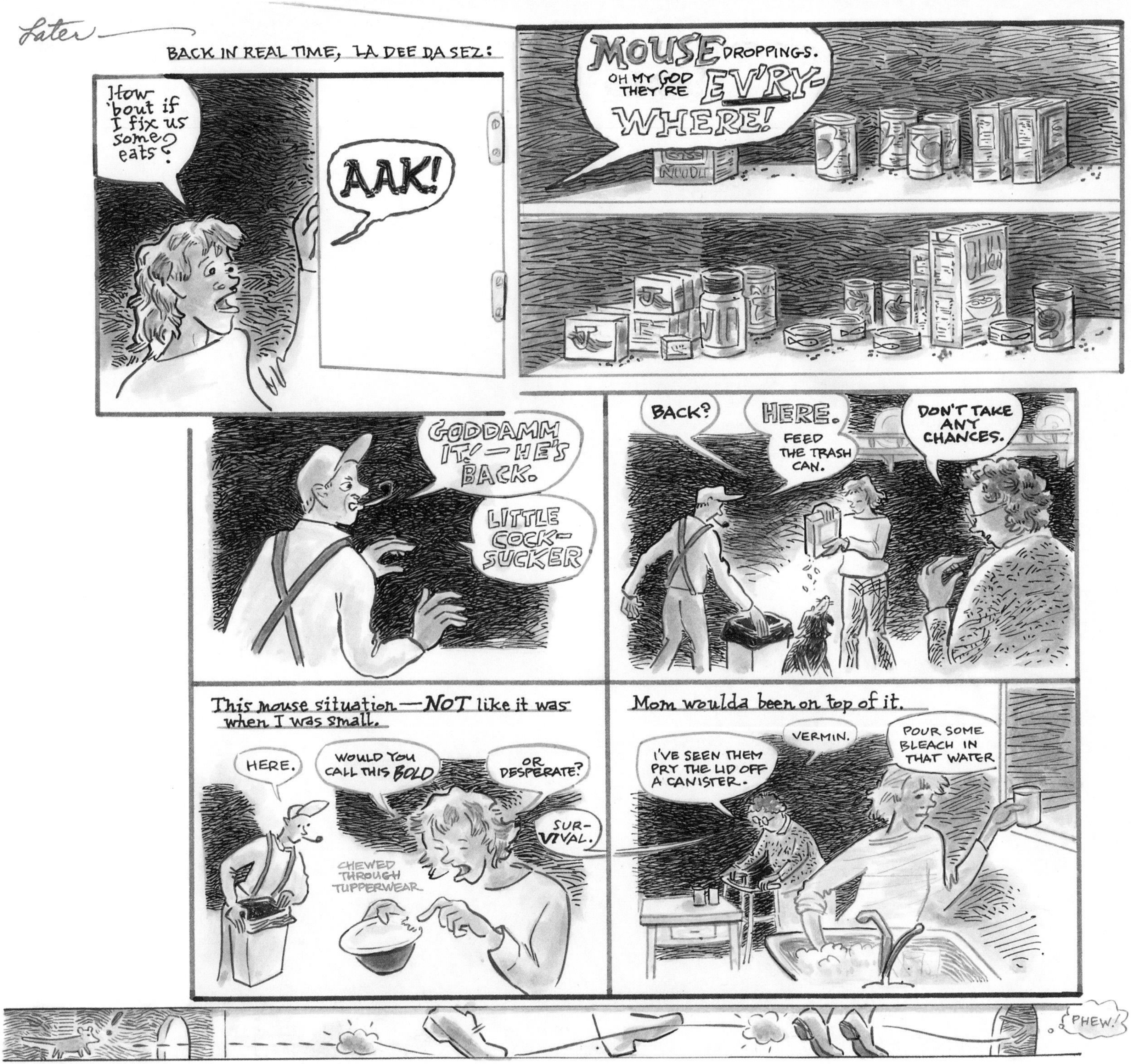
Later
BACK IN REAL TIME, LA DEE DA SEZ:
How 'bout if I fix us some eats?
AAK!
MOUSE DROPPINGS. OH MY GOD THEY'RE EV'RY-WHERE!
GODDAMM IT! — HE'S BACK.
LITTLE COCK-SUCKER
BACK?
HERE. FEED THE TRASH CAN.
DON'T TAKE ANY CHANCES.
This mouse situation — NOT like it was when I was small.
HERE.
WOULD YOU CALL THIS BOLD
OR DESPERATE?
SUR-VIVAL.
CHEWED THROUGH TUPPERWEAR
Mom woulda been on top of it.
I'VE SEEN THEM PRY THE LID OFF A CANISTER.
VERMIN.
POUR SOME BLEACH IN THAT WATER
PHEW!

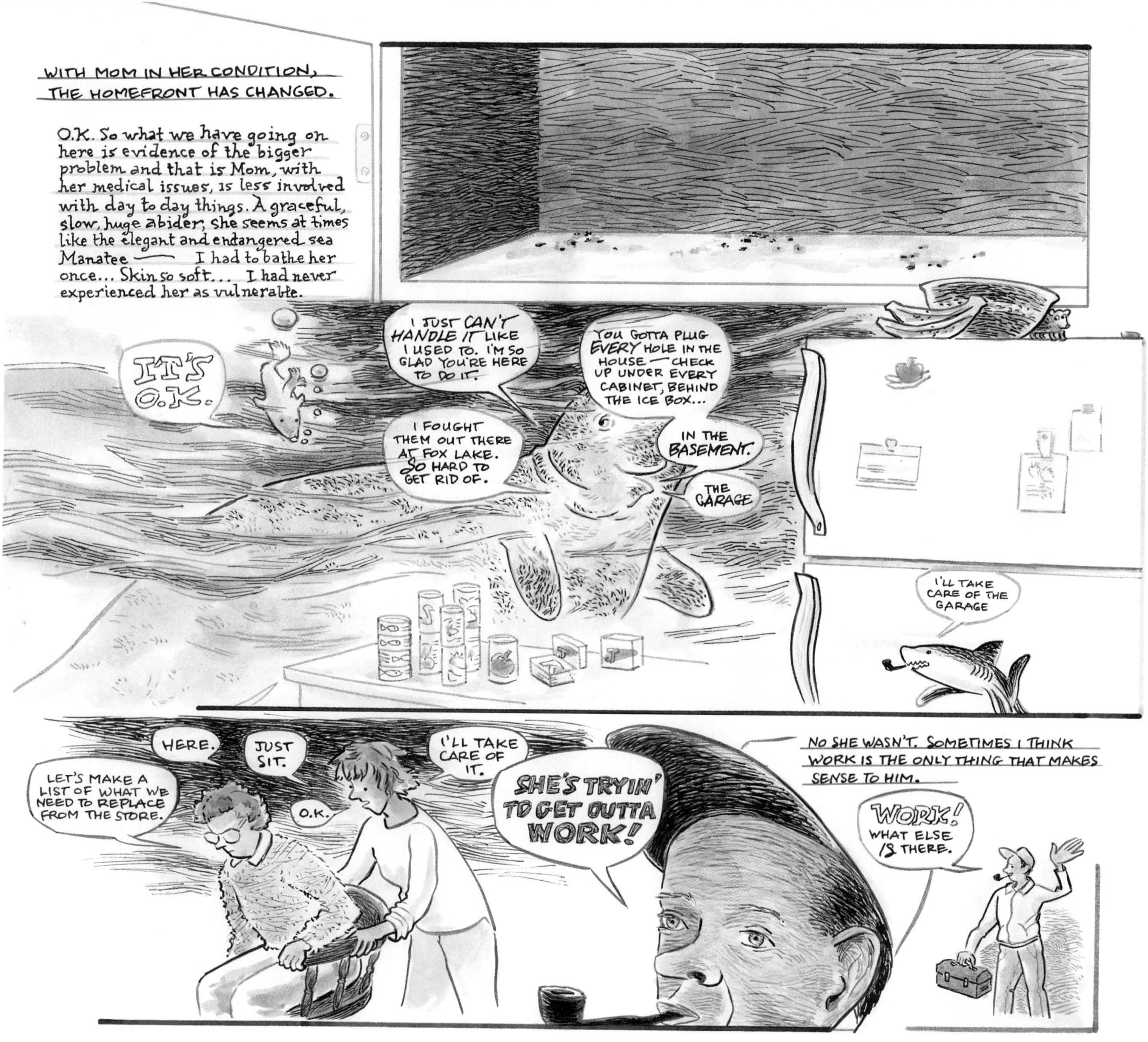
WITH MOM IN HER CONDITION, THE HOMEFRONT HAS CHANGED.
O.K. So what we have going on here is evidence of the bigger problem and that is Mom, with her medical issues, is less involved with day to day things. A graceful, slow, huge abider, she seems at times like the elegant and entangered sea Manatee — I had to bathe her once... Skin so soft... I had never experienced her as vulnerable.
IT'S O.K.
I JUST CAN'T HANDLE IT LIKE I USED TO. I'M SO GLAD YOU'RE HERE TO DO IT.
I FOUGHT THEM OUT THERE AT FOX LAKE. SO HARD TO GET RID OF.
YOU GOTTA PLUG EVERY HOLE IN THE HOUSE — CHECK UP UNDER EVERY CABINET, BEHIND THE ICE BOX...
IN THE BASEMENT.
THE GARAGE
I'LL TAKE CARE OF THE GARAGE
LET'S MAKE A LIST OF WHAT WE NEED TO REPLACE FROM THE STORE.
HERE.
JUST SIT.
O.K.
I'LL TAKE CARE OF IT.
SHE'S TRYIN' TO GET OUTTA WORK!
NO SHE WASN'T. SOMETIMES I THINK WORK IS THE ONLY THING THAT MAKES SENSE TO HIM.
WORK! WHAT ELSE IS THERE.

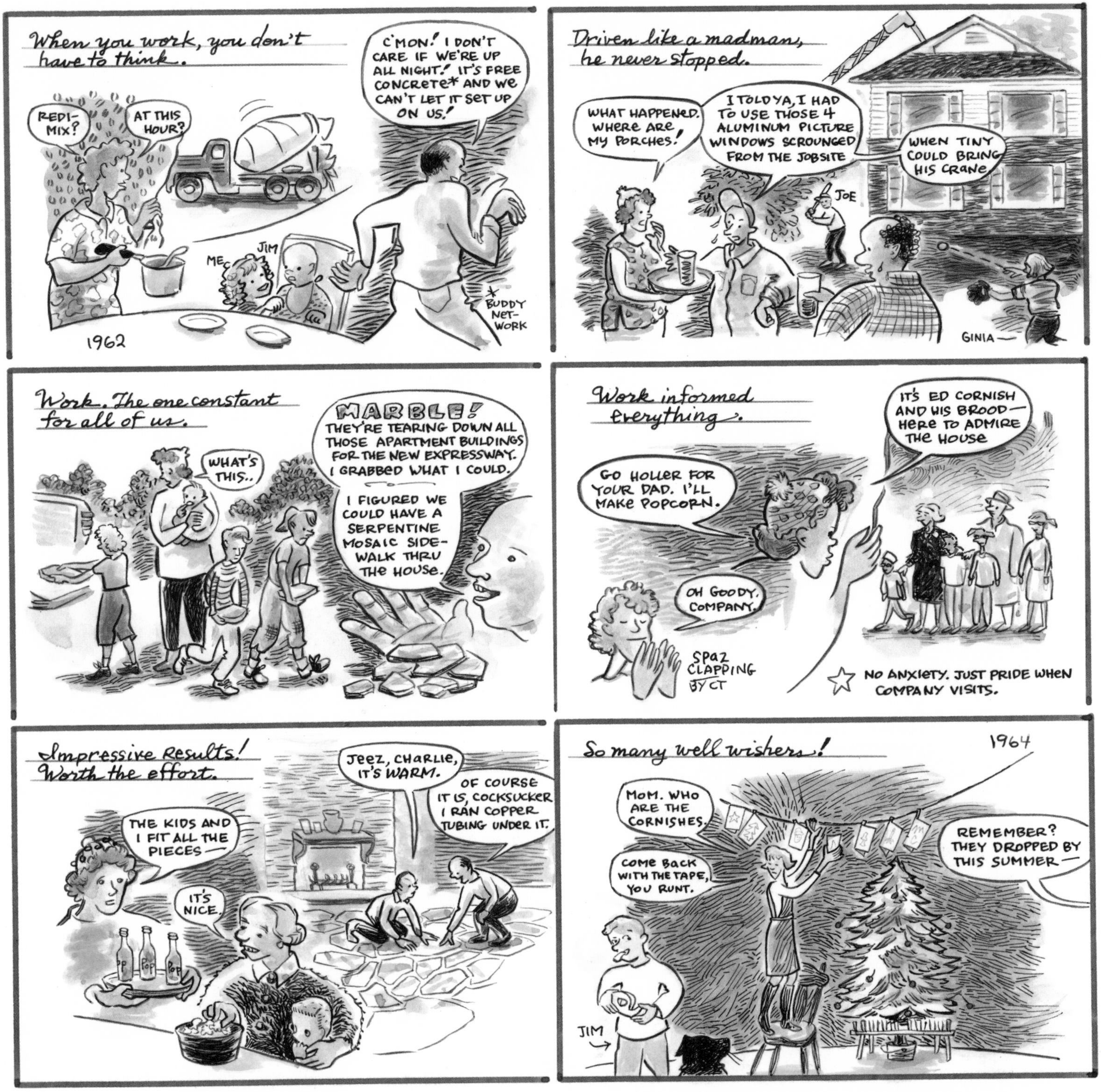
When you work, you don't have to think.
REDI-MIX?
AT THIS HOUR?
C'MON! I DON'T CARE IF WE'RE UP ALL NIGHT! IT'S FREE CONCRETE* AND WE CAN'T LET IT SET UP ON US!
ME
JIM
*BUDDY NET-WORK
1962
Driven like a madman, he never stopped.
WHAT HAPPENED. WHERE ARE MY PORCHES!
I TOLDYA, I HAD TO USE THOSE 4 ALUMINUM PICTURE WINDOWS SCROUNGED FROM THE JOBSITE
WHEN TINY COULD BRING HIS CRANE
JOE
GINIA
Work. The one constant for all of us.
WHAT'S THIS..
MARBLE! THEY'RE TEARING DOWN ALL THOSE APARTMENT BUILDINGS FOR THE NEW EXPRESSWAY. I GRABBED WHAT I COULD.
I FIGURED WE COULD HAVE A SERPENTINE MOSAIC SIDE-WALK THRU THE HOUSE.
Work informed everything.
IT'S ED CORNISH AND HIS BROOD— HERE TO ADMIRE THE HOUSE
GO HOLLER FOR YOUR DAD. I'LL MAKE POPCORN.
OH GOODY. COMPANY.
SPAZ CLAPPING BY CT
NO ANXIETY. JUST PRIDE WHEN COMPANY VISITS.
Impressive Results! Worth the effort.
JEEZ, CHARLIE, IT'S WARM.
OF COURSE IT IS, COCKSUCKER I RAN COPPER TUBING UNDER IT.
THE KIDS AND I FIT ALL THE PIECES—
IT'S NICE.
POP
POP
POP
So many well wishers!
1964
MOM. WHO ARE THE CORNISHES.
COME BACK WITH THE TAPE, YOU RUNT.
REMEMBER? THEY DROPPED BY THIS SUMMER—
JIM

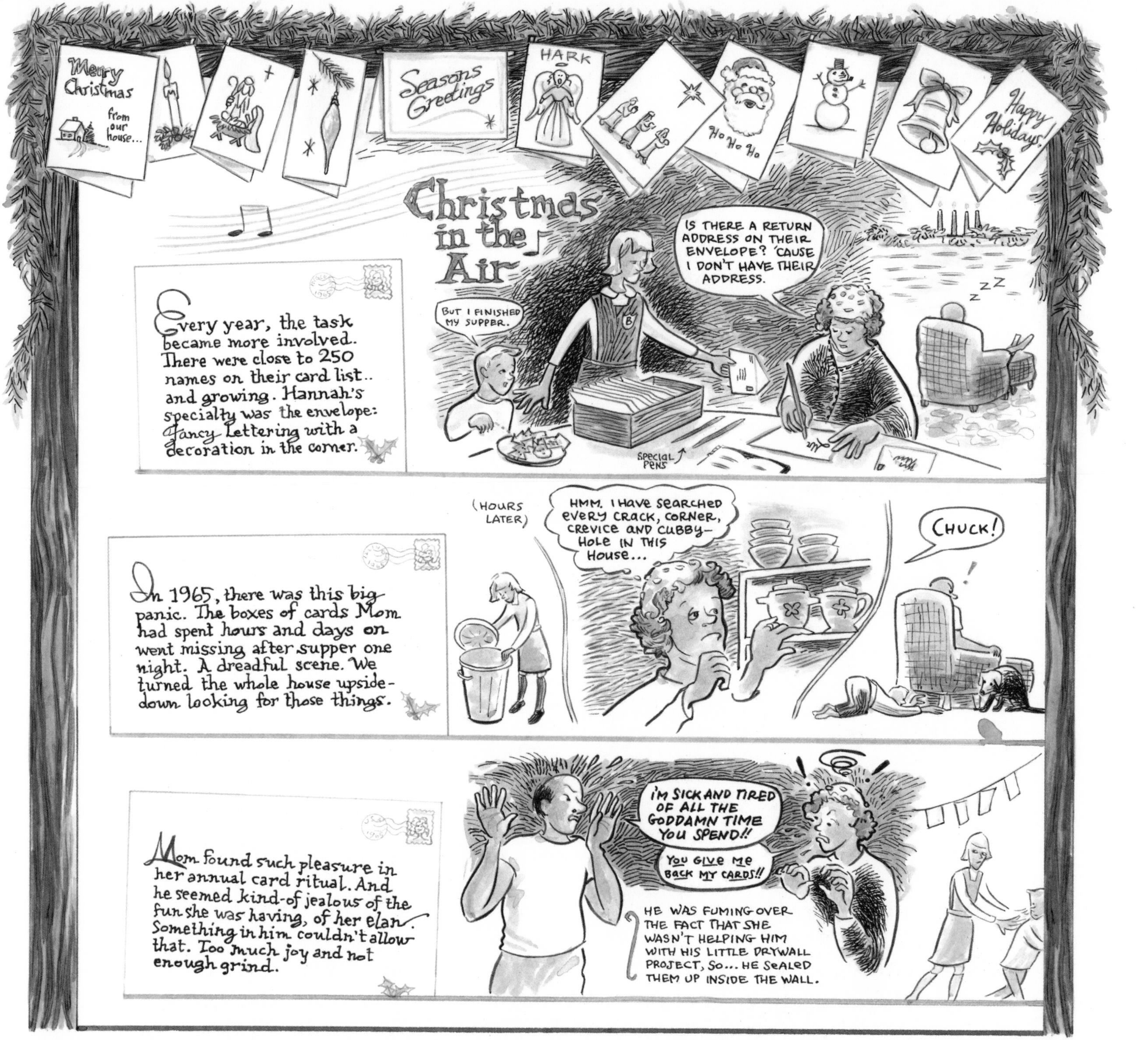

Merry Christmas from our house...
Seasons Greetings
HARK
Ho Ho Ho
Happy Holidays!
Christmas in the Air
Every year, the task became more involved. There were close to 250 names on their card list.. and growing. Hannah's specialty was the envelope: Fancy Lettering with a decoration in the corner.
BUT I FINISHED MY SUPPER.
IS THERE A RETURN ADDRESS ON THEIR ENVELOPE? 'CAUSE I DON'T HAVE THEIR ADDRESS.
ZZZ
SPECIAL PENS
In 1965, there was this big panic. The boxes of cards Mom had spent hours and days on went missing after supper one night. A dreadful scene. We turned the whole house upside-down looking for those things.
(HOURS LATER)
HMM. I HAVE SEARCHED EVERY CRACK, CORNER, CREVICE AND CUBBY-HOLE IN THIS HOUSE...
CHUCK!
Mom found such pleasure in her annual card ritual. And he seemed kind-of jealous of the fun she was having, of her elan. Something in him couldn't allow that. Too much joy and not enough grind.
I'M SICK AND TIRED OF ALL THE GODDAMN TIME YOU SPEND!!
YOU GIVE ME BACK MY CARDS!!
HE WAS FUMING OVER THE FACT THAT SHE WASN'T HELPING HIM WITH HIS LITTLE DRYWALL PROJECT, SO... HE SEALED THEM UP INSIDE THE WALL.

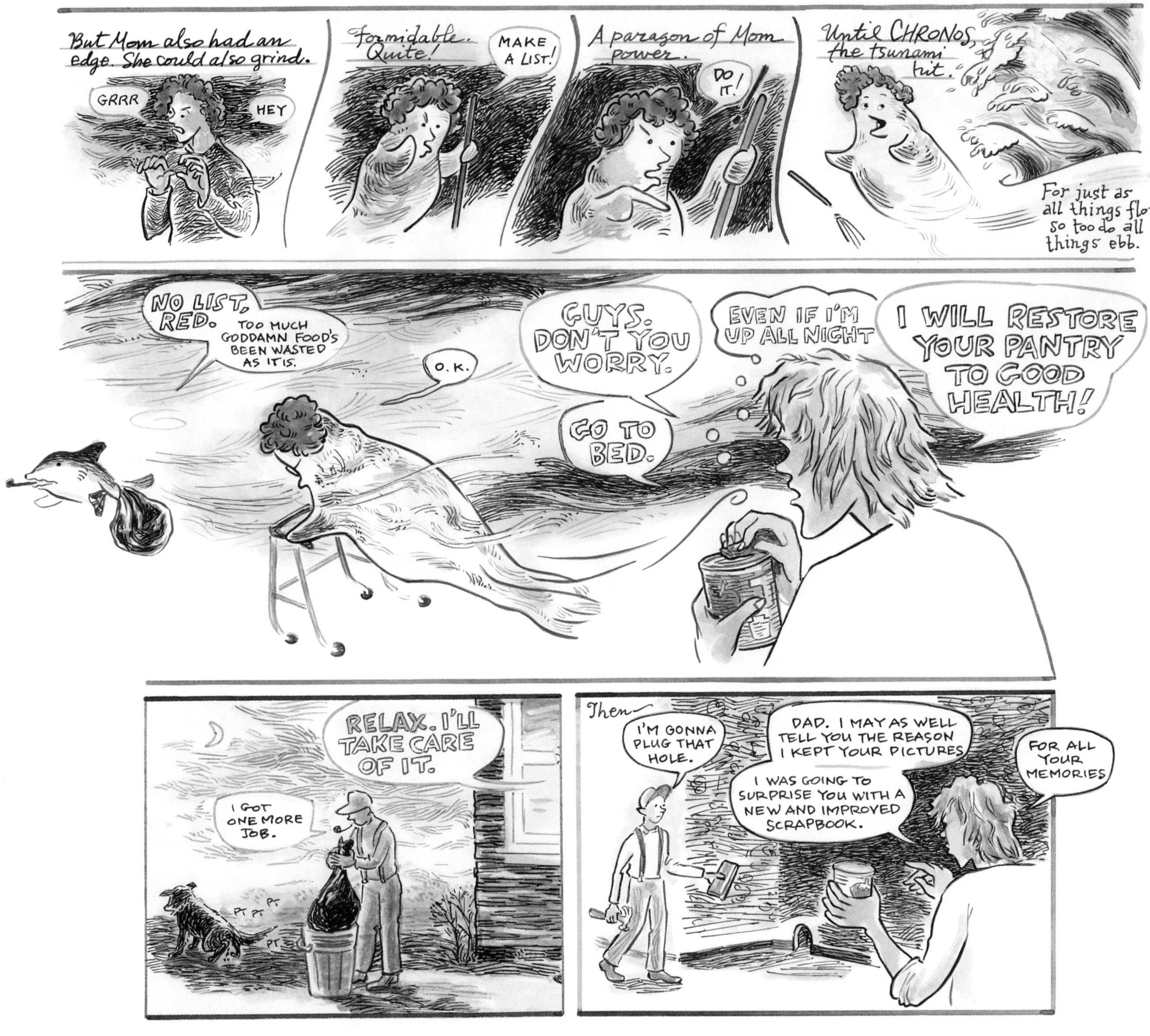

But Mom also had an edge. She could also grind.
GRRR
HEY
Formidable. Quite!
MAKE A LIST!
A paragon of Mom power.
DO IT!
Until CHRONOS, the tsunami hit.
For just as all things flow, so too do all things ebb.
NO LIST, RED.
TOO MUCH GODDAMN FOOD'S BEEN WASTED AS IT IS.
O.K.
GUYS. DON'T YOU WORRY.
GO TO BED.
EVEN IF I'M UP ALL NIGHT
I WILL RESTORE YOUR PANTRY TO GOOD HEALTH!
RELAX. I'LL TAKE CARE OF IT.
I GOT ONE MORE JOB.
PT PT PT
PT
Then—
I'M GONNA PLUG THAT HOLE.
DAD. I MAY AS WELL TELL YOU THE REASON I KEPT YOUR PICTURES
I WAS GOING TO SURPRISE YOU WITH A NEW AND IMPROVED SCRAPBOOK.
FOR ALL YOUR MEMORIES

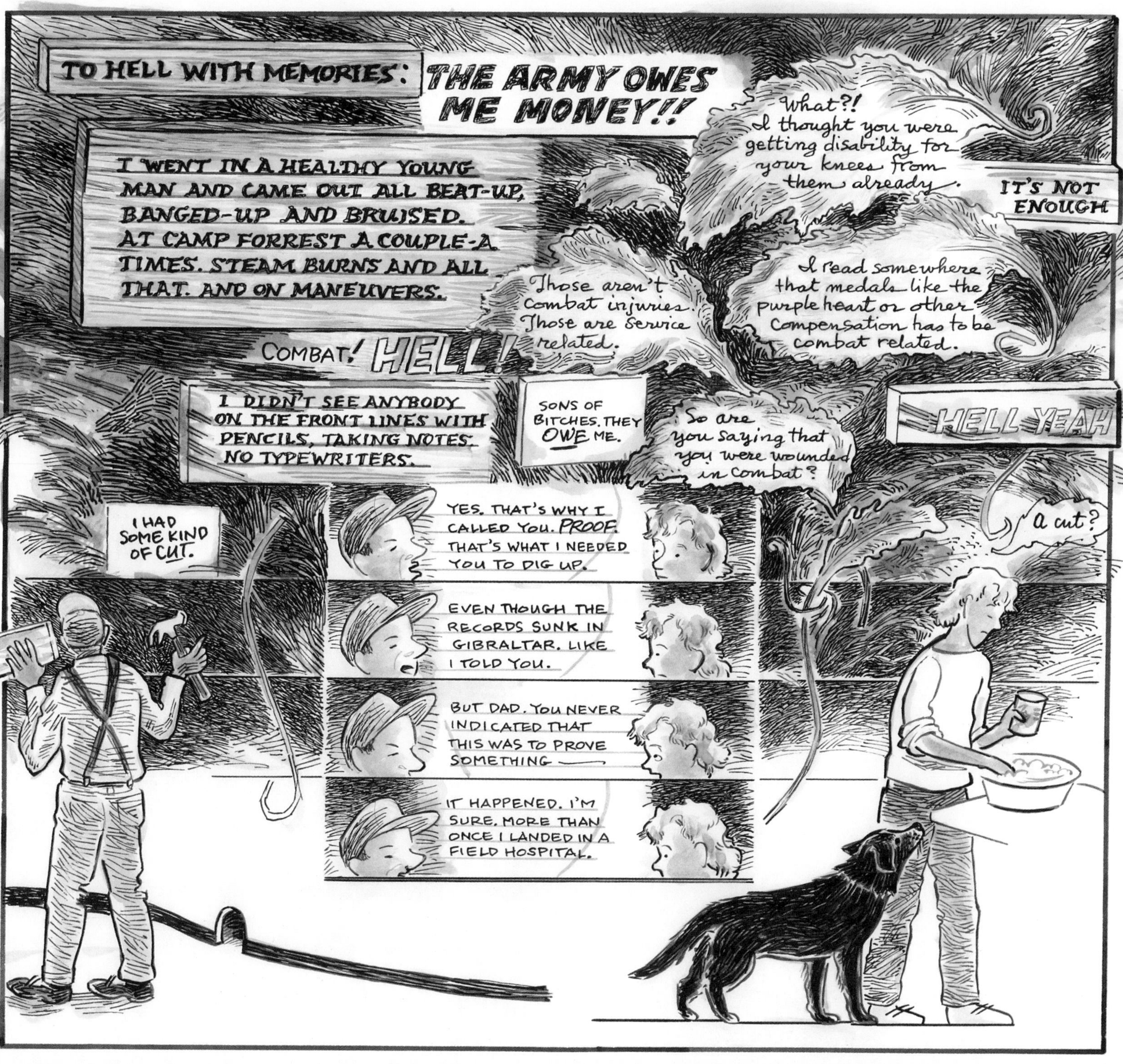
TO HELL WITH MEMORIES: THE ARMY OWES ME MONEY!!
I WENT IN A HEALTHY YOUNG MAN AND CAME OUT ALL BEAT-UP, BANGED-UP AND BRUISED. AT CAMP FORREST A COUPLE-A TIMES. STEAM BURNS AND ALL THAT. AND ON MANEUVERS.
What?! I thought you were getting disability for your knees from them already.
IT'S NOT ENOUGH
Those aren't combat injuries. Those are service related.
I read somewhere that medals like the purple heart or other compensation has to be combat related.
COMBAT! HELL!
I DIDN'T SEE ANYBODY ON THE FRONT LINES WITH PENCILS, TAKING NOTES. NO TYPEWRITERS.
SONS OF BITCHES. THEY OWE ME.
So are you saying that you were wounded in combat?
HELL YEAH
I HAD SOME KIND OF CUT.
a cut?
YES. THAT'S WHY I CALLED YOU. PROOF. THAT'S WHAT I NEEDED YOU TO DIG UP.
EVEN THOUGH THE RECORDS SUNK IN GIBRALTAR. LIKE I TOLD YOU.
BUT DAD. YOU NEVER INDICATED THAT THIS WAS TO PROVE SOMETHING—
IT HAPPENED. I'M SURE. MORE THAN ONCE I LANDED IN A FIELD HOSPITAL.

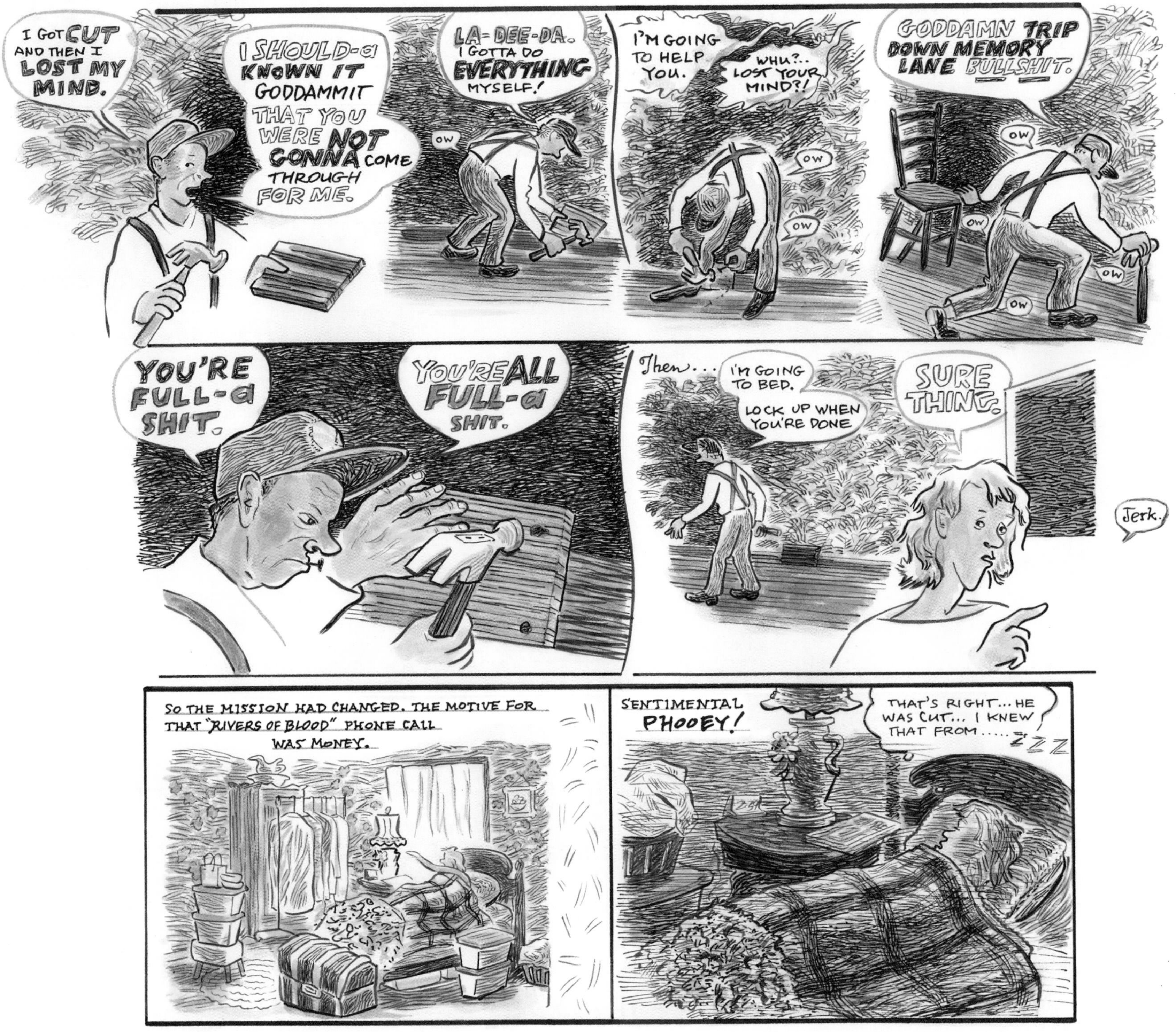

I GOT CUT AND THEN I LOST MY MIND.
I SHOULD-a KNOWN IT GODDAMMIT THAT YOU WERE NOT GONNA COME THROUGH FOR ME.
LA-DEE-DA. I GOTTA DO EVERYTHING MYSELF!
OW
I'M GOING TO HELP YOU.
WHU?.. LOST YOUR MIND?!
OW
OW
GODDAMN TRIP DOWN MEMORY LANE BULLSHIT.
OW
OW
OW
OW
YOU'RE FULL-a SHIT.
YOU'RE ALL FULL-a SHIT.
Then...
I'M GOING TO BED. LOCK UP WHEN YOU'RE DONE
SURE THING.
Jerk.
SO THE MISSION HAD CHANGED. THE MOTIVE FOR THAT "RIVERS OF BLOOD" PHONE CALL WAS MONEY.
SENTIMENTAL PHOOEY!
THAT'S RIGHT... HE WAS CUT... I KNEW THAT FROM..... ZZZ

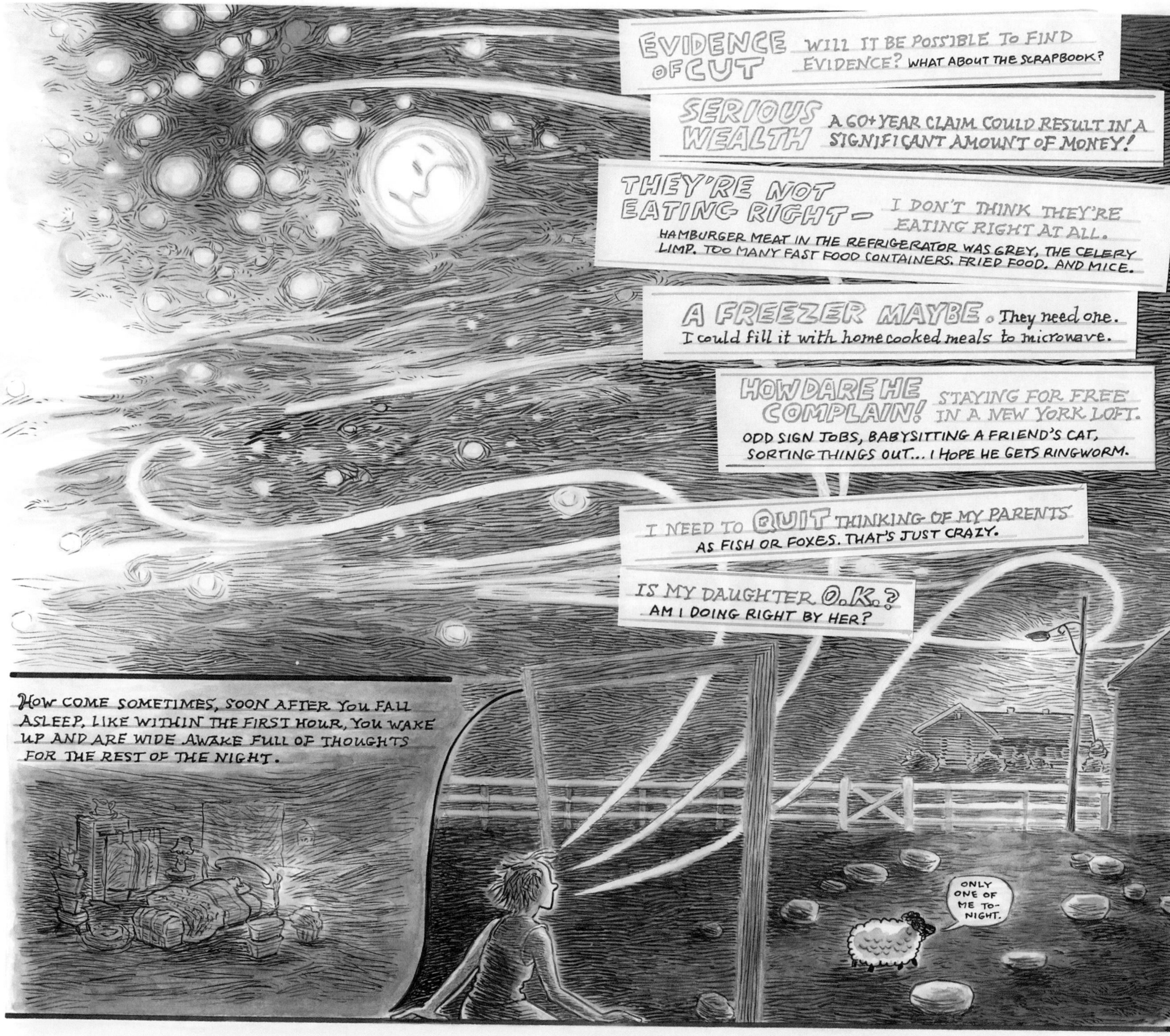

EVIDENCE OF CUT WILL IT BE POSSIBLE TO FIND EVIDENCE? WHAT ABOUT THE SCRAPBOOK?
SERIOUS WEALTH A 60+ YEAR CLAIM COULD RESULT IN A SIGNIFICANT AMOUNT OF MONEY!
THEY'RE NOT EATING RIGHT — I DON'T THINK THEY'RE EATING RIGHT AT ALL.
HAMBURGER MEAT IN THE REFRIGERATOR WAS GREY, THE CELERY LIMP. TOO MANY FAST FOOD CONTAINERS. FRIED FOOD. AND MICE.
A FREEZER MAYBE. They need one. I could fill it with home cooked meals to microwave.
HOW DARE HE COMPLAIN! STAYING FOR FREE IN A NEW YORK LOFT.
ODD SIGN JOBS, BABYSITTING A FRIEND'S CAT, SORTING THINGS OUT... I HOPE HE GETS RINGWORM.
I NEED TO QUIT THINKING OF MY PARENTS AS FISH OR FOXES. THAT'S JUST CRAZY.
IS MY DAUGHTER O.K.? AM I DOING RIGHT BY HER?
HOW COME SOMETIMES, SOON AFTER YOU FALL ASLEEP, LIKE WITHIN THE FIRST HOUR, YOU WAKE UP AND ARE WIDE AWAKE FULL OF THOUGHTS FOR THE REST OF THE NIGHT.
ONLY ONE OF ME TO-NIGHT.

Next Morning

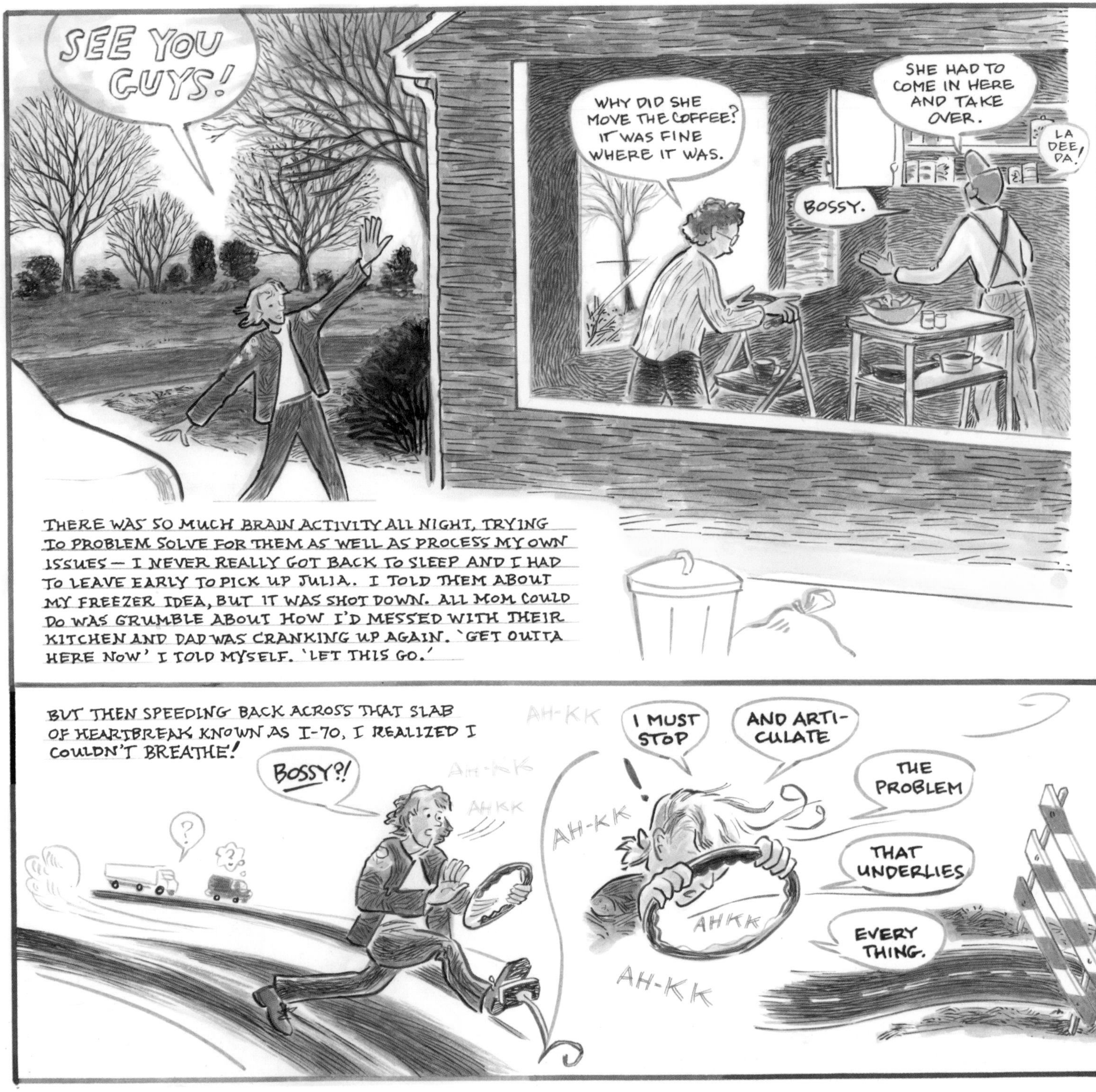
SEE YOU GUYS!
WHY DID SHE MOVE THE COFFEE? IT WAS FINE WHERE IT WAS.
SHE HAD TO COME IN HERE AND TAKE OVER.
LA DEE DA!
BOSSY.
THERE WAS SO MUCH BRAIN ACTIVITY ALL NIGHT, TRYING TO PROBLEM SOLVE FOR THEM AS WELL AS PROCESS MY OWN ISSUES — I NEVER REALLY GOT BACK TO SLEEP AND I HAD TO LEAVE EARLY TO PICK UP JULIA. I TOLD THEM ABOUT MY FREEZER IDEA, BUT IT WAS SHOT DOWN. ALL MOM COULD DO WAS GRUMBLE ABOUT HOW I'D MESSED WITH THEIR KITCHEN AND DAD WAS CRANKING UP AGAIN. 'GET OUTTA HERE NOW' I TOLD MYSELF. 'LET THIS GO.'
BUT THEN SPEEDING BACK ACROSS THAT SLAB OF HEARTBREAK KNOWN AS I-70, I REALIZED I COULDN'T BREATHE!
AH-KK
AH-KK
BOSSY?!
AHKK
AH-KK
I MUST STOP
AND ARTI-CULATE
THE PROBLEM
THAT UNDERLIES
EVERY THING.
AHKK
AH-KK

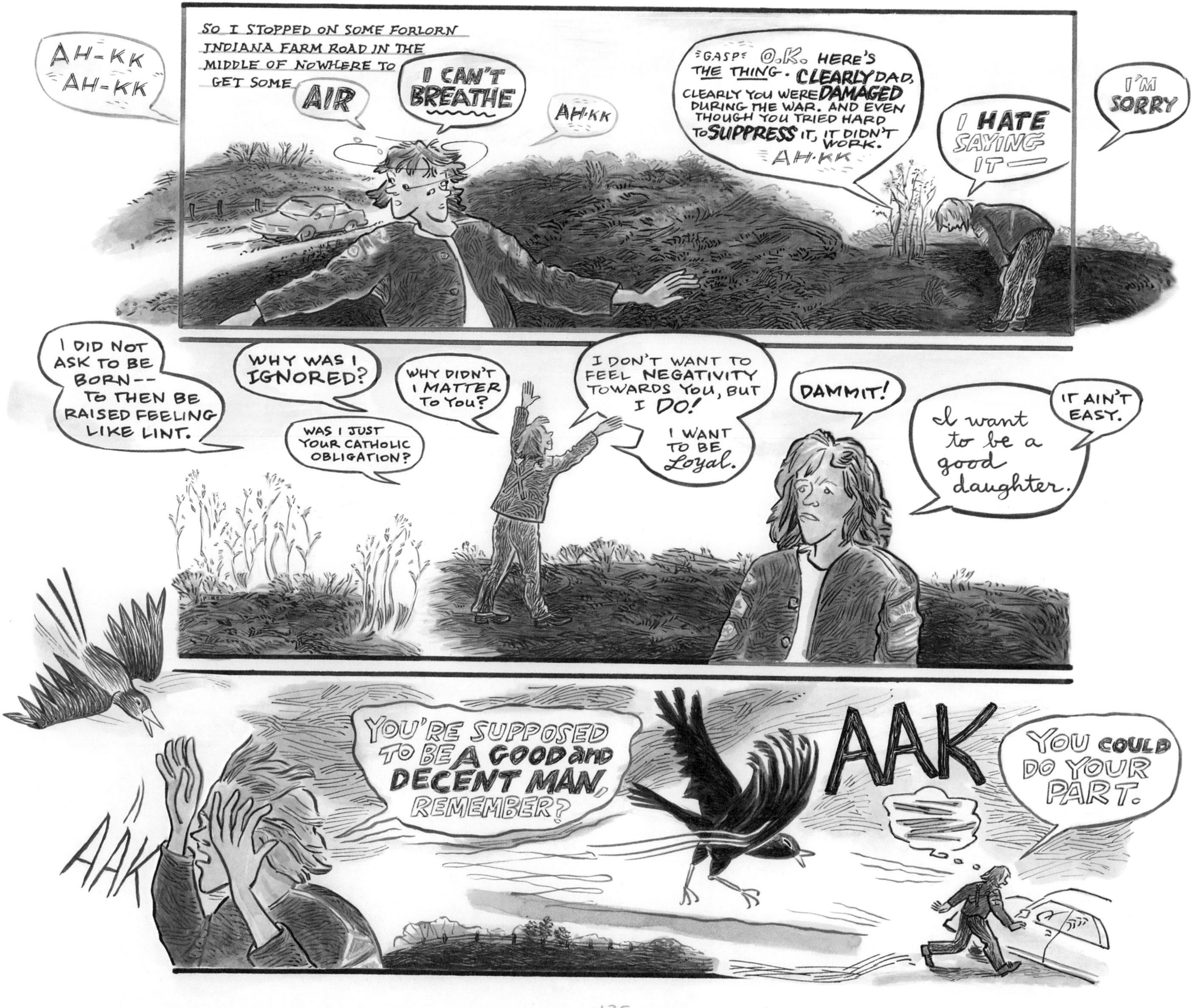

SO I STOPPED ON SOME FORLORN INDIANA FARM ROAD IN THE MIDDLE OF NOWHERE TO GET SOME AIR
AH-KK AH-KK
I CAN'T BREATHE
AH-KK
GASP O.K. HERE'S THE THING. CLEARLY DAD, CLEARLY YOU WERE DAMAGED DURING THE WAR. AND EVEN THOUGH YOU TRIED HARD TO SUPPRESS IT, IT DIDN'T WORK. AH-KK
I HATE SAYING IT—
I'M SORRY
I DID NOT ASK TO BE BORN-- TO THEN BE RAISED FEELING LIKE LINT.
WHY WAS I IGNORED?
WAS I JUST YOUR CATHOLIC OBLIGATION?
WHY DIDN'T I MATTER TO YOU?
I DON'T WANT TO FEEL NEGATIVITY TOWARDS YOU, BUT I DO!
I WANT TO BE Loyal.
DAMMIT!
I want to be a good daughter.
IT AIN'T EASY.
AAK
YOU'RE SUPPOSED TO BE A GOOD and DECENT MAN, REMEMBER?
AAK
YOU COULD DO YOUR PART.

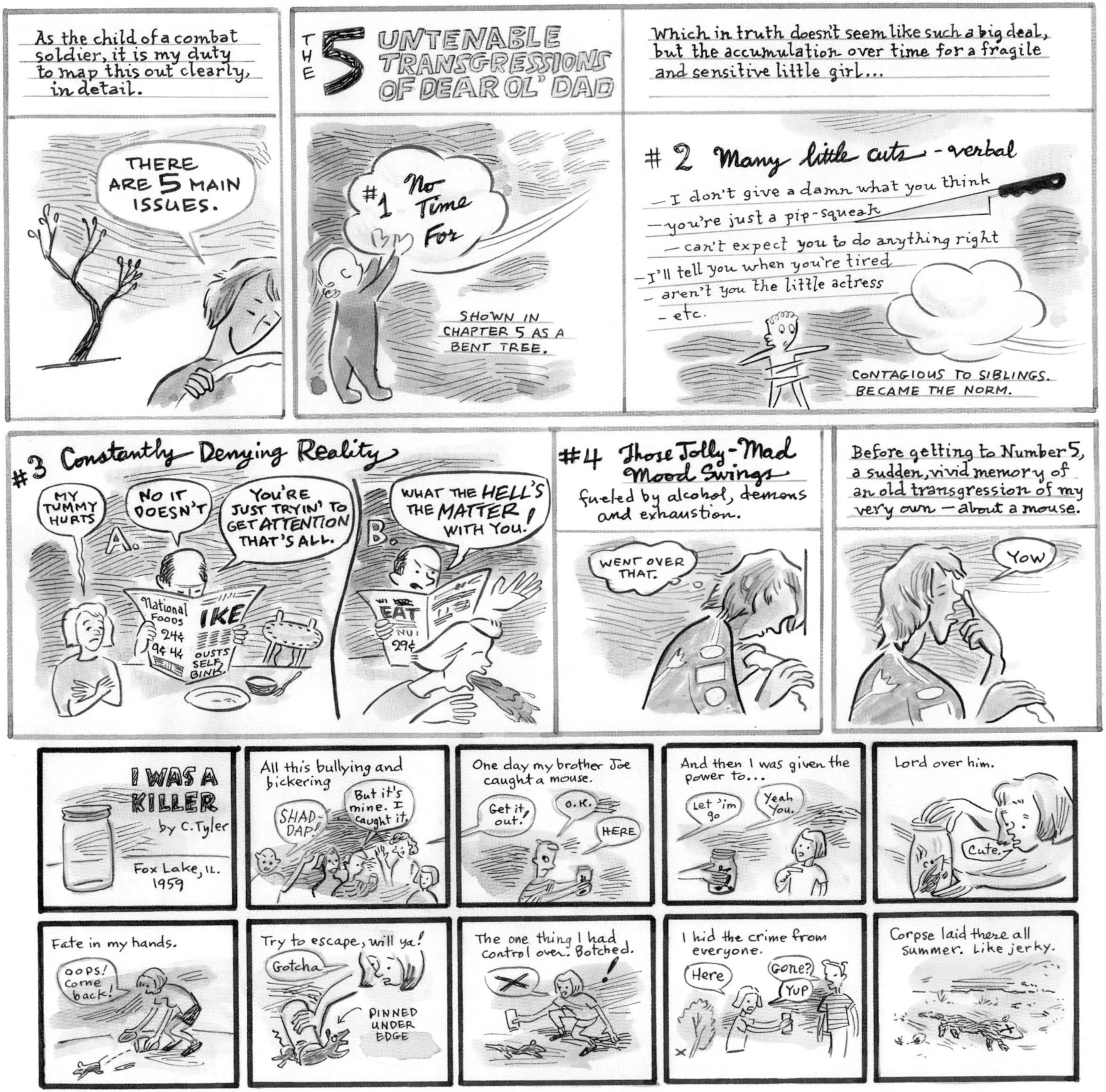
As the child of a combat soldier, it is my duty to map this out clearly, in detail.
THERE ARE 5 MAIN ISSUES.
THE 5 UNTENABLE TRANSGRESSIONS OF DEAR OL' DAD
#1 No Time For
SHOWN IN CHAPTER 5 AS A BENT TREE.
Which in truth doesn't seem like such a big deal, but the accumulation over time for a fragile and sensitive little girl...
2 Many little cuts - verbal
— I don't give a damn what you think
— you're just a pip-squeak
— can't expect you to do anything right
— I'll tell you when you're tired
— aren't you the little actress
— etc.
CONTAGIOUS TO SIBLINGS. BECAME THE NORM.
#3 Constantly Denying Reality
MY TUMMY HURTS
NO IT DOESN'T
YOU'RE JUST TRYIN' TO GET ATTENTION THAT'S ALL.
A.
National Foods 24¢ 9¢ 4¢
IKE OUSTS SELF
B.
WHAT THE HELL'S THE MATTER WITH YOU!
EAT 29¢
#4 Those Jolly-Mad Mood Swings fueled by alcohol, demons and exhaustion.
WENT OVER THAT.
Before getting to Number 5, a sudden, vivid memory of an old transgression of my very own — about a mouse.
YOW
I WAS A KILLER by C. Tyler
Fox Lake, IL. 1959
All this bullying and bickering
SHAD-DAP!
But it's mine. I caught it.
One day my brother Joe caught a mouse.
Get it out.
O.K.
HERE
And then I was given the power to...
Let 'im go
Yeah You.
Lord over him.
Cute.
Fate in my hands.
OOPS! come back!
Try to escape, will ya!
Gotcha
PINNED UNDER EDGE
The one thing I had control over. Botched.
I hid the crime from everyone.
Here
GONE?
YUP
Corpse laid there all summer. Like jerky.

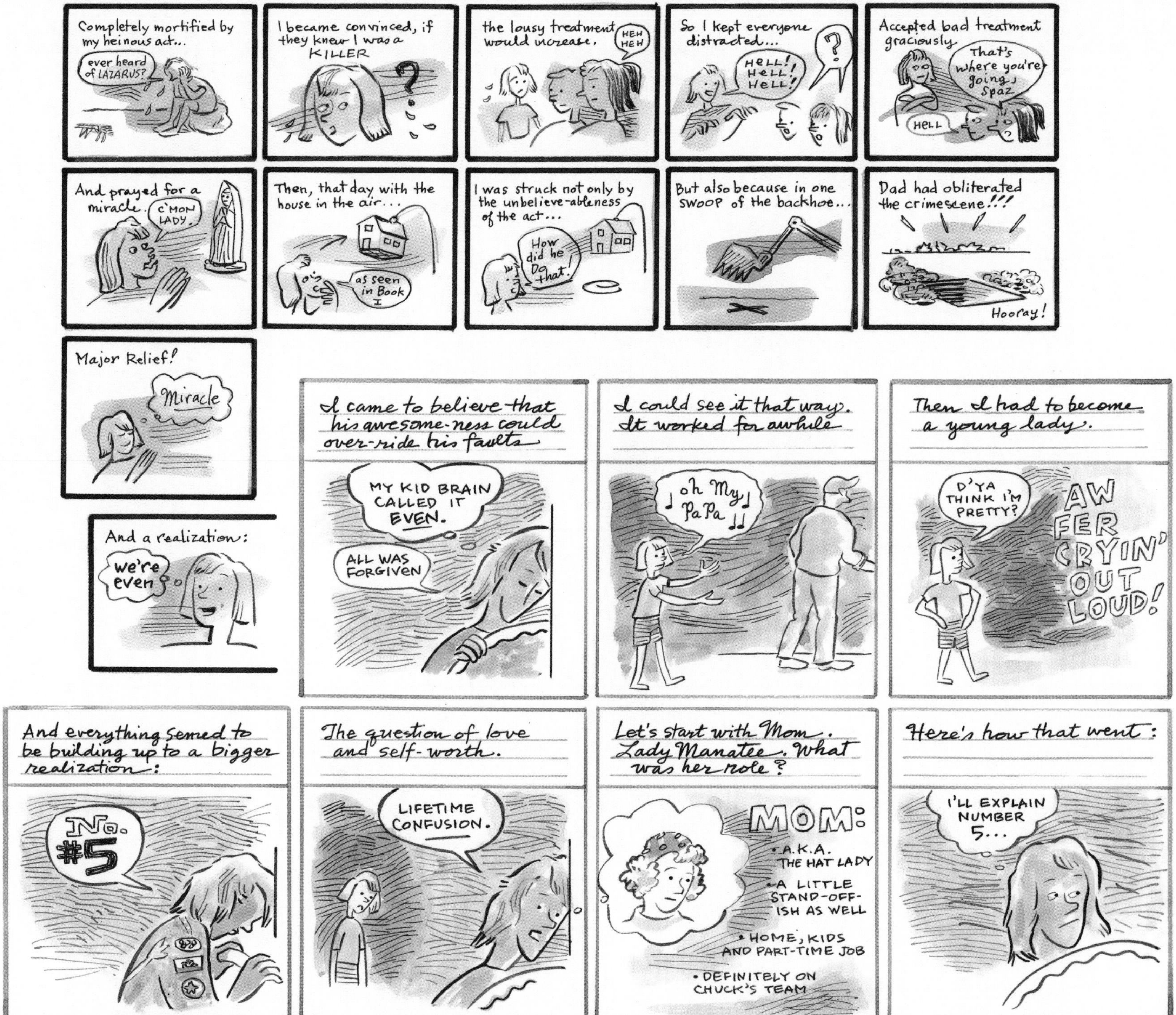
Completely mortified by my heinous act...
ever heard of LAZARUS?
I became convinced, if they knew I was a KILLER
?
the lousy treatment would increase.
HEH HEH
So I kept everyone distracted...
HELL! HELL! HELL!
?
Accepted bad treatment graciously
That's where you're going, Spaz
HELL
And prayed for a miracle.
C'MON LADY.
Then, that day with the house in the air...
as seen in Book I
I was struck not only by the unbelieve-ableness of the act...
How did he Do that!
But also because in one SWOOP of the backhoe...
Dad had obliterated the crimescene!!!
Hooray!
Major Relief!
Miracle
And a realization:
we're even
I came to believe that his awesome-ness could over-ride his faults
MY KID BRAIN CALLED IT EVEN.
ALL WAS FORGIVEN
I could see it that way. It worked for awhile
oh My PaPa
Then I had to become a young lady.
D'YA THINK I'M PRETTY?
AW FER CRYIN' OUT LOUD!
And everything semed to be building up to a bigger realization:
No. #5
The question of love and self-worth.
LIFETIME CONFUSION.
Let's start with Mom. Lady Manatee. What was her role?
MOM:
• A.K.A. THE HAT LADY
• A LITTLE STAND-OFF-ISH AS WELL
• HOME, KIDS AND PART-TIME JOB
• DEFINITELY ON CHUCK'S TEAM
Here's how that went:
I'LL EXPLAIN NUMBER 5...

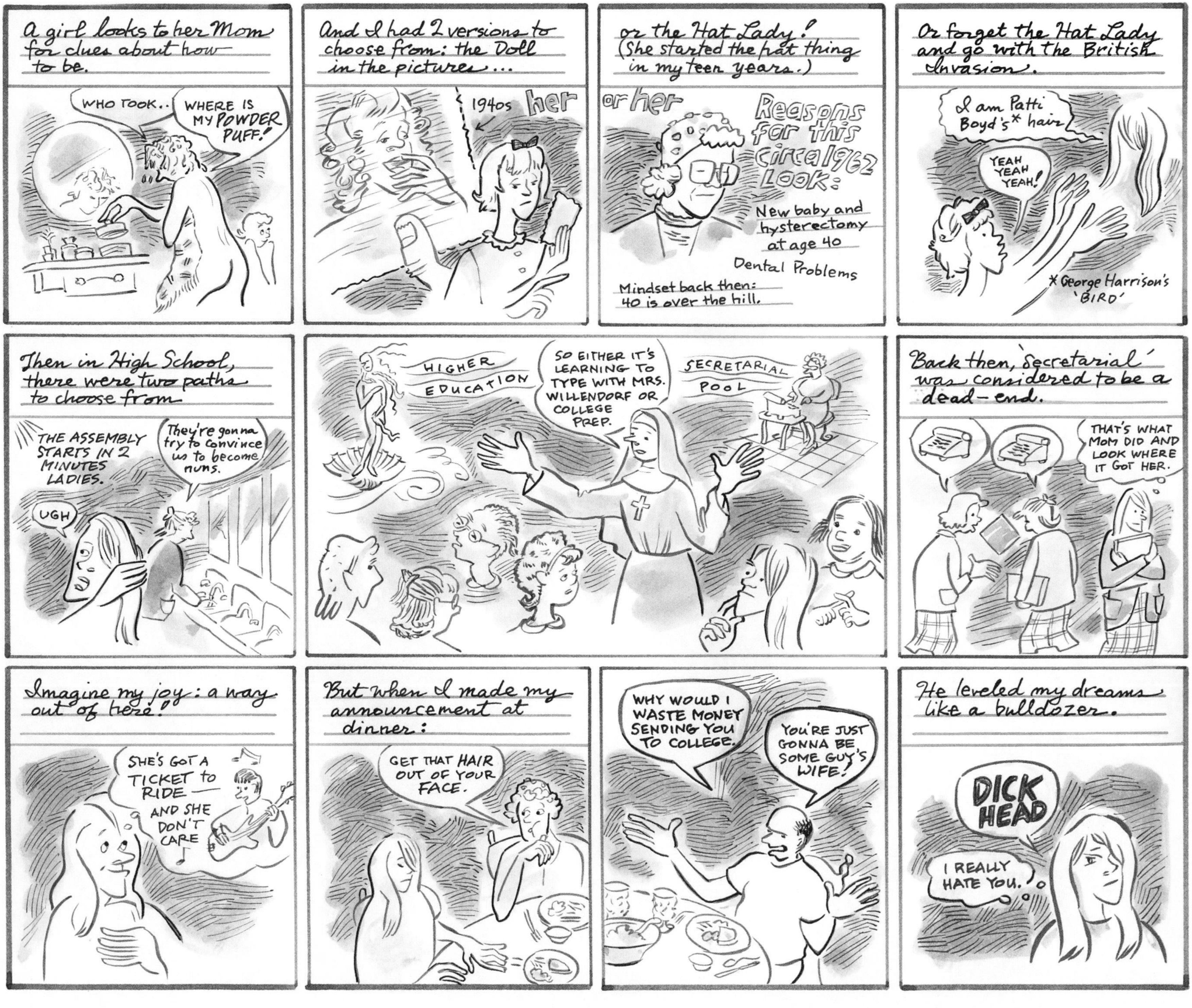
a girl looks to her Mom for clues about how to be.
WHO TOOK..
WHERE IS MY POWDER PUFF!
And I had 2 versions to choose from: the Doll in the pictures...
1940s
her
or the Hat Lady! (She started the hat thing in my teen years.)
or her
Reasons for this circa 1962 Look:
New baby and hysterectomy at age 40
Dental Problems
Mindset back then: 40 is over the hill.
Or forget the Hat Lady and go with the British Invasion.
I am Patti Boyd's* hair
YEAH YEAH YEAH!
* George Harrison's 'BIRD'
Then in High School, there were two paths to choose from
THE ASSEMBLY STARTS IN 2 MINUTES LADIES.
They're gonna try to convince us to become nuns.
UGH
HIGHER EDUCATION
SO EITHER IT'S LEARNING TO TYPE WITH MRS. WILLENDORF OR COLLEGE PREP.
SECRETARIAL POOL
Back then, 'secretarial' was considered to be a dead-end.
THAT'S WHAT MOM DID AND LOOK WHERE IT GOT HER.
Imagine my joy: a way out of here!
SHE'S GOT A TICKET TO RIDE — AND SHE DON'T CARE
But when I made my announcement at dinner:
GET THAT HAIR OUT OF YOUR FACE.
WHY WOULD I WASTE MONEY SENDING YOU TO COLLEGE.
YOU'RE JUST GONNA BE SOME GUY'S WIFE!
He leveled my dreams like a bulldozer.
DICK HEAD
I REALLY HATE YOU.

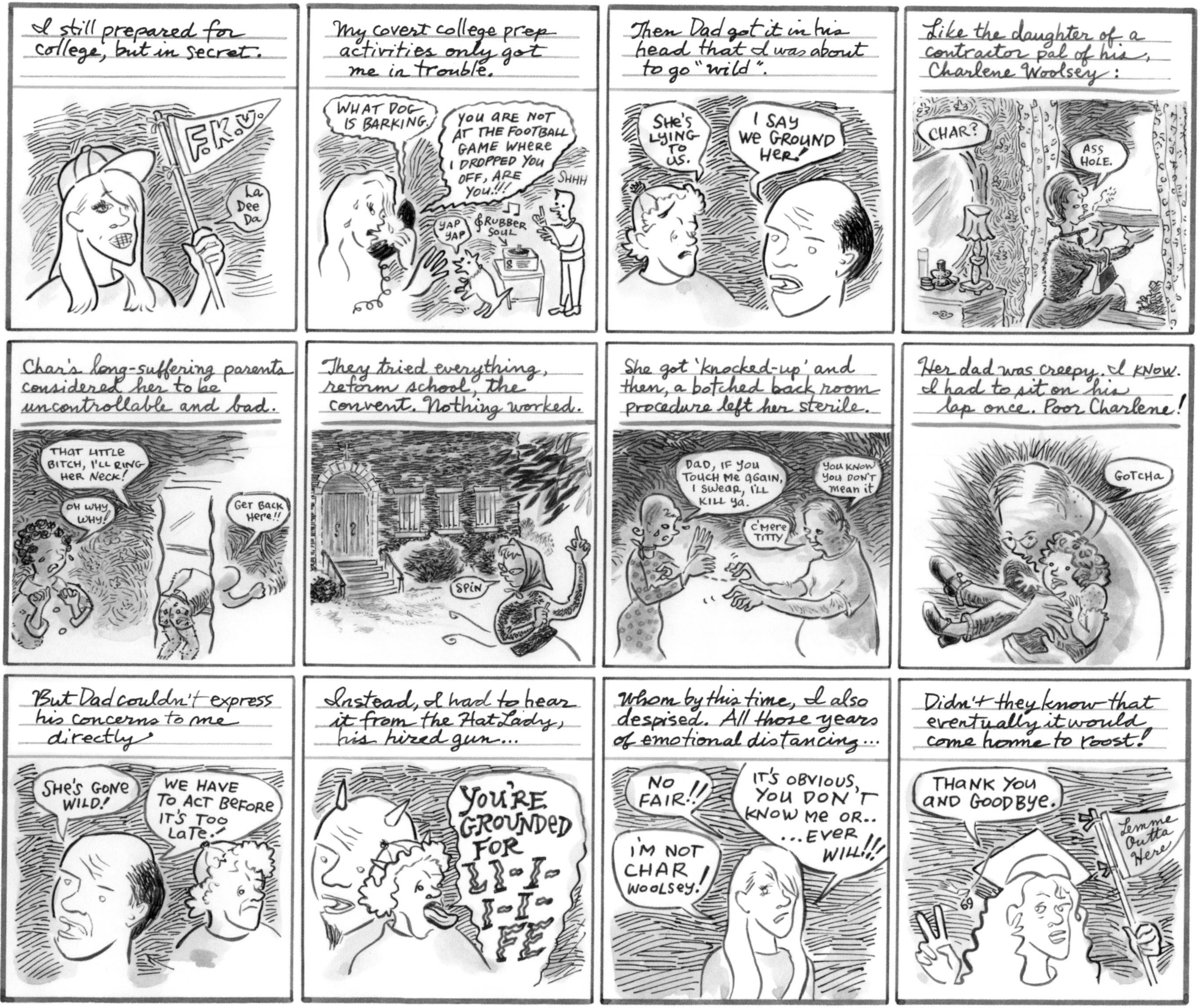
I still prepared for college, but in secret.
F.K.U.
La Dee Da
My covert college prep activities only got me in trouble.
WHAT DOG IS BARKING.
YOU ARE NOT AT THE FOOTBALL GAME WHERE I DROPPED YOU OFF, ARE YOU!!!
SHHH
YAP YAP
RUBBER SOUL
Then Dad got it in his head that I was about to go "wild".
SHE'S LYING TO US.
I SAY WE GROUND HER!
Like the daughter of a contractor pal of his, Charlene Woolsey:
CHAR?
ASS HOLE.
Char's long-suffering parents considered her to be uncontrollable and bad.
THAT LITTLE BITCH, I'LL RING HER NECK!
OH WHY, WHY!
GET BACK HERE!!
They tried everything, reform school, the convent. Nothing worked.
SPIN
She got 'knocked-up' and then, a botched back room procedure left her sterile.
DAD, IF YOU TOUCH ME AGAIN, I SWEAR, I'LL KILL YA.
YOU KNOW YOU DON'T MEAN IT
C'MERE TITTY
Her dad was creepy. I KNOW. I had to sit on his lap once. Poor Charlene!
GOTCHA
But Dad couldn't express his concerns to me directly
SHE'S GONE WILD!
WE HAVE TO ACT BEFORE IT'S TOO LATE!
Instead, I had to hear it from the Hat Lady, his hired gun...
YOU'RE GROUNDED FOR LI-I-I-I-FE
Whom by this time, I also despised. All those years of emotional distancing...
NO FAIR!!
I'M NOT CHAR WOOLSEY!
IT'S OBVIOUS, YOU DON'T KNOW ME OR.. ...EVER WILL!!!
Didn't they know that eventually it would come home to roost!
THANK YOU AND GOODBYE.
Lemme Outta Here
69

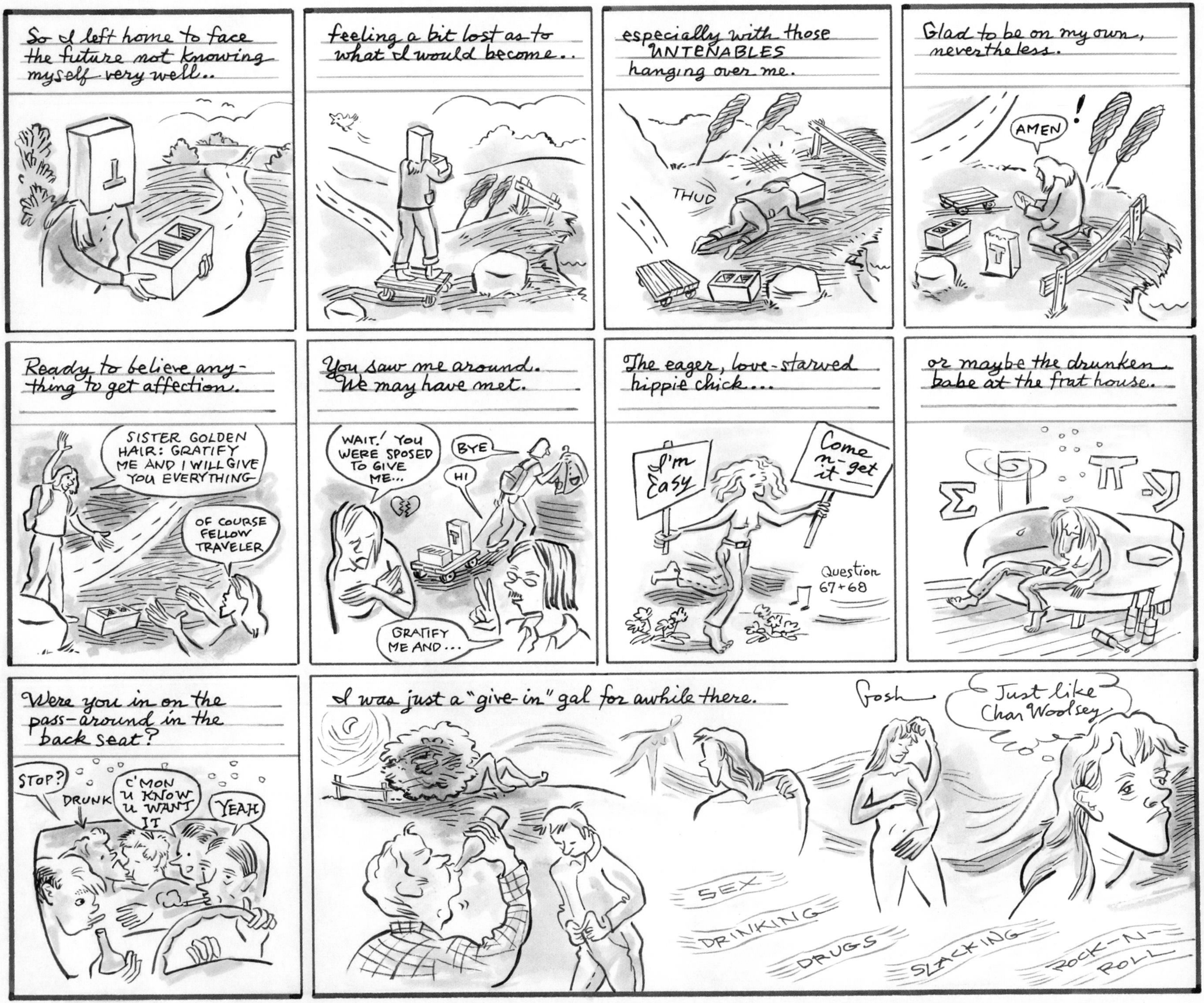
So I left home to face the future not knowing myself very well..
feeling a bit lost as to what I would become..
especially with those UNTENABLES hanging over me.
THUD
Glad to be on my own, nevertheless.
AMEN
Ready to believe anything to get affection.
SISTER GOLDEN HAIR: GRATIFY ME AND I WILL GIVE YOU EVERYTHING
OF COURSE FELLOW TRAVELER
You saw me around. We may have met.
WAIT! YOU WERE SPOSED TO GIVE ME...
BYE
HI
GRATIFY ME AND...
The eager, love-starved hippie chick...
I'm Easy
Come n-get it
Question 67+68
or maybe the drunken babe at the frat house.
Were you in on the pass-around in the back seat?
STOP?
DRUNK
C'MON U KNOW U WANT IT
YEAH
I was just a "give-in" gal for awhile there.
Gosh
Just like Char Woolsey
SEX
DRINKING
DRUGS
SLACKING
ROCK-N-ROLL

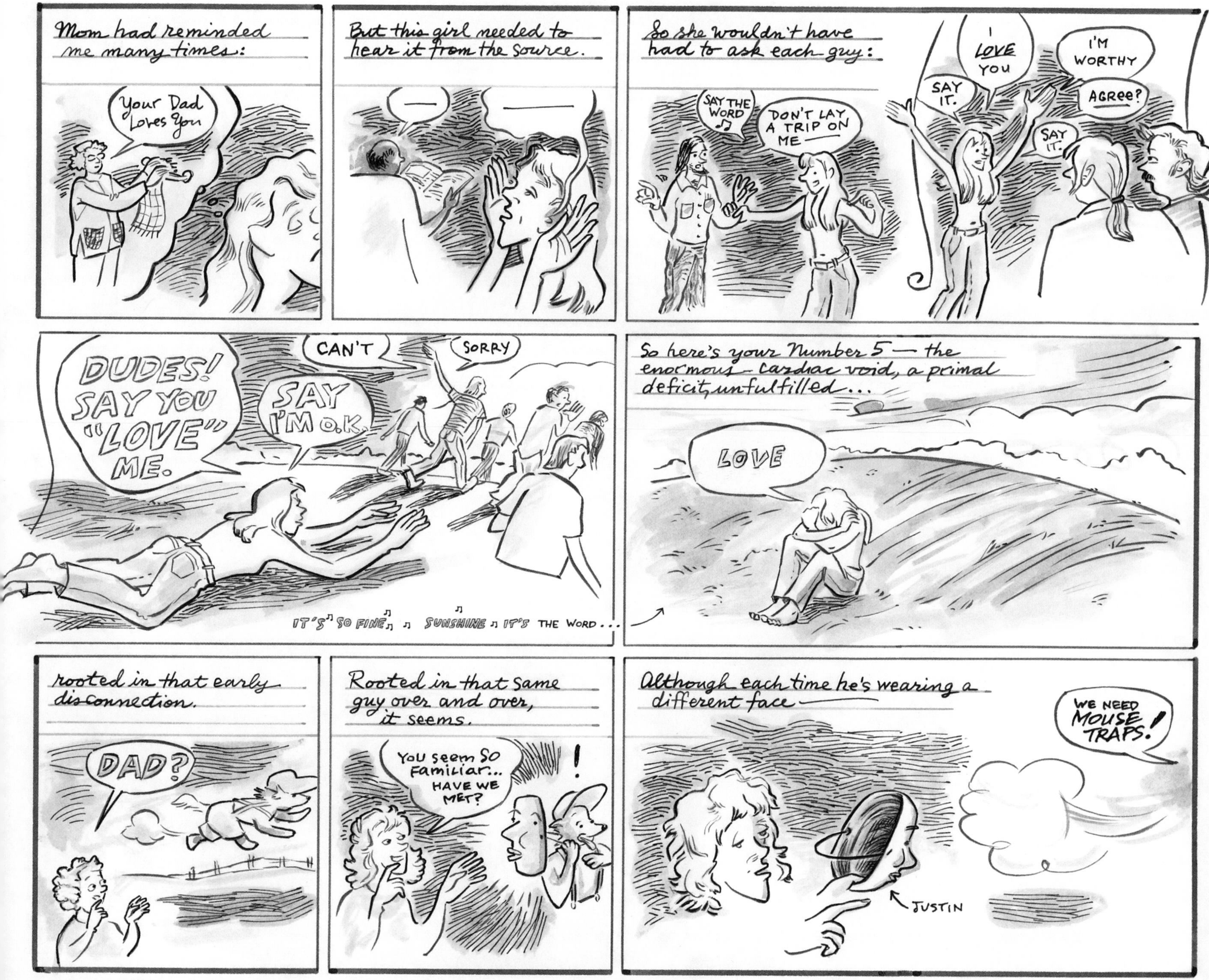
Mom had reminded me many times:
Your Dad Loves You
But this girl needed to hear it from the source.
So she wouldn't have had to ask each guy:
SAY THE WORD ♫
DON'T LAY A TRIP ON ME—
SAY IT.
I LOVE YOU
I'M WORTHY
AGREE?
SAY IT.
DUDES! SAY YOU "LOVE" ME.
SAY I'M O.K.
CAN'T
SORRY
IT'S ♫ SO FINE ♫ ♫ SUNSHINE ♫ IT'S THE WORD...
So here's your Number 5 — the enormous — cardiac void, a primal deficit, unfulfilled...
LOVE
rooted in that early disconnection.
DAD?
Rooted in that same guy over and over, it seems.
YOU SEEM SO FAMILIAR... HAVE WE MET?
!
Although each time he's wearing a different face—
WE NEED MOUSE TRAPS!
JUSTIN

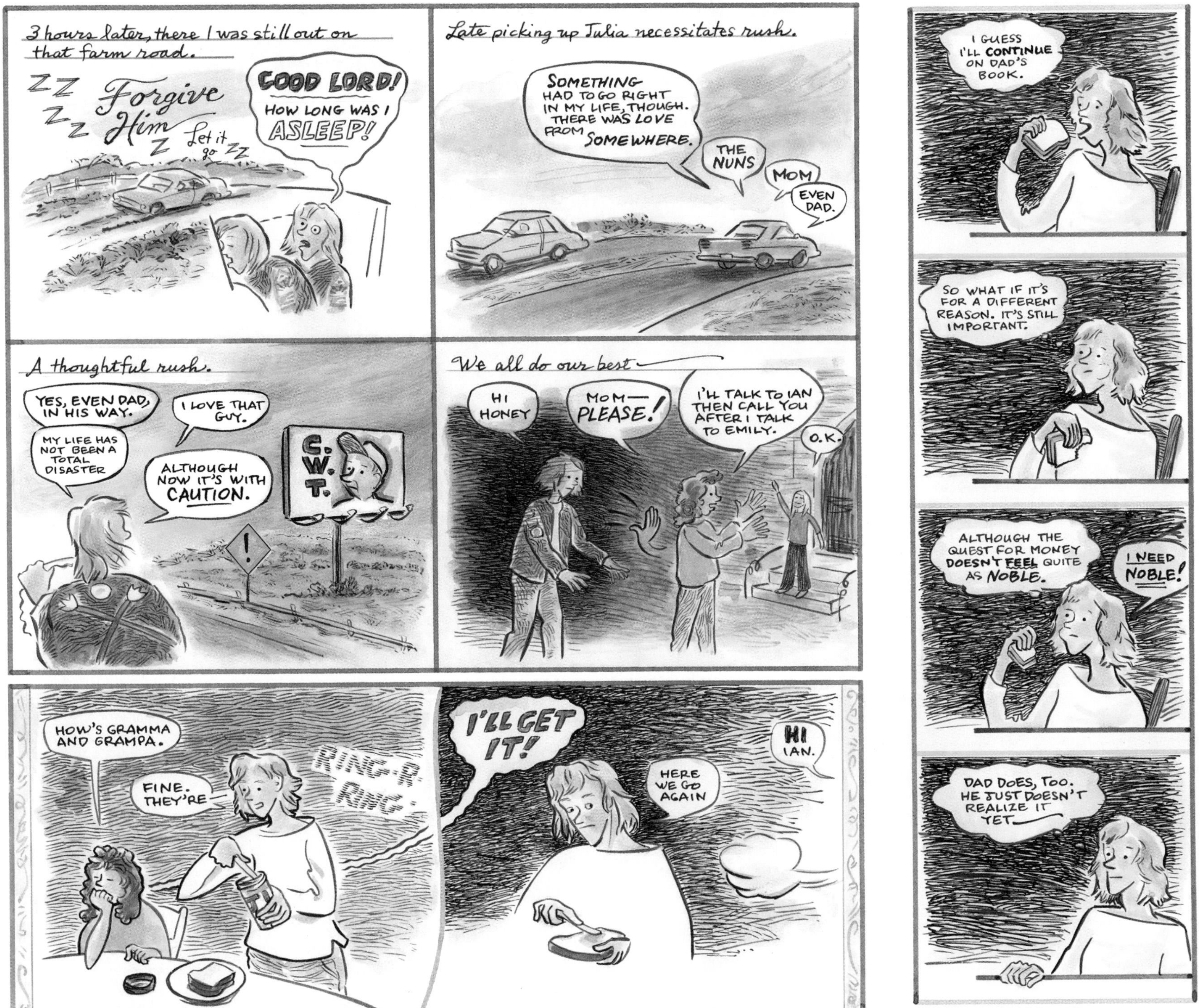
3 hours later, there I was still out on that farm road.
ZZ ZZ Forgive Him Z Let it go ZZ
GOOD LORD! HOW LONG WAS I ASLEEP!
Late picking up Julia necessitates rush.
SOMETHING HAD TO GO RIGHT IN MY LIFE, THOUGH. THERE WAS LOVE FROM SOMEWHERE.
THE NUNS
MOM
EVEN DAD.
A thoughtful rush.
YES, EVEN DAD, IN HIS WAY.
MY LIFE HAS NOT BEEN A TOTAL DISASTER
I LOVE THAT GUY.
ALTHOUGH NOW IT'S WITH CAUTION.
C. W. T.
!
We all do our best
HI HONEY
MOM— PLEASE!
I'LL TALK TO IAN THEN CALL YOU AFTER I TALK TO EMILY.
O.K.
HOW'S GRAMMA AND GRAMPA.
FINE. THEY'RE—
RING-R RING
I'LL GET IT!
HERE WE GO AGAIN
HI IAN.
I GUESS I'LL CONTINUE ON DAD'S BOOK.
SO WHAT IF IT'S FOR A DIFFERENT REASON. IT'S STILL IMPORTANT.
ALTHOUGH THE QUEST FOR MONEY DOESN'T FEEL QUITE AS NOBLE.
I NEED NOBLE!
DAD DOES, TOO. HE JUST DOESN'T REALIZE IT YET—

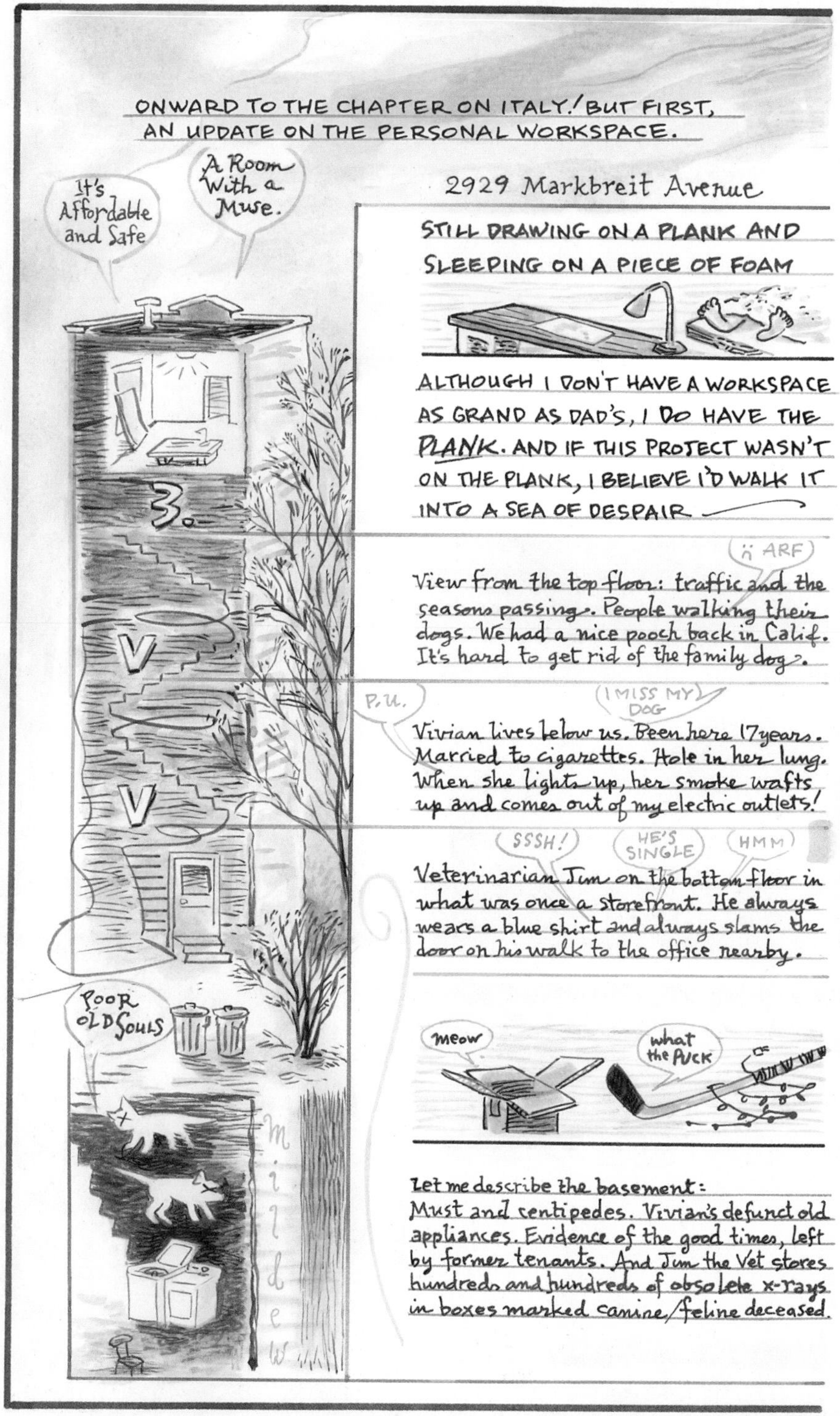
ONWARD TO THE CHAPTER ON ITALY! BUT FIRST, AN UPDATE ON THE PERSONAL WORKSPACE.
It's Affordable and Safe
A Room With a Muse.
2929 Markbreit Avenue
STILL DRAWING ON A PLANK AND SLEEPING ON A PIECE OF FOAM
ALTHOUGH I DON'T HAVE A WORKSPACE AS GRAND AS DAD'S, I DO HAVE THE PLANK. AND IF THIS PROJECT WASN'T ON THE PLANK, I BELIEVE I'D WALK IT INTO A SEA OF DESPAIR
3.
ARF
View from the top floor: traffic and the seasons passing. People walking their dogs. We had a nice pooch back in Calif. It's hard to get rid of the family dog.
P.U.
I MISS MY DOG
Vivian lives below us. Been here 17 years. Married to cigarettes. Hole in her lung. When she lights up, her smoke wafts up and comes out of my electric outlets!
SSSH!
HE'S SINGLE
HMM
Veterinarian Jim on the bottom floor in what was once a storefront. He always wears a blue shirt and always slams the door on his walk to the office nearby.
POOR OLD SOULS
meow
what the PUCK
Let me describe the basement:
Must and centipedes. Vivian's defunct old appliances. Evidence of the good times, left by former tenants. And Jim the Vet stores hundreds and hundreds of obsolete x-rays in boxes marked canine/feline deceased.
Mildew

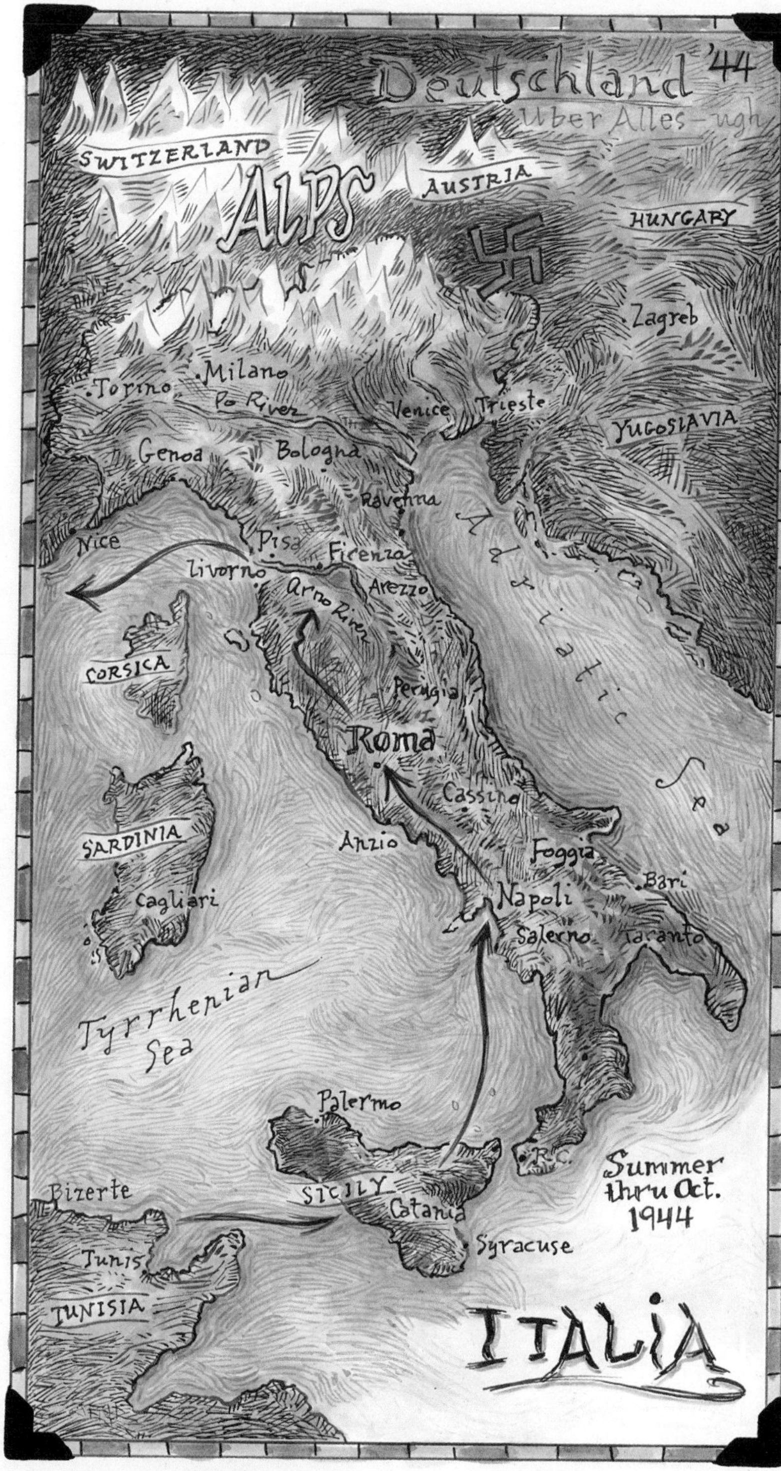
Deutschland '44
Uber Alles - ugh
SWITZERLAND
ALPS
AUSTRIA
HUNGARY
Zagreb
Torino
Milano
Po River
Venice
Trieste
YUGOSLAVIA
Genoa
Bologna
Ravenna
Adriatic Sea
Nice
Pisa
Firenze
Livorno
Arno River
Arezzo
CORSICA
Perugia
Roma
Cassino
SARDINIA
Anzio
Foggia
Bari
Cagliari
Napoli
Salerno
Taranto
Tyrrhenian Sea
Palermo
R.C.
Summer thru Oct. 1944
Bizerte
SICILY
Catania
Syracuse
Tunis
TUNISIA
ITALIA

DAD'S ARMY SCRAPBOOK
AND
TOUR OF DUTY HIGHLIGHTS

PART III

ITALY

JULY 1944 – OCTOBER 1944

Only THIS time,
I'm looking for
EVIDENCE.

Knee Deep

"On the boat over to Italy, all the talk was about Normandy. Rumor had it that the war wouldn't last very much longer. Just a little mopping up, that's all. With Jerry on the run, victory was at hand.

"Going past Sicily, we saw people coming out in their litte boats to greet us. So we got excited and threw our bars of soap to them. A funny thing happened: they started eating the soap thinking they were candy bars.

"Naples — big harbor. That's where we docked."

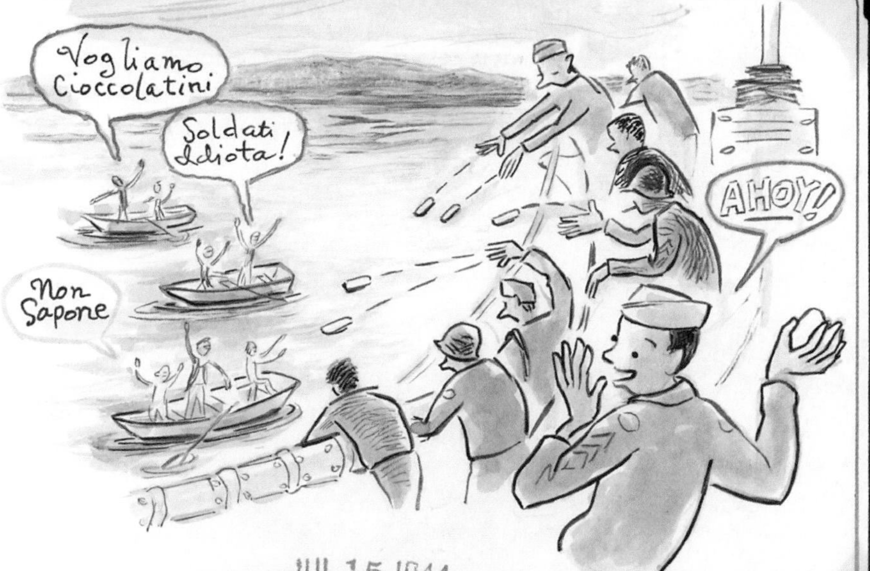
Vogliamo Cioccolatini
Soldati Idiota!
Non Sapone
AHOY!

JUL 15 1944

38

"Hurry up and wait, with a little shot of SNAFU. This was Naples. *Napoli*. Right away when I figured out, it wasn't plumbing they needed me for... I was on hold in a 'Repple Depple.'" (Short for Personnel Replacement Depot — a system to replace casualties, the wounded and the dead.) "We were fresh meat."

"Your life ain't worth a damn. We were there waiting while they were digging trenches for the poor bastards that didn't make it. Our turn was coming so the vino was flowing. We drank like there was no tomorrow."

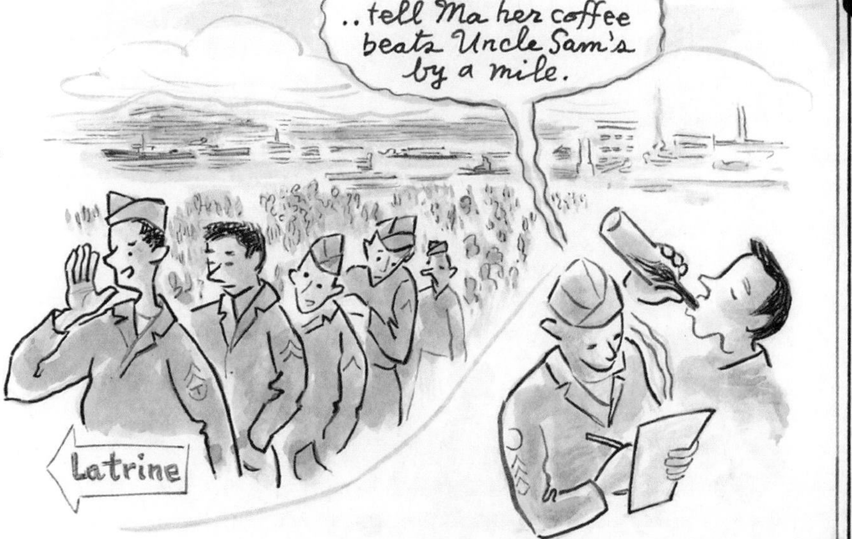
..tell Ma her coffee beats Uncle Sam's by a mile.
Latrine

39

"Liquor— now *THAT* was something else. Vino was cheap, beer too. But liquor— that was the way to go alright.

"Next thing 'What's this?' 'Get up there Jack,* we want you drivingus.' It turns out that the officers needed my truck to sneak their cases of liquor off of the Navy ships. That's how I had access to the good stuff. Of course. So I slipped off a case or two of my own and sold it on the black market. That's how you did it. Everybody did it. Us hunks of meat had to make some extra money somehow."

*everyone calls everyone else 'Jack'.

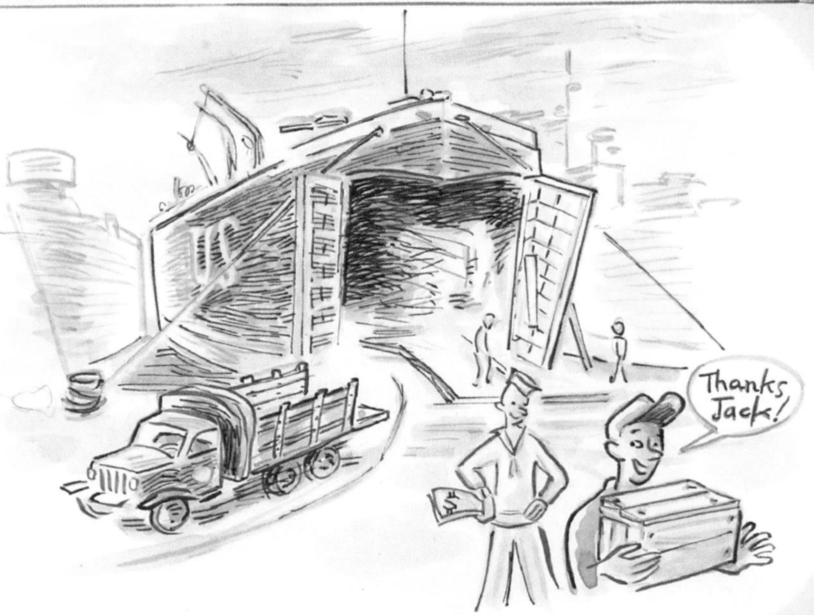
Thanks Jack!

40

"This buddy I met in the Repple Depple—SNOOSE I called him. From Red Lake, Minnesota. Well, we decided we needed something to keep the booze cold. So we went back to the Navy ship— as a construction foreman, I had access. And the truck they gave me. I lied like a son-of-a-bitch to get what we needed.

"They gave us blocks of ice and we stole wood from the quartermaster. We built this giant ice house, there in Naples, Italy— in the middle of summer. 12" thick walls. Hoo hoo, two boys from the mid-west. I imagine it's still there."

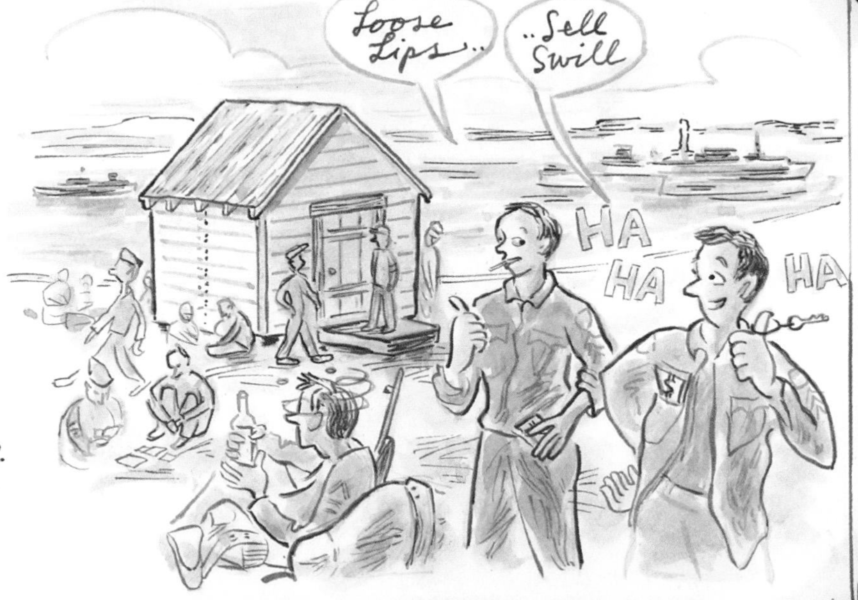
Loose Lips...
..Sell Swill
HA
HA
HA

41

"Somebody had set up three blankets for hookers out in a field — one each for a blonde, a brunette and a redhead. Guys would stand in line and when it was their turn, they'd put their bills down on the blanket. This had nothing to do with love. Strictly wartime survival for the dames.

"Snoose and I, we were married men, but that didn't keep us from snatching up a few stray bills while those broads weren't lookin'. That's how we paid the Navy guys for all that ice."

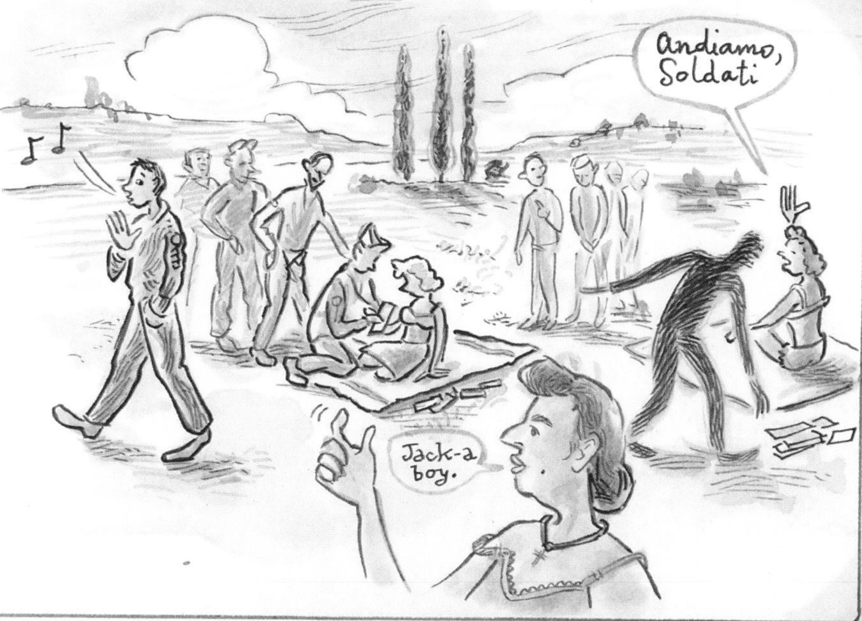
Andiamo, Soldati
Jack-a boy.

42

"There in Naples, picking up ammo for a dump — 3 shells in a pack piled up there as high as you could throw it onto a 6×6 (truck) 9' high and a block square.

"We put a couple of Italians to watch it one night. See, they used to be our enemies, but now they were on our side. So one of those guys shot at somebody, hit the dump and up it went! Boy, we had the wildest bunch of fireworks you'd ever seen! Next thing I know, I'm under Mark Clark headed up to what was called the 'Purple Heart Valley.'"

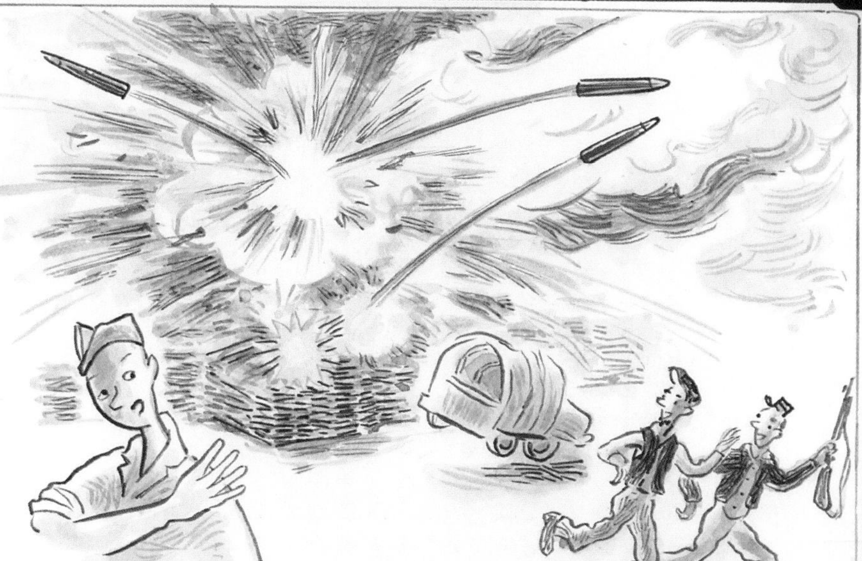

43

"I had a speedboat up there supposedly for hunting mines. Just goofing off, that's all.

"I asked this guy I'd met in Africa—he was in real estate—to get me a boat. Every fence post or building we nicked or banged up, he took note of it and I guess the United States paid for it. We paid in full.

"So I asked this guy could he get me a casa. Wouldn't you know next thing I've got a nice house with a boat on a river in Italy. Wow. Who it belonged to, I'll never know."

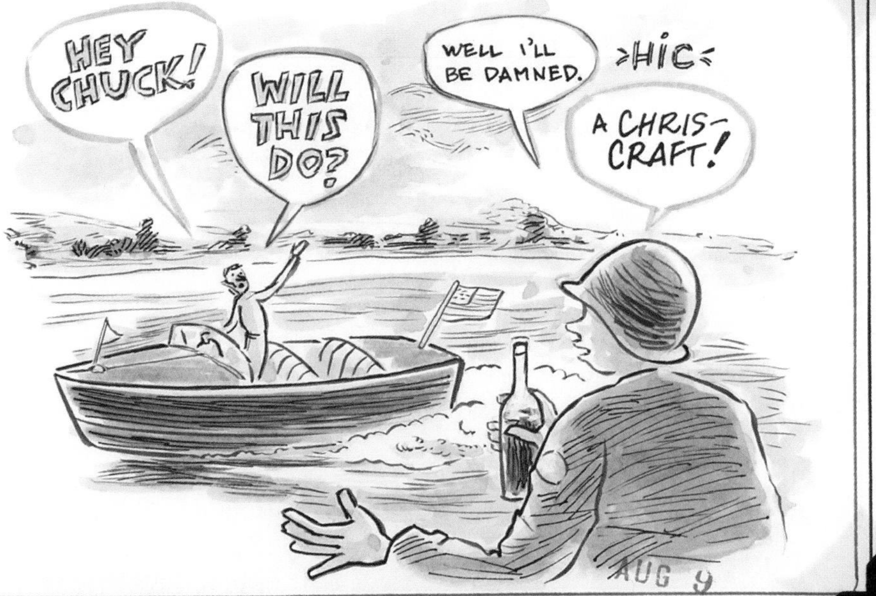
HEY CHUCK!
WILL THIS DO?
WELL I'LL BE DAMNED.
HIC
A CHRIS-CRAFT!
AUG 9

44

"There we were for a few days at my casa. How about a nice dinner before moving on? A little fish with your vino? Except that fishing in Italy wasn't like fishing at home. We decided to throw a grenade into the water and then catch the fish as they came flying out. Great idea, except that some son-of-a-bitch happened to toss in a shrapnel grenade. Holy shit we ran for cover!

"We were just a bunch of crazy kids having a blast over there."

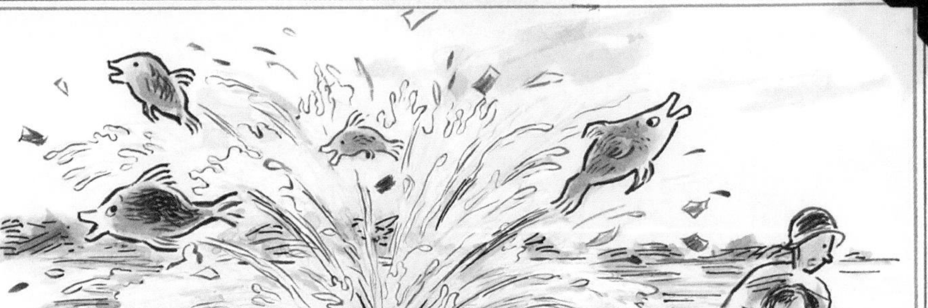

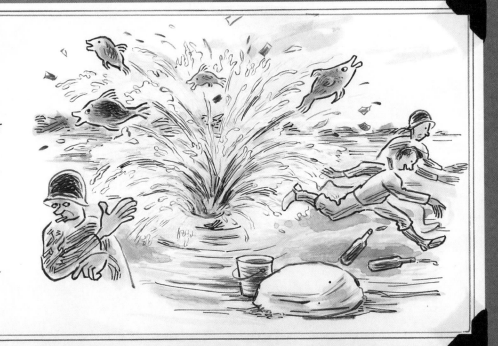

45

By mid-August, three Army infantry Divisions were pulled out of Italy for the invasion of Southern France, and left behind were the smaller rag-tag repple units and far fewer resources. Their mission was to push past the Arno River, up into the impossible terrain of the Apennines Mountains and drive the Nazis off the cliffs and into hell.

A miserable landscape: craggy hills and passes and countless unnamed creeks that could in an instant after a downpour become raging torrents. Fall starts the rainy season.

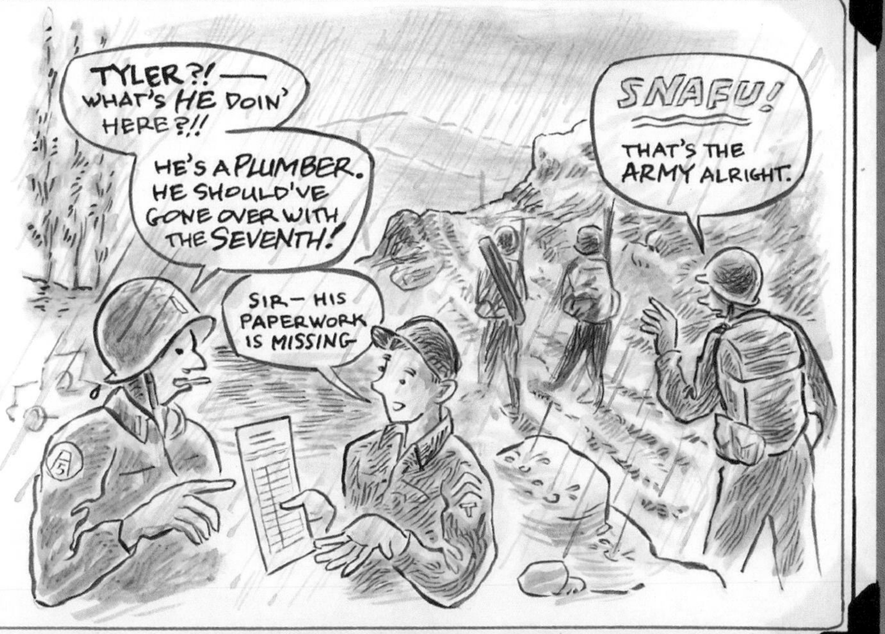
TYLER?! — WHAT'S HE DOIN' HERE?!!
HE'S A PLUMBER. HE SHOULD'VE GONE OVER WITH THE SEVENTH!
SIR— HIS PAPERWORK IS MISSING
SNAFU!
THAT'S THE ARMY ALRIGHT.

46

Certainly more than one of these creeks ran red with blood, and which one Chuck encountered, we'll never know.

"The Germans... we couldn't get them out. Shooting the shit out of us from the hills. We crossed the river with fixed bayonettes. (a blade at the end of a rifle, which means close contact with the enemy). Krauts: they hated bayonettes.

"The river turnt red. I'll never forget that."

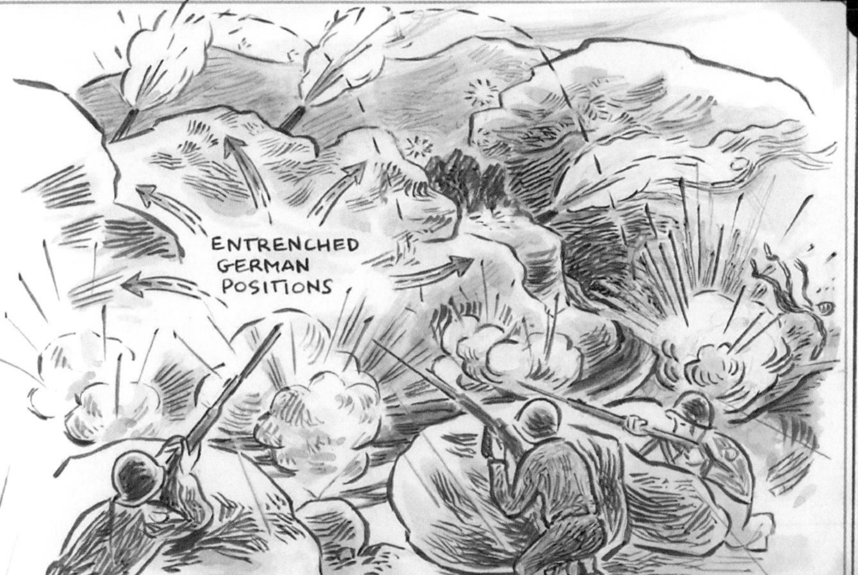
ENTRENCHED GERMAN POSITIONS

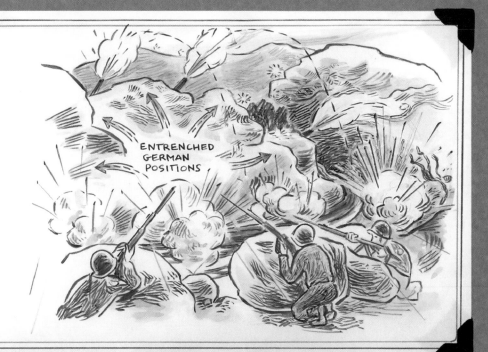

47

"You never knew if you were gonna catch a bullet or get stung by a bee. Hunched over in the rain, I bit into a marmalade sandwich and got stung in the mouth 4 times. My whole face swelled up and I landed over in the sickbay.

"No rest there. Circus Sally kept strafing the hospital *Roop Roop Roop*— with his machine gun. You could hear him coming. I didn't like being a sitting duck, but being laid up gave me a chance to catch up on my mail."

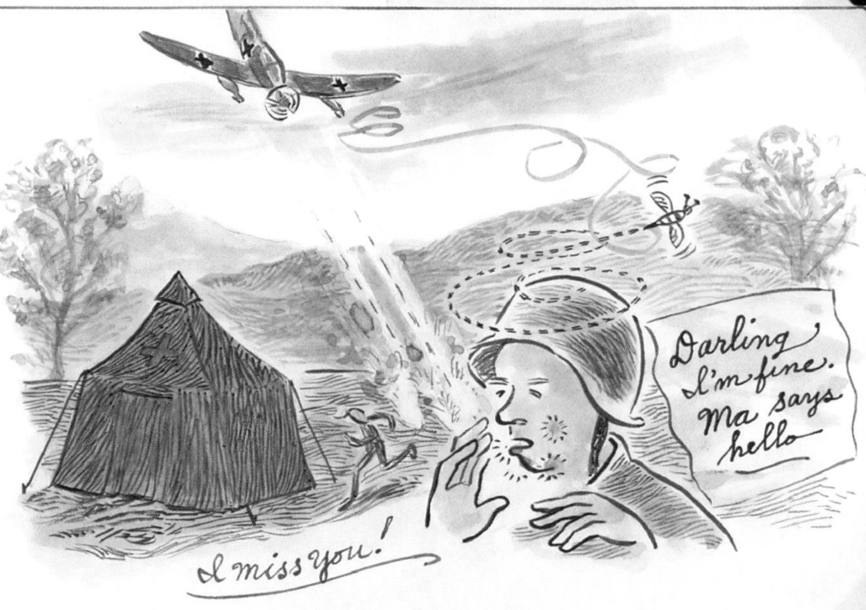
Darling I'm fine. Ma says hello
I miss you!

48

"Soon enough, I was back in a truck, hauling artillery up to the front in a blackout. In a convoy, following the little 1"x2" teardrop tail lights all night while fighting the god-dam mud in my 12 wheel vehicle, sinking up to the axles. They were always moving the road because of mud holes that could swallow up a truck in no time.

"I kept a pistol on my lap, not a rifle—not handy in the cab of a truck. And if I needed bullets, I could get 'em off a dead guy. The bodies were everywhere."

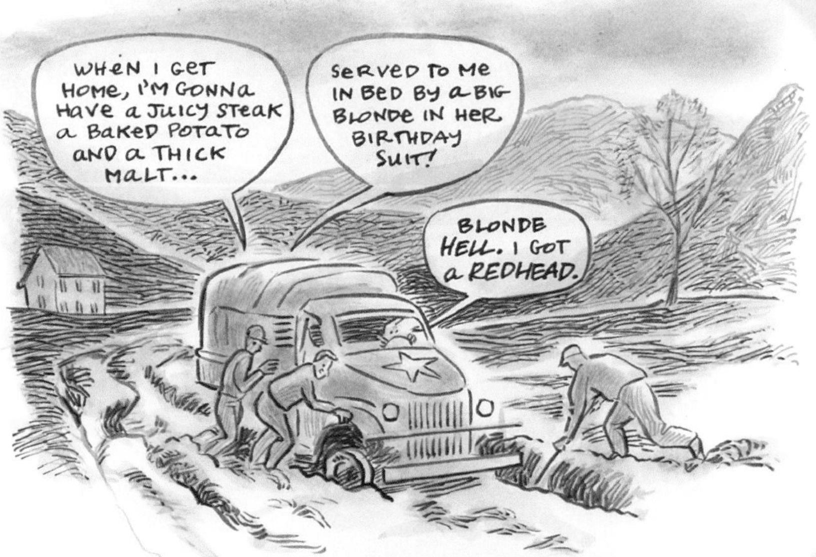
WHEN I GET HOME, I'M GONNA HAVE A JUICY STEAK A BAKED POTATO AND A THICK MALT...
SERVED TO ME IN BED BY A BIG BLONDE IN HER BIRTHDAY SUIT!
BLONDE HELL. I GOT A REDHEAD.

49

"Mud. Knee deep. So much mud that the legs of our cots were on planks. Couldn't wiggle or it would slide off and you'd be up to your neck, wet and filthy. A little stream ran up through the middle of our tent and that's where to aim while peeing off the side of a cot." As long as it runs downhill...

"Laid up there, we couldn't move off the cots so we used our little pill cups as ships to send messages back and forth on the stream. 'Fuck you' the notes would say. 'Kilroy was here' and all that."

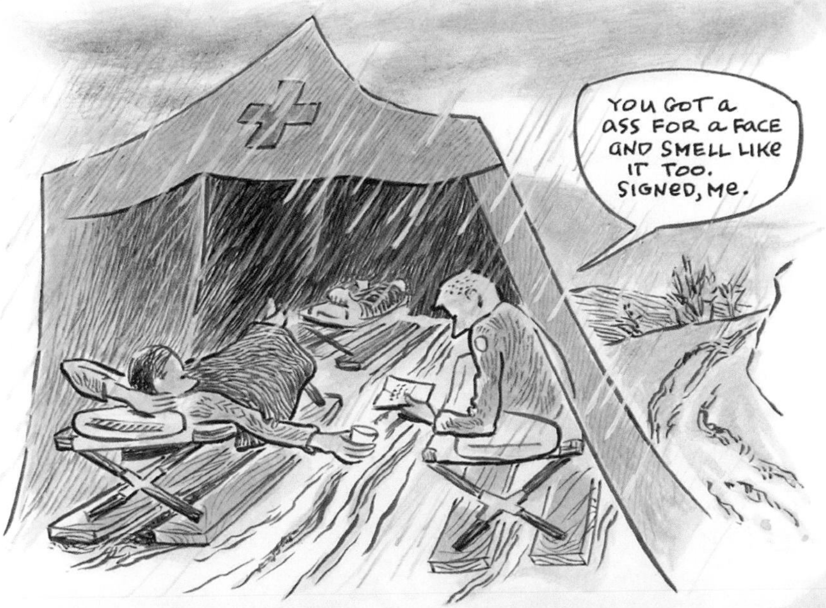
YOU GOT A ASS FOR A FACE AND SMELL LIKE IT TOO. SIGNED, ME.

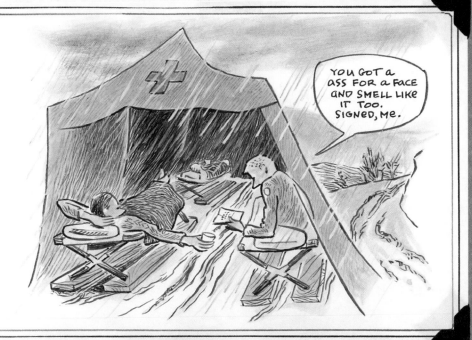

50

"The people buried everything to keep the enemy from getting it: cars, jewelry, sugar. They hid up in the hills until the Germans left and then they would come down waving a flag of whatever country, loyal to whomever just to survive. They were disappointed with us a bit. We were the beat-and-tired grunts rolling in after driving all night, after the stateside commandos had come through there handing out chocolates ahead of us. You know, those desk jockeys in clean uniforms who zip in on a Jeep after the enemy leaves. We had no such treats."

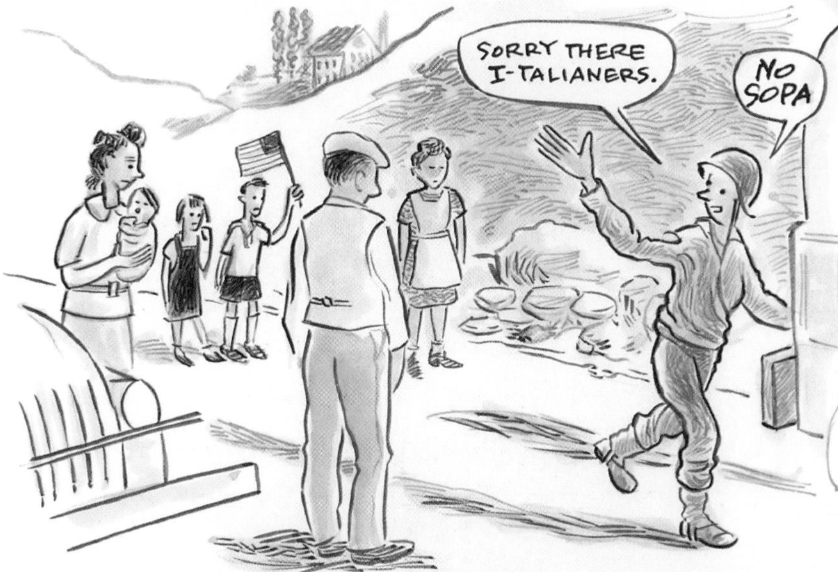
SORRY THERE I-TALIANERS.
NO SOPA

OCT 14

51

"I noticed while driving that the men made the women walk out in front. Was this some custom or *Kaboom*— land mines. 30-40 paces behind, the men stayed.

"So many people out on the roads! They wouldn't get out of the way! We'd honk and they'd just stand there, so we had to knock 'em over. 'Hey, here's some butter, now *MOVE*' but they'd just grease their axles with it so their wagons wouldn't squeak. No stopping the army convoy. We must have knocked over a hundred guys. They didn't listen to us. Things of war, I guess."

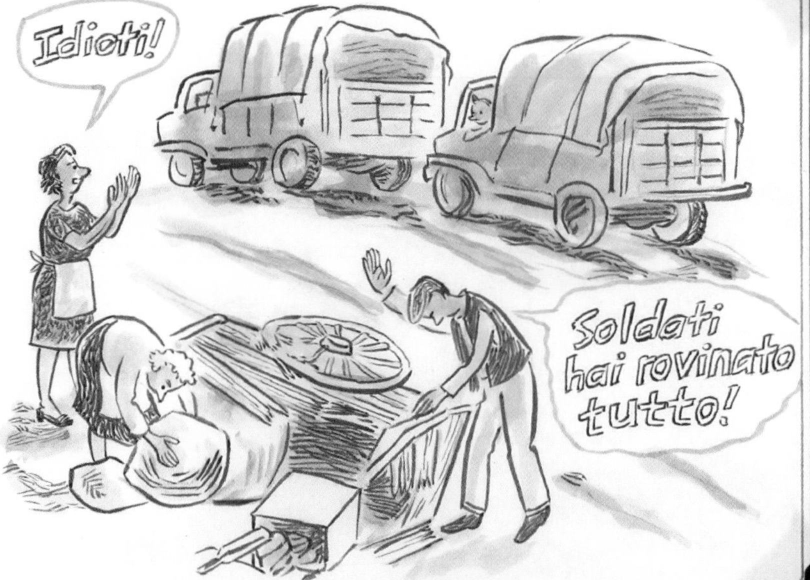
Idioti!
Soldati hai rovinato tutto!

52

Civilians were getting it as bad as the soldiers. Worse, because women and children were involved. Families. Old people. Animals. Rotting dead animals everywhere— This was their homes, roads, villages. This was their land being trampled upon. People caught between armies, coming and going.

"Pretty soon I got word that my bunch was due to leave Italy. Being sent to France to do what, I didn't know. All I could think was that nothing could be worse than this god-forsaken mud hole!"

OCT 16

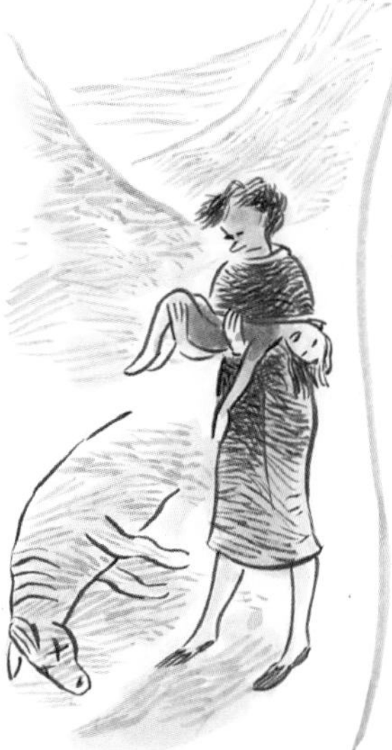

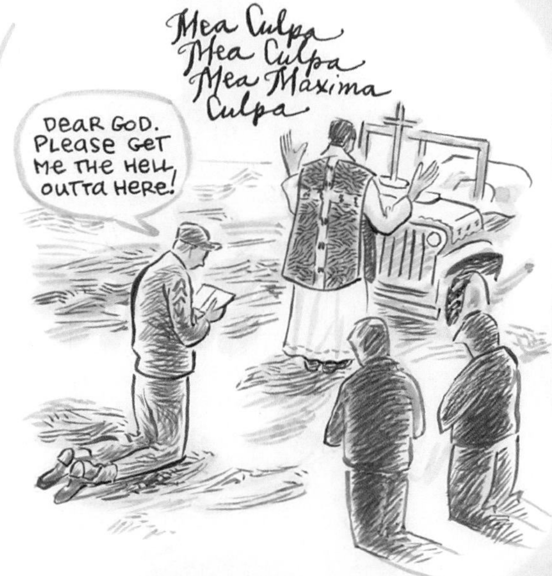
Mea Culpa
Mea Culpa
Mea Maxima Culpa
DEAR GOD. PLEASE GET ME THE HELL OUTTA HERE!

AS HE RELAYED IT, DAD'S STORY OF ITALY REVEALED NOTHING ABOUT A **CUT.** THAT DOESN'T MEAN IT DIDN'T HAPPEN. JUST NEED TO **DIG A LITTLE DEEPER.** BUT I **DO** UNDERSTAND HIS RELUCTANCE TO RECALL THINGS.

IT'S JUST SO SAD AND AWFUL

NOBODY TOLD US KIDS WHEN WE SIGNED UP THAT WE MIGHT HAVE TO GO **RUN OVER** CIVILIANS. **PEOPLE..** ..THAT INNOCENT **PEOPLE** WOULD GET HURT. **KILL THE ENEMY.** THAT'S WHAT WE WERE TRYING TO DO, BUT PEOPLE GOT IN THE WAY.

8.

PITY THE POOR CHILDREN

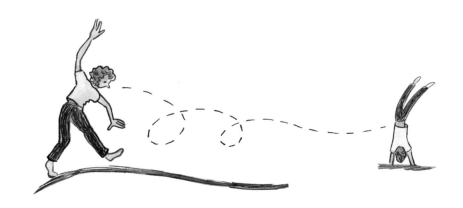

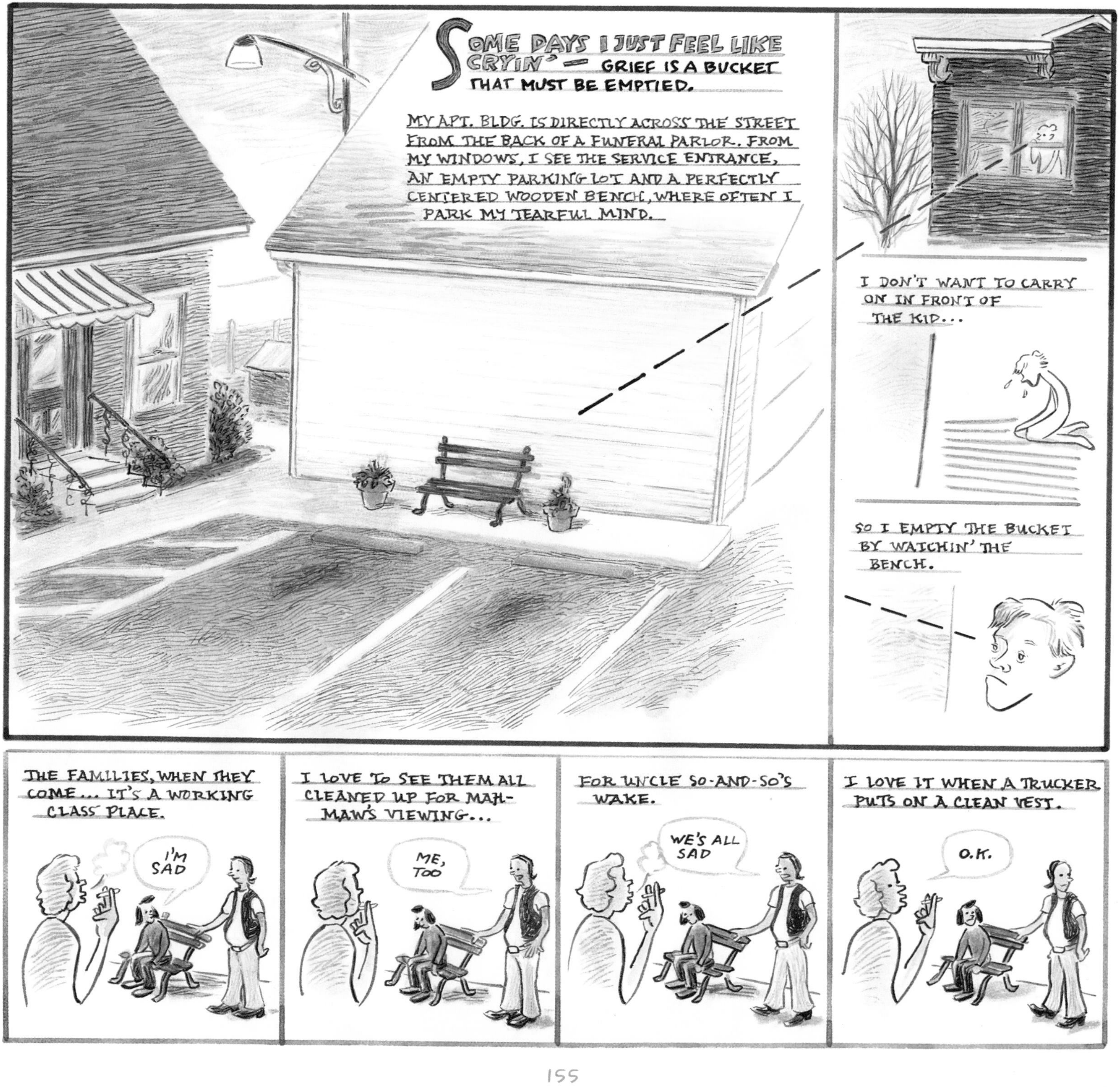
SOME DAYS I JUST FEEL LIKE CRYIN' — GRIEF IS A BUCKET THAT MUST BE EMPTIED.
MY APT. BLDG. IS DIRECTLY ACROSS THE STREET FROM THE BACK OF A FUNERAL PARLOR. FROM MY WINDOWS, I SEE THE SERVICE ENTRANCE, AN EMPTY PARKING LOT AND A PERFECTLY CENTERED WOODEN BENCH, WHERE OFTEN I PARK MY TEARFUL MIND.
I DON'T WANT TO CARRY ON IN FRONT OF THE KID...
SO I EMPTY THE BUCKET BY WATCHIN' THE BENCH.
THE FAMILIES, WHEN THEY COME... IT'S A WORKING CLASS PLACE.
I'M SAD
I LOVE TO SEE THEM ALL CLEANED UP FOR MAH-MAW'S VIEWING...
ME, TOO
FOR UNCLE SO-AND-SO'S WAKE.
WE'S ALL SAD
I LOVE IT WHEN A TRUCKER PUTS ON A CLEAN VEST.
O.K.

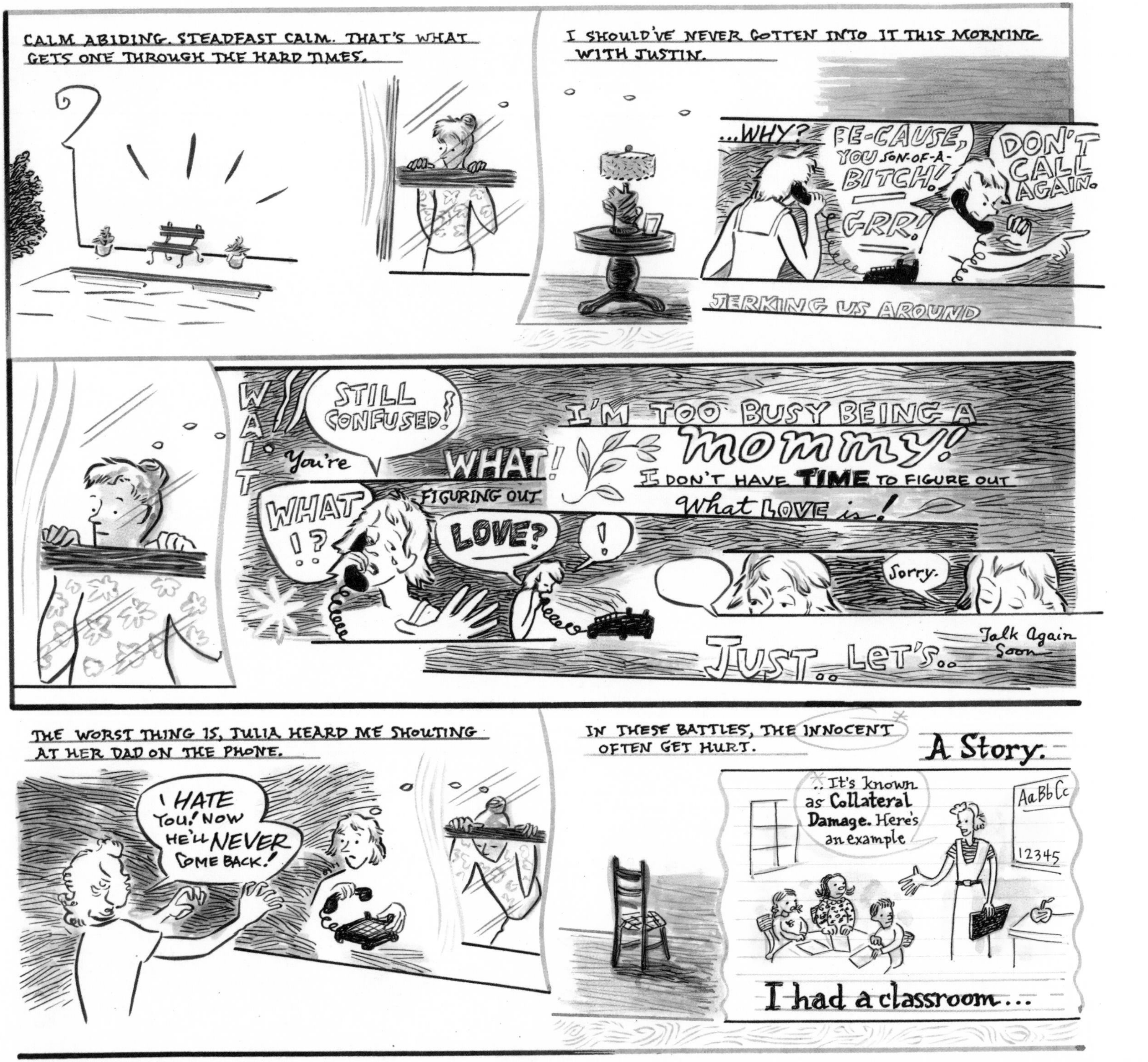
CALM ABIDING. STEADFAST CALM. THAT'S WHAT GETS ONE THROUGH THE HARD TIMES.
I SHOULD'VE NEVER GOTTEN INTO IT THIS MORNING WITH JUSTIN.
...WHY?
BE-CAUSE, YOU SON-OF-A-BITCH!
GRR!
DON'T CALL AGAIN.
JERKING US AROUND
WAIT
You're STILL CONFUSED!
WHAT!
FIGURING OUT
WHAT !?
LOVE?
!
I'M TOO BUSY BEING A mommy!
I DON'T HAVE TIME TO FIGURE OUT what LOVE is!
Sorry.
JUST.. LET'S..
Talk again soon
THE WORST THING IS, JULIA HEARD ME SHOUTING AT HER DAD ON THE PHONE.
I HATE YOU! NOW HE'LL NEVER COME BACK!
IN THESE BATTLES, THE INNOCENT OFTEN GET HURT.
A Story.
..It's known as Collateral Damage. Here's an example
AaBbCc
12345
I had a classroom...

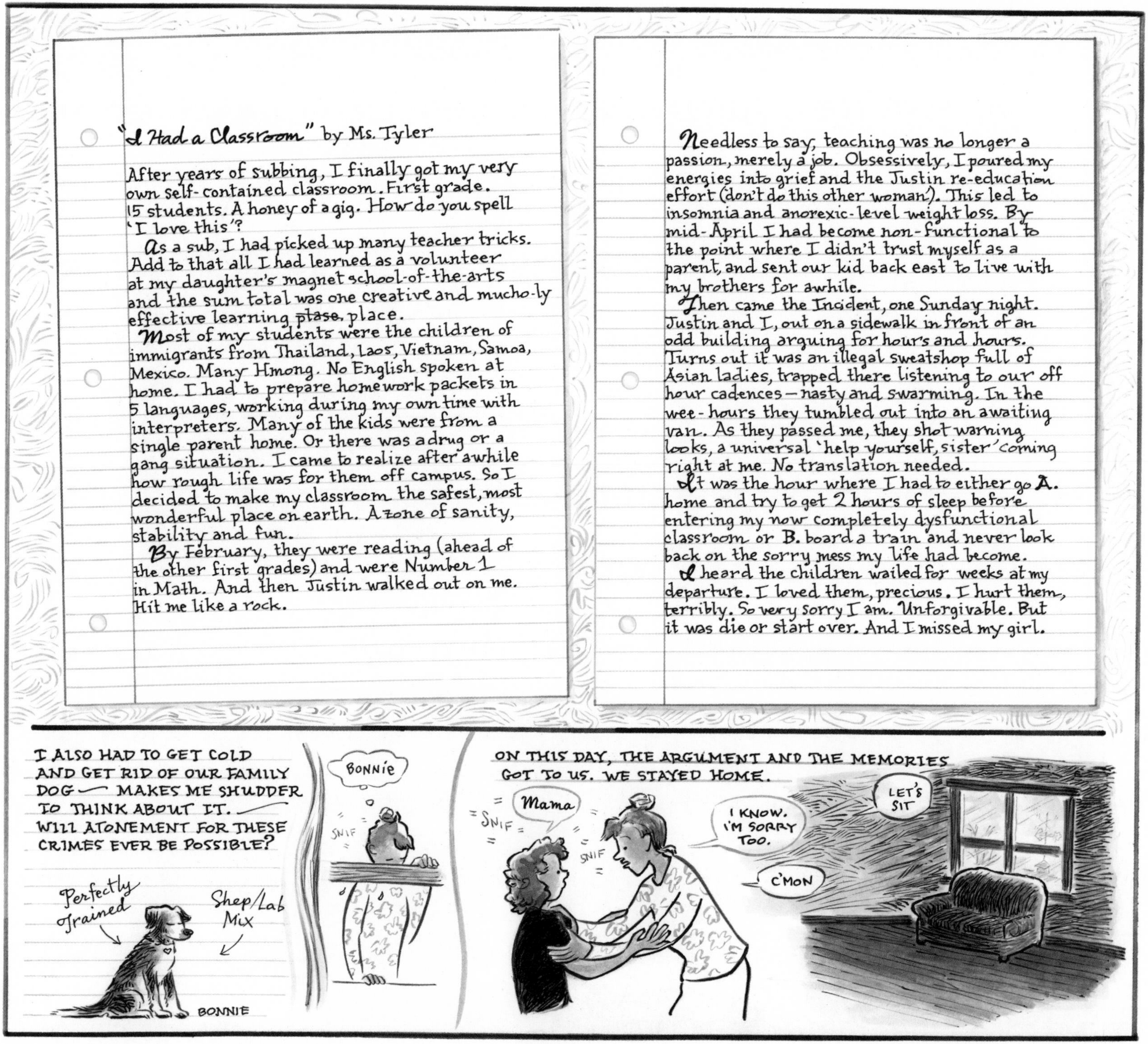
"I Had a Classroom" by Ms. Tyler
After years of subbing, I finally got my very own self-contained classroom. First grade. 15 students. A honey of a gig. How do you spell 'I love this'?
As a sub, I had picked up many teacher tricks. Add to that all I had learned as a volunteer at my daughter's magnet school-of-the-arts and the sum total was one creative and mucho-ly effective learning ~~plase~~ place.
Most of my students were the children of immigrants from Thailand, Laos, Vietnam, Samoa, Mexico. Many Hmong. No English spoken at home. I had to prepare homework packets in 5 languages, working during my own time with interpreters. Many of the kids were from a single parent home. Or there was a drug or a gang situation. I came to realize after awhile how rough life was for them off campus. So I decided to make my classroom the safest, most wonderful place on earth. A zone of sanity, stability and fun.
By February, they were reading (ahead of the other first grades) and were Number 1 in Math. And then Justin walked out on me. Hit me like a rock.
Needless to say, teaching was no longer a passion, merely a job. Obsessively, I poured my energies into grief and the Justin re-education effort (don't do this other woman). This led to insomnia and anorexic-level weight loss. By mid-April I had become non-functional to the point where I didn't trust myself as a parent, and sent our kid back east to live with my brothers for awhile.
Then came the Incident, one Sunday night. Justin and I, out on a sidewalk in front of an odd building arguing for hours and hours. Turns out it was an illegal sweatshop full of Asian ladies, trapped there listening to our off hour cadences — nasty and swarming. In the wee-hours they tumbled out into an awaiting van. As they passed me, they shot warning looks, a universal 'help yourself, sister' coming right at me. No translation needed.
It was the hour where I had to either go A. home and try to get 2 hours of sleep before entering my now completely dysfunctional classroom or B. board a train and never look back on the sorry mess my life had become.
I heard the children wailed for weeks at my departure. I loved them, precious. I hurt them, terribly. So very sorry I am. Unforgivable. But it was die or start over. And I missed my girl.
I ALSO HAD TO GET COLD AND GET RID OF OUR FAMILY DOG — MAKES ME SHUDDER TO THINK ABOUT IT. — WILL ATONEMENT FOR THESE CRIMES EVER BE POSSIBLE?
Perfectly Trained
Shep/Lab Mix
BONNIE
BONNIE
SNIF
ON THIS DAY, THE ARGUMENT AND THE MEMORIES GOT TO US. WE STAYED HOME.
SNIF
Mama
SNIF
I KNOW. I'M SORRY TOO.
LET'S SIT
C'MON

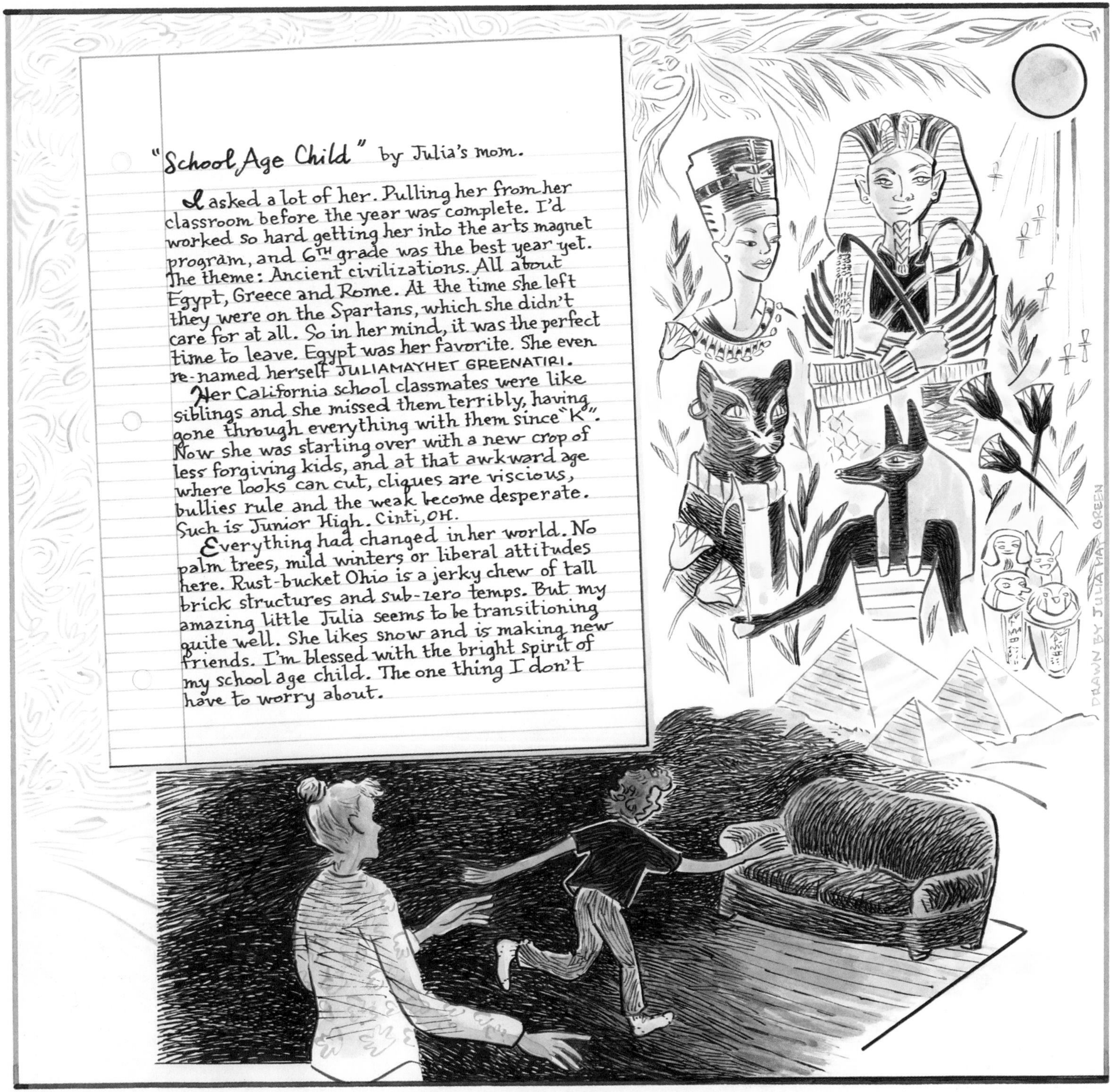
"School Age Child" by Julia's mom.
I asked a lot of her. Pulling her from her classroom before the year was complete. I'd worked so hard getting her into the arts magnet program, and 6TH grade was the best year yet. The theme: Ancient civilizations. All about Egypt, Greece and Rome. At the time she left they were on the Spartans, which she didn't care for at all. So in her mind, it was the perfect time to leave. Egypt was her favorite. She even re-named herself JULIAMAYHET GREENATIRI.
Her California school classmates were like siblings and she missed them terribly, having gone through everything with them since "K". Now she was starting over with a new crop of less forgiving kids, and at that awkward age where looks can cut, cliques are viscious, bullies rule and the weak become desperate. Such is Junior High. Cinti, OH.
Everything had changed in her world. No palm trees, mild winters or liberal attitudes here. Rust-bucket Ohio is a jerky chew of tall brick structures and sub-zero temps. But my amazing little Julia seems to be transitioning quite well. She likes snow and is making new friends. I'm blessed with the bright spirit of my school age child. The one thing I don't have to worry about.
DRAWN BY JULIA MAY GREEN

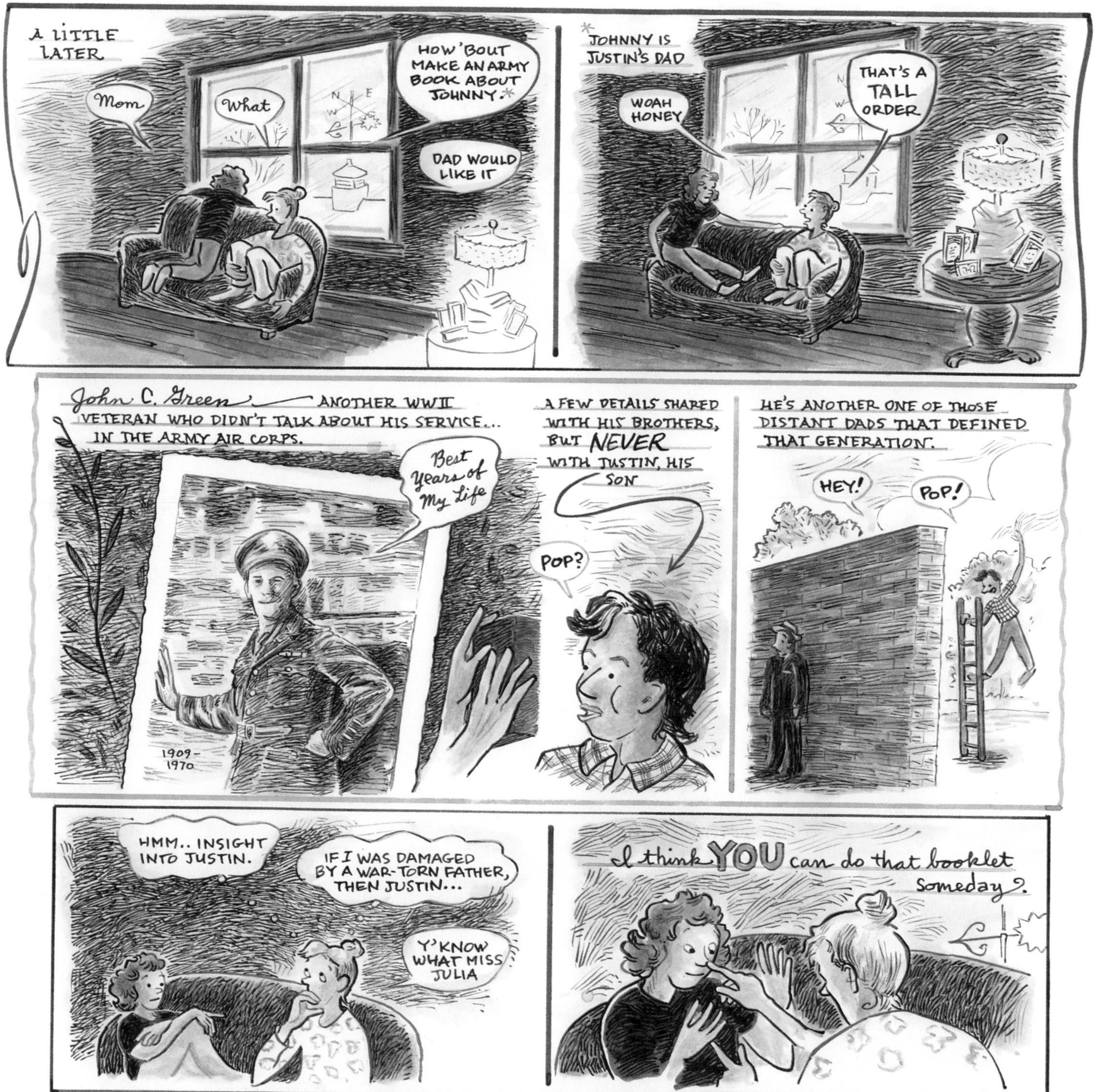
A LITTLE LATER
Mom
What
HOW 'BOUT MAKE AN ARMY BOOK ABOUT JOHNNY.*
DAD WOULD LIKE IT
* JOHNNY IS JUSTIN'S DAD
WOAH HONEY
THAT'S A TALL ORDER
John C. Green — ANOTHER WWII VETERAN WHO DIDN'T TALK ABOUT HIS SERVICE... IN THE ARMY AIR CORPS.
Best Years of My Life
1909-1970
A FEW DETAILS SHARED WITH HIS BROTHERS, BUT NEVER WITH JUSTIN, HIS SON
POP?
HE'S ANOTHER ONE OF THOSE DISTANT DADS THAT DEFINED THAT GENERATION.
HEY!
POP!
HMM.. INSIGHT INTO JUSTIN.
IF I WAS DAMAGED BY A WAR-TORN FATHER, THEN JUSTIN...
Y'KNOW WHAT MISS JULIA
I think YOU can do that booklet someday?

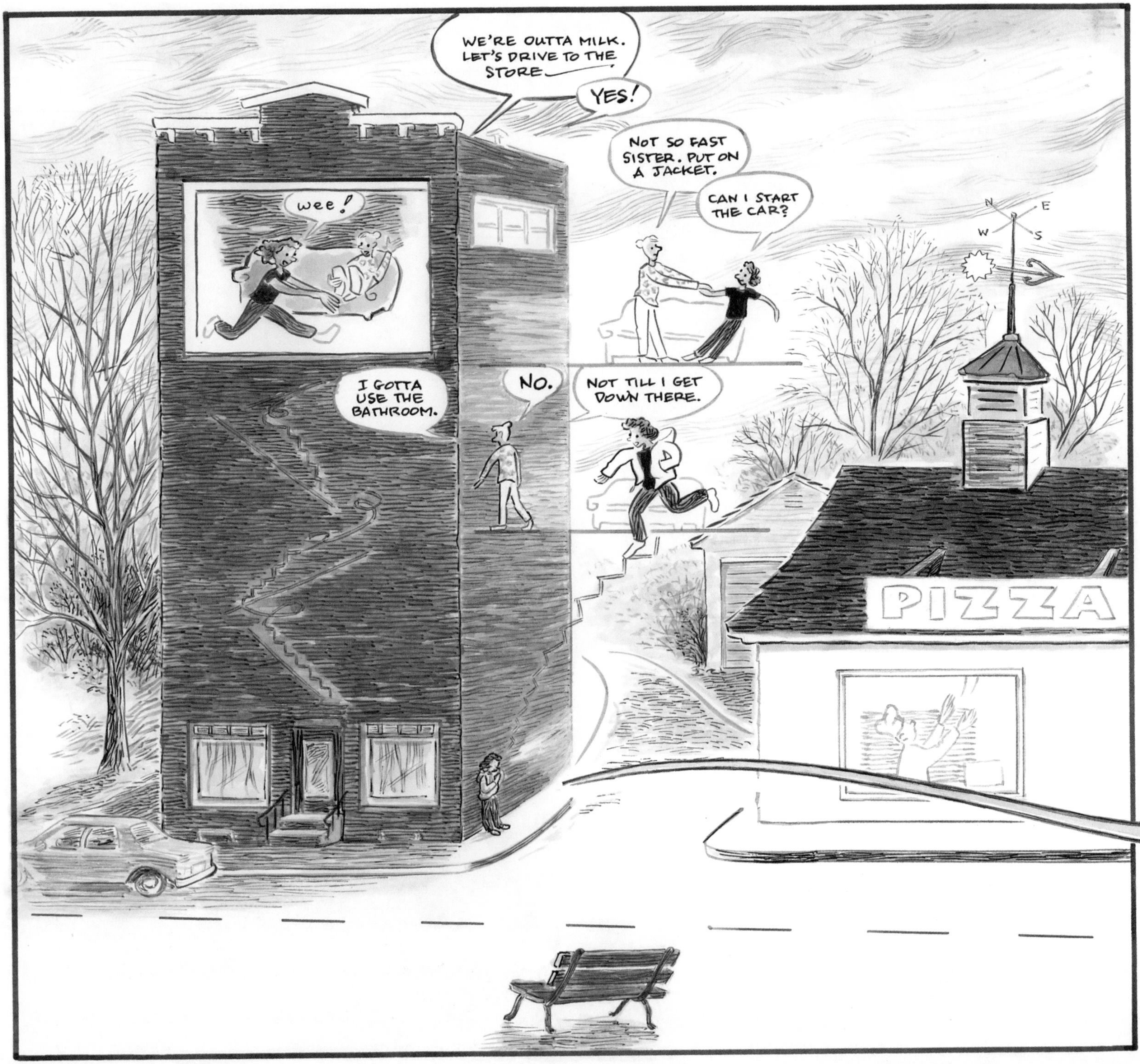
WE'RE OUTTA MILK. LET'S DRIVE TO THE STORE
YES!
wee!
NOT SO FAST SISTER. PUT ON A JACKET.
CAN I START THE CAR?
I GOTTA USE THE BATHROOM.
NO.
NOT TILL I GET DOWN THERE.
N
E
W
S
PIZZA

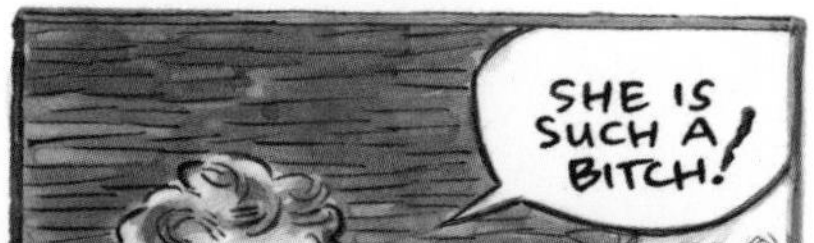
SHE IS SUCH A BITCH!

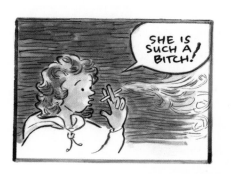

O.K. SO NOW LET'S SEE WHAT'S BEEN ESTABLISHED SO FAR: LOOKING AT THE LIVES OF 5 PEOPLE... DAD WAS IN THE ARMY AND THERE WERE, AND STILL ARE, BIG SECRETS AND MANY UNKNOWNS... THAT ESSENTIALLY, HE'S A GOOD AND DECENT MAN WHO'S BEEN *DAMAGED* — JUST HOW, WE'RE NOT SURE. HE CAME HOME FROM WAR AND *CAUSED* DAMAGE. STILL DOES, UNINTENTIONALLY, OF COURSE. WE'VE ALL BEEN AFFECTED. COLLATERAL DAMAGE

ALSO SHOWN, MY CHALLENGES AS A SORT-OF SINGLE MOM...

FROM HERE I WANT TO SHOW THE FRAGILITY OF THESE CHARACTERS, FROM AGE, HEALTH, AND MENTAL ILLNESS FACTORS.

9.

CAMP CHEMO

FUNNY TO SAY 'CHARACTERS' WHEN ONE OF THEM IS ME.

READERS:

CAMP CHEMO IS A BACKSTORY. IT HELPS EXPLAIN HOW CHUCK CAME TO KNOW ABOUT HIS CUT. CAMP CHEMO WAS THE START OF HIS QUEST TO FIND OUT HOW IT HAPPENED, AND LED, FIVE YEARS LATER, TO THAT 'RIVERS OF BLOOD' PHONE CALL.

SO BETWEEN HIS CHEMO PHASE AND THE PHONE CALL, MY CALIFORNIA HEARTBREAK AND OHIO RELOCATION OCCURRED.

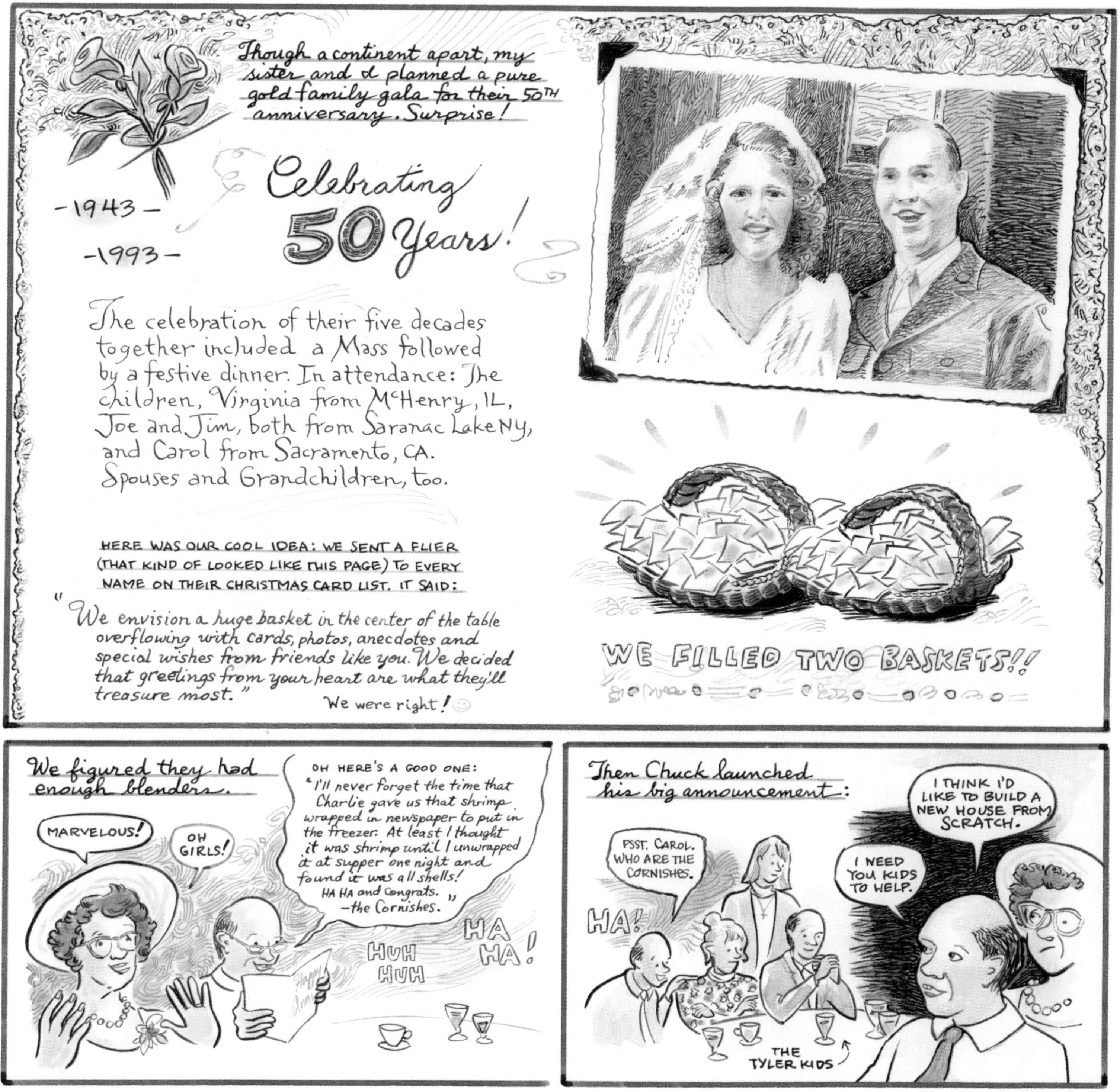
Though a continent apart, my sister and I planned a pure gold family gala for their 50TH anniversary. Surprise!
Celebrating 50 Years!
-1943-
-1993-
The celebration of their five decades together included a Mass followed by a festive dinner. In attendance: The children, Virginia from McHenry, IL, Joe and Jim, both from Saranac Lake NY, and Carol from Sacramento, CA. Spouses and Grandchildren, too.
HERE WAS OUR COOL IDEA: WE SENT A FLIER (THAT KIND OF LOOKED LIKE THIS PAGE) TO EVERY NAME ON THEIR CHRISTMAS CARD LIST. IT SAID:
"We envision a huge basket in the center of the table overflowing with cards, photos, anecdotes and special wishes from friends like you. We decided that greetings from your heart are what they'll treasure most."
We were right!
WE FILLED TWO BASKETS!!
We figured they had enough blenders.
MARVELOUS!
OH GIRLS!
OH HERE'S A GOOD ONE: "I'll never forget the time that Charlie gave us that shrimp wrapped in newspaper to put in the freezer. At least I thought it was shrimp until I unwrapped it at supper one night and found it was all shells! HA HA and Congrats. —the Cornishes."
HUH HUH
HA HA!
Happy Anni
Then Chuck launched his big announcement:
HA!
PSST. CAROL. WHO ARE THE CORNISHES.
I THINK I'D LIKE TO BUILD A NEW HOUSE FROM SCRATCH.
I NEED YOU KIDS TO HELP.
THE TYLER KIDS

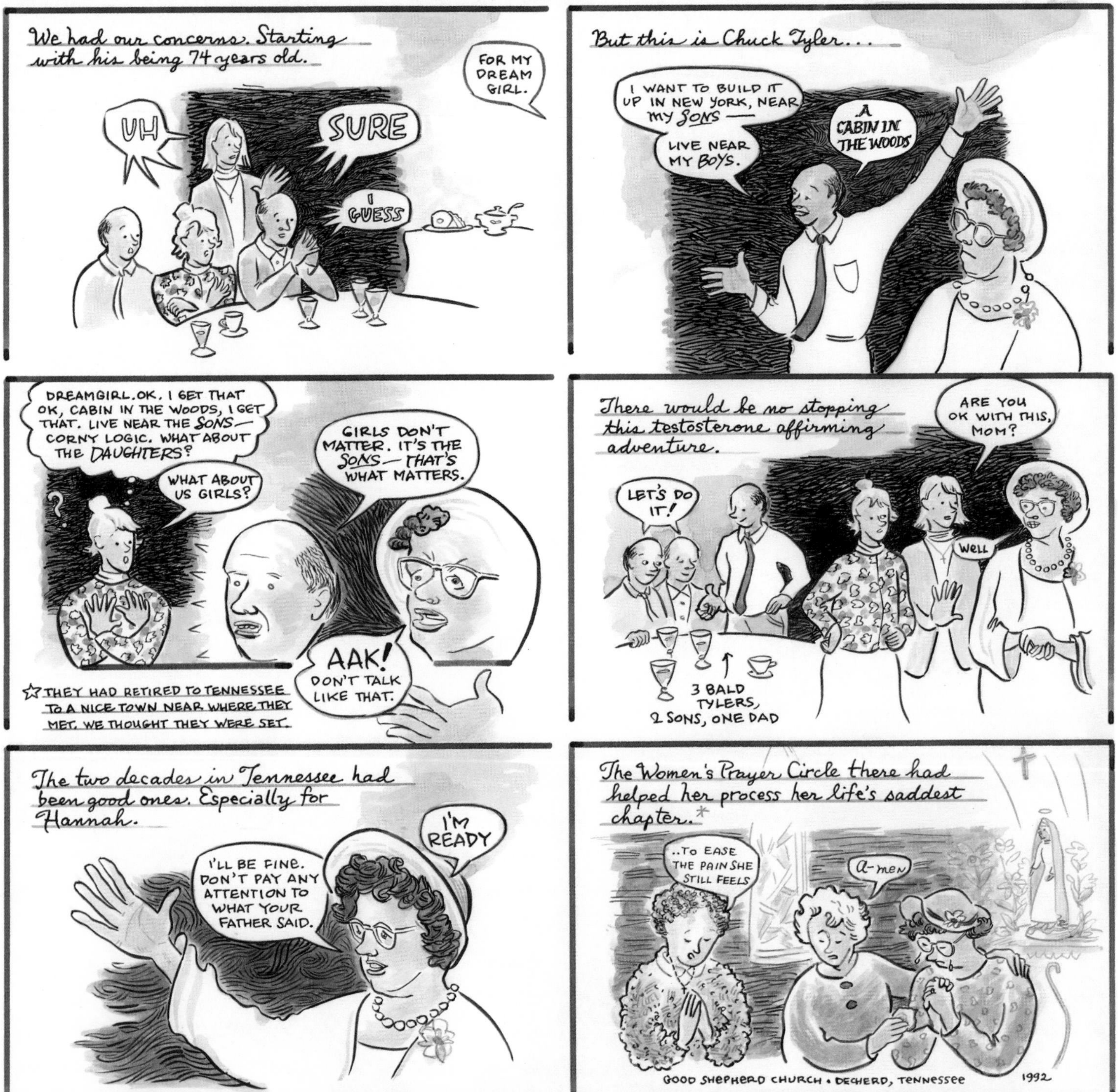
We had our concerns. Starting with his being 74 years old.
UH
SURE
I GUESS
FOR MY DREAM GIRL.
But this is Chuck Tyler...
I WANT TO BUILD IT UP IN NEW YORK, NEAR MY SONS —
LIVE NEAR MY BOYS.
A CABIN IN THE WOODS
DREAMGIRL. OK. I GET THAT OK, CABIN IN THE WOODS, I GET THAT. LIVE NEAR THE SONS — CORNY LOGIC. WHAT ABOUT THE DAUGHTERS?
?
WHAT ABOUT US GIRLS?
GIRLS DON'T MATTER. IT'S THE SONS — THAT'S WHAT MATTERS.
AAK! DON'T TALK LIKE THAT.
☆ THEY HAD RETIRED TO TENNESSEE TO A NICE TOWN NEAR WHERE THEY MET. WE THOUGHT THEY WERE SET.
There would be no stopping this testosterone affirming adventure.
ARE YOU OK WITH THIS, MOM?
LET'S DO IT!
WELL
3 BALD TYLERS, 2 SONS, ONE DAD
The two decades in Tennessee had been good ones. Especially for Hannah.
I'M READY
I'LL BE FINE. DON'T PAY ANY ATTENTION TO WHAT YOUR FATHER SAID.
The Women's Prayer Circle there had helped her process her life's saddest chapter.*
..TO EASE THE PAIN SHE STILL FEELS
A-men
GOOD SHEPHERD CHURCH • DECHERD, TENNESSEE
1992

* which appears later in this book

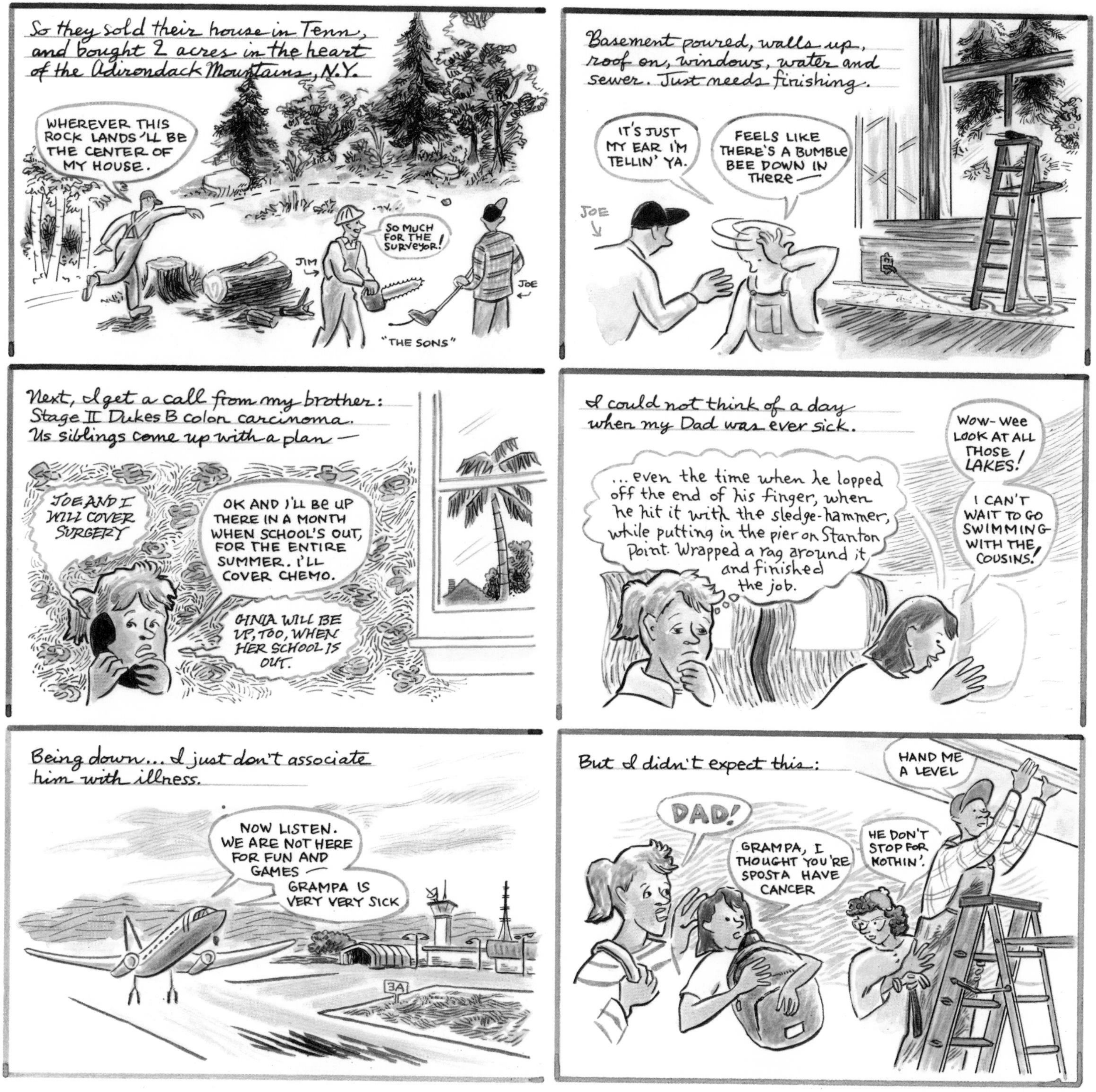

So they sold their house in Tenn, and bought 2 acres in the heart of the Adirondack Mountains, N.Y.
WHEREVER THIS ROCK LANDS'LL BE THE CENTER OF MY HOUSE.
SO MUCH FOR THE SURVEYOR!
JIM
JOE
"THE SONS"
Basement poured, walls up, roof on, windows, water and sewer. Just needs finishing.
IT'S JUST MY EAR I'M TELLIN' YA.
FEELS LIKE THERE'S A BUMBLE BEE DOWN IN THERE—
JOE
Next, I get a call from my brother: Stage II Dukes B colon carcinoma. Us siblings come up with a plan—
JOE AND I WILL COVER SURGERY
OK AND I'LL BE UP THERE IN A MONTH WHEN SCHOOL'S OUT, FOR THE ENTIRE SUMMER. I'LL COVER CHEMO.
GINIA WILL BE UP, TOO, WHEN HER SCHOOL IS OUT.
I could not think of a day when my Dad was ever sick.
...even the time when he lopped off the end of his finger, when he hit it with the sledge-hammer, while putting in the pier on Stanton Point. Wrapped a rag around it and finished the job.
WOW-WEE LOOK AT ALL THOSE LAKES!
I CAN'T WAIT TO GO SWIMMING WITH THE COUSINS!
Being down... I just don't associate him with illness.
NOW LISTEN. WE ARE NOT HERE FOR FUN AND GAMES—
GRAMPA IS VERY VERY SICK
3A
But I didn't expect this:
HAND ME A LEVEL
DAD!
GRAMPA, I THOUGHT YOU'RE SPOSTA HAVE CANCER
HE DON'T STOP FOR NOTHIN'.

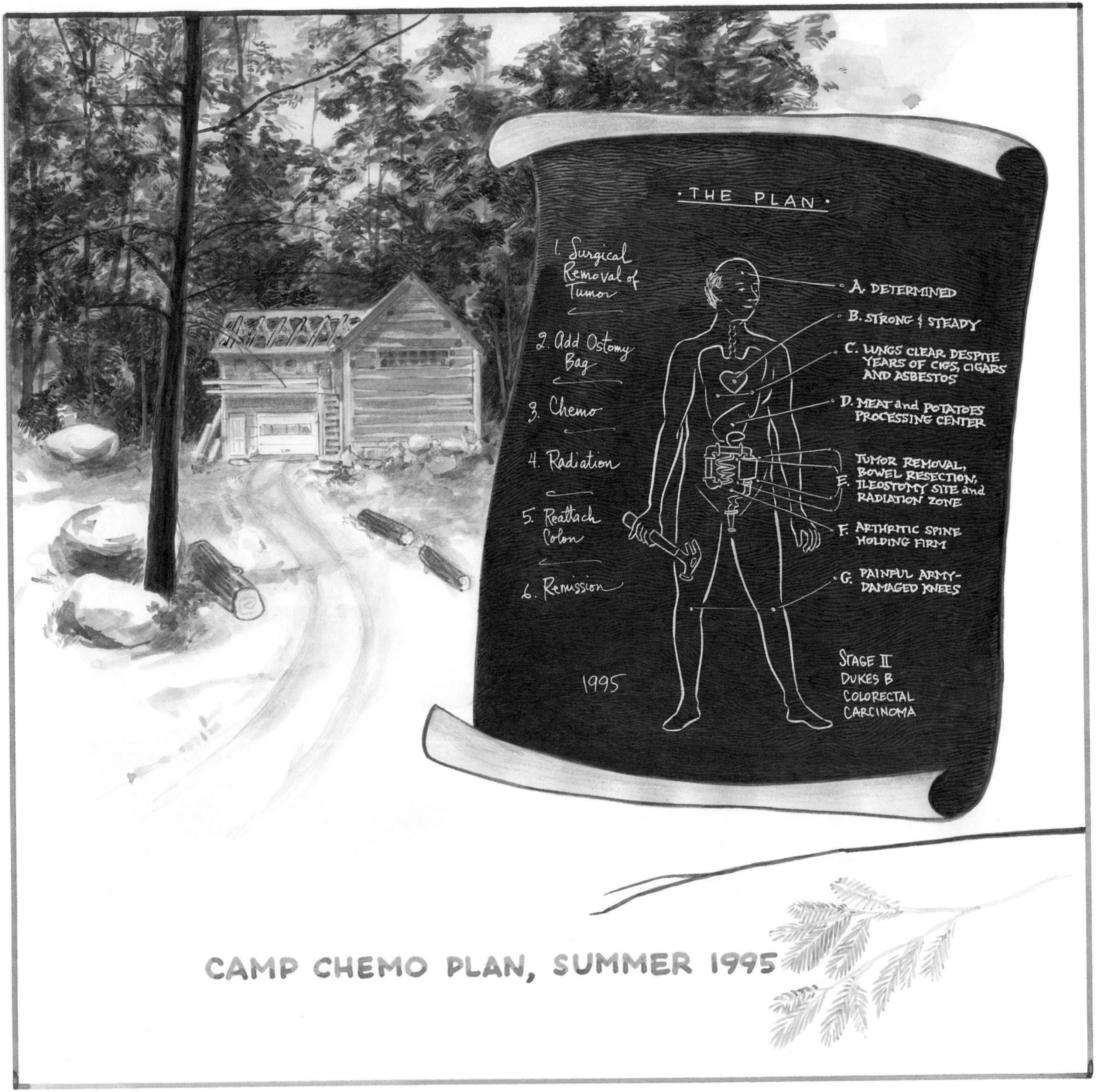
·THE PLAN·
1. Surgical Removal of Tumor
2. Add Ostomy Bag
3. Chemo
4. Radiation
5. Reattach Colon
6. Remission
A. DETERMINED
B. STRONG & STEADY
C. LUNGS CLEAR DESPITE YEARS OF CIGS, CIGARS AND ASBESTOS
D. MEAT and POTATOES PROCESSING CENTER
E. TUMOR REMOVAL, BOWEL RESECTION, ILEOSTOMY SITE and RADIATION ZONE
F. ARTHRITIC SPINE HOLDING FIRM
G. PAINFUL ARMY-DAMAGED KNEES
1995
STAGE II DUKES B COLORECTAL CARCINOMA
CAMP CHEMO PLAN, SUMMER 1995

Over the next few months, it kinda went like this: go for some chemo, then come home and get busy with some drywall. Few days later, go for another treatment, come home and get busy again. He simply stayed focused on the house. Certainly no reason to focus on hair loss.

This was the deal at Camp Chemo.

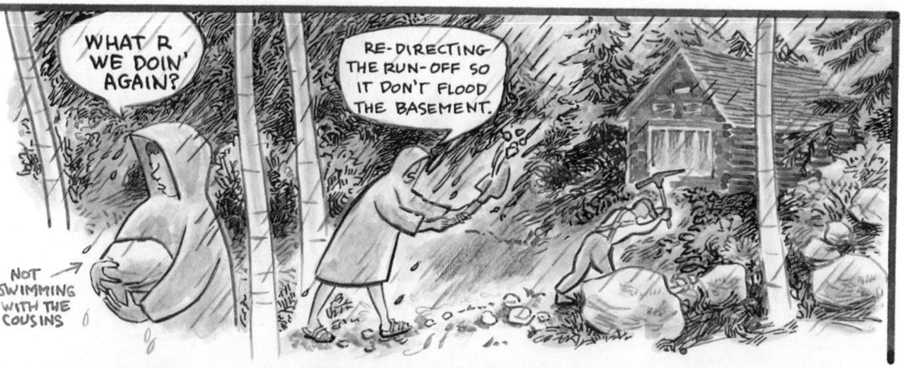
WHAT R WE DOIN' AGAIN?
RE-DIRECTING THE RUN-OFF SO IT DON'T FLOOD THE BASEMENT.
NOT SWIMMING WITH THE COUSINS

He sure didn't act sick, although if he felt bad, he sure wouldn't have told me about it. It's possible to guage how somebody's feeling by how they look, but he just looked like a 75 year old. Another way to tell would be the activity level, and well... hey. This is Chuck Tyler. One of Georgie's boys (Patton that is). That means he's unstoppable.

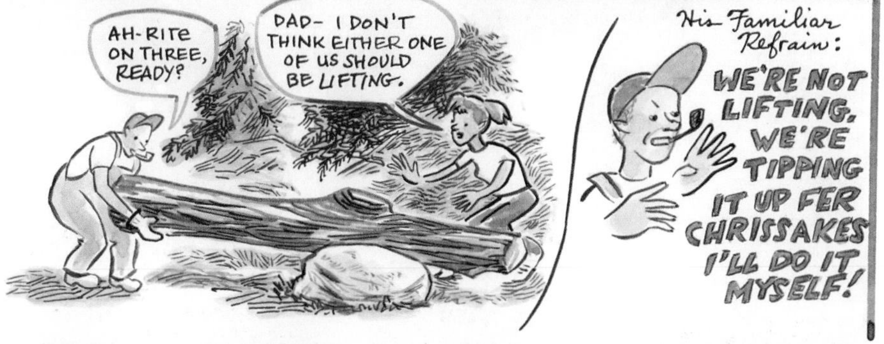
AH-RITE ON THREE, READY?
DAD- I DON'T THINK EITHER ONE OF US SHOULD BE LIFTING.
His Familiar Refrain:
WE'RE NOT LIFTING. WE'RE TIPPING IT UP FER CHRISSAKES I'LL DO IT MYSELF!

So I set up a card table and worked on my comics, there, under the 'floor to ceiling' windows of the "great room." The windows that mother insisted we cover with drapes, so she didn't feel so all exposed out there in the woods (?). I mainly played a supportive role and helped whenever they'd let me. (For some reason, I wasn't allowed to drive the car!)!

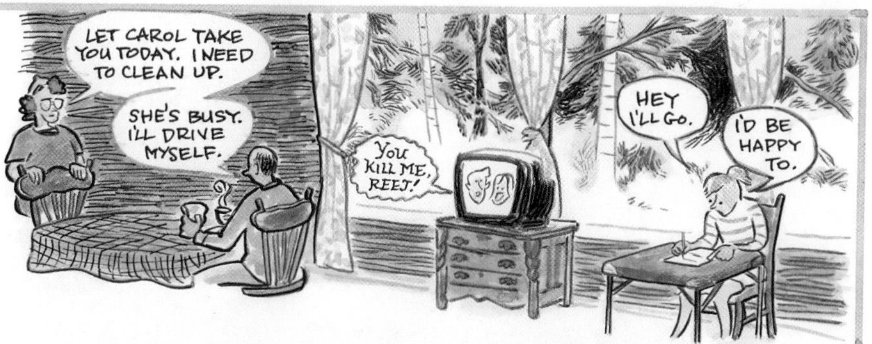
LET CAROL TAKE YOU TODAY. I NEED TO CLEAN UP.
SHE'S BUSY. I'LL DRIVE MYSELF.
YOU KILL ME, REET!
HEY I'LL GO.
I'D BE HAPPY TO.

A patch of illness can mark a time of vulnerability, when people step in to help and show their love. But Chuck had that invisible brick wall, and while heroically coping with the side effects of his treatment, it was very difficult to deal with the raging, pissy stalwart he had become. He did let the medical people in — a pussycat with the nurses..

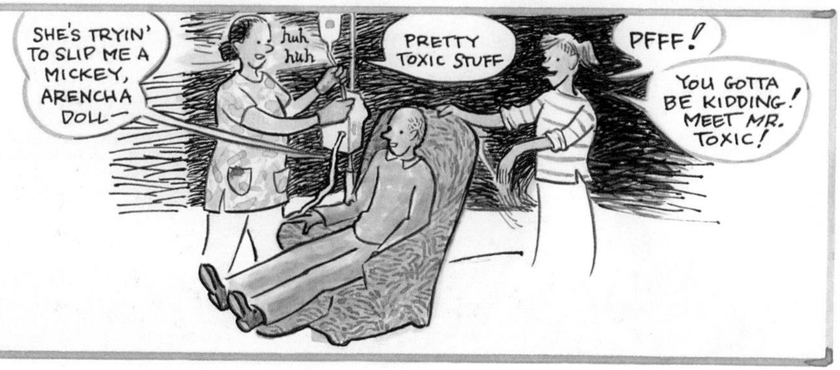
SHE'S TRYIN' TO SLIP ME A MICKEY, ARENCHA DOLL—
huh huh
PRETTY TOXIC STUFF
PFFF!
YOU GOTTA BE KIDDING! MEET MR. TOXIC!

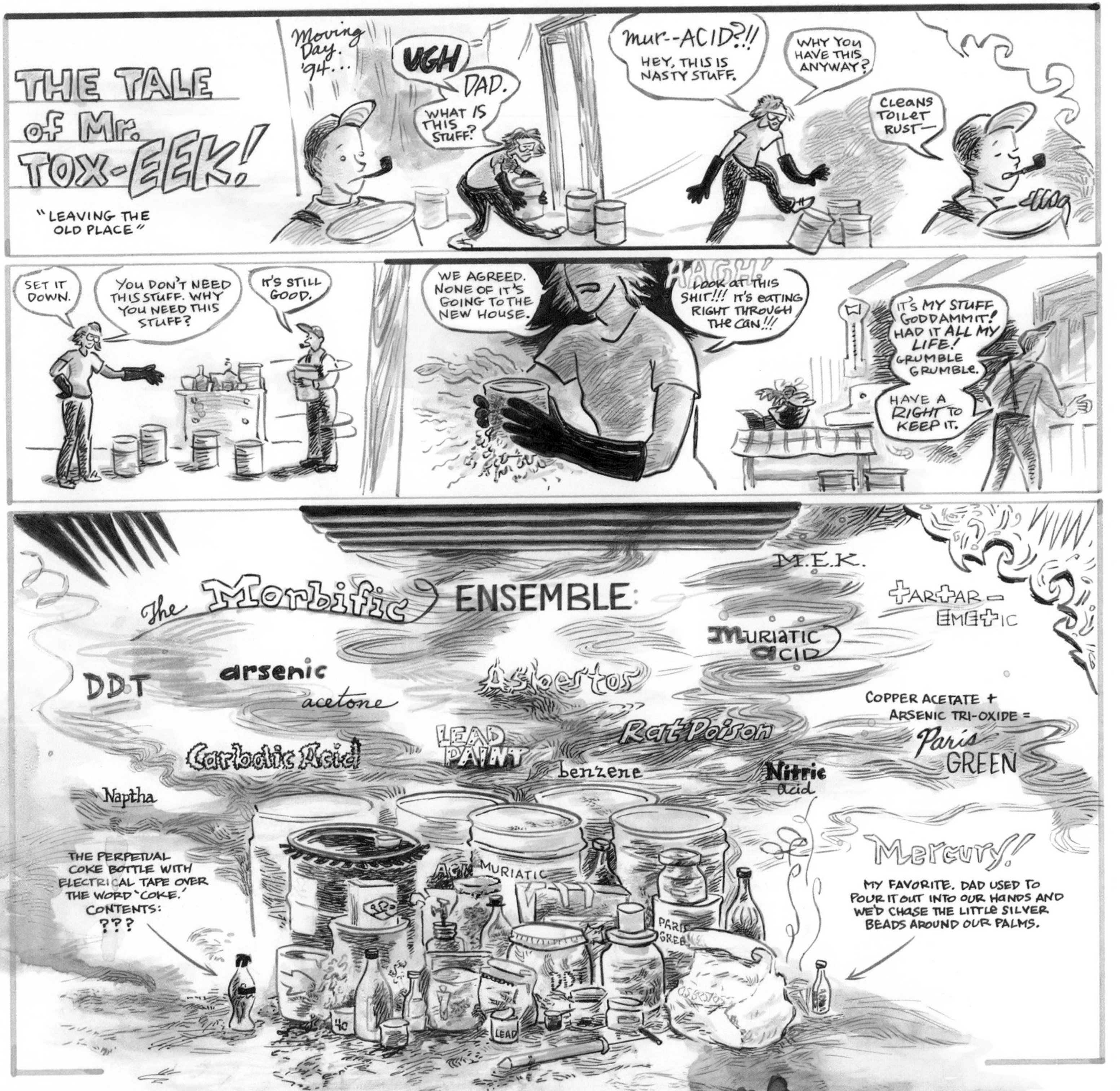
THE TALE of Mr. TOX-EEK!
"LEAVING THE OLD PLACE"
Moving Day. '94…
UGH
DAD.
WHAT IS THIS STUFF?
mur--ACID?!!
HEY, THIS IS NASTY STUFF.
WHY YOU HAVE THIS ANYWAY?
CLEANS TOILET RUST—
SET IT DOWN.
YOU DON'T NEED THIS STUFF. WHY YOU NEED THIS STUFF?
IT'S STILL GOOD.
WE AGREED. NONE OF IT'S GOING TO THE NEW HOUSE.
AAGH!
LOOK AT THIS SHIT!!! IT'S EATING RIGHT THROUGH THE CAN!!!
IT'S MY STUFF GODDAMMIT! HAD IT ALL MY LIFE! GRUMBLE GRUMBLE.
HAVE A RIGHT TO KEEP IT.
The Morbific ENSEMBLE:
M.E.K.
TARTAR-EMETIC
Muriatic Acid
DDT
arsenic
acetone
Asbestos
COPPER ACETATE + ARSENIC TRI-OXIDE = Paris GREEN
Rat Poison
LEAD PAINT
Carbolic Acid
benzene
Nitric Acid
Naptha
Mercury!
THE PERPETUAL COKE BOTTLE WITH ELECTRICAL TAPE OVER THE WORD 'COKE.' CONTENTS: ???
MY FAVORITE. DAD USED TO POUR IT OUT INTO OUR HANDS AND WE'D CHASE THE LITTLE SILVER BEADS AROUND OUR PALMS.
MURIATIC
PARIS GREEN
DDT
LEAD
ASBESTOS

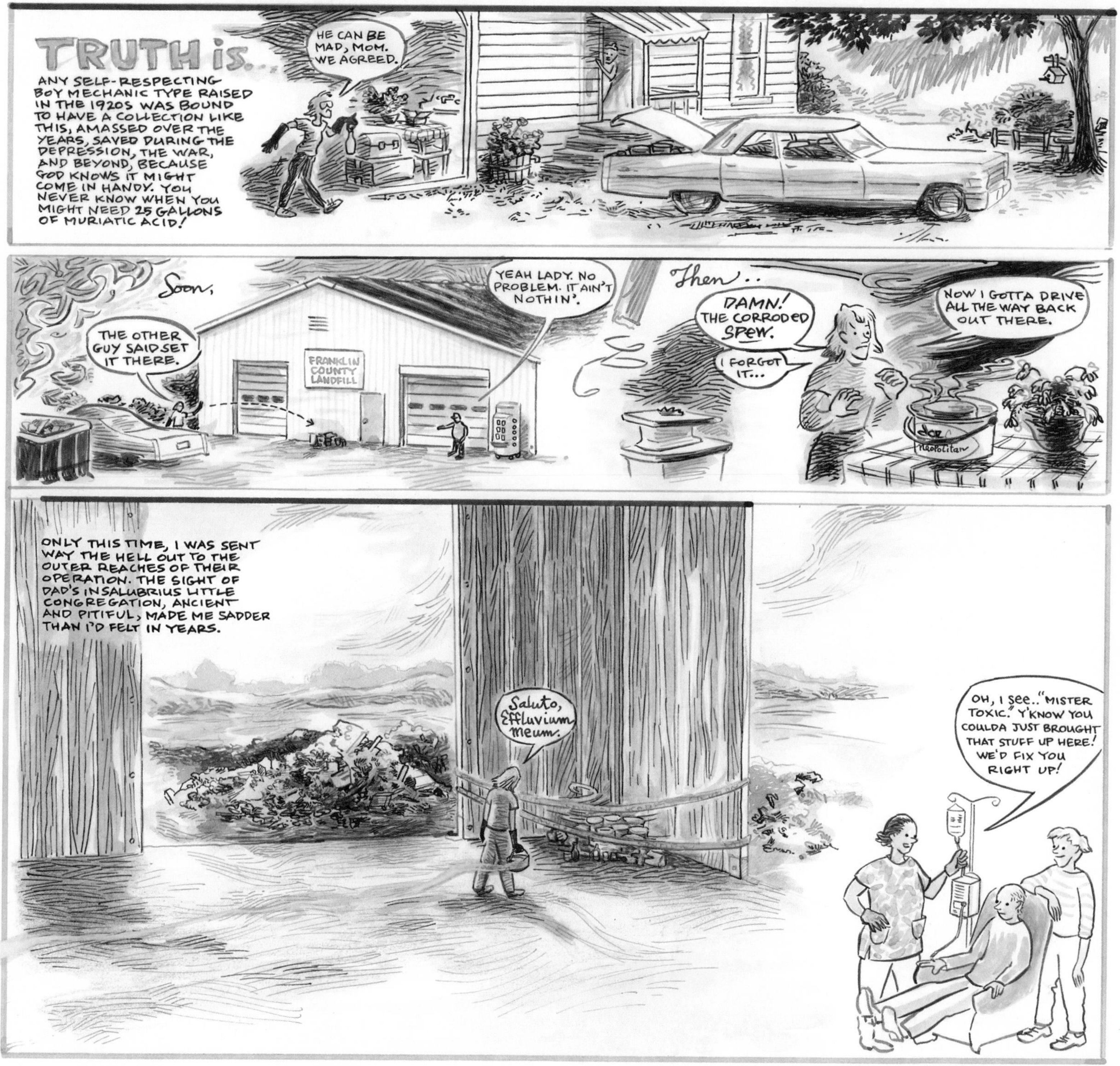
TRUTH is...
ANY SELF-RESPECTING BOY MECHANIC TYPE RAISED IN THE 1920S WAS BOUND TO HAVE A COLLECTION LIKE THIS, AMASSED OVER THE YEARS, SAVED DURING THE DEPRESSION, THE WAR, AND BEYOND, BECAUSE GOD KNOWS IT MIGHT COME IN HANDY. YOU NEVER KNOW WHEN YOU MIGHT NEED 25 GALLONS OF MURIATIC ACID!
HE CAN BE MAD, MOM. WE AGREED.
Soon,
THE OTHER GUY SAID SET IT THERE.
FRANKLIN COUNTY LANDFILL
YEAH LADY. NO PROBLEM. IT AIN'T NOTHIN'.
Then..
DAMN! THE CORRODED SPEW.
I FORGOT IT...
NOW I GOTTA DRIVE ALL THE WAY BACK OUT THERE.
ONLY THIS TIME, I WAS SENT WAY THE HELL OUT TO THE OUTER REACHES OF THEIR OPERATION. THE SIGHT OF DAD'S INSALUBRIUS LITTLE CONGREGATION, ANCIENT AND PITIFUL, MADE ME SADDER THAN I'D FELT IN YEARS.
Saluto, Effluvium meum.
OH, I SEE.. "MISTER TOXIC." Y'KNOW YOU COULDA JUST BROUGHT THAT STUFF UP HERE! WE'D FIX YOU RIGHT UP!

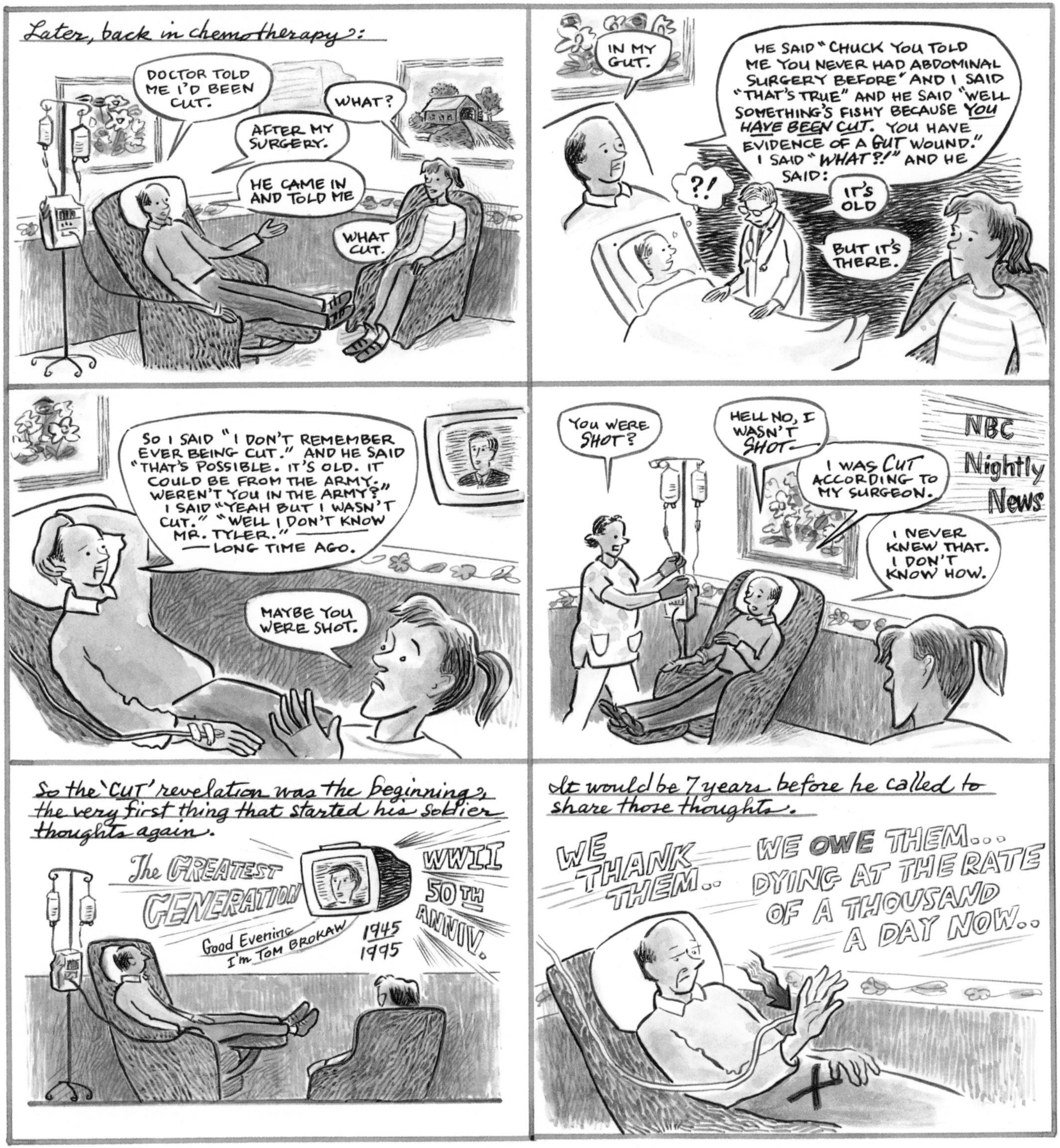
Later, back in chemotherapy:
DOCTOR TOLD ME I'D BEEN CUT.
WHAT?
AFTER MY SURGERY.
HE CAME IN AND TOLD ME
WHAT CUT.
IN MY GUT.
HE SAID "CHUCK YOU TOLD ME YOU NEVER HAD ABDOMINAL SURGERY BEFORE" AND I SAID "THAT'S TRUE" AND HE SAID "WELL SOMETHING'S FISHY BECAUSE YOU HAVE BEEN CUT. YOU HAVE EVIDENCE OF A GUT WOUND." I SAID "WHAT?!" AND HE SAID:
?!
IT'S OLD
BUT IT'S THERE.
SO I SAID "I DON'T REMEMBER EVER BEING CUT." AND HE SAID "THAT'S POSSIBLE. IT'S OLD. IT COULD BE FROM THE ARMY. WEREN'T YOU IN THE ARMY?" I SAID "YEAH BUT I WASN'T CUT." "WELL I DON'T KNOW MR. TYLER." —LONG TIME AGO.
MAYBE YOU WERE SHOT.
YOU WERE SHOT?
HELL NO, I WASN'T SHOT.
I WAS CUT ACCORDING TO MY SURGEON.
I NEVER KNEW THAT. I DON'T KNOW HOW.
NBC Nightly News
So the 'CUT' revelation was the beginning, the very first thing that started his soldier thoughts again.
The GREATEST GENERATION
Good Evening I'm TOM BROKAW
WWII 50TH ANNIV.
1945 1995
It would be 7 years before he called to share those thoughts.
WE THANK THEM..
WE OWE THEM... DYING AT THE RATE OF A THOUSAND A DAY NOW..

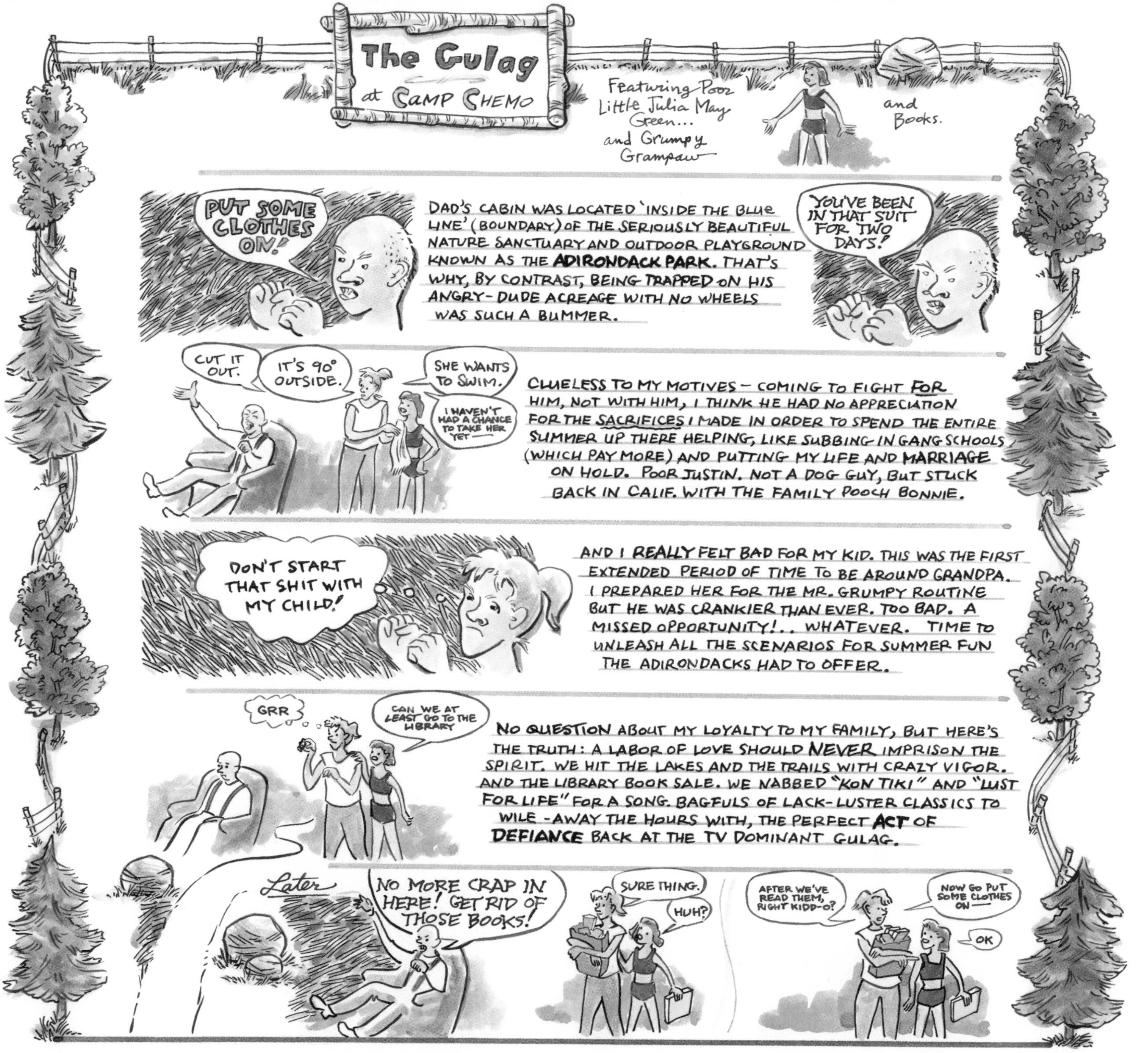
The Gulag
at Camp Chemo
Featuring Poor Little Julia May Green... and Grumpy Grampaw
and Books.
PUT SOME CLOTHES ON!
DAD'S CABIN WAS LOCATED 'INSIDE THE BLUE LINE' (BOUNDARY) OF THE SERIOUSLY BEAUTIFUL NATURE SANCTUARY AND OUTDOOR PLAYGROUND KNOWN AS THE ADIRONDACK PARK. THAT'S WHY, BY CONTRAST, BEING TRAPPED ON HIS ANGRY-DUDE ACREAGE WITH NO WHEELS WAS SUCH A BUMMER.
YOU'VE BEEN IN THAT SUIT FOR TWO DAYS!
CUT IT OUT.
IT'S 90° OUTSIDE.
SHE WANTS TO SWIM.
I HAVEN'T HAD A CHANCE TO TAKE HER YET—
CLUELESS TO MY MOTIVES – COMING TO FIGHT FOR HIM, NOT WITH HIM, I THINK HE HAD NO APPRECIATION FOR THE SACRIFICES I MADE IN ORDER TO SPEND THE ENTIRE SUMMER UP THERE HELPING, LIKE SUBBING IN GANG SCHOOLS (WHICH PAY MORE) AND PUTTING MY LIFE AND MARRIAGE ON HOLD. POOR JUSTIN. NOT A DOG GUY, BUT STUCK BACK IN CALIF. WITH THE FAMILY POOCH BONNIE.
DON'T START THAT SHIT WITH MY CHILD!
AND I REALLY FELT BAD FOR MY KID. THIS WAS THE FIRST EXTENDED PERIOD OF TIME TO BE AROUND GRANDPA. I PREPARED HER FOR THE MR. GRUMPY ROUTINE BUT HE WAS CRANKIER THAN EVER. TOO BAD. A MISSED OPPORTUNITY!.. WHATEVER. TIME TO UNLEASH ALL THE SCENARIOS FOR SUMMER FUN THE ADIRONDACKS HAD TO OFFER.
GRR
CAN WE AT LEAST GO TO THE LIBRARY
NO QUESTION ABOUT MY LOYALTY TO MY FAMILY, BUT HERE'S THE TRUTH: A LABOR OF LOVE SHOULD NEVER IMPRISON THE SPIRIT. WE HIT THE LAKES AND THE TRAILS WITH CRAZY VIGOR. AND THE LIBRARY BOOK SALE. WE NABBED "KON TIKI" AND "LUST FOR LIFE" FOR A SONG. BAGFULS OF LACK-LUSTER CLASSICS TO WILE-AWAY THE HOURS WITH, THE PERFECT ACT OF DEFIANCE BACK AT THE TV DOMINANT GULAG.
Later
NO MORE CRAP IN HERE! GET RID OF THOSE BOOKS!
SURE THING.
HUH?
AFTER WE'VE READ THEM, RIGHT KIDD-O?
NOW GO PUT SOME CLOTHES ON—
OK

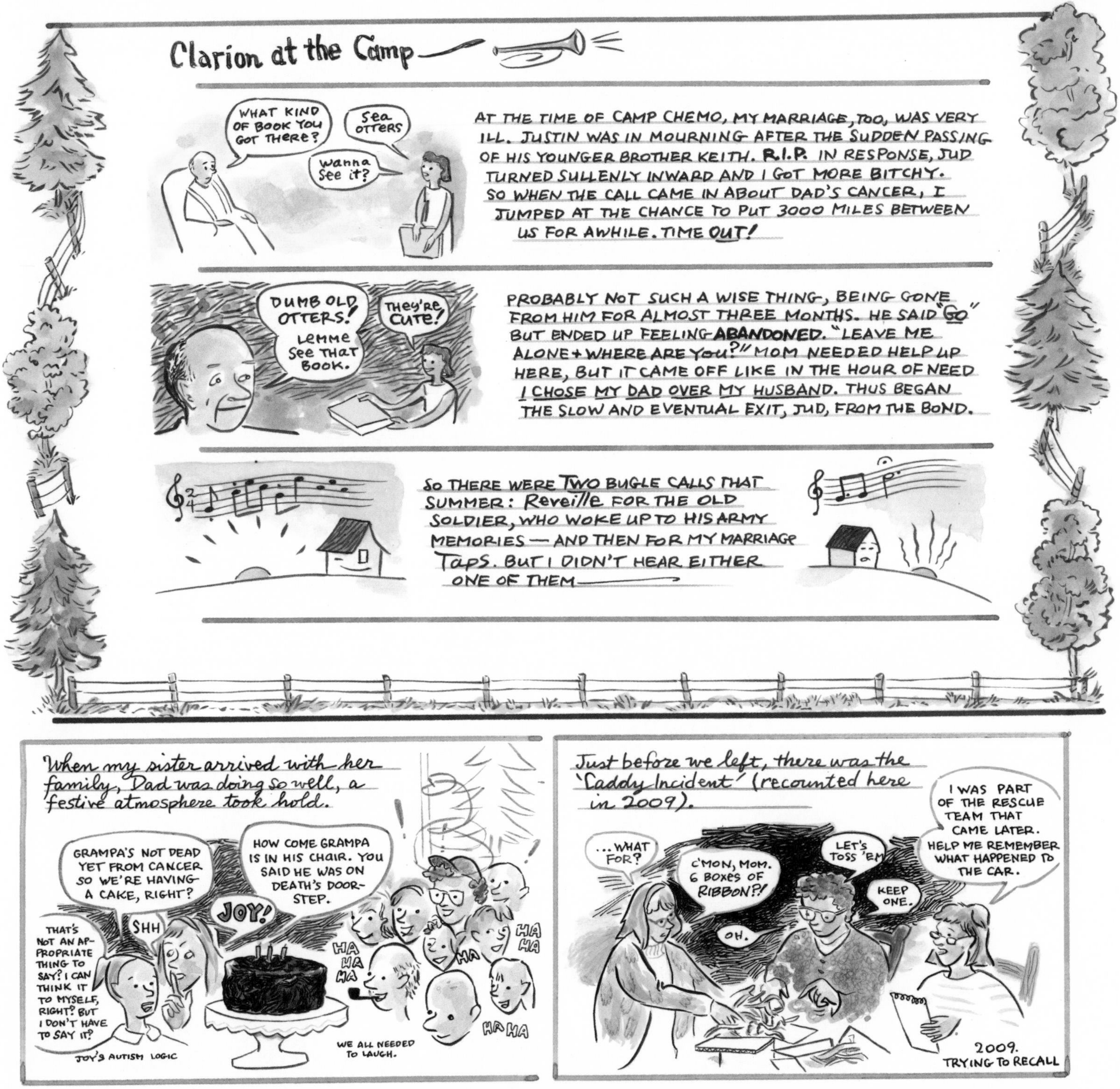

Clarion at the Camp
WHAT KIND OF BOOK YOU GOT THERE?
Sea otters
wanna see it?
AT THE TIME OF CAMP CHEMO, MY MARRIAGE, TOO, WAS VERY ILL. JUSTIN WAS IN MOURNING AFTER THE SUDDEN PASSING OF HIS YOUNGER BROTHER KEITH. R.I.P. IN RESPONSE, JUD TURNED SULLENLY INWARD AND I GOT MORE BITCHY. SO WHEN THE CALL CAME IN ABOUT DAD'S CANCER, I JUMPED AT THE CHANCE TO PUT 3000 MILES BETWEEN US FOR AWHILE. TIME OUT!
DUMB OLD OTTERS! Lemme see that book.
They're CUTE!
PROBABLY NOT SUCH A WISE THING, BEING GONE FROM HIM FOR ALMOST THREE MONTHS. HE SAID "GO" BUT ENDED UP FEELING ABANDONED. "LEAVE ME ALONE + WHERE ARE YOU?" MOM NEEDED HELP UP HERE, BUT IT CAME OFF LIKE IN THE HOUR OF NEED I CHOSE MY DAD OVER MY HUSBAND. THUS BEGAN THE SLOW AND EVENTUAL EXIT, JUD, FROM THE BOND.
SO THERE WERE TWO BUGLE CALLS THAT SUMMER: Reveille FOR THE OLD SOLDIER, WHO WOKE UP TO HIS ARMY MEMORIES — AND THEN FOR MY MARRIAGE Taps. BUT I DIDN'T HEAR EITHER ONE OF THEM
When my sister arrived with her family, Dad was doing so well, a festive atmosphere took hold.
GRAMPA'S NOT DEAD YET FROM CANCER SO WE'RE HAVING A CAKE, RIGHT?
HOW COME GRAMPA IS IN HIS CHAIR. YOU SAID HE WAS ON DEATH'S DOOR-STEP.
SHH
JOY!
THAT'S NOT AN AP-PROPRIATE THING TO SAY? I CAN THINK IT TO MYSELF, RIGHT? BUT I DON'T HAVE TO SAY IT?
HA HA HA
HA HA
HA
HA HA
JOY'S AUTISM LOGIC
WE ALL NEEDED TO LAUGH.
Just before we left, there was the 'Caddy Incident' (recounted here in 2009).
...WHAT FOR?
C'MON, MOM. 6 BOXES OF RIBBON?!
LET'S TOSS 'EM
KEEP ONE.
OH.
I WAS PART OF THE RESCUE TEAM THAT CAME LATER. HELP ME REMEMBER WHAT HAPPENED TO THE CAR.
2009. TRYING TO RECALL

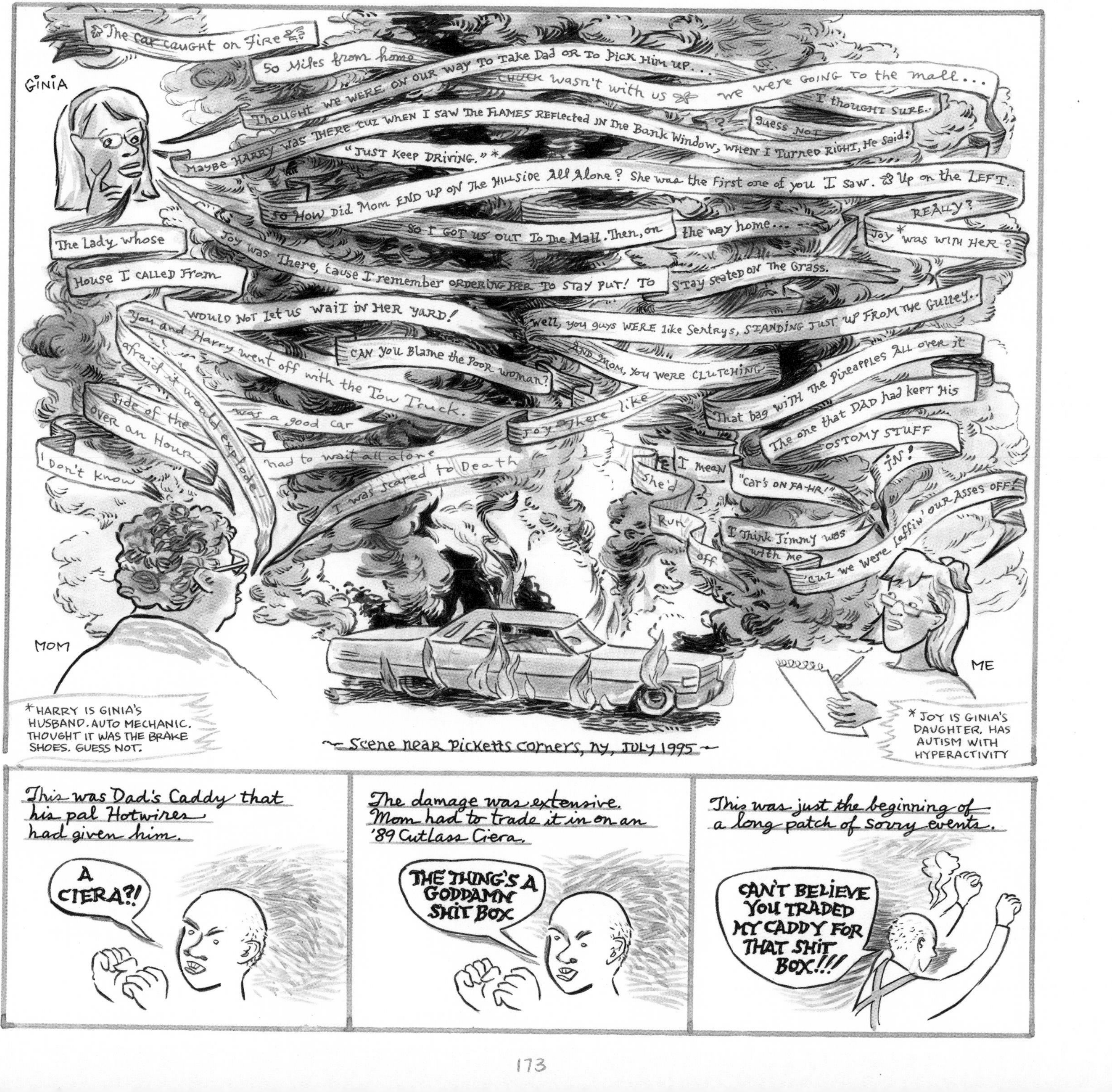
The car caught on Fire
50 Miles from home
Thought we were on our way to take Dad or to pick him up...
Chuck wasn't with us
we were going to the mall...
I thought sure..
guess not
Maybe Harry was there 'cuz when I saw the Flames reflected in the Bank Window, when I turned right, He said:
"Just keep driving." *
So how did Mom end up on the Hillside All Alone? She was the first one of you I saw. Up on the LEFT..
So I got us out to the Mall. Then, on the way home...
REALLY?
Joy * was with her?
The Lady whose House I called From
Joy was there, cause I remember ordering her to stay put! To stay seated on the Grass.
would not let us wait in her yard!
Well, you guys were like Sentrys, standing just up from the Gulley..
Can you blame the poor woman?
And Mom, you were clutching
that bag with the Pineapples all over it
The one that Dad had kept his ostomy stuff in!
You and Harry went off with the Tow Truck.
afraid it would explode!
Side of the
over an Hour
I don't know
was a good car
Joy There like
had to wait all alone
I was scared to Death
I mean
She'd Run off
"Car's on fa-hr."
I think Jimmy was with me
'cuz we were laffin' our Asses off!
GINIA
MOM
ME
* Harry is Ginia's husband. Auto mechanic. Thought it was the brake shoes. Guess not.
~ Scene near Picketts Corners, NY, July 1995 ~
* Joy is Ginia's daughter, has autism with hyperactivity
This was Dad's Caddy that his pal Hotwires had given him.
A CIERA?!
The damage was extensive. Mom had to trade it in on an '89 Cutlass Ciera.
THE THING'S A GODDAMN SHIT BOX
This was just the beginning of a long patch of sorry events.
CAN'T BELIEVE YOU TRADED MY CADDY FOR THAT SHIT BOX!!!

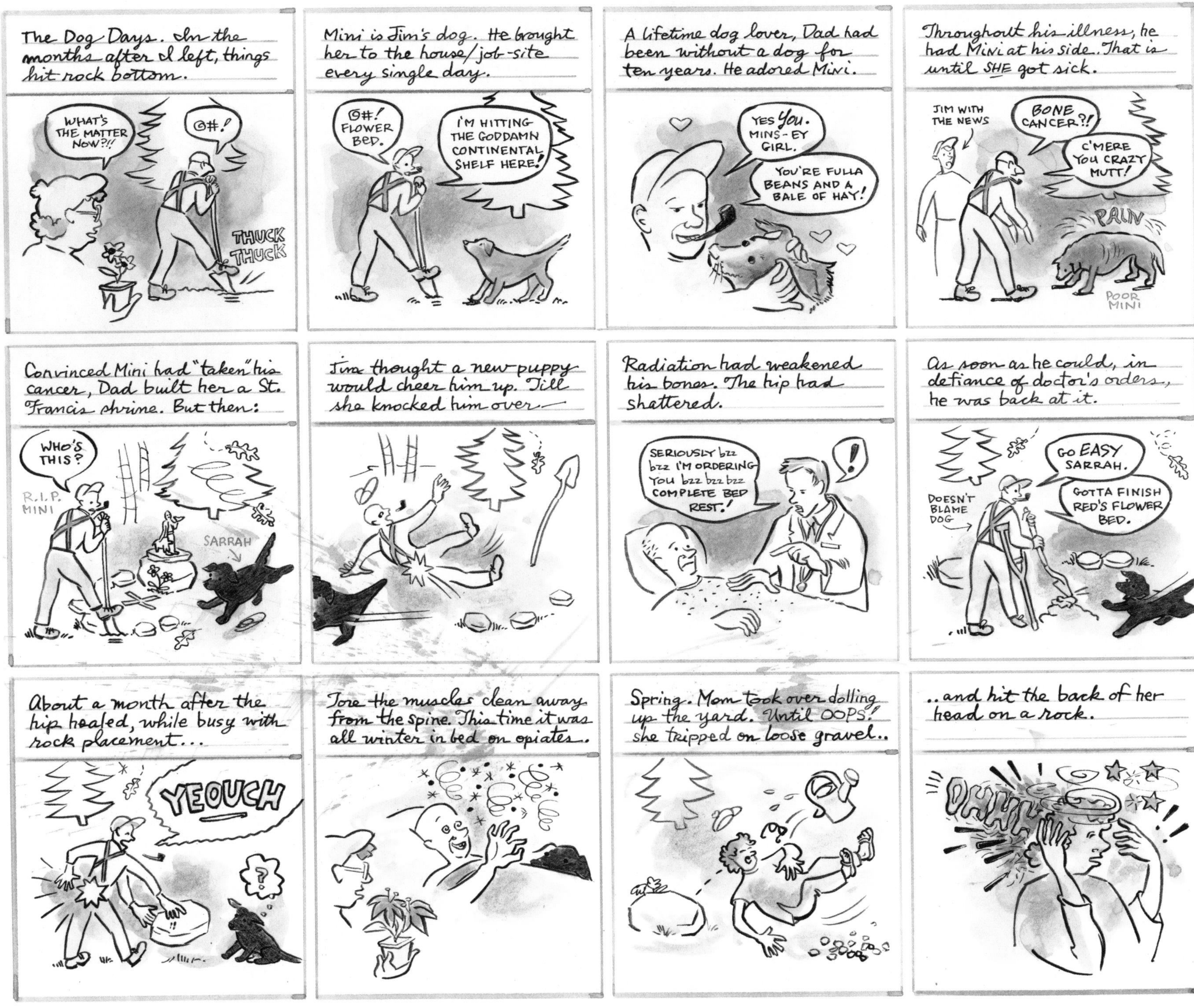

The Dog Days. In the months after I left, things hit rock bottom.
WHAT'S THE MATTER NOW?!!
@#!
THUCK THUCK
Mini is Jim's dog. He brought her to the house/job-site every single day.
@#! FLOWER BED.
I'M HITTING THE GODDAMN CONTINENTAL SHELF HERE!
A lifetime dog lover, Dad had been without a dog for ten years. He adored Mini.
YES YOU. MINS-EY GIRL.
YOU'RE FULLA BEANS AND A BALE OF HAY!
Throughout his illness, he had Mini at his side. That is until SHE got sick.
JIM WITH THE NEWS
BONE CANCER?!
C'MERE YOU CRAZY MUTT!
PAIN
POOR MINI
Convinced Mini had "taken" his cancer, Dad built her a St. Francis shrine. But then:
WHO'S THIS?
R.I.P. MINI
SARRAH
Jim thought a new puppy would cheer him up. Till she knocked him over—
Radiation had weakened his bones. The hip had shattered.
SERIOUSLY bzz bzz I'M ORDERING YOU bzz bzz bzz COMPLETE BED REST!
!
As soon as he could, in defiance of doctor's orders, he was back at it.
GO EASY SARRAH.
GOTTA FINISH RED'S FLOWER BED.
DOESN'T BLAME DOG
About a month after the hip healed, while busy with rock placement...
YEOUCH
?
Tore the muscles clean away from the spine. This time it was all winter in bed on opiates.
Spring. Mom took over dolling up the yard. Until OOPS! she tripped on loose gravel..
..and hit the back of her head on a rock.

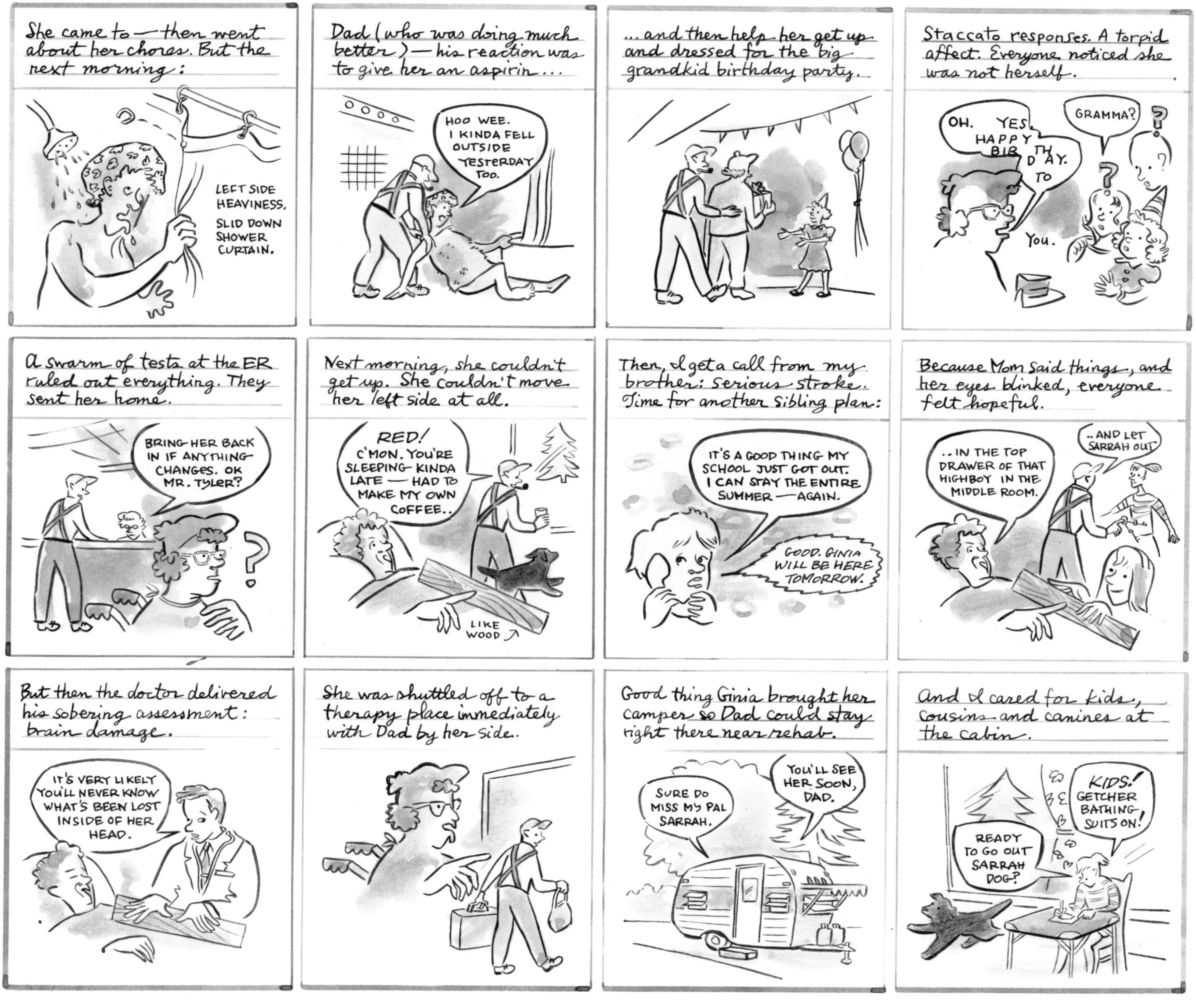
She came to — then went about her chores. But the next morning:
LEFT SIDE HEAVINESS.
SLID DOWN SHOWER CURTAIN.
Dad (who was doing much better) — his reaction was to give her an aspirin...
HOO WEE. I KINDA FELL OUTSIDE YESTERDAY TOO.
...and then help her get up and dressed for the big grandkid birthday party.
Staccato responses. A torpid affect. Everyone noticed she was not herself.
OH. YES. HAPPY BIR TH DAY. TO YOU.
GRAMMA?
A swarm of tests at the ER ruled out everything. They sent her home.
BRING HER BACK IN IF ANYTHING CHANGES. OK MR. TYLER?
Next morning, she couldn't get up. She couldn't move her left side at all.
RED! C'MON. YOU'RE SLEEPING KINDA LATE — HAD TO MAKE MY OWN COFFEE..
LIKE WOOD
Then, I get a call from my brother: Serious stroke. Time for another sibling plan:
IT'S A GOOD THING MY SCHOOL JUST GOT OUT. I CAN STAY THE ENTIRE SUMMER — AGAIN.
GOOD. GINIA WILL BE HERE TOMORROW.
Because Mom said things, and her eyes blinked, everyone felt hopeful.
..IN THE TOP DRAWER OF THAT HIGHBOY IN THE MIDDLE ROOM.
..AND LET SARRAH OUT
But then the doctor delivered his sobering assessment: brain damage.
IT'S VERY LIKELY YOU'LL NEVER KNOW WHAT'S BEEN LOST INSIDE OF HER HEAD.
She was shuttled off to a therapy place immediately with Dad by her side.
Good thing Ginia brought her camper so Dad could stay right there near rehab.
SURE DO MISS MY PAL SARRAH.
YOU'LL SEE HER SOON, DAD.
And I cared for kids, cousins and canines at the cabin.
KIDS! GETCHER BATHING SUITS ON!
READY TO GO OUT SARRAH DOG?

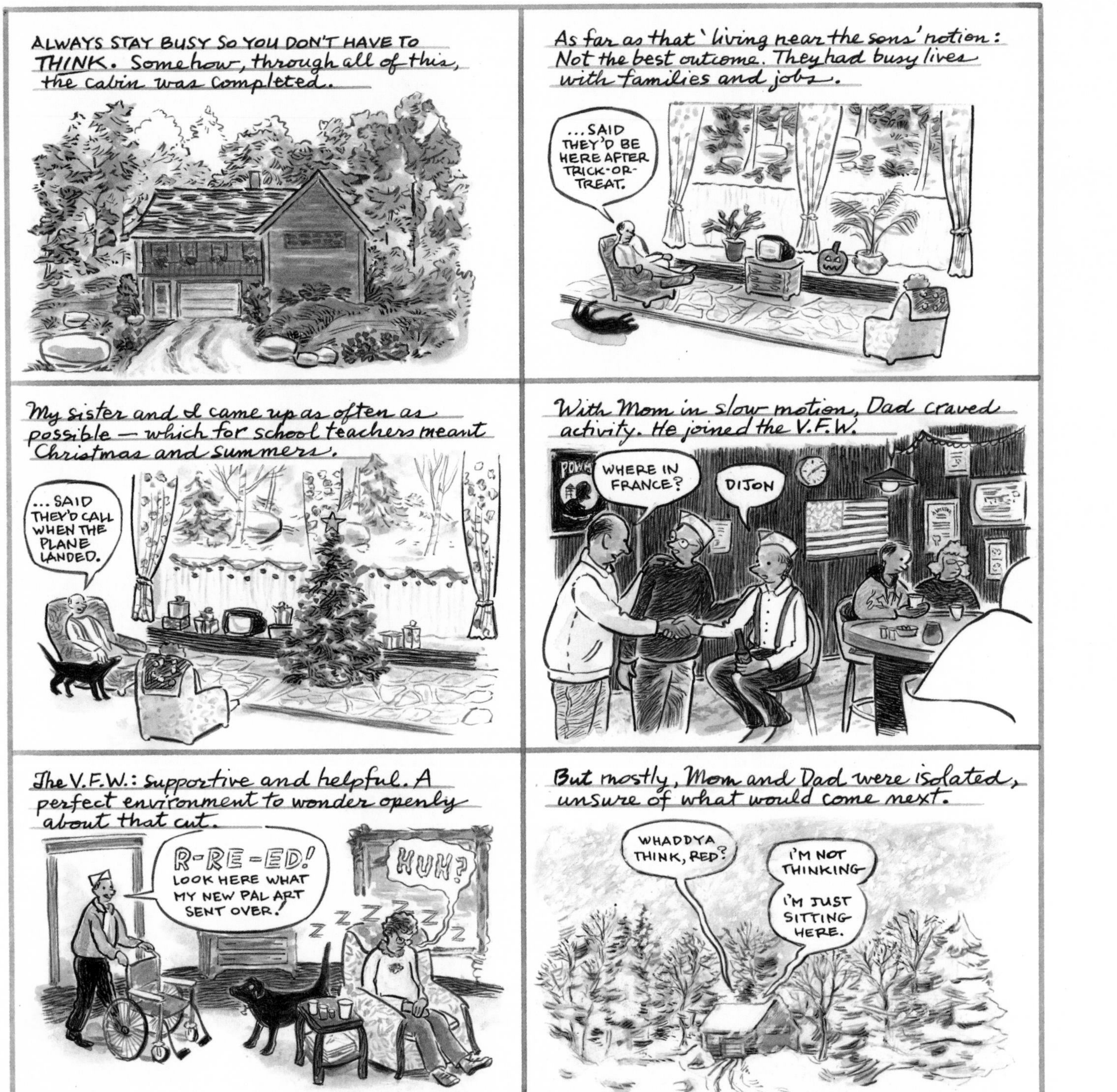
ALWAYS STAY BUSY SO YOU DON'T HAVE TO THINK. Somehow, through all of this, the cabin was completed.
As far as that 'living near the sons' notion: Not the best outcome. They had busy lives with families and jobs.
...SAID THEY'D BE HERE AFTER TRICK-OR-TREAT.
My sister and I came up as often as possible — which for school teachers meant Christmas and summers.
...SAID THEY'D CALL WHEN THE PLANE LANDED.
With Mom in slow motion, Dad craved activity. He joined the V.F.W.
WHERE IN FRANCE?
DIJON
The V.F.W.: supportive and helpful. A perfect environment to wonder openly about that cut.
R-RE-ED! LOOK HERE WHAT MY NEW PAL ART SENT OVER!
HUH?
ZZZZZZZ
But mostly, Mom and Dad were isolated, unsure of what would come next.
WHADDYA THINK, RED?
I'M NOT THINKING
I'M JUST SITTING HERE.

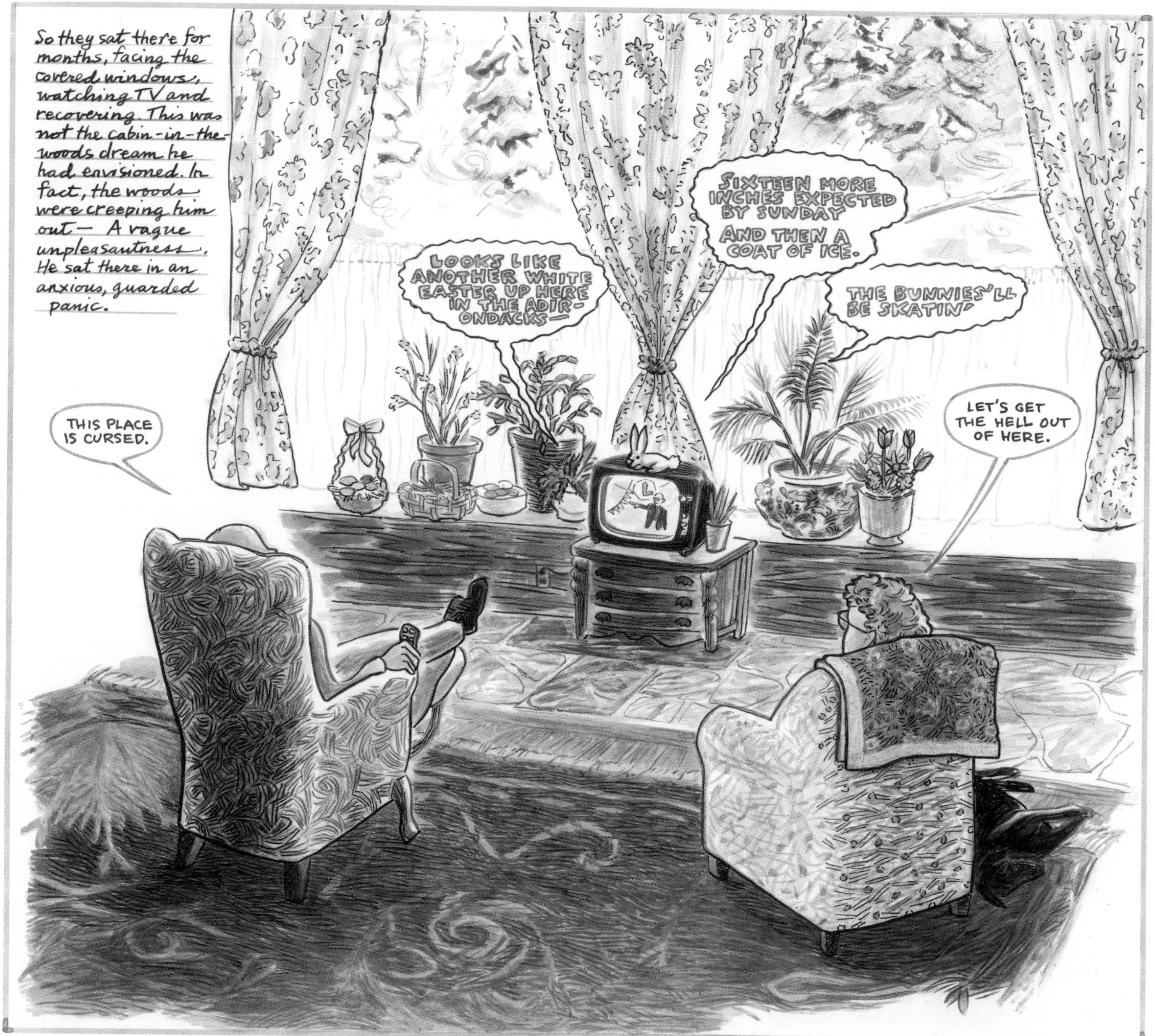

So they sat there for months, facing the covered windows, watching TV and recovering. This was not the cabin-in-the-woods dream he had envisioned. In fact, the woods were creeping him out— A vague unpleasantness. He sat there in an anxious, guarded panic.
THIS PLACE IS CURSED.
LOOKS LIKE ANOTHER WHITE EASTER UP HERE IN THE ADIRONDACKS—
SIXTEEN MORE INCHES EXPECTED BY SUNDAY
AND THEN A COAT OF ICE.
THE BUNNIES'LL BE SKATIN'
LET'S GET THE HELL OUT OF HERE.

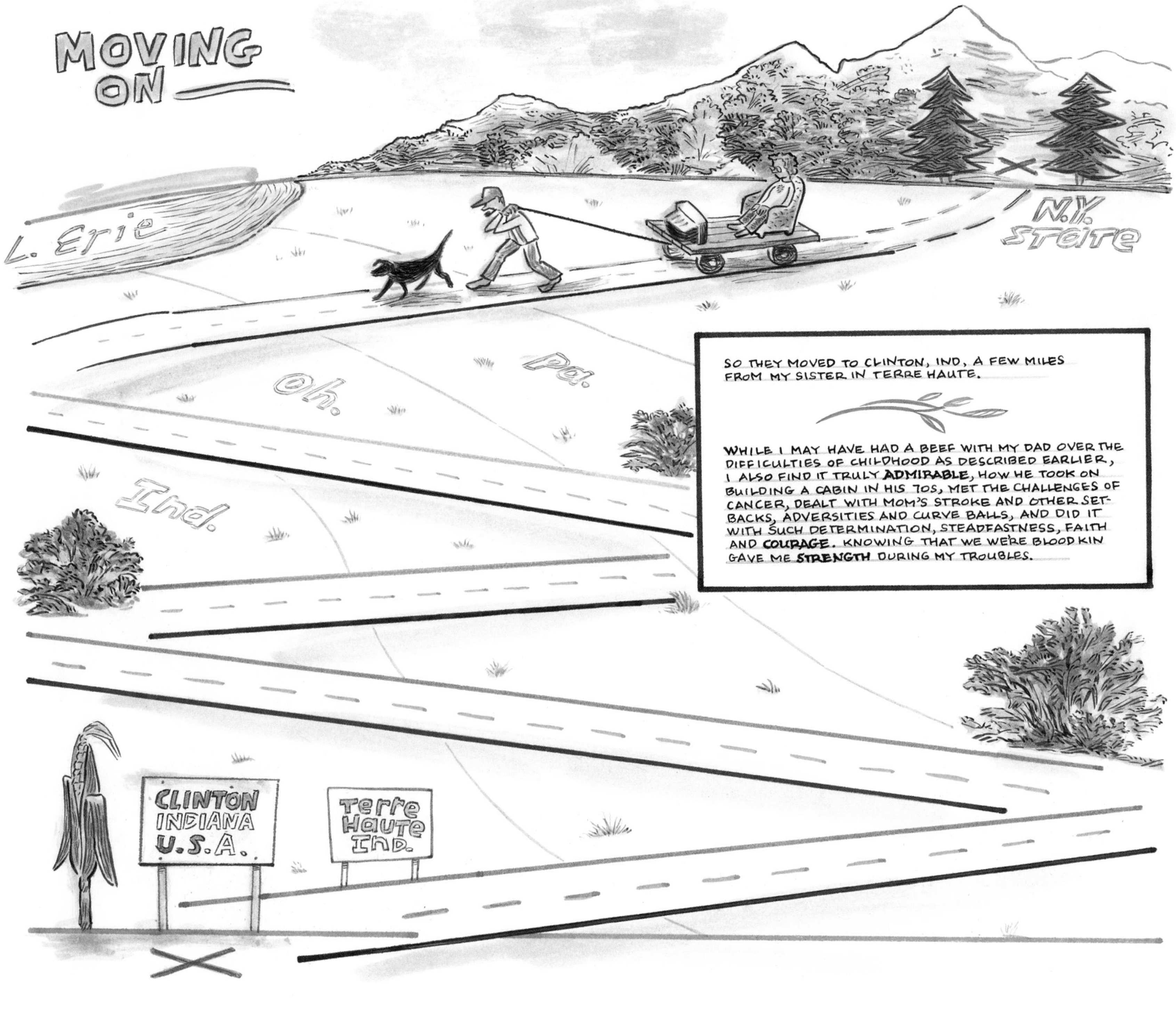
MOVING ON
L. Erie
N.Y. State
Pa.
Oh.
Ind.
SO THEY MOVED TO CLINTON, IND, A FEW MILES FROM MY SISTER IN TERRE HAUTE.
WHILE I MAY HAVE HAD A BEEF WITH MY DAD OVER THE DIFFICULTIES OF CHILDHOOD AS DESCRIBED EARLIER, I ALSO FIND IT TRULY **ADMIRABLE**, HOW HE TOOK ON BUILDING A CABIN IN HIS 70s, MET THE CHALLENGES OF CANCER, DEALT WITH MOM'S STROKE AND OTHER SET-BACKS, ADVERSITIES AND CURVE BALLS, AND DID IT WITH SUCH DETERMINATION, STEADFASTNESS, FAITH AND **COURAGE**. KNOWING THAT WE WERE BLOOD KIN GAVE ME **STRENGTH** DURING MY TROUBLES.
CLINTON INDIANA U.S.A.
Terre Haute Ind.

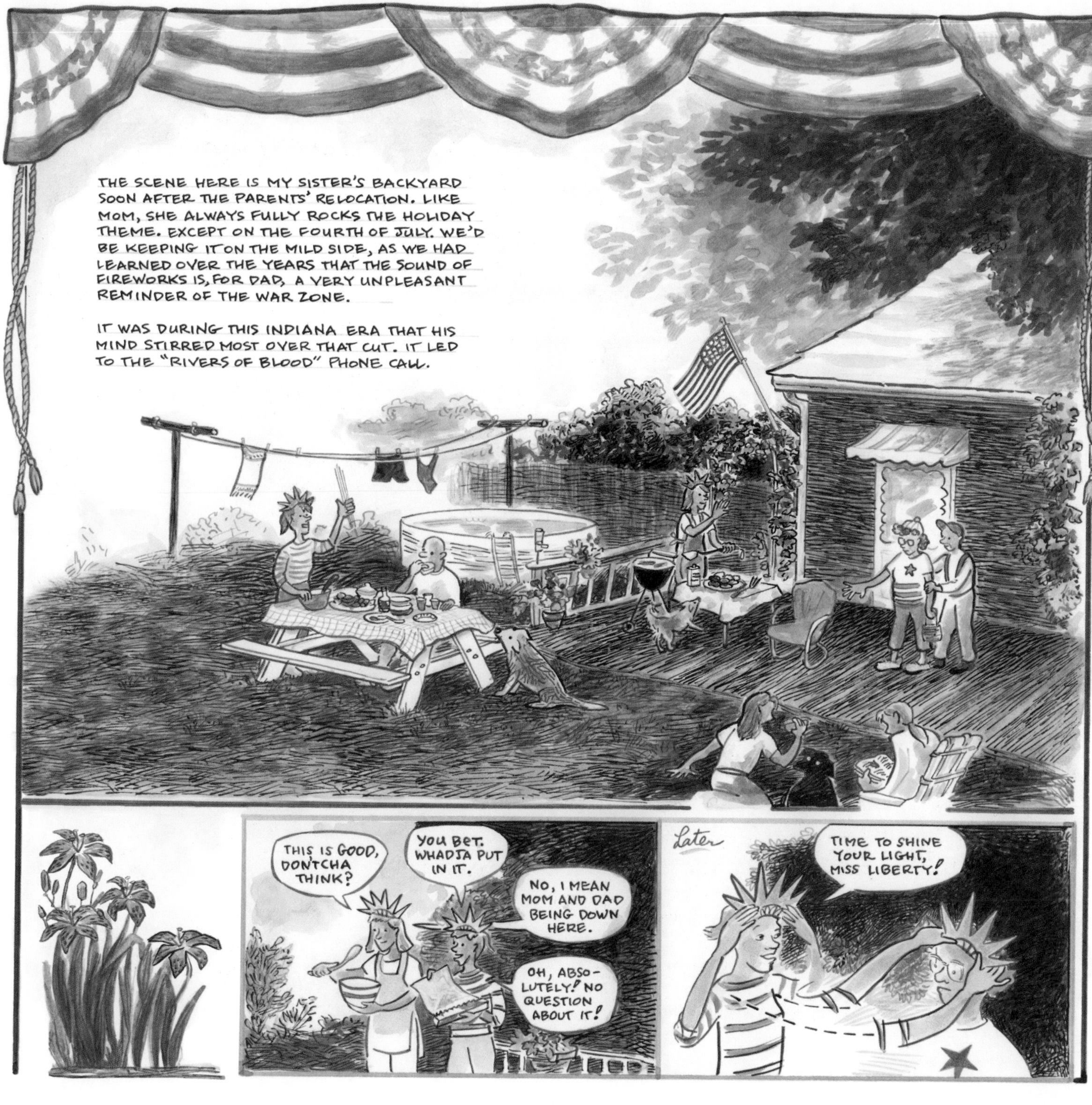
THE SCENE HERE IS MY SISTER'S BACKYARD SOON AFTER THE PARENTS' RELOCATION. LIKE MOM, SHE ALWAYS FULLY ROCKS THE HOLIDAY THEME. EXCEPT ON THE FOURTH OF JULY. WE'D BE KEEPING IT ON THE MILD SIDE, AS WE HAD LEARNED OVER THE YEARS THAT THE SOUND OF FIREWORKS IS, FOR DAD, A VERY UNPLEASANT REMINDER OF THE WAR ZONE.
IT WAS DURING THIS INDIANA ERA THAT HIS MIND STIRRED MOST OVER THAT CUT. IT LED TO THE "RIVERS OF BLOOD" PHONE CALL.
THIS IS GOOD, DON'TCHA THINK?
YOU BET. WHADJA PUT IN IT.
NO, I MEAN MOM AND DAD BEING DOWN HERE.
OH, ABSOLUTELY! NO QUESTION ABOUT IT!
Later
TIME TO SHINE YOUR LIGHT, MISS LIBERTY!

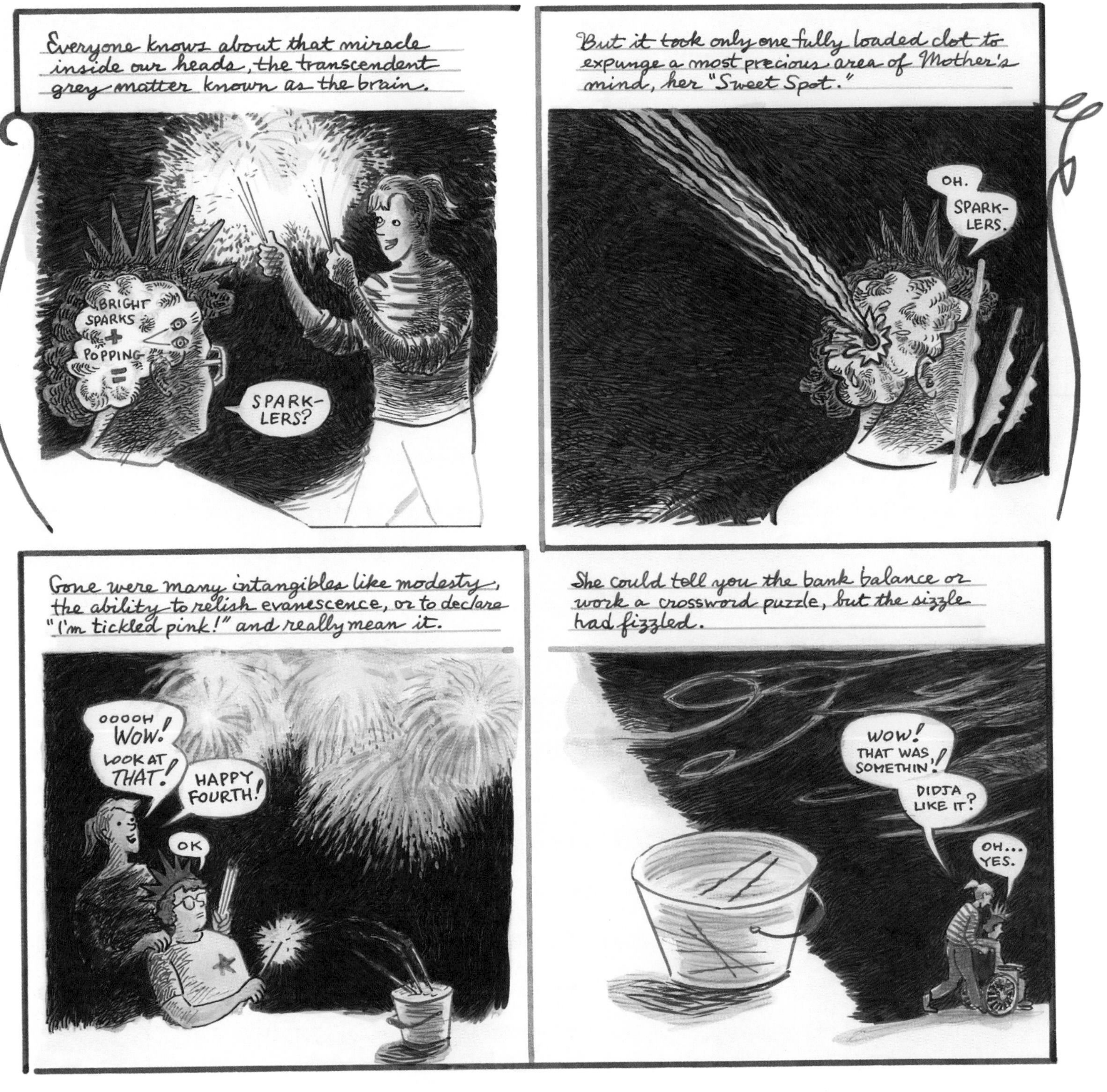
Everyone knows about that miracle inside our heads, the transcendent grey matter known as the brain.
BRIGHT SPARKS + POPPING =
SPARKLERS?
But it took only one fully loaded clot to expunge a most precious area of Mother's mind, her "Sweet Spot."
OH. SPARKLERS.
Gone were many intangibles like modesty, the ability to relish evanescence, or to declare "I'm tickled pink!" and really mean it.
OOOOH WOW! LOOK AT THAT!
HAPPY FOURTH!
OK
She could tell you the bank balance or work a crossword puzzle, but the sizzle had fizzled.
WOW! THAT WAS SOMETHIN'!
DIDJA LIKE IT?
OH... YES.

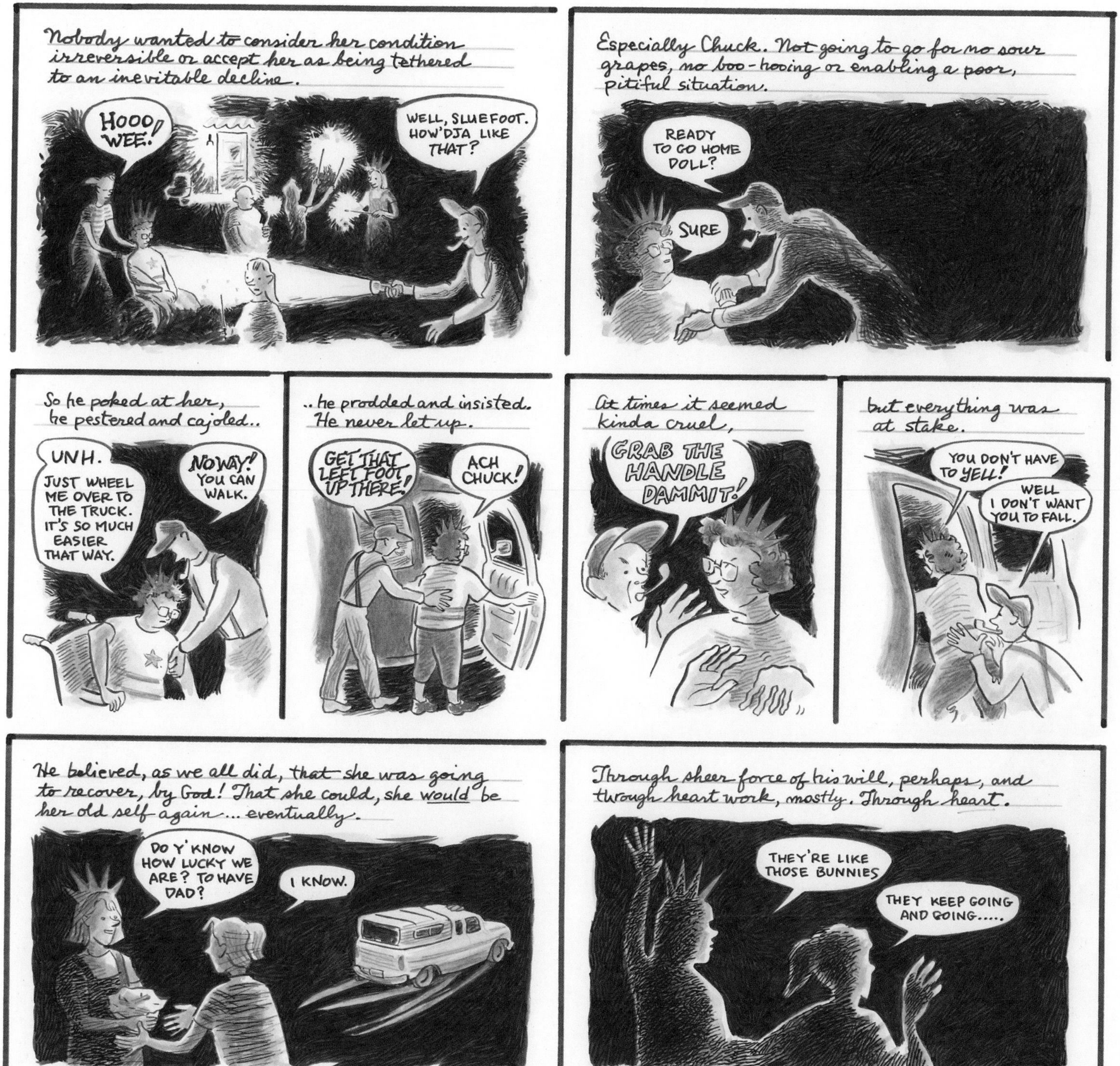
Nobody wanted to consider her condition irreversible or accept her as being tethered to an inevitable decline.
HOOO WEE!
WELL, SLUEFOOT. HOW'DJA LIKE THAT?
Especially Chuck. Not going to go for no sour grapes, no boo-hooing or enabling a poor, pitiful situation.
READY TO GO HOME DOLL?
SURE
So he poked at her, he pestered and cajoled..
UNH. JUST WHEEL ME OVER TO THE TRUCK. IT'S SO MUCH EASIER THAT WAY.
NO WAY! YOU CAN WALK.
..he prodded and insisted. He never let up.
GET THAT LEFT FOOT UP THERE!
ACH CHUCK!
At times it seemed kinda cruel,
GRAB THE HANDLE DAMMIT!
but everything was at stake.
YOU DON'T HAVE TO YELL!
WELL I DON'T WANT YOU TO FALL.
He believed, as we all did, that she was going to recover, by God! That she could, she would be her old self again... eventually.
DO Y'KNOW HOW LUCKY WE ARE? TO HAVE DAD?
I KNOW.
Through sheer force of his will, perhaps, and through heart work, mostly. Through heart.
THEY'RE LIKE THOSE BUNNIES
THEY KEEP GOING AND GOING.....

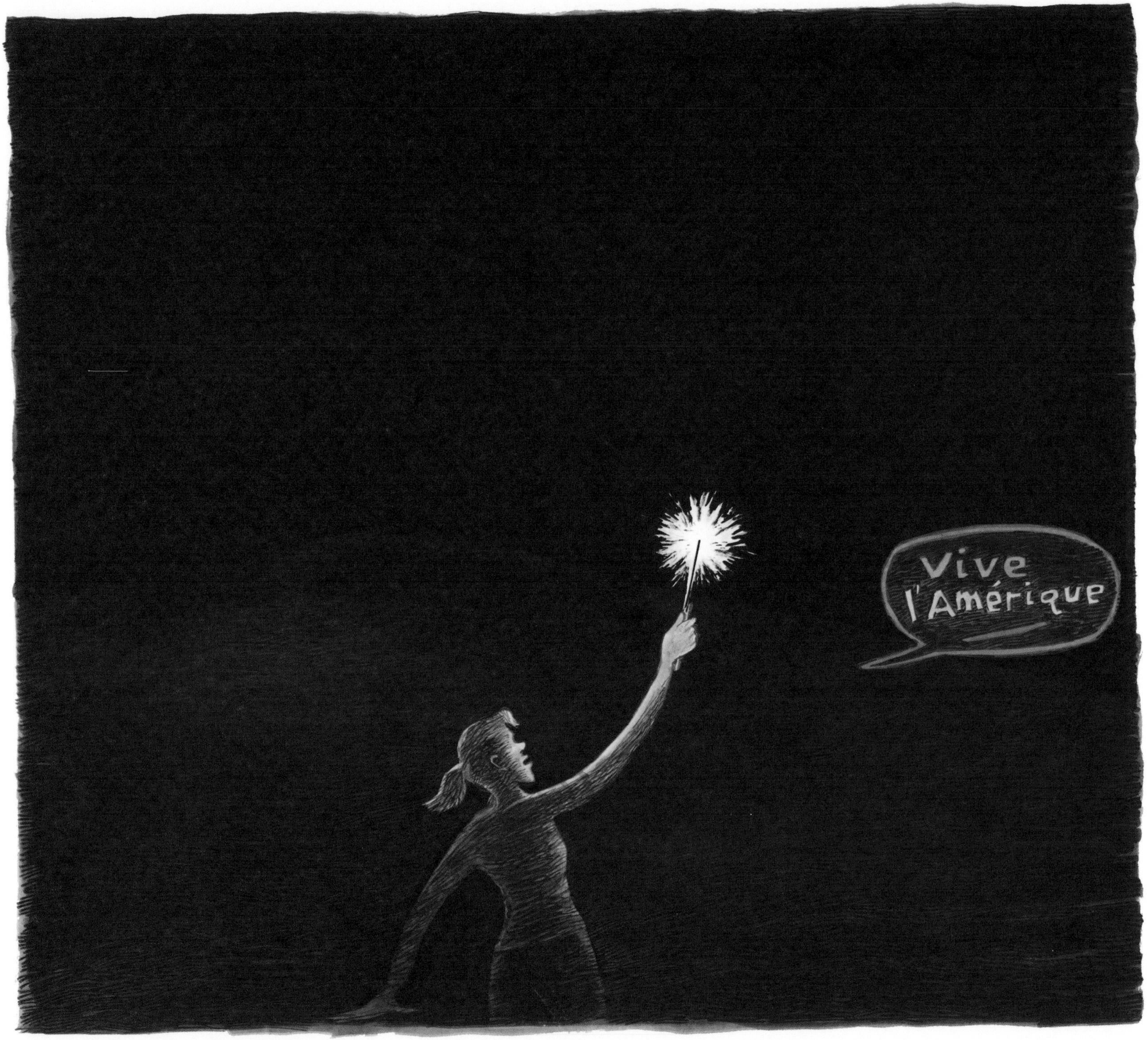
Vive l'Amérique

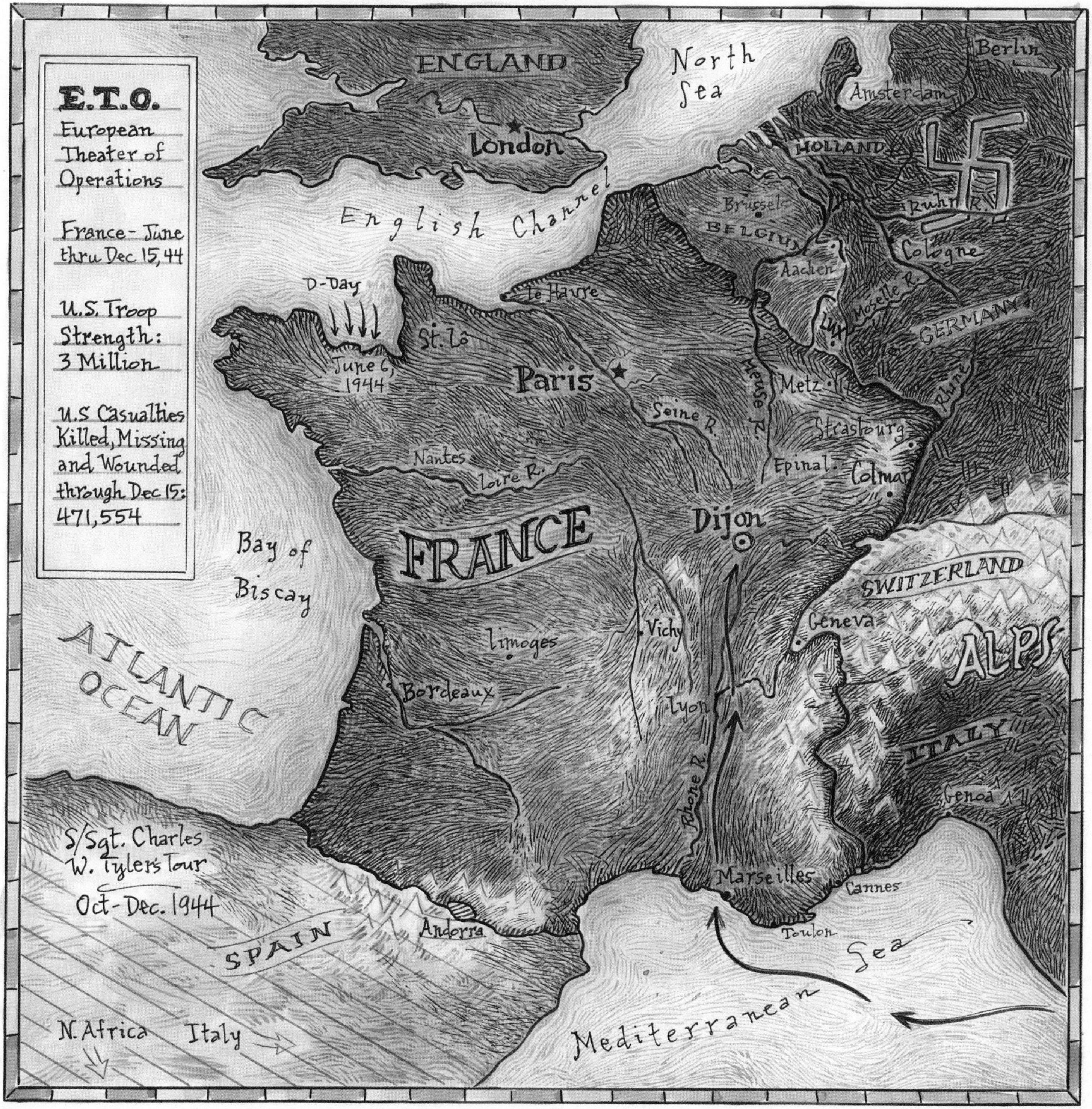
E.T.O.
European Theater of Operations
France - June thru Dec 15, 44
U.S. Troop Strength: 3 Million
U.S Casualties Killed, Missing and Wounded through Dec 15: 471,554
ENGLAND
London
North Sea
English Channel
Amsterdam
Berlin
HOLLAND
Brussels
BELGIUM
Ruhr R.
Cologne
Aachen
Le Havre
D-Day
June 6, 1944
St. Lô
Paris
Moselle R.
GERMANY
Metz
Meuse R.
Seine R.
Rhine
Strasbourg
Nantes
Loire R.
Epinal
Colmar
Dijon
FRANCE
Bay of Biscay
SWITZERLAND
Geneva
Vichy
Limoges
ALPS
ATLANTIC OCEAN
Bordeaux
Lyon
ITALY
Rhone R.
Genoa
S/Sgt. Charles W. Tyler's Tour Oct-Dec. 1944
Marseilles
Cannes
Andorra
Toulon
SPAIN
Sea
Mediterranean
N. Africa
Italy

DAD'S ARMY SCRAPBOOK
AND
TOUR OF DUTY HIGHLIGHTS

PART IV

FRANCE

OCTOBER 1944 – DECEMBER 1944

Hi-Hi-Hee

"Going from Italy to Southern France, we were on one of the big English ships. It wasn't the Queen, but it was a big one, tho. Real delicacy — they're gonna treat us extra nice and so they give us fish eyes and fish eggs. Sour.. Pickled. For *BREAKFAST!* We threw that shit all over that ship and had to stay in that mess for 3 days. Stink! Flies! Oh you never <u>seen</u> such a mess!"

"The only thing that kept me going through all this was Red. If it wasn't for her, I don't know what I woulda done."

OCT 17 1944

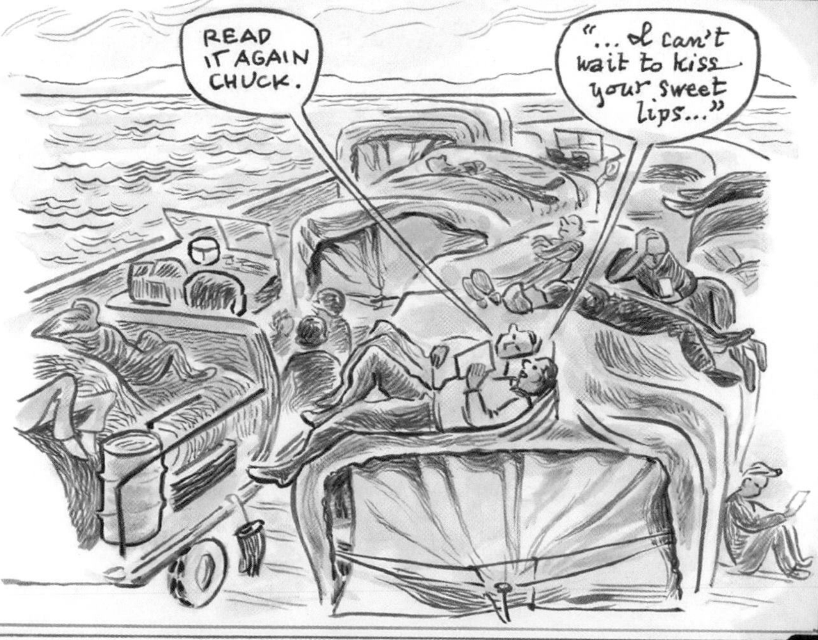
READ IT AGAIN CHUCK.
"...I can't wait to kiss your sweet lips..."

54

"Got off the boat in Marseilles. And lo and behold, that real estate guy hollers at me, 'Hey Chuck! Come with me. You c'n catch up to your unit later. Bivouacked up a short way.' He had a Jeep with a 55 gallon drum of gas in the back. We drove up to the right someplace on some road, met some guy and sold the Jeep and the 55 gallons of gas. Gas was more valuable than anything.

"So there I was, not 2 minutes in France and in the black market again, right off the bat, without even asking for it."

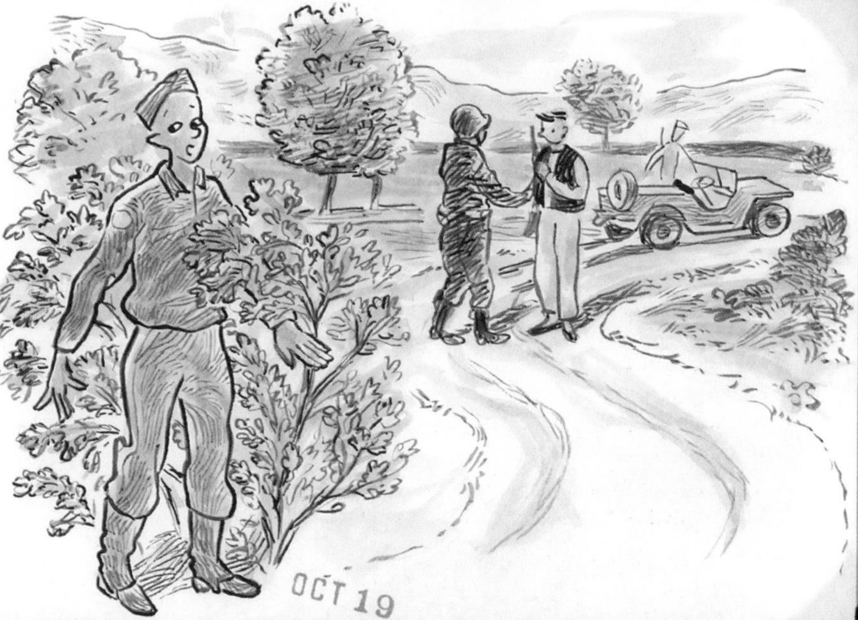

OCT 19

55

"Held up in Marseilles for a couple-a days because our guys were still clearing the Rhone valley. Our staging area was an old armory type building that had the roof blown away. Barrels here and there for fires. The place was full of the walking wounded. The sergeant there says to me, 'It's a bit chilly, so when you go out, bring some firewood home.'

"Later, I got all hepped-up on champagne blanc and drove a streetcar into an ammo truck. I went through the windshield."

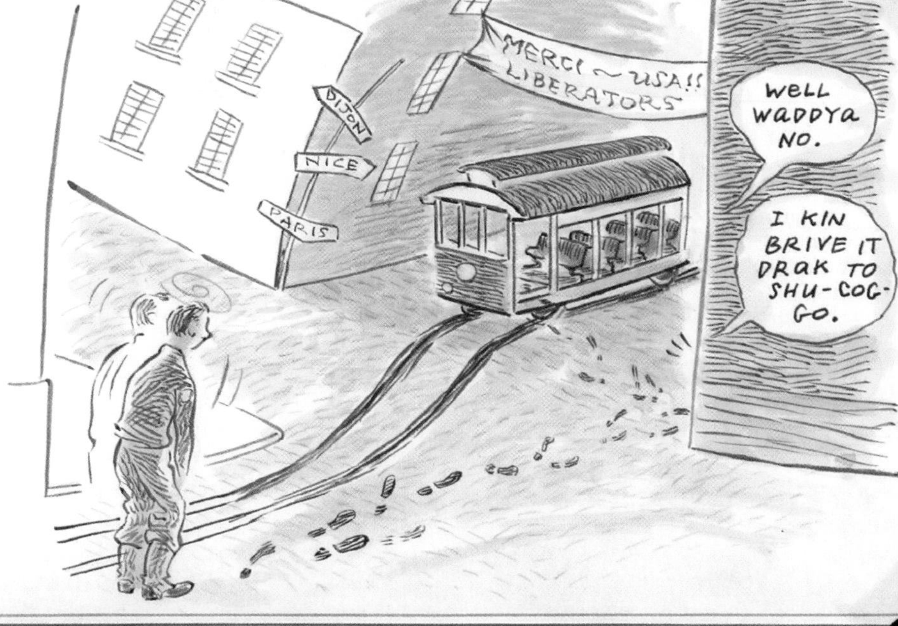
DIJON
NICE
PARIS
MERCI ~ USA!!
LIBERATORS
WELL WADDYA NO.
I KIN BRIVE IT DRAK TO SHU-COG-GO.

56

"On the way back to the armory, I'm thinkin' 'Oh boy. I gotta bring some firewood for the walking wounded.' So I drug back some 2x4s, some 12-15' long with sticks on them. Like it must've been somebody's fence post I got a hold of. I was drunk. It was dark.

"Before I go to sleep, I pack the barrels good with this stuff and the next thing I know, the barrels are flaming up, burning straight up like wild, sparks falling on these poor bastards, sick and they're burning up—oh we had a hell of an awful time that night."

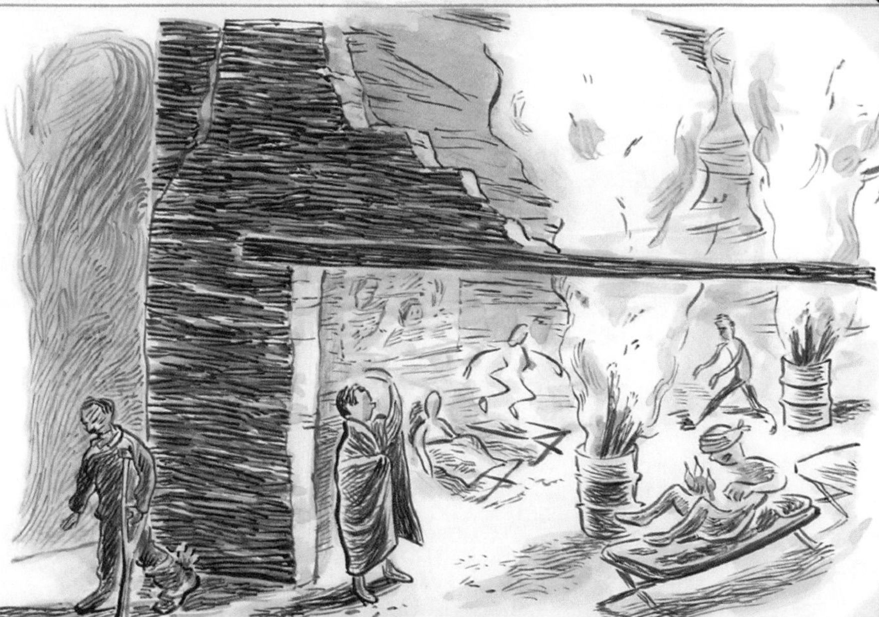

57

"Up the Rhone from Marseilles — total destruction. Our job was to pick up ammo on the side of the road. We didn't have such an easy time of it. What a mangled mess! Tanks, Renaults, carts. Our Air Force had strafed it bad. And what we didn't destroy, the Germans when they left, tore everything to pieces. Then everything was bulldozed off onto the shoulders by our engineers. This went on for miles, a hundred miles. I thought Italy was a mess. Frying pan to the fire."

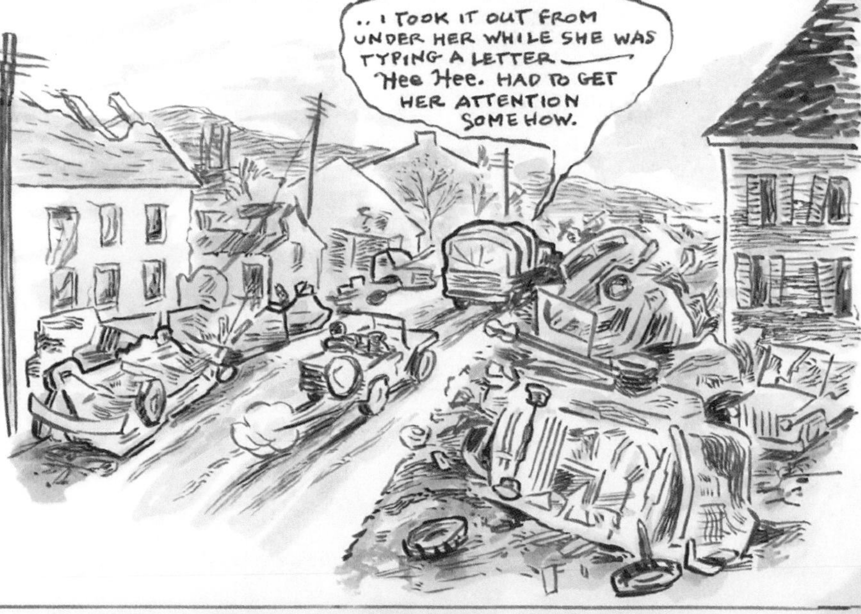
.. I TOOK IT OUT FROM UNDER HER WHILE SHE WAS TYPING A LETTER — Hee Hee. HAD TO GET HER ATTENTION SOMEHOW.

58

I wound up at the American Standard Factory, where they put me in charge of repairing blown out tires. In Dijon. With POW labor. I had 509 Germans, 200 some Italians and 169 Hungarians. Every 2 weeks or so we'd send a cab-over engine truck to Heidelberg maybe to get beer. We had it on tap, 24/7. They all drank it. The Germans would sing and march MACH SCHNELL! The Hungarians were cryin' all the time and the I-talians were f**ing through the fence."

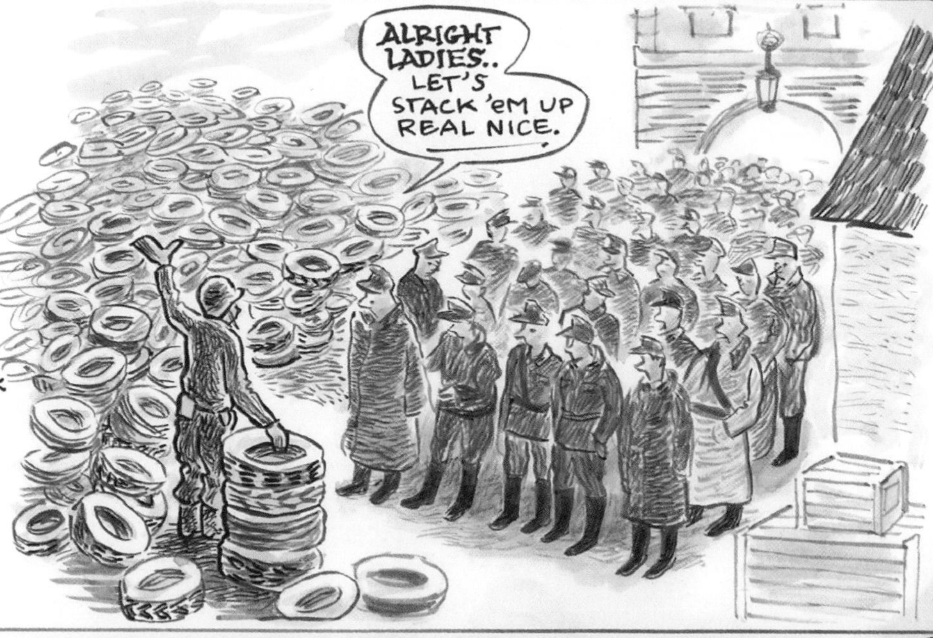
ALRIGHT LADIES.. LET'S STACK 'EM UP REAL NICE.

59

"This buddy of mine says, 'Chuck, you don't want to stay with the prisoners. Stay off the post.' So he got me a 22 room hotel for my little gang. I think there were 8 soldiers, 8 of us. We each had our own private room and I was in charge of the place.

"I run a good depot. We fixed 100,000 tires in 6 weeks. I know 'cause I made note of that. They promoted me to Master Sgt., but I didn't like the extra paperwork. I'm not a pencil-pusher, so they dropped me back down to Staff Sergeant."

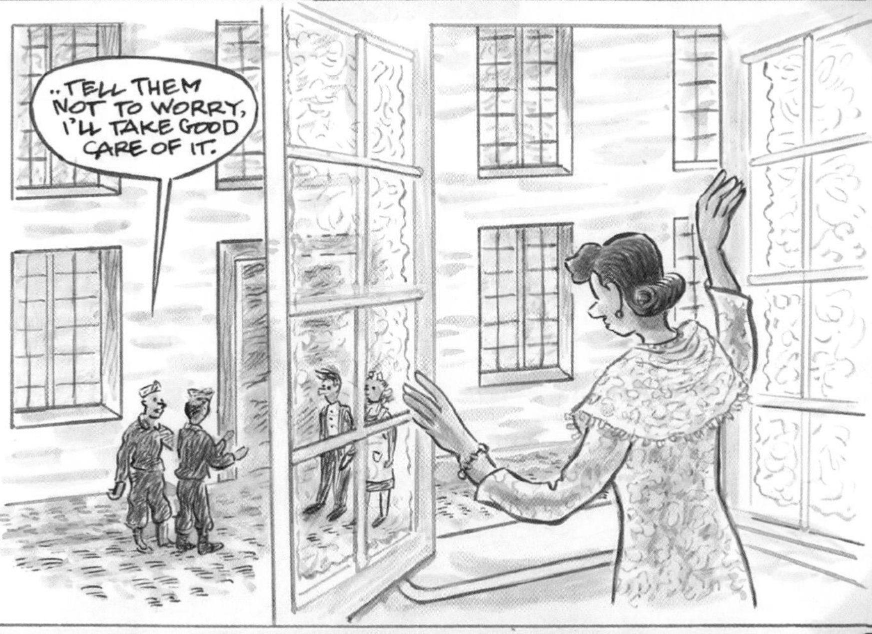
..TELL THEM NOT TO WORRY, I'LL TAKE GOOD CARE OF IT.

60

"I took up smoking cigars in France because I could make money selling my cigarettes. Everybody wanted our U.S. smokes, but no interest in cigars. So I made money that way. And when I went out, I would sell my spare tire because I could always come back to the depot for another one. I guess I could still get in trouble for that. — We got paid with invasion money, not the Yankee dollar. All deals were done with it, even on the black market. We'd take it to a tavern to exchange it at whatever percentage because local money, the Lira or the Franc were better to have."

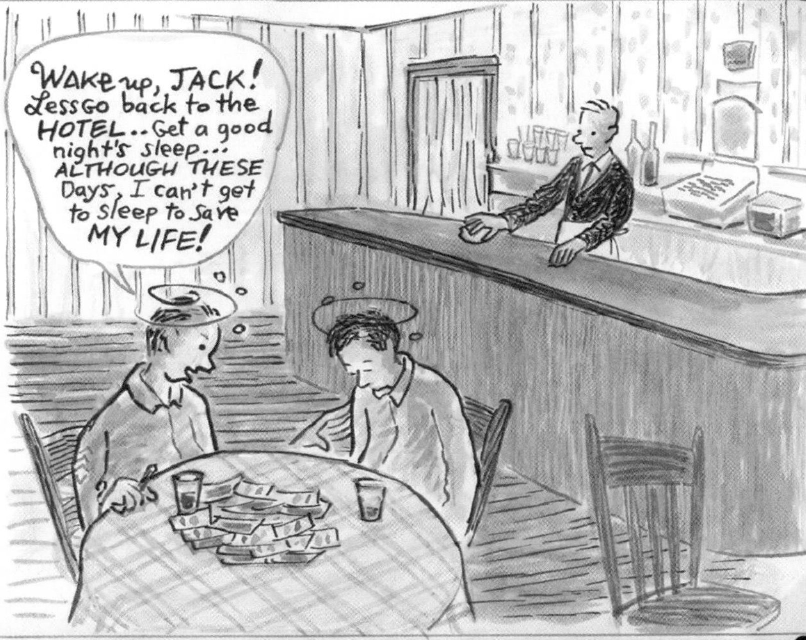
WAKE up, JACK! Lessgo back to the HOTEL.. Get a good night's sleep... ALTHOUGH THESE Days, I can't get to sleep to save MY LIFE!

61

"I took a 3 day leave to see Paris. I drove around. It wasn't nothin'. The Eiffel Tower— closed. Sent post cards. Never felt so lonely as I did in Paris. — So I come home early to find my hotel in shambles! Across the street was the medical station for all the whores in town and apparently my guys had invited them over to our hotel. They were eating all our food, drinking, tore everything to hell. Biggest whore house you ever seen! I run everybody out, made 'em buy all new dishes and got the Germans to clean up."

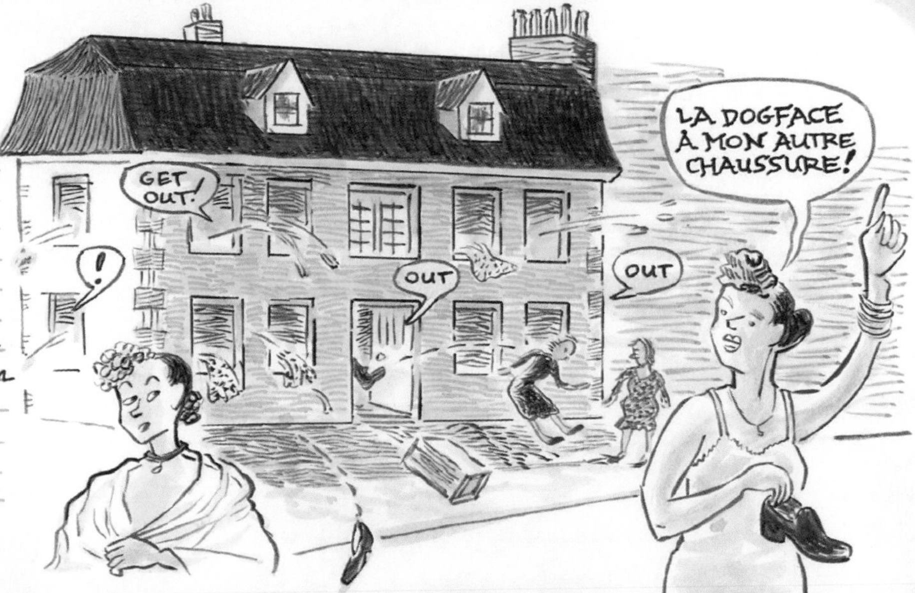

GET OUT!
!
OUT
OUT
LA DOGFACE À MON AUTRE CHAUSSURE!

62

"I guess one night I had a little too much to drink and passed out in the Tire Depot. I'll never forget the German officers. They had a lot of respect for me. They knew I was fair. So they cleaned me up, washed me, polished my boots without being asked... never used being drunk against me, never mentioned it as far as I knew.

"I had a lot of respect for them, too. They kept clean and busy. Hard to think of them sometimes as the enemy. But I never forgot that they were."

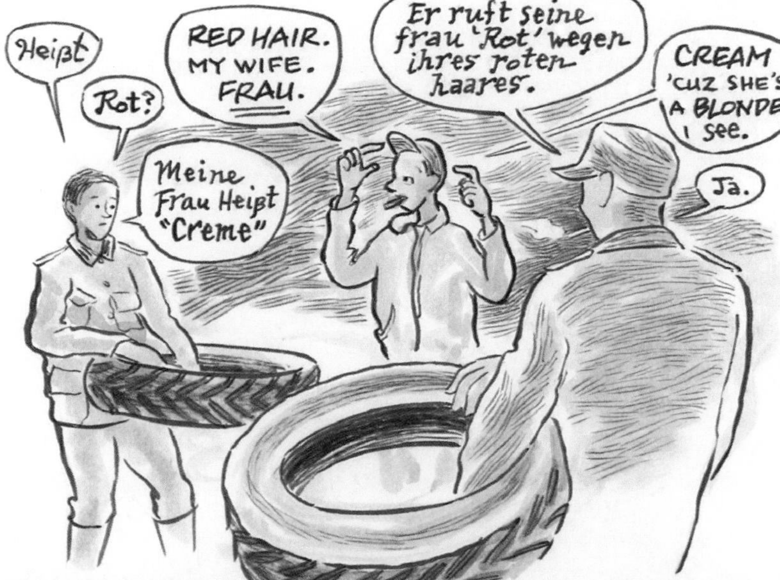

Heißt
Rot?
RED HAIR. MY WIFE. FRAU.
Er ruft seine frau 'Rot' wegen ihres roten haares.
CREAM 'CUZ SHE'S A BLONDE. I see.
Meine Frau Heißt "Creme"
Ja.

63

"'Killer Kane', this guy I knew, comes to see me. 'Let's go to Lausanne, Switzerland for a few days. R&R.' He had a couple of girls in the car— but I was a married man. But I wanted to go for a ride. See something nice besides tires and prisoners. So we're going around these mountain switchbacks. He's a little sauced and takes a curve too fast. Next thing I know, we're teetering on a cliff. And then he starts to go psycho, just like in combat. I wasn't gonna die like this. Because Red would have thought I was cheating on her when really, I was just out ridin'."

NOV 17

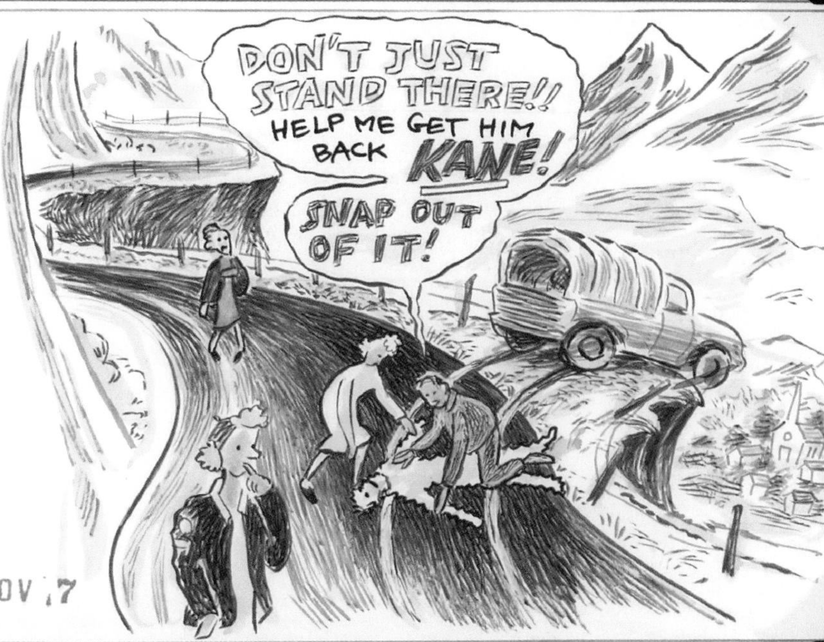

DON'T JUST STAND THERE!! HELP ME GET HIM BACK KANE!
SNAP OUT OF IT!

64

"Around Thanksgiving, here come 2 Frogs in a Renault (French officers) with a couple of gals. Headed for the Riviera. They needed gas.

"There was this great big bottle with wicker around it on top of their car. I really wanted that bottle. 'No. No' Finally, I filled his tank and gave him 2 5 gallon jerry cans extra. Not what I wanted but whatever, you know, hoping, bartering— He gave me that bottle. Then I discovered it was full of cognac! We drank that up in one day."

NOV 20

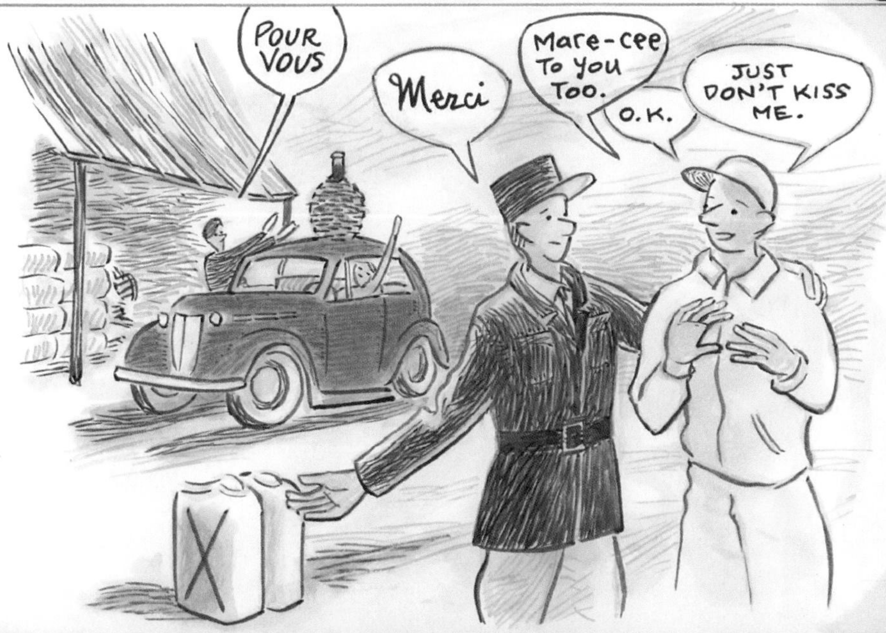

POUR VOUS
Merci
Mare-cee To you Too.
O.K.
JUST DON'T KISS ME.

65

"Around this time, I got word from home. From Red. We had been out of touch for so long with the mail being crossed up and all. I couldn't for the life of me figure out her message. Finally one of the guys said it looked to him like a stork notice. That 'she' looked like me. Congrats and all that. I sipped my cognac, convinced that since now I was a daddy and the war was just about over, they'd ship me home for the holidays. But — no such luck. Funny thing, though: That picture I lost in Africa, of Red — It got sent to me in Dijon."

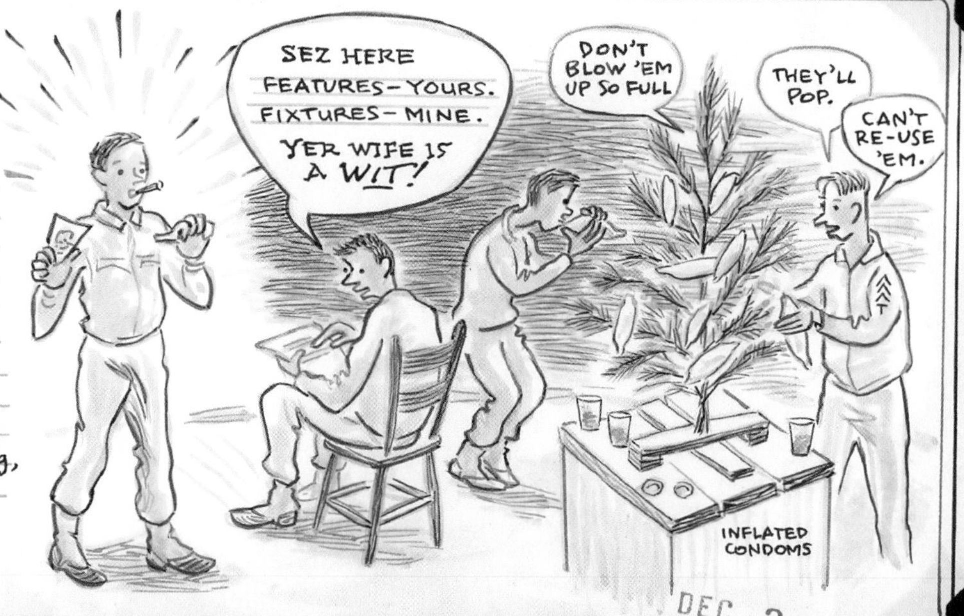
SEZ HERE FEATURES – YOURS. FIXTURES – MINE. YER WIFE IS A WIT!
DON'T BLOW 'EM UP SO FULL
THEY'LL POP.
CAN'T RE-USE 'EM.
INFLATED CONDOMS

DEC 2

66

However, he was not getting shipped home any time soon. In fact, just the opposite. "You see, those Frogs with the cognac, they said they seen piles of our uniforms and ammo up on the front lines for I guess our final big push up into Germany after our G.I.s finished their Christmas R and R. Our line was skimpy and the Germans knew it. Next thing I know, I'm dumping gas for Patton, around the clock, out the back of a truck convoy. I pretty much gave up on sleep or the idea I was ever gonna get any rest."

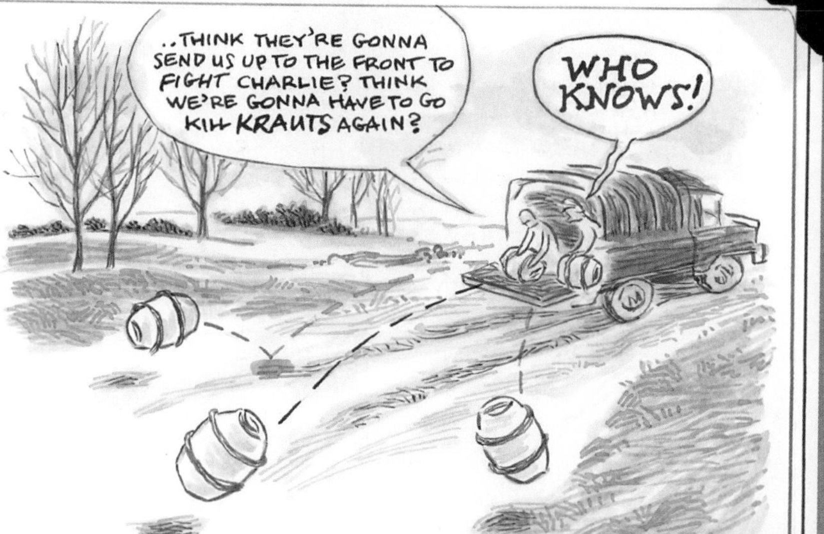
..THINK THEY'RE GONNA SEND US UP TO THE FRONT TO FIGHT CHARLIE? THINK WE'RE GONNA HAVE TO GO KILL KRAUTS AGAIN?
WHO KNOWS!

DEC 19 1944

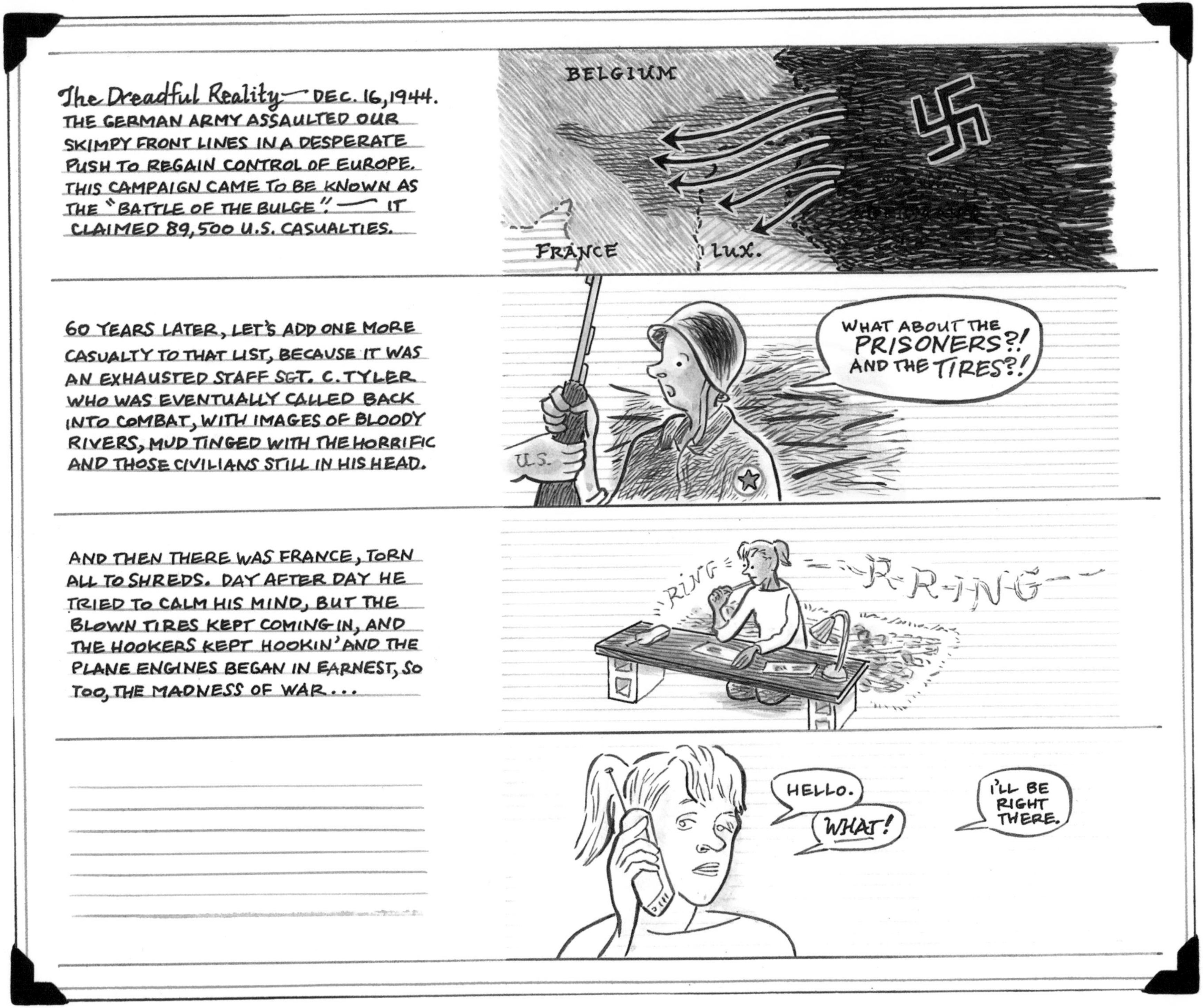
The Dreadful Reality — DEC. 16, 1944. THE GERMAN ARMY ASSAULTED OUR SKIMPY FRONT LINES IN A DESPERATE PUSH TO REGAIN CONTROL OF EUROPE. THIS CAMPAIGN CAME TO BE KNOWN AS THE "BATTLE OF THE BULGE." — IT CLAIMED 89,500 U.S. CASUALTIES.
BELGIUM
FRANCE
LUX.
60 YEARS LATER, LET'S ADD ONE MORE CASUALTY TO THAT LIST, BECAUSE IT WAS AN EXHAUSTED STAFF SGT. C. TYLER WHO WAS EVENTUALLY CALLED BACK INTO COMBAT, WITH IMAGES OF BLOODY RIVERS, MUD TINGED WITH THE HORRIFIC AND THOSE CIVILIANS STILL IN HIS HEAD.
U.S.
WHAT ABOUT THE PRISONERS?! AND THE TIRES?!
AND THEN THERE WAS FRANCE, TORN ALL TO SHREDS. DAY AFTER DAY HE TRIED TO CALM HIS MIND, BUT THE BLOWN TIRES KEPT COMING IN, AND THE HOOKERS KEPT HOOKIN' AND THE PLANE ENGINES BEGAN IN EARNEST, SO TOO, THE MADNESS OF WAR...
RING
R-R-I-N-G
HELLO.
WHAT!
I'LL BE RIGHT THERE.

I WISH I COULD SAY IT WAS THE FIRST TIME I'D GOTTEN A CALL FROM MY CHILD'S SCHOOL. SEEMS LIKE ONCE OR TWICE A WEEK LATELY — EVERYTHING FROM SASSING THE TEACHER TO SKIPPING CLASS. AND IT'S BEEN GOING ON EVER SINCE SHE STARTED HANGING AROUND WITH THAT AVERY BENNETT. I KNEW SHE WAS TROUBLE. FROM THAT VERY FIRST TIME JULIA WENT OVER THERE.

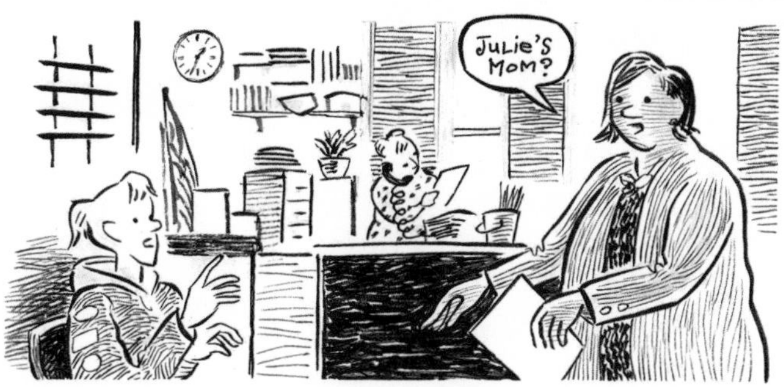
JULIE'S MOM?

THOSE OTHER CALLS: AGE APPROPRIATE. BUT THIS TIME SHE WENT TOO FAR. SHE TRIPPED THE CIRCUIT BREAKER FOR THE ENTIRE SCHOOL. ON A DARE. SO NOW SHE'S BEEN SUSPENDED FOR A WEEK — I MADE MY APOLOGIES TO THE VICE PRINCIPAL (AGAIN) AND WAS ALL SET TO TAKE HER HOME. JUST ONE LITTLE PROBLEM: SHE WAS IN THE RESTROOM VOMITING — APPARENTLY MY LITTLE DARLING WAS PLASTERED.

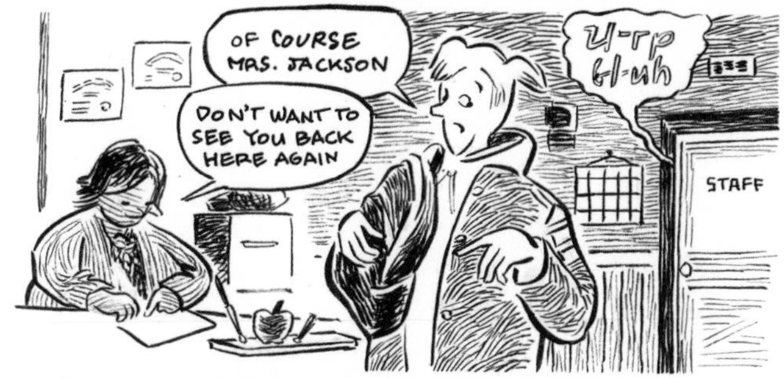
OF COURSE MRS. JACKSON
DON'T WANT TO SEE YOU BACK HERE AGAIN
U-rp bl-uh
STAFF

BEING DRUNK WASN'T THE *HALF* OF IT! WHEN I GOT HER IN THE CAR, I DEMANDED SHE SPILL OUT THE CONTENTS OF HER BACK-PACK: OH MY GOD, REEFER, CONDOMS, RAZOR BLADES, CIGARETTES, PURPLE HAIR DYE AND A HALF EMPTY PINT OF JACK-IN-THE-BLACK THAT SHE *CLAIMS* HAD BEEN PARKED THERE BY AVERY (WHOSE MOM WOULD KILL HER IF SHE FOUND OUT SO COULD I *PLEASE* NOT SAY ANYTHING.)

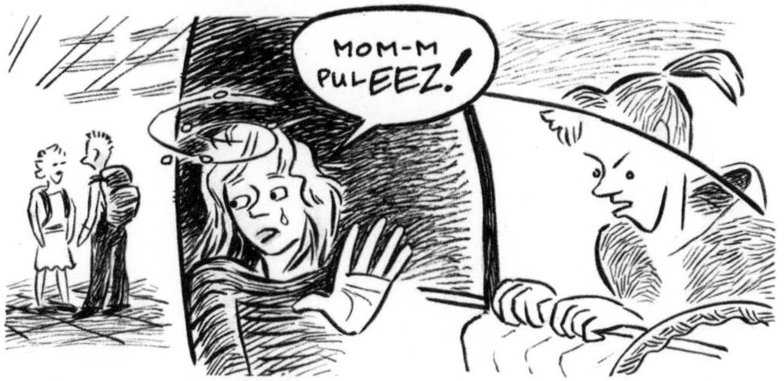
MOM-M PULEEZ!

AS IF I WAS GOING TO COVER FOR THAT LITTLE *BRAT!* SO I READ MISS JULIA THE RIOT ACT BETWEEN EVERY STOP-AND-OPEN-THE-DOOR-SO-SHE-CAN-VOMIT STOP ON THE WAY HOME. IT'S A SHOCKER TO BE SURE, SEEING YOUR KID IN SUCH A SORRY STATE. I'M NOT SURE WHAT GOOD IT DOES TO CURSE THE "EX" (IF HE IS MY "EX"), BUT DOING SO, EVEN IN MY MIND ONLY, SEEMED TO HELP MY DRIVING.

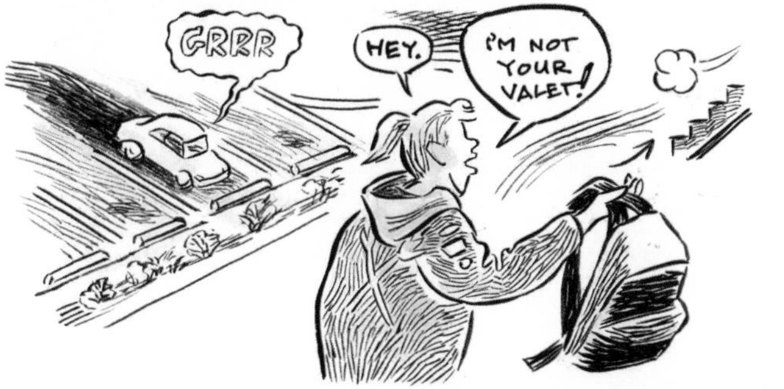
GRRR
HEY.
I'M NOT YOUR VALET!

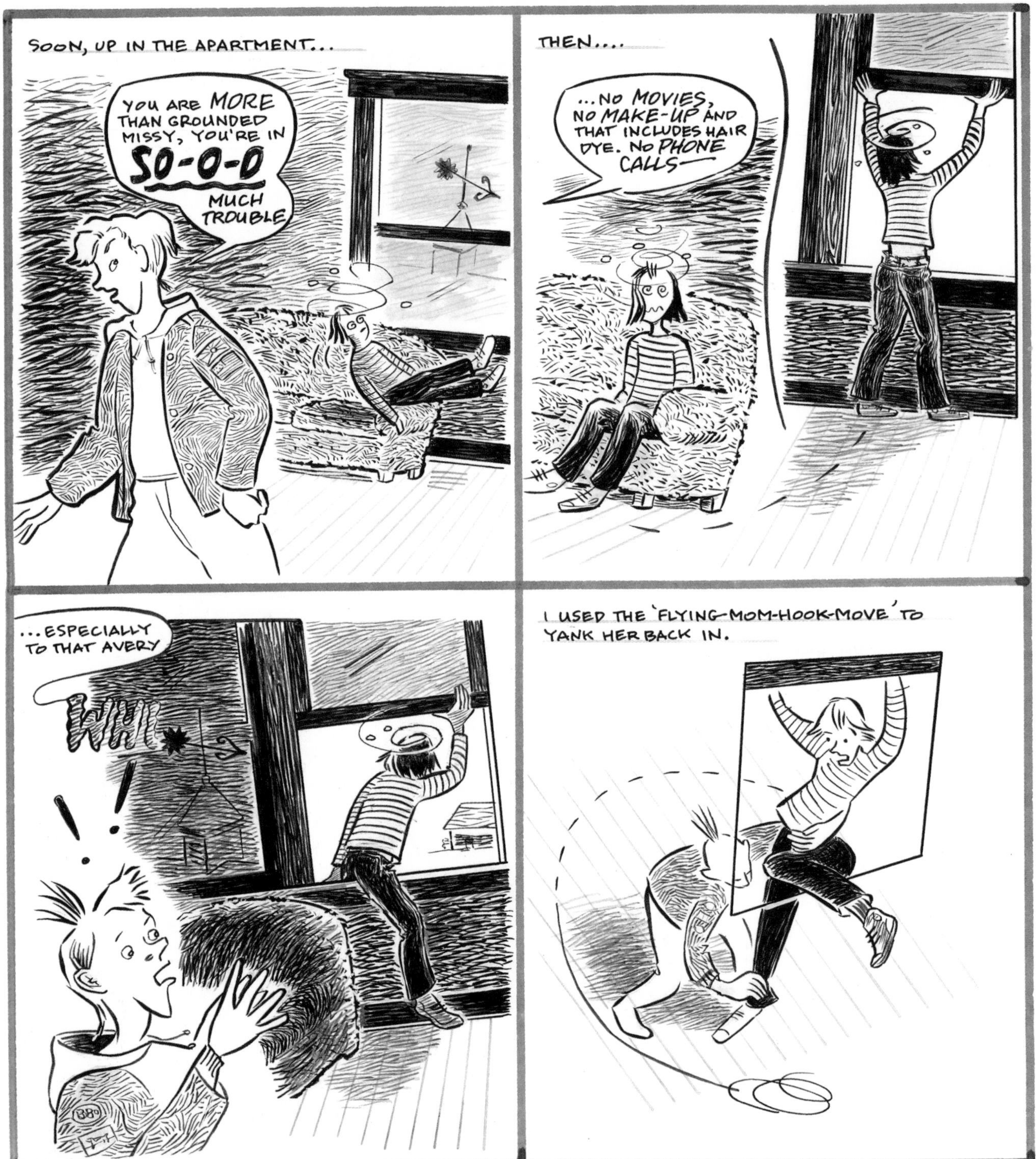
SOON, UP IN THE APARTMENT...
YOU ARE MORE THAN GROUNDED MISSY, YOU'RE IN SO-O-O MUCH TROUBLE
THEN....
...NO MOVIES, NO MAKE-UP AND THAT INCLUDES HAIR DYE. NO PHONE CALLS—
...ESPECIALLY TO THAT AVERY
WH
I USED THE 'FLYING-MOM-HOOK-MOVE' TO YANK HER BACK IN.

AFTER WE CAUGHT OUR BREATH AND SHE THREW UP ON ME, I MADE HER SPILL IT OVER WHAT THE HELL WAS GOING ON. 'I NEED AIR' SHE WHINED BUT I WASN'T BUYING IT. SO IT CAME DOWN TO THE MOST CHILLING REVELATION. "I'M NOT SUPPOSED TO TELL YOU BECAUSE HE'LL GET MAD AT ME." "OH YEAH? WHO'S THAT?" HER RUEFUL RETORT "THE BIRD MAN INSIDE MY HEAD. THE ONE WHO TOLD ME TO SUCK IN AIR BY JUMPING."

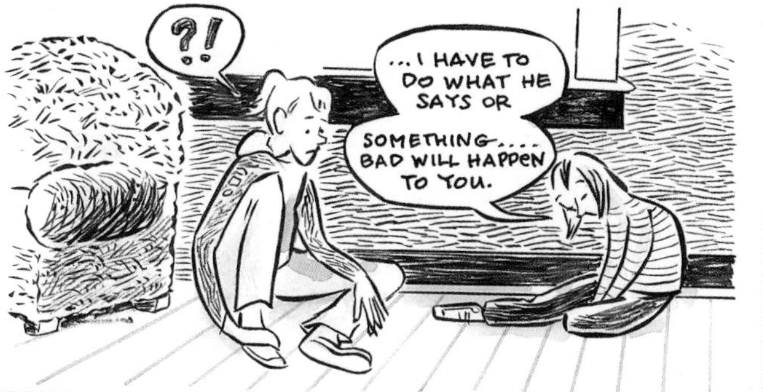
?!
...I HAVE TO DO WHAT HE SAYS OR
SOMETHING.... BAD WILL HAPPEN TO YOU.

NEEDLESS TO SAY, I RAN HER TO THE ER IMMEDIATELY. SAT THERE IN SHOCK. WAITED AND WAITED AND WAITED. SAT THERE AND WAITED. NURSE COMES IN, TAKES NOTES AND VITALS, GOES OUT. COMES BACK IN TO CHECK. GOES BACK OUT. IT'S CHIPPER HERE, FOR THE KIDS' SAKE. EVERYONE'S CHIPPER, AS OPPOSED TO **WEIGHTY**, WHICH IS WHAT THE REAL SITUATION IS.

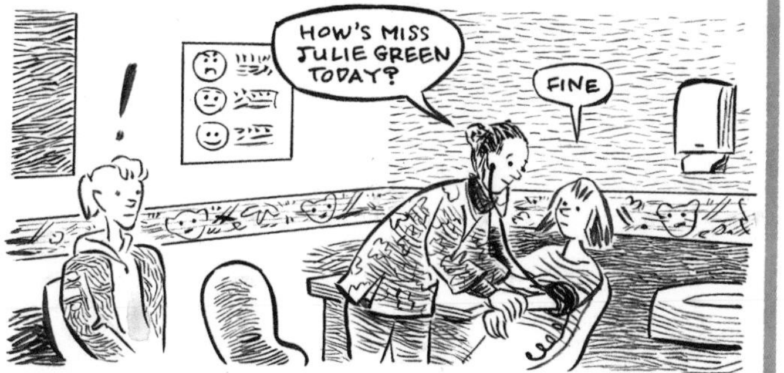
!
HOW'S MISS JULIE GREEN TODAY?
FINE

HOW COULD SHE BE HEARING A *VOICE*? IT'S JUST NOT TRUE! I KNOW MY CHILD. IT'S THE **BOOZE** MOST LIKELY. OR THE WEED. OR LORD KNOWS WHATEVER ELSE SHE'S UP TO.— I AM ***REALLY*** GOING AFTER THAT AVERY. TRACK DOWN HER MOTHER IN EUROPE SOMEWHERE... STEP-MOM MAYBE? STAFF? DAMMIT, I WANT A DIAGNOSIS ***NOW*** SO WE CAN GET OUT OF HERE. *I* NEED TO SUCK IN AIR... NEAR A TREE-TRUNK.

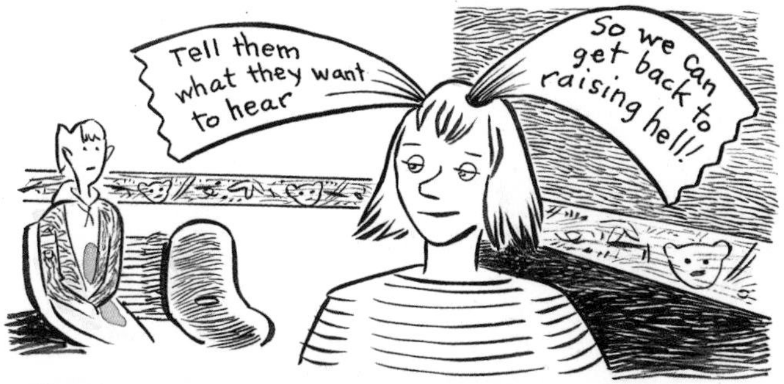
Tell them what they want to hear
So we can get back to raising hell!!

FINALLY, THE DOCTOR COMES IN. MORE TESTS NEED TO RULE OUT THIS AND THAT. WHAT'S CAUSING HER BEHAVIOR CHANGES. ORDERED A COMPLETE PSYCH EVALUATION TO FIGURE OUT THE VOICE. DEPRESSION? ANXIETY? HE CAN'T SAY. SO, SHE'S BEING ADMITTED FOR A FEW DAYS IN A 24 HOUR SECURITY WATCH UNIT DUE TO THE WINDOW INCIDENT. I'M WELCOME TO STAY....

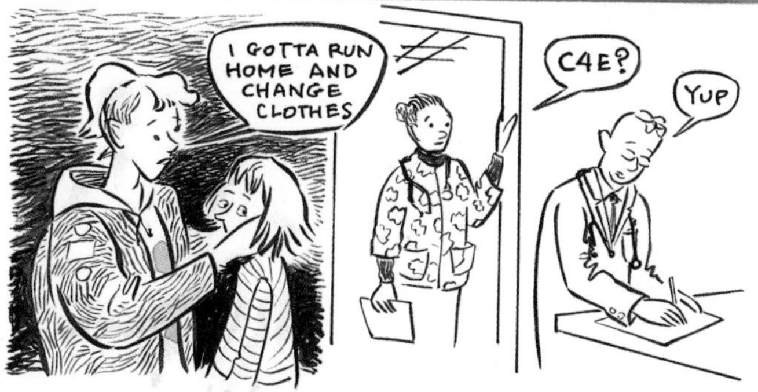
I GOTTA RUN HOME AND CHANGE CLOTHES
C4E?
YUP

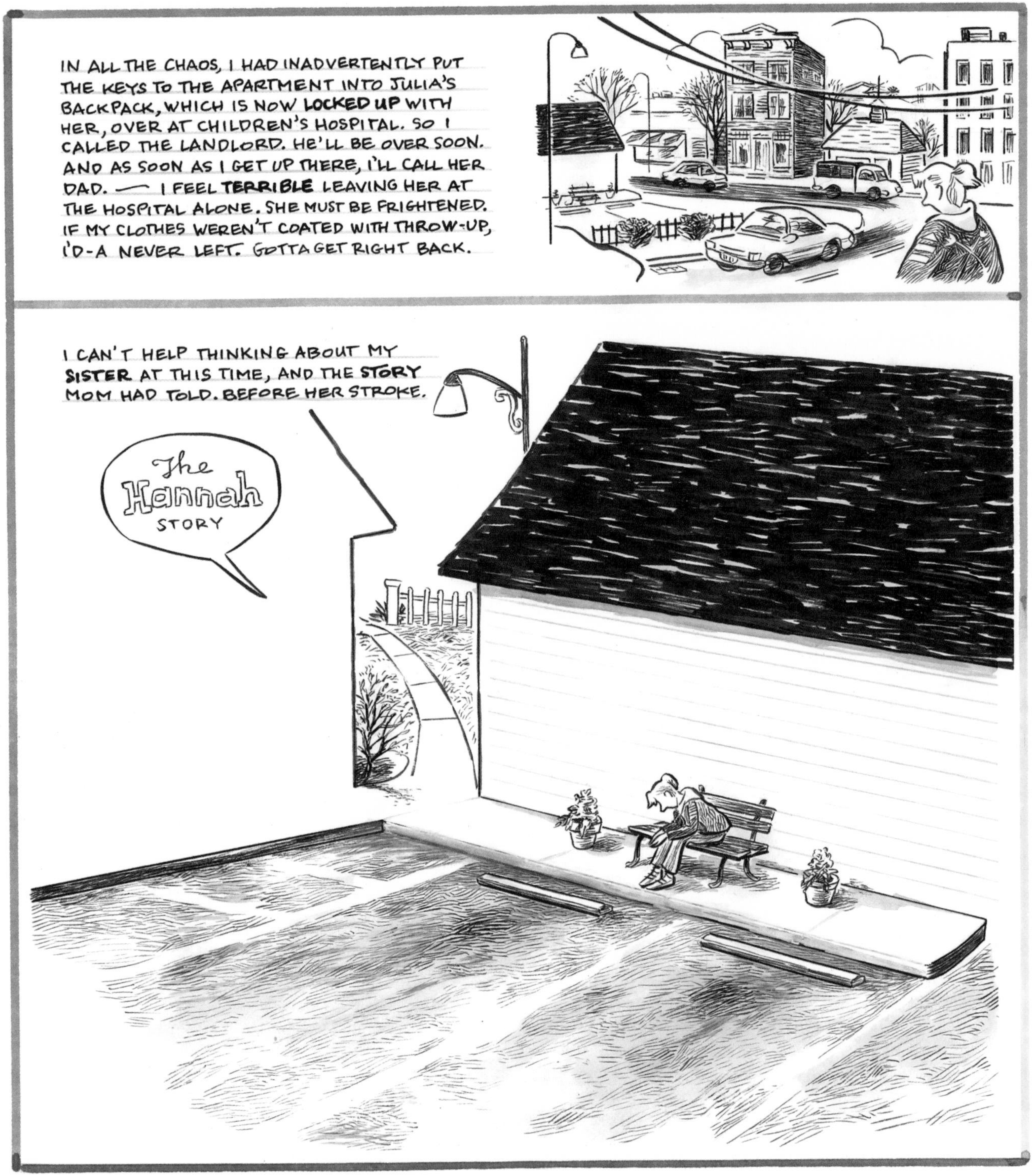
IN ALL THE CHAOS, I HAD INADVERTENTLY PUT THE KEYS TO THE APARTMENT INTO JULIA'S BACKPACK, WHICH IS NOW LOCKED UP WITH HER, OVER AT CHILDREN'S HOSPITAL. SO I CALLED THE LANDLORD. HE'LL BE OVER SOON. AND AS SOON AS I GET UP THERE, I'LL CALL HER DAD. — I FEEL TERRIBLE LEAVING HER AT THE HOSPITAL ALONE. SHE MUST BE FRIGHTENED. IF MY CLOTHES WEREN'T COATED WITH THROW-UP, I'D-A NEVER LEFT. GOTTA GET RIGHT BACK.
I CAN'T HELP THINKING ABOUT MY SISTER AT THIS TIME, AND THE STORY MOM HAD TOLD. BEFORE HER STROKE.
The Hannah STORY

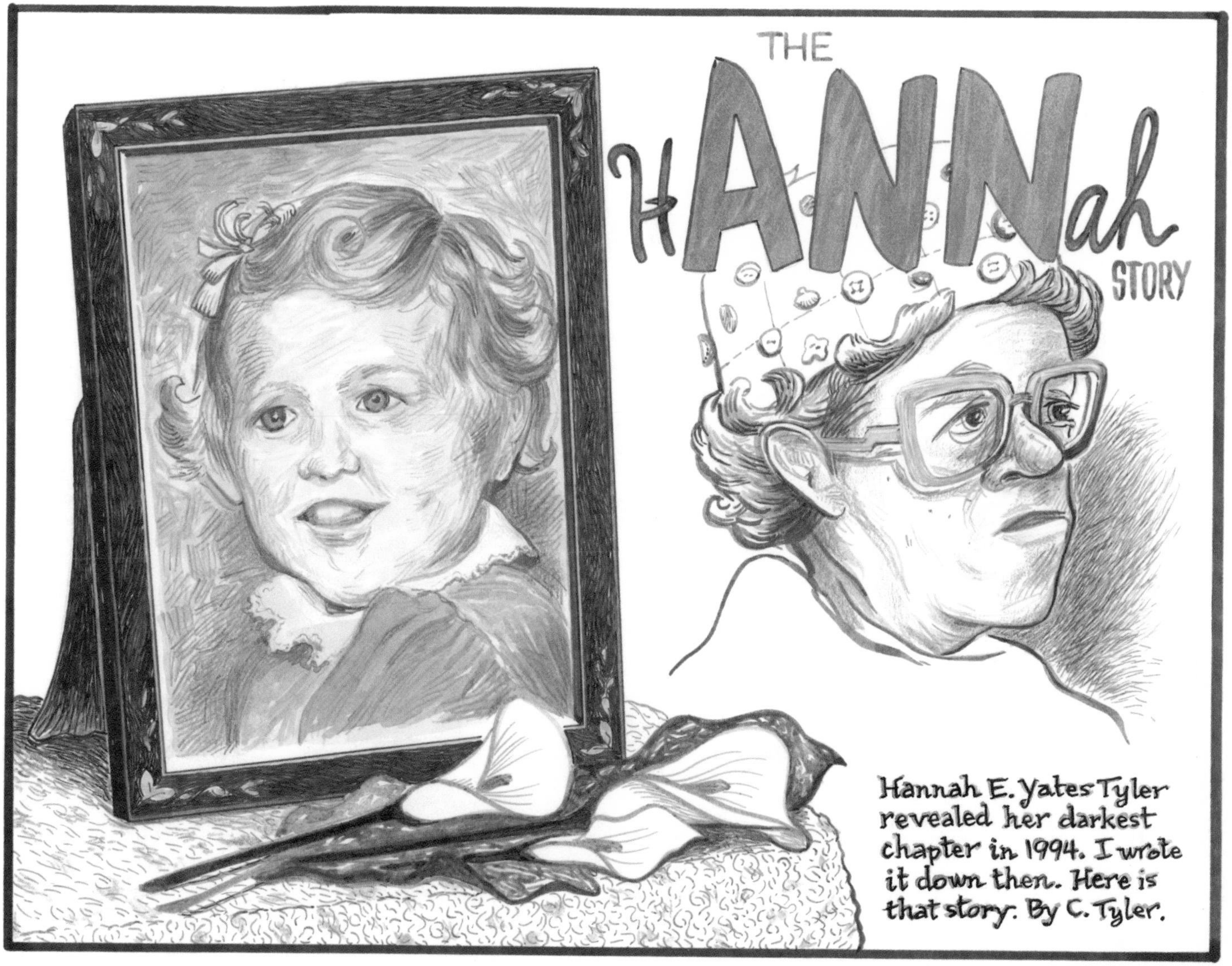
THE
HANNah
STORY
Hannah E. Yates Tyler revealed her darkest chapter in 1994. I wrote it down then. Here is that story: By C. Tyler.

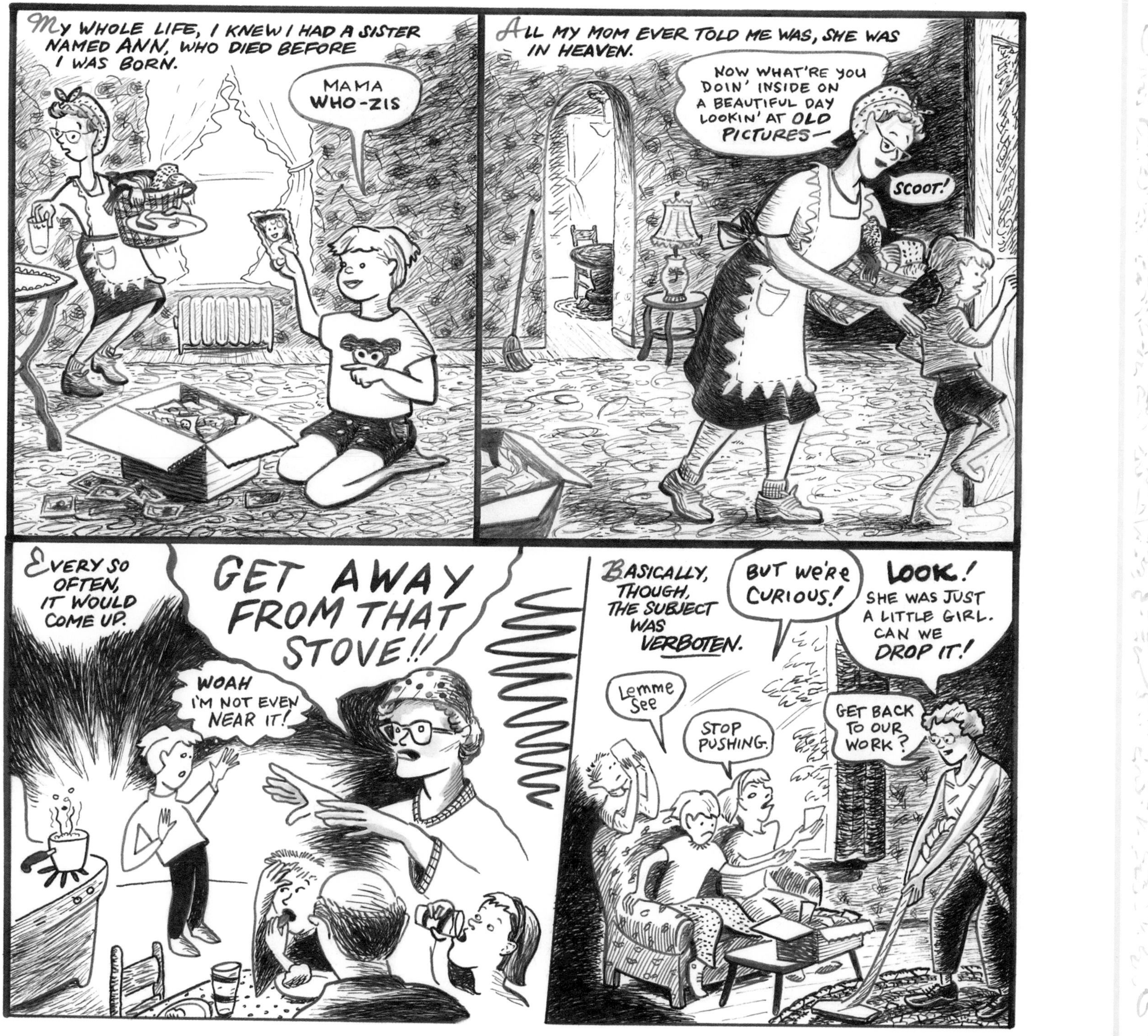
MY WHOLE LIFE, I KNEW I HAD A SISTER NAMED ANN, WHO DIED BEFORE I WAS BORN.
MAMA WHO-ZIS
ALL MY MOM EVER TOLD ME WAS, SHE WAS IN HEAVEN.
NOW WHAT'RE YOU DOIN' INSIDE ON A BEAUTIFUL DAY LOOKIN' AT OLD PICTURES—
SCOOT!
EVERY SO OFTEN, IT WOULD COME UP.
GET AWAY FROM THAT STOVE!!
WOAH I'M NOT EVEN NEAR IT!
BASICALLY, THOUGH, THE SUBJECT WAS VERBOTEN.
BUT WE'RE CURIOUS!
LOOK! SHE WAS JUST A LITTLE GIRL. CAN WE DROP IT!
Lemme See
STOP PUSHING.
GET BACK TO OUR WORK?

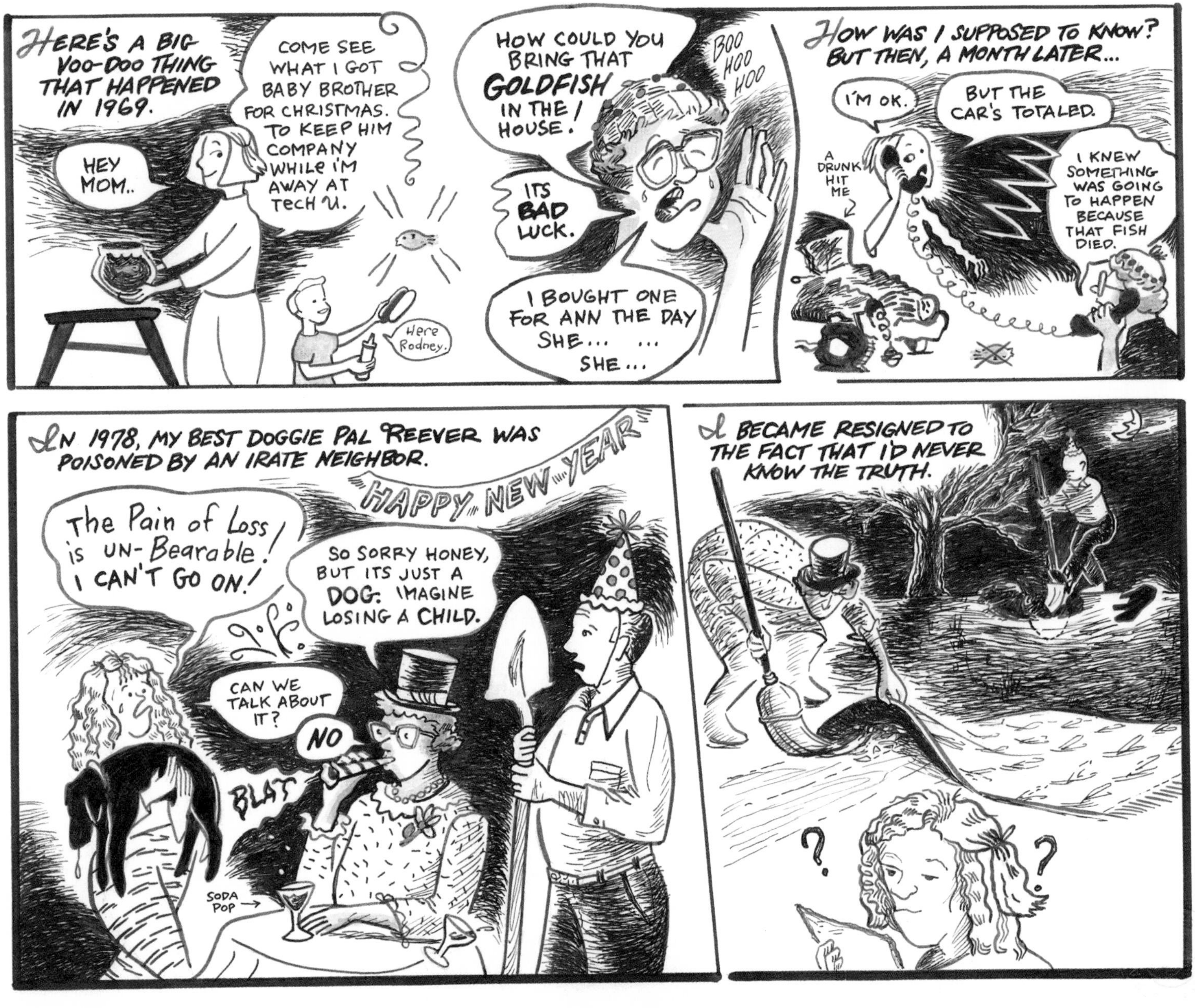

HERE'S A BIG VOO-DOO THING THAT HAPPENED IN 1969.
HEY MOM..
COME SEE WHAT I GOT BABY BROTHER FOR CHRISTMAS. TO KEEP HIM COMPANY WHILE I'M AWAY AT TECH U.
Here Rodney.
HOW COULD YOU BRING THAT GOLDFISH IN THE HOUSE.
BOO HOO HOO
ITS BAD LUCK.
I BOUGHT ONE FOR ANN THE DAY SHE... ... SHE...
HOW WAS I SUPPOSED TO KNOW? BUT THEN, A MONTH LATER...
I'M OK.
BUT THE CAR'S TOTALED.
A DRUNK HIT ME
I KNEW SOMETHING WAS GOING TO HAPPEN BECAUSE THAT FISH DIED.
IN 1978, MY BEST DOGGIE PAL REEVER WAS POISONED BY AN IRATE NEIGHBOR.
HAPPY NEW YEAR
The Pain of Loss is UN-Bearable! I CAN'T GO ON!
SO SORRY HONEY, BUT ITS JUST A DOG: IMAGINE LOSING A CHILD.
CAN WE TALK ABOUT IT?
NO
BLAT
SODA POP
I BECAME RESIGNED TO THE FACT THAT I'D NEVER KNOW THE TRUTH.
? ?

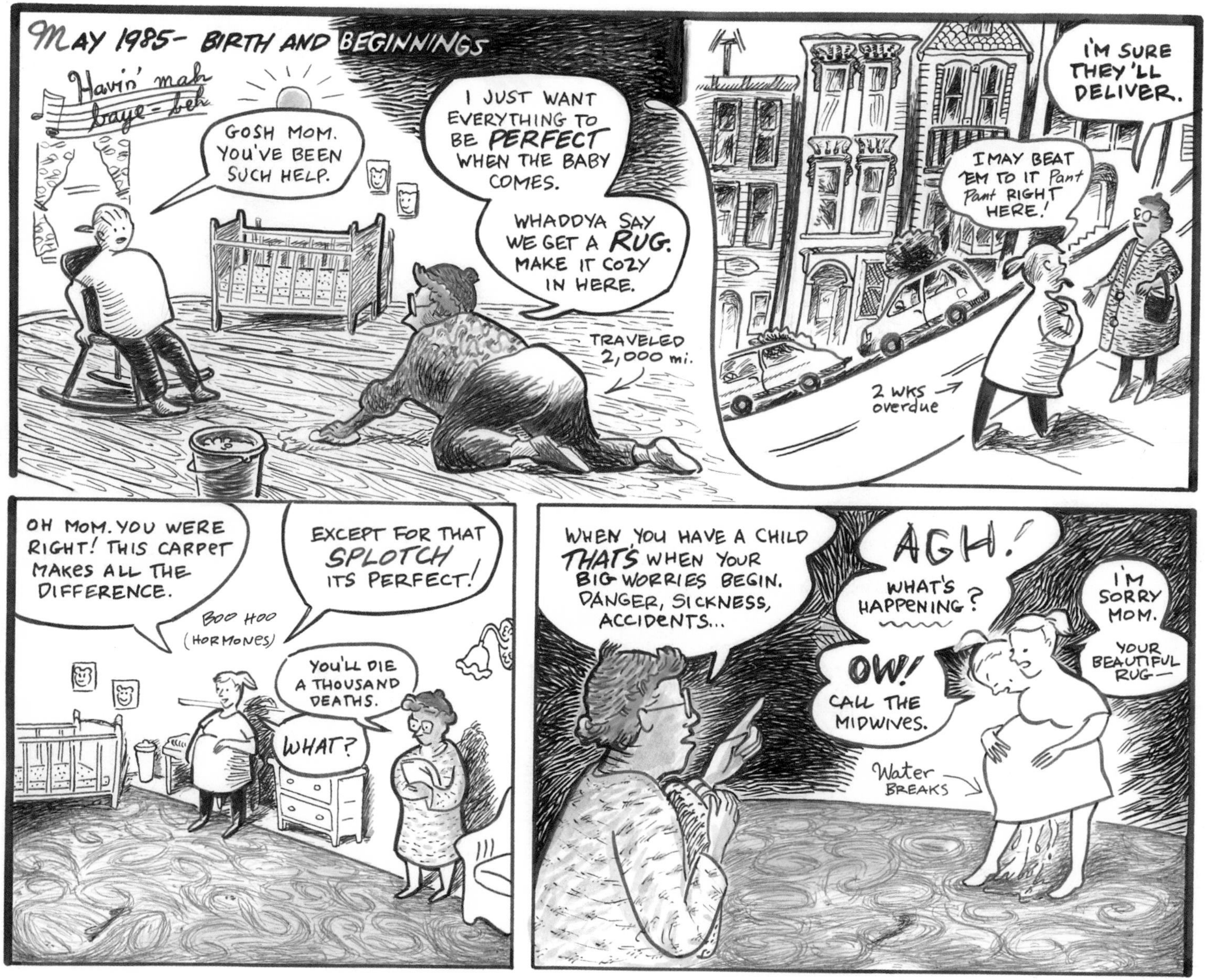
May 1985- BIRTH AND BEGINNINGS
Havin' mah baye-beh
GOSH MOM. YOU'VE BEEN SUCH HELP.
I JUST WANT EVERYTHING TO BE PERFECT WHEN THE BABY COMES.
WHADDYA SAY WE GET A RUG. MAKE IT COZY IN HERE.
TRAVELED 2,000 mi.
I'M SURE THEY'LL DELIVER.
I MAY BEAT 'EM TO IT Pant Pant RIGHT HERE!
2 WKS overdue
OH MOM. YOU WERE RIGHT! THIS CARPET MAKES ALL THE DIFFERENCE.
EXCEPT FOR THAT SPLOTCH ITS PERFECT!
BOO HOO (HORMONES)
YOU'LL DIE A THOUSAND DEATHS.
WHAT?
WHEN YOU HAVE A CHILD THAT'S WHEN YOUR BIG WORRIES BEGIN. DANGER, SICKNESS, ACCIDENTS...
AGH! WHAT'S HAPPENING?
OW! CALL THE MIDWIVES.
I'M SORRY MOM. YOUR BEAUTIFUL RUG—
Water BREAKS

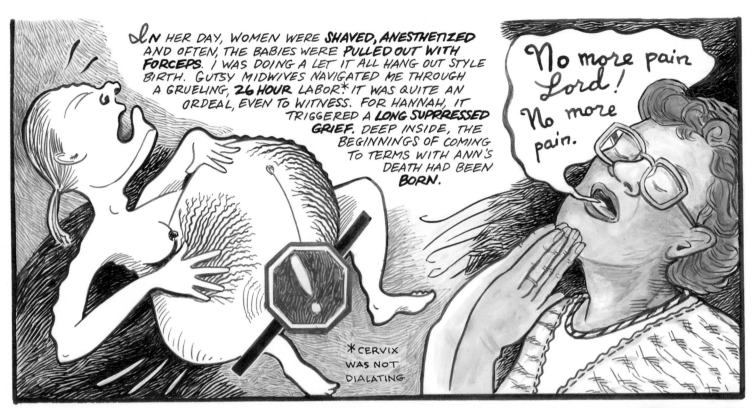

IN HER DAY, WOMEN WERE **SHAVED, ANESTHETIZED** AND OFTEN, THE BABIES WERE **PULLED OUT WITH FORCEPS**. I WAS DOING A LET IT ALL HANG OUT STYLE BIRTH. GUTSY MIDWIVES NAVIGATED ME THROUGH A GRUELING, **26 HOUR** LABOR* IT WAS QUITE AN ORDEAL, EVEN TO WITNESS. FOR HANNAH, IT TRIGGERED A **LONG SUPPRESSED GRIEF**. DEEP INSIDE, THE BEGINNINGS OF COMING TO TERMS WITH ANN'S DEATH HAD BEEN **BORN**.

*CERVIX WAS NOT DIALATING

No more pain Lord! No more pain.

THE BABY HAD STRIDOR* AND HAD TO BE WHEELED OFF TO THE NURSERY FOR OBSERVATION.

Whew! I'm exhausted! Get me a steak!

where are they taking JULIA?

SFGH

*A COMMON NEWBORN RESPIRATORY PROBLEM

HANNAH FREAKED OUT.

ALL I CAN SAY IS, IF ANYTHING HAPPENS TO MY LITTLE GIRL... I MEAN... I'LL NOT ENDURE ANOTHER **NURSERY TRAGEDY**.

OH NO YOU DON'T

ANN

?

HUH

(NURSES)

202

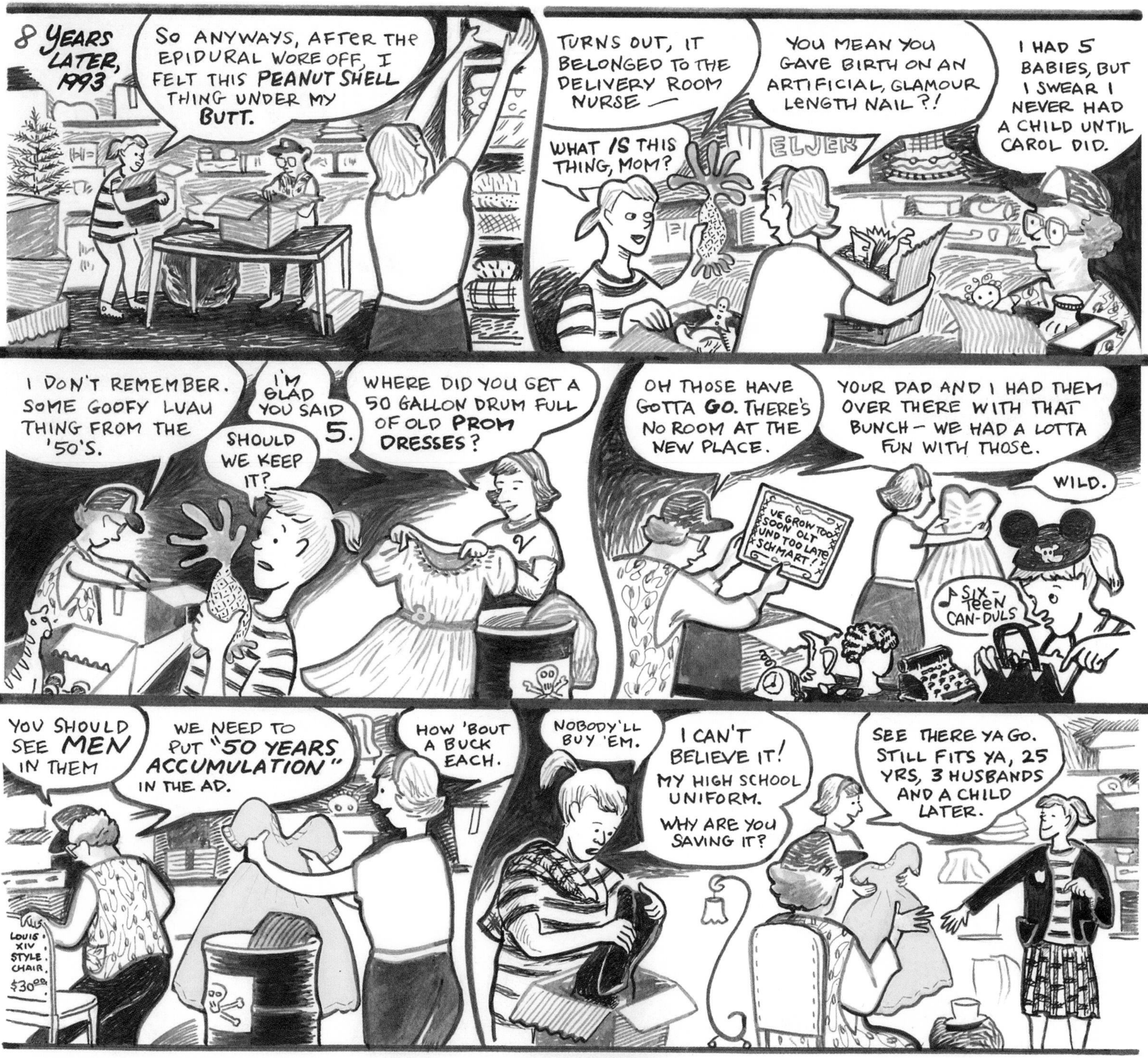

8 YEARS LATER, 1993
SO ANYWAYS, AFTER THE EPIDURAL WORE OFF, I FELT THIS PEANUT SHELL THING UNDER MY BUTT.
TURNS OUT, IT BELONGED TO THE DELIVERY ROOM NURSE —
WHAT IS THIS THING, MOM?
YOU MEAN YOU GAVE BIRTH ON AN ARTIFICIAL, GLAMOUR LENGTH NAIL?!
I HAD 5 BABIES, BUT I SWEAR I NEVER HAD A CHILD UNTIL CAROL DID.
ELJER
I DON'T REMEMBER. SOME GOOFY LUAU THING FROM THE '50'S.
I'M GLAD YOU SAID 5.
SHOULD WE KEEP IT?
WHERE DID YOU GET A 50 GALLON DRUM FULL OF OLD PROM DRESSES?
OH THOSE HAVE GOTTA GO. THERE'S NO ROOM AT THE NEW PLACE.
VE GROW TOO SOON OLT UND TOO LATE SCHMART!
YOUR DAD AND I HAD THEM OVER THERE WITH THAT BUNCH – WE HAD A LOTTA FUN WITH THOSE.
WILD.
♪ SIX-TEEN CAN-DULS
YOU SHOULD SEE MEN IN THEM
WE NEED TO PUT "50 YEARS ACCUMULATION" IN THE AD.
HOW 'BOUT A BUCK EACH.
LOUIS XIV STYLE CHAIR. $30.00
NOBODY'LL BUY 'EM.
I CAN'T BELIEVE IT! MY HIGH SCHOOL UNIFORM.
WHY ARE YOU SAVING IT?
SEE THERE YA GO. STILL FITS YA, 25 YRS, 3 HUSBANDS AND A CHILD LATER.

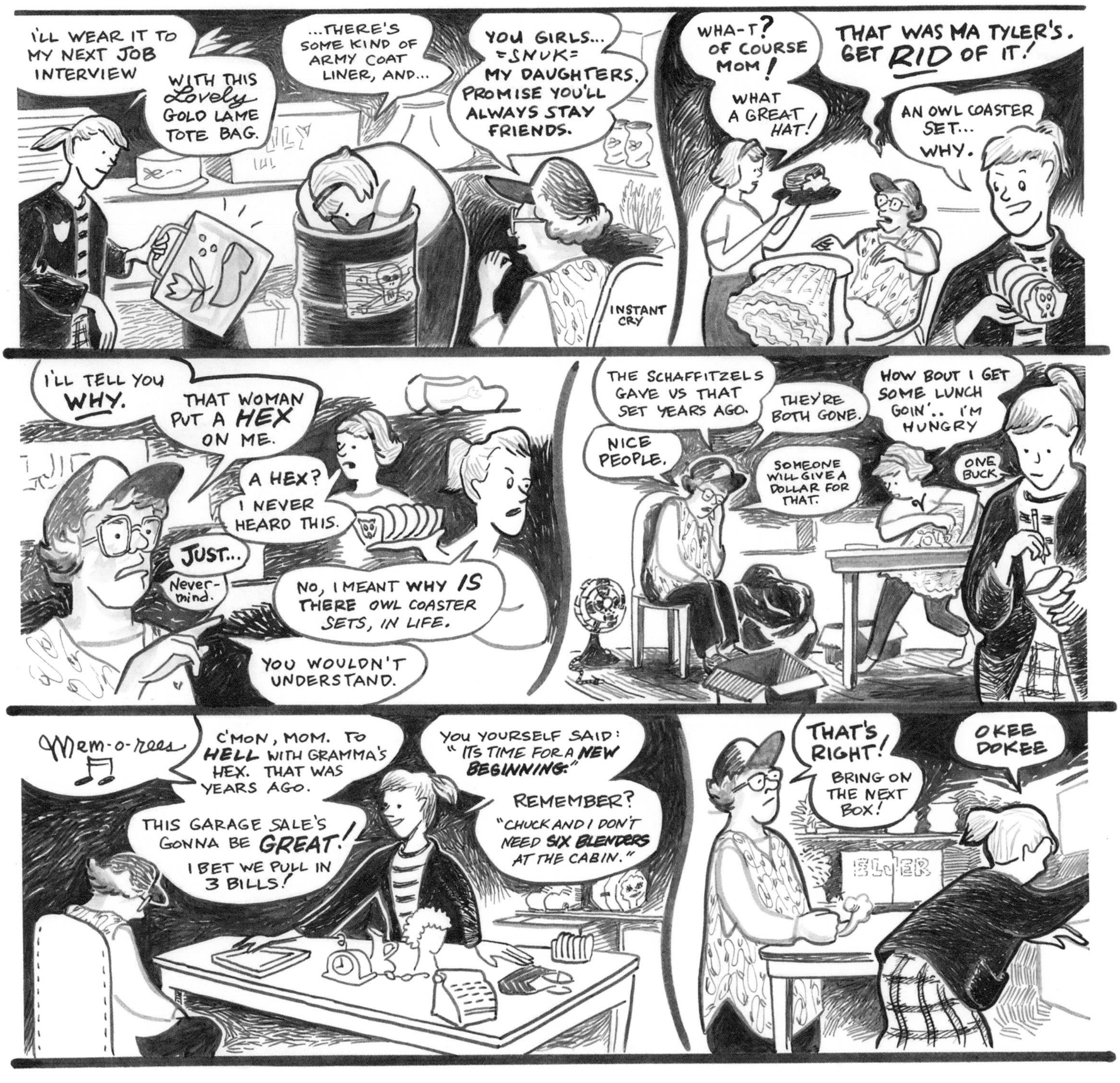
I'LL WEAR IT TO MY NEXT JOB INTERVIEW
WITH THIS Lovely GOLD LAME TOTE BAG.
...THERE'S SOME KIND OF ARMY COAT LINER, AND...
YOU GIRLS... =SNUK= MY DAUGHTERS. PROMISE YOU'LL ALWAYS STAY FRIENDS.
INSTANT CRY
WHA-T? OF COURSE MOM!
WHAT A GREAT HAT!
THAT WAS MA TYLER'S. GET RID OF IT!
AN OWL COASTER SET... WHY.
I'LL TELL YOU WHY.
THAT WOMAN PUT A HEX ON ME.
A HEX? I NEVER HEARD THIS.
JUST...
Never-mind.
NO, I MEANT WHY IS THERE OWL COASTER SETS, IN LIFE.
YOU WOULDN'T UNDERSTAND.
THE SCHAFFITZELS GAVE US THAT SET YEARS AGO.
NICE PEOPLE.
THEY'RE BOTH GONE.
SOMEONE WILL GIVE A DOLLAR FOR THAT.
HOW BOUT I GET SOME LUNCH GOIN'.. I'M HUNGRY
ONE BUCK.
Mem-o-rees
C'MON, MOM. TO HELL WITH GRAMMA'S HEX. THAT WAS YEARS AGO.
THIS GARAGE SALE'S GONNA BE GREAT! I BET WE PULL IN 3 BILLS!
YOU YOURSELF SAID: "ITS TIME FOR A NEW BEGINNING."
REMEMBER? "CHUCK AND I DON'T NEED SIX BLENDERS AT THE CABIN."
THAT'S RIGHT! BRING ON THE NEXT BOX!
OKEE DOKEE

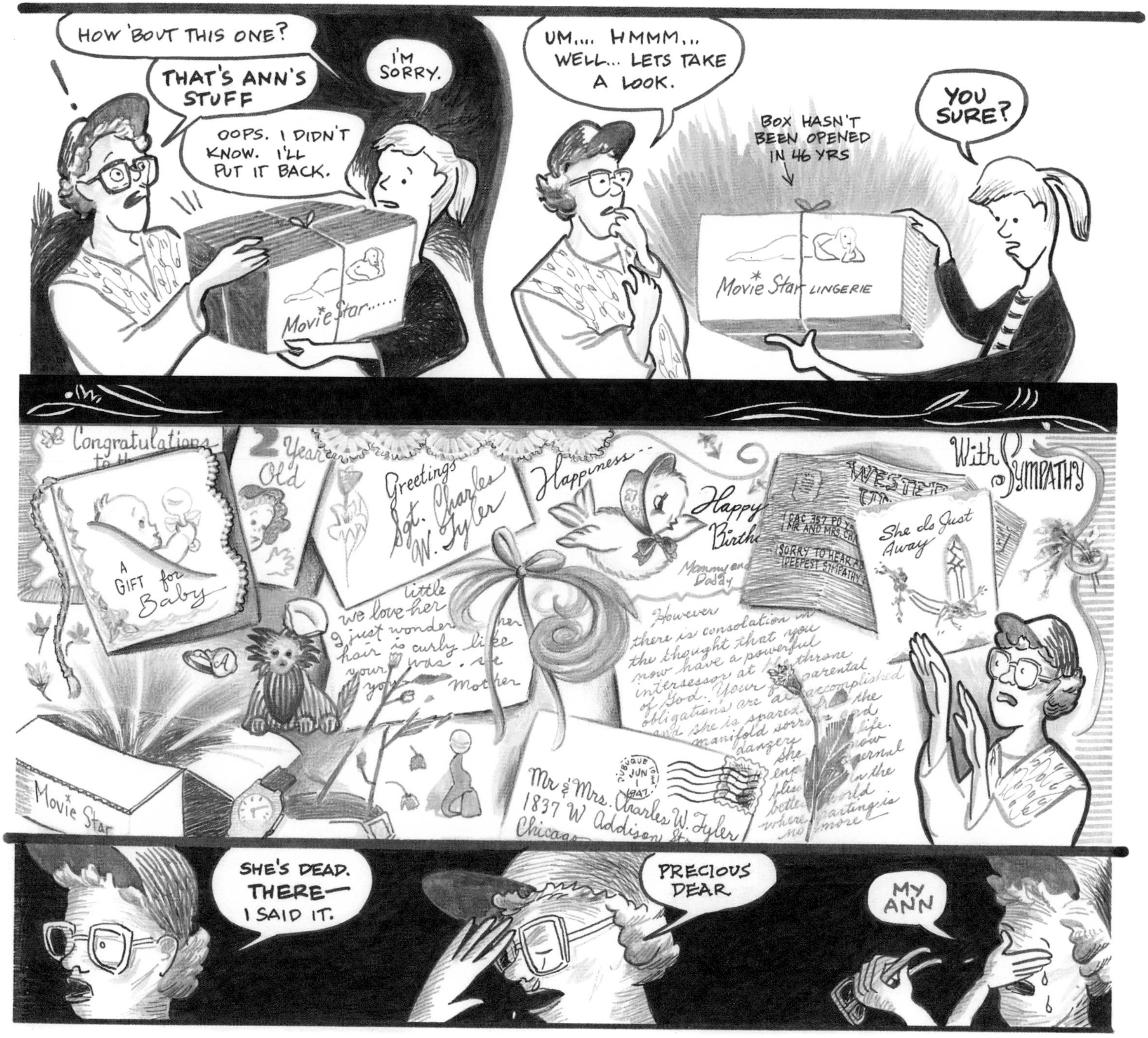

HOW 'BOUT THIS ONE?
!
THAT'S ANN'S STUFF
OOPS. I DIDN'T KNOW. I'LL PUT IT BACK.
I'M SORRY.
Movie Star......
UM.... HMMM... WELL... LETS TAKE A LOOK.
BOX HASN'T BEEN OPENED IN 46 YRS
YOU SURE?
Movie Star LINGERIE
Congratulations
A GIFT for Baby
2 Years Old
Greetings Sgt. Charles W. Tyler
Happiness...
Happy
Mommy and Daddy
With Sympathy
However there is consolation in the thought that you now have a powerful intersessor at the throne of God.
Mr & Mrs. Charles W. Tyler
1837 W Addison St.
Movie Star
SHE'S DEAD. THERE— I SAID IT.
PRECIOUS DEAR
MY ANN

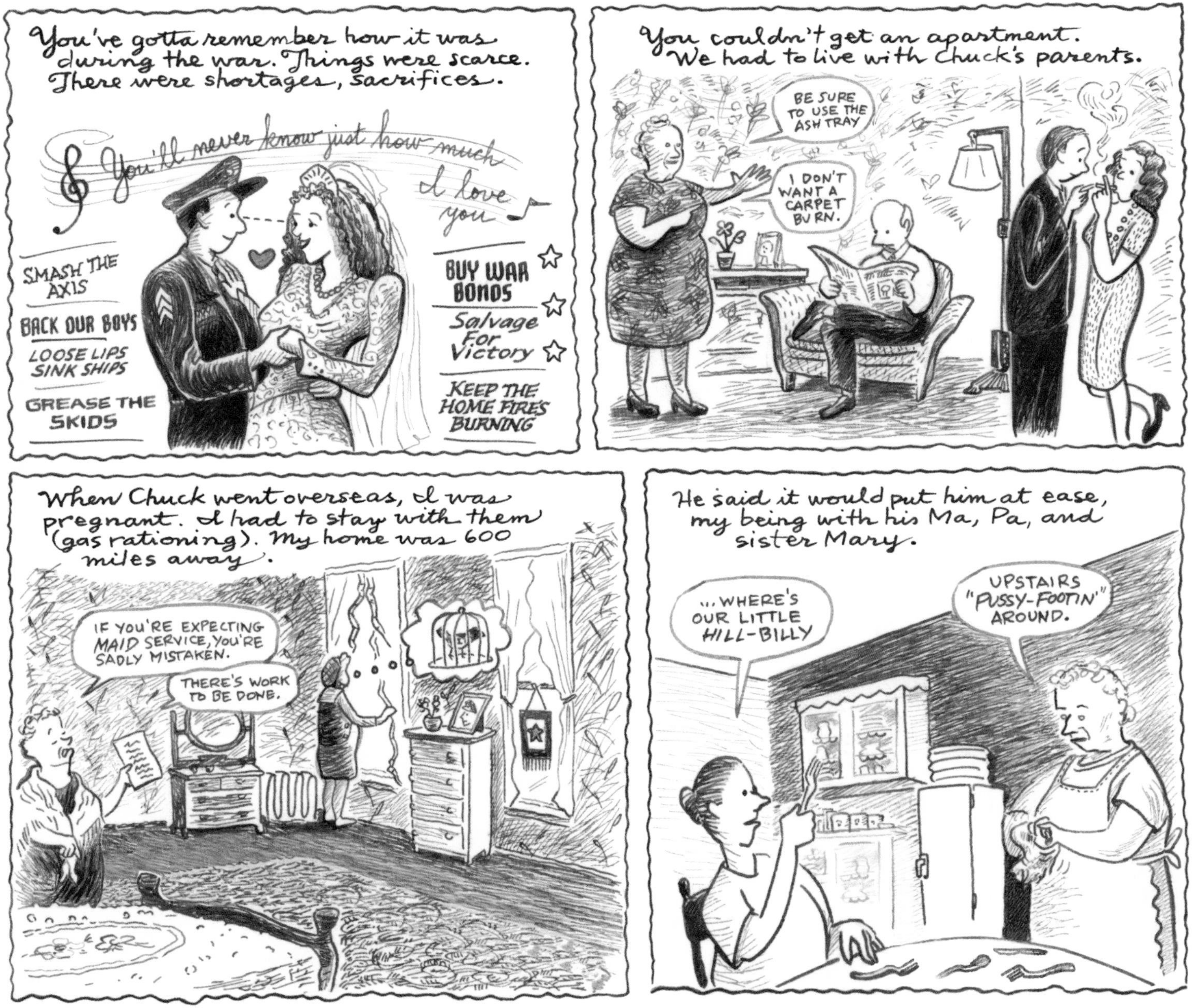
You've gotta remember how it was during the war. Things were scarce. There were shortages, sacrifices.
You'll never know just how much I love you
SMASH THE AXIS
BACK OUR BOYS
LOOSE LIPS SINK SHIPS
GREASE THE SKIDS
BUY WAR BONDS
Salvage For Victory
KEEP THE HOME FIRES BURNING
You couldn't get an apartment. We had to live with Chuck's parents.
BE SURE TO USE THE ASH TRAY
I DON'T WANT A CARPET BURN.
When Chuck went overseas, I was pregnant. I had to stay with them (gas rationing). My home was 600 miles away.
IF YOU'RE EXPECTING MAID SERVICE, YOU'RE SADLY MISTAKEN.
THERE'S WORK TO BE DONE.
He said it would put him at ease, my being with his Ma, Pa, and sister Mary.
...WHERE'S OUR LITTLE HILL-BILLY
UPSTAIRS "PUSSY-FOOTIN" AROUND.

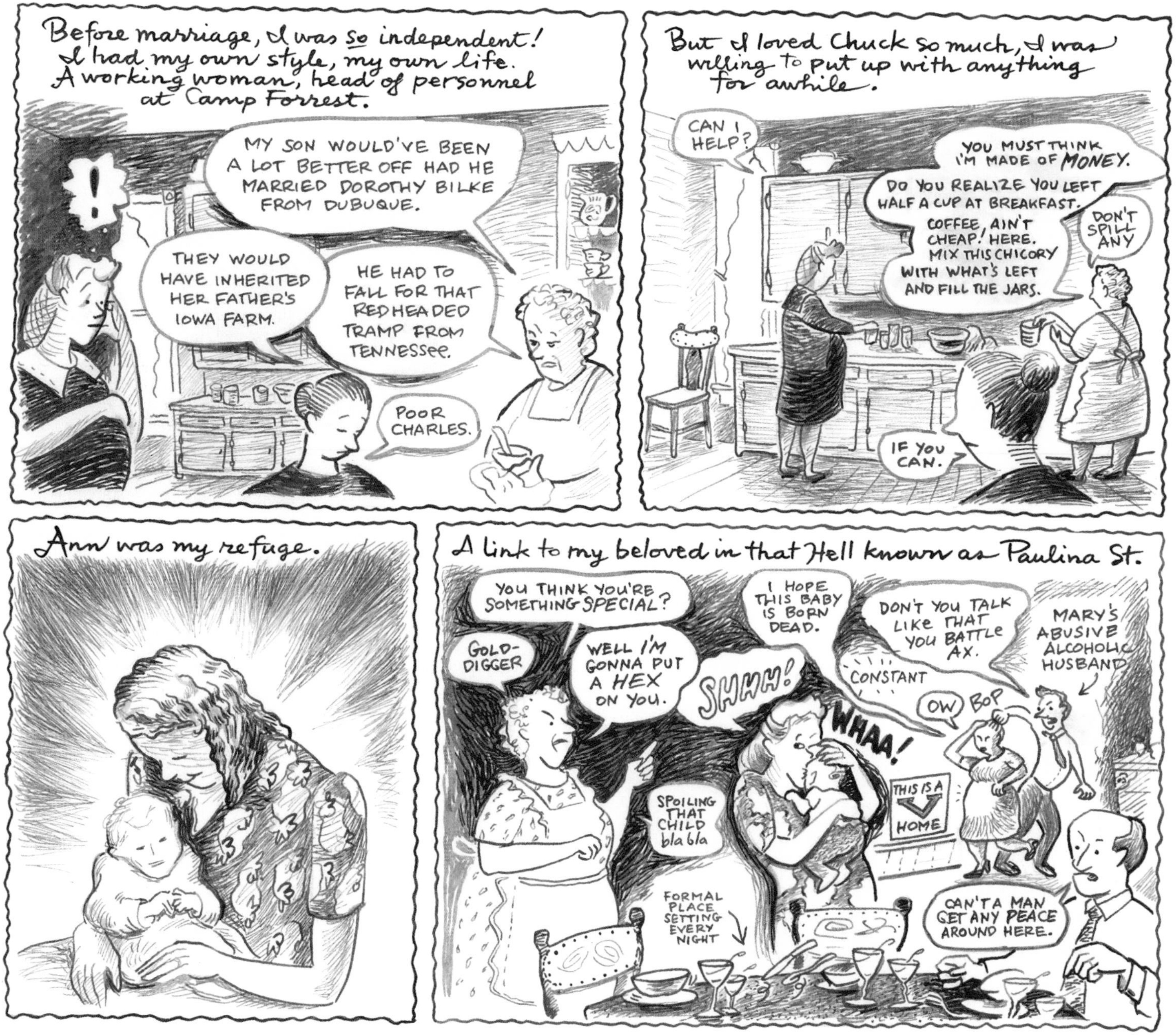
Before marriage, I was so independent! I had my own style, my own life. A working woman, head of personnel at Camp Forrest.
!
MY SON WOULD'VE BEEN A LOT BETTER OFF HAD HE MARRIED DOROTHY BILKE FROM DUBUQUE.
THEY WOULD HAVE INHERITED HER FATHER'S IOWA FARM.
HE HAD TO FALL FOR THAT REDHEADED TRAMP FROM TENNESSEE.
POOR CHARLES.
But I loved Chuck so much, I was willing to put up with anything for awhile.
CAN I HELP?
YOU MUST THINK I'M MADE OF MONEY.
DO YOU REALIZE YOU LEFT HALF A CUP AT BREAKFAST.
COFFEE, AIN'T CHEAP. HERE. MIX THIS CHICORY WITH WHAT'S LEFT AND FILL THE JARS.
DON'T SPILL ANY
IF YOU CAN.
Ann was my refuge.
A link to my beloved in that Hell known as Paulina St.
YOU THINK YOU'RE SOMETHING SPECIAL?
GOLD-DIGGER
WELL I'M GONNA PUT A HEX ON YOU.
I HOPE THIS BABY IS BORN DEAD.
SHHH!
DON'T YOU TALK LIKE THAT YOU BATTLE AX.
MARY'S ABUSIVE ALCOHOLIC HUSBAND
CONSTANT
OW
BOP
WHAA!
THIS IS A HOME
SPOILING THAT CHILD bla bla
FORMAL PLACE SETTING EVERY NIGHT
CAN'T A MAN GET ANY PEACE AROUND HERE.

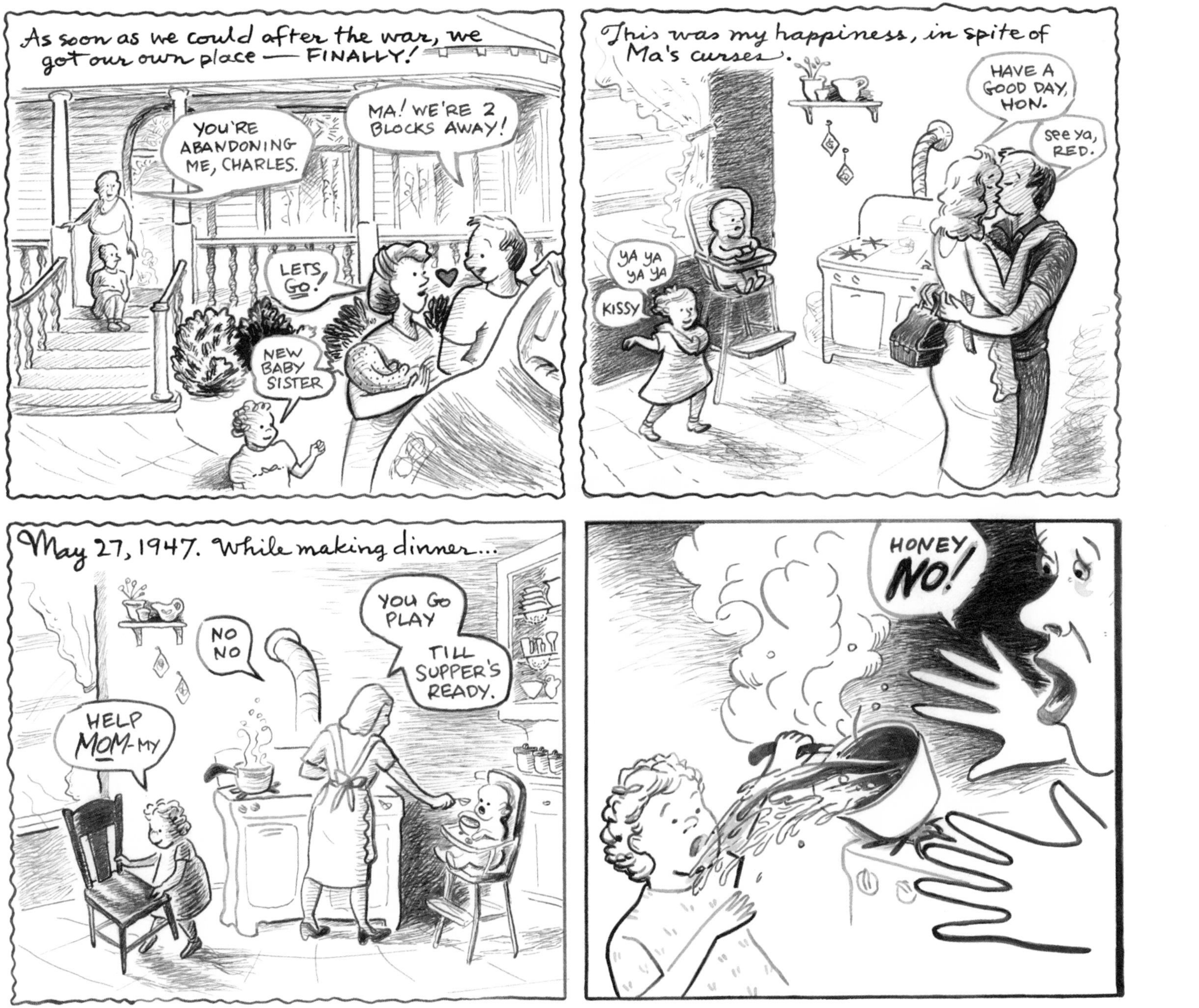
As soon as we could after the war, we got our own place — FINALLY!
YOU'RE ABANDONING ME, CHARLES.
MA! WE'RE 2 BLOCKS AWAY!
LETS GO!
NEW BABY SISTER
This was my happiness, in spite of Ma's curses.
HAVE A GOOD DAY, HON.
SEE YA, RED.
YA YA YA YA
KISSY
May 27, 1947. While making dinner...
NO NO
YOU GO PLAY
TILL SUPPER'S READY.
HELP MOM-MY
HONEY NO!

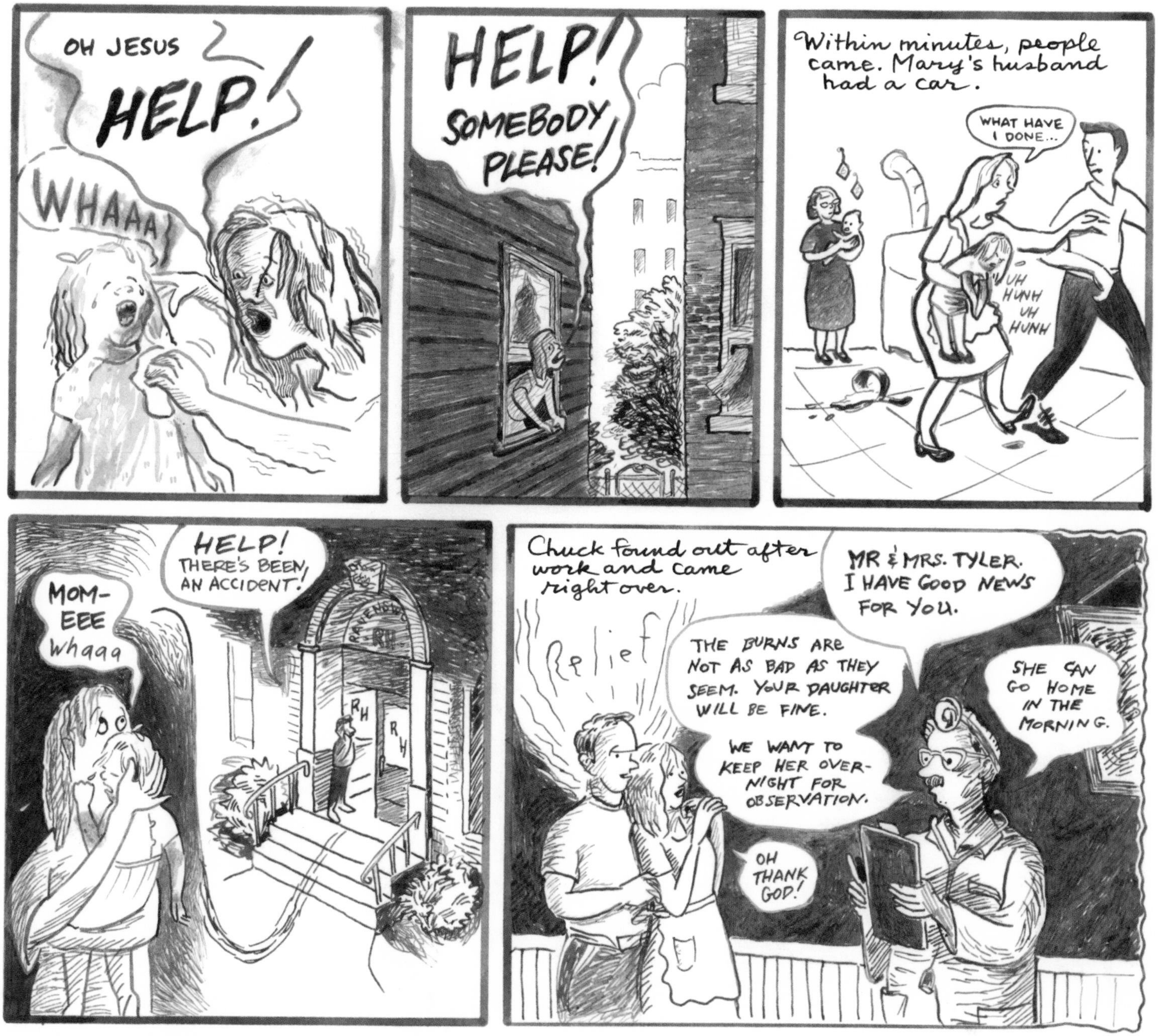
OH JESUS
HELP!
WHAAA
HELP! SOMEBODY PLEASE!
Within minutes, people came. Mary's husband had a car.
WHAT HAVE I DONE...
UH HUNH UH HUNH
MOM-EEE Whaaa
HELP! THERE'S BEEN AN ACCIDENT!
RH
RH
Chuck found out after work and came right over.
Relief
MR & MRS. TYLER. I HAVE GOOD NEWS FOR YOU.
THE BURNS ARE NOT AS BAD AS THEY SEEM. YOUR DAUGHTER WILL BE FINE.
WE WANT TO KEEP HER OVER-NIGHT FOR OBSERVATION.
SHE CAN GO HOME IN THE MORNING.
OH THANK GOD!

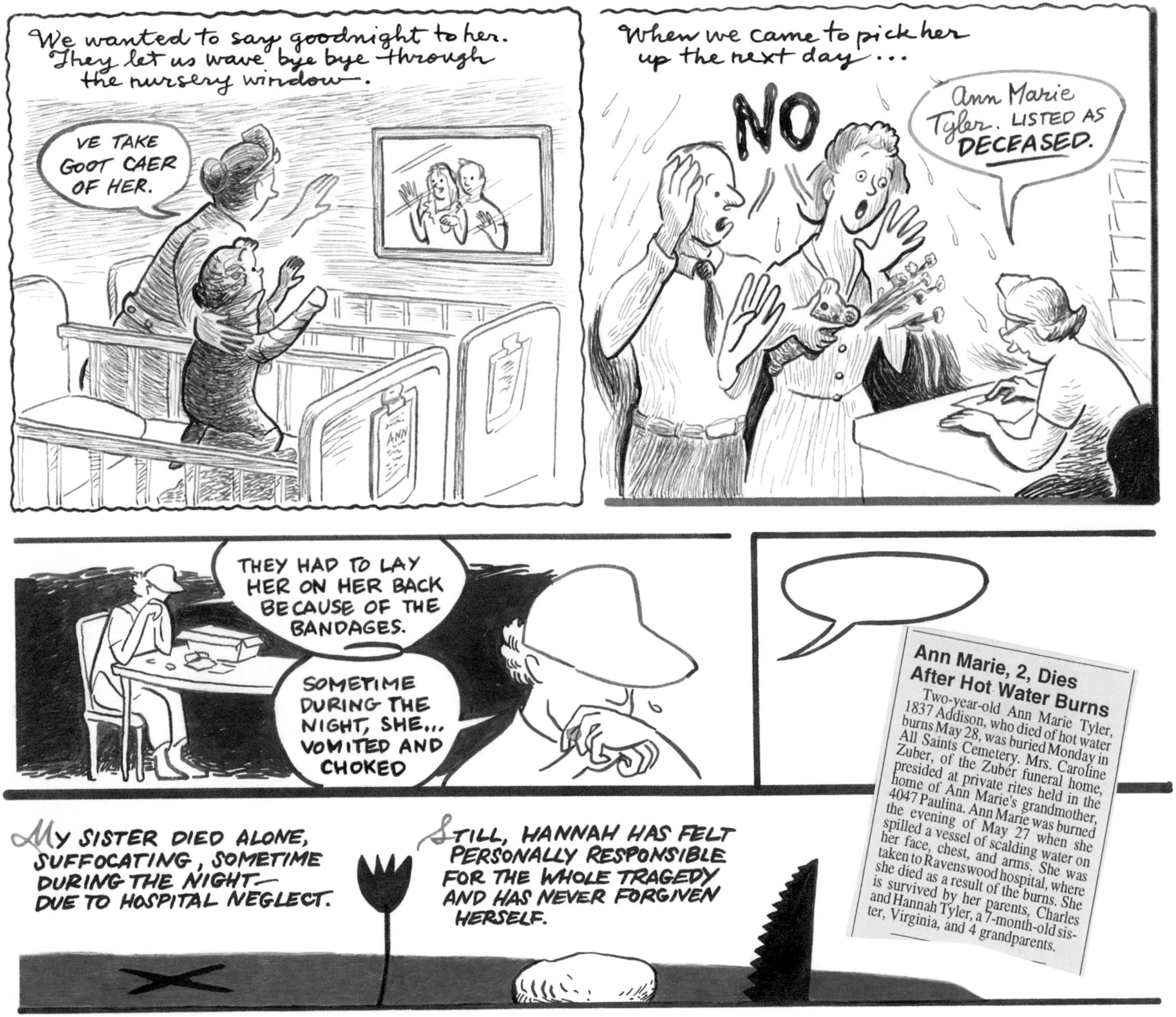
We wanted to say goodnight to her. They let us wave bye bye through the nursery window.
VE TAKE GOOT CAER OF HER.
ANN
When we came to pick her up the next day...
NO
Ann Marie Tyler. LISTED AS DECEASED.
THEY HAD TO LAY HER ON HER BACK BECAUSE OF THE BANDAGES.
SOMETIME DURING THE NIGHT, SHE... VOMITED AND CHOKED
Ann Marie, 2, Dies After Hot Water Burns
Two-year-old Ann Marie Tyler, 1837 Addison, who died of hot water burns May 28, was buried Monday in All Saints Cemetery. Mrs. Caroline Zuber, of the Zubér funeral home, presided at private rites held in the home of Ann Marie's grandmother, 4047 Paulina. Ann Marie was burned the evening of May 27 when she spilled a vessel of scalding water on her face, chest, and arms. She was taken to Ravenswood hospital, where she died as a result of the burns. She is survived by her parents, Charles and Hannah Tyler, a 7-month-old sister, Virginia, and 4 grandparents.
MY SISTER DIED ALONE, SUFFOCATING, SOMETIME DURING THE NIGHT— DUE TO HOSPITAL NEGLECT.
STILL, HANNAH HAS FELT PERSONALLY RESPONSIBLE FOR THE WHOLE TRAGEDY AND HAS NEVER FORGIVEN HERSELF.

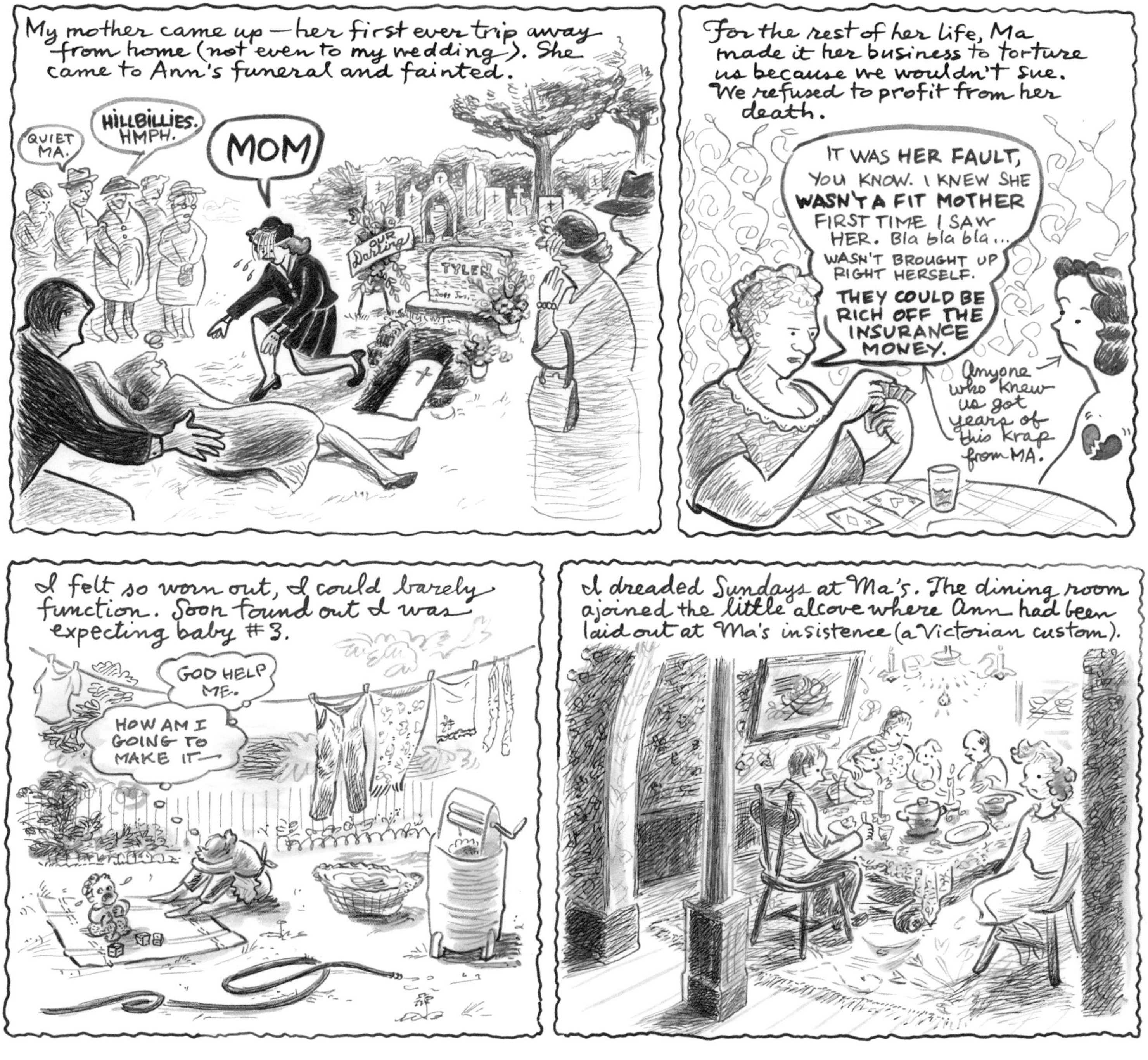
My mother came up — her first ever trip away from home (not even to my wedding). She came to Ann's funeral and fainted.
QUIET MA.
HILLBILLIES. HMPH.
MOM
OUR Darling
TYLER
For the rest of her life, Ma made it her business to torture us because we wouldn't sue. We refused to profit from her death.
IT WAS HER FAULT, YOU KNOW. I KNEW SHE WASN'T A FIT MOTHER FIRST TIME I SAW HER. Bla bla bla... WASN'T BROUGHT UP RIGHT HERSELF. THEY COULD BE RICH OFF THE INSURANCE MONEY.
Anyone who knew us got years of this Krap from MA.
I felt so worn out, I could barely function. Soon found out I was expecting baby #3.
GOD HELP ME.
HOW AM I GOING TO MAKE IT—
I dreaded Sundays at Ma's. The dining room ajoined the little alcove where Ann had been laid out at Ma's insistence (a Victorian custom).

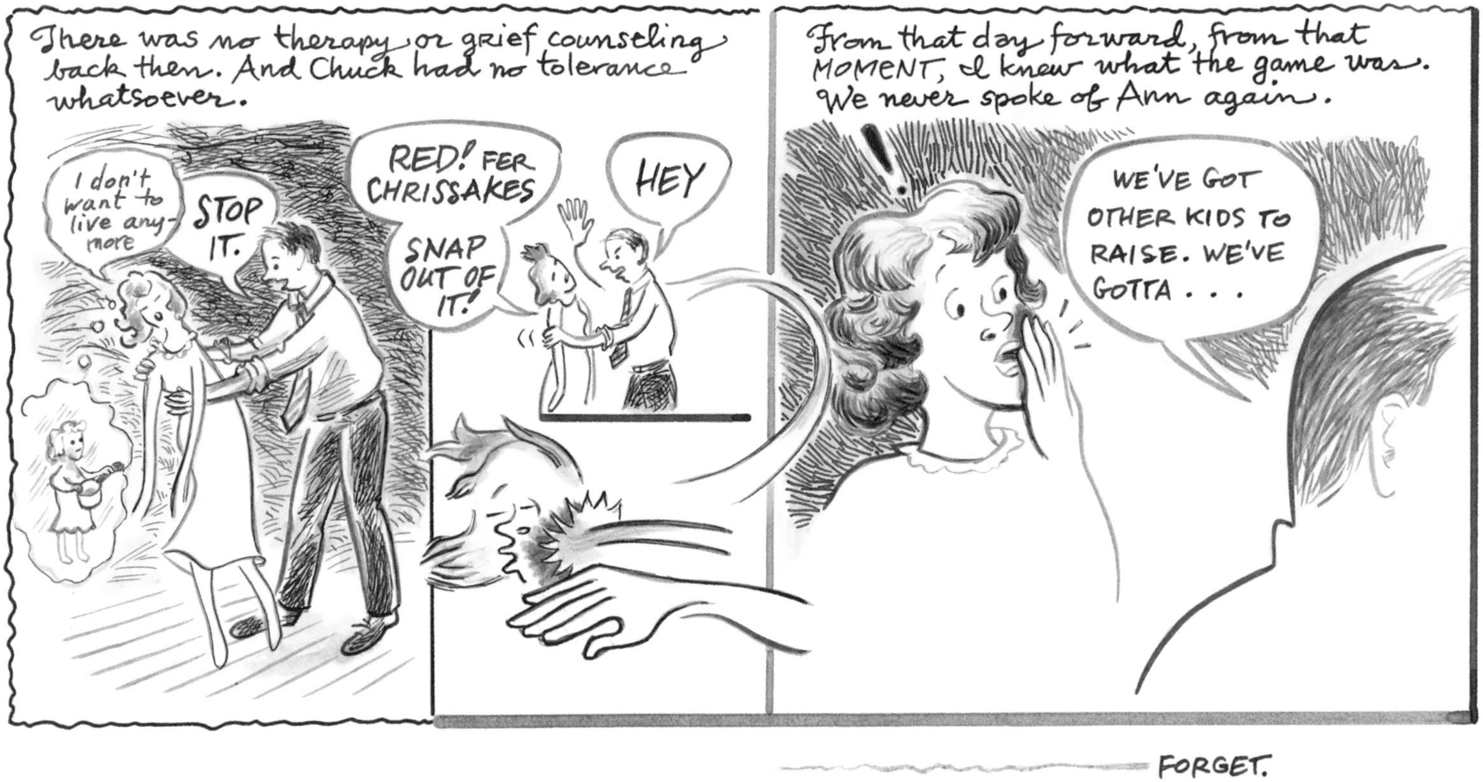
There was no therapy or grief counseling back then. And Chuck had no tolerance whatsoever.
I don't want to live any-more
STOP IT.
RED! FER CHRISSAKES
SNAP OUT OF IT!
HEY
From that day forward, from that MOMENT, I knew what the game was. We never spoke of Ann again.
WE'VE GOT OTHER KIDS TO RAISE. WE'VE GOTTA . . .
FORGET.

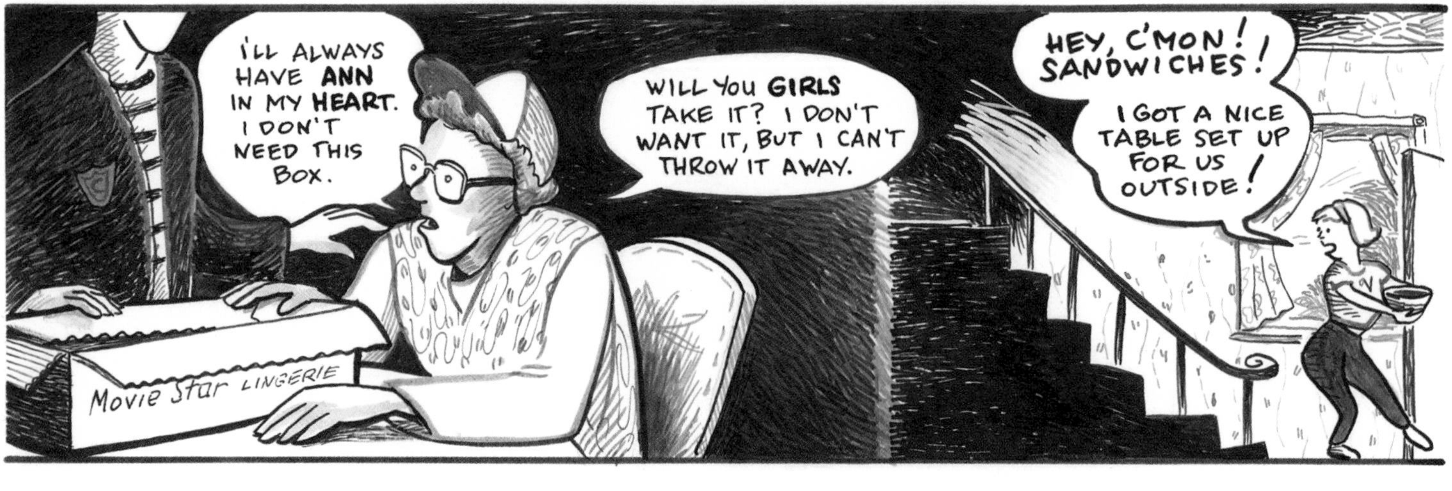
I'LL ALWAYS HAVE ANN IN MY HEART. I DON'T NEED THIS BOX.
WILL YOU GIRLS TAKE IT? I DON'T WANT IT, BUT I CAN'T THROW IT AWAY.
HEY, C'MON! SANDWICHES!
I GOT A NICE TABLE SET UP FOR US OUTSIDE!
Movie Star LINGERIE

THE BABY AND THE BATHWATER.

1945. DID I EVER TELL YOU ABOUT MY GREAT SUMMER?

I had Ann in November. As soon as spring broke, we got out of the Hell House and came home by bus.

WE'RE SURE PROUD YOU'VE COME, HANNAH

AW... GIVE HER HERE TO ME—

Tenn.

Mom took charge of Ann so I could just BE.

Peek-A-Boo
HA
HA HA

All the hometown boys had gone to war. It was peaceful -- just old men, babies women and children.

HI, MRS. HASTON.

WHY HEL-LO THERE, HANNAH. I HEARD YOU WUZ BACK.

Farm Feed

HOW'S VOLLIE BELLE?

SHE'S JUST FINE.

SHE'S DYIN' T' SEE YA

YOUR BABY'S SO SWEET!

SHE FAVORS YOU, HANNAH.

HAVE YOU MET M' GRANDSON?

COME EAT DINNER WITH US SUNDEE.

AW-RAHT

213

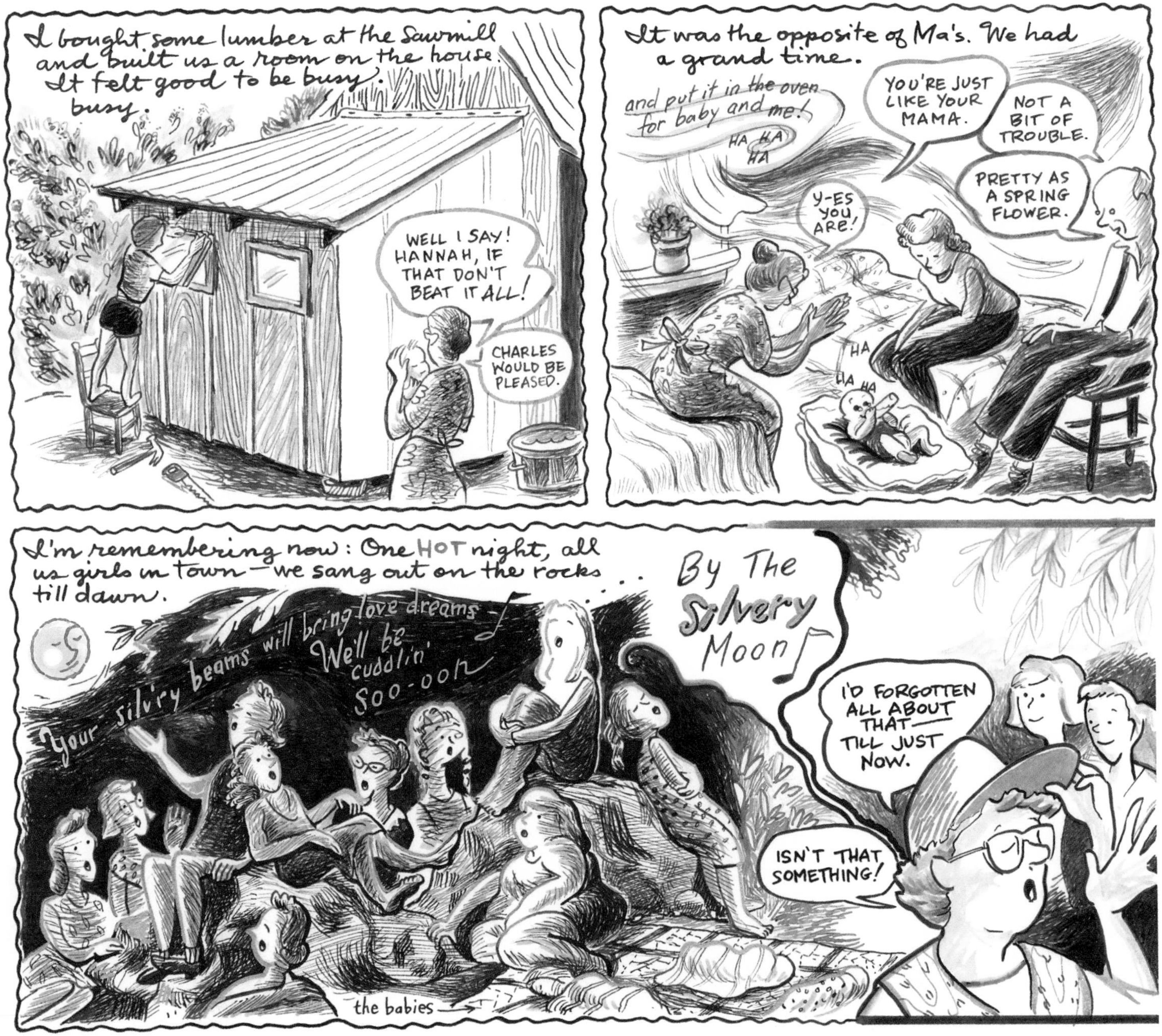

I bought some lumber at the sawmill and built us a room on the house. It felt good to be busy
busy.
WELL I SAY! HANNAH, IF THAT DON'T BEAT IT ALL!
CHARLES WOULD BE PLEASED.
It was the opposite of Ma's. We had a grand time.
and put it in the oven for baby and me!
HA HA HA
YOU'RE JUST LIKE YOUR MAMA.
NOT A BIT OF TROUBLE.
Y-ES YOU ARE!
PRETTY AS A SPRING FLOWER.
HA
HA HA
I'm remembering now: One HOT night, all us girls in town — we sang out on the rocks till dawn. . .
By The Silvery Moon
Your silvery beams will bring love dreams
We'll be cuddlin' Soo-oon
I'D FORGOTTEN ALL ABOUT THAT — TILL JUST NOW.
ISN'T THAT SOMETHING!
the babies

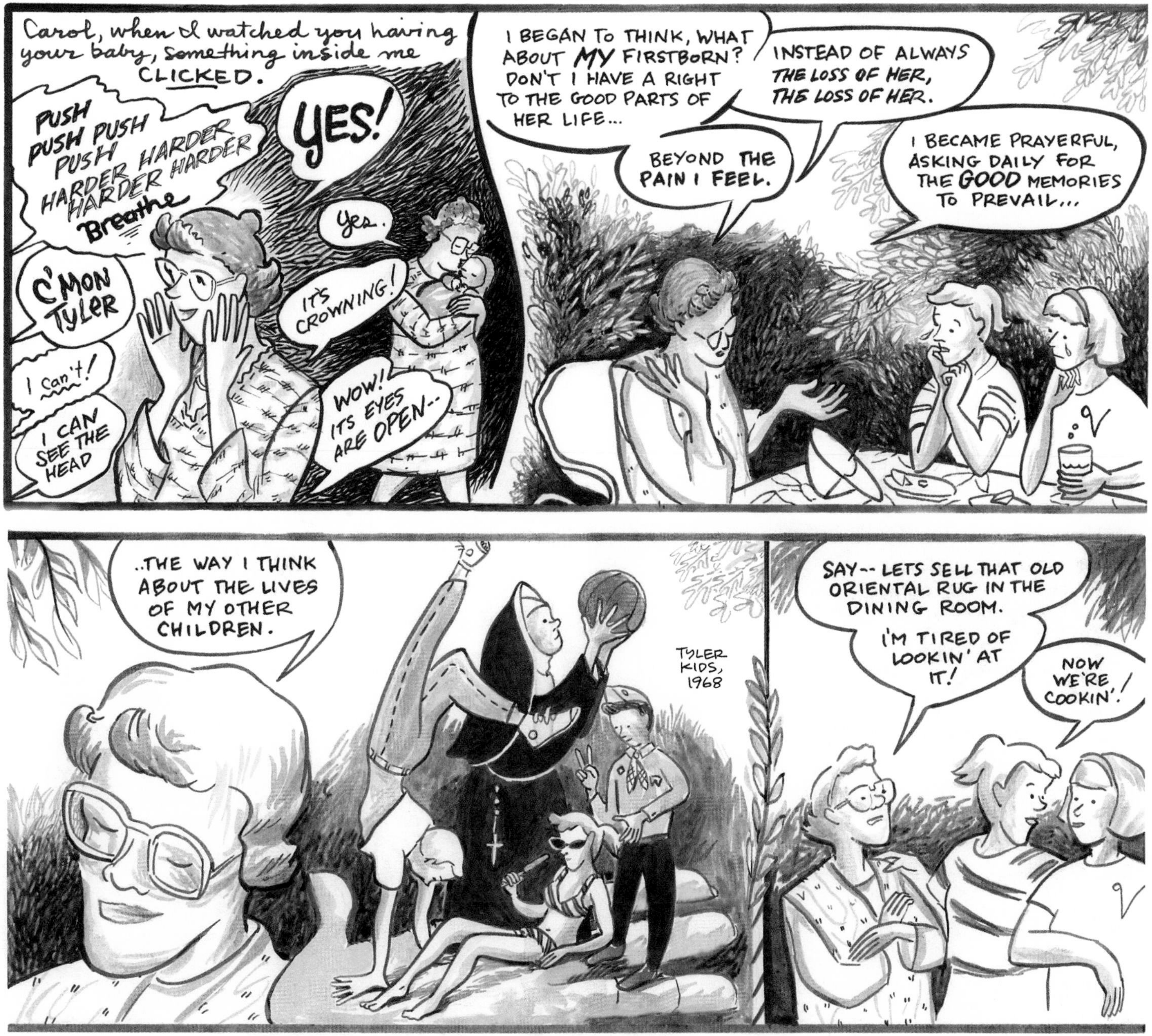
Carol, when I watched you having your baby, something inside me CLICKED.
PUSH PUSH PUSH PUSH HARDER HARDER HARDER HARDER Breathe
YES!
Yes.
C'MON TYLER
IT'S CROWNING!
I can't!
I CAN SEE THE HEAD
WOW! ITS EYES ARE OPEN--
I BEGAN TO THINK, WHAT ABOUT MY FIRSTBORN? DON'T I HAVE A RIGHT TO THE GOOD PARTS OF HER LIFE...
INSTEAD OF ALWAYS THE LOSS OF HER, THE LOSS OF HER.
BEYOND THE PAIN I FEEL.
I BECAME PRAYERFUL, ASKING DAILY FOR THE GOOD MEMORIES TO PREVAIL...
..THE WAY I THINK ABOUT THE LIVES OF MY OTHER CHILDREN.
TYLER KIDS, 1968
SAY-- LETS SELL THAT OLD ORIENTAL RUG IN THE DINING ROOM.
I'M TIRED OF LOOKIN' AT IT!
NOW WE'RE COOKIN'!

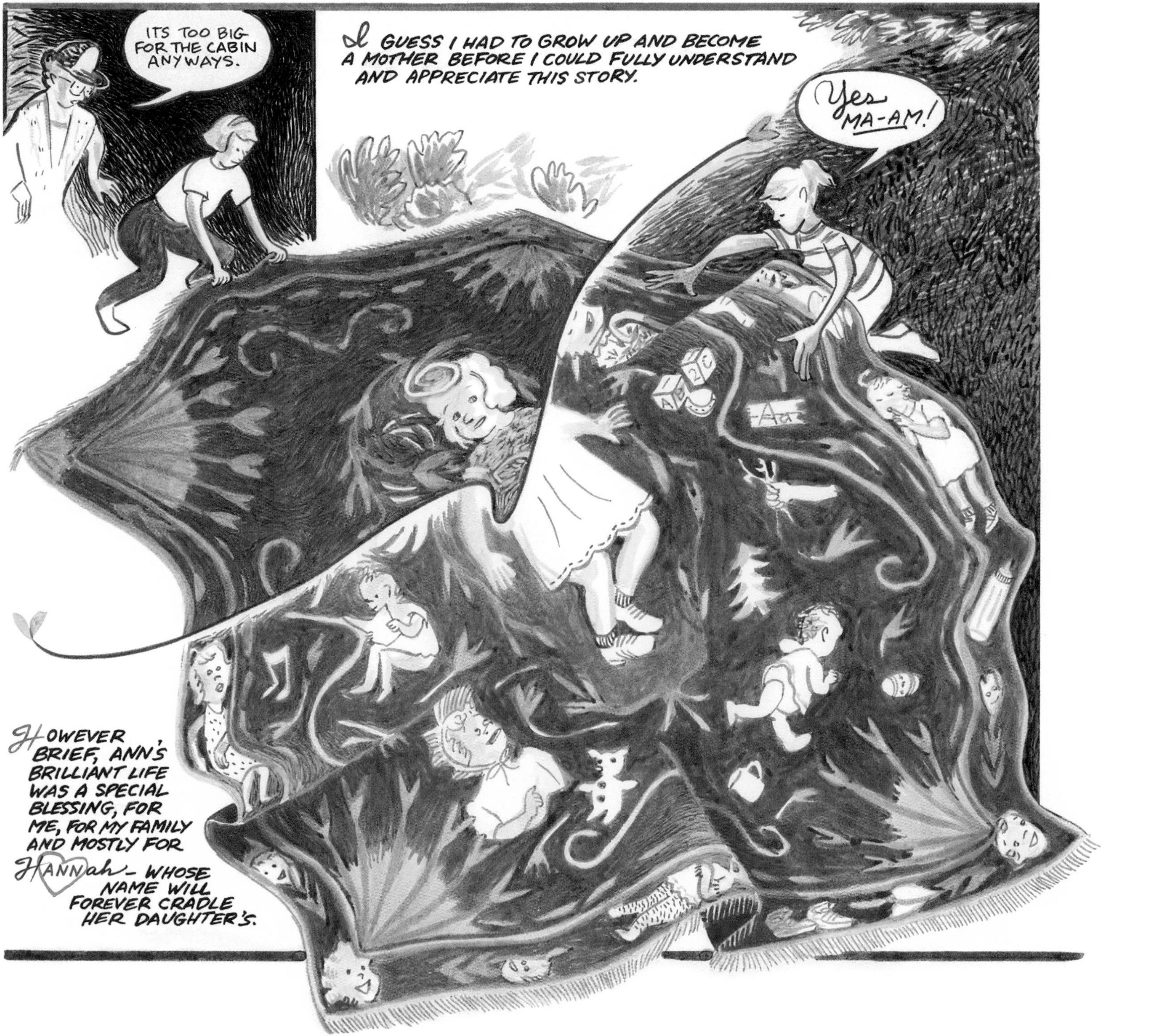
ITS TOO BIG FOR THE CABIN ANYWAYS.
I GUESS I HAD TO GROW UP AND BECOME A MOTHER BEFORE I COULD FULLY UNDERSTAND AND APPRECIATE THIS STORY.
Yes MA-AM!
HOWEVER BRIEF, ANN'S BRILLIANT LIFE WAS A SPECIAL BLESSING, FOR ME, FOR MY FAMILY AND MOSTLY FOR HANNAH- WHOSE NAME WILL FOREVER CRADLE HER DAUGHTER'S.

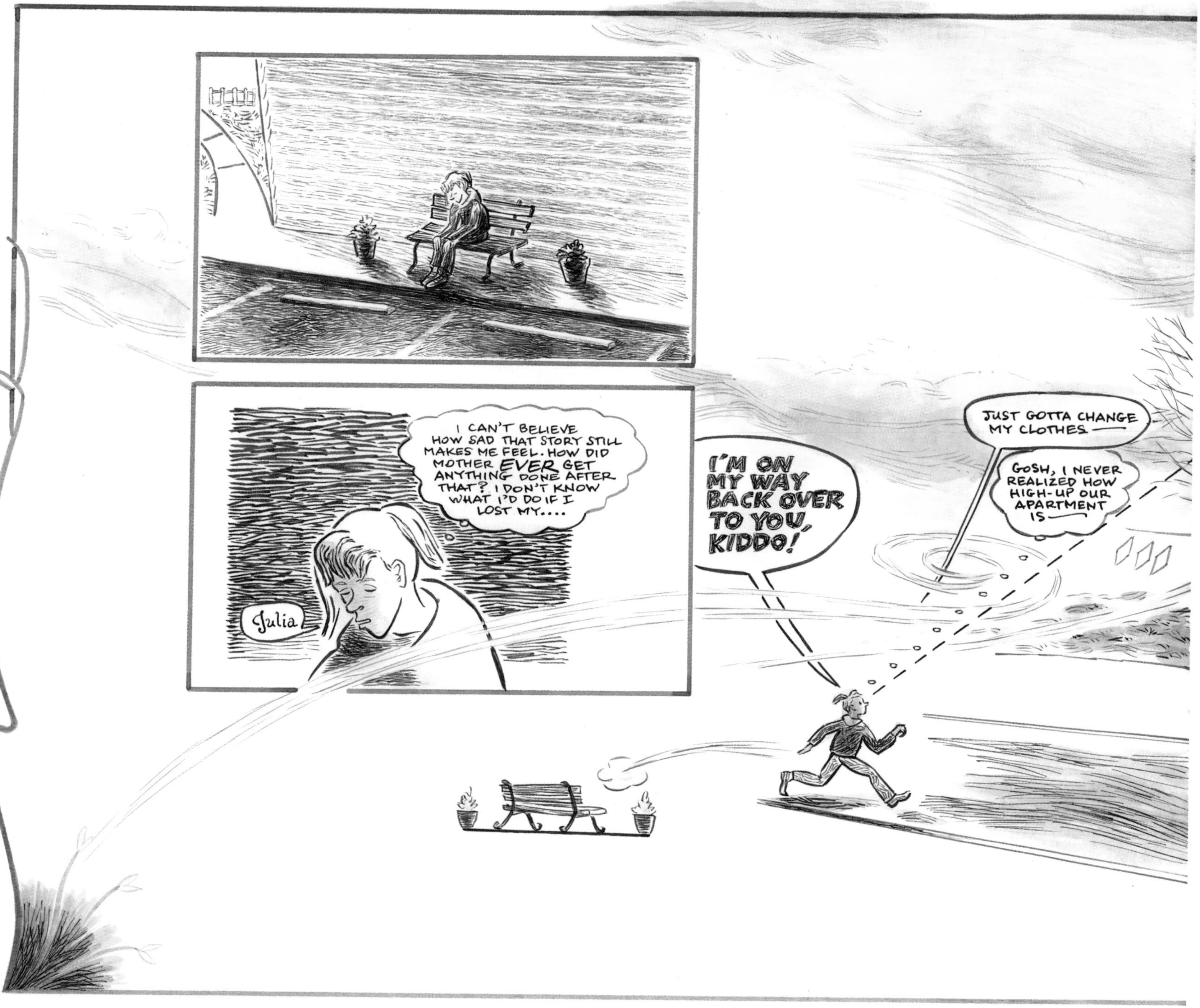
I CAN'T BELIEVE HOW SAD THAT STORY STILL MAKES ME FEEL. HOW DID MOTHER EVER GET ANYTHING DONE AFTER THAT? I DON'T KNOW WHAT I'D DO IF I LOST MY....
Julia
I'M ON MY WAY BACK OVER TO YOU, KIDDO!
JUST GOTTA CHANGE MY CLOTHES—
GOSH, I NEVER REALIZED HOW HIGH-UP OUR APARTMENT IS—

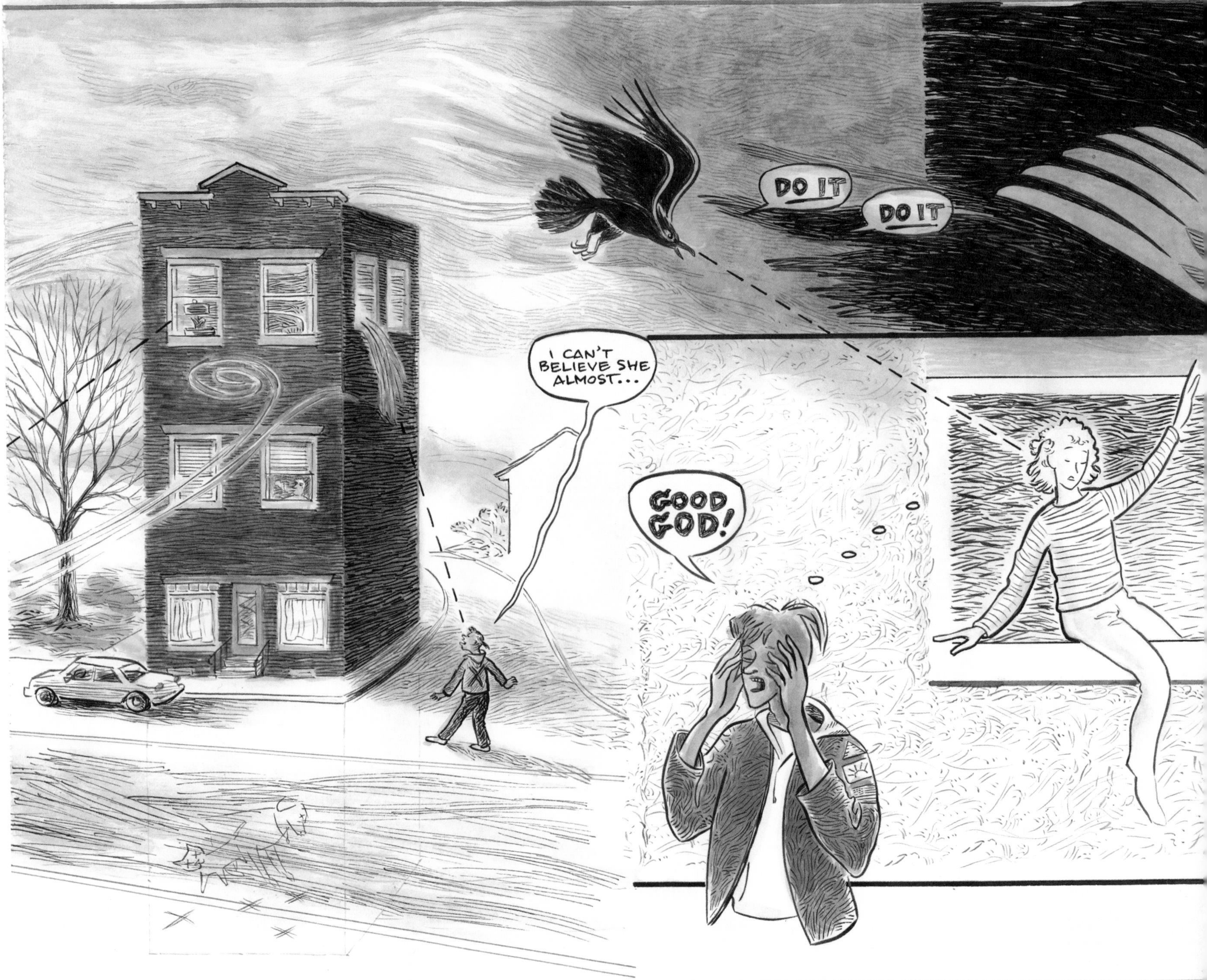
DO IT
DO IT
I CAN'T BELIEVE SHE ALMOST...
GOOD GOD!

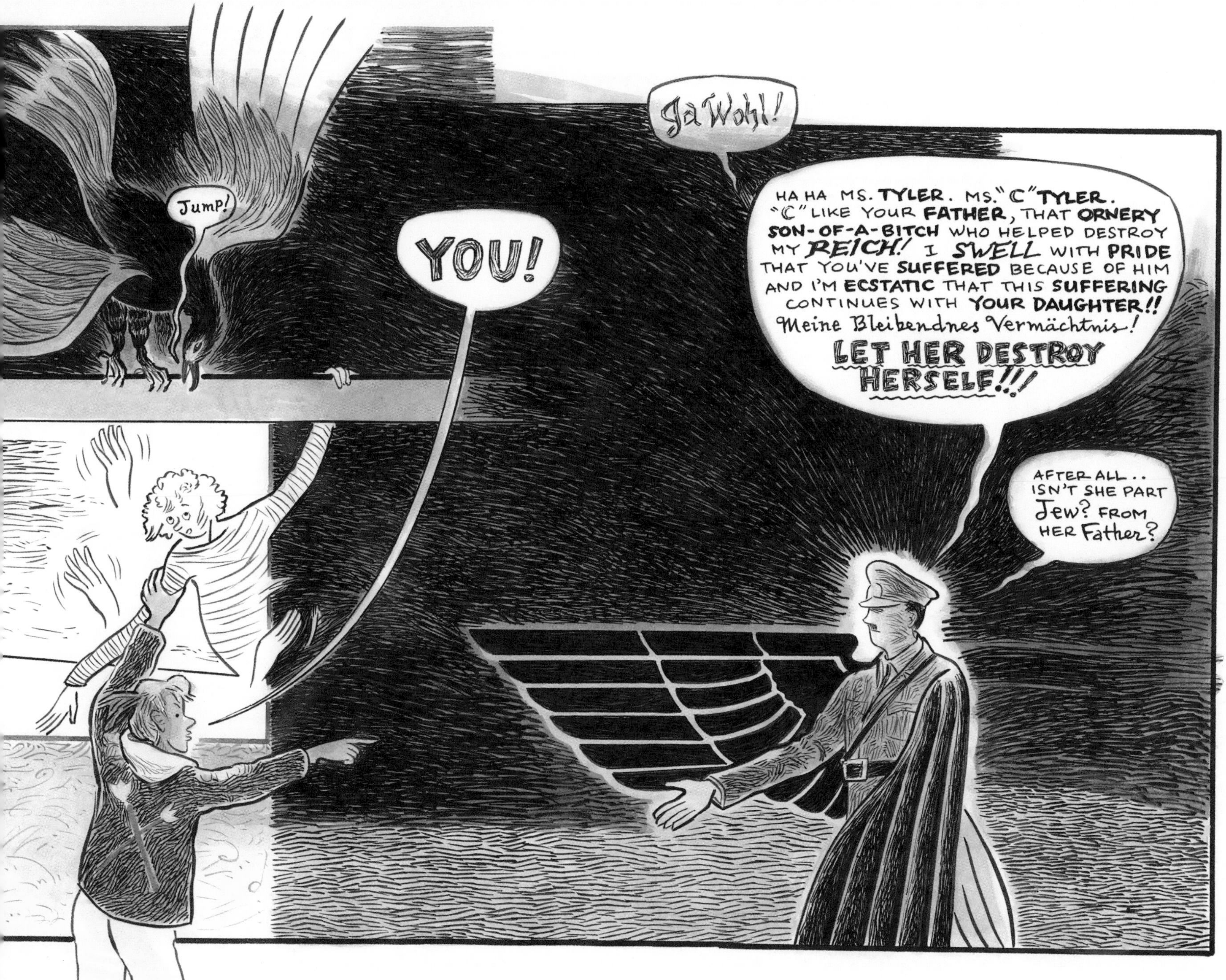
JUMP!
YOU!
Ja Wohl!
HA HA MS. TYLER. MS. "C" TYLER. "C" LIKE YOUR FATHER, THAT ORNERY SON-OF-A-BITCH WHO HELPED DESTROY MY REICH! I SWELL WITH PRIDE THAT YOU'VE SUFFERED BECAUSE OF HIM AND I'M ECSTATIC THAT THIS SUFFERING CONTINUES WITH YOUR DAUGHTER!! Meine Bleibendnes Vermächtnis! LET HER DESTROY HERSELF!!!
AFTER ALL.. ISN'T SHE PART Jew? FROM HER Father?

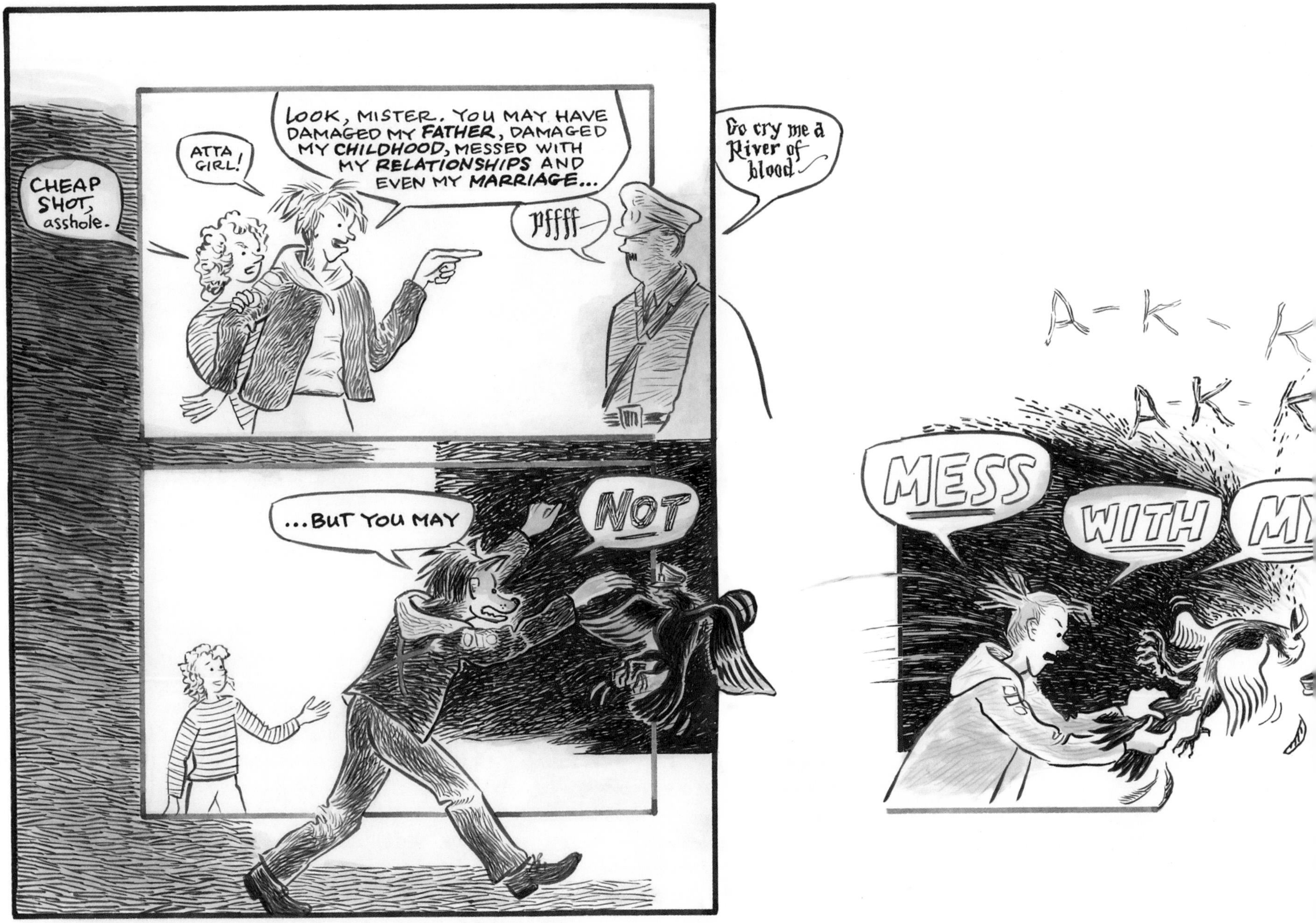

CHEAP SHOT, asshole.
ATTA GIRL!
LOOK, MISTER. YOU MAY HAVE DAMAGED MY FATHER, DAMAGED MY CHILDHOOD, MESSED WITH MY RELATIONSHIPS AND EVEN MY MARRIAGE...
Pffff—
Go cry me a River of blood
...BUT YOU MAY
NOT
MESS
WITH

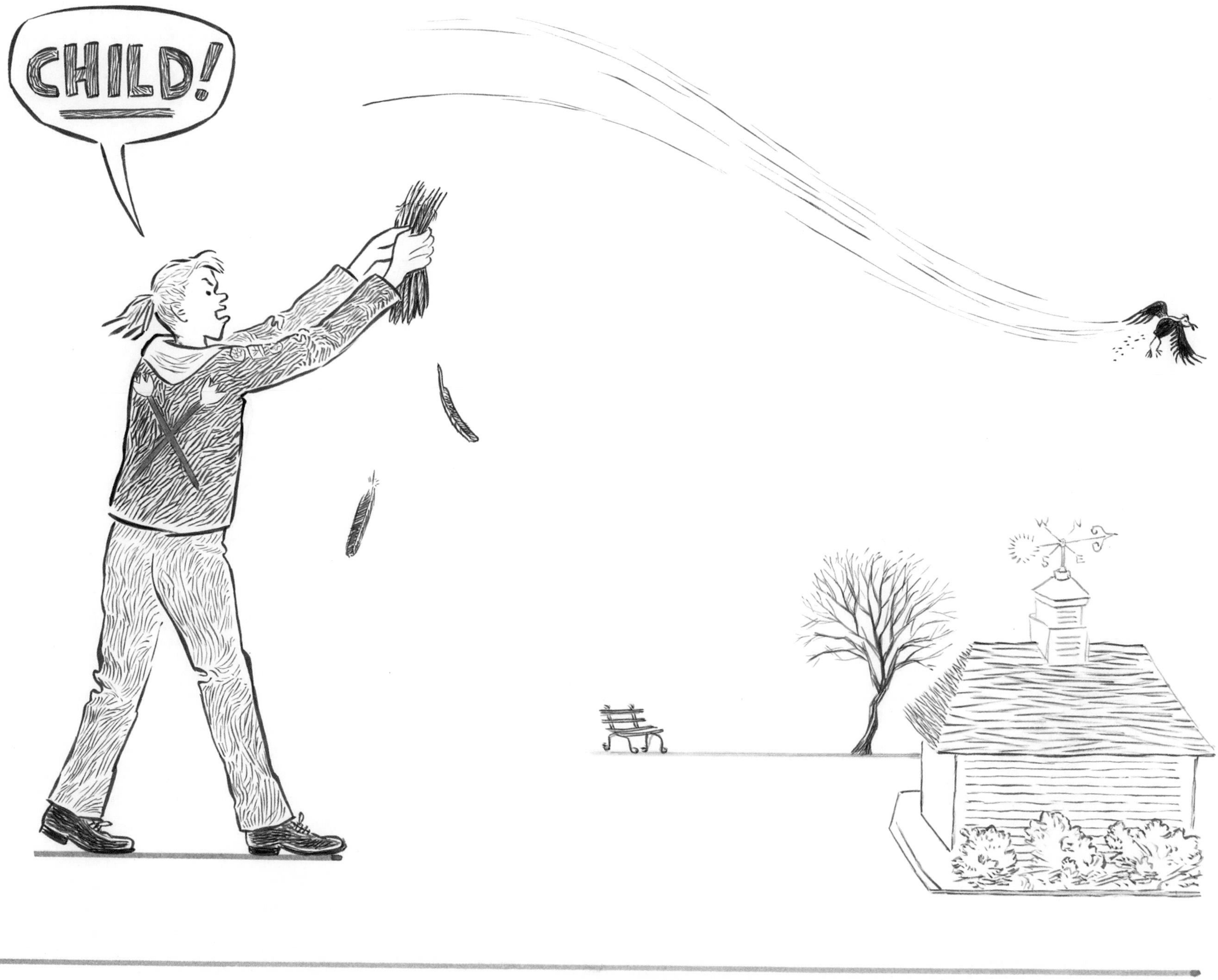
CHILD!

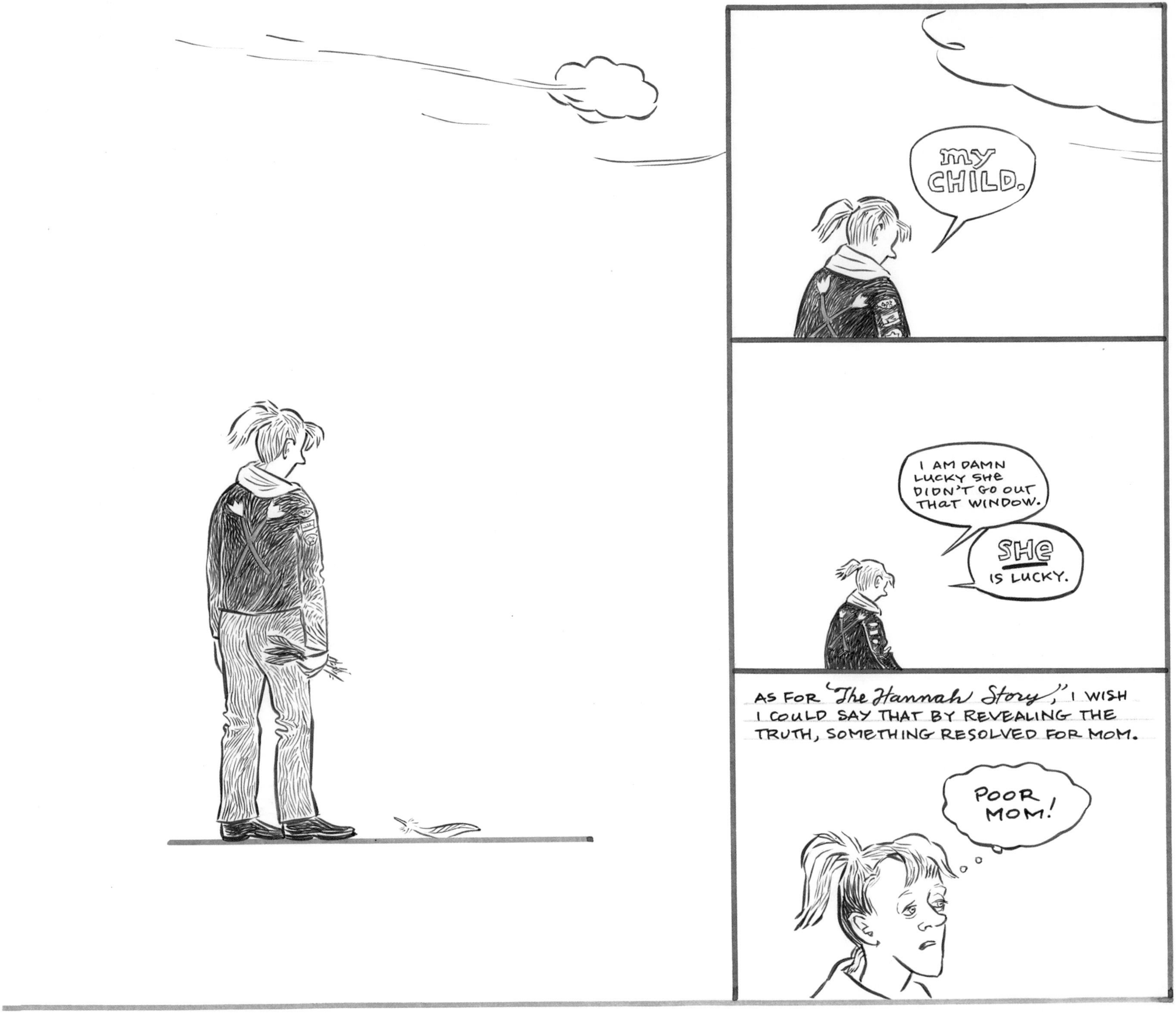
MY CHILD.
I AM DAMN LUCKY SHE DIDN'T GO OUT THAT WINDOW.
SHE IS LUCKY.
AS FOR 'The Hannah Story,' I WISH I COULD SAY THAT BY REVEALING THE TRUTH, SOMETHING RESOLVED FOR MOM.
POOR MOM!

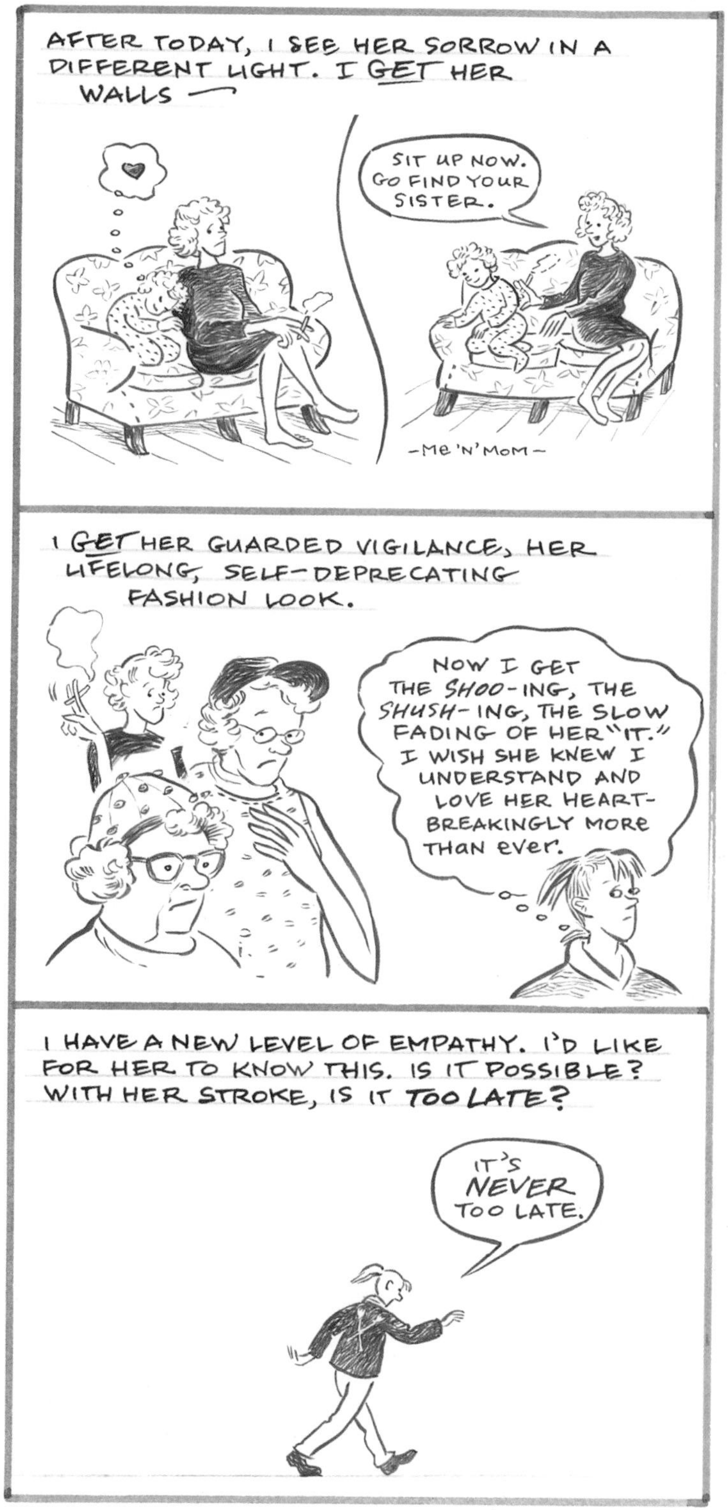
AFTER TODAY, I SEE HER SORROW IN A DIFFERENT LIGHT. I GET HER WALLS —
SIT UP NOW. GO FIND YOUR SISTER.
-ME 'N' MOM-
I GET HER GUARDED VIGILANCE, HER LIFELONG, SELF-DEPRECATING FASHION LOOK.
NOW I GET THE SHOO-ING, THE SHUSH-ING, THE SLOW FADING OF HER "IT." I WISH SHE KNEW I UNDERSTAND AND LOVE HER HEART-BREAKINGLY MORE THAN EVER.
I HAVE A NEW LEVEL OF EMPATHY. I'D LIKE FOR HER TO KNOW THIS. IS IT POSSIBLE? WITH HER STROKE, IS IT TOO LATE?
IT'S NEVER TOO LATE.

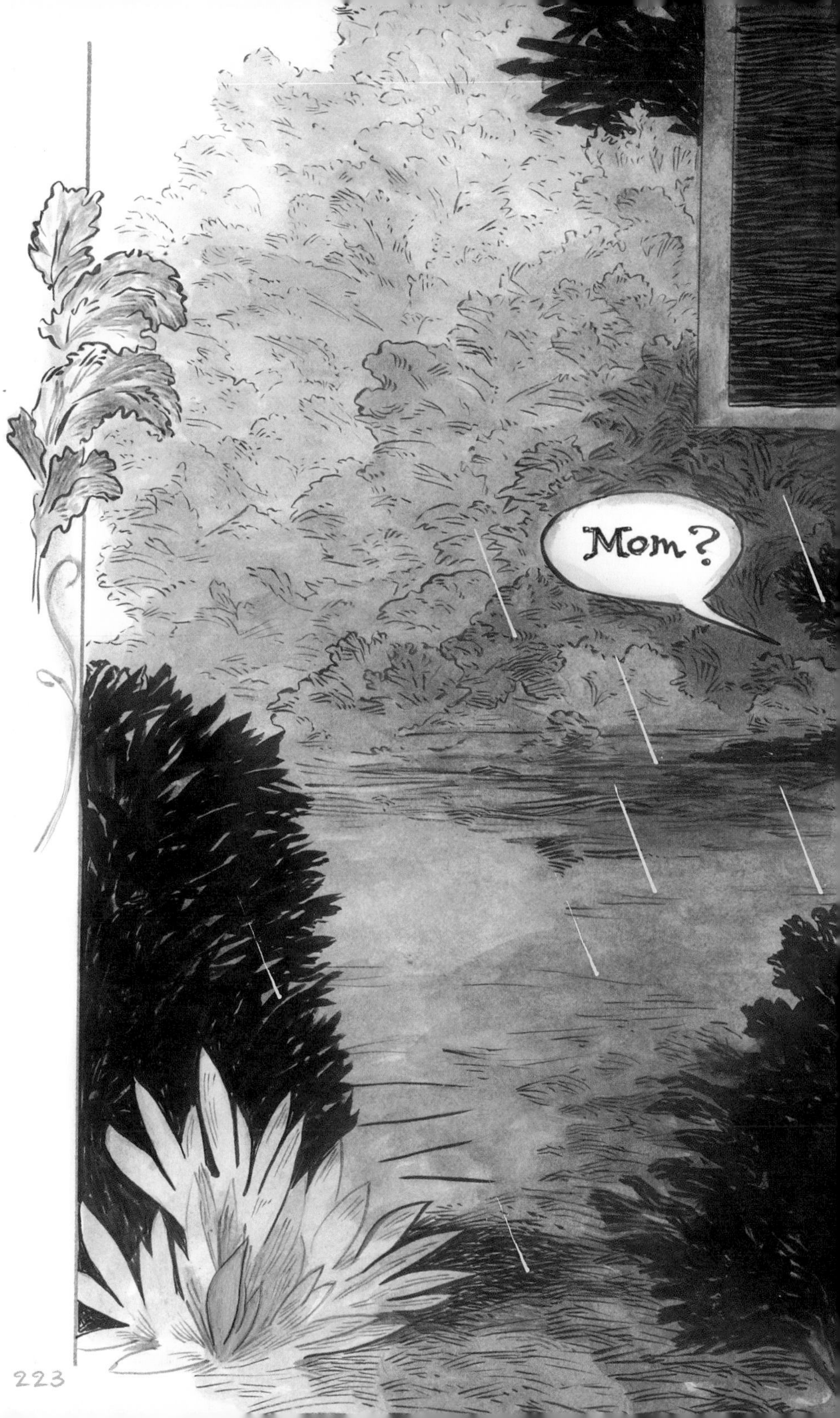
Mom?

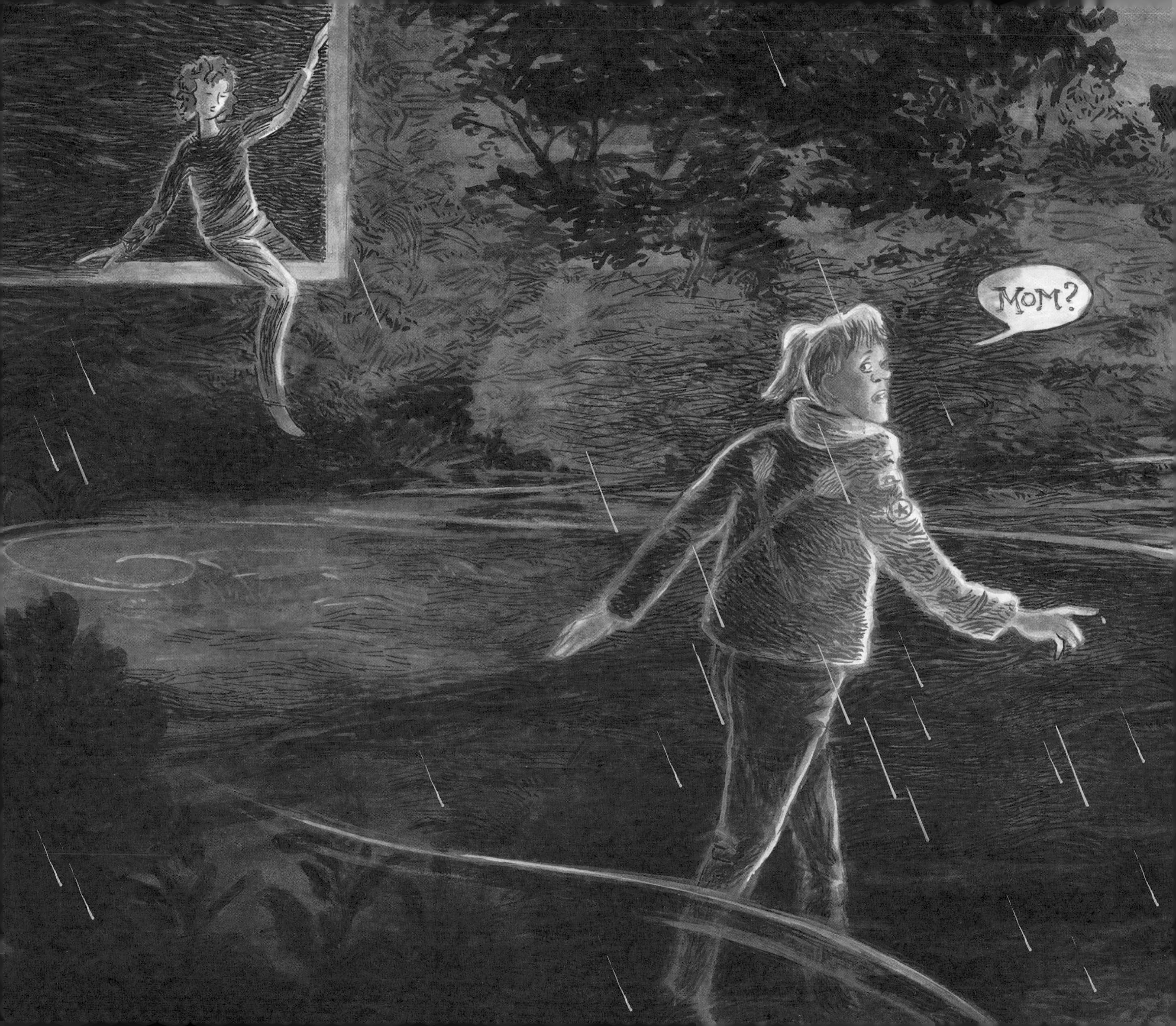
MOM?

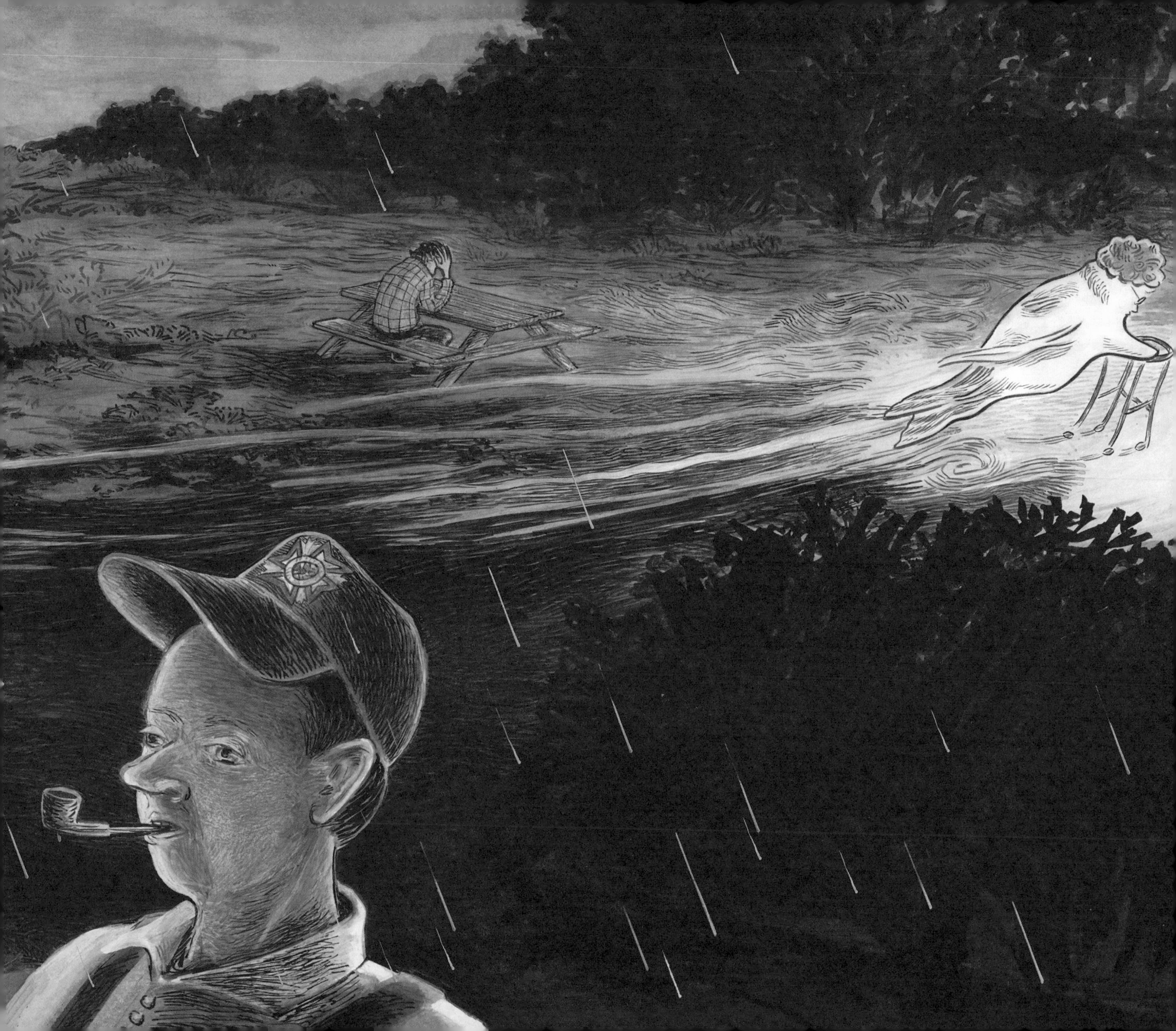

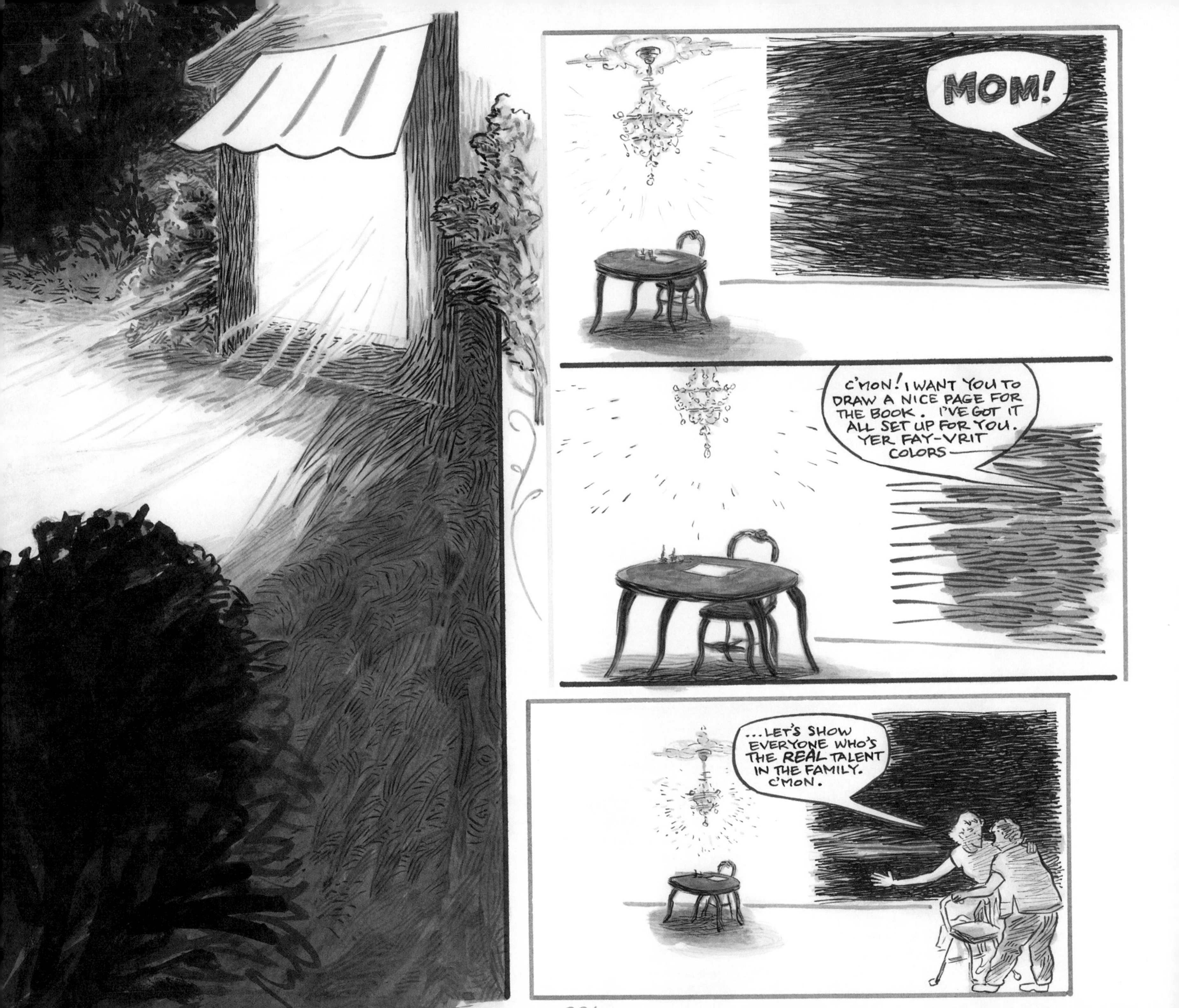
MOM!
C'MON! I WANT YOU TO DRAW A NICE PAGE FOR THE BOOK. I'VE GOT IT ALL SET UP FOR YOU. YER FAY-VRIT COLORS
...LET'S SHOW EVERYONE WHO'S THE REAL TALENT IN THE FAMILY. C'MON.

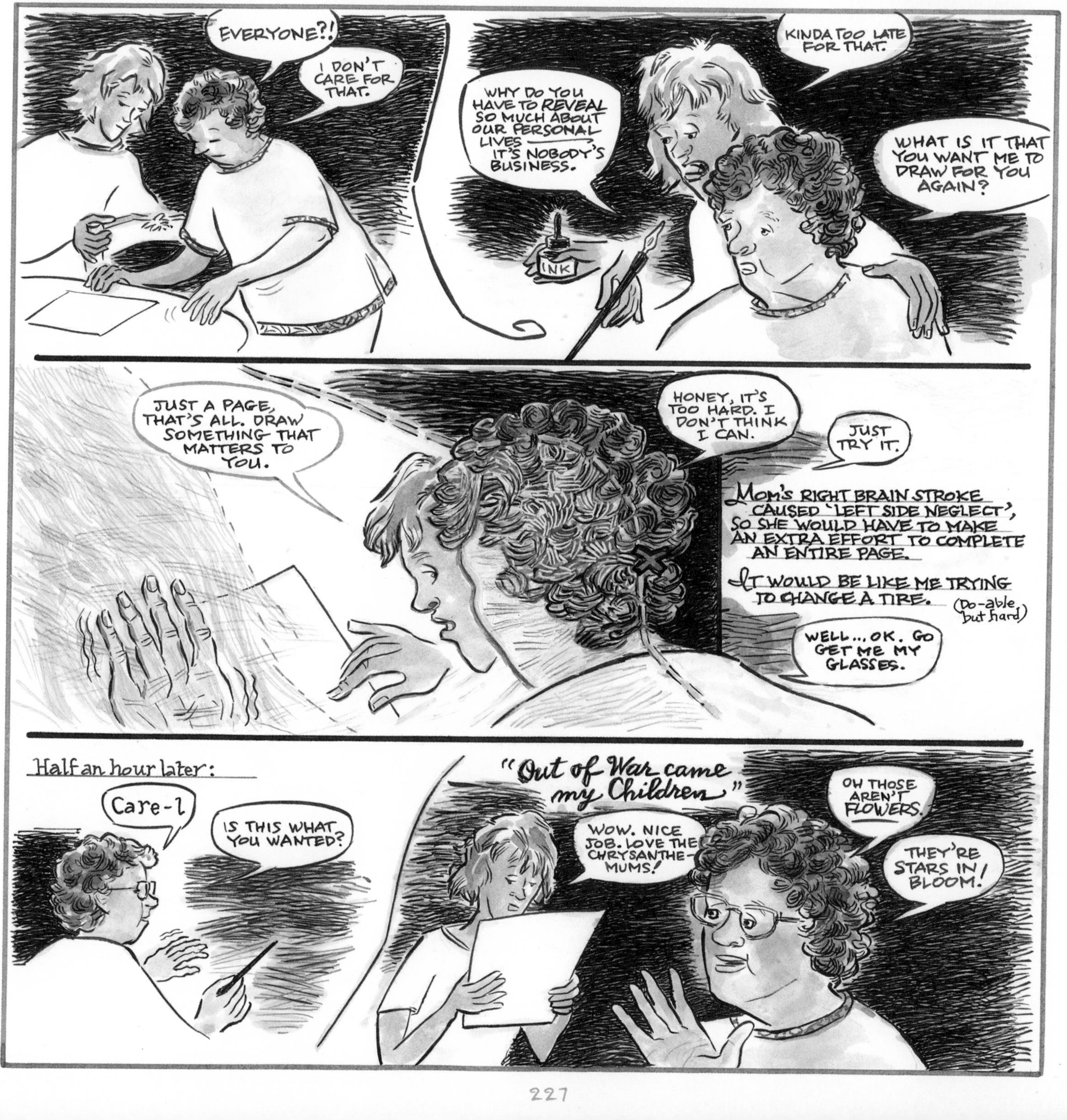
EVERYONE?!
I DON'T CARE FOR THAT.
WHY DO YOU HAVE TO REVEAL SO MUCH ABOUT OUR PERSONAL LIVES — IT'S NOBODY'S BUSINESS.
KINDA TOO LATE FOR THAT.
WHAT IS IT THAT YOU WANT ME TO DRAW FOR YOU AGAIN?
INK
JUST A PAGE, THAT'S ALL. DRAW SOMETHING THAT MATTERS TO YOU.
HONEY, IT'S TOO HARD. I DON'T THINK I CAN.
JUST TRY IT.
MOM'S RIGHT BRAIN STROKE CAUSED 'LEFT SIDE NEGLECT', SO SHE WOULD HAVE TO MAKE AN EXTRA EFFORT TO COMPLETE AN ENTIRE PAGE.
IT WOULD BE LIKE ME TRYING TO CHANGE A TIRE. (Do-able but hard)
WELL... OK. GO GET ME MY GLASSES.
Half an hour later:
Care-l
IS THIS WHAT YOU WANTED?
"Out of War came my Children"
WOW. NICE JOB. LOVE THE CHRYSANTHE-MUMS!
OH THOSE AREN'T FLOWERS.
THEY'RE STARS IN BLOOM!

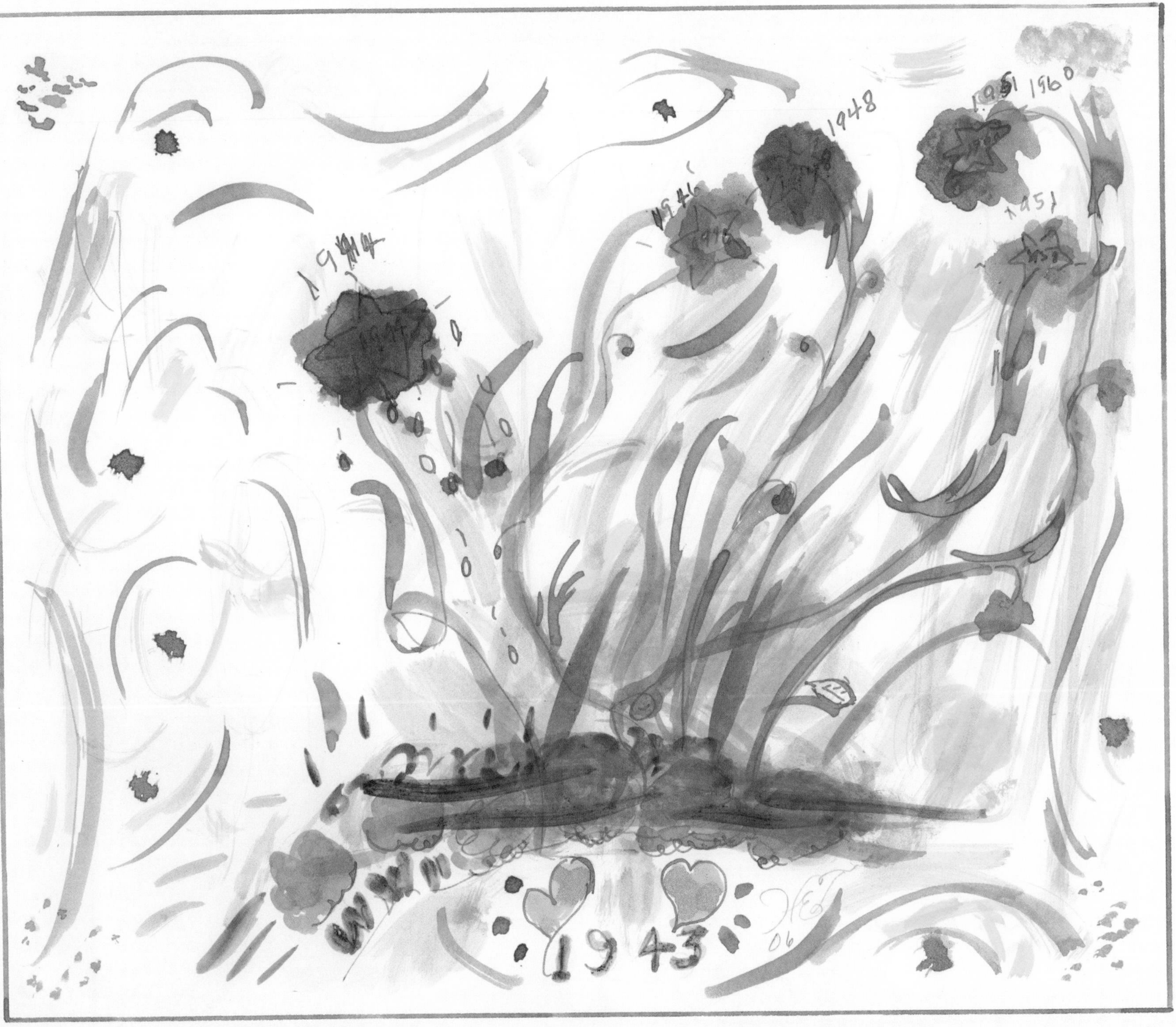
1948
1960
1951
1943

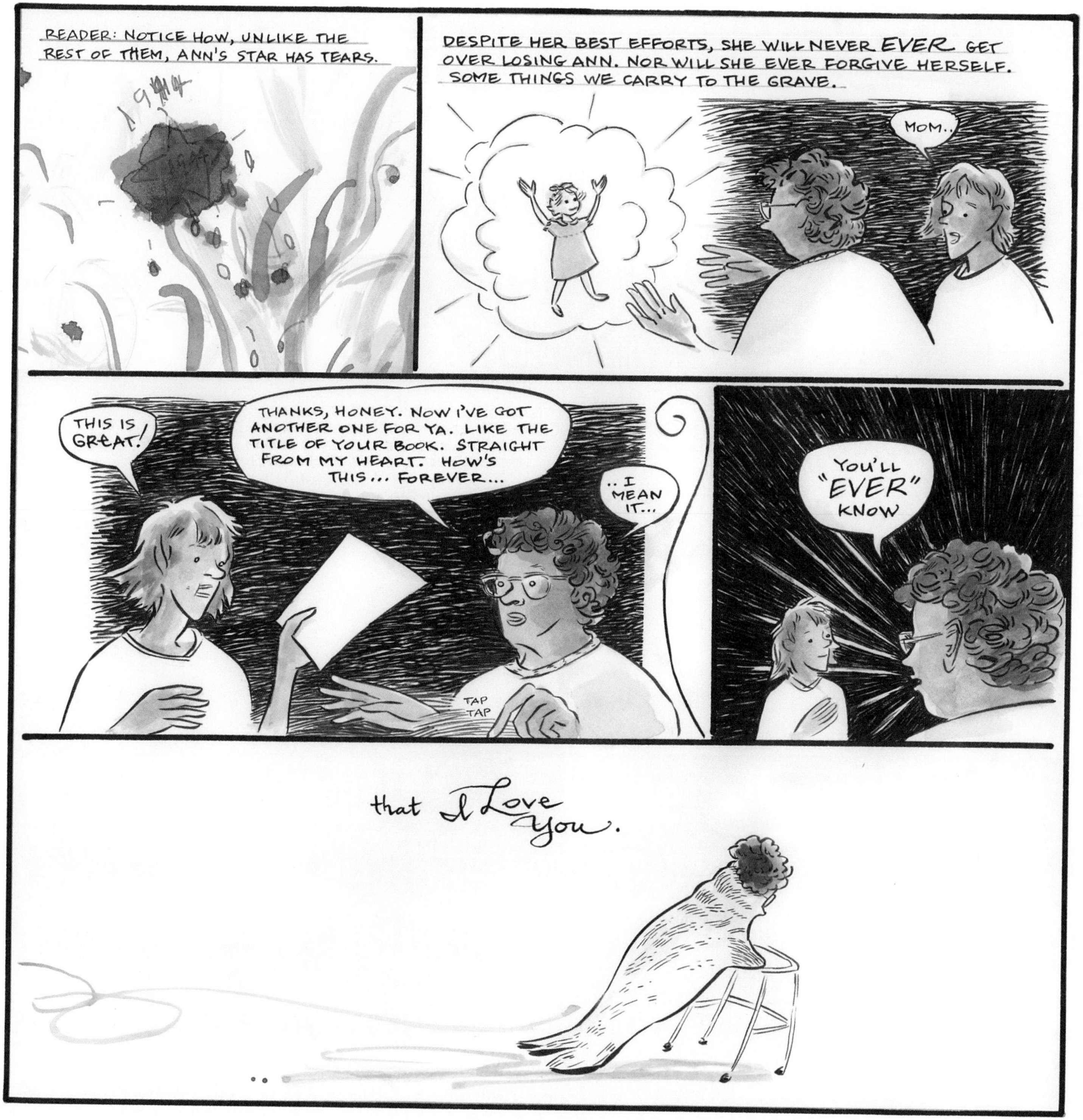
READER: NOTICE HOW, UNLIKE THE REST OF THEM, ANN'S STAR HAS TEARS.
DESPITE HER BEST EFFORTS, SHE WILL NEVER EVER GET OVER LOSING ANN. NOR WILL SHE EVER FORGIVE HERSELF. SOME THINGS WE CARRY TO THE GRAVE.
MOM..
THIS IS GREAT!
THANKS, HONEY. NOW I'VE GOT ANOTHER ONE FOR YA. LIKE THE TITLE OF YOUR BOOK. STRAIGHT FROM MY HEART. HOW'S THIS... FOREVER...
..I MEAN IT...
TAP TAP
YOU'LL "EVER" KNOW
that I Love You.

10.

IN GEAR

O.K....

So NOW YOU KNOW FROM READING BOOKS I + II THAT I WAS RAISED BY A NICE COUPLE WHO HAD SUFFERED SIGNIFICANT EMOTIONAL TRAUMA DUE TO WAR AND TRAGIC LOSS. AND THAT THIS TRAUMA STAINED MY CHILDHOOD. I DID NOT WANT THIS PATHOLOGY TO CYCLE THROUGH YET ANOTHER GENERATION AND STAIN MY CHILD. BUT SADLY, BECAUSE OF THE DRAMA BETWEEN ME AND HER DAD, IT HAPPENED. SO I'M GOING TO CALL HIM IN *N.Y.* AND INSIST HE COME HERE *Now!*

ALRIGHT. SO ONCE I GOT TURNED AROUND, I HEADED BACK OVER TO BE WITH MY GIRL. WHATEVER SUBSTANCE SHE WAS ON, WELL... SHE SEEMED BETTER. SO MUCH WAS BEING REVEALED: THE EXTENT OF HER RISKY BEHAVIOR AND ITS BASIS IN HER SADNESS OVER THIS WHOLE DAMN MESS WITH HER DAD LEAVING, AND ME YANKING HER OUT OF HER CALIFORNIA LIFE. BLESS HER HEART, SHE HELD IT TOGETHER AS LONG AS SHE COULD.

DADDY'LL BE HERE FRIDAY.

Liar

GOING ON DAY 3 AT CHILDREN'S AND THE DOCTORS WERE STILL NOT READY TO PUT A LABEL ON HER CONDITION. MY MOM HUNCH, AFTER ALL THESE TESTS AND EXCEPT FOR THE VOICE — I'D SAY SHE HAS DEPRESSION. I SHOULD'A SEEN IT COMING. I MEAN I WENT *NUTS* FOR AWHILE THERE. BUT THEN I THREW MYSELF INTO PARENTAL RESPONSIBILITIES. AND DAD'S *BOOK* — I MEAN, DAD'S *CLAIM*.

SO TALENTED! IS THAT A HORSE?

OY.

IT'S THE VOICE GUY

SEEING JUSTIN THERE AT THE NURSES STATION... AND AFTER SO MANY MONTHS...THE RELIEF I FELT WAS DEEP, LIKE NOURISHMENT TO THE STARVED. BUT THEN IT WAS AS IF SOMEONE POURED A CAN OF SALTY BROWN GRAVY ON ME, BECAUSE I KNEW WHY HE HAD COME AND I KNEW HOW THE GRAVITY OF WHAT I HAD TO TELL HIM WOULD BREAK HIS HEART — REGARDLESS, I EMBRACED HIM AS ONE DOES POSSIBILITY: WITH HOPEFULNESS AND A *SMILE*.

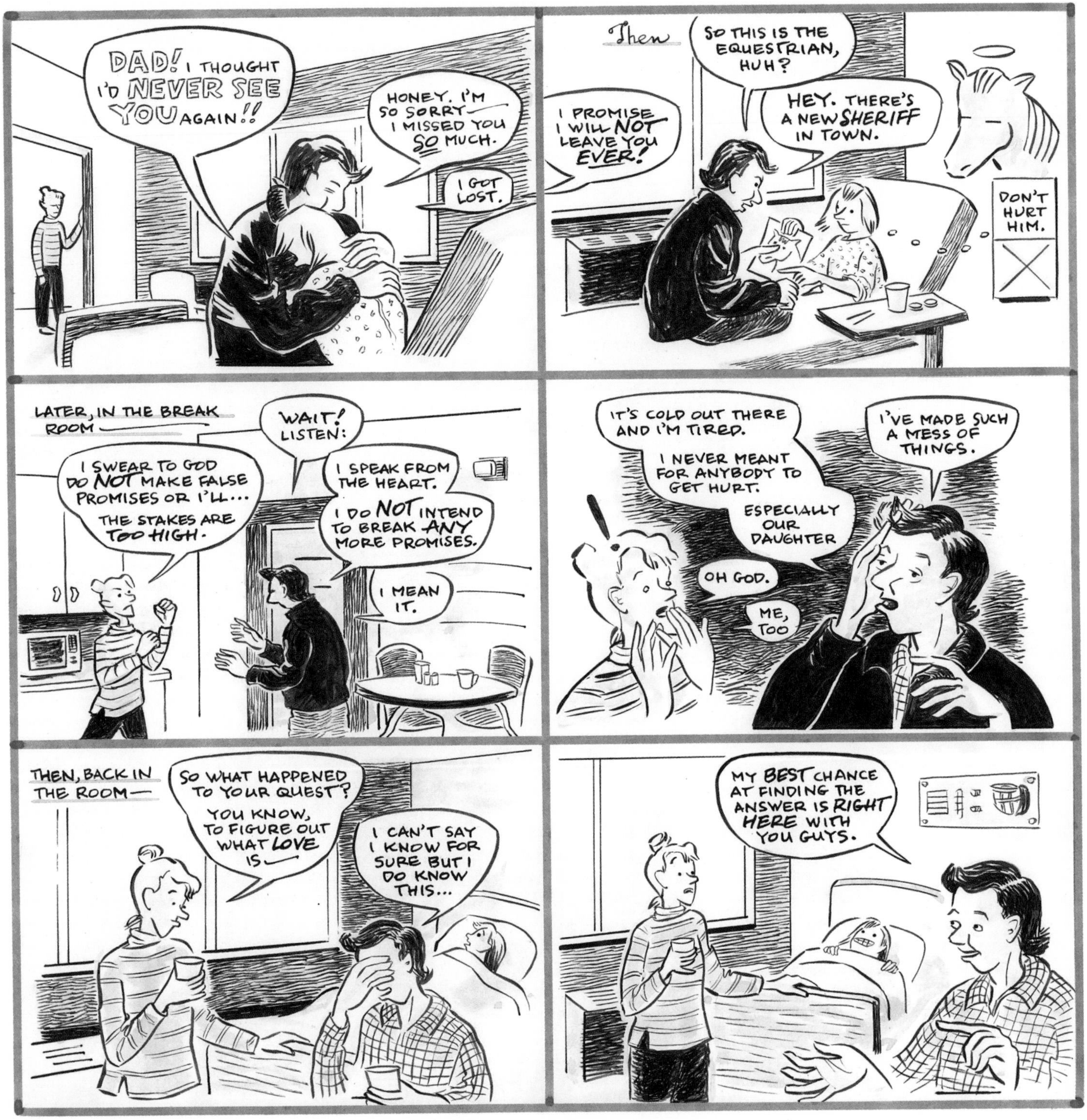
DAD! I THOUGHT I'D NEVER SEE YOU AGAIN!!
HONEY. I'M SO SORRY— I MISSED YOU SO MUCH.
I GOT LOST.
Then
SO THIS IS THE EQUESTRIAN, HUH?
I PROMISE I WILL NOT LEAVE YOU EVER!
HEY. THERE'S A NEW SHERIFF IN TOWN.
DON'T HURT HIM.
LATER, IN THE BREAK ROOM
WAIT! LISTEN:
I SWEAR TO GOD DO NOT MAKE FALSE PROMISES OR I'LL...
THE STAKES ARE TOO HIGH.
I SPEAK FROM THE HEART.
I DO NOT INTEND TO BREAK ANY MORE PROMISES.
I MEAN IT.
IT'S COLD OUT THERE AND I'M TIRED.
I NEVER MEANT FOR ANYBODY TO GET HURT.
ESPECIALLY OUR DAUGHTER
I'VE MADE SUCH A MESS OF THINGS.
OH GOD.
ME, TOO
THEN, BACK IN THE ROOM—
SO WHAT HAPPENED TO YOUR QUEST?
YOU KNOW, TO FIGURE OUT WHAT LOVE IS—
I CAN'T SAY I KNOW FOR SURE BUT I DO KNOW THIS...
MY BEST CHANCE AT FINDING THE ANSWER IS RIGHT HERE WITH YOU GUYS.

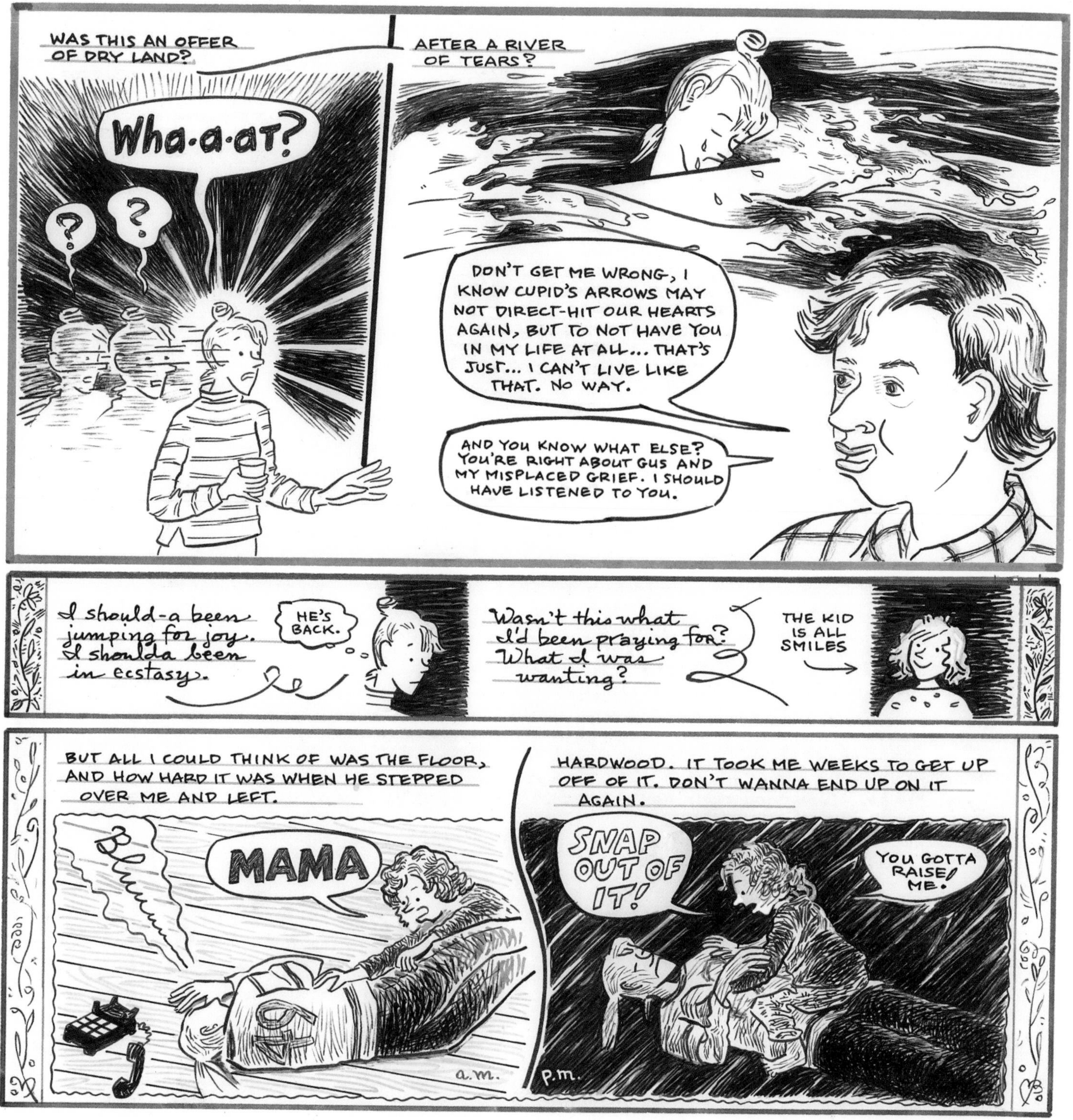
WAS THIS AN OFFER OF DRY LAND?
Wha-a-at?
AFTER A RIVER OF TEARS?
DON'T GET ME WRONG, I KNOW CUPID'S ARROWS MAY NOT DIRECT-HIT OUR HEARTS AGAIN, BUT TO NOT HAVE YOU IN MY LIFE AT ALL... THAT'S JUST... I CAN'T LIVE LIKE THAT. NO WAY.
AND YOU KNOW WHAT ELSE? YOU'RE RIGHT ABOUT GUS AND MY MISPLACED GRIEF. I SHOULD HAVE LISTENED TO YOU.
I should-a been jumping for joy. I shoulda been in ecstasy.
HE'S BACK.
Wasn't this what I'd been praying for? What I was wanting?
THE KID IS ALL SMILES
BUT ALL I COULD THINK OF WAS THE FLOOR, AND HOW HARD IT WAS WHEN HE STEPPED OVER ME AND LEFT.
MAMA
a.m.
HARDWOOD. IT TOOK ME WEEKS TO GET UP OFF OF IT. DON'T WANNA END UP ON IT AGAIN.
SNAP OUT OF IT!
YOU GOTTA RAISE ME!
p.m.

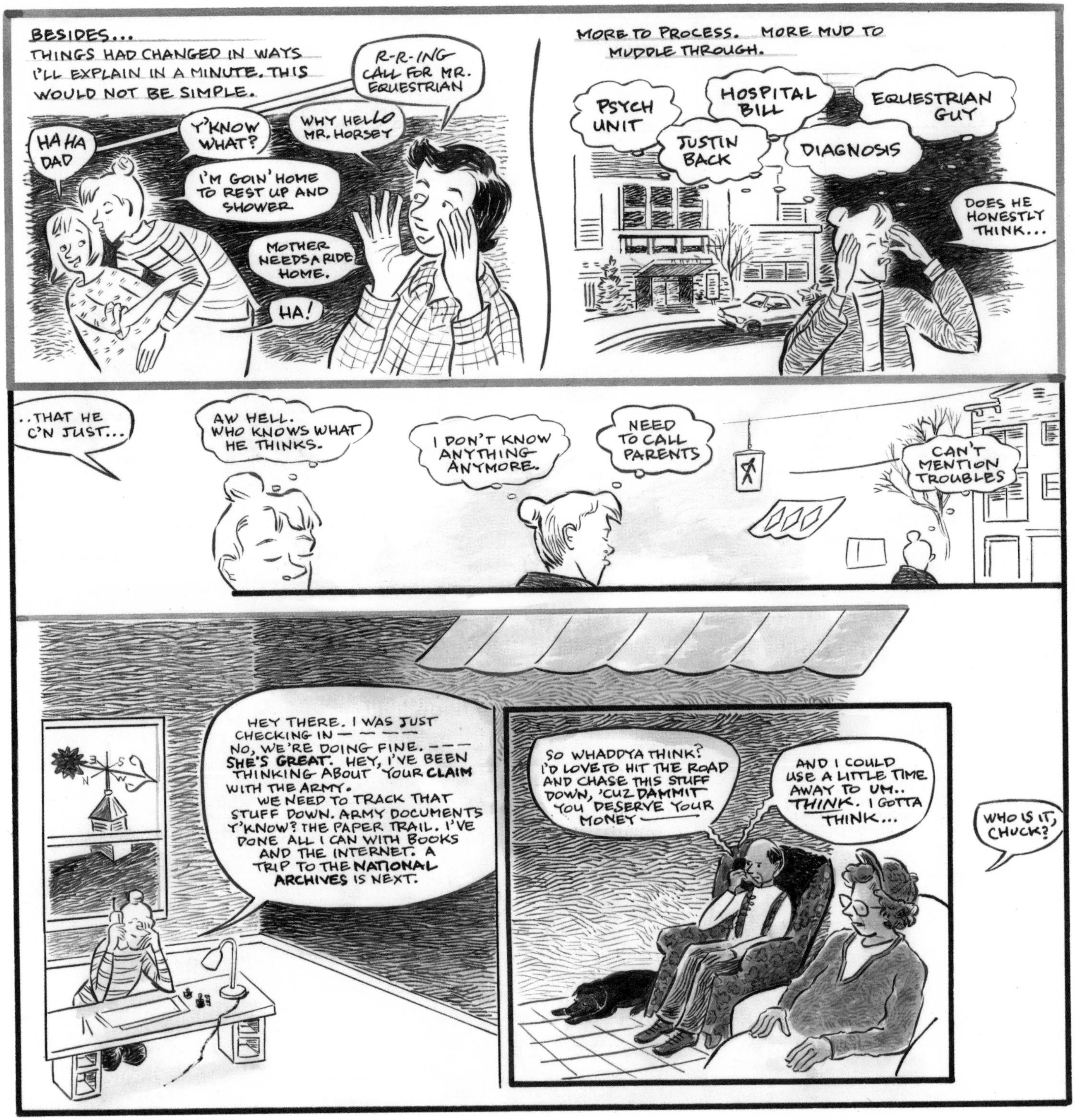
BESIDES... THINGS HAD CHANGED IN WAYS I'LL EXPLAIN IN A MINUTE. THIS WOULD NOT BE SIMPLE.
R-R-ING CALL FOR MR. EQUESTRIAN
HA HA DAD
Y'KNOW WHAT?
WHY HELLO MR. HORSEY
I'M GOIN' HOME TO REST UP AND SHOWER
MOTHER NEEDS A RIDE HOME.
HA!
MORE TO PROCESS. MORE MUD TO MUDDLE THROUGH.
PSYCH UNIT
HOSPITAL BILL
EQUESTRIAN GUY
JUSTIN BACK
DIAGNOSIS
DOES HE HONESTLY THINK...
..THAT HE C'N JUST...
AW HELL. WHO KNOWS WHAT HE THINKS.
I DON'T KNOW ANYTHING ANYMORE.
NEED TO CALL PARENTS
CAN'T MENTION TROUBLES
HEY THERE. I WAS JUST CHECKING IN— — — — NO, WE'RE DOING FINE. — — — SHE'S GREAT. HEY, I'VE BEEN THINKING ABOUT YOUR CLAIM WITH THE ARMY. WE NEED TO TRACK THAT STUFF DOWN. ARMY DOCUMENTS Y'KNOW? THE PAPER TRAIL. I'VE DONE ALL I CAN WITH BOOKS AND THE INTERNET. A TRIP TO THE NATIONAL ARCHIVES IS NEXT.
SO WHADDYA THINK? I'D LOVE TO HIT THE ROAD AND CHASE THIS STUFF DOWN, 'CUZ DAMMIT YOU DESERVE YOUR MONEY——
AND I COULD USE A LITTLE TIME AWAY TO UM.. THINK. I GOTTA THINK...
WHO IS IT, CHUCK?

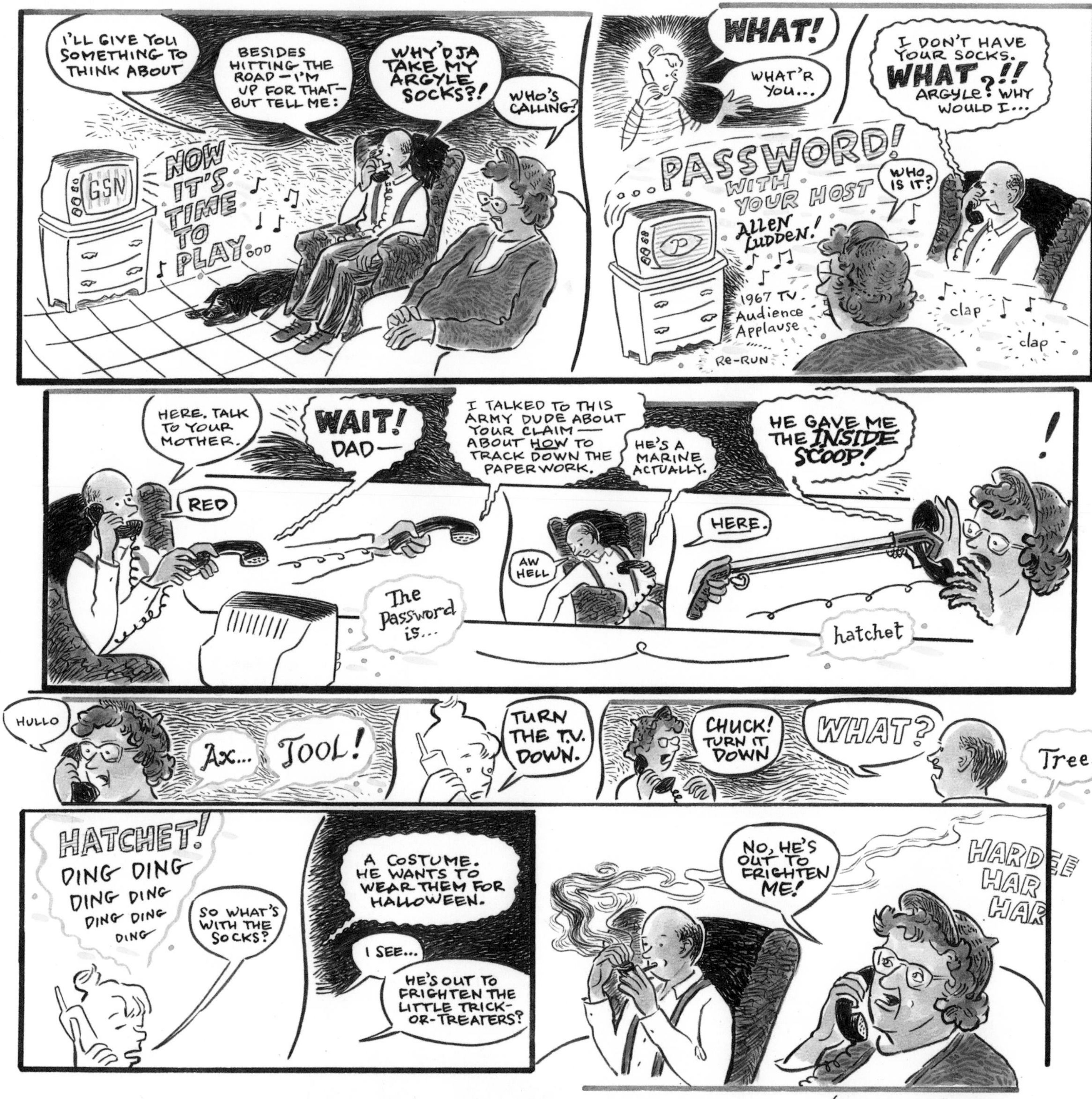
I'LL GIVE YOU SOMETHING TO THINK ABOUT
BESIDES HITTING THE ROAD — I'M UP FOR THAT — BUT TELL ME:
WHY'D JA TAKE MY ARGYLE SOCKS?!
WHO'S CALLING?
GSN
NOW IT'S TIME TO PLAY...
WHAT!
WHAT'R YOU...
I DON'T HAVE YOUR SOCKS. WHAT?!! ARGYLE? WHY WOULD I...
PASSWORD! WITH YOUR HOST ALLEN LUDDEN!
WHO IS IT?
1967 TV Audience Applause
RE-RUN
clap
clap
HERE. TALK TO YOUR MOTHER.
RED
WAIT! DAD —
I TALKED TO THIS ARMY DUDE ABOUT YOUR CLAIM — ABOUT HOW TO TRACK DOWN THE PAPERWORK.
HE'S A MARINE ACTUALLY.
AW HELL
HE GAVE ME THE INSIDE SCOOP!
!
HERE.
The Password is...
hatchet
HULLO
Ax... TOOL!
TURN THE T.V. DOWN.
CHUCK! TURN IT DOWN
WHAT?
Tree...
HATCHET!
DING DING DING DING DING DING DING
SO WHAT'S WITH THE SOCKS?
A COSTUME. HE WANTS TO WEAR THEM FOR HALLOWEEN.
I SEE...
HE'S OUT TO FRIGHTEN THE LITTLE TRICK-OR-TREATERS?
NO, HE'S OUT TO FRIGHTEN ME!
HARDEE HAR HAR

(Sometimes I forget how NUTTY these two are!)

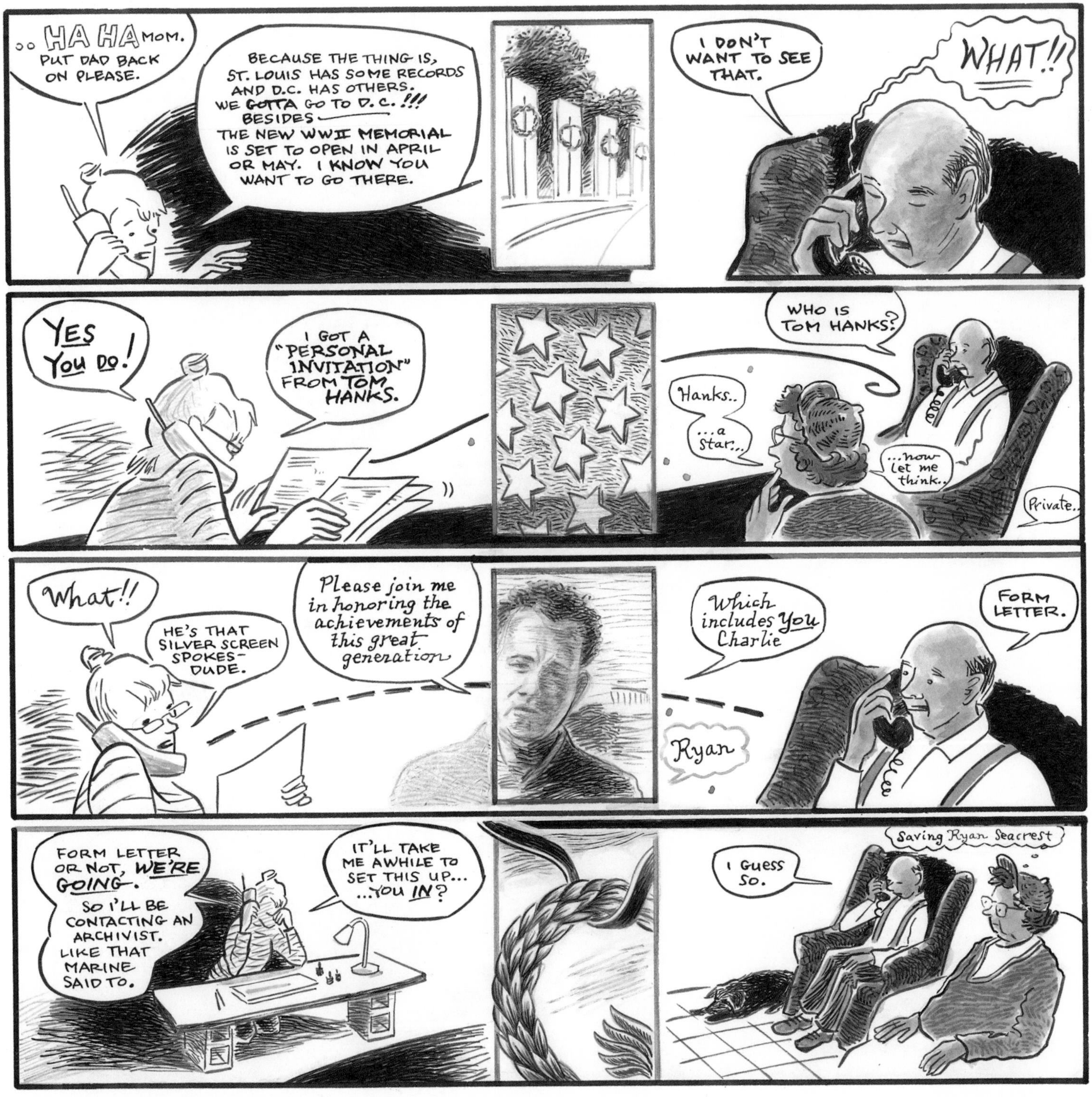
..HA HA MOM. PUT DAD BACK ON PLEASE.
BECAUSE THE THING IS, ST. LOUIS HAS SOME RECORDS AND D.C. HAS OTHERS. WE GOTTA GO TO D.C.!!! BESIDES— THE NEW WWII MEMORIAL IS SET TO OPEN IN APRIL OR MAY. I KNOW YOU WANT TO GO THERE.
I DON'T WANT TO SEE THAT.
WHAT!!
YES YOU DO!
I GOT A "PERSONAL INVITATION" FROM TOM HANKS.
WHO IS TOM HANKS?
Hanks..
...a Star...
...now let me think..
Private..
What!!
HE'S THAT SILVER SCREEN SPOKES-DUDE.
Please join me in honoring the achievements of this great generation
Which includes You Charlie
FORM LETTER.
Ryan
FORM LETTER OR NOT, WE'RE GOING. SO I'LL BE CONTACTING AN ARCHIVIST. LIKE THAT MARINE SAID TO.
IT'LL TAKE ME AWHILE TO SET THIS UP... ...YOU IN?
Saving Ryan Seacrest
I GUESS SO.

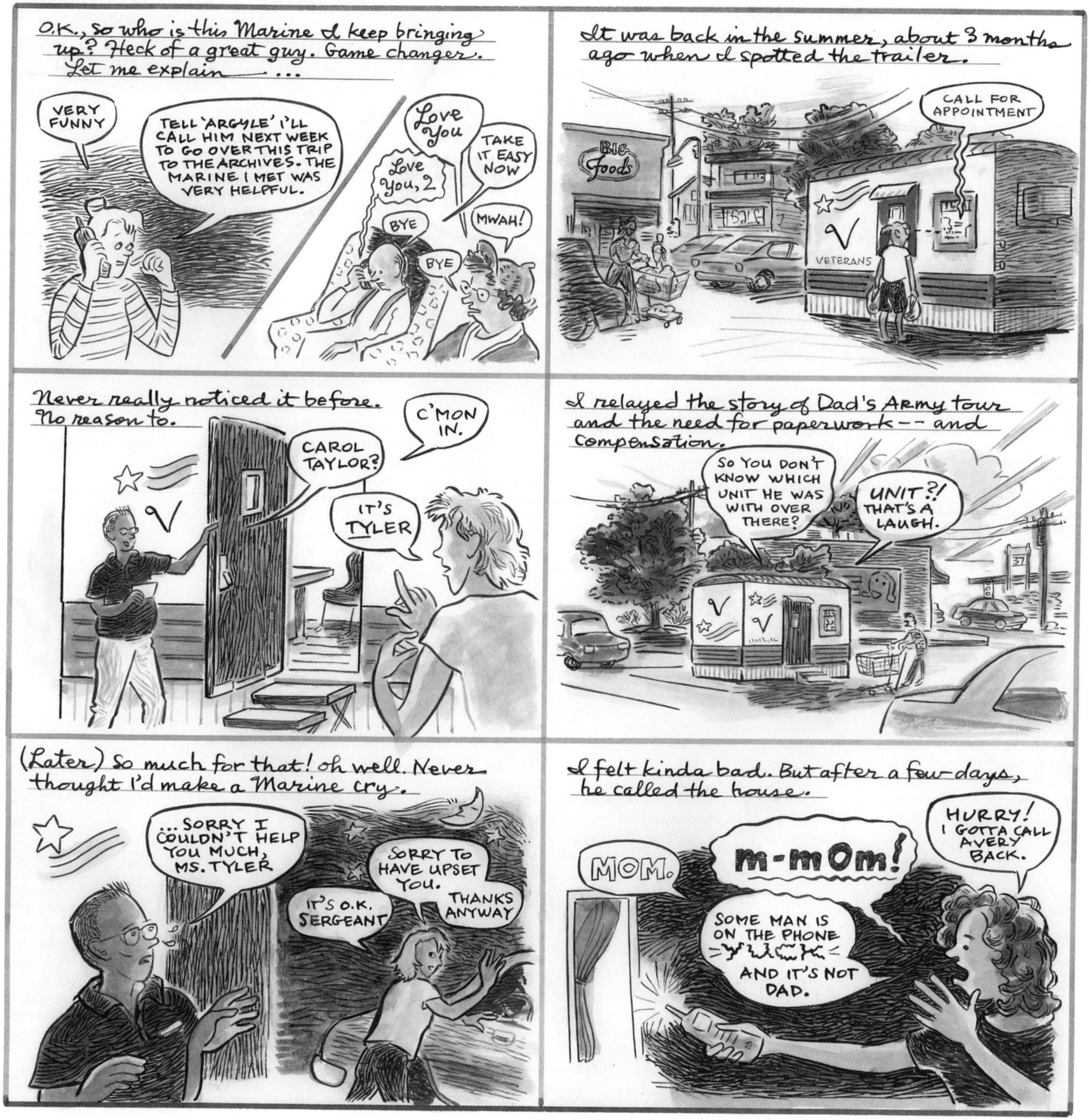
O.K., so who is this Marine I keep bringing up? Heck of a great guy. Game changer. Let me explain ...
VERY FUNNY
TELL 'ARGYLE' I'LL CALL HIM NEXT WEEK TO GO OVER THIS TRIP TO THE ARCHIVES. THE MARINE I MET WAS VERY HELPFUL.
Love You
Love You, 2
TAKE IT EASY NOW
BYE
MWAH!
BYE
It was back in the summer, about 3 months ago when I spotted the trailer.
CALL FOR APPOINTMENT
BIG Foods
VETERANS
Never really noticed it before. No reason to.
C'MON IN.
CAROL TAYLOR?
IT'S TYLER
I relayed the story of Dad's Army tour and the need for paperwork -- and compensation.
SO YOU DON'T KNOW WHICH UNIT HE WAS WITH OVER THERE?
UNIT?! THAT'S A LAUGH.
(Later) So much for that! oh well. Never thought I'd make a Marine cry.
...SORRY I COULDN'T HELP YOU MUCH, MS. TYLER
SORRY TO HAVE UPSET YOU.
IT'S O.K. SERGEANT
THANKS ANYWAY
I felt kinda bad. But after a few days, he called the house.
MOM.
m-mOm!
HURRY! I GOTTA CALL AVERY BACK.
SOME MAN IS ON THE PHONE AND IT'S NOT DAD.

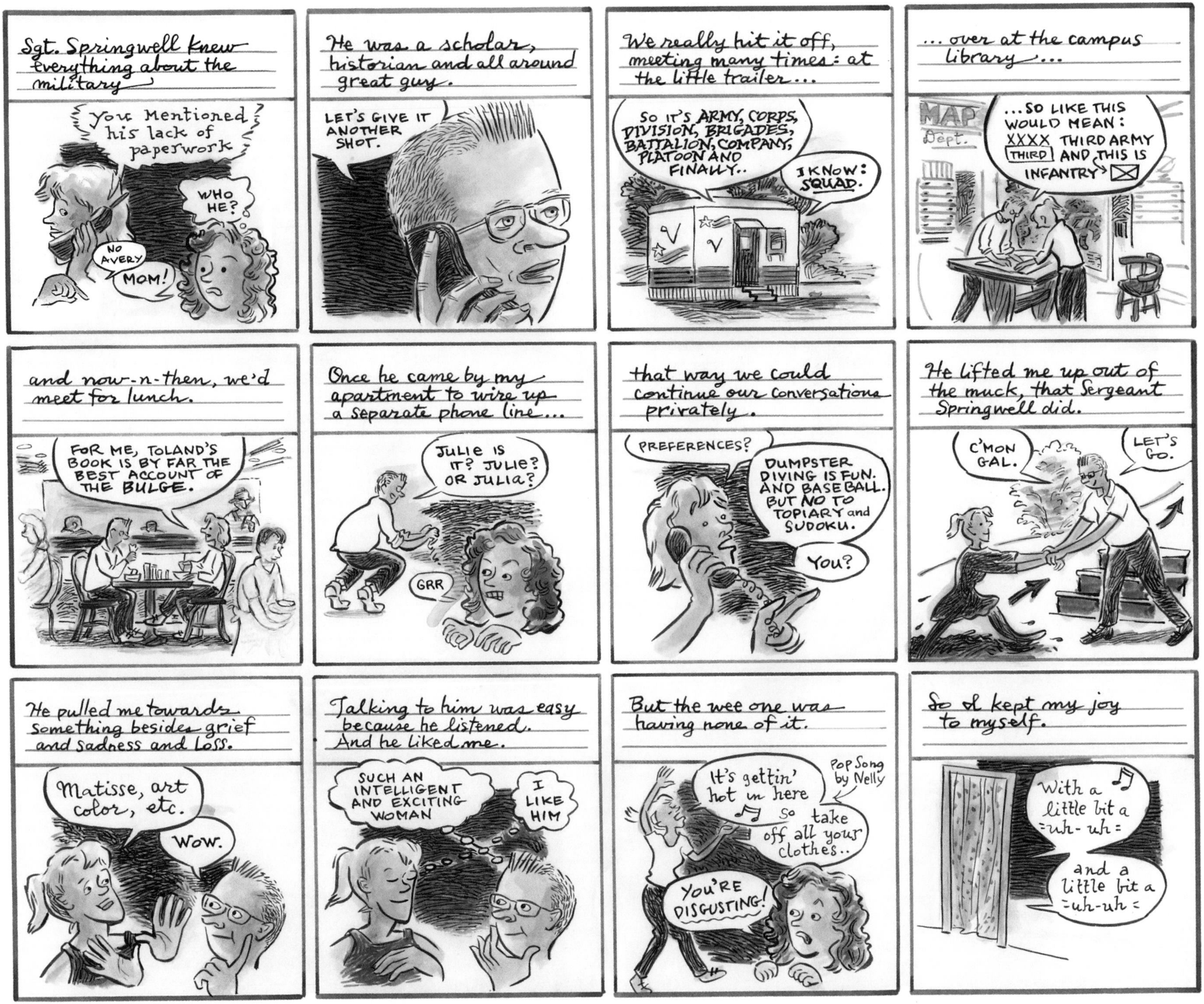
Sgt. Springwell knew everything about the military
You mentioned his lack of paperwork
WHO HE?
NO AVERY
MOM!
He was a scholar, historian and all around great guy.
LET'S GIVE IT ANOTHER SHOT.
We really hit it off, meeting many times: at the little trailer...
SO IT'S ARMY, CORPS, DIVISION, BRIGADES, BATTALION, COMPANY, PLATOON AND FINALLY..
I KNOW: SQUAD.
... over at the campus library...
MAP Dept.
...SO LIKE THIS WOULD MEAN: XXXX THIRD ARMY THIRD AND THIS IS INFANTRY
and now-n-then, we'd meet for lunch.
FOR ME, TOLAND'S BOOK IS BY FAR THE BEST ACCOUNT OF THE BULGE.
Once he came by my apartment to wire up a separate phone line...
JULIE IS IT? JULIE? OR JULIA?
GRR
that way we could continue our conversations privately.
PREFERENCES?
DUMPSTER DIVING IS FUN. AND BASEBALL. BUT NO TO TOPIARY and SUDOKU.
YOU?
He lifted me up out of the muck, that Sergeant Springwell did.
C'MON GAL.
LET'S GO.
He pulled me towards something besides grief and sadness and loss.
Matisse, art color, etc.
WOW.
Talking to him was easy because he listened. And he liked me.
SUCH AN INTELLIGENT AND EXCITING WOMAN
I LIKE HIM
But the wee one was having none of it.
It's gettin' hot in here so take off all your clothes..
Pop Song by Nelly
YOU'RE DISGUSTING!
So I kept my joy to myself.
With a little bit a =uh-uh=
and a little bit a =uh-uh=

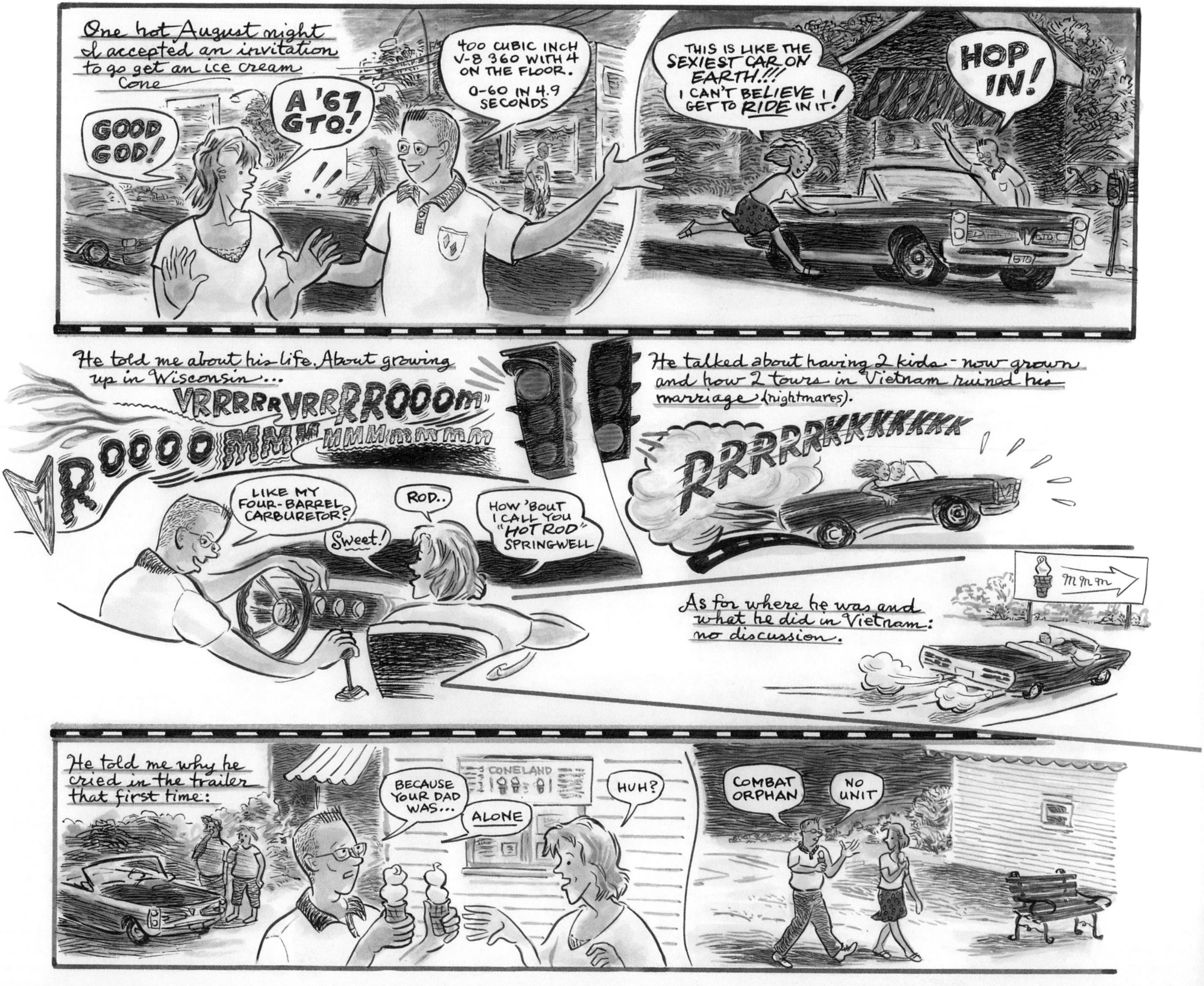
One hot August night I accepted an invitation to go get an ice cream cone
GOOD GOD!
A '67 GTO!
400 CUBIC INCH V-8 360 WITH 4 ON THE FLOOR. 0-60 IN 4.9 SECONDS
THIS IS LIKE THE SEXIEST CAR ON EARTH!!!! I CAN'T BELIEVE I GET TO RIDE IN IT!
HOP IN!
He told me about his life. About growing up in Wisconsin...
VRRRRR VRRRROOOm
ROOOOO MMMMMMMMMMM
LIKE MY FOUR-BARREL CARBURETOR?
Sweet!
ROD..
HOW 'BOUT I CALL YOU "HOT ROD" SPRINGWELL
He talked about having 2 kids - now grown and how 2 tours in Vietnam ruined his marriage (nightmares).
RRRRRKKKKKKK
MMM
As for where he was and what he did in Vietnam: no discussion.
He told me why he cried in the trailer that first time:
CONELAND
BECAUSE YOUR DAD WAS...
ALONE
HUH?
COMBAT ORPHAN
NO UNIT

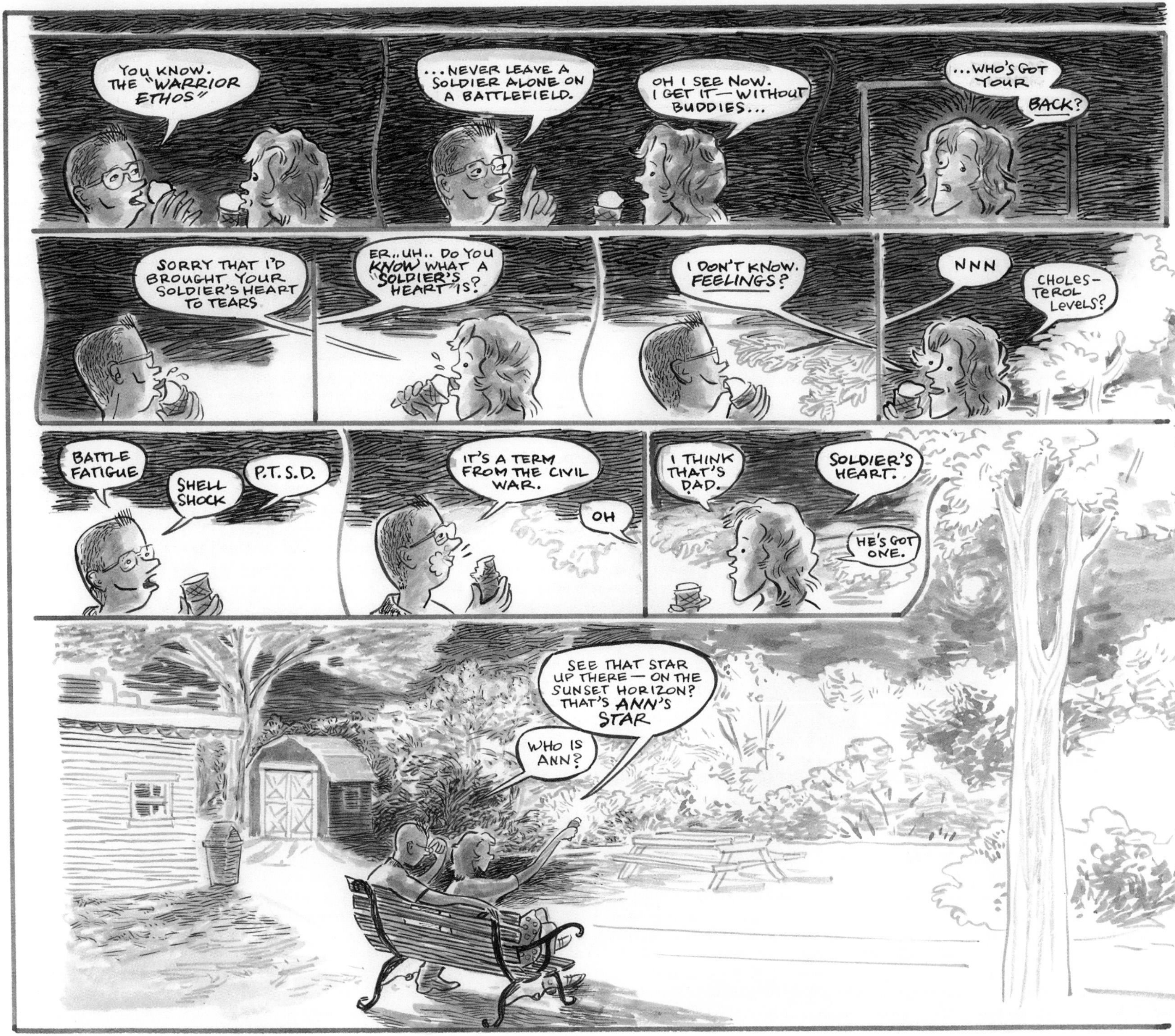

YOU KNOW. THE "WARRIOR ETHOS"
...NEVER LEAVE A SOLDIER ALONE ON A BATTLEFIELD.
OH I SEE NOW. I GET IT— WITHOUT BUDDIES...
...WHO'S GOT YOUR BACK?
SORRY THAT I'D BROUGHT YOUR SOLDIER'S HEART TO TEARS
ER.. UH.. DO YOU KNOW WHAT A "SOLDIER'S HEART" IS?
I DON'T KNOW. FEELINGS?
NNN
CHOLES-TEROL LEVELS?
BATTLE FATIGUE
SHELL SHOCK
P.T.S.D.
IT'S A TERM FROM THE CIVIL WAR.
OH
I THINK THAT'S DAD.
SOLDIER'S HEART.
HE'S GOT ONE.
SEE THAT STAR UP THERE— ON THE SUNSET HORIZON? THAT'S ANN'S STAR
WHO IS ANN?

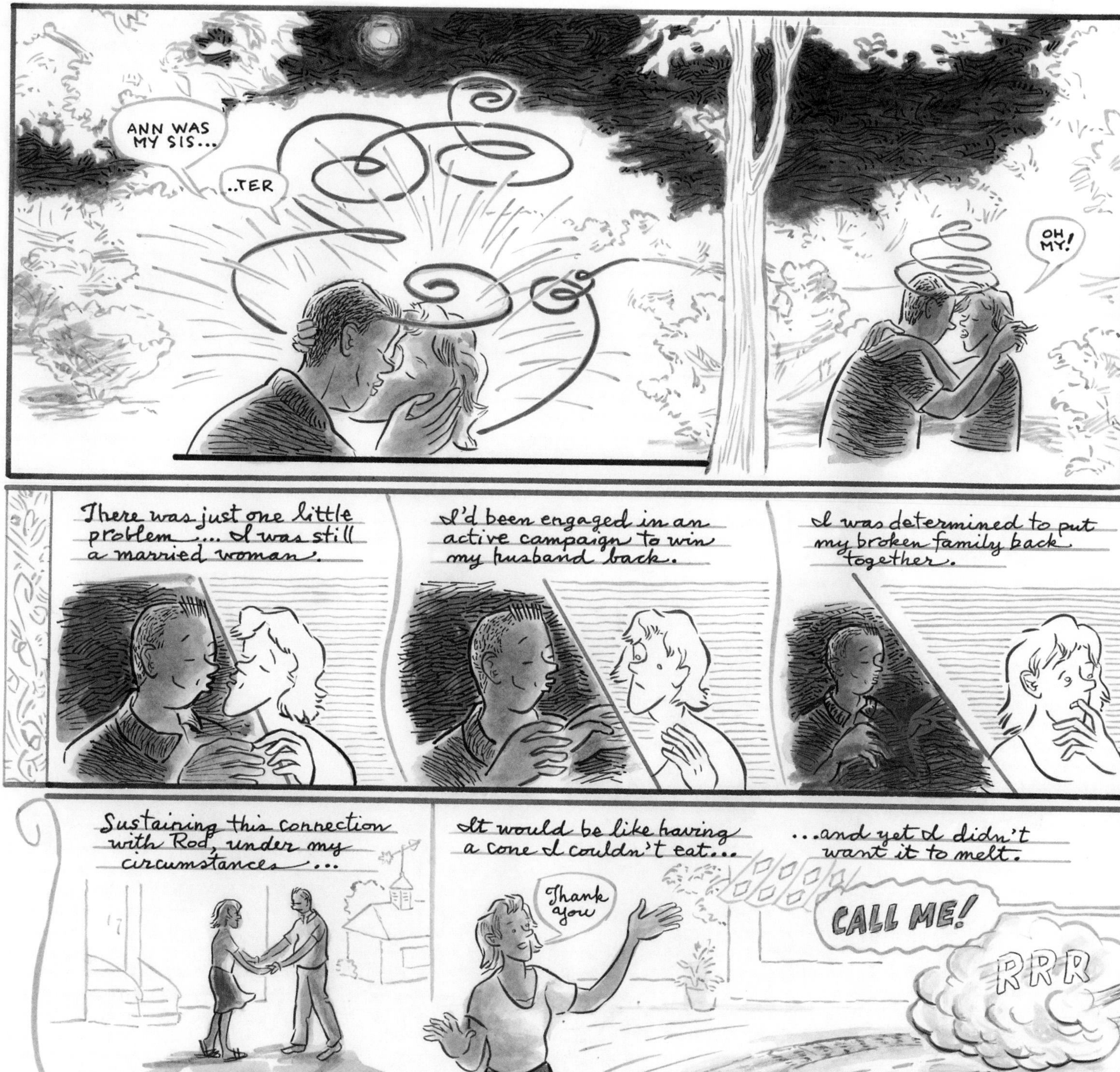
ANN WAS MY SIS...
..TER
OH MY!
There was just one little problem... I was still a married woman.
I'd been engaged in an active campaign to win my husband back.
I was determined to put my broken family back together.
Sustaining this connection with Rod, under my circumstances...
It would be like having a cone I couldn't eat...
...and yet I didn't want it to melt.
Thank you
CALL ME!
RRR

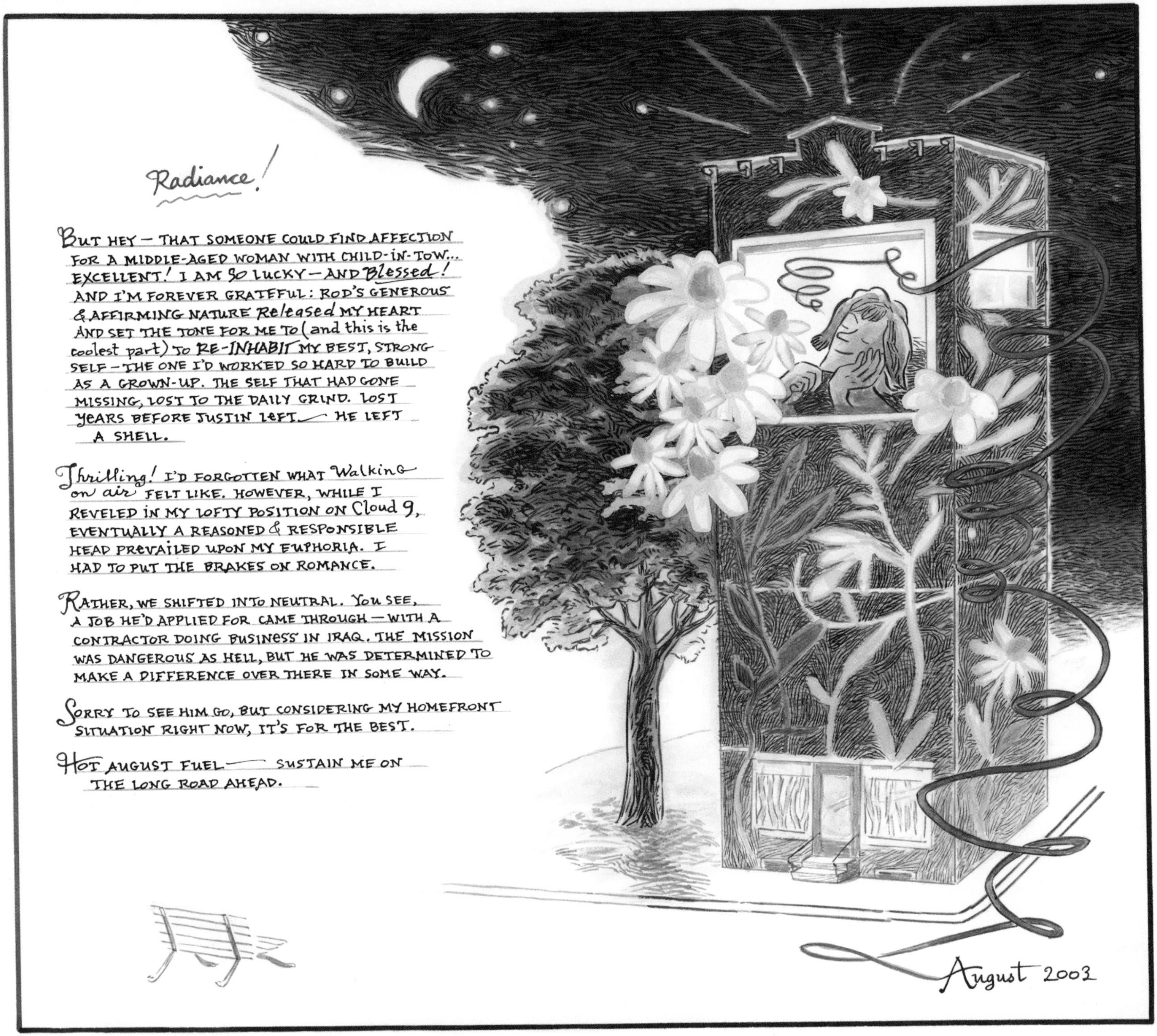
Radiance!
But hey — that someone could find affection for a middle-aged woman with child-in-tow... Excellent! I am so lucky — and Blessed! And I'm forever grateful: Rod's generous & affirming nature Released my heart and set the tone for me to (and this is the coolest part) to RE-INHABIT my best, strong self — the one I'd worked so hard to build as a grown-up. The self that had gone missing, lost to the daily grind. Lost years before Justin left — he left a shell.
Thrilling! I'd forgotten what Walking on air felt like. However, while I reveled in my lofty position on Cloud 9, eventually a reasoned & responsible head prevailed upon my euphoria. I had to put the brakes on romance.
Rather, we shifted into neutral. You see, a job he'd applied for came through — with a contractor doing business in Iraq. The mission was dangerous as hell, but he was determined to make a difference over there in some way.
Sorry to see him go, but considering my homefront situation right now, it's for the best.
Hot August fuel — sustain me on the long road ahead.
August 2003

11.

BREATHING ROOM

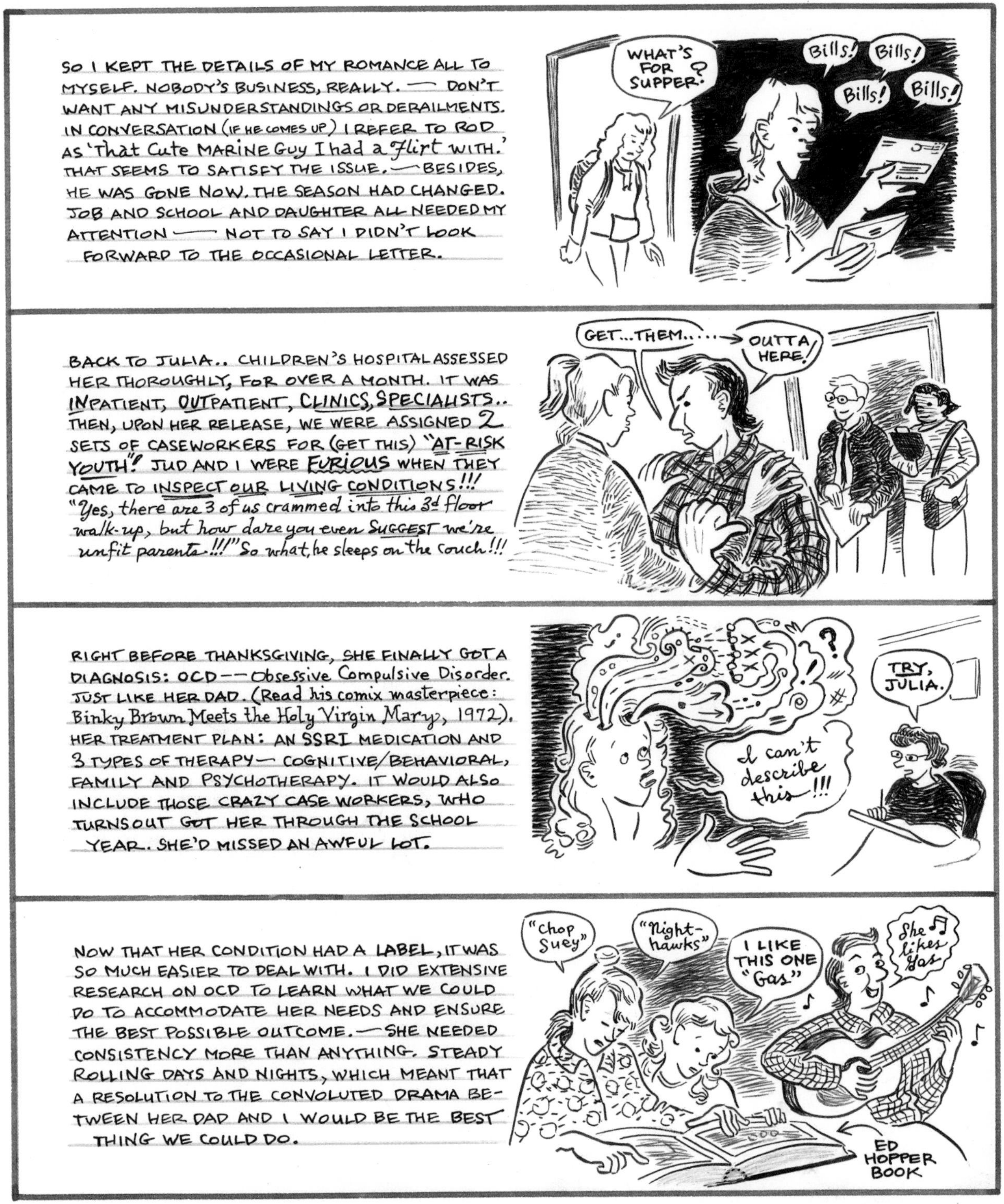
SO I KEPT THE DETAILS OF MY ROMANCE ALL TO MYSELF. NOBODY'S BUSINESS, REALLY. — DON'T WANT ANY MISUNDERSTANDINGS OR DERAILMENTS. IN CONVERSATION (IF HE COMES UP) I REFER TO ROD AS 'That Cute MARINE Guy I had a Flirt WITH.' THAT SEEMS TO SATISFY THE ISSUE. — BESIDES, HE WAS GONE NOW. THE SEASON HAD CHANGED. JOB AND SCHOOL AND DAUGHTER ALL NEEDED MY ATTENTION — NOT TO SAY I DIDN'T LOOK FORWARD TO THE OCCASIONAL LETTER.
WHAT'S FOR SUPPER?
Bills!
Bills!
Bills!
Bills!
BACK TO JULIA.. CHILDREN'S HOSPITAL ASSESSED HER THOROUGHLY, FOR OVER A MONTH. IT WAS INPATIENT, OUTPATIENT, CLINICS, SPECIALISTS.. THEN, UPON HER RELEASE, WE WERE ASSIGNED 2 SETS OF CASEWORKERS FOR (GET THIS) "AT-RISK YOUTH"! JUD AND I WERE FURIOUS WHEN THEY CAME TO INSPECT OUR LIVING CONDITIONS!!! "Yes, there are 3 of us crammed into this 3d floor walk-up, but how dare you even SUGGEST we're unfit parents!!!" So what, he sleeps on the couch!!!
GET...THEM.....
OUTTA HERE!
RIGHT BEFORE THANKSGIVING, SHE FINALLY GOT A DIAGNOSIS: OCD — Obsessive Compulsive Disorder. JUST LIKE HER DAD. (Read his comix masterpiece: Binky Brown Meets the Holy Virgin Mary, 1972). HER TREATMENT PLAN: AN SSRI MEDICATION AND 3 TYPES OF THERAPY — COGNITIVE/BEHAVIORAL, FAMILY AND PSYCHOTHERAPY. IT WOULD ALSO INCLUDE THOSE CRAZY CASE WORKERS, WHO TURNS OUT GOT HER THROUGH THE SCHOOL YEAR. SHE'D MISSED AN AWFUL LOT.
TRY, JULIA.
I can't describe this!!!
NOW THAT HER CONDITION HAD A LABEL, IT WAS SO MUCH EASIER TO DEAL WITH. I DID EXTENSIVE RESEARCH ON OCD TO LEARN WHAT WE COULD DO TO ACCOMMODATE HER NEEDS AND ENSURE THE BEST POSSIBLE OUTCOME. — SHE NEEDED CONSISTENCY MORE THAN ANYTHING. STEADY ROLLING DAYS AND NIGHTS, WHICH MEANT THAT A RESOLUTION TO THE CONVOLUTED DRAMA BETWEEN HER DAD AND I WOULD BE THE BEST THING WE COULD DO.
"Chop Suey"
"Night-hawks"
I LIKE THIS ONE "Gas"
She likes Gas
ED HOPPER BOOK

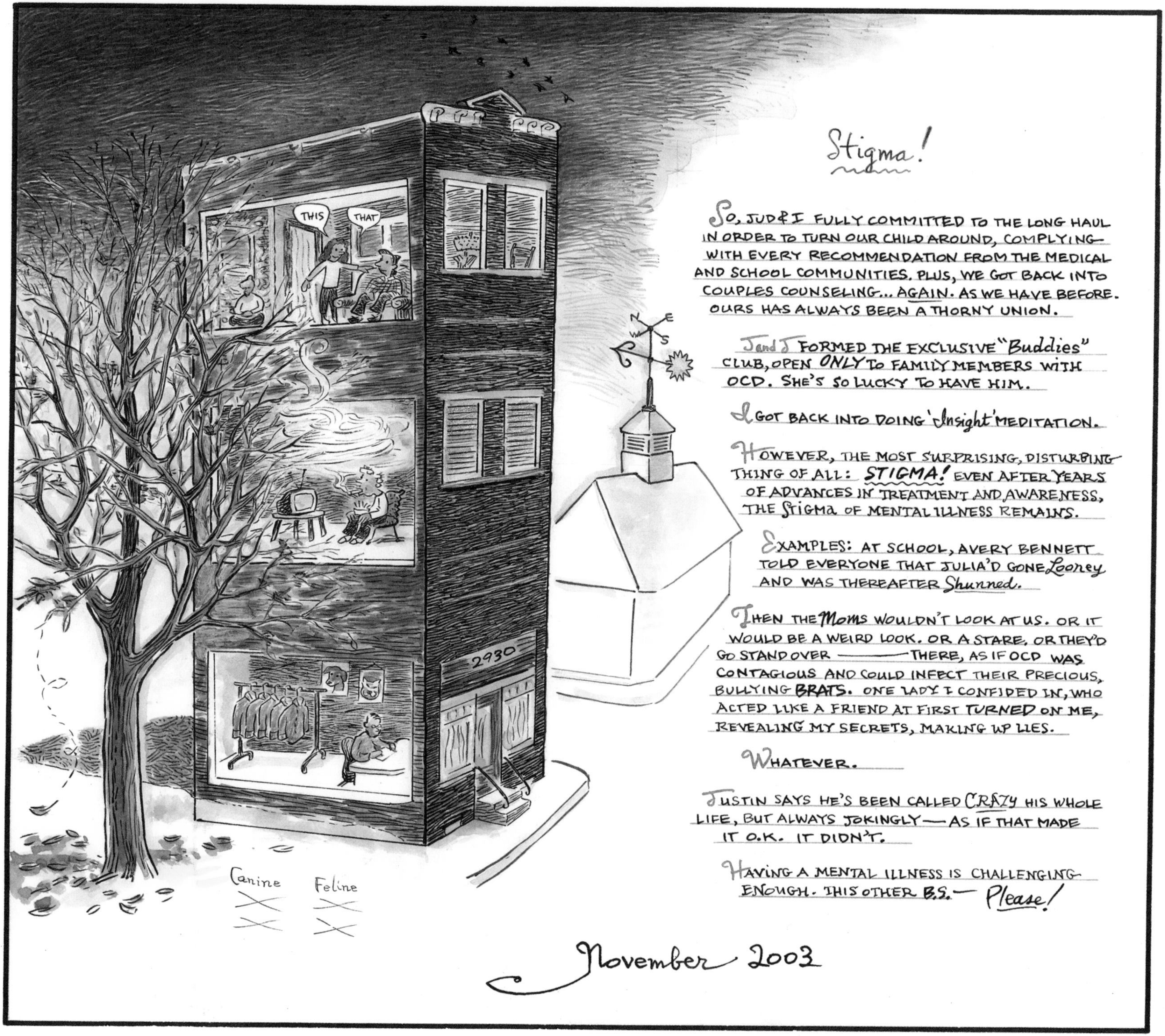
THIS
THAT
2930
N
E
W
S
Canine
Feline
Stigma!
So, Jud & I fully committed to the long haul in order to turn our child around, complying with every recommendation from the medical and school communities. Plus, we got back into couples counseling... AGAIN. As we have before. Ours has always been a thorny union.
J and J formed the exclusive "Buddies" club, open ONLY to family members with OCD. She's so lucky to have him.
I got back into doing 'Insight' meditation.
However, the most surprising, disturbing thing of all: STIGMA! Even after years of advances in treatment and awareness, the stigma of mental illness remains.
Examples: at school, Avery Bennett told everyone that Julia'd gone Looney and was thereafter Shunned.
Then the Moms wouldn't look at us. Or it would be a weird look. Or a stare. Or they'd go stand over —— there, as if OCD was contagious and could infect their precious, bullying BRATS. One lady I confided in, who acted like a friend at first turned on me, revealing my secrets, making up lies.
Whatever.
Justin says he's been called CRAZY his whole life, but always jokingly — as if that made it O.K. It didn't.
Having a mental illness is challenging enough. This other B.S. — Please!
November 2003

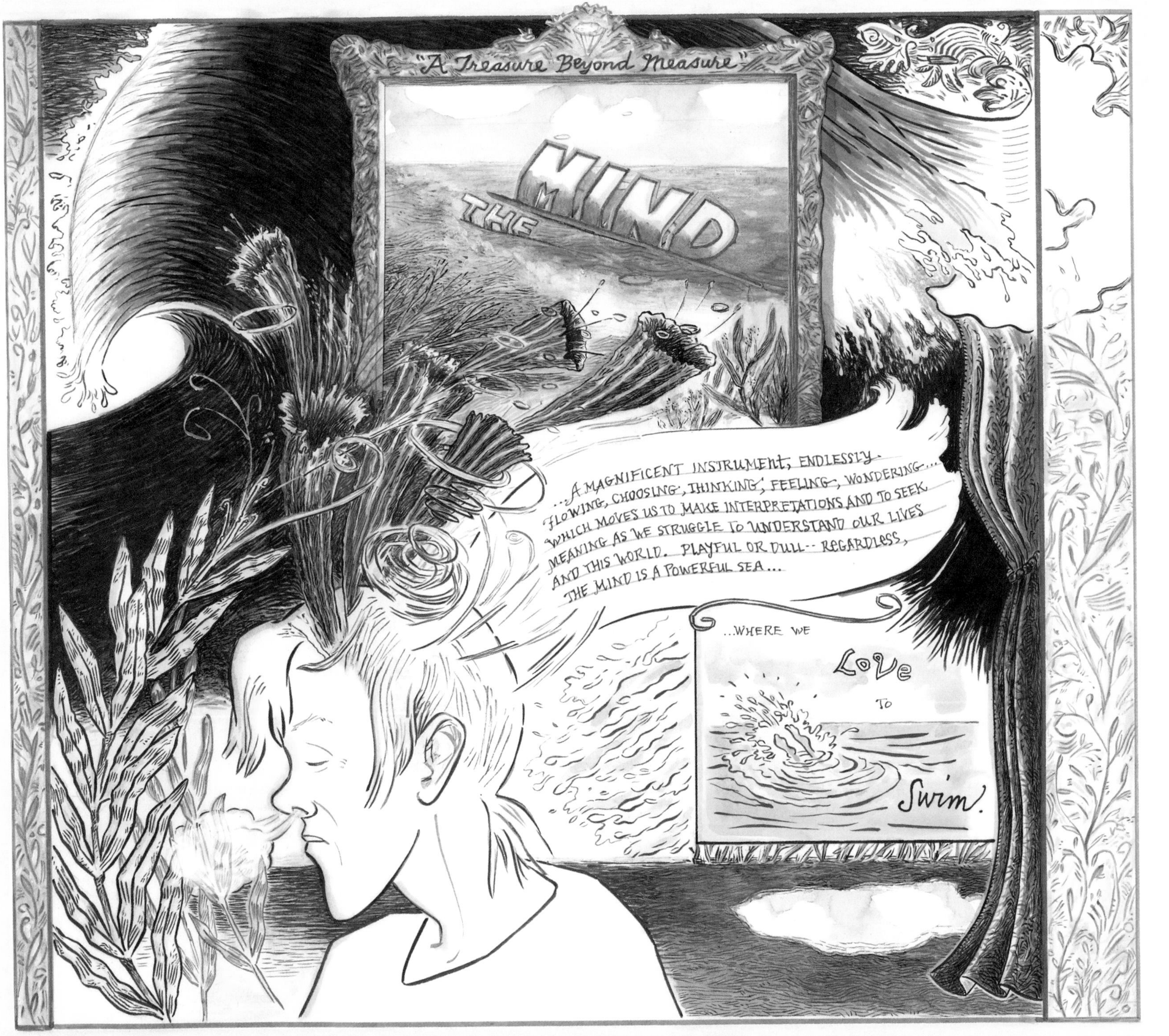
"A Treasure Beyond Measure"
THE MIND
...A MAGNIFICENT INSTRUMENT, ENDLESSLY FLOWING, CHOOSING, THINKING, FEELING, WONDERING... WHICH MOVES US TO MAKE INTERPRETATIONS AND TO SEEK MEANING AS WE STRUGGLE TO UNDERSTAND OUR LIVES AND THIS WORLD. PLAYFUL OR DULL-- REGARDLESS, THE MIND IS A POWERFUL SEA...
...WHERE WE
LOVE
TO
Swim.

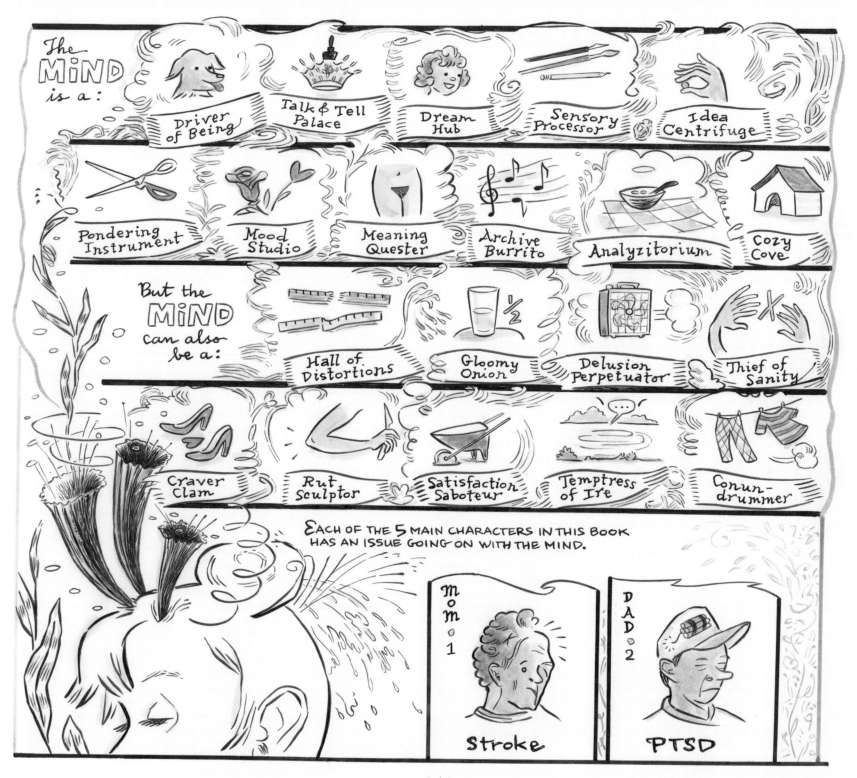

The MiND is a:

Driver of Being

Talk & Tell Palace

Dream Hub

Sensory Processor

Idea Centrifuge

Pondering Instrument

Mood Studio

Meaning Quester

Archive Burrito

Analyzitorium

Cozy Cove

But the MiND can also be a:

Hall of Distortions

Gloomy Onion

Delusion Perpetuator

Thief of Sanity

Craver Clam

Rut Sculptor

Satisfaction Saboteur

Temptress of Ire

Conun-drummer

EACH OF THE 5 MAIN CHARACTERS IN THIS BOOK HAS AN ISSUE GOING ON WITH THE MIND.

MOM 1 — Stroke

DAD 2 — PTSD

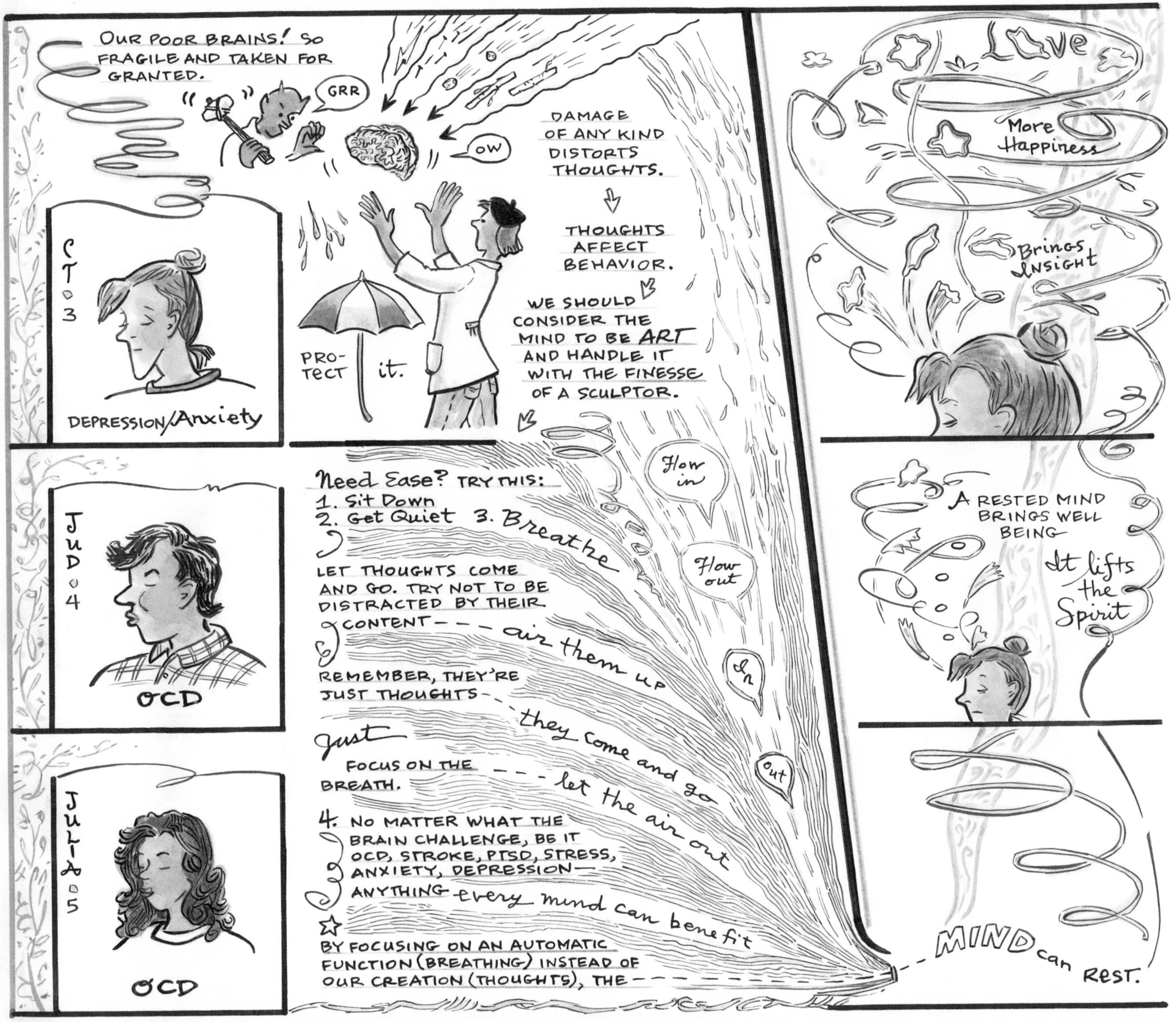

OUR POOR BRAINS! SO FRAGILE AND TAKEN FOR GRANTED.
GRR
OW
DAMAGE OF ANY KIND DISTORTS THOUGHTS.
THOUGHTS AFFECT BEHAVIOR.
WE SHOULD CONSIDER THE MIND TO BE ART AND HANDLE IT WITH THE FINESSE OF A SCULPTOR.
PRO-TECT it.
CT 3
DEPRESSION/Anxiety
Love
More Happiness
Brings Insight
Need Ease? TRY THIS:
1. Sit Down
2. Get Quiet 3. Breathe
Flow in
Flow out
LET THOUGHTS COME AND GO. TRY NOT TO BE DISTRACTED BY THEIR CONTENT--- air them up
REMEMBER, THEY'RE JUST THOUGHTS--- they come and go
In
Just FOCUS ON THE BREATH. --- let the air out
out
4. NO MATTER WHAT THE BRAIN CHALLENGE, BE IT OCD, STROKE, PTSD, STRESS, ANXIETY, DEPRESSION— ANYTHING every mind can benefit
BY FOCUSING ON AN AUTOMATIC FUNCTION (BREATHING) INSTEAD OF OUR CREATION (THOUGHTS), THE --- MIND can REST.
JUD 4
OCD
JULIA 5
OCD
A RESTED MIND BRINGS WELL BEING
It lifts the Spirit

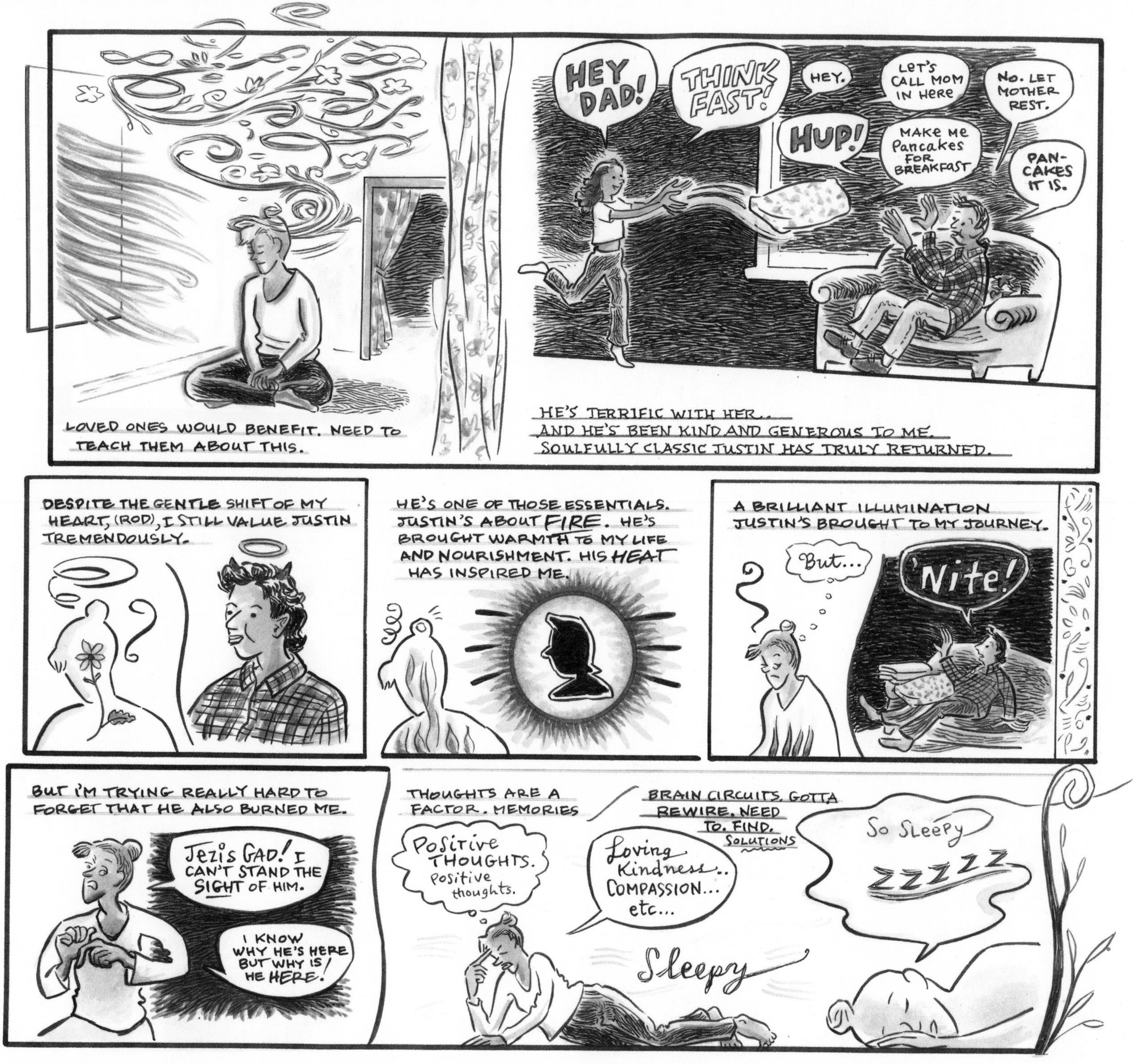

LOVED ONES WOULD BENEFIT. NEED TO TEACH THEM ABOUT THIS.
HEY DAD!
THINK FAST!
HEY.
HUP!
LET'S CALL MOM IN HERE
MAKE ME Pancakes FOR BREAKFAST
NO. LET MOTHER REST.
PAN-CAKES IT IS.
HE'S TERRIFIC WITH HER.
AND HE'S BEEN KIND AND GENEROUS TO ME.
SOULFULLY CLASSIC JUSTIN HAS TRULY RETURNED.
DESPITE THE GENTLE SHIFT OF MY HEART, (ROD), I STILL VALUE JUSTIN TREMENDOUSLY.
HE'S ONE OF THOSE ESSENTIALS. JUSTIN'S ABOUT FIRE. HE'S BROUGHT WARMTH TO MY LIFE AND NOURISHMENT. HIS HEAT HAS INSPIRED ME.
A BRILLIANT ILLUMINATION JUSTIN'S BROUGHT TO MY JOURNEY.
But...
'Nite!
BUT I'M TRYING REALLY HARD TO FORGET THAT HE ALSO BURNED ME.
Jezis GAD! I CAN'T STAND THE SIGHT OF HIM.
I KNOW WHY HE'S HERE BUT WHY IS HE HERE!
THOUGHTS ARE A FACTOR. MEMORIES
BRAIN CIRCUITS. GOTTA REWIRE. NEED TO. FIND. SOLUTIONS
Positive THOUGHTS. Positive thoughts.
Loving Kindness... COMPASSION... etc...
Sleepy
So Sleepy
ZZZZZZ

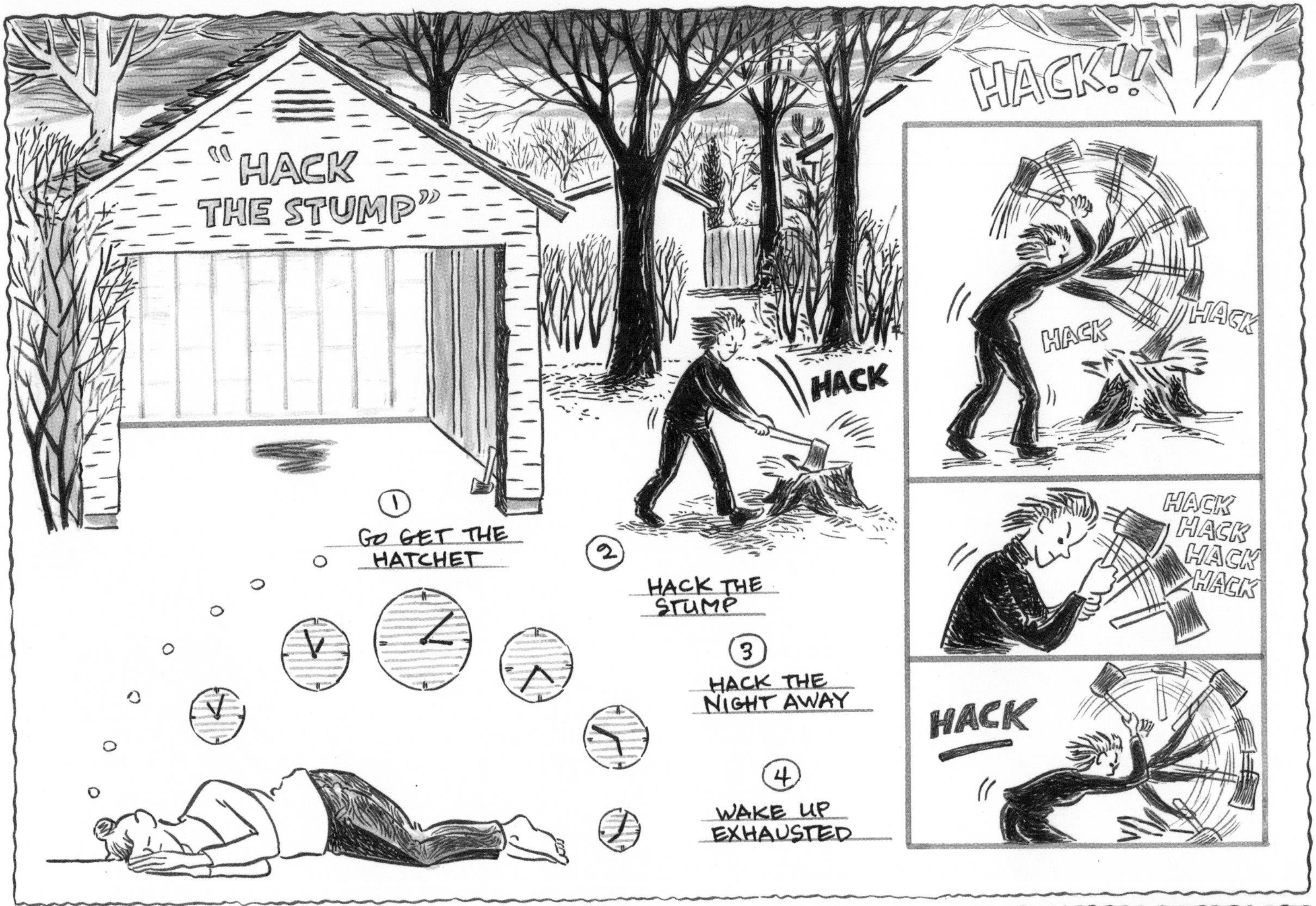
"HACK THE STUMP"
HACK!!
HACK
1 GO GET THE HATCHET
2 HACK THE STUMP
3 HACK THE NIGHT AWAY
4 WAKE UP EXHAUSTED
HACK
HACK
HACK HACK HACK HACK
HACK

BORN OUT OF THE FRUSTRATIONS I FELT WHEN JUSTIN LEFT, THIS REOCCURRING RAGE DREAM CAME NIGHTLY. MY UNRELENTING ATTACK ON THE POOR, BENIGN STUMP WAS NOT INTENDED TO OBLITERATE IT, BUT TO PROVIDE AN OUTLET FOR MY WEARY-WORN PSYCHE. — IT TAPERED OFF SOMEWHAT DURING DAD'S PROJECT AND STOPPED ALTOGETHER WHEN I MET ROD. NOW JUSTIN WAS BACK AND SO WAS THE DREAM. BUT TONIGHT, THE OUTCOME WOULD BE DIFFERENT.

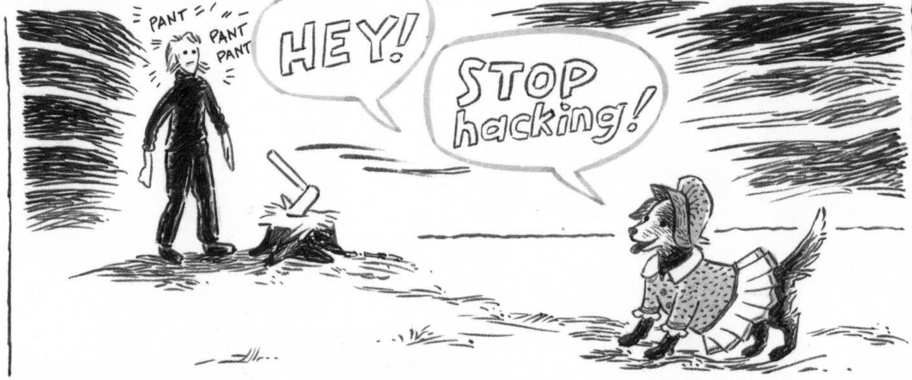
PANT
PANT PANT
HEY!
STOP hacking!

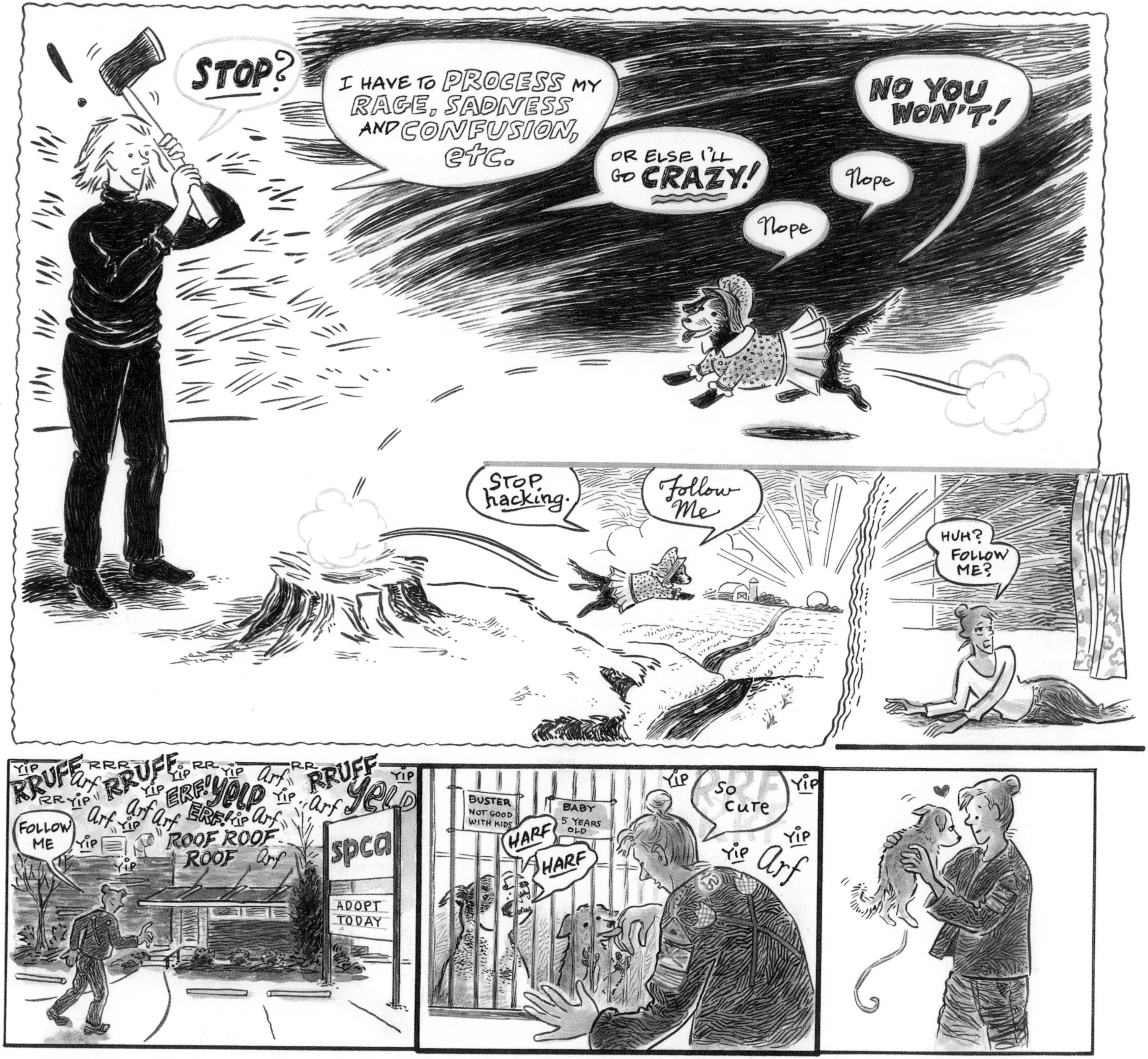
!
STOP?
I HAVE TO PROCESS MY RAGE, SADNESS AND CONFUSION, etc.
OR ELSE I'LL GO CRAZY!
NO YOU WON'T!
Nope
Nope
STOP hacking.
Follow Me
HUH? FOLLOW ME?
YIP RRUFF RRR arf RRUFF YIP RR YIP arf RR RRUFF YIP
RR YIP arf ERF! yelp YIP ERF! YIP arf arf arf YIP arf yelp
FOLLOW ME
YIP ROOF ROOF ROOF arf YIP
spca
ADOPT TODAY
BUSTER NOT GOOD WITH KIDS
BABY 5 YEARS OLD
HARF
HARF
YIP
So cute
YIP
YIP
YIP
arf

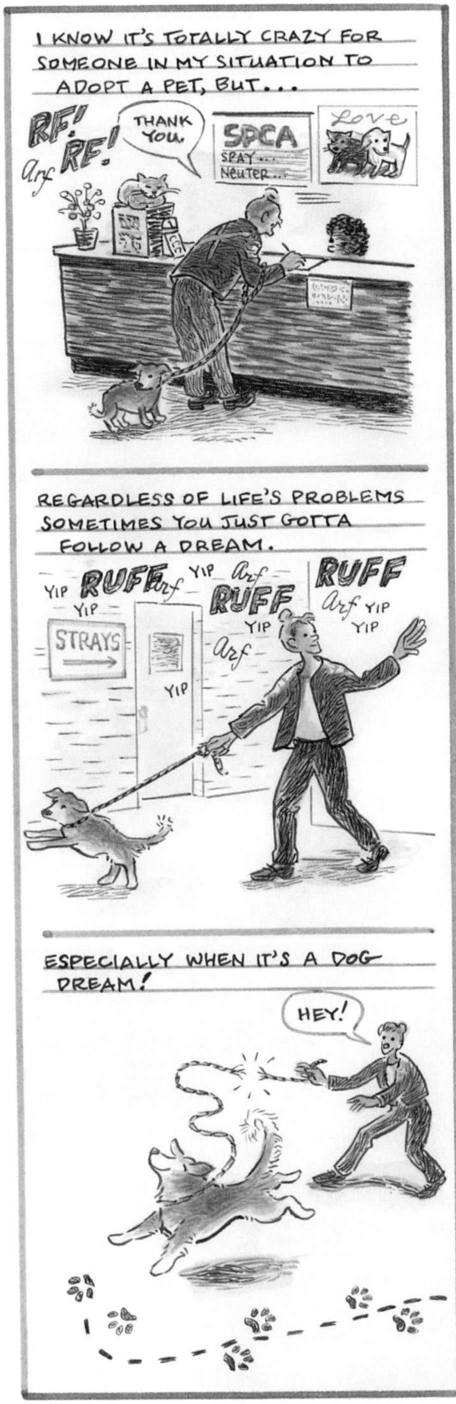
I KNOW IT'S TOTALLY CRAZY FOR SOMEONE IN MY SITUATION TO ADOPT A PET, BUT...
RF! RF!
Arf
THANK YOU.
SPCA
SPAY...
NEUTER...
Love
REGARDLESS OF LIFE'S PROBLEMS SOMETIMES YOU JUST GOTTA FOLLOW A DREAM.
YIP RUFF Arf YIP Arf RUFF RUFF
YIP YIP Arf YIP YIP
STRAYS
Arf
YIP
ESPECIALLY WHEN IT'S A DOG DREAM!
HEY!

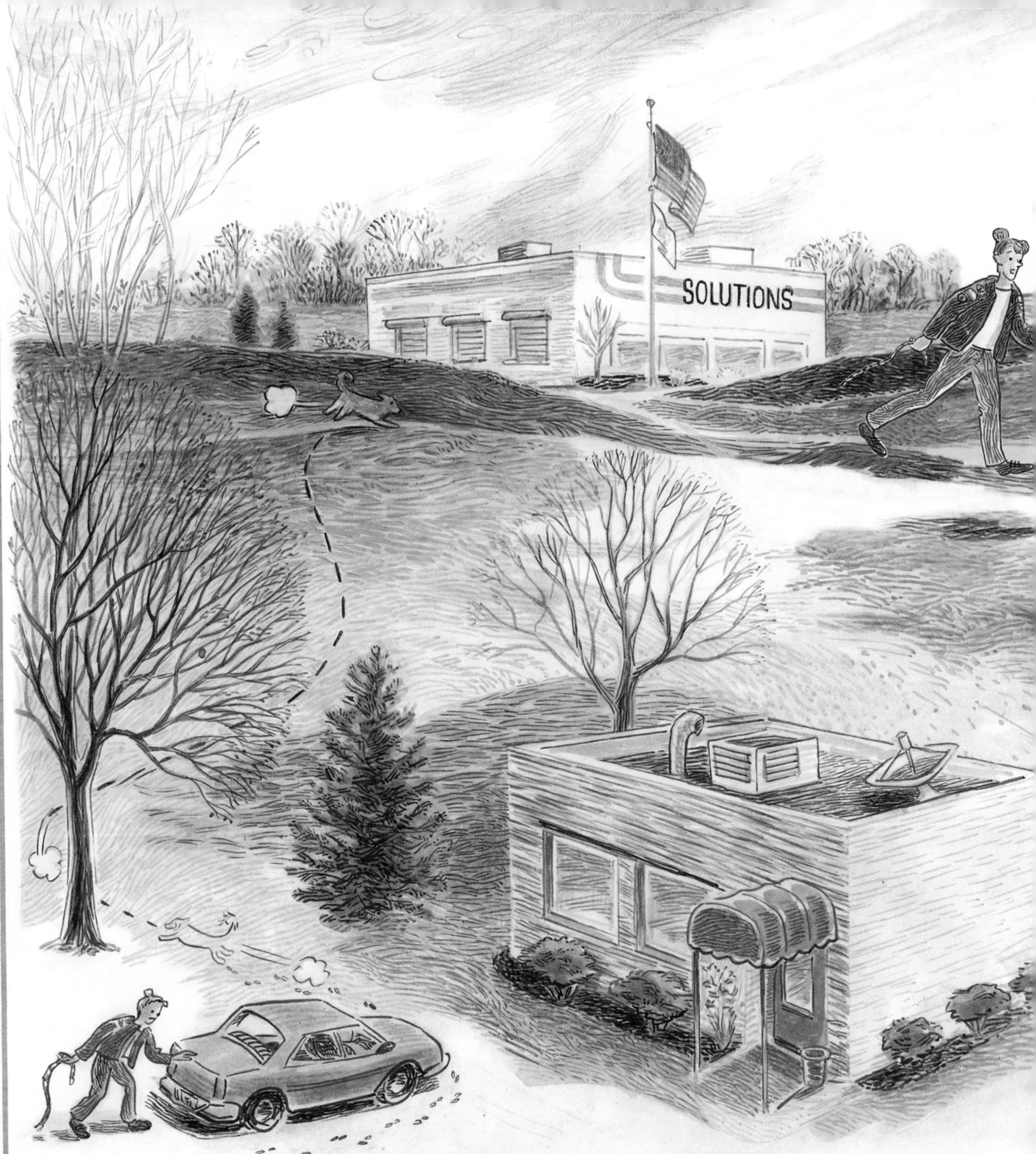
SOLUTIONS

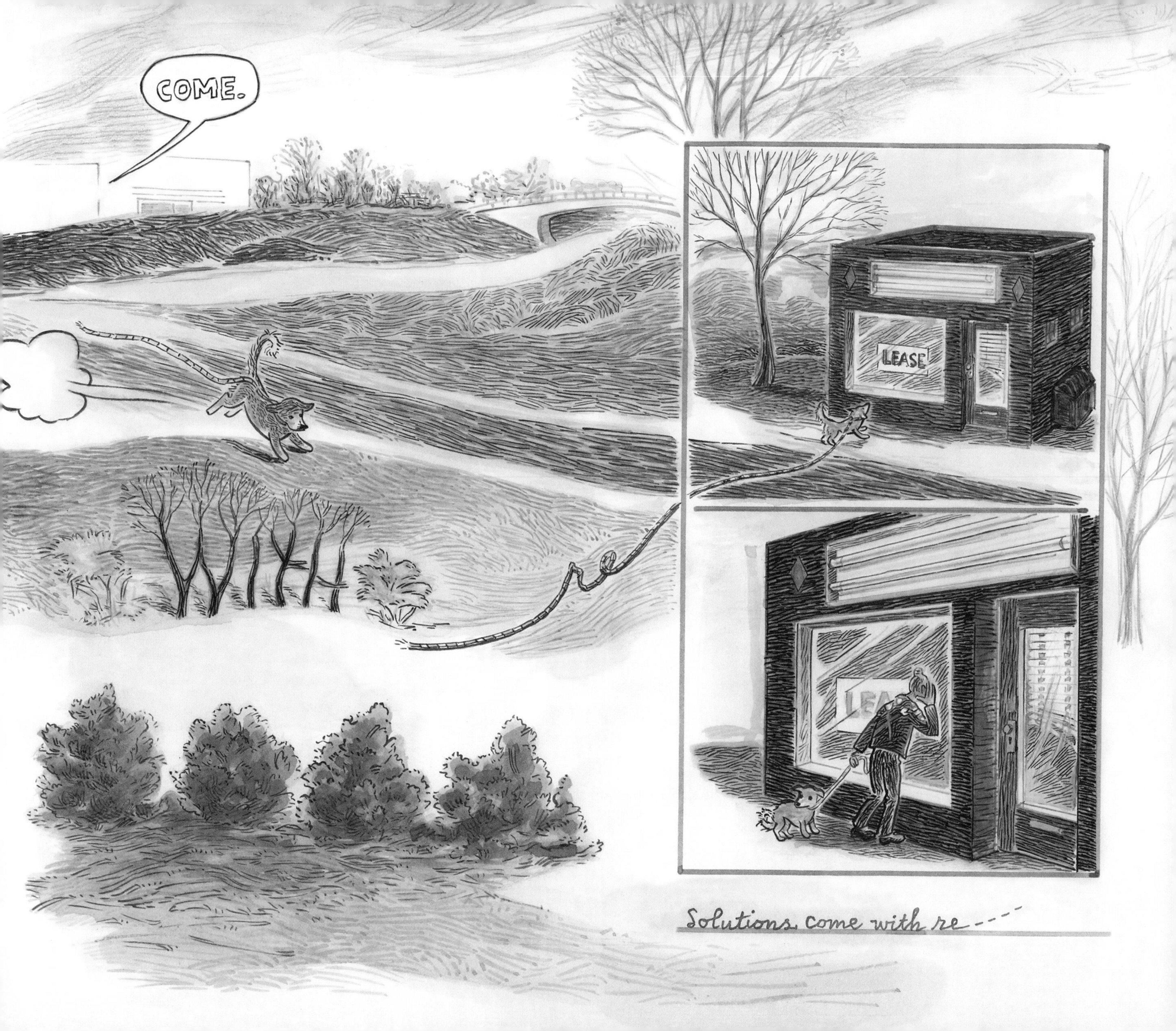
COME.
LEASE
Solutions come with re- - - -

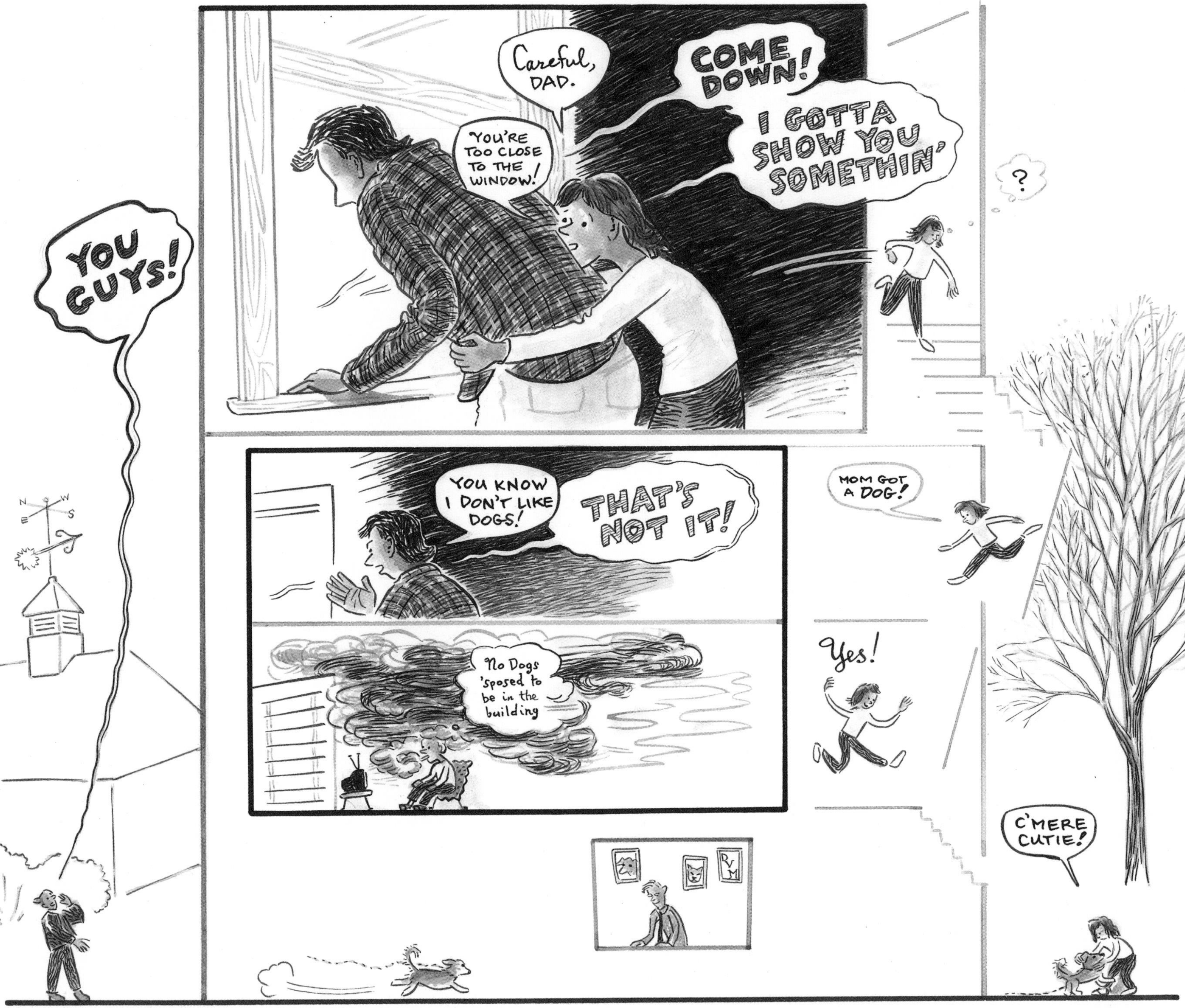
YOU GUYS!
Careful, DAD.
YOU'RE TOO CLOSE TO THE WINDOW!
COME DOWN!
I GOTTA SHOW YOU SOMETHIN'
?
YOU KNOW I DON'T LIKE DOGS!
THAT'S NOT IT!
MOM GOT A DOG!
No Dogs 'sposed to be in the building
Yes!
DVM
C'MERE CUTIE!
N W E S

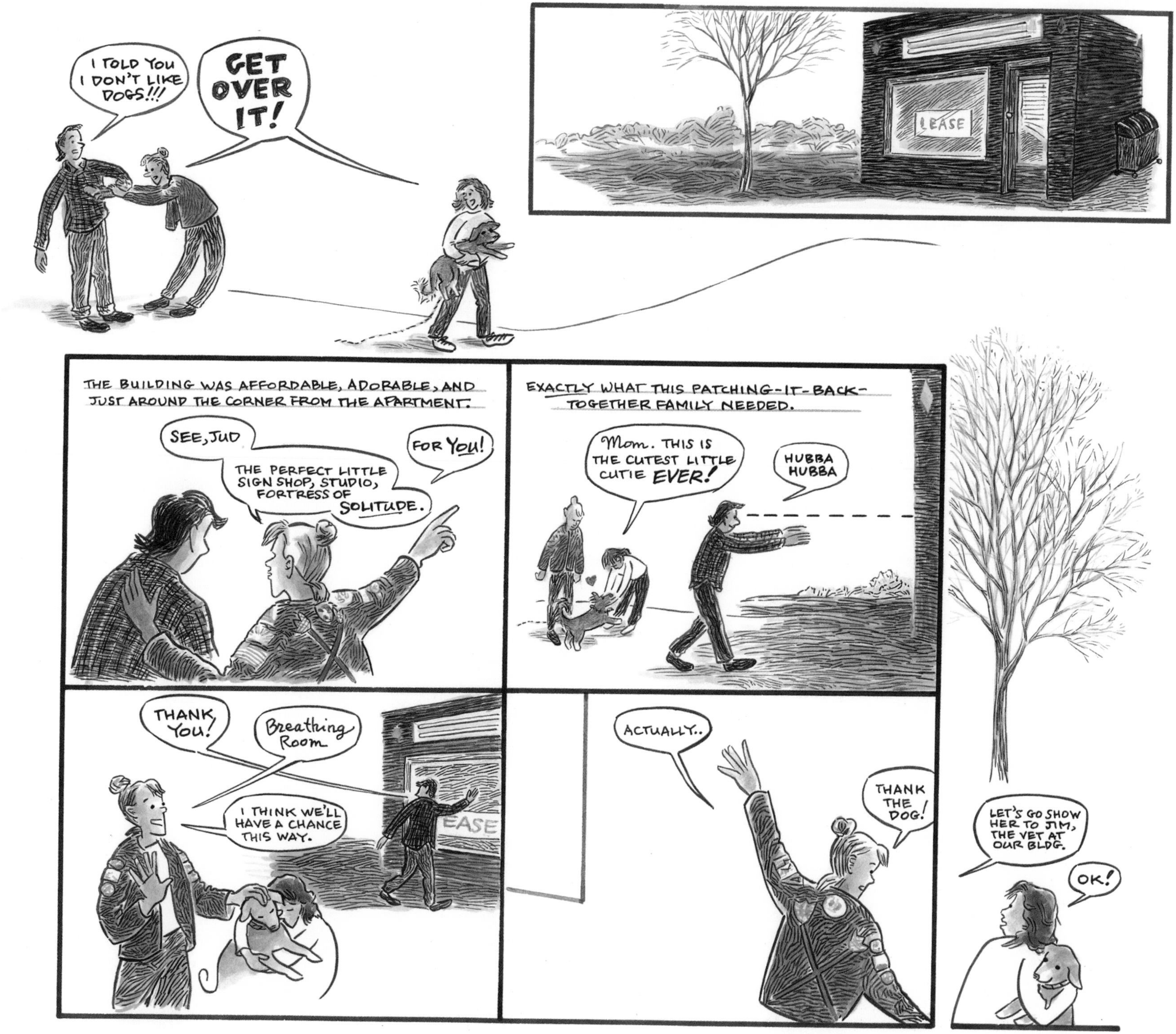

I TOLD YOU I DON'T LIKE DOGS!!!
GET OVER IT!
LEASE
THE BUILDING WAS AFFORDABLE, ADORABLE, AND JUST AROUND THE CORNER FROM THE APARTMENT.
SEE, JUD
THE PERFECT LITTLE SIGN SHOP, STUDIO, FORTRESS OF SOLITUDE.
FOR YOU!
EXACTLY WHAT THIS PATCHING-IT-BACK-TOGETHER FAMILY NEEDED.
Mom. THIS IS THE CUTEST LITTLE CUTIE EVER!
HUBBA HUBBA
THANK YOU!
Breathing Room
I THINK WE'LL HAVE A CHANCE THIS WAY.
EASE
ACTUALLY..
THANK THE DOG!
LET'S GO SHOW HER TO JIM, THE VET AT OUR BLDG.
OK!

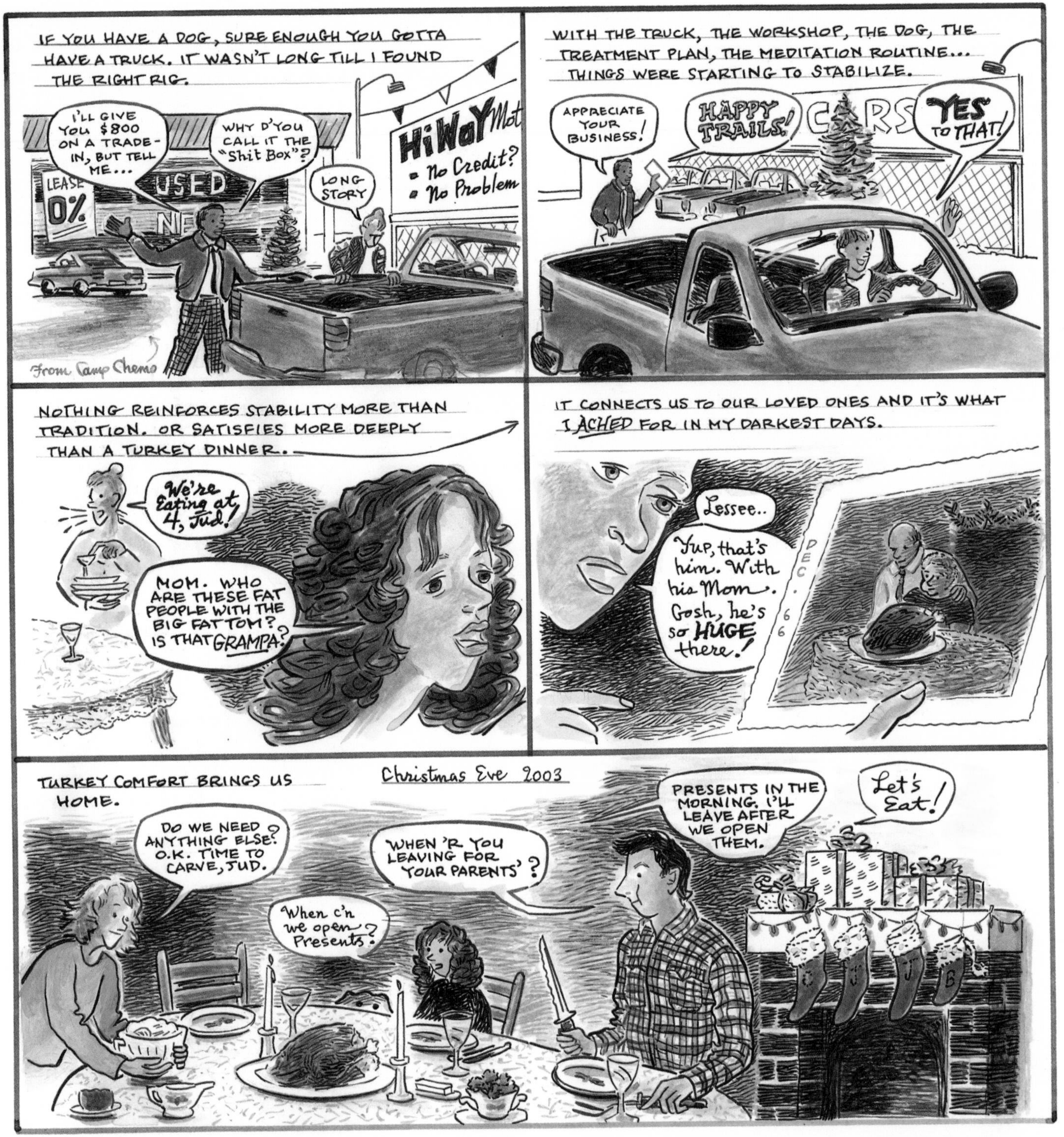
IF YOU HAVE A DOG, SURE ENOUGH YOU GOTTA HAVE A TRUCK. IT WASN'T LONG TILL I FOUND THE RIGHT RIG.
I'LL GIVE YOU $800 ON A TRADE-IN, BUT TELL ME...
WHY D'YOU CALL IT THE "Shit Box"?
LONG STORY
LEASE 0%
USED
HiWay Mot
No Credit?
No Problem
From Camp Chemo
WITH THE TRUCK, THE WORKSHOP, THE DOG, THE TREATMENT PLAN, THE MEDITATION ROUTINE... THINGS WERE STARTING TO STABILIZE.
APPRECIATE YOUR BUSINESS!
HAPPY TRAILS!
CARS
YES TO THAT!
NOTHING REINFORCES STABILITY MORE THAN TRADITION. OR SATISFIES MORE DEEPLY THAN A TURKEY DINNER.
We're Eating at 4, Jud!
MOM. WHO ARE THESE FAT PEOPLE WITH THE BIG FAT TOM? IS THAT GRAMPA?
IT CONNECTS US TO OUR LOVED ONES AND IT'S WHAT I ACHED FOR IN MY DARKEST DAYS.
Lessee..
Yup, that's him. With his Mom. Gosh, he's so HUGE there!
DEC. 66
TURKEY COMFORT BRINGS US HOME.
Christmas Eve 2003
DO WE NEED ANYTHING ELSE? O.K. TIME TO CARVE, JUD.
When c'n we open Presents?
WHEN 'R YOU LEAVING FOR YOUR PARENTS'?
PRESENTS IN THE MORNING. I'LL LEAVE AFTER WE OPEN THEM.
Let's Eat!

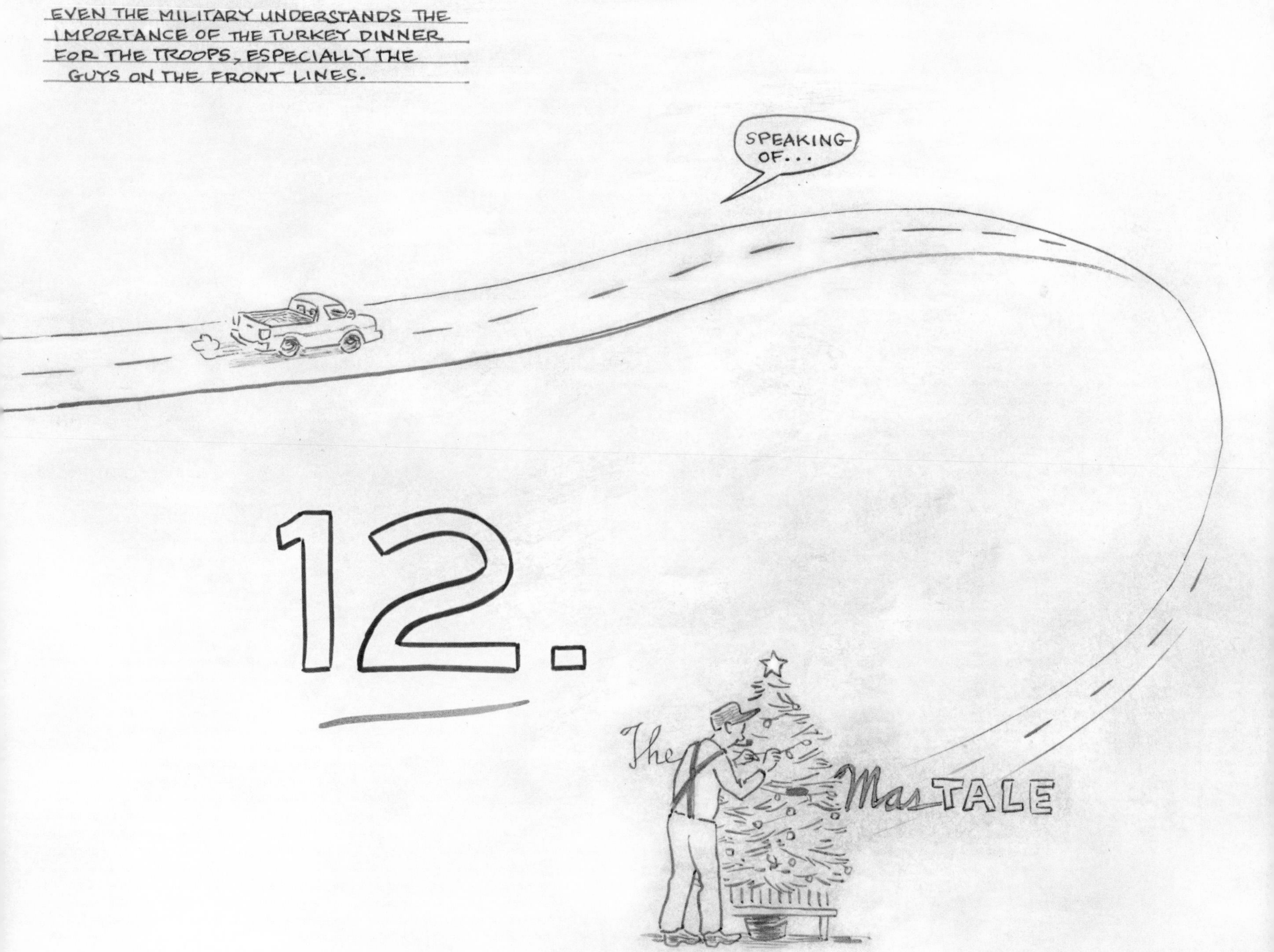
EVEN THE MILITARY UNDERSTANDS THE IMPORTANCE OF THE TURKEY DINNER FOR THE TROOPS, ESPECIALLY THE GUYS ON THE FRONT LINES.
SPEAKING OF...
12.
The
Mas TALE

Baby

Ginja's dog Cleo

Sarrah

The Great Ornament Bat Down, 2003

O Tannenbaum! O Tannenbaum! Wie treu sind deine Blätter! Your ornaments are dazzle-ing, til dog tails almost chaos bring! ～ Oh Christmas tree, oh Christmas tree ～ How ever green your branches!

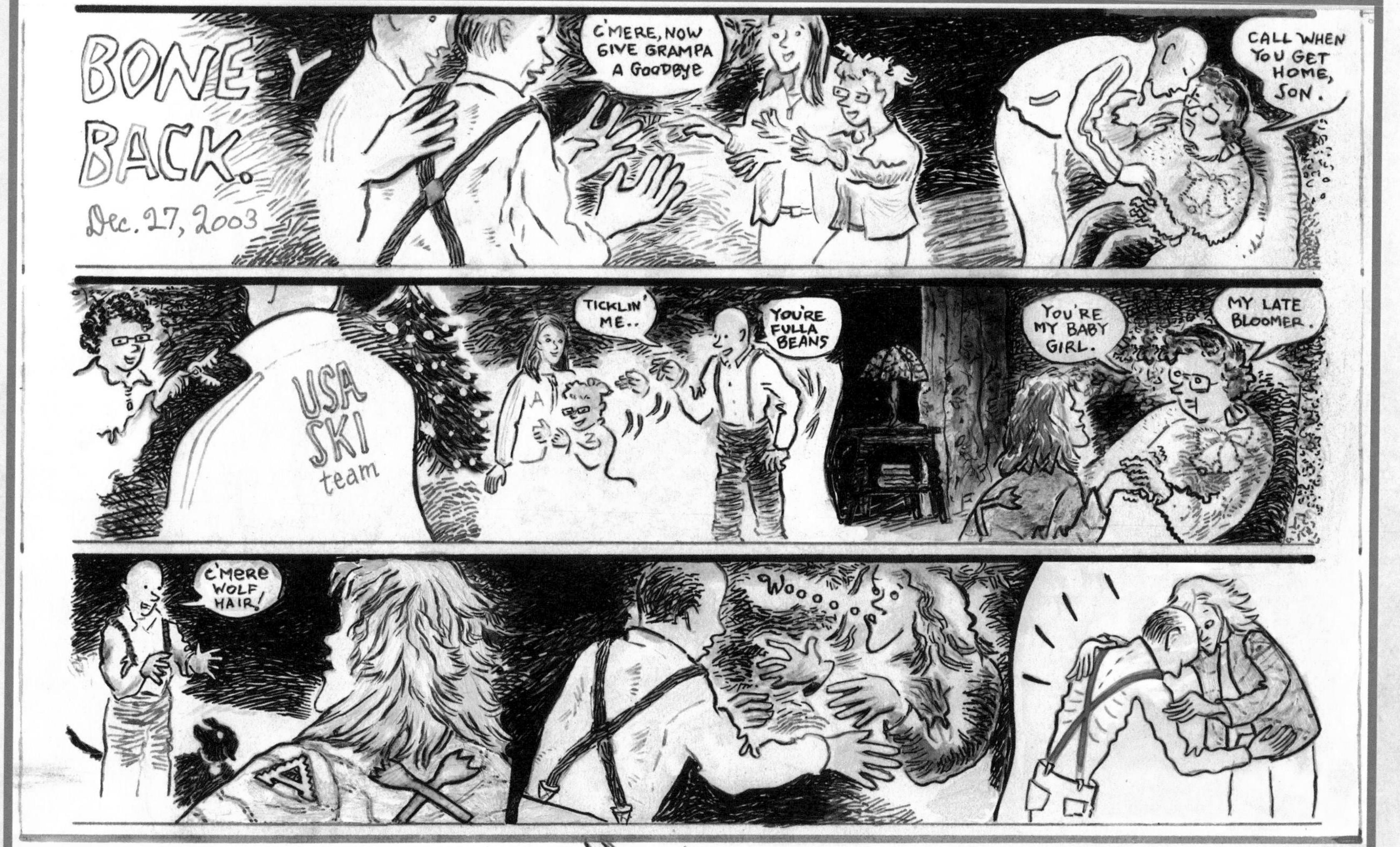
BONE-Y BACK.
Dec. 27, 2003
C'MERE, NOW GIVE GRAMPA A GOODBYE
CALL WHEN YOU GET HOME, SON.
USA SKI team
TICKLIN' ME..
YOU'RE FULLA BEANS
YOU'RE MY BABY GIRL.
MY LATE BLOOMER.
C'MERE WOLF HAIR!
Woooooo

DAD TRIES. HE REALLY DOES. BUT WHY IN THE HECK WOULD ANYONE PUT DELICATE HAND-BLOWN DANGLERS LOW ENOUGH FOR DOG TAILS TO **LOFT** THEM ACROSS THE ROOM LIKE **MISSILES**? STILL, YOU GOTTA GIVE IT TO CHUCK BECAUSE THE TREE TRIMMING TORCH HAD RATHER ABRUPTLY BEEN PASSED TO HIM UPON **CHRISTMAS LOVIN' MOM'S** INCAPACITATION. HIS CONTRIBUTION TO THE YULETIDE TRADITION: CUSS DECORATING.

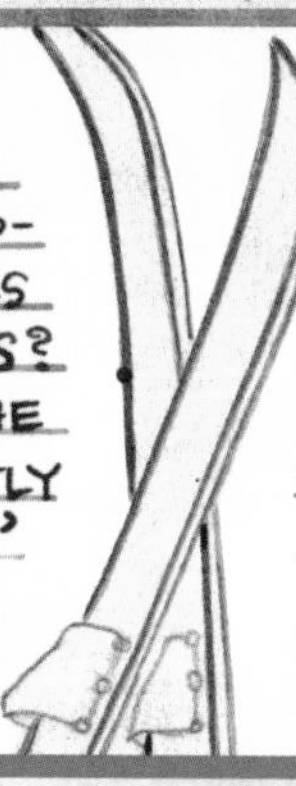

TODAY IS DEC. 27. MY BROTHER JIM AND HIS FAMILY ARE HEADED BACK UP TO N.Y. I WAS OUT THE DOOR, TOO, HAVING DRIVEN OVER FROM CINCI ON X-MAS MORNING. CHRISTMAS EVE WAS SPENT WITH **JUSTIN** and **JULIA** HAVING A NICE MEAL. JIM AND I WOULD GO IN TANDEM TO INDY, STOP FOR A MILKSHAKE, THEN GO OUR SEPARATE WAYS — OH YEAH. SOMETHING TO NOTE: WHILE LOOKING AROUND FOR BLEACH TO CLEAN UP DOG VOMIT (BABY GOT INTO SOME GARBAGE) JIM CAME ACROSS A **HUGE** MOUSE HOLE.

How loyal I am to the winter landscape! Graphically exquisite like an expensive Tiffany lamp. I especially like it on the cusp between 'all that's been known in daylight' and 'yield to sobering dusk.' Fall in.

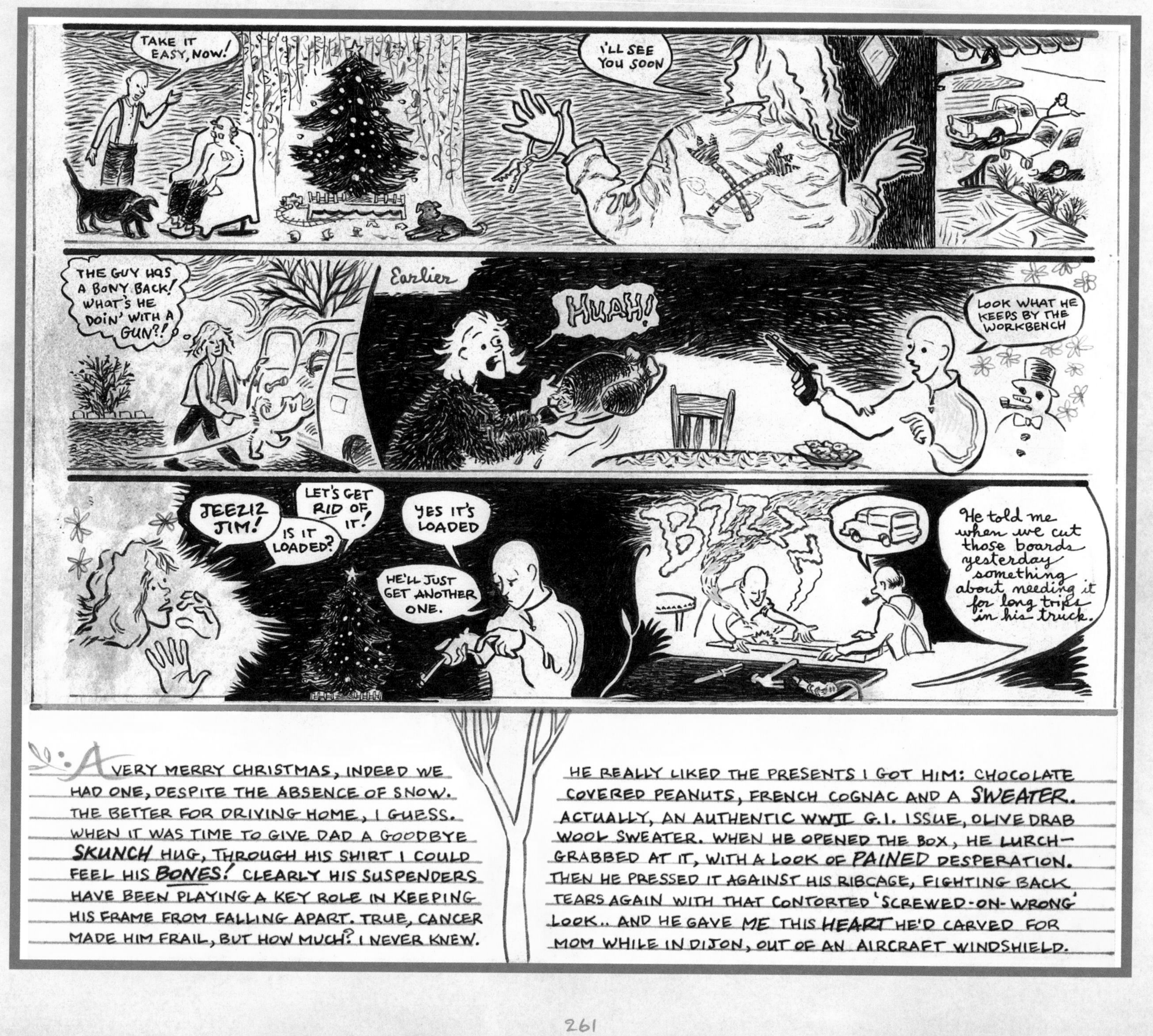
TAKE IT EASY, NOW!
I'LL SEE YOU SOON
THE GUY HAS A BONY BACK! WHAT'S HE DOIN' WITH A GUN?!
Earlier
HUAH!
LOOK WHAT HE KEEPS BY THE WORKBENCH
JEEZIZ JIM!
IS IT LOADED?
LET'S GET RID OF IT!
YES IT'S LOADED
HE'LL JUST GET ANOTHER ONE.
He told me when we cut those boards yesterday something about needing it for long trips in his truck.

A VERY MERRY CHRISTMAS, INDEED WE HAD ONE, DESPITE THE ABSENCE OF SNOW. THE BETTER FOR DRIVING HOME, I GUESS. WHEN IT WAS TIME TO GIVE DAD A GOODBYE *SKUNCH* HUG, THROUGH HIS SHIRT I COULD FEEL HIS *BONES!* CLEARLY HIS SUSPENDERS HAVE BEEN PLAYING A KEY ROLE IN KEEPING HIS FRAME FROM FALLING APART. TRUE, CANCER MADE HIM FRAIL, BUT HOW MUCH? I NEVER KNEW.

HE REALLY LIKED THE PRESENTS I GOT HIM: CHOCOLATE COVERED PEANUTS, FRENCH COGNAC AND A **SWEATER.** ACTUALLY, AN AUTHENTIC WWII G.I. ISSUE, OLIVE DRAB WOOL SWEATER. WHEN HE OPENED THE BOX, HE LURCH-GRABBED AT IT, WITH A LOOK OF *PAINED* DESPERATION. THEN HE PRESSED IT AGAINST HIS RIBCAGE, FIGHTING BACK TEARS AGAIN WITH THAT CONTORTED 'SCREWED-ON-WRONG' LOOK.. AND HE GAVE ME THIS **HEART** HE'D CARVED FOR MOM WHILE IN DIJON, OUT OF AN AIRCRAFT WINDSHIELD.

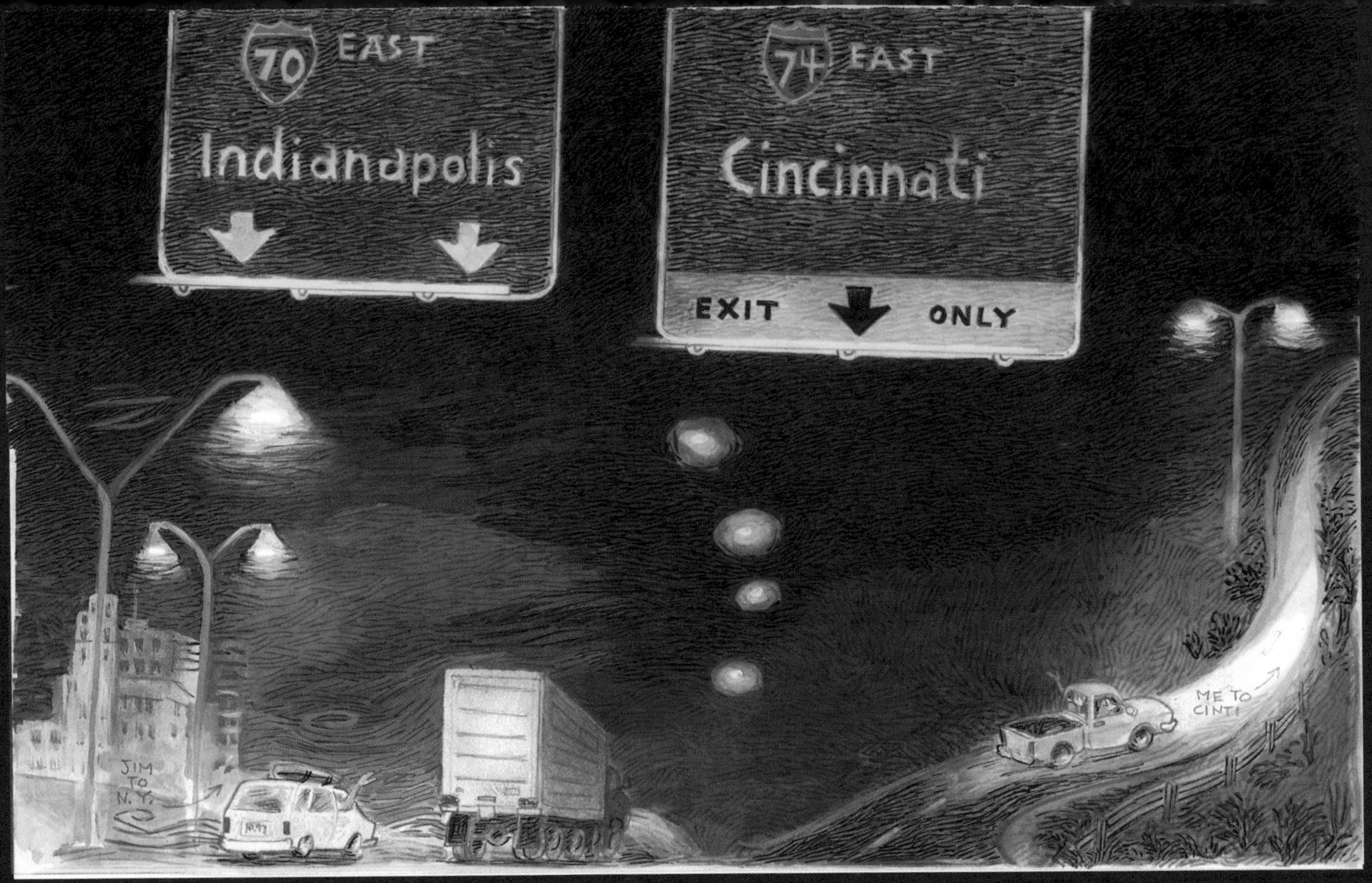
70 EAST
Indianapolis
74 EAST
Cincinnati
EXIT ONLY
JIM TO N.Y.
ME TO CINTI

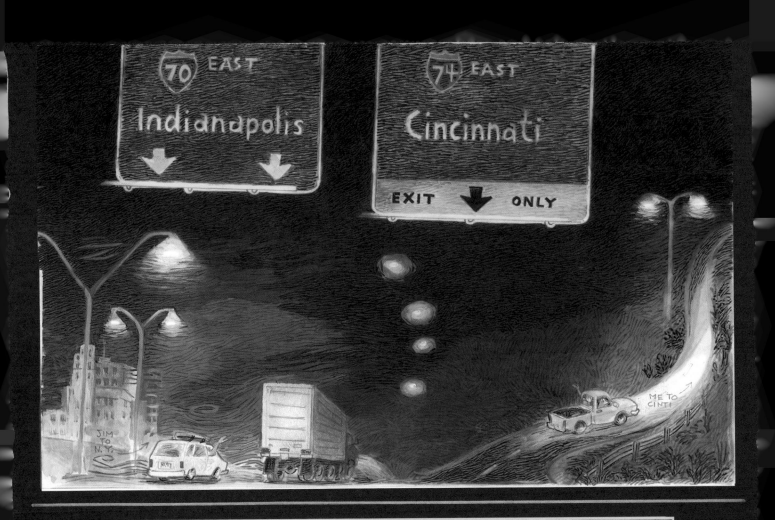

Yield to the municipal pink sky, its atmospheric opalescence, its favorable, cost-saving glow. Are your bricks dissolving, fair city? And how clever to challenge my assumption that 'black' top really is.

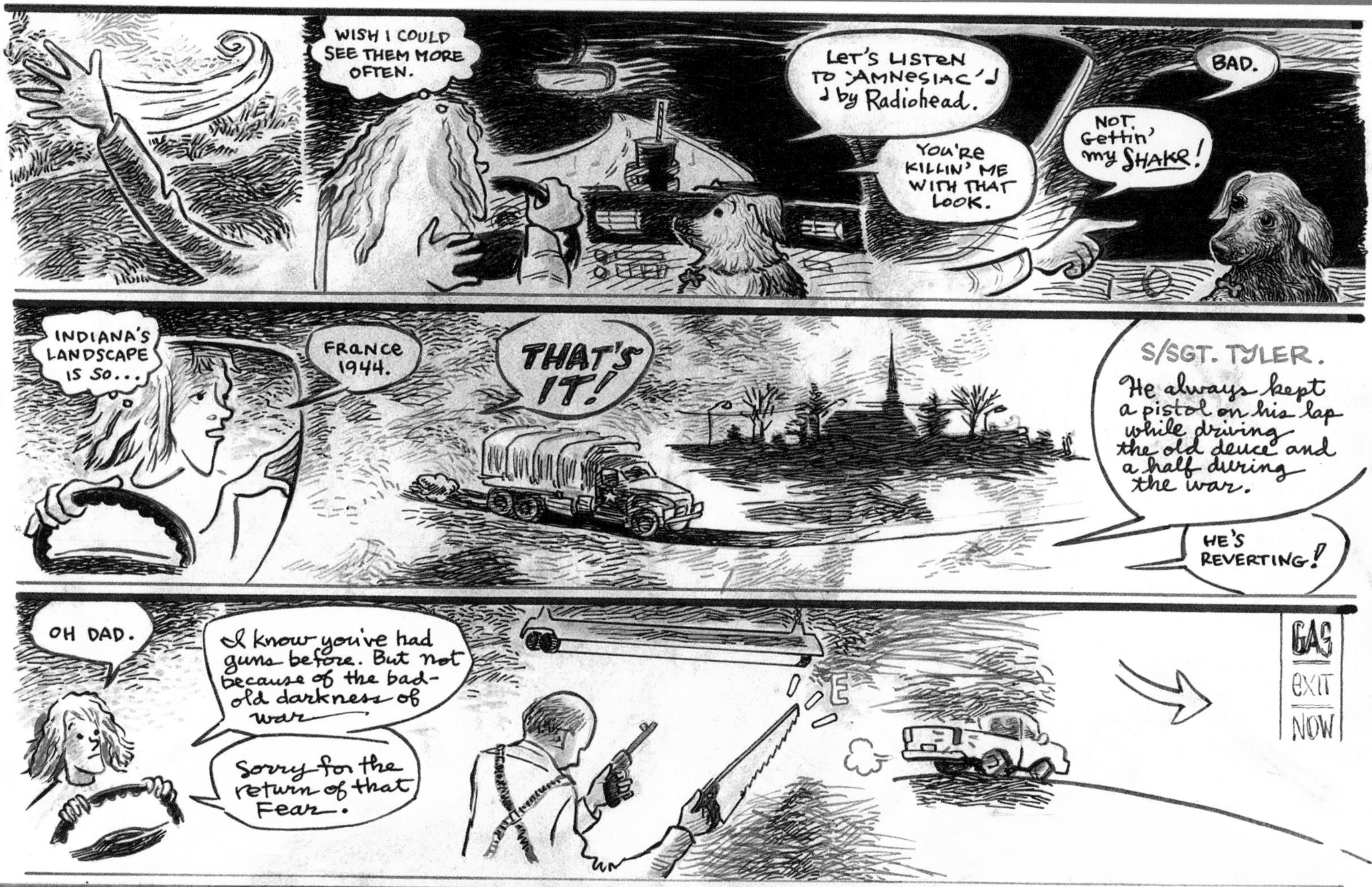
WISH I COULD SEE THEM MORE OFTEN.
LET'S LISTEN TO 'AMNESIAC' by Radiohead.
YOU'RE KILLIN' ME WITH THAT LOOK.
BAD.
NOT GETTIN' MY SHAKE!
INDIANA'S LANDSCAPE IS SO...
France 1944.
THAT'S IT!
S/SGT. TYLER.
He always kept a pistol on his lap while driving the old deuce and a half during the war.
HE'S REVERTING!
OH DAD.
I know you've had guns before. But not because of the bad-old darkness of war.
Sorry for the return of that Fear.
E
GAS
EXIT
NOW

LAST SUMMER, CHUCK TOLD ME 'THE DAY MY DAD LAID DOWN HIS TOOLS WAS THE DAY HE GAVE UP ON LIFE.' SAME FOR HIM, I WOULD SAY. ONLY ADD **KEYS**. FOR DAD TO STOP DRIVING—THAT WOULD SURELY SIGNAL HIS DEMISE. A LOVE AFFAIR THAT BEGAN WITH THE **MODEL 'T'** IN THE 1920S. DRIVING HAS BEEN HIS LIFELONG SURE THING. I CAN RELATE. I ♥ DRIVING. REMEMBER THE 'SHIT BOX' FROM CAMP CHEMO?

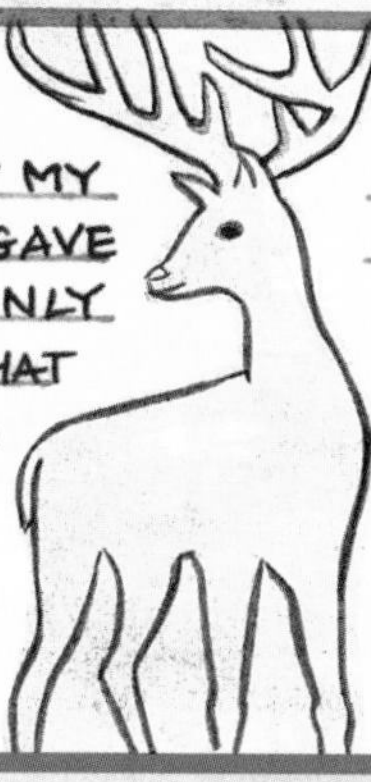

DAD GOT RID OF IT BECAUSE ONE NIGHT, WHILE PUSHING 80 MPH, A DEER **DARTED** ACROSS. SO HE UPGRADED TO THIS ENORMOUS GMC SIERRA. SO BIG THAT LITTLE MR. PEANUT GUY HAD TO BUILD A **STEP-STOOL** TO GET UP INTO THE DAMN THING! THE SIERRA IS SIMILAR IN SIZE TO THE TRUCKS HE DROVE IN EUROPE. IT COULD HAVE TRIGGERED HIS DESIRE FOR A **GUN**. ALTHOUGH HE CLAIMS THAT WITH OIL AND GAS PRICES GOING UP THERE'S BOUND TO BE TROUBLE AT THE FILLING STATION.

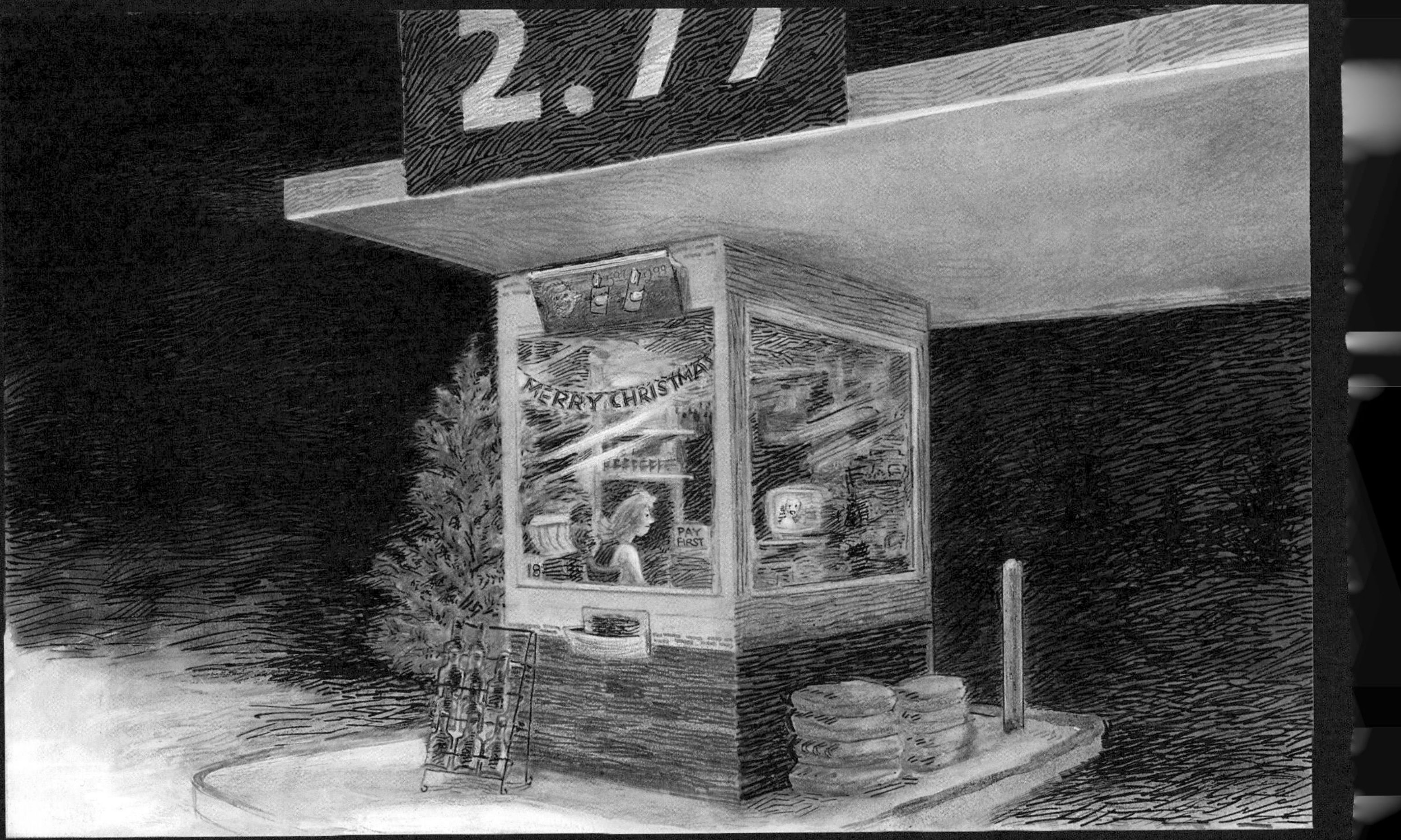
MERRY CHRISTMAS
PAY FIRST

Assume night is black and you'll miss its cloak of sapphire. But no matter the color of darkness, there's no denying the bright prairie pop-ups that anchor freeway off-ramps like rivets on dungarees.

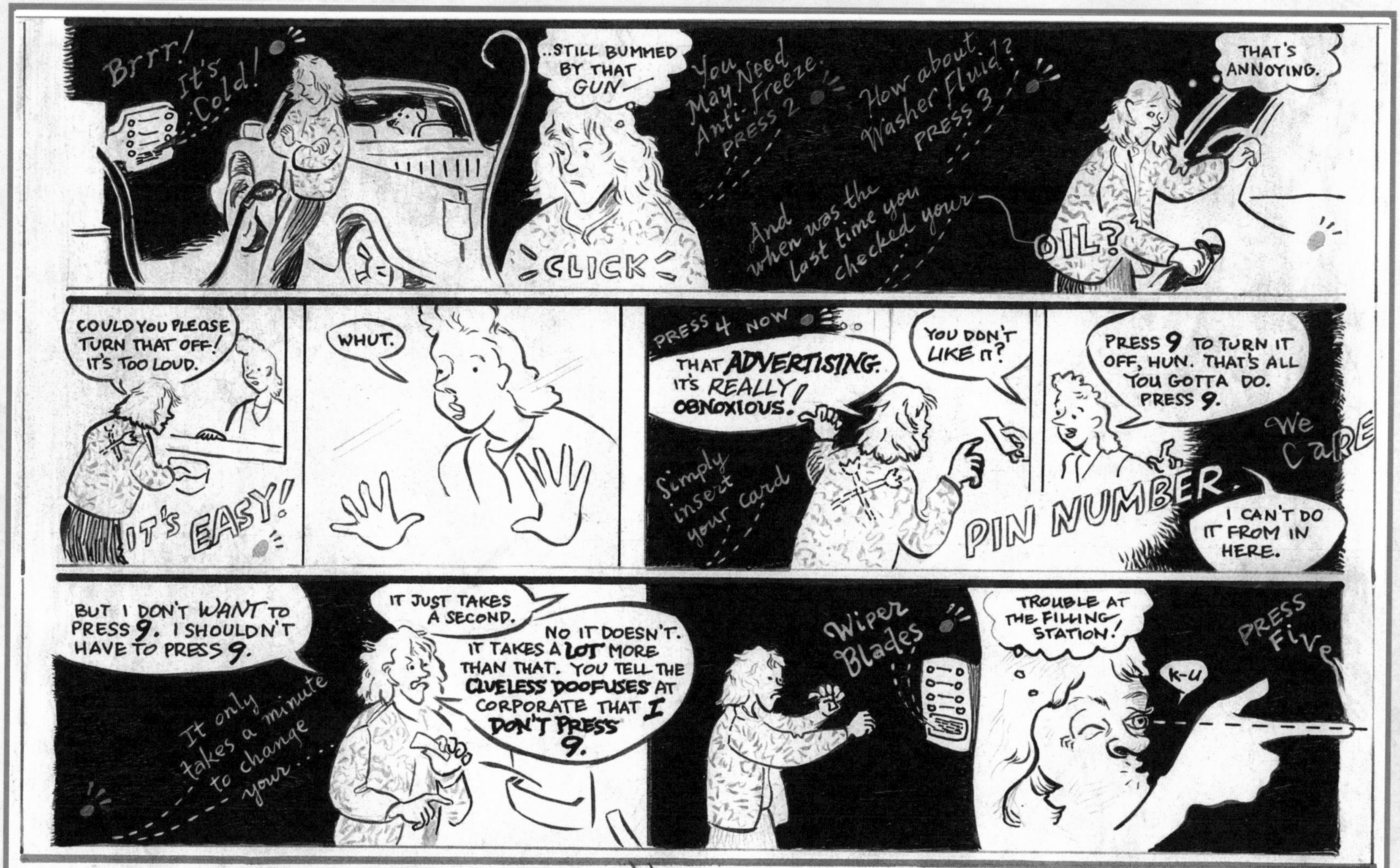
Brrr! It's Cold!
...STILL BUMMED BY THAT GUN
You May Need Anti-Freeze. PRESS 2
How about Washer Fluid? PRESS 3
And when was the last time you checked your
CLICK!
OIL?
THAT'S ANNOYING.
COULD YOU PLEASE TURN THAT OFF! IT'S TOO LOUD.
IT'S EASY!
WHUT.
PRESS 4 NOW
THAT ADVERTISING. IT'S REALLY OBNOXIOUS!
YOU DON'T LIKE IT?
Simply insert your card
PIN NUMBER.
PRESS 9 TO TURN IT OFF, HUN. THAT'S ALL YOU GOTTA DO. PRESS 9.
We Care
I CAN'T DO IT FROM IN HERE.
BUT I DON'T WANT TO PRESS 9. I SHOULDN'T HAVE TO PRESS 9.
It only takes a minute to change your...
IT JUST TAKES A SECOND.
NO IT DOESN'T. IT TAKES A LOT MORE THAN THAT. YOU TELL THE CLUELESS DOOFUSES AT CORPORATE THAT I DON'T PRESS 9.
Wiper Blades
TROUBLE AT THE FILLING STATION!
PRESS Five
K-U

A FEW WEEKS AGO, I WENT WITH DAD TO THE V.A. FOR HIS ANNUAL CHECK UP. MANAGED TO GET A PRIVATE CONSULTATION WITH HIS DOCTOR. THE DIAGNOSIS: DEGENERATIVE ARTHRITIS OF THE KNEES AND SPINE. (HE'S 5" SHORTER THAN HIS YOUNGER SELF). AND HIS CT SCAN SHOWED THAT HIS BRAIN WAS SHRINKING AWAY FROM THE SKULL! MEANING IT'S THE BASAL GANGLIA CALLING FOR SURVIVAL. HENCE, THE GUN, SWEATER AND THE MONSTER TRUCK.

YET HE MUSTERED ENOUGH BRAIN POWER TO THINK OF THE PERFECT GIFT FOR ME: THAT CARVED HEART (GIVEN WITH MOM'S BLESSING). AND I AM SO GLAD HE LIKED THE SWEATER. FINALLY, FOR THE FIRST TIME IN POSSIBLY OUR WHOLE LIVES, WE HIT THE BULLSEYE ON GIFT EXCHANGE. WHO COULD ASK FOR ANYTHING MORE? WELL, I COULD. THERE IS ONE MORE ITEM ON MY X-MAS LIST: FOR MY BIG STRONG DADDY NOT TO HAVE A BONE-Y BACK!

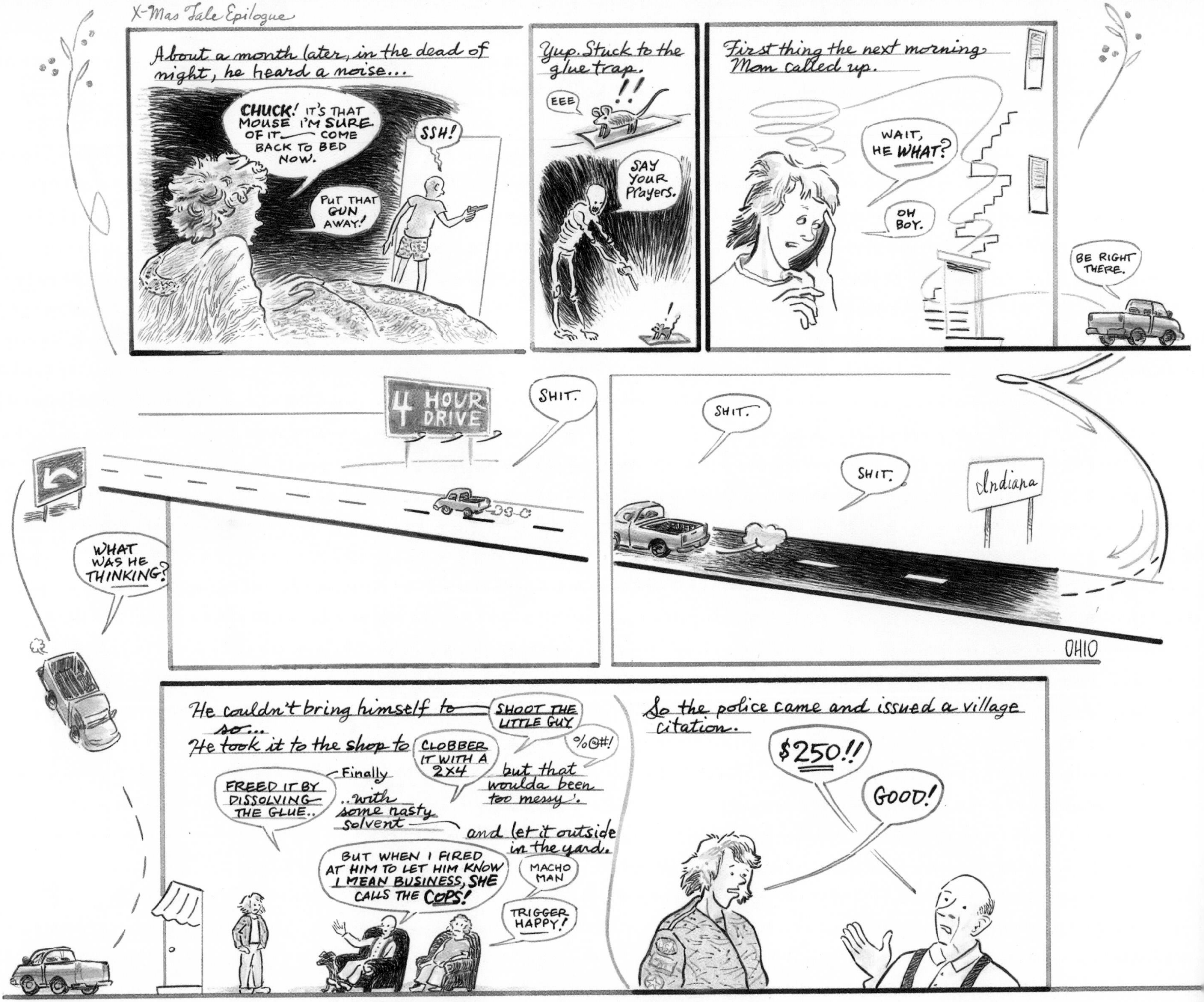

X-Mas Tale Epilogue
About a month later, in the dead of night, he heard a noise...
CHUCK! IT'S THAT MOUSE I'M SURE OF IT. COME BACK TO BED NOW.
SSH!
PUT THAT GUN AWAY!
Yup. Stuck to the glue trap.
EEE
!!
SAY YOUR PRAYERS.
First thing the next morning Mom called up.
WAIT, HE WHAT?
OH BOY.
BE RIGHT THERE.
4 HOUR DRIVE
SHIT.
SHIT.
SHIT.
Indiana
OHIO
WHAT WAS HE THINKING?
He couldn't bring himself to
SHOOT THE LITTLE GUY
so...
He took it to the shop to
CLOBBER IT WITH A 2X4
%@#!
but that woulda been too messy.
Finally
FREED IT BY DISSOLVING THE GLUE..
..with some nasty solvent
and let it outside in the yard.
BUT WHEN I FIRED AT HIM TO LET HIM KNOW I MEAN BUSINESS, SHE CALLS THE COPS!
MACHO MAN
TRIGGER HAPPY!
So the police came and issued a village citation.
$250!!
GOOD!

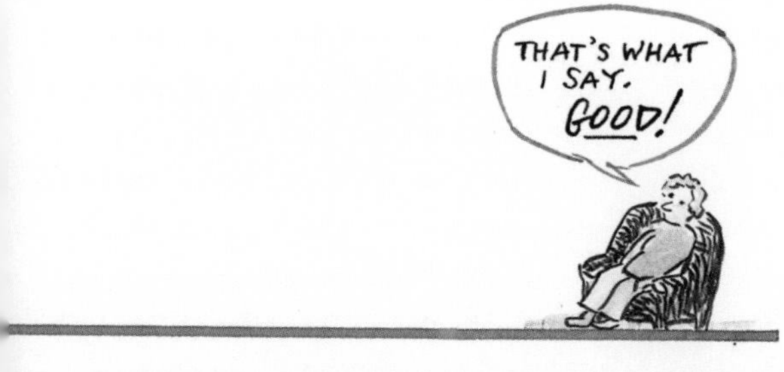
THAT'S WHAT I SAY. GOOD!

13.

WALKING THE MAT

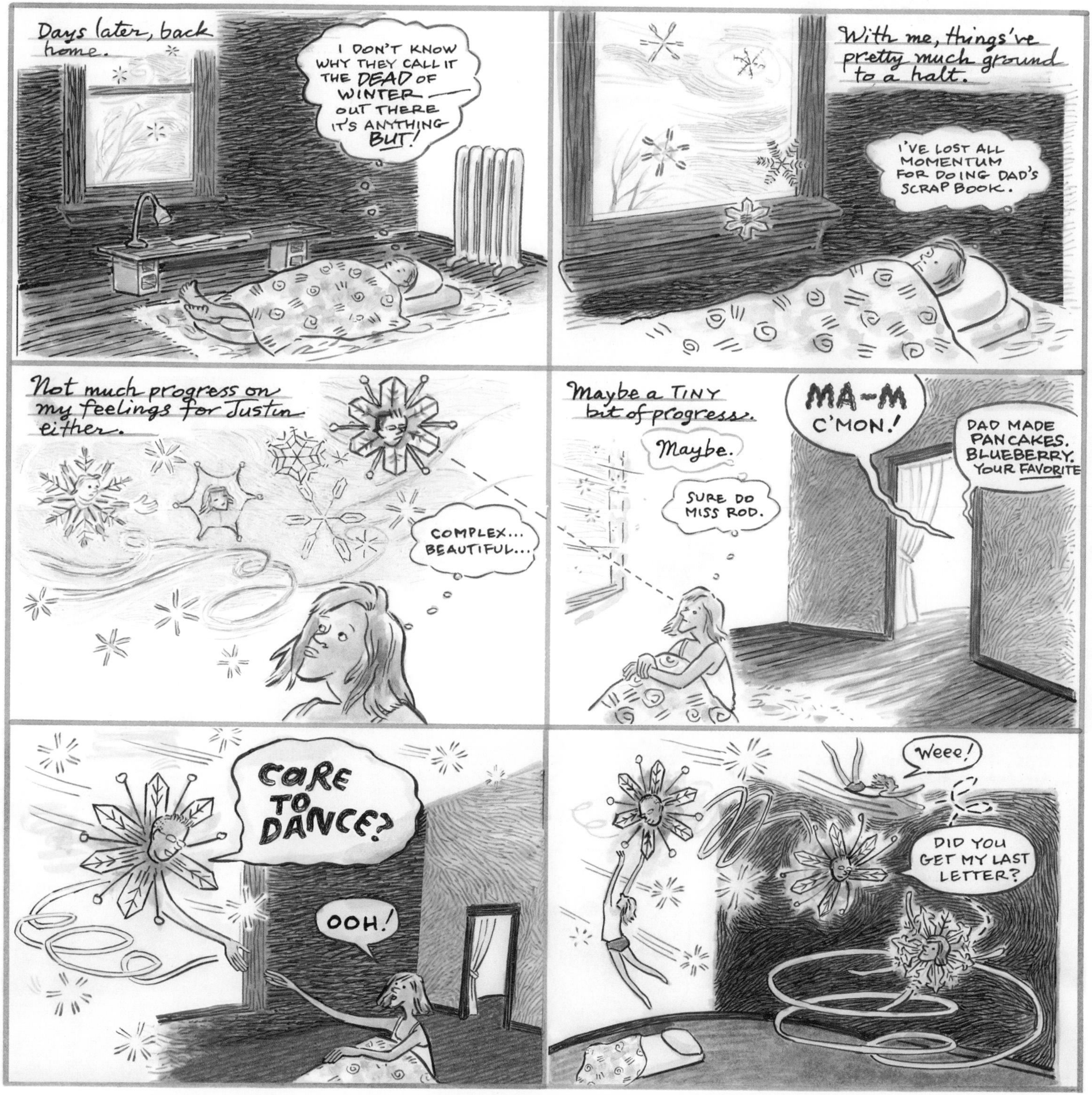
Days later, back home.
I DON'T KNOW WHY THEY CALL IT THE DEAD OF WINTER — OUT THERE IT'S ANYTHING BUT!
With me, things've pretty much ground to a halt.
I'VE LOST ALL MOMENTUM FOR DOING DAD'S SCRAP BOOK.
Not much progress on my feelings for Justin either.
COMPLEX... BEAUTIFUL...
Maybe a TINY bit of progress.
Maybe.
SURE DO MISS ROD.
MA-M C'MON!
DAD MADE PANCAKES. BLUEBERRY. YOUR FAVORITE
CARE TO DANCE?
OOH!
Weee!
DID YOU GET MY LAST LETTER?

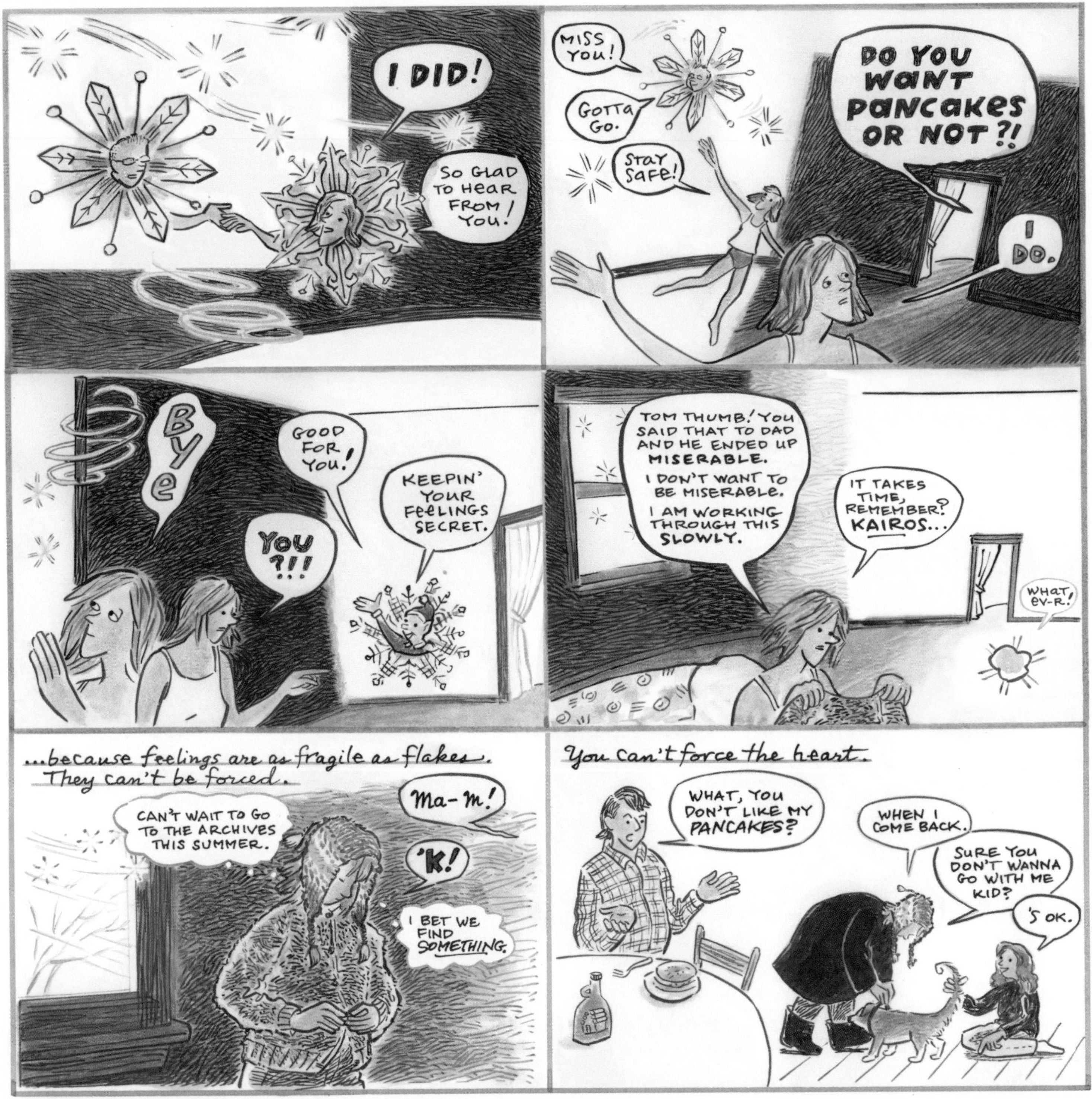
I DID!
SO GLAD TO HEAR FROM YOU!
MISS YOU!
GOTTA GO.
STAY SAFE!
DO YOU WANT PANCAKES OR NOT?!
I DO.
BYE
GOOD FOR YOU!
YOU ?!!
KEEPIN' YOUR FEELINGS SECRET.
TOM THUMB! YOU SAID THAT TO DAD AND HE ENDED UP MISERABLE.
I DON'T WANT TO BE MISERABLE.
I AM WORKING THROUGH THIS SLOWLY.
IT TAKES TIME, REMEMBER? KAIROS...
WHAT, EV-R!
...because feelings are as fragile as flakes. They can't be forced.
CAN'T WAIT TO GO TO THE ARCHIVES THIS SUMMER.
Ma-m!
'K!
I BET WE FIND SOMETHING.
You can't force the heart.
WHAT, YOU DON'T LIKE MY PANCAKES?
WHEN I COME BACK.
SURE YOU DON'T WANNA GO WITH ME KID?
'S OK.

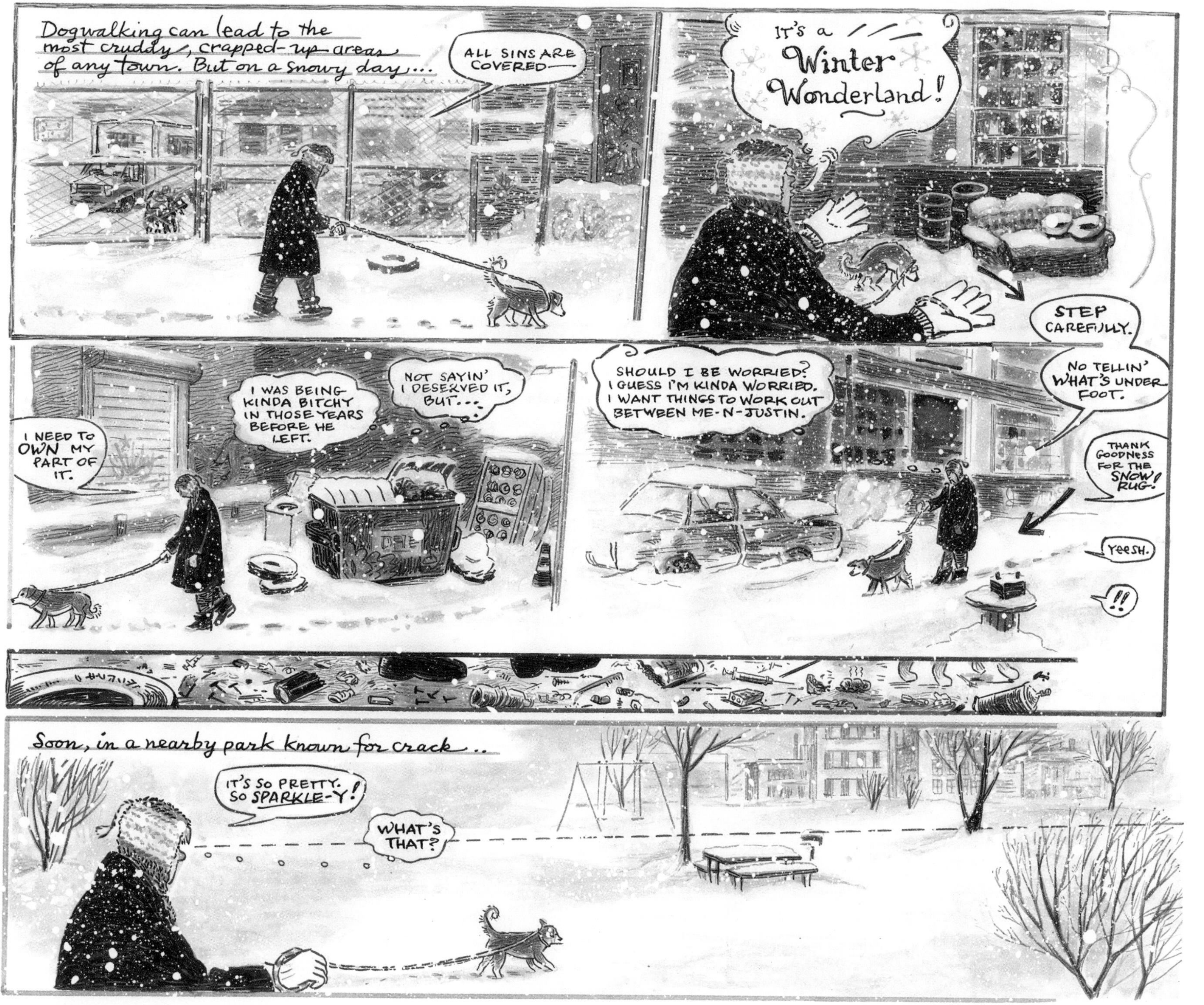

Dogwalking can lead to the most cruddy, crapped-up areas of any town. But on a snowy day...
ALL SINS ARE COVERED—
IT'S a Winter Wonderland!
STEP CAREFULLY.
I NEED TO OWN MY PART OF IT.
I WAS BEING KINDA BITCHY IN THOSE YEARS BEFORE HE LEFT.
NOT SAYIN' I DESERVED IT, BUT...
SHOULD I BE WORRIED? I GUESS I'M KINDA WORRIED. I WANT THINGS TO WORK OUT BETWEEN ME-N-JUSTIN.
NO TELLIN' WHAT'S UNDER FOOT.
THANK GOODNESS FOR THE SNOW RUG!
YEESH.
!!
Soon, in a nearby park known for crack..
IT'S SO PRETTY. SO SPARKLE-Y!
WHAT'S THAT?

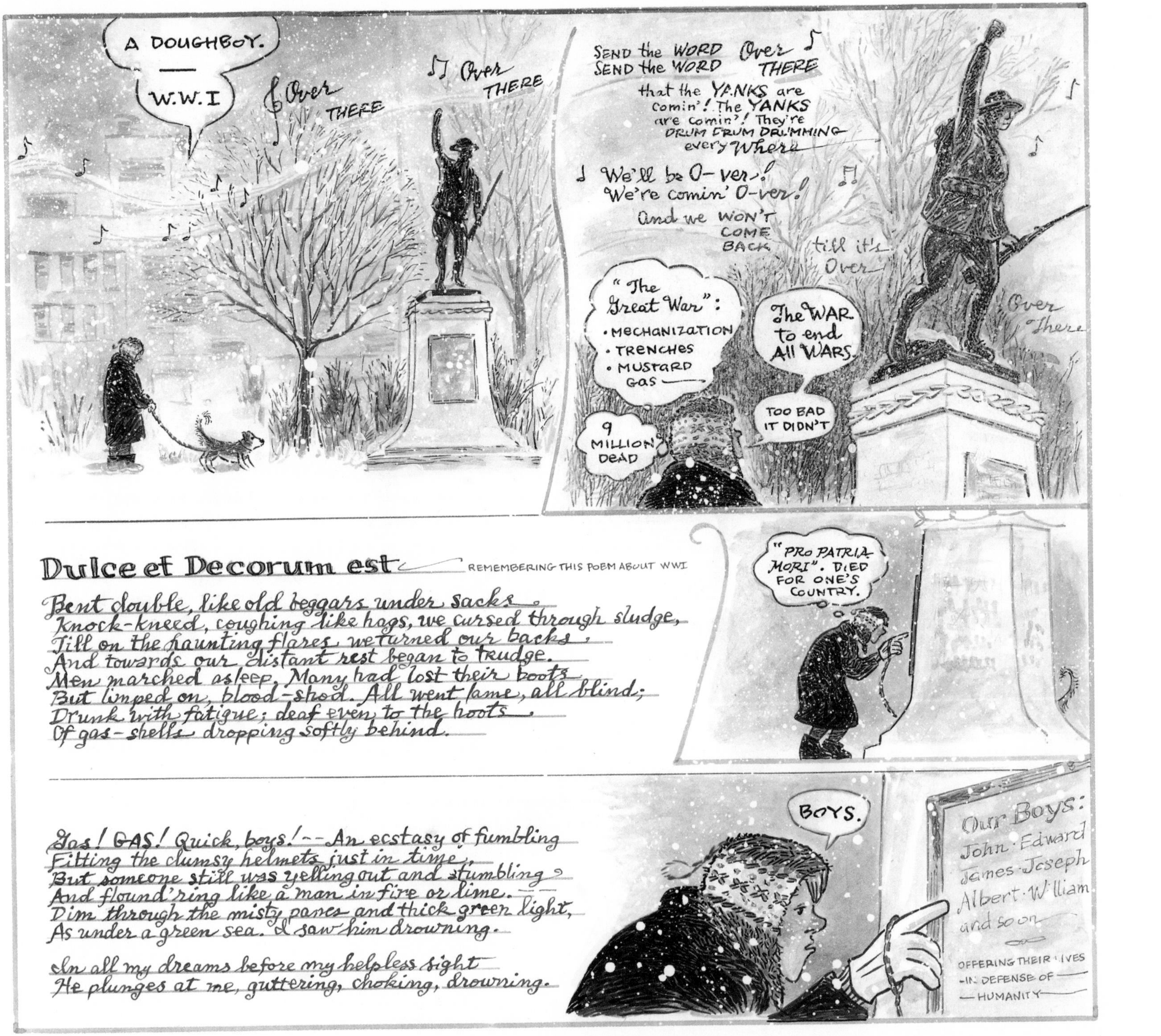
A DOUGHBOY.
W.W.I
Over THERE
Over THERE
SEND the WORD SEND the WORD Over THERE
that the YANKS are comin'! The YANKS are comin'! They're DRUM DRUM DRUMMING every Where
We'll be O-ver! We're comin' O-ver!
And we WON'T COME BACK till it's Over
Over There
"The Great War":
• MECHANIZATION
• TRENCHES
• MUSTARD GAS
9 MILLION DEAD
The WAR to end All WARS.
TOO BAD IT DIDN'T
Dulce et Decorum est
REMEMBERING THIS POEM ABOUT WWI
Bent double, like old beggars under sacks,
Knock-kneed, coughing like hags, we cursed through sludge,
Till on the haunting flares we turned our backs
And towards our distant rest began to trudge.
Men marched asleep. Many had lost their boots
But limped on, blood-shod. All went lame, all blind;
Drunk with fatigue; deaf even to the hoots
Of gas-shells dropping softly behind.
"PRO PATRIA MORI". DIED FOR ONE'S COUNTRY.
Gas! GAS! Quick, boys!-- An ecstasy of fumbling
Fitting the clumsy helmets just in time,
But someone still was yelling out and stumbling
And flound'ring like a man in fire or lime.--
Dim through the misty panes and thick green light,
As under a green sea, I saw him drowning.
In all my dreams before my helpless sight
He plunges at me, guttering, choking, drowning.
BOYS.
Our Boys:
John · Edward
James · Joseph
Albert · William
and so on
OFFERING THEIR LIVES
IN DEFENSE OF
HUMANITY

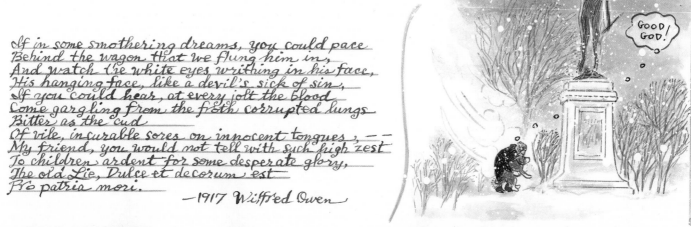

If in some smothering dreams, you could pace
Behind the wagon that we flung him in,
And watch the white eyes writhing in his face,
His hanging face, like a devil's sick of sin,
If you could hear, at every jolt the blood
Come gargling from the froth corrupted lungs
Bitter as the cud
Of vile, incurable sores on innocent tongues, — —
My friend, you would not tell with such high zest
To children ardent for some desperate glory,
The old Lie, Dulce et decorum est
Pro patria mori.

            —1917 Wilfred Owen

GOOD
GOD!

TO THE BATTLEFIELDS WE SEND OUR BEAUTIFUL BOYS.

OUR MEN AND WOMEN

STILL!

AT THIS TIME FEB. 2004, IT'S Fallujah IRAQ

BUT AS LONG AS THERE ARE BAD GUYS...

..AND POLITICS

UGH

YEAH. I NEED YOU TO GUARD THAT STATUE.

YOU NEED SOMETHIN' LADY?

OXYS? PERCS?

HATE IT.

THOSE BOYS DESERVE IT!

?
!

YIKES—IT'S GETTING COLDER!

SPEAKING OF GUARDS.. HOW DO THEY DO IT?

THOSE TOMB GUARDS IN WASHINGTON.

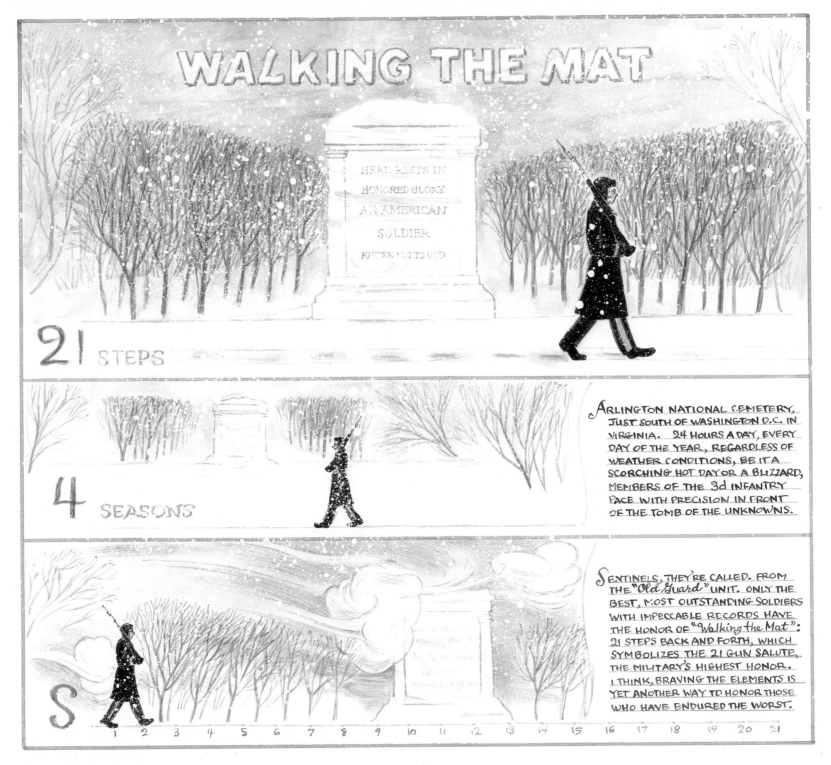

WALKING THE MAT

HERE RESTS IN
HONORED GLORY
AN AMERICAN
SOLDIER
KNOWN BUT TO GOD

21 STEPS

4 SEASONS

ARLINGTON NATIONAL CEMETERY, JUST SOUTH OF WASHINGTON D.C. IN VIRGINIA. 24 HOURS A DAY, EVERY DAY OF THE YEAR, REGARDLESS OF WEATHER CONDITIONS, BE IT A SCORCHING HOT DAY OR A BLIZZARD, MEMBERS OF THE 3d INFANTRY PACE WITH PRECISION IN FRONT OF THE TOMB OF THE UNKNOWNS.

S

SENTINELS, THEY'RE CALLED. FROM THE "Old Guard" UNIT. ONLY THE BEST, MOST OUTSTANDING SOLDIERS WITH IMPECCABLE RECORDS HAVE THE HONOR OF "Walking the Mat": 21 STEPS BACK AND FORTH, WHICH SYMBOLIZES THE 21 GUN SALUTE, THE MILITARY'S HIGHEST HONOR. I THINK, BRAVING THE ELEMENTS IS YET ANOTHER WAY TO HONOR THOSE WHO HAVE ENDURED THE WORST.

1 2 3 4 5 6 7 8 9 10 11 12 13 14 15 16 17 18 19 20 21

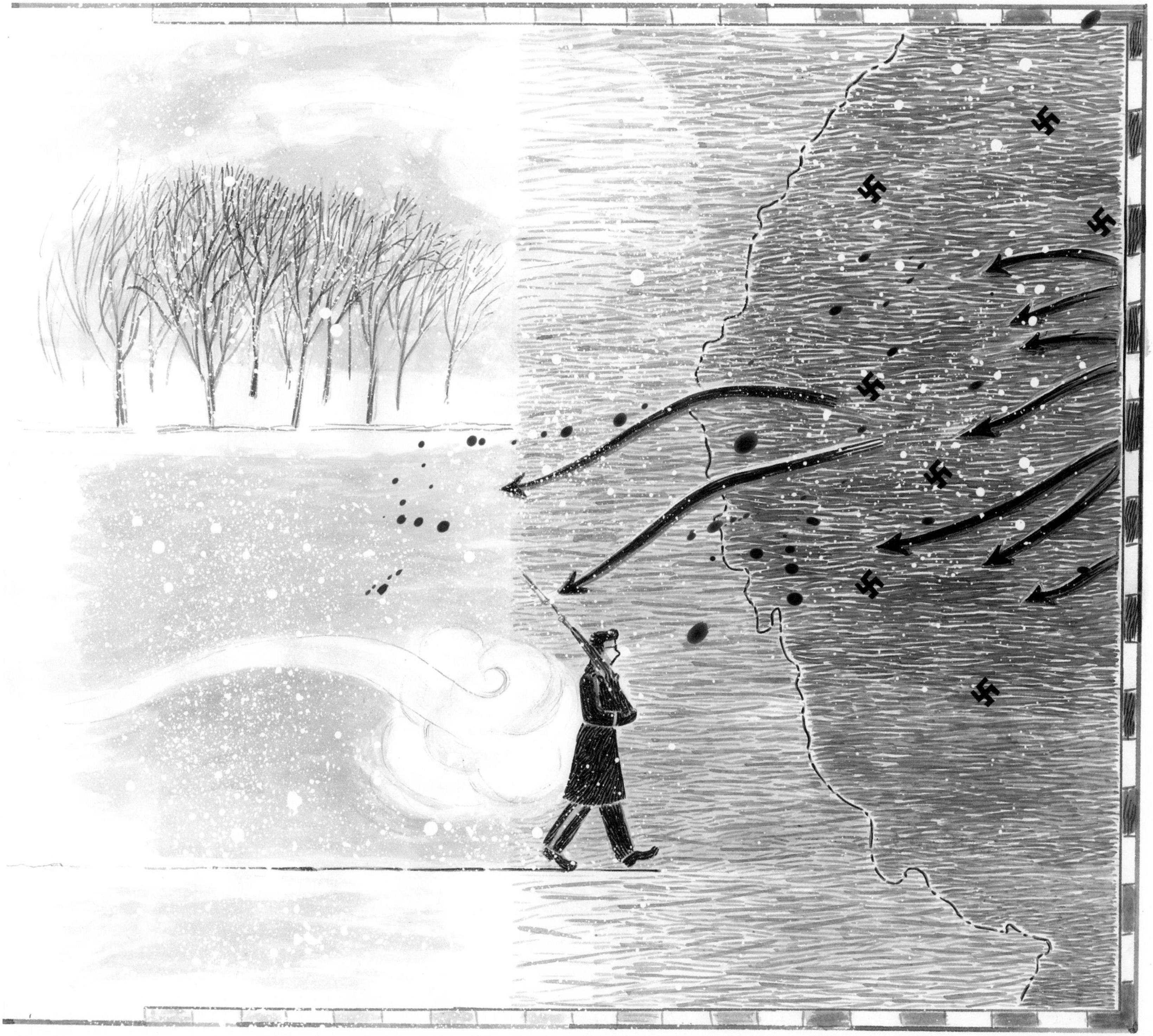

DAD'S ARMY SCRAPBOOK
AND
TOUR OF DUTY HIGHLIGHTS

PART V

RHINELAND

DECEMBER 1944 –
MARCH 1945

67

It was Field Marshal von Rundstedt that used the phrase 'Es Geht Ums Ganze' as a way of firing-up what was left of Hitler's fighting elite before the Dec. 16 push to take back Europe. Rout the Allies and take no prisoners. 'Give all you've got.' Ultra fanatic Hitler youth also signed on for the campaign, although according to Chuck: "The Germans we fought against were starving. They were hurting. They didn't have nothing left except to fight for the Fatherland. So many of them were just kids."

I DON'T KNOW WHO FOUND IT OR HOW COME, BUT IT GOT SENT TO ME AT THE DEPOT. I MUST-A SHOWED IT TO SOMEBODY. LUCKY ME.

To the Ardennes
(with Red's picture.)

68

"Then I got sent up there along with clerks and cooks — it didn't matter. Warm bodies with guns, that's what was needed most. "So you've got a bunch of guys that had never been together, never trained together, scared to death and going into battle. Piled into troop trucks and driven up to the front.

"Everybody went to the Bulge because things were desperate. The people were hurting and there was that damn frost and cold. It was Christmastime, cold and snowy."

YOU ARE ONE LUCKY SON-OF-A-BITCH TO HAVE A DAME LIKE THIS!

69

"They had our uniforms on! We never knew if they were them or us. We'd holler at them and if they didn't answer right back, we'd shoot 'em. Take no chances. Shoot anything that moves. We'd say 'This is it!'"

"We loaded airplanes, B-29s, with those gas drums. They ran low, 200 feet over the 101st Airborne at Bastogne. We let the drums roll out the back." Bastogne was surrounded. When given the option of, the mandate of surrender, General Anthony McAuliffe famously replied: 'Nuts'. "This made us bolder."

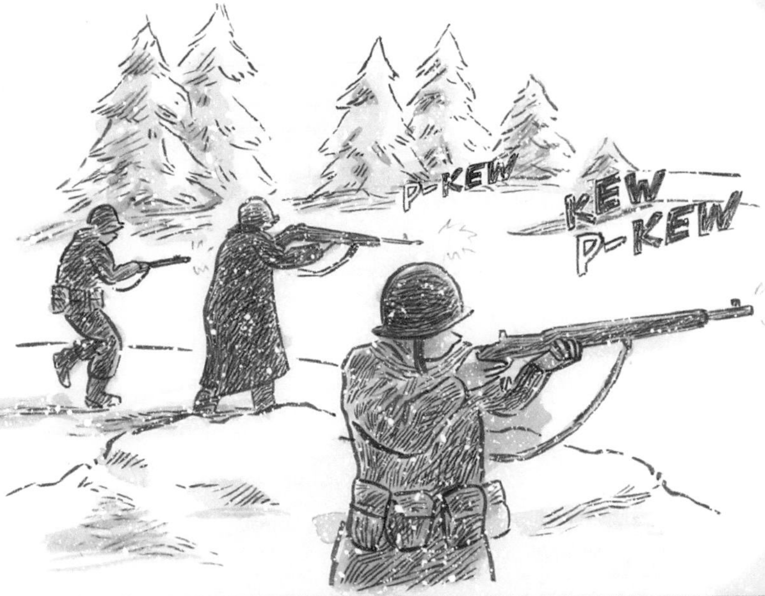
P-KEW
KEW
P-KEW

70

"No doubt about it. We were fighting an evil force bent on world domination, but up close to a German soldier, dead or alive, that idea didn't seem real. My Great-Grandparents came from Germany, which meant I could have been shootin' at my kin.

"The Germans I had as prisoners at the depot talked about the Jews and how the war was their fault. Then up there at the Bulge, we had heard rumors about large scale extermination camps But I never knew to what extent until after I got home and saw the pictures in LIFE magazine."

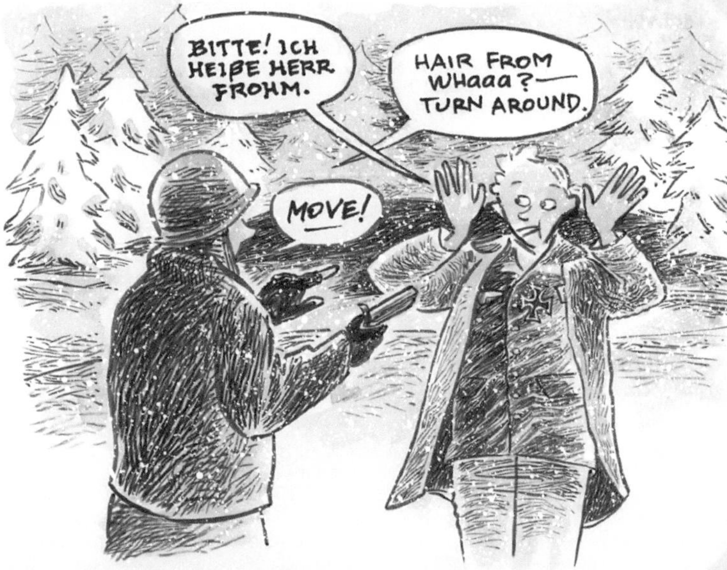
BITTE! ICH HEIßE HERR FROHM.
HAIR FROM WHaaa?— TURN AROUND.
MOVE!

71

"It was hard to think at all. Even about the littlest things. Everything I did functioned on automatic: eat, shit, load the gun.

" I have a lot of trouble remembering the details of that time or where I was even. I had no maps. The towns, roads, rivers and the countryside all frozen up — it all looked the same. There were no signs. They'd been blown to bits or had been changed to mix us up. I never knew where the hell I was or what day it was. France? luxembourg? Belgium? Nobody knew."

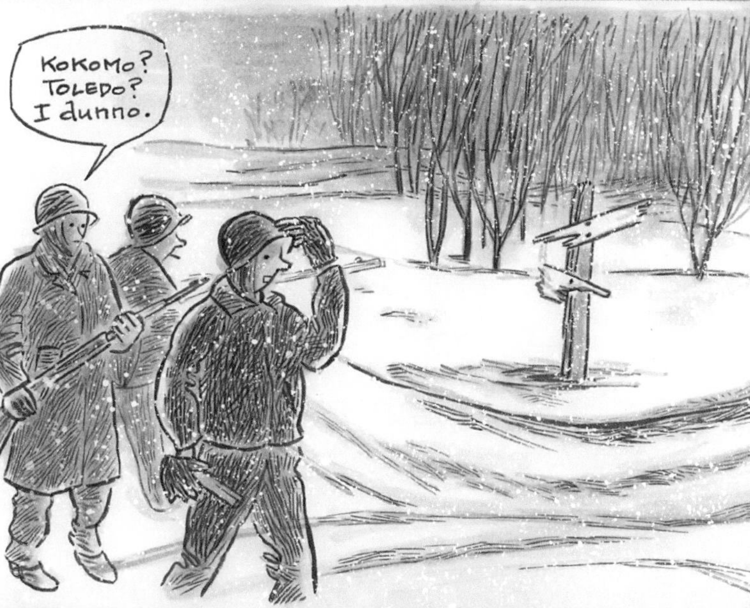
KOKOMO? TOLEDO? I dunno.

72

"The most important thing now was to survive. Hunker down, stay warm and try not to catch a bullet. Oh yeah, and Pray. I couldn't sleep but maybe an hour or two here and there.

" I did pray whenever I could and tried to think of home, my parents and friends. I tried to remember anything — it was all so long ago and far away. I tried extra hard to bring that redhead to mind and imagine my new little girl, but then POOF. Gone."

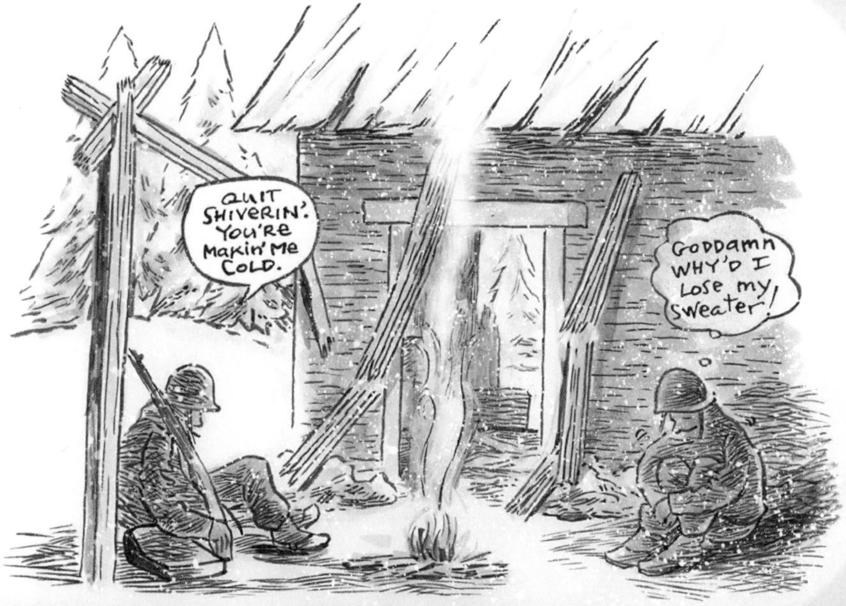
QUIT SHIVERIN'. YOU'RE MAKIN' ME COLD.
GODDAMN WHY'D I LOSE MY SWEATER!

73

Back on the Homefront, life may have been quieter and a little less harrowing but still rife with anxiety. It was difficult to know exactly what was going on with a loved one because of censored mail. You could read accounts of the war's progress or watch a newsreel. Life magazine brought the war home in a big way. Everyone read LIFE.

The most troublesome sight, however, was the humble Western Union telegram delivery boy bearing the awful news.

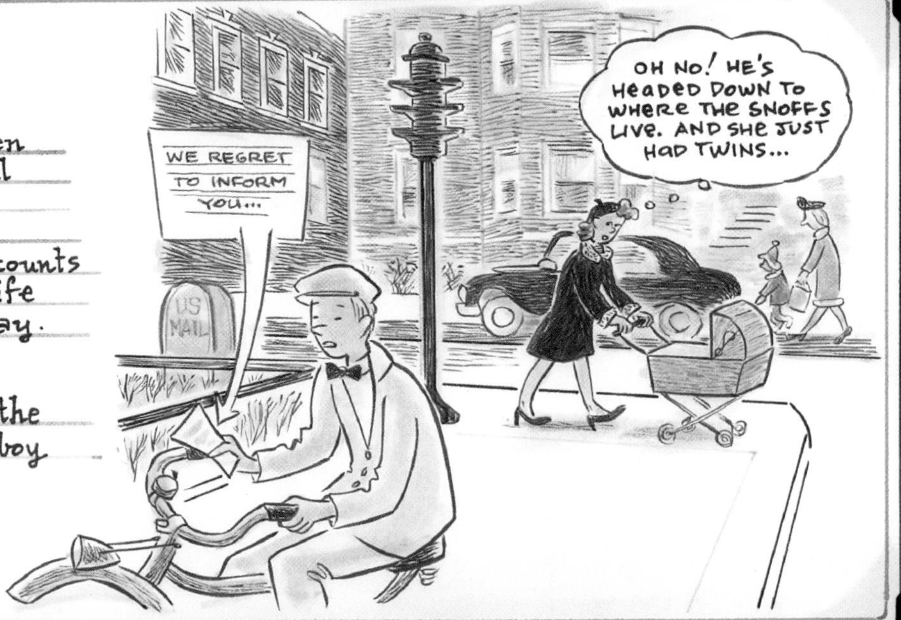

WE REGRET TO INFORM YOU...
US MAIL
OH NO! HE'S HEADED DOWN TO WHERE THE SNOFFS LIVE. AND SHE JUST HAD TWINS...

74

"The noise up there in the Bulge, all the loud shelling, gunfire and explosions, never ever stopped. Day and night. I don't know who captured it, my squad or one of 'em, but we had a German 88 that didn't blow the breech on us. That screaming mee-mee son-of-a-bitch — an eerie sound, you couldn't sleep. That thing would scream and scream. Run you NUTS! But if you couldn't hear it, that was your shell, 'cuz otherwise it was going by you.

"That's why I don't go to fireworks shows on the 4TH. Too much random noise."

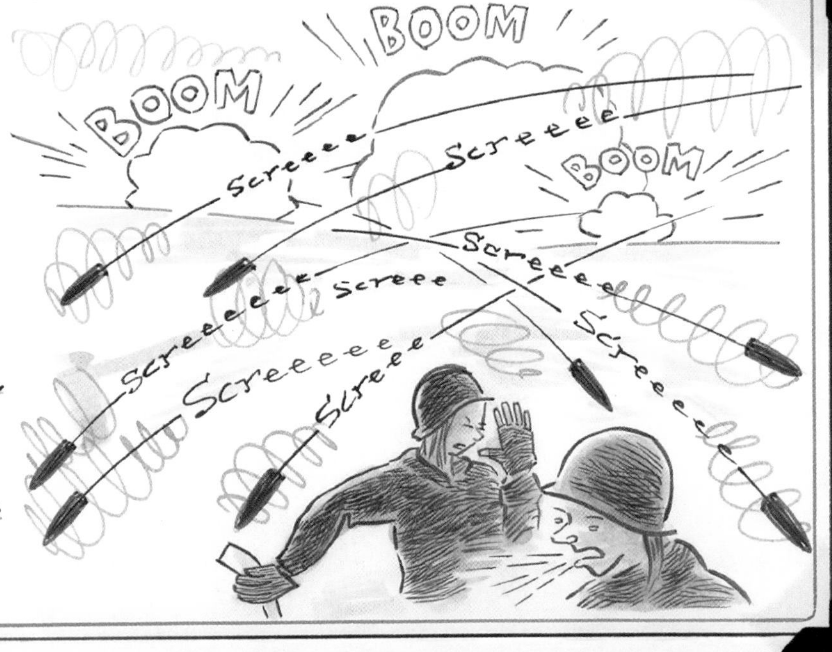

BOOM
BOOM
BOOM
Screeee
Screeeee
Screee
Screeeeeeee
Screeeeeee
Screee
Screeeeee

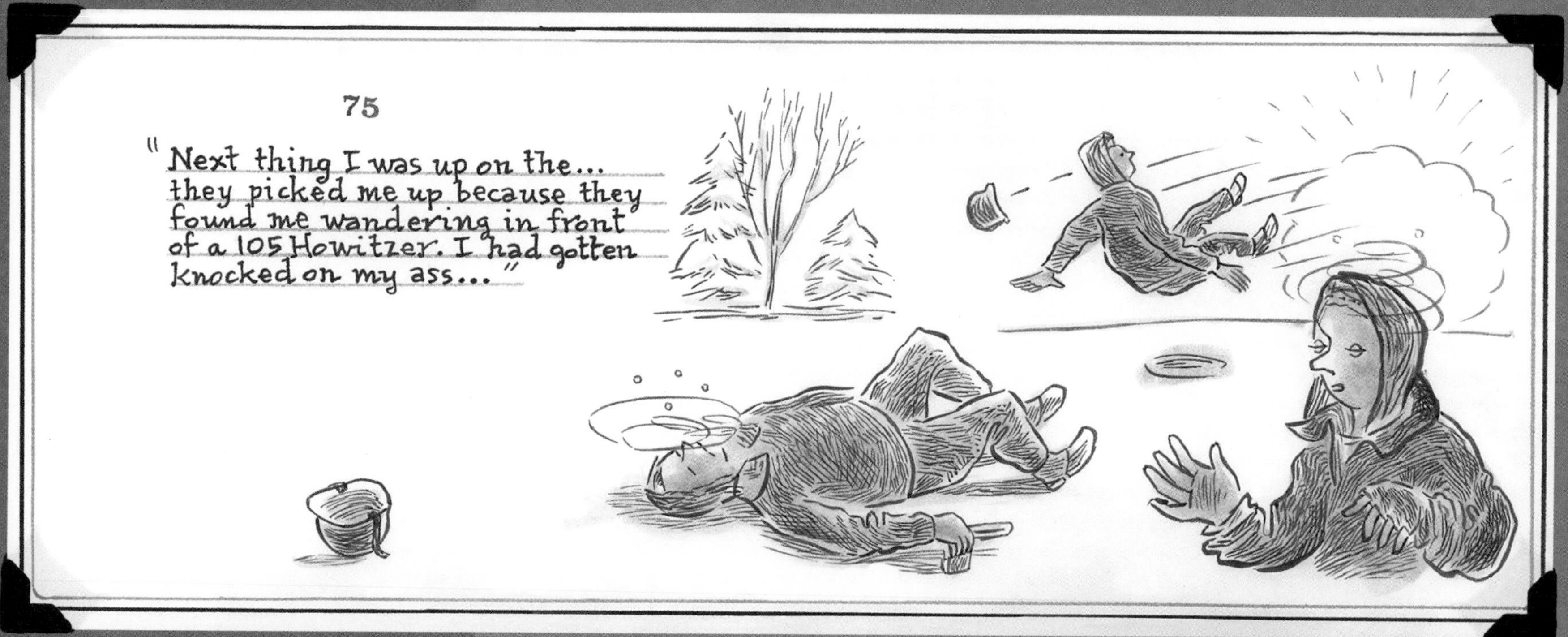
75
"Next thing I was up on the... they picked me up because they found me wandering in front of a 105 Howitzer. I had gotten knocked on my ass..."

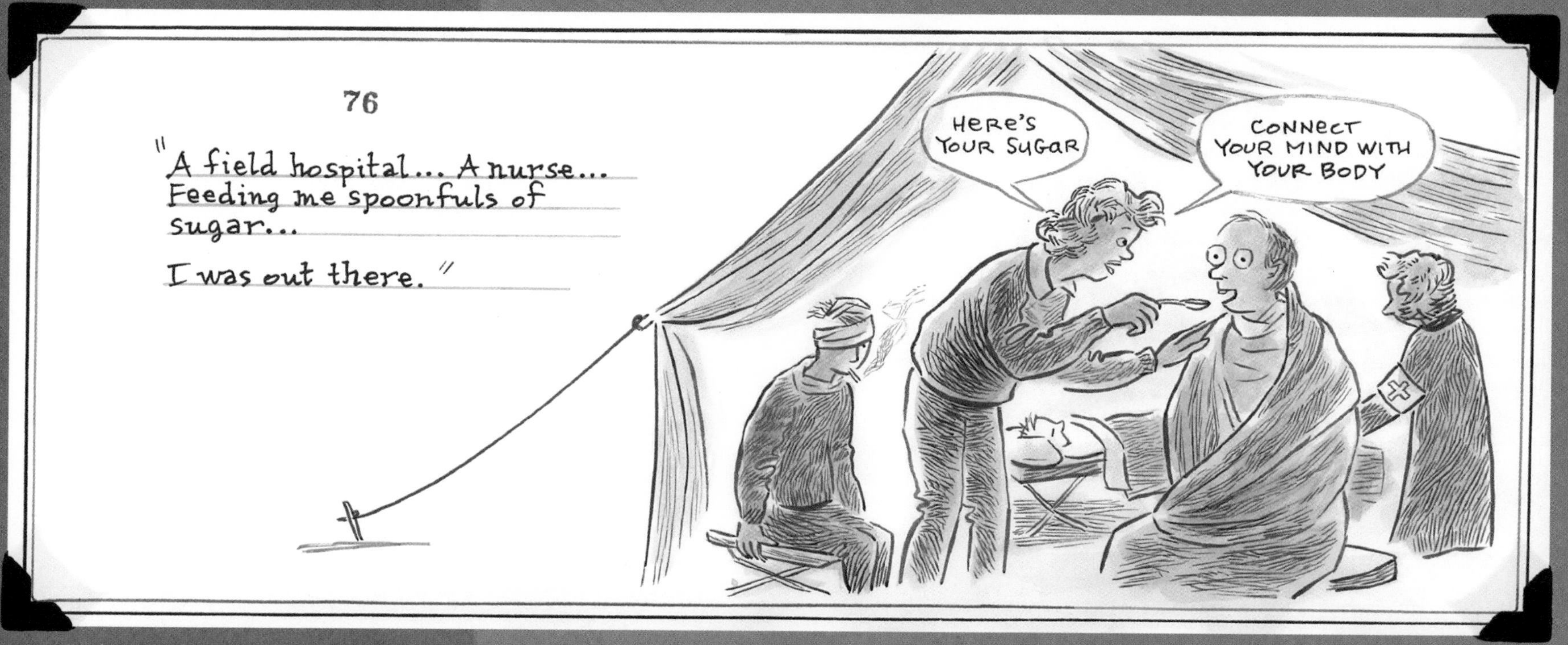
76
"A field hospital... A nurse... Feeding me spoonfuls of sugar...
I was out there."
HERE'S YOUR SUGAR
CONNECT YOUR MIND WITH YOUR BODY

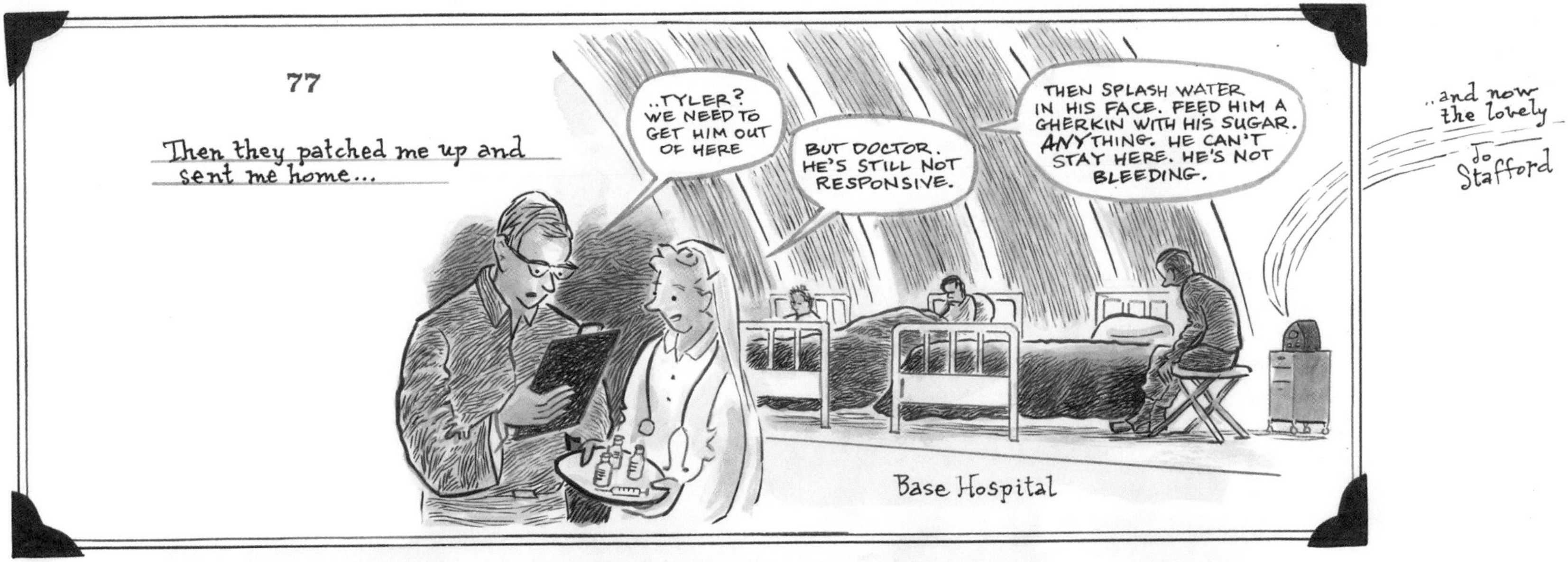
77
Then they patched me up and sent me home...
..TYLER? WE NEED TO GET HIM OUT OF HERE
BUT DOCTOR. HE'S STILL NOT RESPONSIVE.
THEN SPLASH WATER IN HIS FACE. FEED HIM A GHERKIN WITH HIS SUGAR. ANYTHING. HE CAN'T STAY HERE. HE'S NOT BLEEDING.
..and now the lovely Jo Stafford
Base Hospital

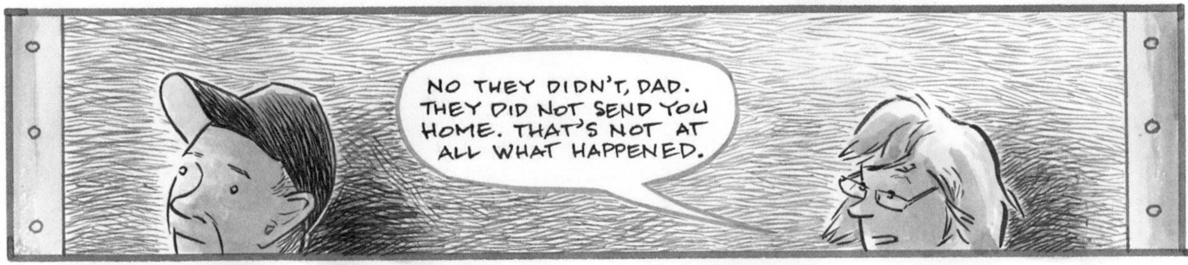
NO THEY DIDN'T, DAD. THEY DID NOT SEND YOU HOME. THAT'S NOT AT ALL WHAT HAPPENED.

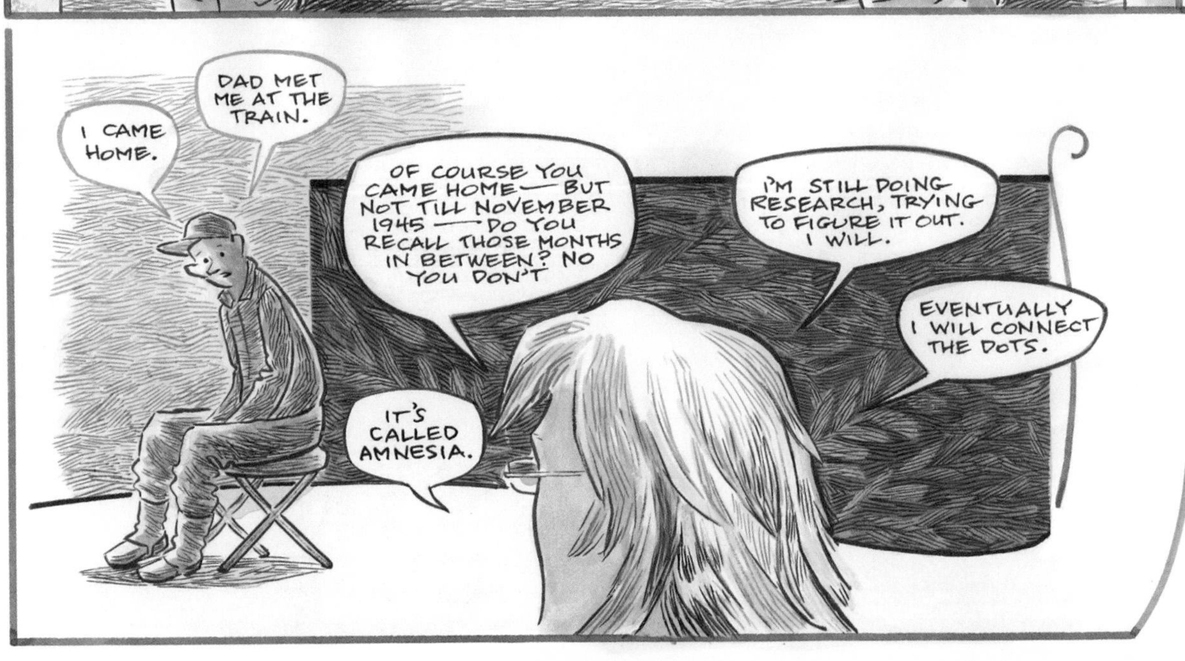
I CAME HOME.
DAD MET ME AT THE TRAIN.
OF COURSE YOU CAME HOME— BUT NOT TILL NOVEMBER 1945 — DO YOU RECALL THOSE MONTHS IN BETWEEN? NO YOU DON'T
IT'S CALLED AMNESIA.
I'M STILL DOING RESEARCH, TRYING TO FIGURE IT OUT. I WILL.
EVENTUALLY I WILL CONNECT THE DOTS.

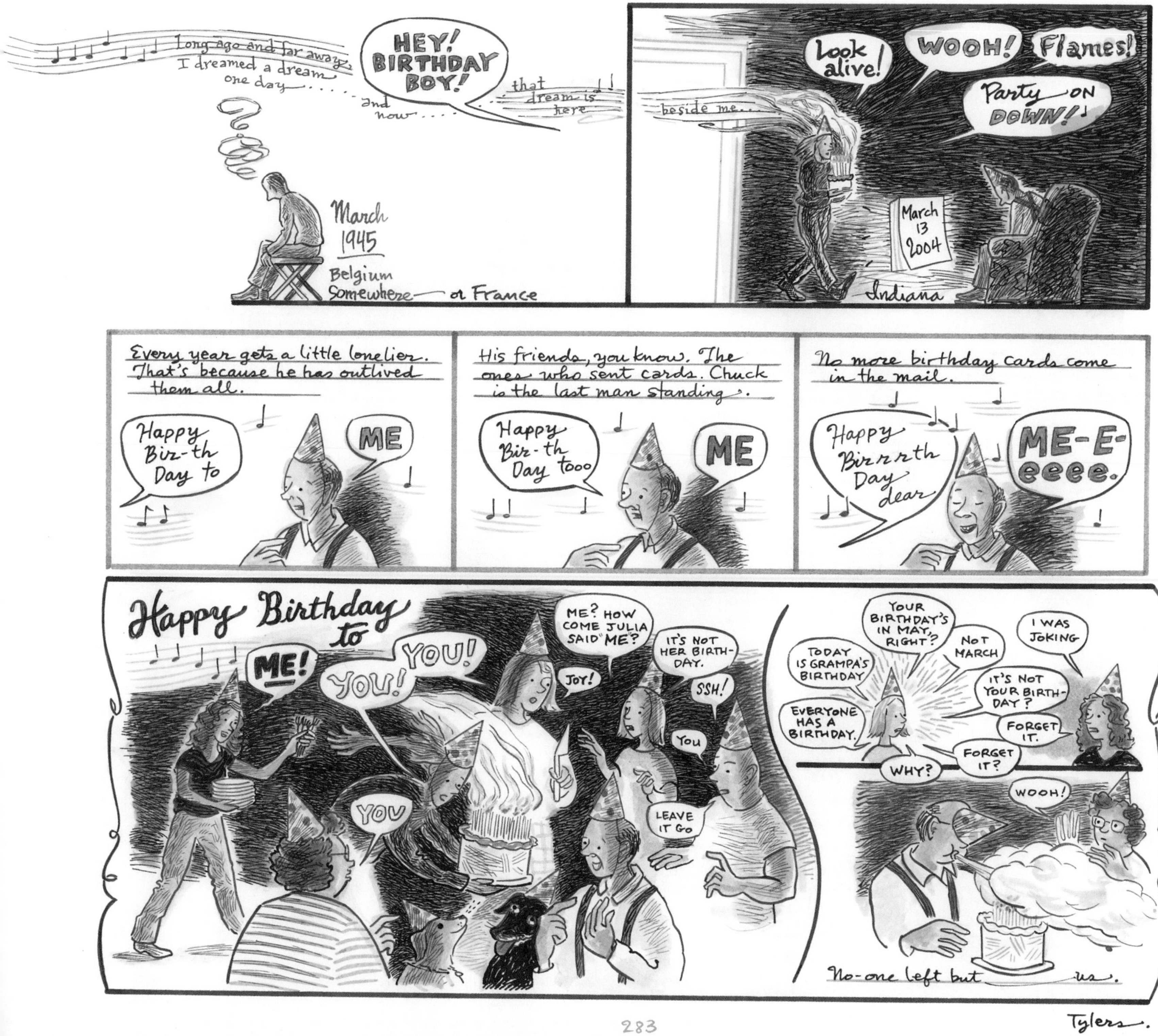

Long ago and far away,
I dreamed a dream one day
and now
HEY! BIRTHDAY BOY!
that dream is here
beside me....
March 1945
Belgium
Somewhere — or France
Look alive!
WOOH!
Flames!
Party ON DOWN!
March 13 2004
Indiana
Every year gets a little lonelier. That's because he has outlived them all.
Happy Birz-th Day to
ME
His friends, you know. The ones who sent cards. Chuck is the last man standing.
Happy Bir-th Day tooo
ME
No more birthday cards come in the mail.
Happy Birrrth Day dear
ME-E-eeee.
Happy Birthday to
ME!
YOU!
YOU!
ME? HOW COME JULIA SAID "ME"?
JOY!
IT'S NOT HER BIRTH-DAY.
SSH!
You
YOU
LEAVE IT GO
YOUR BIRTHDAY'S IN MAY, RIGHT?
TODAY IS GRAMPA'S BIRTHDAY
NOT MARCH
I WAS JOKING
IT'S NOT YOUR BIRTH-DAY?
EVERYONE HAS A BIRTHDAY.
FORGET IT.
FORGET IT?
WHY?
WOOH!
No-one left but us.
Tylers.

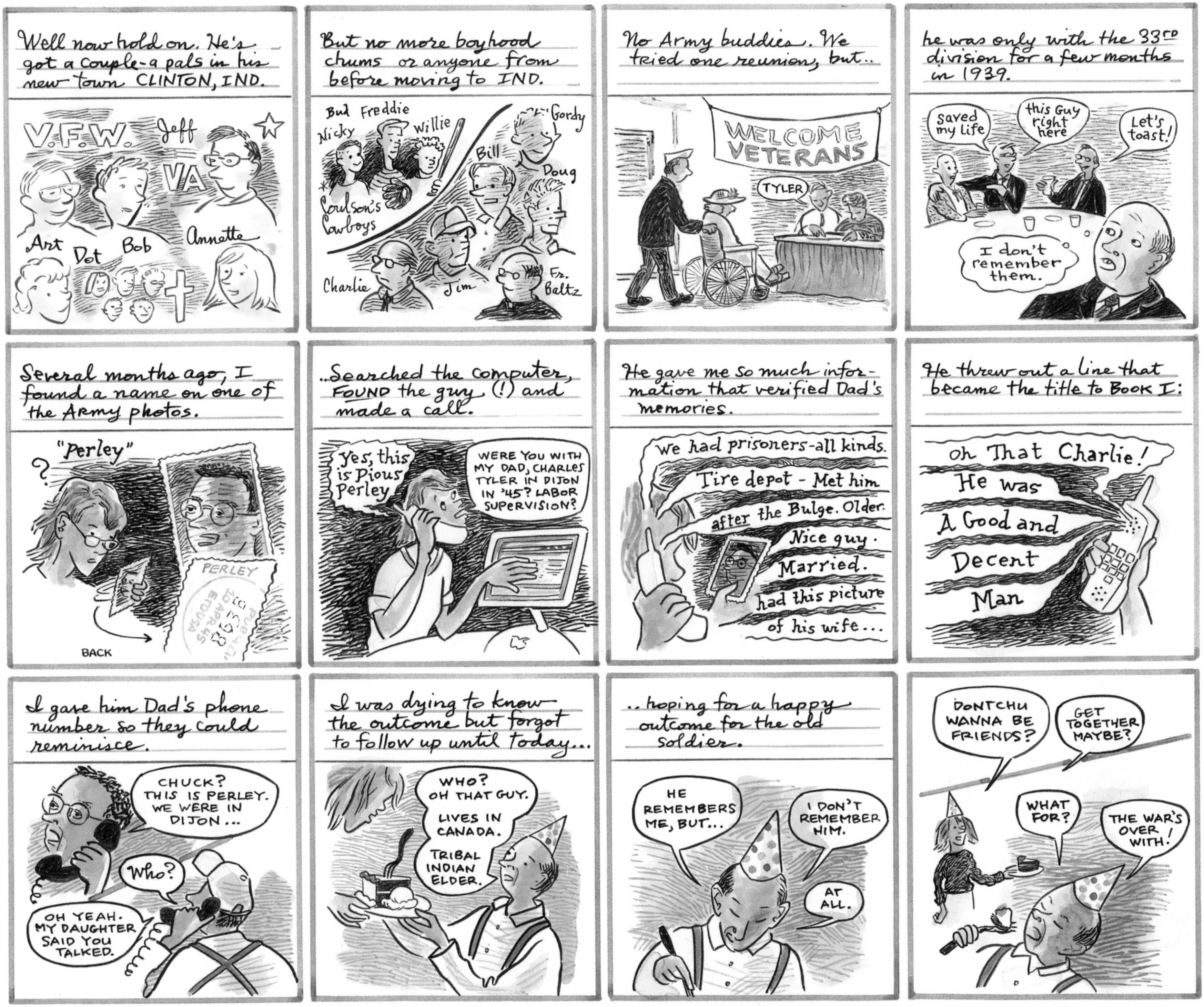
Well now hold on. He's got a couple-a pals in his new town CLINTON, IND.
V.F.W.
Jeff
VA
Art
Dot
Bob
Annette
But no more boyhood chums or anyone from before moving to IND.
Bud
Freddie
Nicky
Willie
Coulson's Cowboys
Bill
Gordy
Doug
Charlie
Jim
Fr. Baltz
No Army buddies. We tried one reunion, but..
WELCOME VETERANS
TYLER
he was only with the 33rd division for a few months in 1939.
Saved my life
this Guy right here
Let's toast!
I don't remember them.
Several months ago, I found a name on one of the Army photos.
"Perley"
?
PERLEY
BACK
..Searched the computer, FOUND the guy (!) and made a call.
Yes, this is Pious Perley
WERE YOU WITH MY DAD, CHARLES TYLER IN DIJON IN '45? LABOR SUPERVISION?
He gave me so much information that verified Dad's memories.
We had prisoners-all kinds.
Tire depot - Met him after the Bulge. Older.
Nice guy.
Married.
had this picture of his wife...
He threw out a line that became the title to Book I:
Oh That Charlie!
He was
A Good and
Decent
Man
I gave him Dad's phone number so they could reminisce.
CHUCK? THIS IS PERLEY. WE WERE IN DIJON...
Who?
OH YEAH. MY DAUGHTER SAID YOU TALKED.
I was dying to know the outcome but forgot to follow up until today...
WHO? OH THAT GUY.
LIVES IN CANADA.
TRIBAL INDIAN ELDER.
..hoping for a happy outcome for the old soldier.
HE REMEMBERS ME, BUT...
I DON'T REMEMBER HIM.
AT ALL.
DONTCHU WANNA BE FRIENDS?
GET TOGETHER MAYBE?
WHAT FOR?
THE WAR'S OVER WITH!

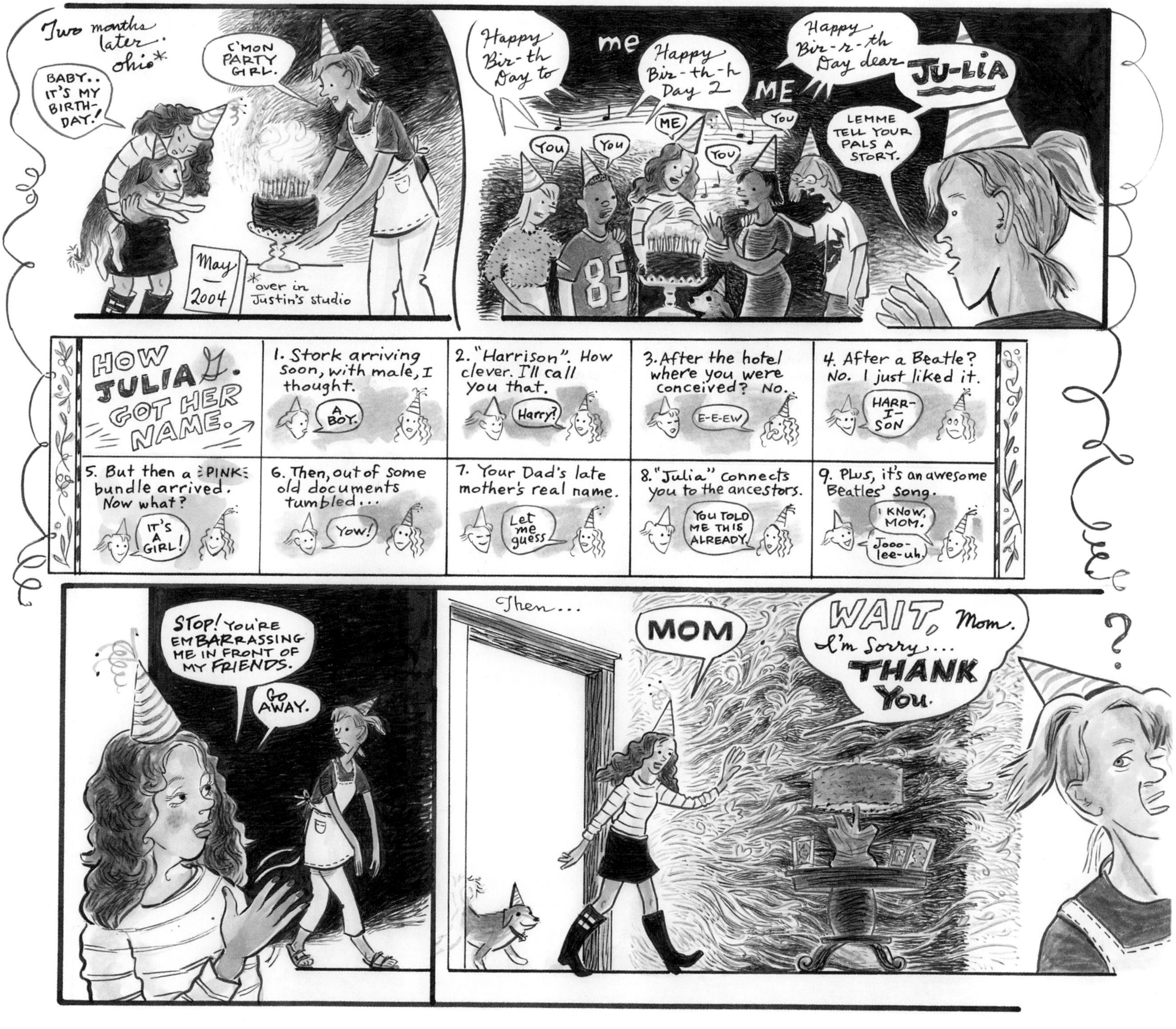
Two months later. ohio*
BABY.. IT'S MY BIRTH-DAY!
C'MON PARTY GIRL.
May 2004
*over in Justin's studio
Happy Bir-th Day to
me
Happy Bir-th-h Day 2
ME
Happy Bir-r-th Day dear
JU-LIA
You
You
ME
You
You
LEMME TELL YOUR PALS A STORY.
HOW JULIA G. GOT HER NAME.
1. Stork arriving soon, with male, I thought.
A BOY.
2. "Harrison". How clever. I'll call you that.
Harry?
3. After the hotel where you were conceived? No.
E-E-EW
4. After a Beatle? No. I just liked it.
HARR-I-SON
5. But then a PINK bundle arrived. Now what?
IT'S A GIRL!
6. Then, out of some old documents tumbled...
YOW!
7. Your Dad's late mother's real name.
Let me guess
8. "Julia" connects you to the ancestors.
YOU TOLD ME THIS ALREADY.
9. Plus, it's an awesome Beatles' song.
I KNOW, MOM.
Jooo-lee-uh.
STOP! YOU'RE EMBARRASSING ME IN FRONT OF MY FRIENDS.
GO AWAY.
Then...
MOM
WAIT, Mom. I'm Sorry... THANK You.
?

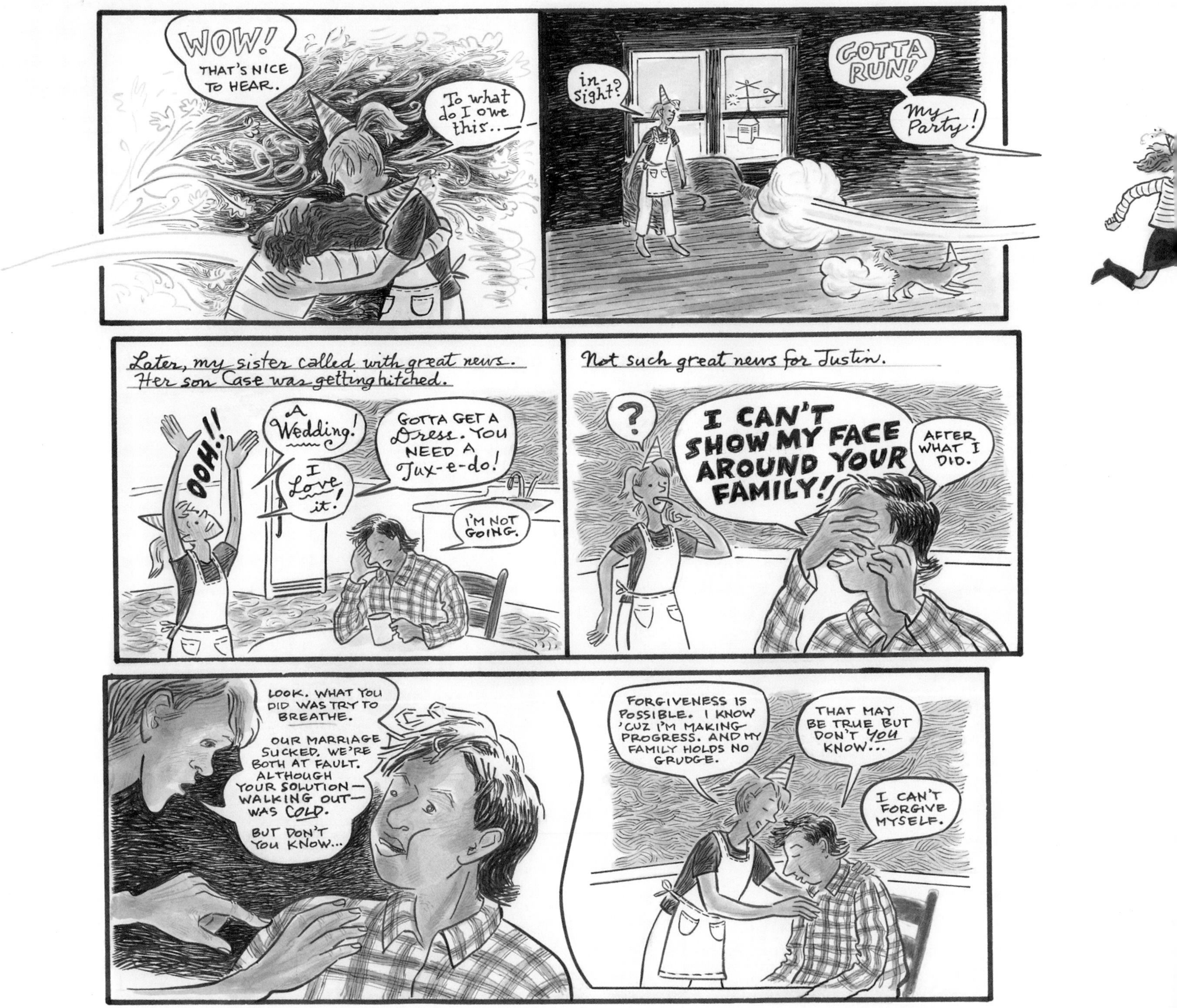
WOW! THAT'S NICE TO HEAR.
To what do I owe this...
in-sight?
GOTTA RUN!
My Party!
Later, my sister called with great news. Her son Case was getting hitched.
OOH!!
A Wedding!
I Love it!
GOTTA GET A Dress. YOU NEED A Tux-e-do!
I'M NOT GOING.
Not such great news for Justin.
?
I CAN'T SHOW MY FACE AROUND YOUR FAMILY!
AFTER WHAT I DID.
LOOK. WHAT YOU DID WAS TRY TO BREATHE.
OUR MARRIAGE SUCKED. WE'RE BOTH AT FAULT. ALTHOUGH YOUR SOLUTION— WALKING OUT— WAS COLD.
BUT DON'T YOU KNOW...
FORGIVENESS IS POSSIBLE. I KNOW 'CUZ I'M MAKING PROGRESS. AND MY FAMILY HOLDS NO GRUDGE.
THAT MAY BE TRUE BUT DON'T YOU KNOW...
I CAN'T FORGIVE MYSELF.

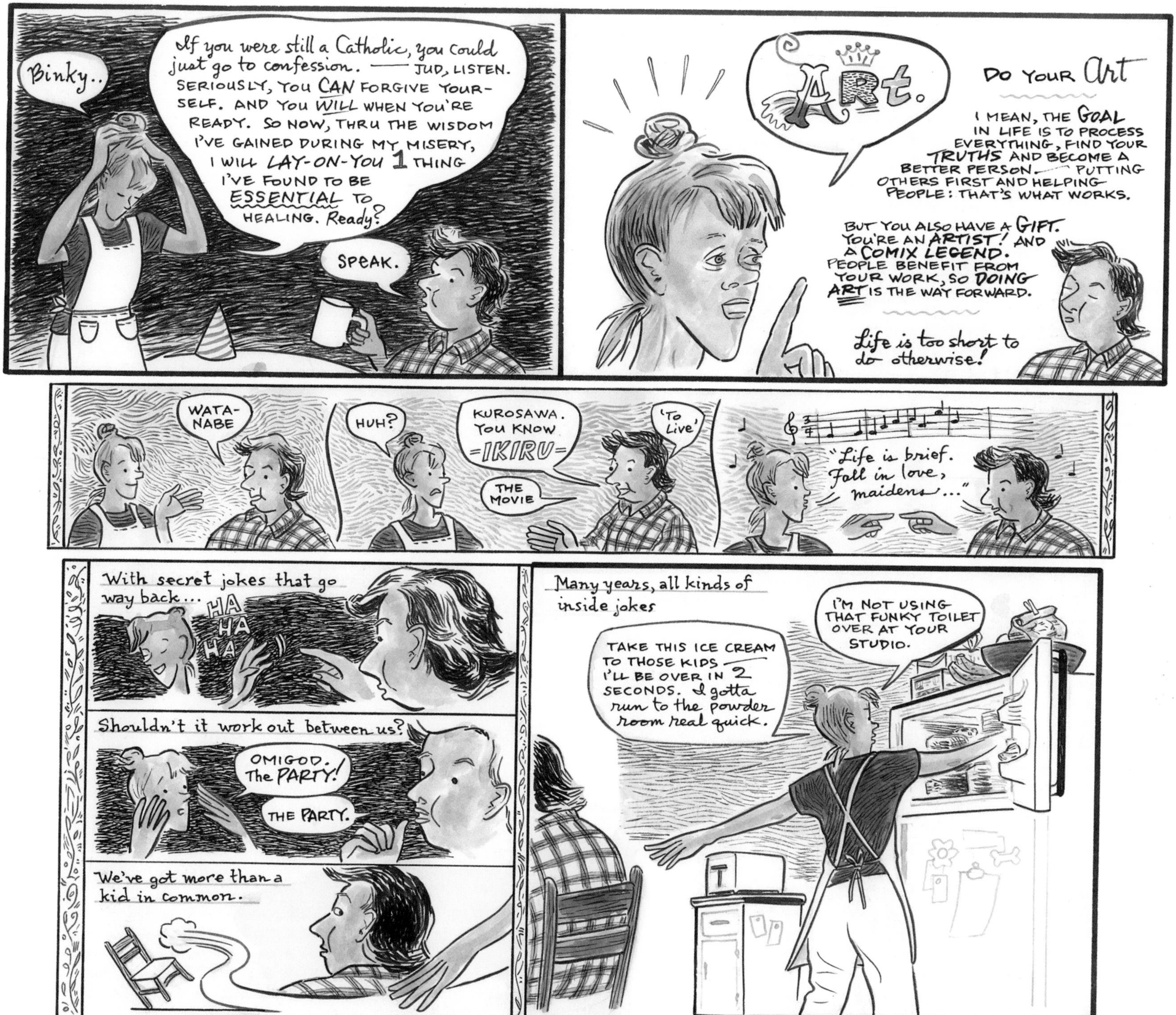
Binky..
If you were still a Catholic, you could just go to confession. — JUD, LISTEN. SERIOUSLY, YOU CAN FORGIVE YOURSELF. AND YOU WILL WHEN YOU'RE READY. SO NOW, THRU THE WISDOM I'VE GAINED DURING MY MISERY, I WILL LAY-ON-YOU 1 THING I'VE FOUND TO BE ESSENTIAL TO HEALING. Ready?
SPEAK.
ART.
DO YOUR Art
I MEAN, THE GOAL IN LIFE IS TO PROCESS EVERYTHING, FIND YOUR TRUTHS AND BECOME A BETTER PERSON. — PUTTING OTHERS FIRST AND HELPING PEOPLE: THAT'S WHAT WORKS.
BUT YOU ALSO HAVE A GIFT. YOU'RE AN ARTIST! AND A COMIX LEGEND. PEOPLE BENEFIT FROM YOUR WORK, SO DOING ART IS THE WAY FORWARD.
Life is too short to do otherwise!
WATA-NABE
HUH?
KUROSAWA. YOU KNOW =IKIRU=
THE MOVIE
'TO Live'
"Life is brief. Fall in love, maidens..."
With secret jokes that go way back...
HA HA HA
Shouldn't it work out between us?
OMIGOD. The PARTY!
THE PARTY.
We've got more than a kid in common.
Many years, all kinds of inside jokes
I'M NOT USING THAT FUNKY TOILET OVER AT YOUR STUDIO.
TAKE THIS ICE CREAM TO THOSE KIDS — I'LL BE OVER IN 2 SECONDS. I gotta run to the powder room real quick.

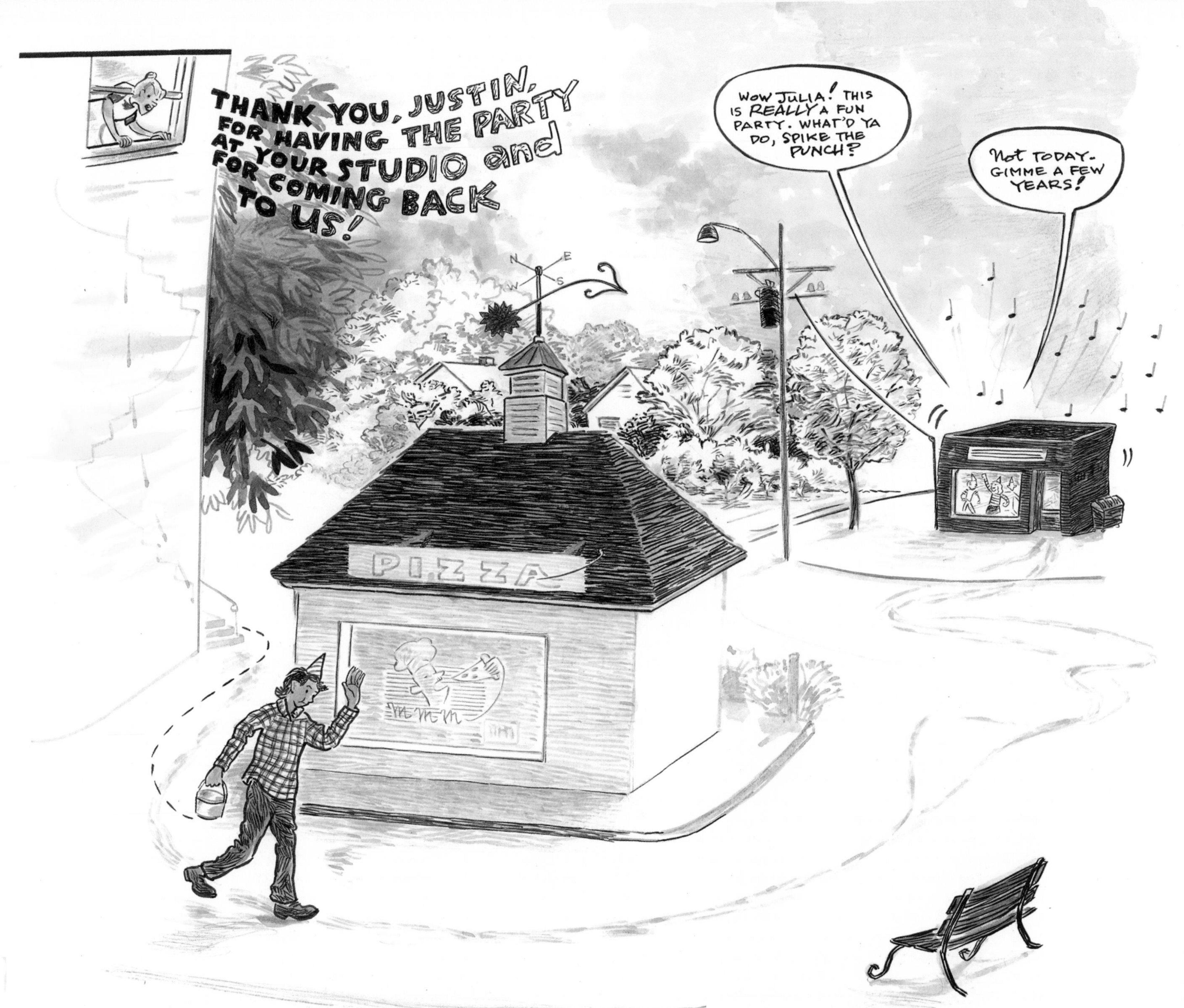

THANK YOU, JUSTIN, FOR HAVING THE PARTY AT YOUR STUDIO and FOR COMING BACK TO US!
WOW JULIA! THIS IS REALLY A FUN PARTY. WHAT'D YA DO, SPIKE THE PUNCH?
Not TODAY- GIMME A FEW YEARS!
PIZZA

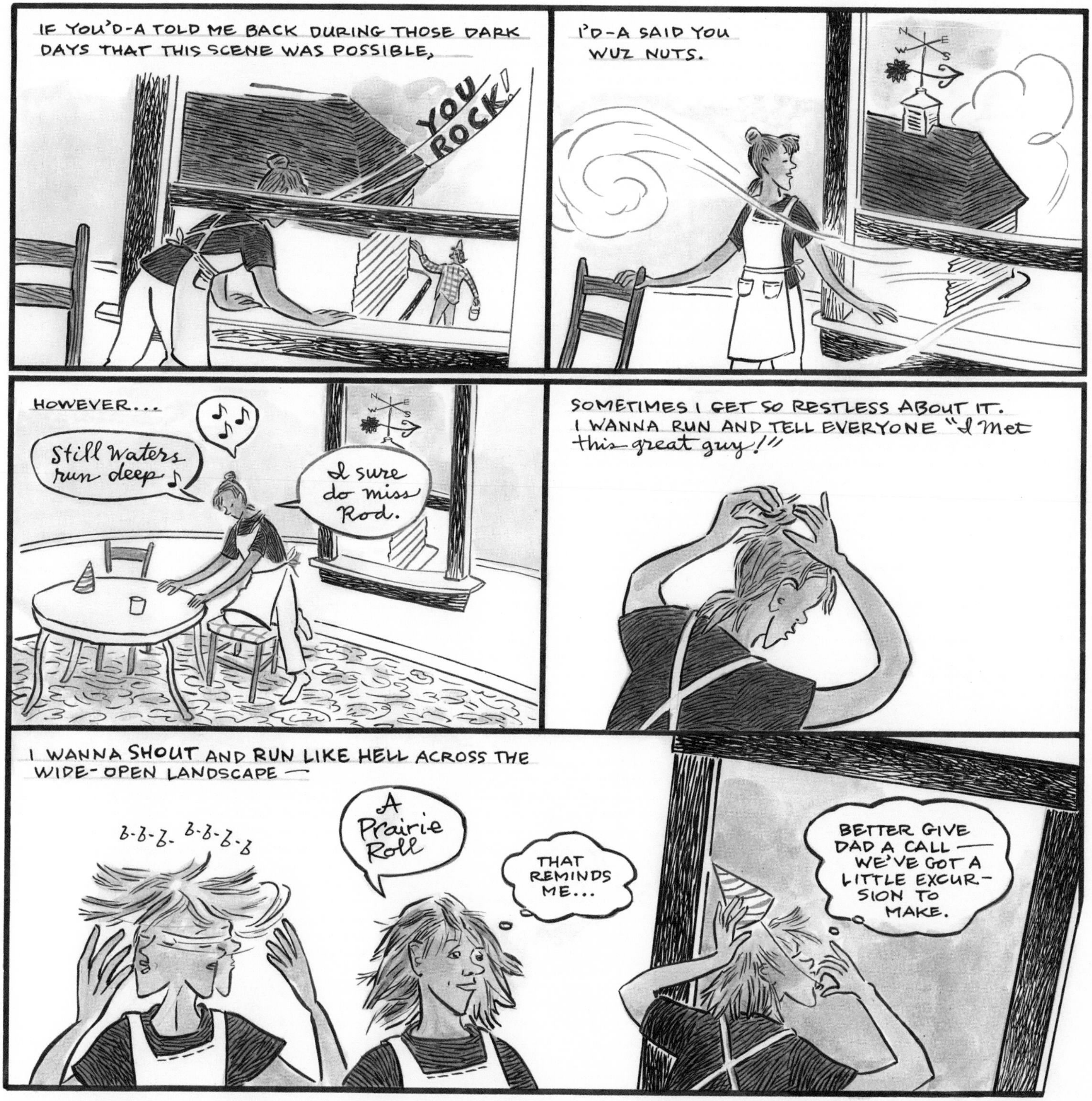

IF YOU'D-A TOLD ME BACK DURING THOSE DARK DAYS THAT THIS SCENE WAS POSSIBLE,
YOU ROCK!
I'D-A SAID YOU WUZ NUTS.
N E W S
HOWEVER...
Still waters run deep
I sure do miss Rod.
SOMETIMES I GET SO RESTLESS ABOUT IT. I WANNA RUN AND TELL EVERYONE "I met this great guy!"
I WANNA SHOUT AND RUN LIKE HELL ACROSS THE WIDE-OPEN LANDSCAPE —
Z-Z-Z- Z-Z-Z-Z
A Prairie Roll
THAT REMINDS ME...
BETTER GIVE DAD A CALL — WE'VE GOT A LITTLE EXCURSION TO MAKE.

14.

CHASING PAPER

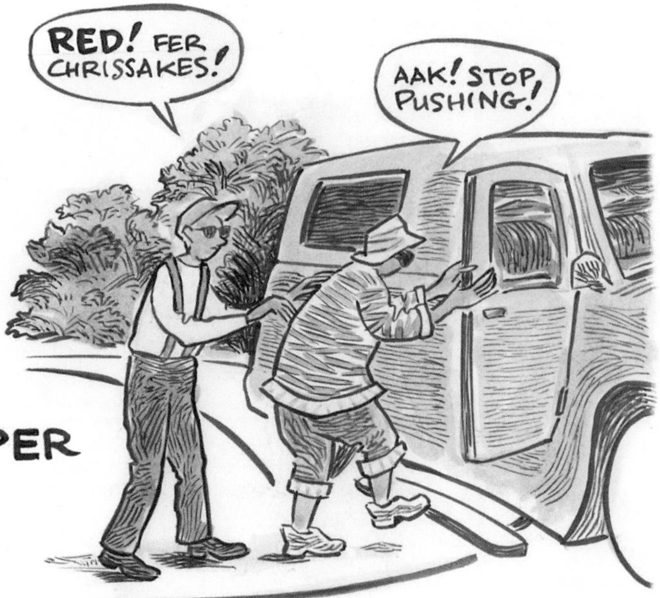
RED! FER CHRISSAKES!
AAK! STOP, PUSHING!

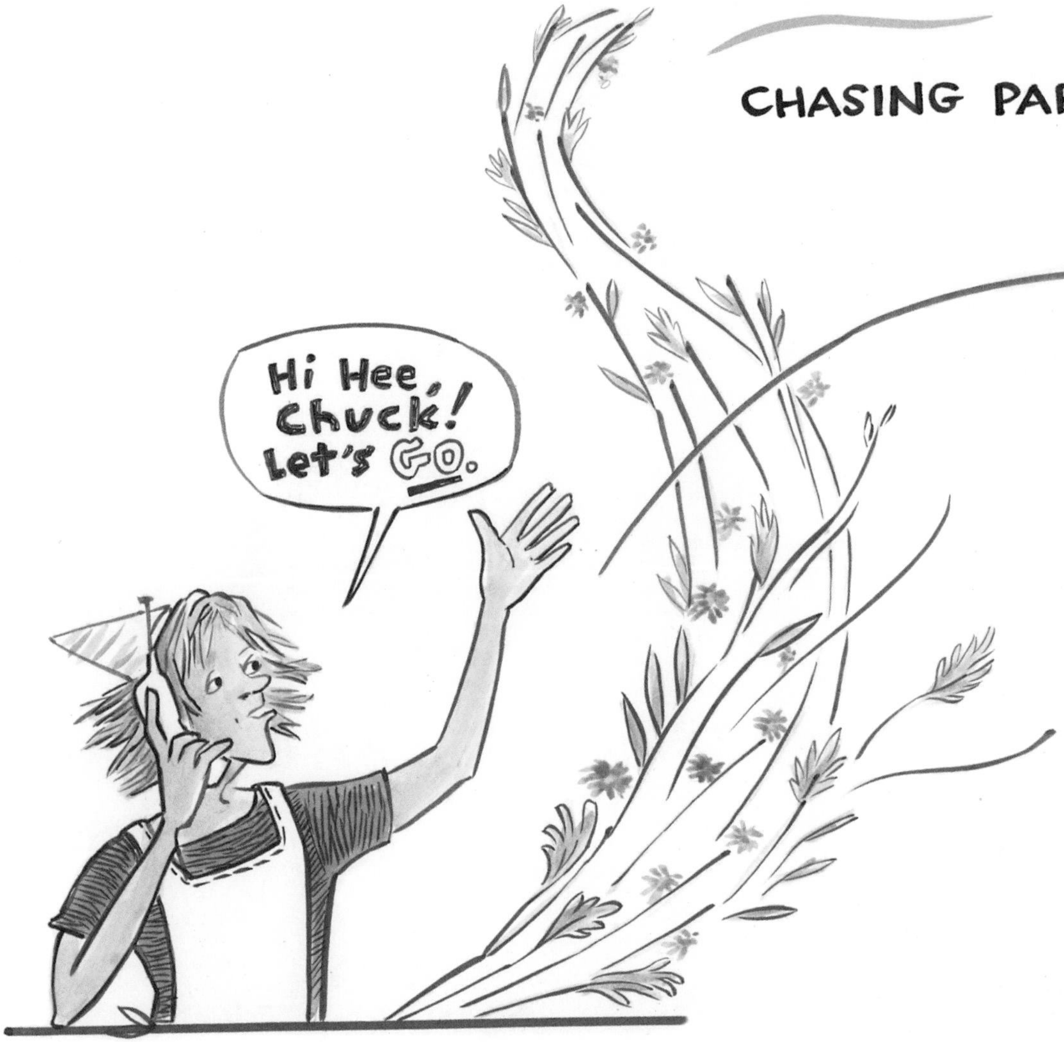
Hi Hee, Chuck! Let's GO.

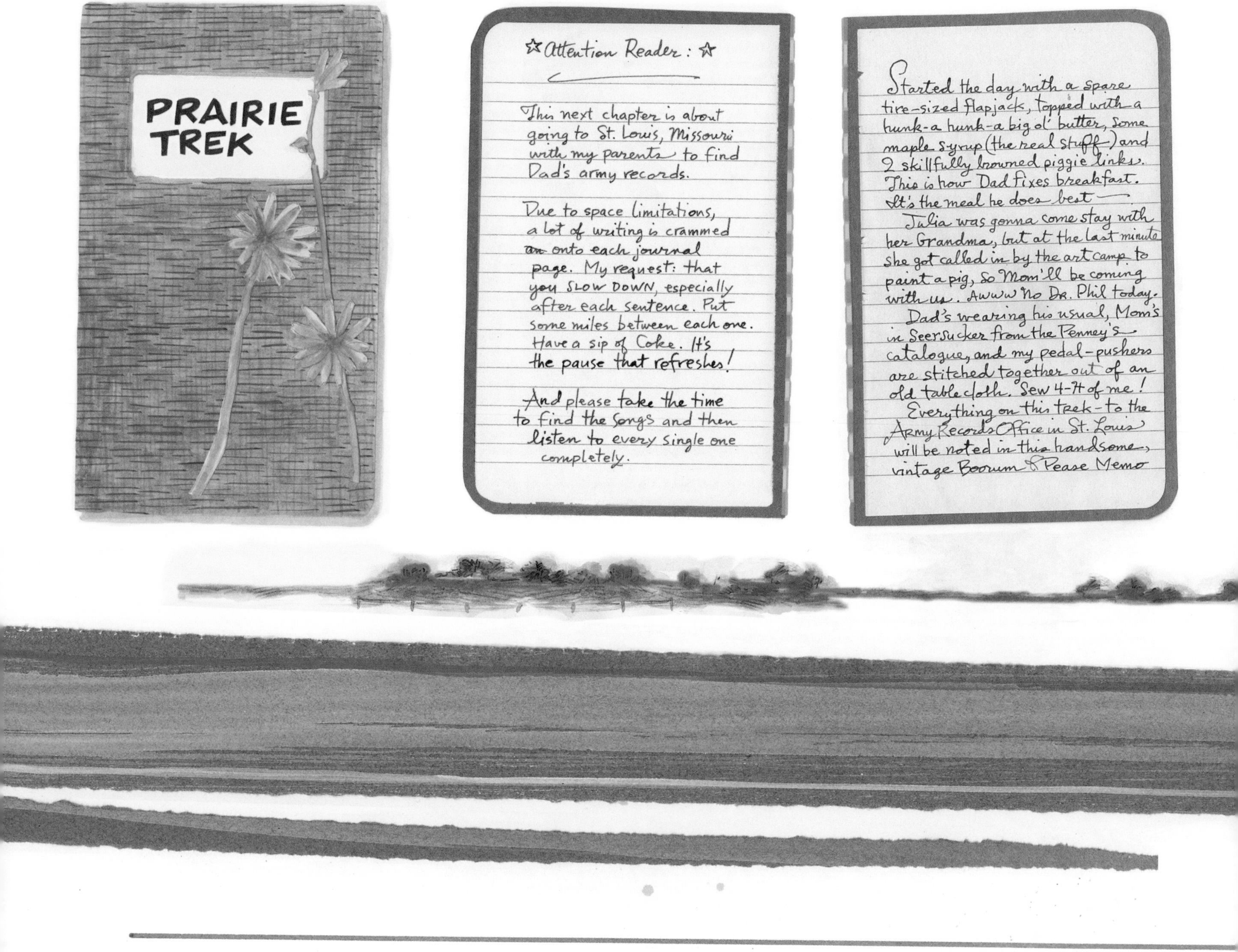
PRAIRIE TREK
☆ Attention Reader: ☆
This next chapter is about going to St. Louis, Missouri with my parents to find Dad's army records.
Due to space limitations, a lot of writing is crammed ~~an~~ onto each journal page. My request: that you SLOW DOWN, especially after each sentence. Put some miles between each one. Have a sip of Coke. It's the pause that refreshes!
And please take the time to find the songs and then listen to every single one completely.
Started the day with a spare tire-sized flapjack, topped with a hunk-a hunk-a big ol' butter, some maple syrup (the real stuff) and 2 skillfully browned piggie links. This is how Dad fixes breakfast. It's the meal he does best —
Julia was gonna come stay with her Grandma, but at the last minute she got called in by the art camp to paint a pig, so Mom'll be coming with us. Awww no Dr. Phil today.
Dad's wearing his usual, Mom's in seersucker from the Penney's catalogue, and my pedal-pushers are stitched together out of an old tablecloth. Sew 4-H of me!
Everything on this trek - to the Army Records Office in St. Louis will be noted in this handsome, vintage Boorum & Pease Memo

book, No. 6553. Got it at a yard sale back in Calif. in the 1980s. Totally rad! They don't make 'em any more. Can't find 'em thriftin' or on the internet. So what I've got here is FINITE and rare, which makes me appreciate it even more. ☼. So—

with a full tank of gas, it's Hi-Hi-Hee as our caisson goes rolling along. I get to be the kid in the back seat again. And with Chuck Tyler at the wheel, there's nothing to fear. He's an EXCELLENT driver. One of Patton's boys, so call this a 'LUCKY FORWARD' roll. This means no STOPPING, no side trips. "Ladies, do what you gotta do while I gas-up."

Control over the wheel includes dominion over the radio...

Turned VERY LOW. Barely audible songs from the American songbook HINT at us. Because, the radio is on "in case of a bulletin from the authorities." Out here. In the middle of nowhere. On a spectacular day. ♫ Whispering towards us now: TRAVELING MAN by Rick Nelson. ♫ ♪ . . .

So much preparation went into this 2 day Road jolly to Missouri. You can't just show up. Micro-Film viewing requires clearance. Something about the FREEDOM of INFORMATION Act. Bunch of forms faxed back and forth, signatures, SSNs. Blood promises. ☞ SIGN HERE

We are running with the big rigs and their naughty mud flaps, to ♫ Terry Stafford's Amarillo by Morning. Unfolding before us is the

great American landscape: waving prairies edging corn, corn, corn and soybeans. The bread basket! One grand country, ours. The one soldiers defend and die for. ~ Just saw a sign that reads GUNS SAVE LIVES. (!)

Mom and I are already SICK of Dad's STINKING pipe. Click the Zippo open. Light the bowl. Clank it SHUT. Fill the bowl again from the tobacco pouch on lap. Click-PUFF-PUFF-Clank. Click-PUFF-PUFF-Clank. At least the window is cracked open just enough to suck out our complaints, along with ♫ Handy Man by ♫ James Taylor. The KHHKHHHKKH noise from the window, clicking, clanking RRR engines WWR wheels. So noisy! I can't ponder my angst over Justin and Rod, I conclude, as George's guitar gently weeps... ♫

St. Louis

Hour 3. Still on the heartland conveyor belt. Remembering 1961... It was cee-gars while driving. Outta the side of his mouth. DAD. He smoked and cussed at Janes for 'sitting on the pot' when they shoulda been speeding like he was. HONK HONK 'Gonna cause a Pile-up for Chrissakes.' Mom's reaction never varied: (sucking sound through her teeth) 'You're taking a chance, Chuck!' and her motion was to hit the fictitious passenger-side brake while tapping a non-existent steering wheel. Still does it.

♫ Lilting on the airwaves now: Gogi Grant ♪ Oh the way-ward wind.. is a restless wind...

Mom is a tree watcher. Not signs, not architecture.

She notices them out loud. "Look how big THAT one is !" OR, of one hacked by a storm, "Oh that poor sad fellow." But out in the wide open she becomes a CLOUD WATCHER. Not so much to shape out a lady's profile, but to marvel at the Magnificence of something so much bigger than she is, with the same awe she has for trees — I didn't know until just recently that she requests to have her ashes buried in a tree trunk. It's in her will.

Dad wishes to be up by his parents in Chicago. Ann is there, too. The plot was paid for years ago, "why waste money", he says. He's ok with Mom's tree wishes. "When you're gone, you're

gone. That's it." ♫♪

♪ ...and she was born the next of kin... to the wayward wind. ♪♪

M: "That blue stuff on the side of the road: CHICORY. Dad complained when they'd use too much of it To stretch coffee during the Depression." Later, Dad (D) says "I'm gonna shoot BUSH if he takes away my Social Security." M: "You can't talk that way any more, Chuck. Zero tolerance. They'll lock you up." D: "Why not! The stock market's gonna go broke and there's no more poor farm. I'll be better off in prison." M: "Maybe. If you like chicory."

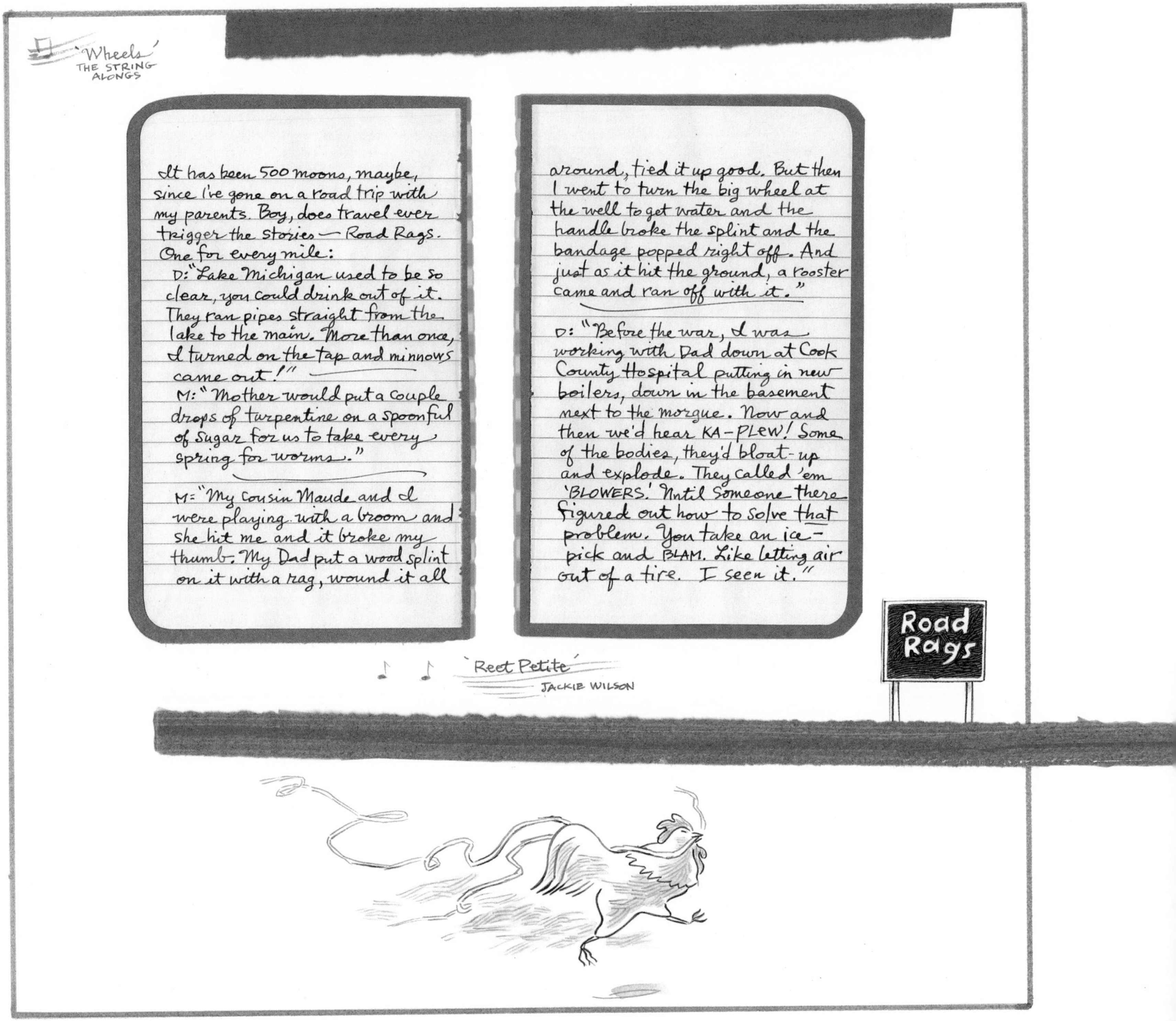
'Wheels'
THE STRING ALONGS
It has been 500 moons, maybe, since I've gone on a road trip with my parents. Boy, does travel ever trigger the stories — Road Rags. One for every mile:
D: "Lake Michigan used to be so clear, you could drink out of it. They ran pipes straight from the lake to the main. More than once, I turned on the tap and minnows came out!"
M: "Mother would put a couple drops of turpentine on a spoonful of sugar for us to take every spring for worms."
M: "My cousin Maude and I were playing with a broom and she hit me and it broke my thumb. My Dad put a wood splint on it with a rag, wound it all around, tied it up good. But then I went to turn the big wheel at the well to get water and the handle broke the splint and the bandage popped right off. And just as it hit the ground, a rooster came and ran off with it."
D: "Before the war, I was working with Dad down at Cook County Hospital putting in new boilers, down in the basement next to the morgue. Now and then we'd hear KA-PLEW! Some of the bodies, they'd bloat-up and explode. They called 'em 'BLOWERS.' Until someone there figured out how to solve that problem. You take an ice-pick and BLAM. Like letting air out of a tire. I seen it."
Road Rags
'Reet Petite'
JACKIE WILSON

'Theme from Airport' VINCE BELL

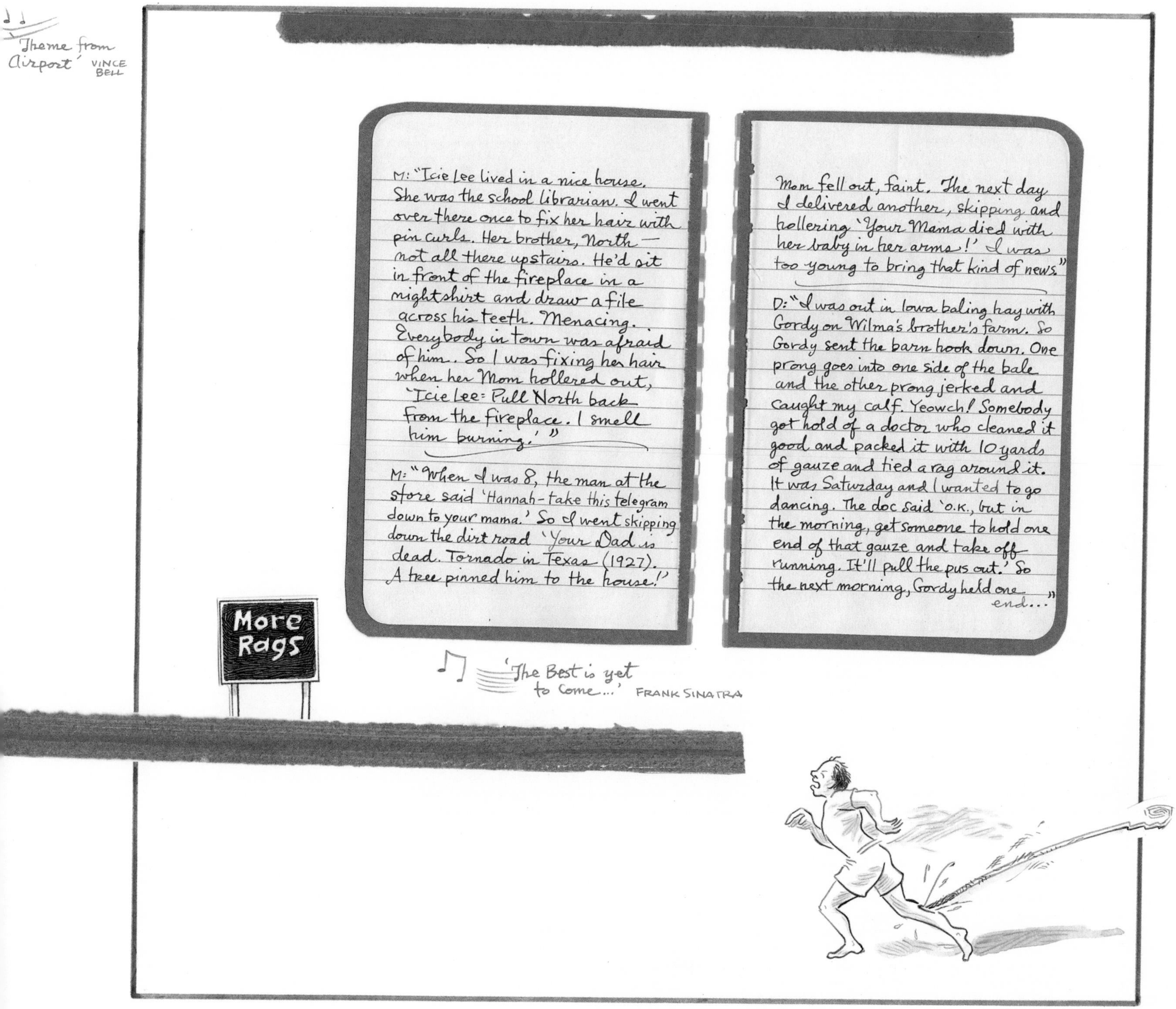
M: "Icie Lee lived in a nice house. She was the school librarian. I went over there once to fix her hair with pin curls. Her brother, North — not all there upstairs. He'd sit in front of the fireplace in a nightshirt and draw a file across his teeth. Menacing. Everybody in town was afraid of him. So I was fixing her hair when her Mom hollered out, 'Icie Lee: Pull North back from the fireplace. I smell him burning.'"
M: "When I was 8, the man at the store said 'Hannah- take this telegram down to your mama.' So I went skipping down the dirt road 'Your Dad is dead. Tornado in Texas (1927). A tree pinned him to the house!' Mom fell out, faint. The next day I delivered another, skipping and hollering 'Your Mama died with her baby in her arms!' I was too young to bring that kind of news."
D: "I was out in Iowa baling hay with Gordy on Wilma's brother's farm. So Gordy sent the barn hook down. One prong goes into one side of the bale and the other prong jerked and caught my calf. Yeowch! Somebody got hold of a doctor who cleaned it good and packed it with 10 yards of gauze and tied a rag around it. It was Saturday and I wanted to go dancing. The doc said 'O.K., but in the morning, get someone to hold one end of that gauze and take off running. It'll pull the pus out.' So the next morning, Gordy held one end..."
More Rags
'The Best is yet to Come...' FRANK SINATRA

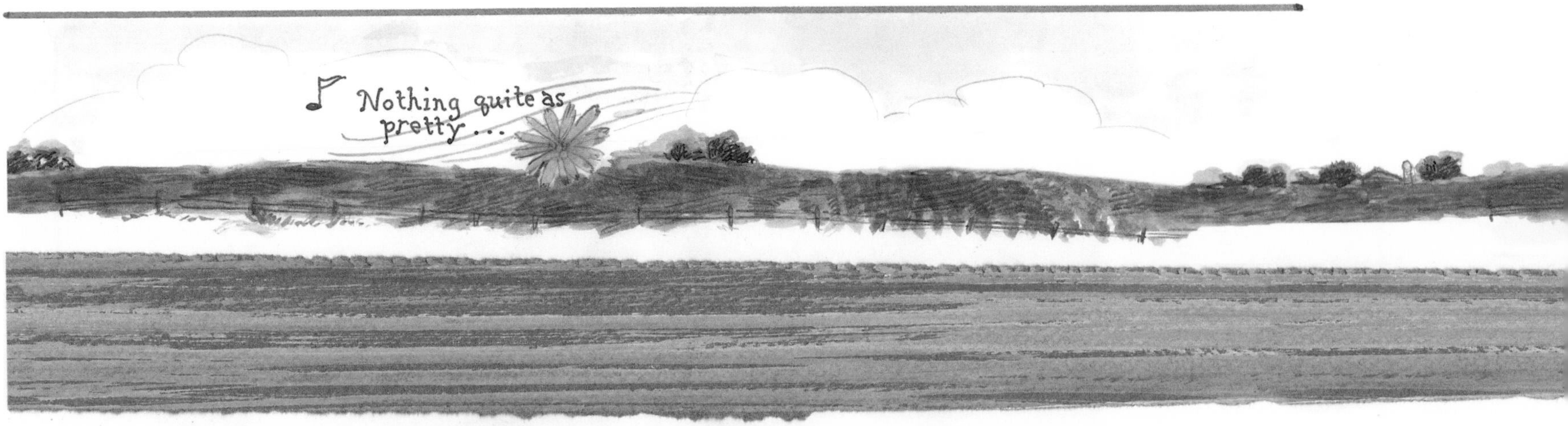
Nothing quite as pretty...

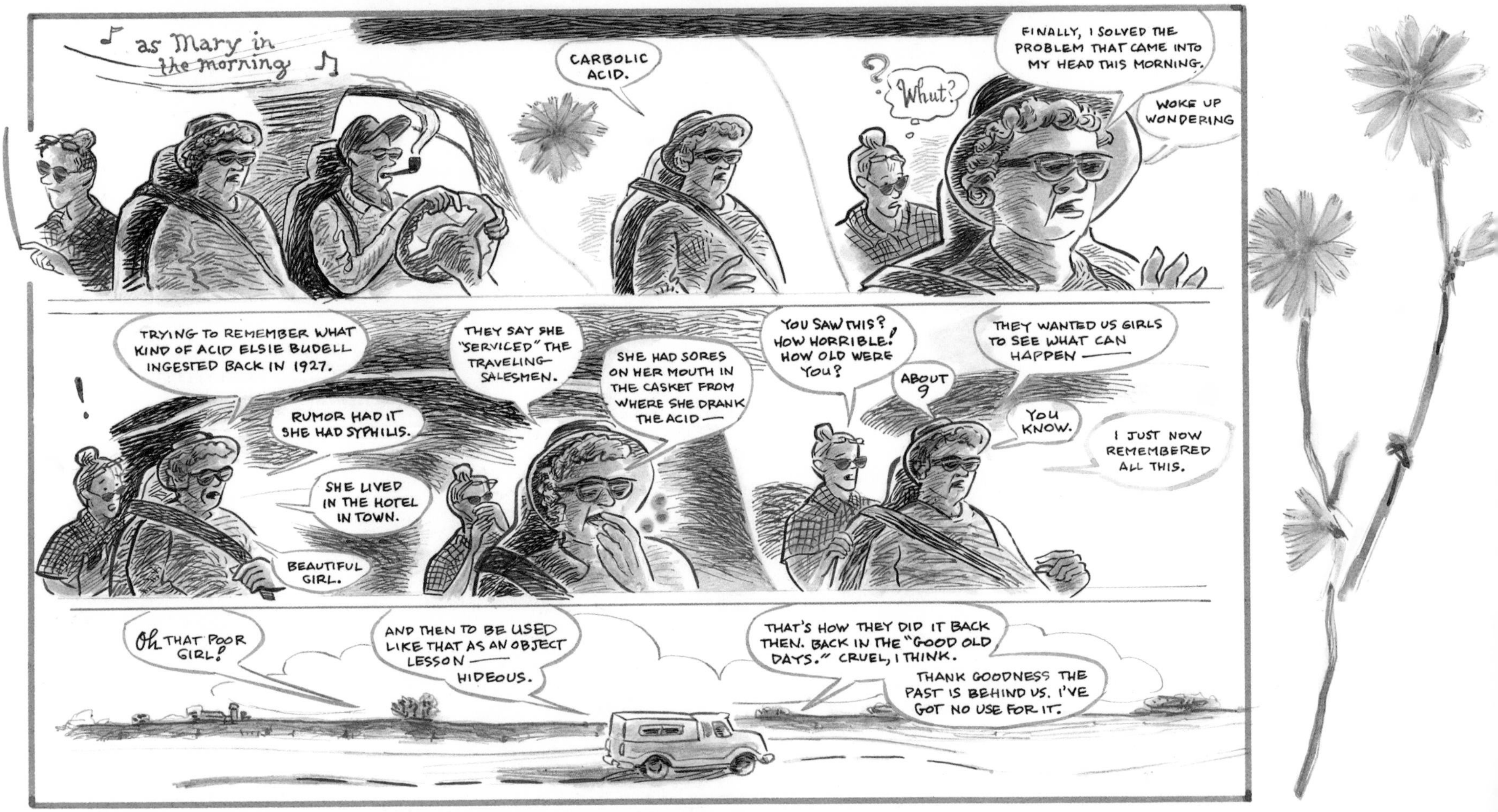
as Mary in the morning
CARBOLIC ACID.
FINALLY, I SOLVED THE PROBLEM THAT CAME INTO MY HEAD THIS MORNING.
Whut?
WOKE UP WONDERING
TRYING TO REMEMBER WHAT KIND OF ACID ELSIE BUDELL INGESTED BACK IN 1927.
RUMOR HAD IT SHE HAD SYPHILIS.
SHE LIVED IN THE HOTEL IN TOWN.
BEAUTIFUL GIRL.
THEY SAY SHE "SERVICED" THE TRAVELING-SALESMEN.
SHE HAD SORES ON HER MOUTH IN THE CASKET FROM WHERE SHE DRANK THE ACID—
YOU SAW THIS? HOW HORRIBLE! HOW OLD WERE YOU?
ABOUT 9
THEY WANTED US GIRLS TO SEE WHAT CAN HAPPEN—
YOU KNOW.
I JUST NOW REMEMBERED ALL THIS.
Oh THAT POOR GIRL!
AND THEN TO BE USED LIKE THAT AS AN OBJECT LESSON— HIDEOUS.
THAT'S HOW THEY DID IT BACK THEN. BACK IN THE "GOOD OLD DAYS." CRUEL, I THINK.
THANK GOODNESS THE PAST IS BEHIND US. I'VE GOT NO USE FOR IT.

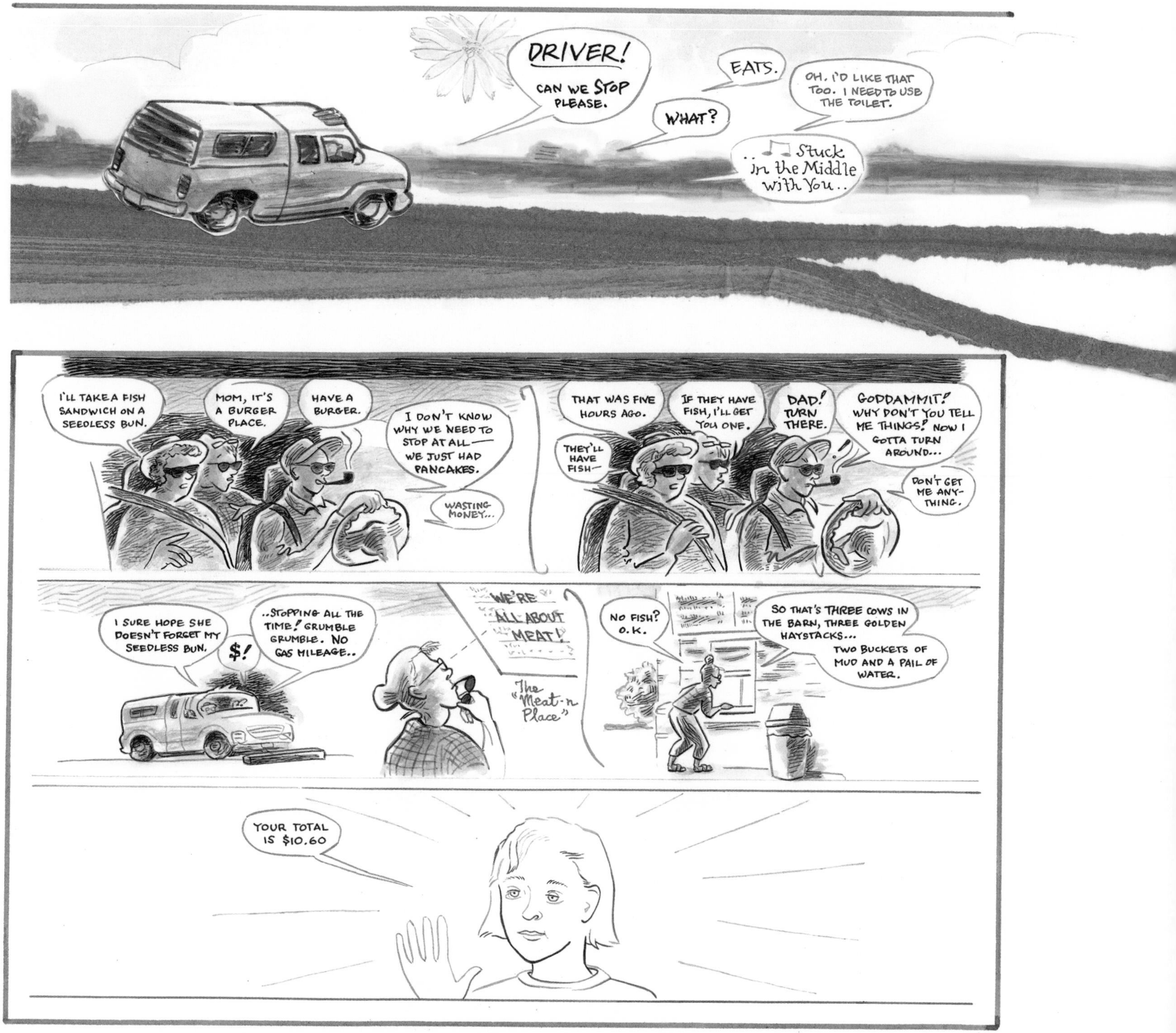
DRIVER!
CAN WE STOP PLEASE.
WHAT?
EATS.
OH, I'D LIKE THAT TOO. I NEED TO USE THE TOILET.
.. Stuck in the Middle with You..
I'LL TAKE A FISH SANDWICH ON A SEEDLESS BUN.
MOM, IT'S A BURGER PLACE.
HAVE A BURGER.
I DON'T KNOW WHY WE NEED TO STOP AT ALL— WE JUST HAD PANCAKES.
WASTING MONEY...
THAT WAS FIVE HOURS AGO.
THEY'LL HAVE FISH—
IF THEY HAVE FISH, I'LL GET YOU ONE.
DAD! TURN THERE.
GODDAMMIT! WHY DON'T YOU TELL ME THINGS! NOW I GOTTA TURN AROUND...
DON'T GET ME ANY-THING.
I SURE HOPE SHE DOESN'T FORGET MY SEEDLESS BUN.
$!
..STOPPING ALL THE TIME! GRUMBLE GRUMBLE. NO GAS MILEAGE..
WE'RE ALL ABOUT MEAT!
The "Meat-n Place"
NO FISH? O.K.
SO THAT'S THREE COWS IN THE BARN, THREE GOLDEN HAYSTACKS...
TWO BUCKETS OF MUD AND A PAIL OF WATER.
YOUR TOTAL IS $10.60

♩ ~~Shoo bop shoo bop~~
~~my baby shoo~~
~~bop shoo bop~~ ♫
♫ Hello Stranger ♫. (Hello
Barbara Lewis!)
That girl back there who
served us: Wearing an expression
I've seen in a painting. The
Mona Lisa, I think. In fact,
I'll call her that. Mona Lisa
of the Midwest, I love you.
Or, she could be someone Dorothea
Lange would have photographed.
~~♫ oooo seems like a~~
mighty long time ... shoo bop
shoo bop
Mom says she's got no use
for the past. It's true that
things have to change, but I
love their stories. I love them
juxtaposed on this prairie
trek. —— Mom and Dad
are so-o-o WPA mural.

They are ART to me, as much as
Grant Wood or Edward Hopper.
American Art, as in Jackson
Pollock. Heartland + Ashcan +
Action + 20TH Century = these
true people. But unlike art,
experience is VAPOR. I'm
doing my best to catch it and
hold it on these pages before it's
out the window with Dad's smoke.
♪ ♪ ♪
♪ On a day - like today -
we'll pass the time away - writing
Love Letters in .. the sand ♪
Pat Boone croons.
M: "I wrote your Dad a letter
every day during the war."
me: "Really? A year and a half?
Wow, that's a lot of letters. What
happened to them?" = INTERRUPTION
D "HEY. Which exit now. We're
here"

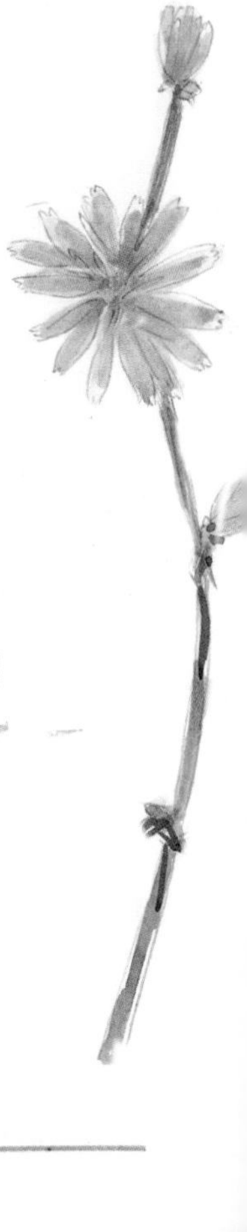

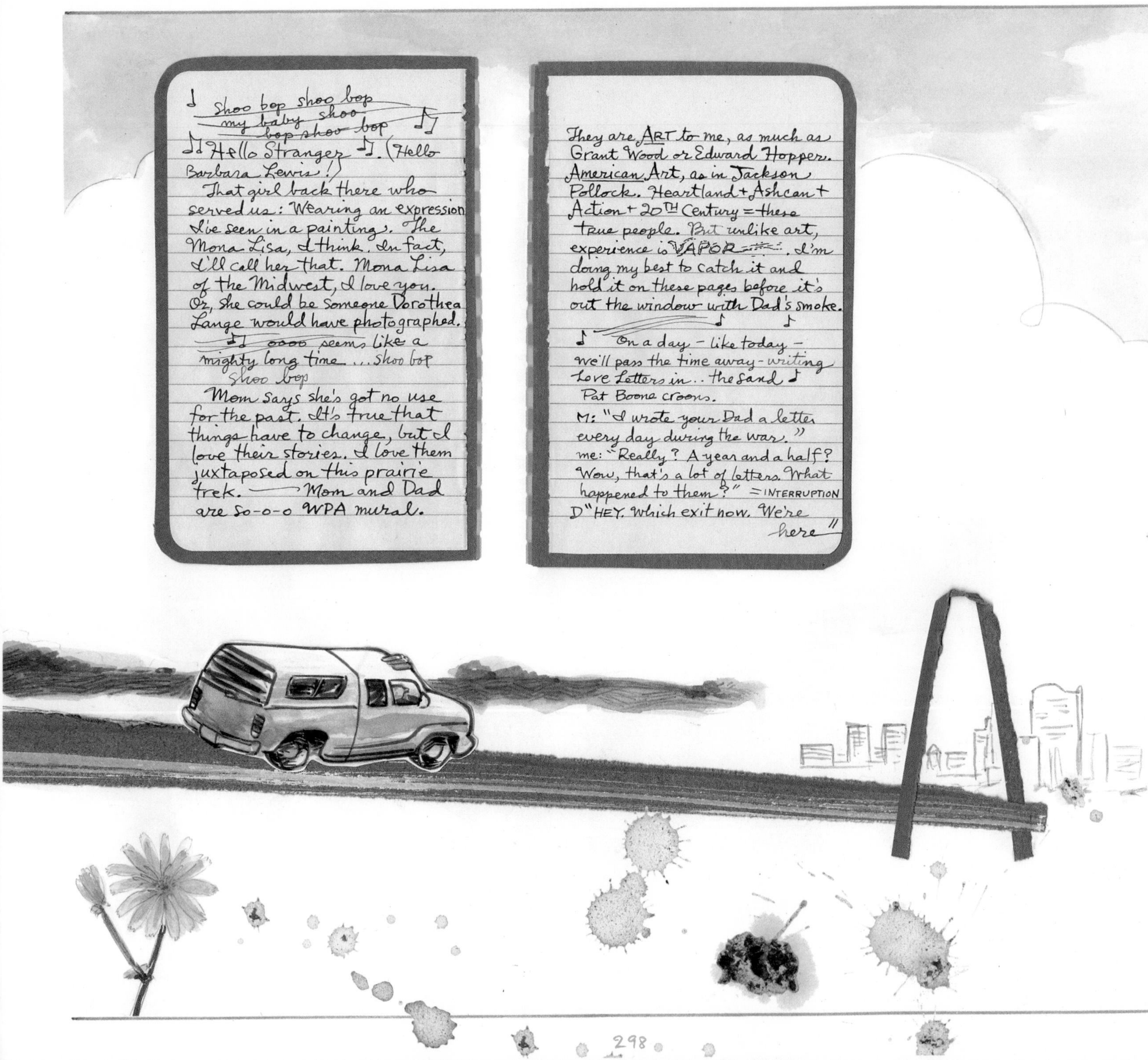

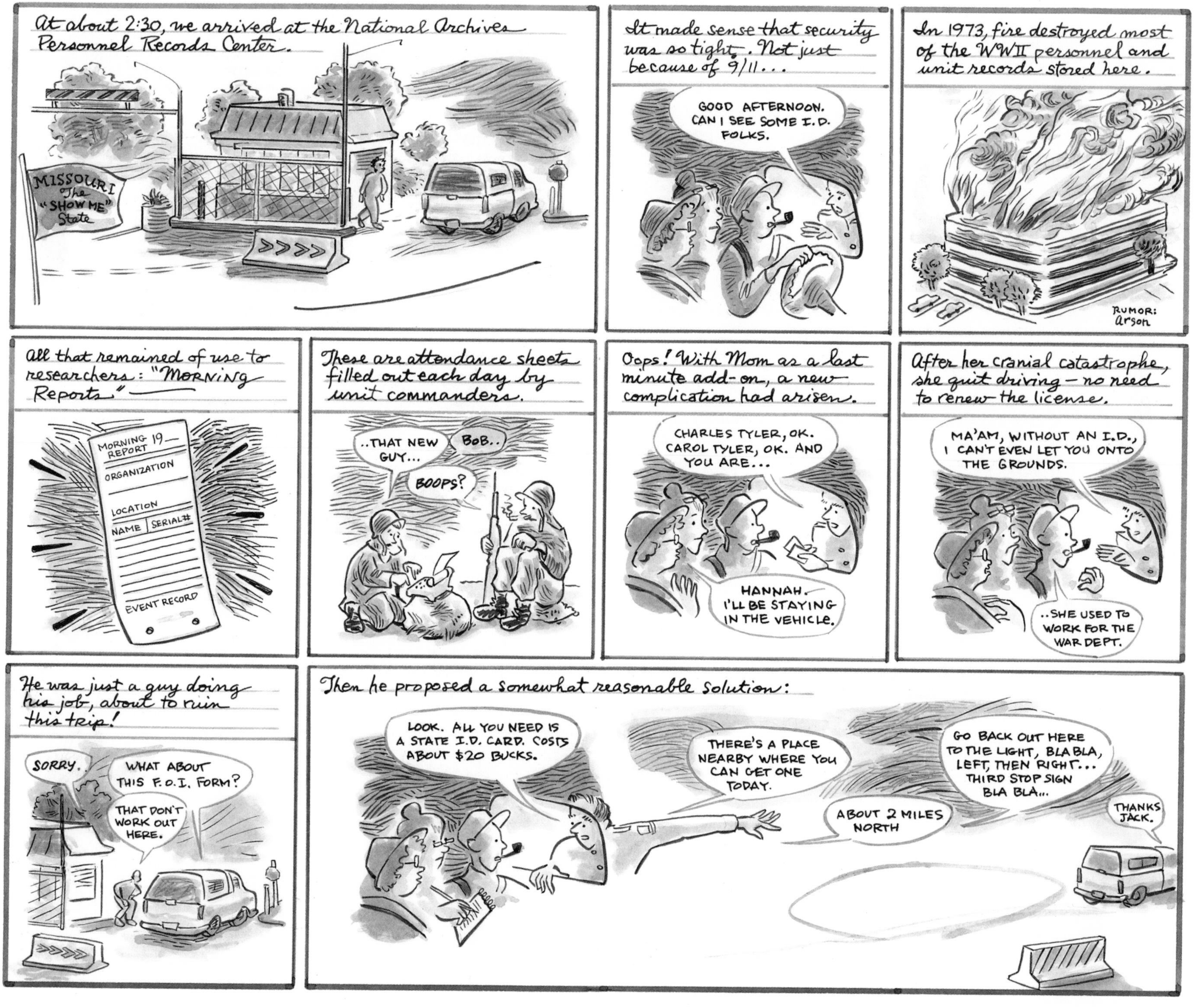
At about 2:30, we arrived at the National Archives Personnel Records Center.
MISSOURI The "SHOW ME" State
>>>>
It made sense that security was so tight. Not just because of 9/11...
GOOD AFTERNOON. CAN I SEE SOME I.D. FOLKS.
In 1973, fire destroyed most of the WWII personnel and unit records stored here.
RUMOR: arson
All that remained of use to researchers: "MORNING Reports"
MORNING REPORT 19__
ORGANIZATION
LOCATION
NAME SERIAL#
EVENT RECORD
These are attendance sheets filled out each day by unit commanders.
..THAT NEW GUY...
BOB..
BOOPS?
Oops! With Mom as a last minute add-on, a new complication had arisen.
CHARLES TYLER, OK. CAROL TYLER, OK. AND YOU ARE...
HANNAH. I'LL BE STAYING IN THE VEHICLE.
After her cranial catastrophe, she quit driving — no need to renew the license.
MA'AM, WITHOUT AN I.D., I CAN'T EVEN LET YOU ONTO THE GROUNDS.
..SHE USED TO WORK FOR THE WAR DEPT.
He was just a guy doing his job, about to ruin this trip!
SORRY.
WHAT ABOUT THIS F.O.I. FORM?
THAT DON'T WORK OUT HERE.
>>>>
Then he proposed a somewhat reasonable solution:
LOOK. ALL YOU NEED IS A STATE I.D. CARD. COSTS ABOUT $20 BUCKS.
THERE'S A PLACE NEARBY WHERE YOU CAN GET ONE TODAY.
ABOUT 2 MILES NORTH
GO BACK OUT HERE TO THE LIGHT, BLA BLA, LEFT, THEN RIGHT... THIRD STOP SIGN BLA BLA...
THANKS JACK.

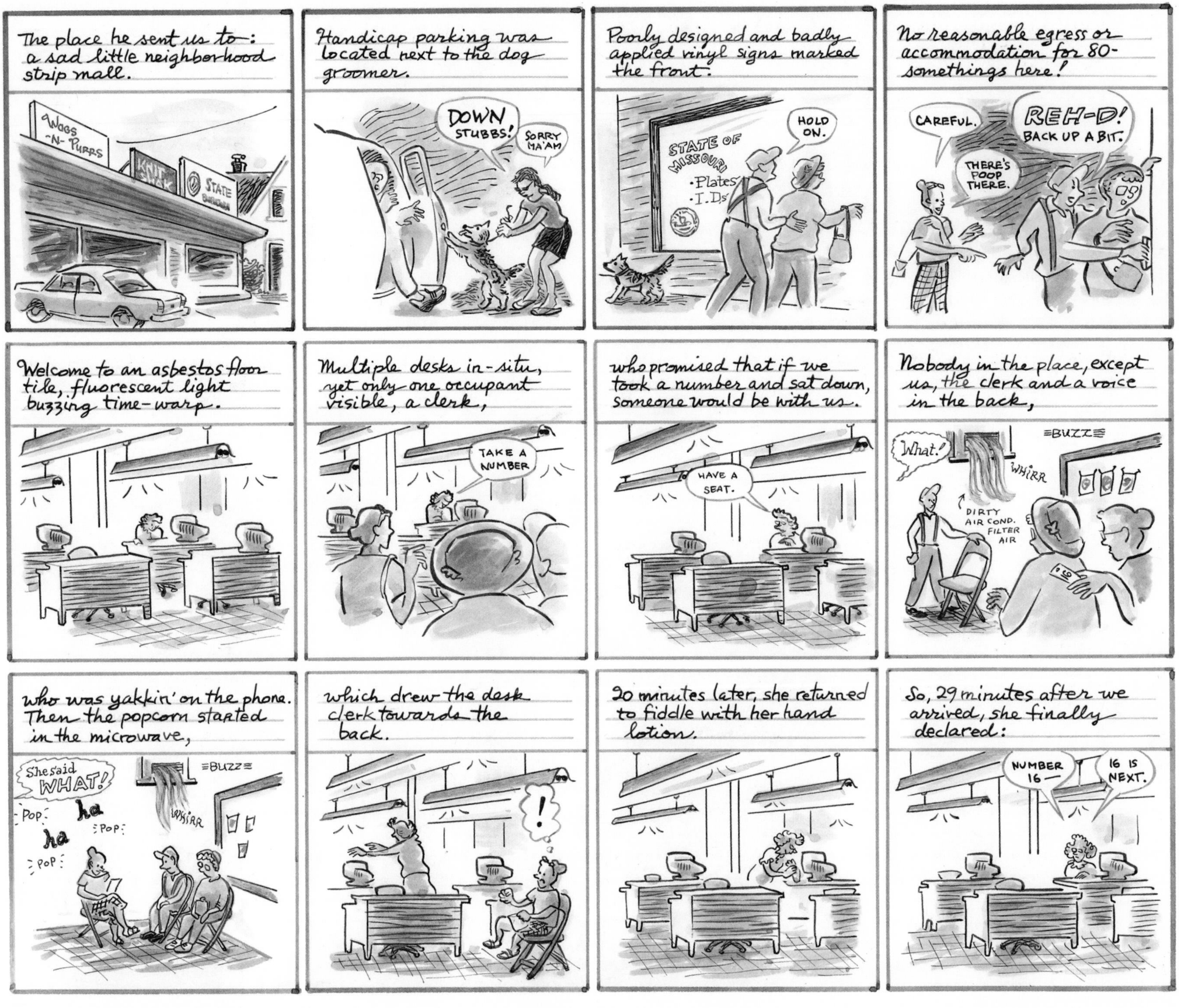

The place he sent us to: a sad little neighborhood strip mall.
WAGS -N- PURRS
KNIT SHACK
STATE
Handicap parking was located next to the dog groomer.
DOWN STUBBS!
SORRY MA'AM
Poorly designed and badly applied vinyl signs marked the front.
HOLD ON.
STATE OF MISSOURI
•Plates
•I.D.s
No reasonable egress or accommodation for 80-somethings here!
CAREFUL.
REH-D!
BACK UP A BIT.
THERE'S POOP THERE.
Welcome to an asbestos floor tile, fluorescent light buzzing time-warp.
Multiple desks in-situ, yet only one occupant visible, a clerk,
TAKE A NUMBER
who promised that if we took a number and sat down, someone would be with us.
HAVE A SEAT.
Nobody in the place, except us, the clerk and a voice in the back,
What!
≡BUZZ≡
WHIRR
DIRTY AIR COND. FILTER AIR
who was yakkin' on the phone. Then the popcorn started in the microwave,
She said WHAT!
≡BUZZ≡
ha
ha
POP
POP
POP
WHIRR
which drew the desk clerk towards the back.
!
20 minutes later, she returned to fiddle with her hand lotion.
So, 29 minutes after we arrived, she finally declared:
NUMBER 16—
16 IS NEXT.

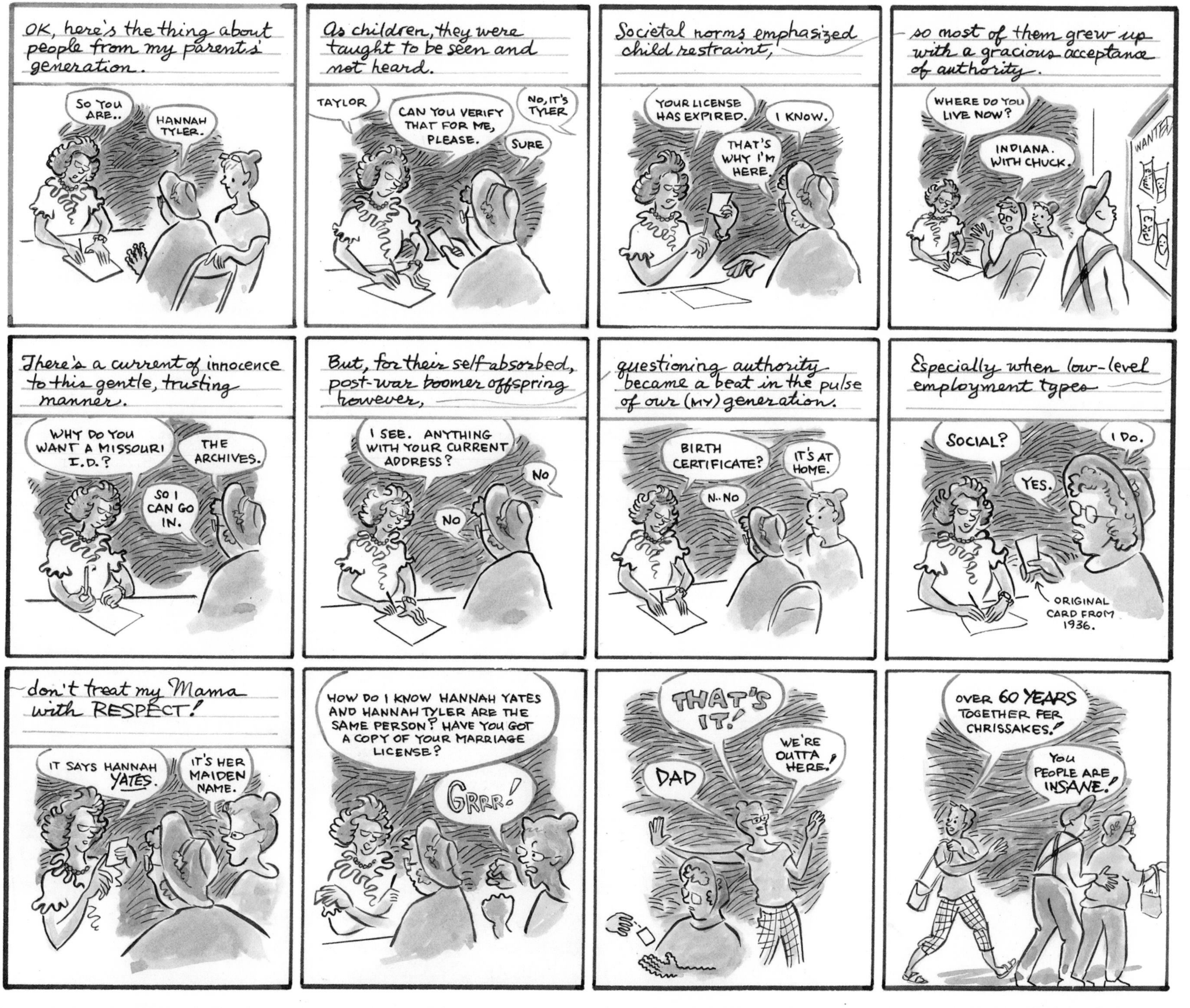
OK, here's the thing about people from my parent's generation.
SO YOU ARE..
HANNAH TYLER.
As children, they were taught to be seen and not heard.
TAYLOR
CAN YOU VERIFY THAT FOR ME, PLEASE.
NO, IT'S TYLER
SURE
Societal norms emphasized child restraint,
YOUR LICENSE HAS EXPIRED.
I KNOW.
THAT'S WHY I'M HERE.
so most of them grew up with a gracious acceptance of authority.
WHERE DO YOU LIVE NOW?
INDIANA. WITH CHUCK.
WANTED
There's a current of innocence to this gentle, trusting manner.
WHY DO YOU WANT A MISSOURI I.D.?
THE ARCHIVES.
SO I CAN GO IN.
But, for their self absorbed, post-war boomer offspring however,
I SEE. ANYTHING WITH YOUR CURRENT ADDRESS?
NO
NO
questioning authority became a beat in the pulse of our (MY) generation.
BIRTH CERTIFICATE?
IT'S AT HOME.
N..NO
Especially when low-level employment types
SOCIAL?
I DO.
YES.
ORIGINAL CARD FROM 1936.
don't treat my Mama with RESPECT!
IT SAYS HANNAH YATES.
IT'S HER MAIDEN NAME.
HOW DO I KNOW HANNAH YATES AND HANNAH TYLER ARE THE SAME PERSON? HAVE YOU GOT A COPY OF YOUR MARRIAGE LICENSE?
GRRR!
THAT'S IT!
DAD
WE'RE OUTTA HERE!
OVER 60 YEARS TOGETHER FER CHRISSAKES!
YOU PEOPLE ARE INSANE!

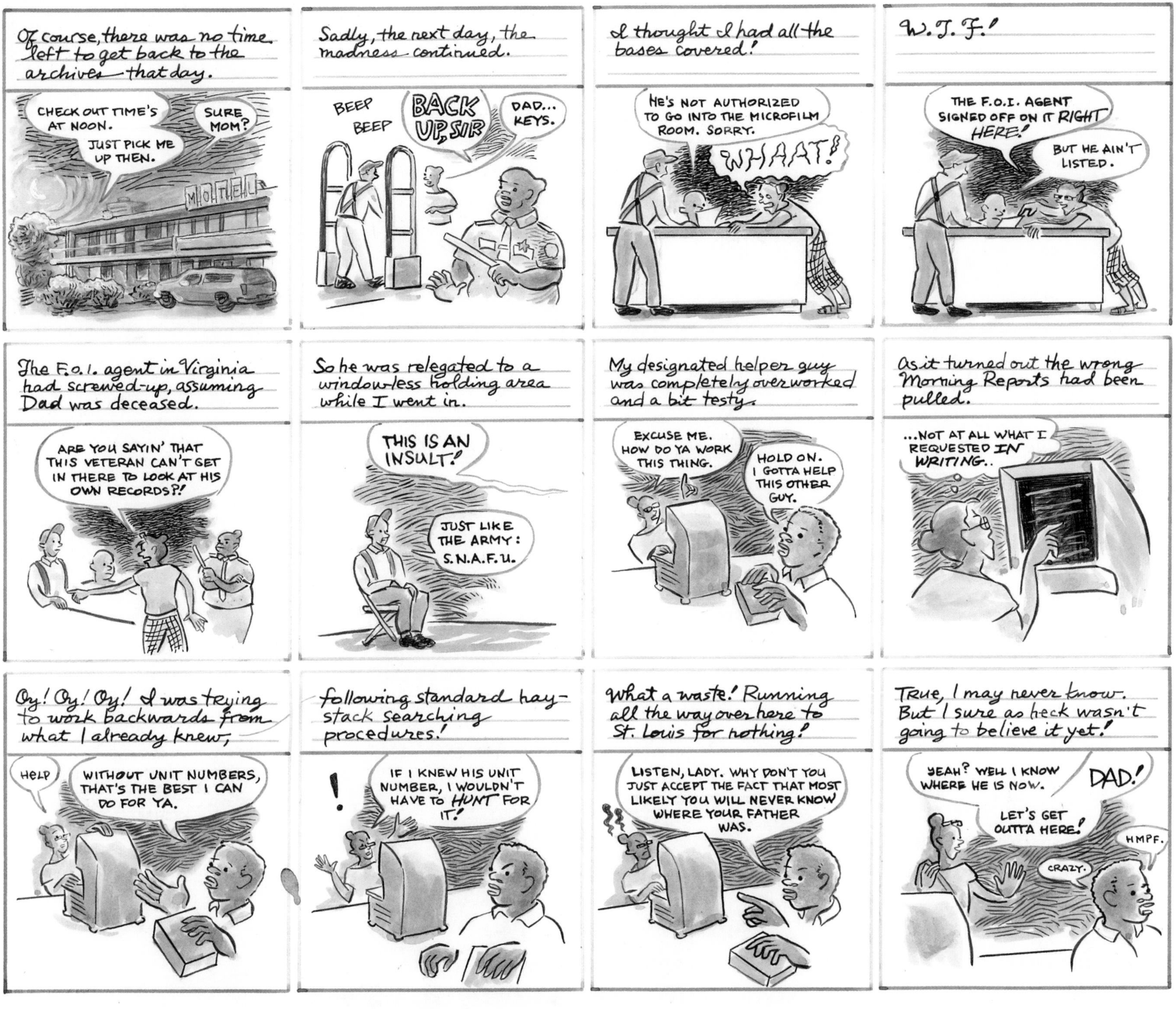
Of course, there was no time left to get back to the archives that day.
CHECK OUT TIME'S AT NOON.
SURE MOM?
JUST PICK ME UP THEN.
MOTEL
Sadly, the next day, the madness continued.
BEEP
BEEP
BACK UP, SIR
DAD... KEYS.
I thought I had all the bases covered!
HE'S NOT AUTHORIZED TO GO INTO THE MICROFILM ROOM. SORRY.
WHAAT!
W.T.F.!
THE F.O.I. AGENT SIGNED OFF ON IT RIGHT HERE!
BUT HE AIN'T LISTED.
The F.O.I. agent in Virginia had screwed-up, assuming Dad was deceased.
ARE YOU SAYIN' THAT THIS VETERAN CAN'T GET IN THERE TO LOOK AT HIS OWN RECORDS?!
So he was relegated to a windowless holding area while I went in.
THIS IS AN INSULT!
JUST LIKE THE ARMY: S.N.A.F.U.
My designated helper guy was completely overworked and a bit testy.
EXCUSE ME. HOW DO YA WORK THIS THING.
HOLD ON. I GOTTA HELP THIS OTHER GUY.
As it turned out the wrong Morning Reports had been pulled.
...NOT AT ALL WHAT I REQUESTED IN WRITING..
Oy! Oy! Oy! I was trying to work backwards from what I already knew,
HELP
WITHOUT UNIT NUMBERS, THAT'S THE BEST I CAN DO FOR YA.
following standard hay-stack searching procedures!
!
IF I KNEW HIS UNIT NUMBER, I WOULDN'T HAVE TO HUNT FOR IT!
What a waste! Running all the way over here to St. Louis for nothing!
LISTEN, LADY. WHY DON'T YOU JUST ACCEPT THE FACT THAT MOST LIKELY YOU WILL NEVER KNOW WHERE YOUR FATHER WAS.
True, I may never know. But I sure as heck wasn't going to believe it yet!
YEAH? WELL I KNOW WHERE HE IS NOW.
DAD!
LET'S GET OUTTA HERE!
HMPF.
CRAZY.

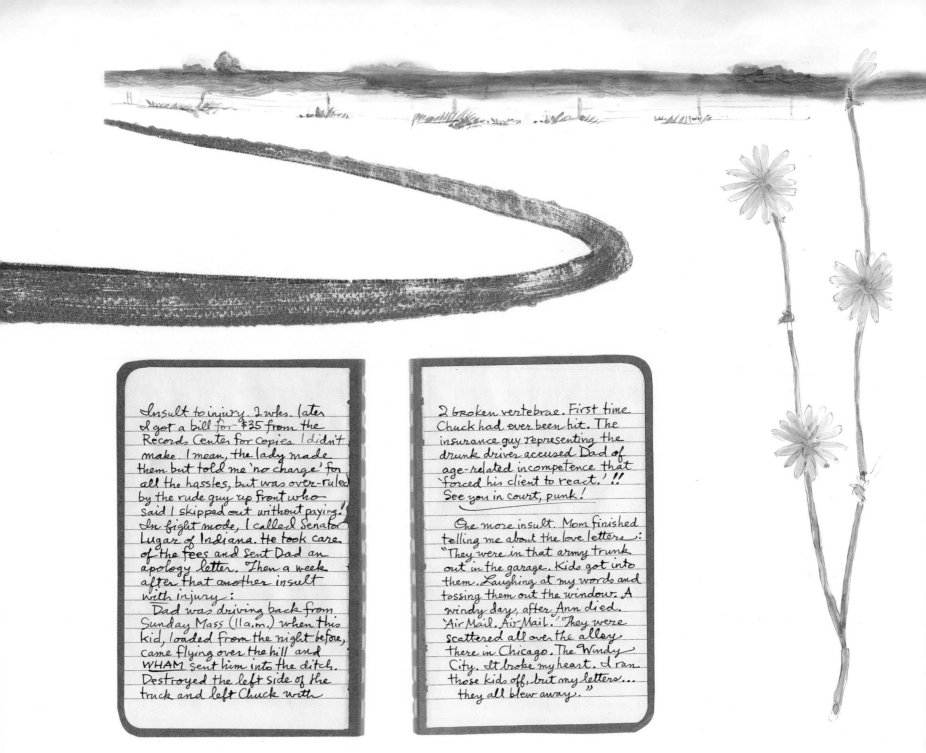

Insult to injury. 2 wks. later I got a bill for $35 from the Records Center for copies I didn't make. I mean, the lady made them but told me 'no charge' for all the hassles, but was over-ruled by the rude guy up front who said I skipped out without paying! In fight mode, I called Senator Lugar of Indiana. He took care of the fees and sent Dad an apology letter. Then a week after that another insult with injury:

Dad was driving back from Sunday Mass (11 a.m.) when this kid, loaded from the night before, came flying over the hill and WHAM sent him into the ditch. Destroyed the left side of the truck and left Chuck with

2 broken vertebrae. First time Chuck had ever been hit. The insurance guy representing the drunk driver accused Dad of age-related incompetence that 'forced his client to react.'!! See you in court, punk!

One more insult. Mom finished telling me about the love letters: "They were in that army trunk out in the garage. Kids got into them. Laughing at my words and tossing them out the window. A windy day, after Ann died. 'Air Mail. Air Mail.' They were scattered all over the alley there in Chicago. The Windy City. It broke my heart. I ran those kids off, but my letters... they all blew away."

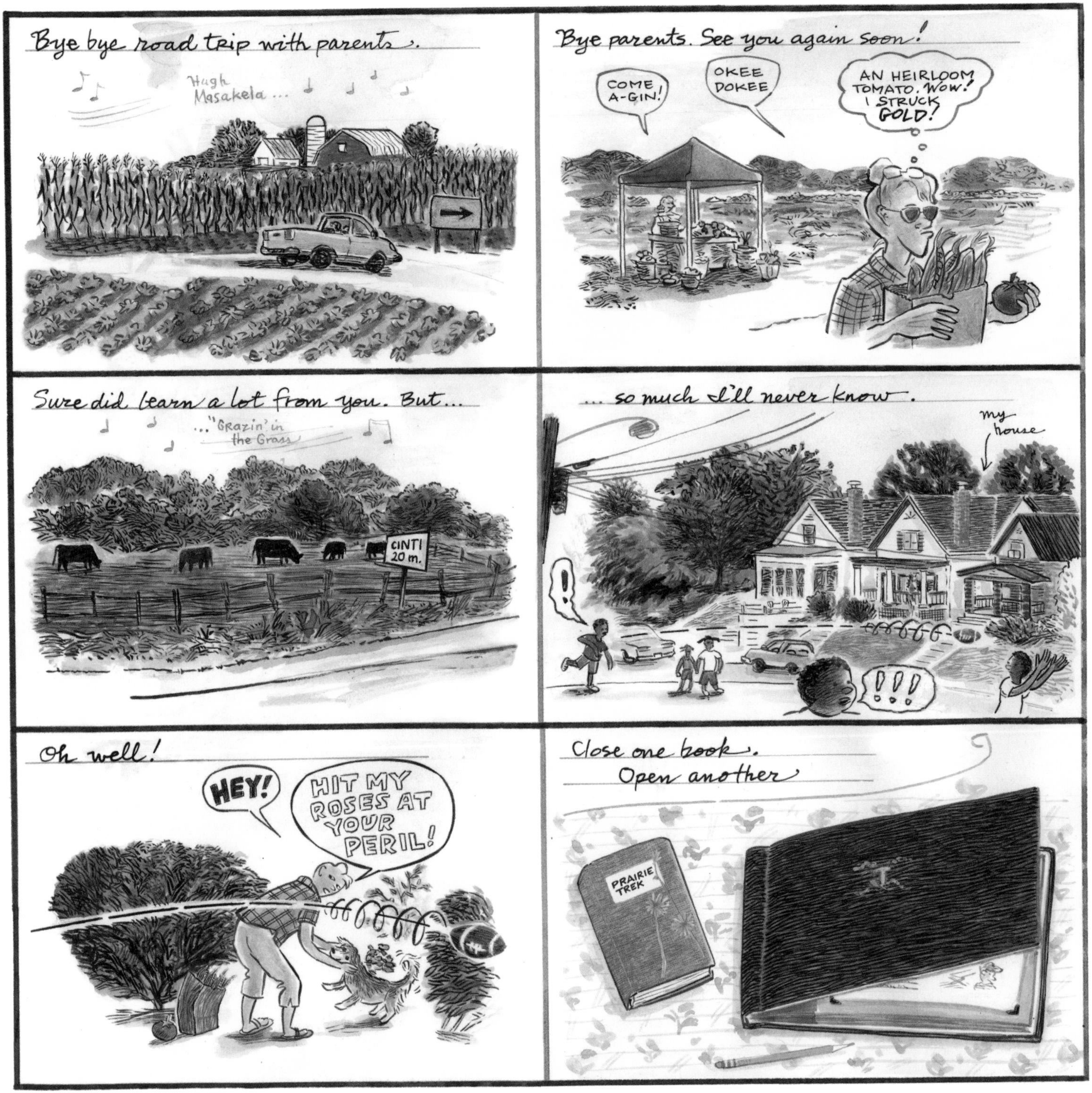
Bye bye road trip with parents.
Hugh Masakela ...
Bye parents. See you again soon!
COME A-GIN!
OKEE DOKEE
AN HEIRLOOM TOMATO. WOW! I STRUCK GOLD!
Sure did learn a lot from you. But...
..."Grazin' in the Grass
CINTI 20 m.
... so much I'll never know.
my house
!
!!!
Oh well!
HEY!
HIT MY ROSES AT YOUR PERIL!
Close one book.
Open another
PRAIRIE TREK

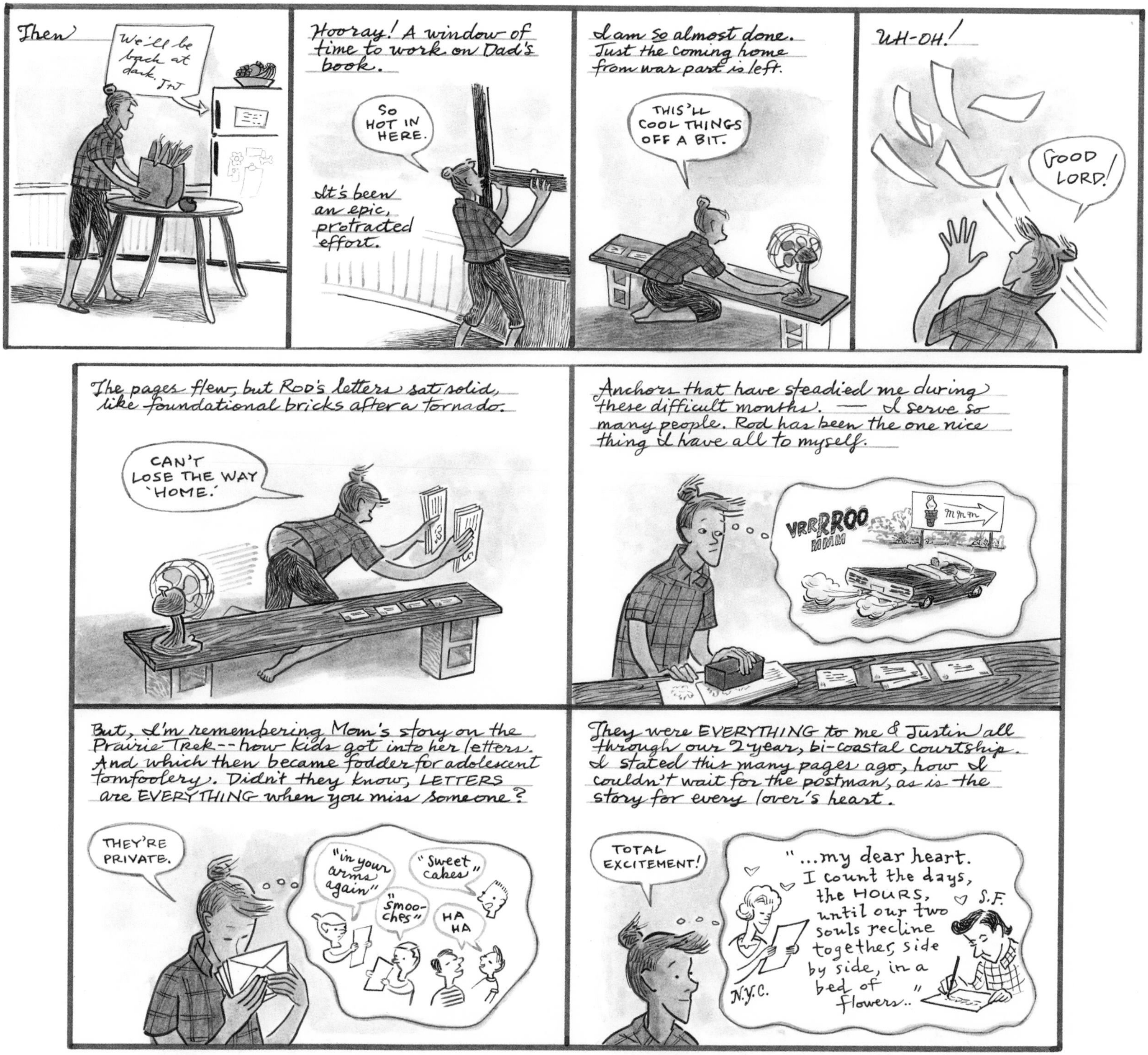
Then
We'll be back at dark.
Hooray! A window of time to work on Dad's book.
SO HOT IN HERE.
It's been an epic, protracted effort.
I am so almost done. Just the coming home from war part is left.
THIS'LL COOL THINGS OFF A BIT.
UH-OH!
GOOD LORD!
The pages flew, but Rod's letters sat solid, like foundational bricks after a tornado.
CAN'T LOSE THE WAY 'HOME.'
Anchors that have steadied me during these difficult months. — I serve so many people. Rod has been the one nice thing I have all to myself.
VRRRROO MMM
mmm
But, I'm remembering Mom's story on the Prairie Trek--how kids got into her letters. And which then became fodder for adolescent tomfoolery. Didn't they know, LETTERS are EVERYTHING when you miss someone?
THEY'RE PRIVATE.
"in your arms again"
"sweet cakes"
"smooches"
HA HA
They were EVERYTHING to me & Justin all through our 2 year, bi-coastal courtship. I stated this many pages ago, how I couldn't wait for the postman, as is the story for every lover's heart.
TOTAL EXCITEMENT!
"...my dear heart. I count the days, the HOURS, until our two souls recline together, side by side, in a bed of flowers.."
N.Y.C.
S.F.

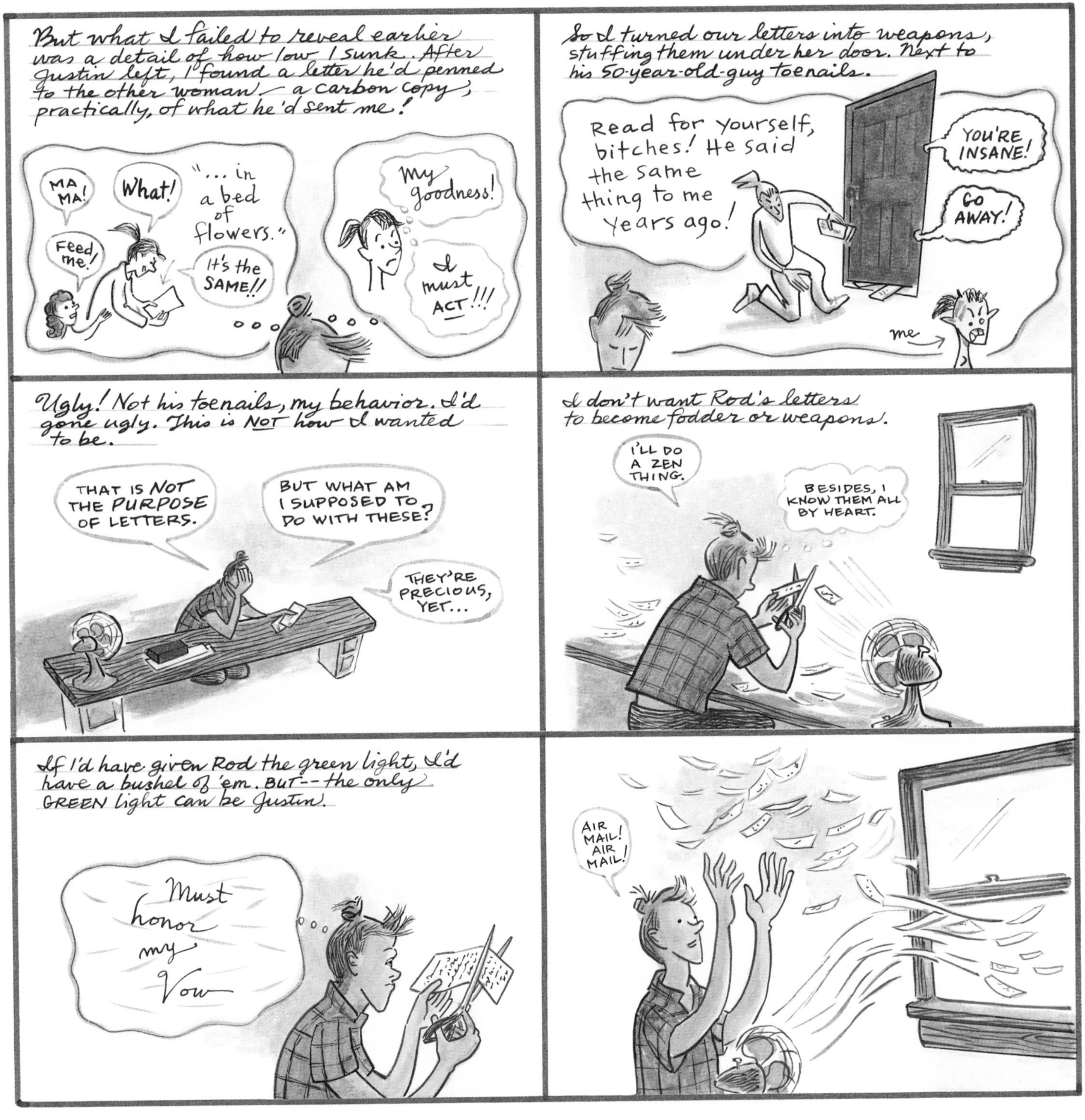
But what I failed to reveal earlier was a detail of how low I sunk. After Justin left, I found a letter he'd penned to the other woman — a carbon copy, practically, of what he'd sent me!
MA MA!
What!
"... in a bed of flowers."
Feed me!
It's the SAME!!
My goodness!
I must ACT!!!
So I turned our letters into weapons, stuffing them under her door. Next to his 50-year-old-guy toenails.
Read for yourself, bitches! He said the same thing to me years ago!
YOU'RE INSANE!
GO AWAY!
me
Ugly! Not his toenails, my behavior. I'd gone ugly. This is NOT how I wanted to be.
THAT IS NOT THE PURPOSE OF LETTERS.
BUT WHAT AM I SUPPOSED TO DO WITH THESE?
THEY'RE PRECIOUS, YET...
I don't want Rod's letters to become fodder or weapons.
I'LL DO A ZEN THING.
BESIDES, I KNOW THEM ALL BY HEART.
If I'd have given Rod the green light, I'd have a bushel of 'em. BUT-- the only GREEN light can be Justin.
Must honor my Vow
AIR MAIL! AIR MAIL!

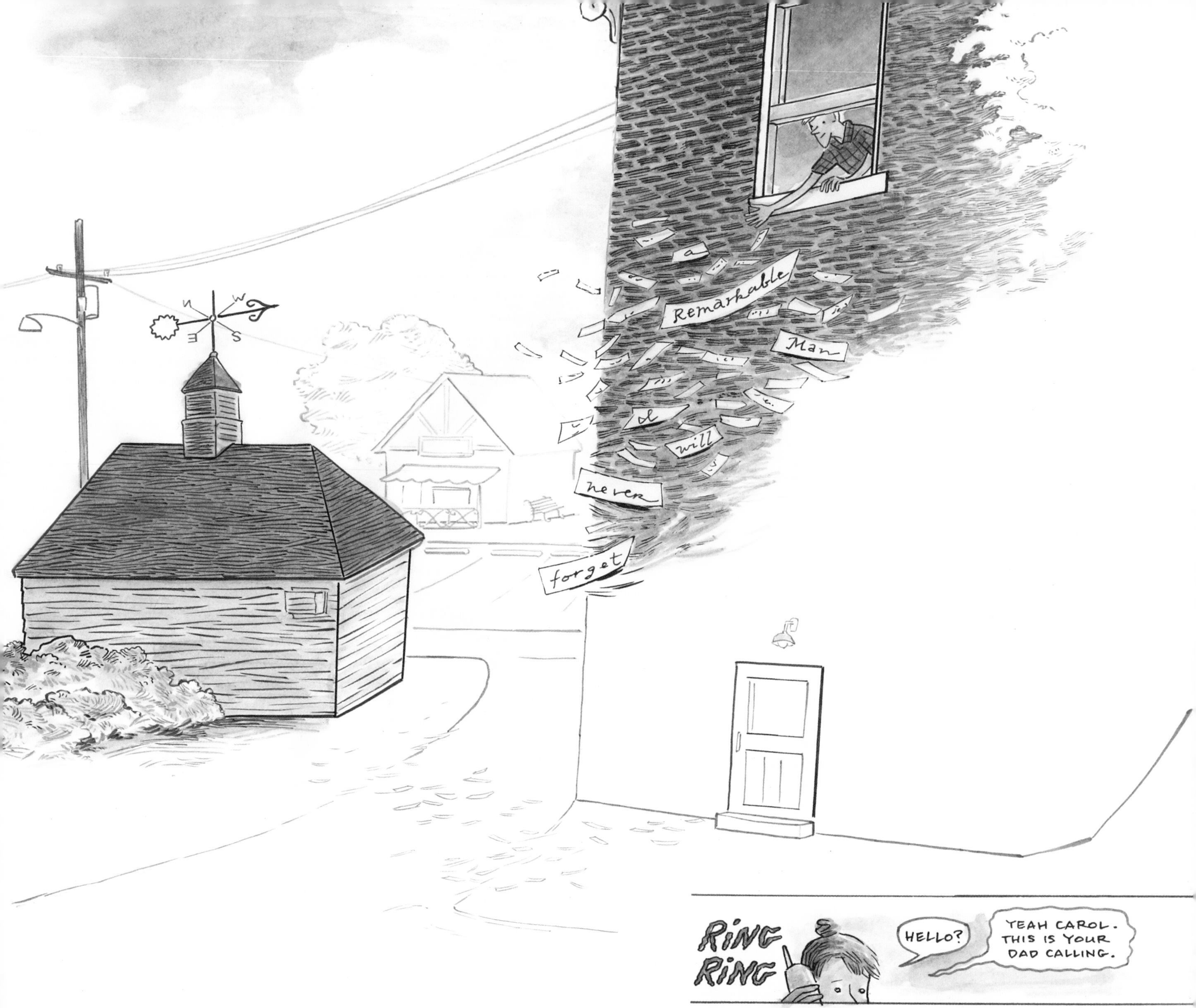
a
Remarkable
Man
will
never
forget
RING RING
HELLO?
YEAH CAROL. THIS IS YOUR DAD CALLING.

15.

GOIN' IN

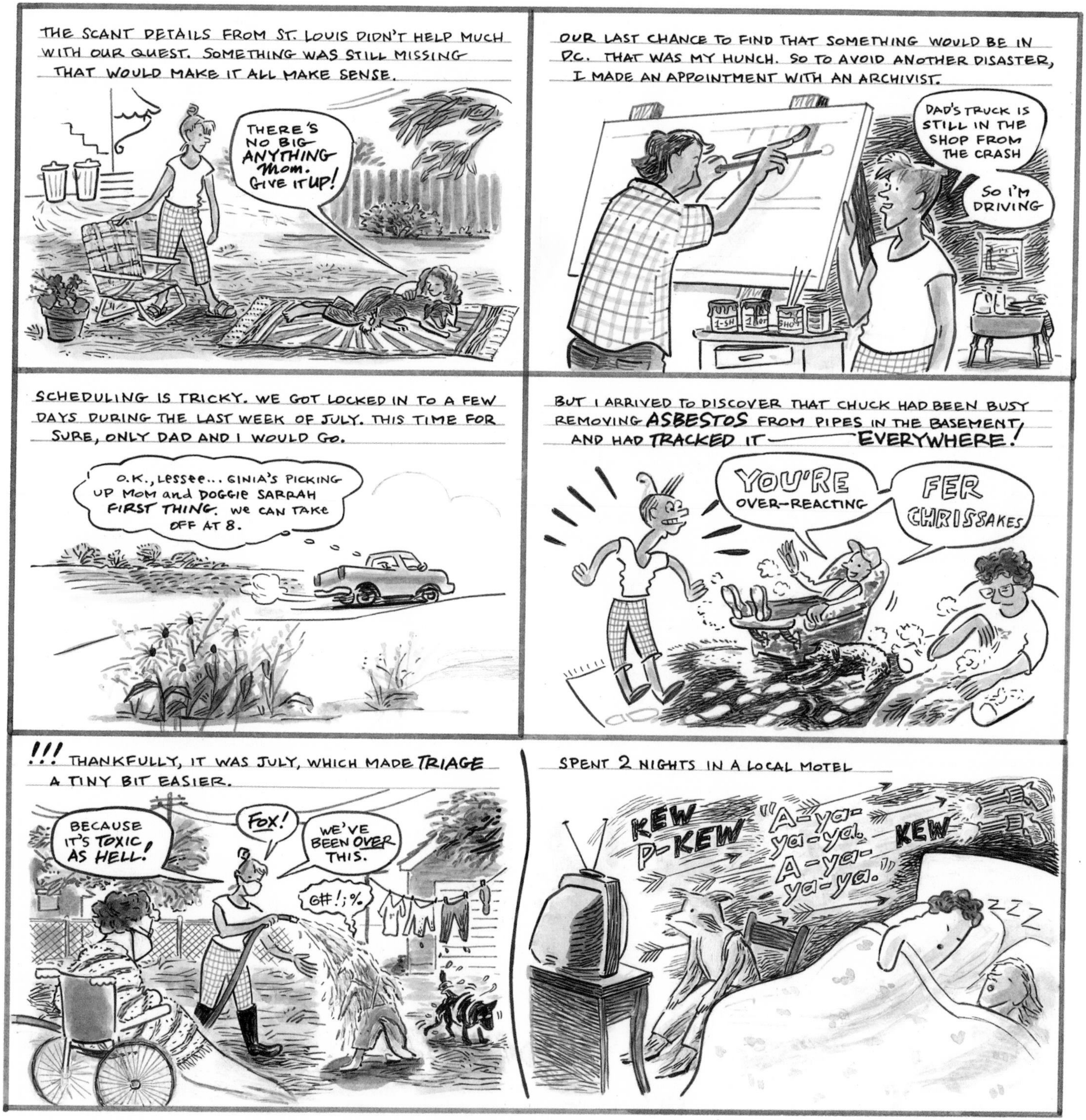
THE SCANT DETAILS FROM ST. LOUIS DIDN'T HELP MUCH WITH OUR QUEST. SOMETHING WAS STILL MISSING THAT WOULD MAKE IT ALL MAKE SENSE.
THERE'S NO BIG ANYTHING Mom. GIVE IT UP!
OUR LAST CHANCE TO FIND THAT SOMETHING WOULD BE IN D.C. THAT WAS MY HUNCH. SO TO AVOID ANOTHER DISASTER, I MADE AN APPOINTMENT WITH AN ARCHIVIST.
DAD'S TRUCK IS STILL IN THE SHOP FROM THE CRASH
SO I'M DRIVING
SCHEDULING IS TRICKY. WE GOT LOCKED IN TO A FEW DAYS DURING THE LAST WEEK OF JULY. THIS TIME FOR SURE, ONLY DAD AND I WOULD GO.
O.K., LESSEE... GINIA'S PICKING UP MOM and DOGGIE SARRAH FIRST THING. WE CAN TAKE OFF AT 8.
BUT I ARRIVED TO DISCOVER THAT CHUCK HAD BEEN BUSY REMOVING ASBESTOS FROM PIPES IN THE BASEMENT, AND HAD TRACKED IT — EVERYWHERE!
YOU'RE OVER-REACTING
FER CHRISSAKES
!!! THANKFULLY, IT WAS JULY, WHICH MADE TRIAGE A TINY BIT EASIER.
BECAUSE IT'S TOXIC AS HELL!
FOX!
WE'VE BEEN OVER THIS.
@#!;%
SPENT 2 NIGHTS IN A LOCAL MOTEL
KEW P-KEW
"A-ya-ya-ya. A-ya-ya-ya."
KEW
ZZZ

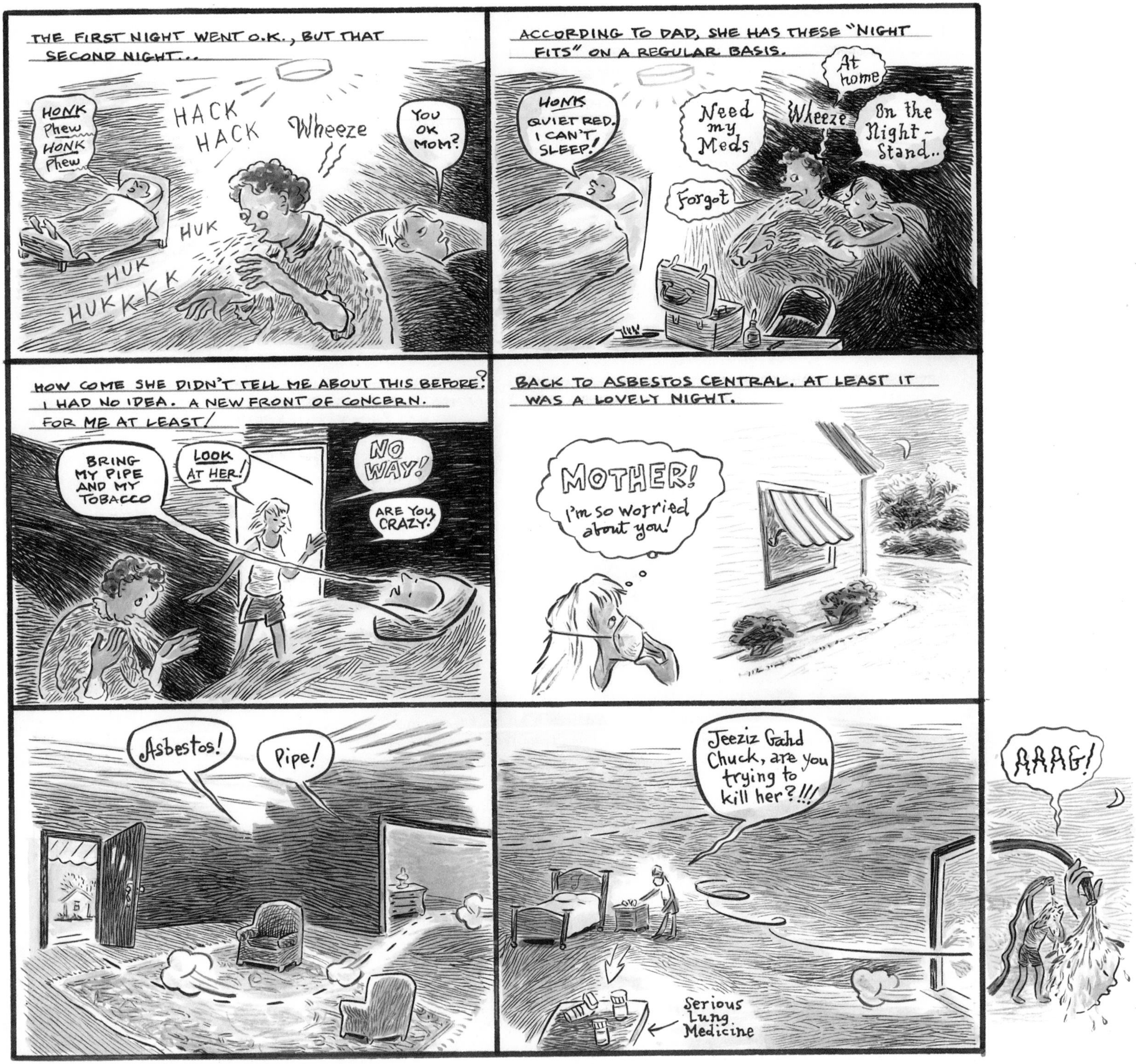
THE FIRST NIGHT WENT O.K., BUT THAT SECOND NIGHT...
HONK Phew HONK Phew
HACK HACK
Wheeze
You OK MOM?
HUK
HUK
HUKKKK
ACCORDING TO DAD, SHE HAS THESE "NIGHT FITS" ON A REGULAR BASIS.
HONK QUIET RED. I CAN'T SLEEP!
Need my Meds
Wheeze
At home
On the Night-Stand..
Forgot
HOW COME SHE DIDN'T TELL ME ABOUT THIS BEFORE? I HAD NO IDEA. A NEW FRONT OF CONCERN. FOR ME AT LEAST!
BRING MY PIPE AND MY TOBACCO
LOOK AT HER!
NO WAY!
ARE YOU CRAZY?
BACK TO ASBESTOS CENTRAL. AT LEAST IT WAS A LOVELY NIGHT.
MOTHER! I'm so worried about you!
Asbestos!
Pipe!
Jeeziz Gahd Chuck, are you trying to kill her?!!!
Serious Lung Medicine
AAAG!

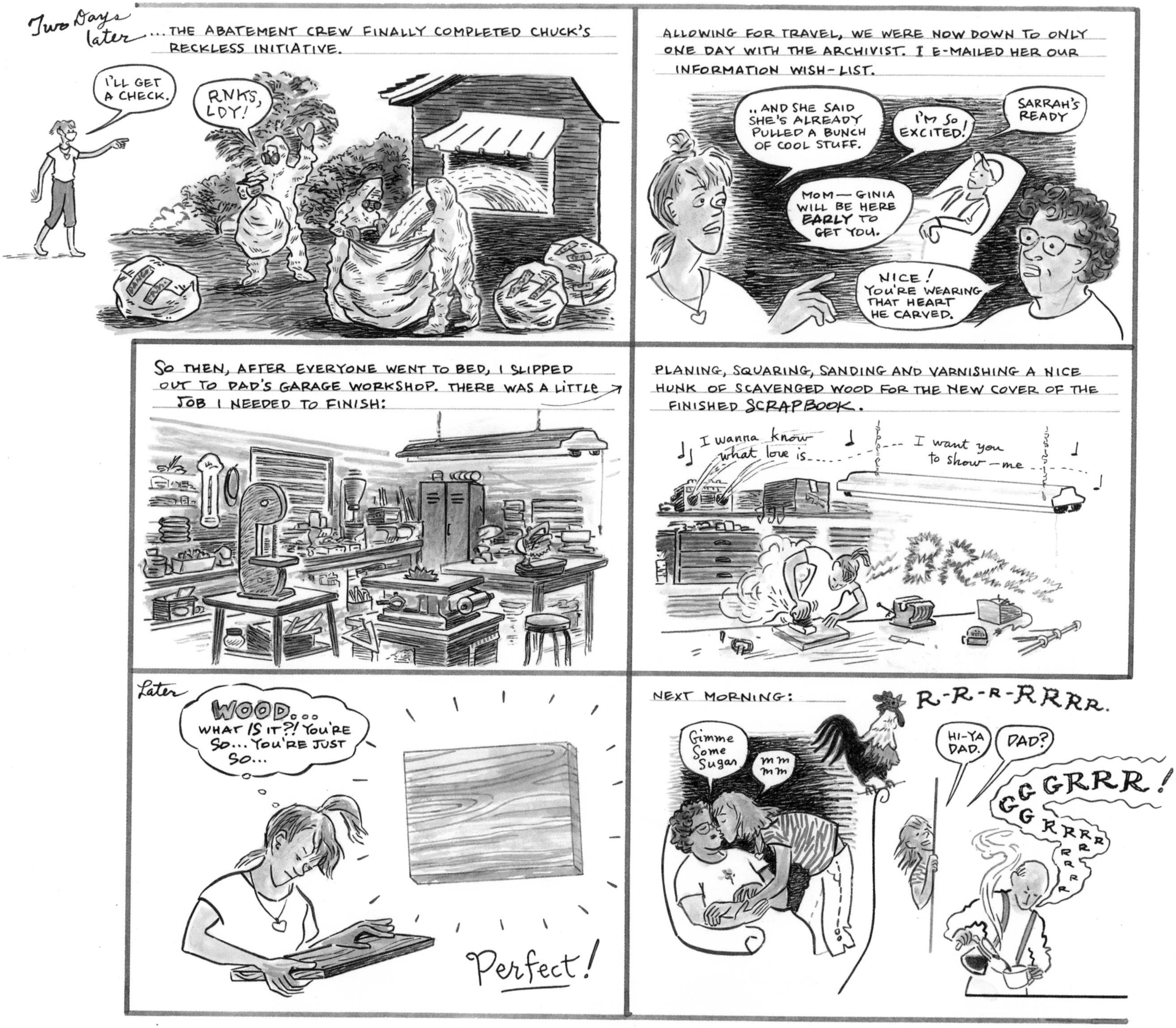

Two Days later ...THE ABATEMENT CREW FINALLY COMPLETED CHUCK'S RECKLESS INITIATIVE.
I'LL GET A CHECK.
RNKS, LDY!
ALLOWING FOR TRAVEL, WE WERE NOW DOWN TO ONLY ONE DAY WITH THE ARCHIVIST. I E-MAILED HER OUR INFORMATION WISH-LIST.
..AND SHE SAID SHE'S ALREADY PULLED A BUNCH OF COOL STUFF.
I'M SO EXCITED!
SARRAH'S READY
MOM—GINIA WILL BE HERE EARLY TO GET YOU.
NICE! YOU'RE WEARING THAT HEART HE CARVED.
SO THEN, AFTER EVERYONE WENT TO BED, I SLIPPED OUT TO DAD'S GARAGE WORKSHOP. THERE WAS A LITTLE JOB I NEEDED TO FINISH:
PLANING, SQUARING, SANDING AND VARNISHING A NICE HUNK OF SCAVENGED WOOD FOR THE NEW COVER OF THE FINISHED SCRAPBOOK.
I wanna know what love is... I want you to show me
BRR
Later
WOOD... WHAT IS IT?! YOU'RE SO... YOU'RE JUST SO...
Perfect!
NEXT MORNING:
R-R-R-RRRR.
Gimme Some Sugar
mm mm
HI-YA DAD.
DAD?
GGGRRR! GRRRRRRRRR

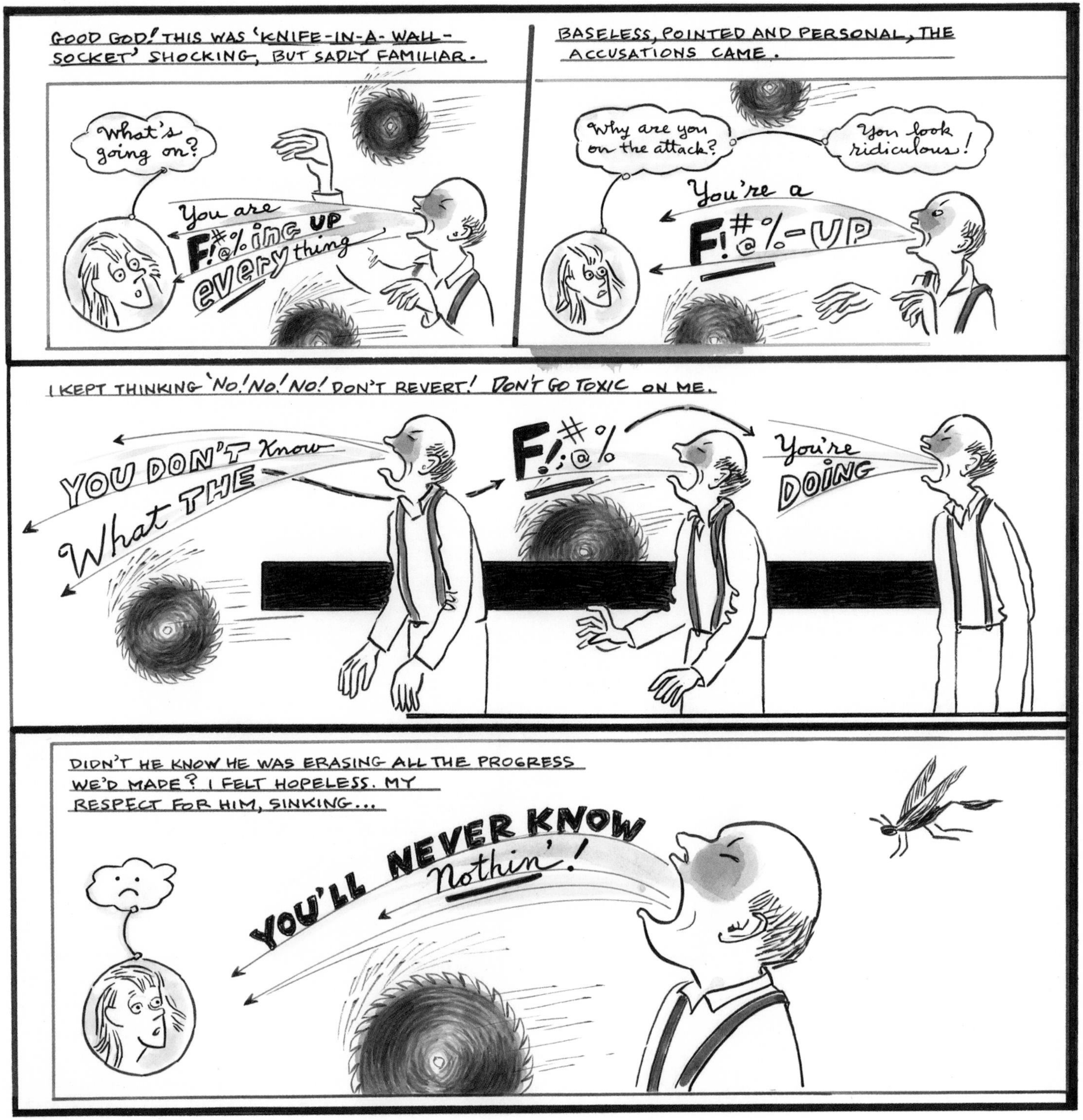
GOOD GOD! THIS WAS 'KNIFE-IN-A-WALL-SOCKET' SHOCKING, BUT SADLY FAMILIAR.
What's going on?
You are F!#@%ing UP everything
BASELESS, POINTED AND PERSONAL, THE ACCUSATIONS CAME.
Why are you on the attack?
You look ridiculous!
You're a F!#@%-UP
I KEPT THINKING 'NO! NO! NO! DON'T REVERT! DON'T GO TOXIC ON ME.
YOU DON'T Know What THE
F!#;@%
You're DOING
DIDN'T HE KNOW HE WAS ERASING ALL THE PROGRESS WE'D MADE? I FELT HOPELESS. MY RESPECT FOR HIM, SINKING...
YOU'LL NEVER KNOW Nothin'!

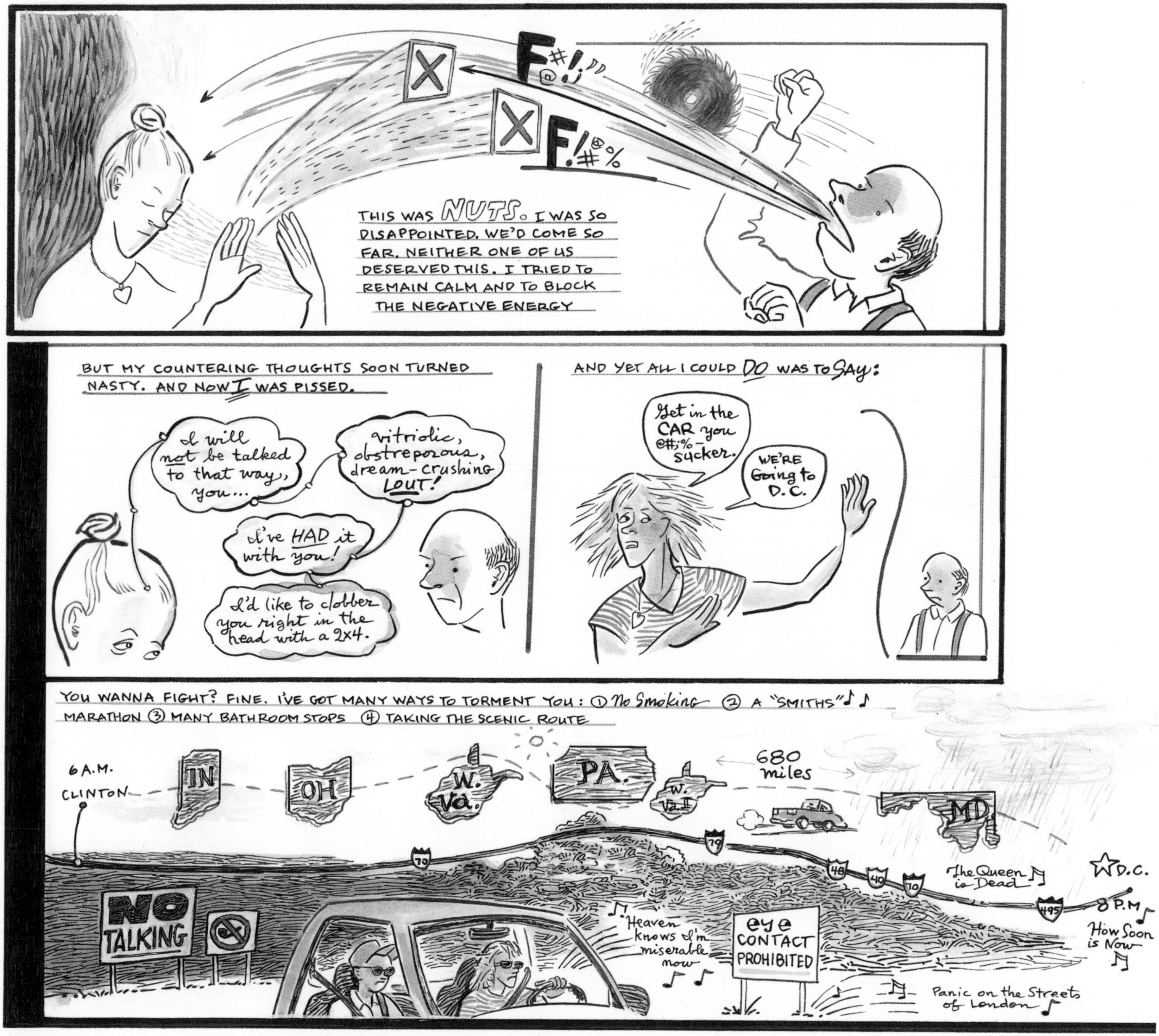
F#!@;"
F!#@%
THIS WAS NUTS. I WAS SO DISAPPOINTED. WE'D COME SO FAR. NEITHER ONE OF US DESERVED THIS. I TRIED TO REMAIN CALM AND TO BLOCK THE NEGATIVE ENERGY
BUT MY COUNTERING THOUGHTS SOON TURNED NASTY. AND NOW I WAS PISSED.
I will not be talked to that way, you...
vitriolic, obstreporous, dream-crushing LOUT!
I've HAD it with you!
I'd like to clobber you right in the head with a 2x4.
AND YET ALL I COULD DO WAS TO SAY:
Get in the CAR you @#;%-sucker.
WE'RE Going to D.C.
YOU WANNA FIGHT? FINE. I'VE GOT MANY WAYS TO TORMENT YOU: ① No Smoking ② A "SMITHS" MARATHON ③ MANY BATHROOM STOPS ④ TAKING THE SCENIC ROUTE
6 A.M. CLINTON
IN
OH
W. Va.
PA.
W. Va. II
680 miles
MD.
70
79
48
40
70
495
D.C.
8 P.M.
The Queen is Dead
How Soon is Now
NO TALKING
Heaven knows I'm miserable now
eye CONTACT PROHIBITED
Panic on the Streets of London

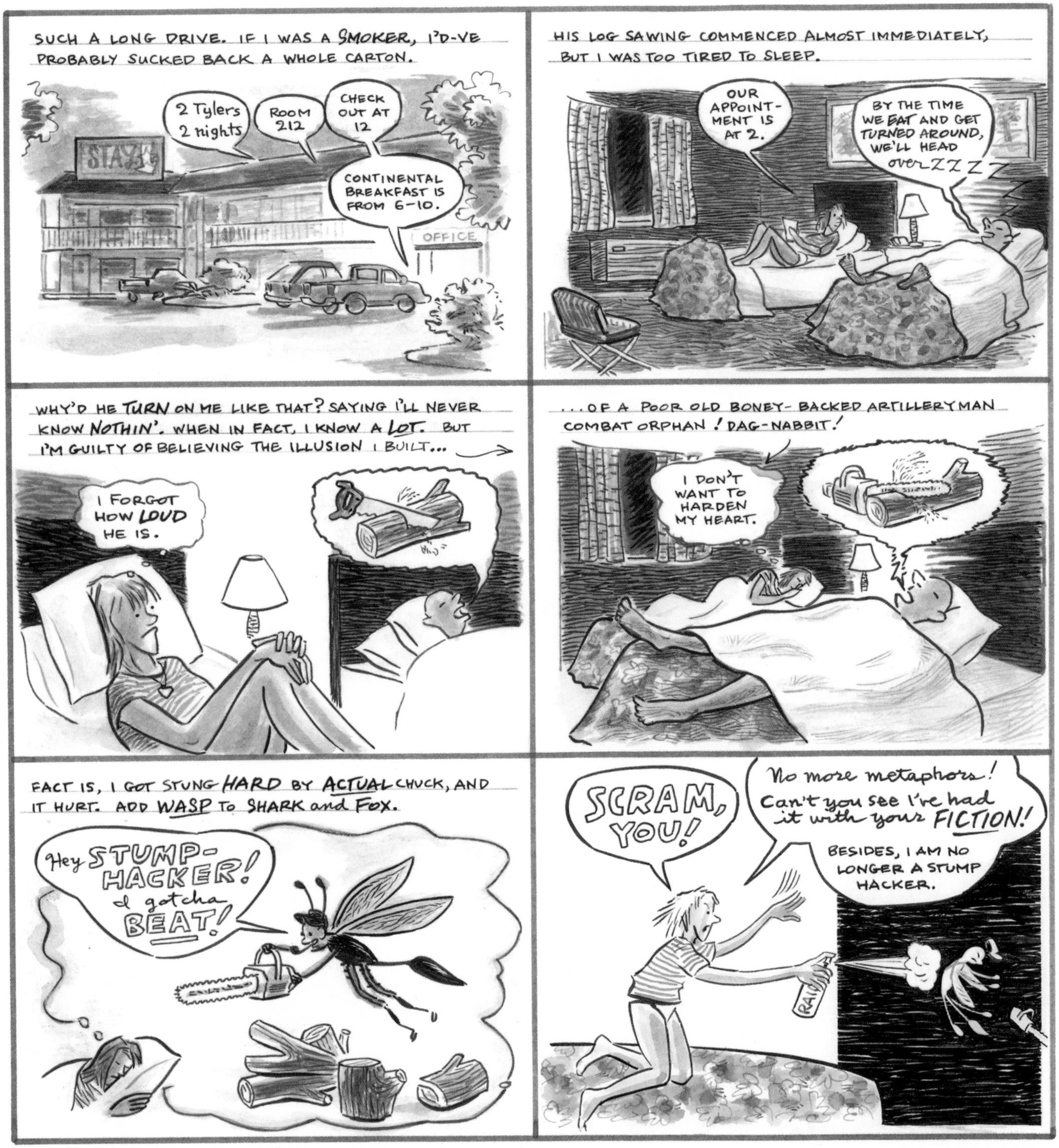
SUCH A LONG DRIVE. IF I WAS A SMOKER, I'D-VE PROBABLY SUCKED BACK A WHOLE CARTON.
2 Tylers 2 nights
ROOM 212
CHECK OUT AT 12
CONTINENTAL BREAKFAST IS FROM 6-10.
STAY
OFFICE
HIS LOG SAWING COMMENCED ALMOST IMMEDIATELY, BUT I WAS TOO TIRED TO SLEEP.
OUR APPOINTMENT IS AT 2.
BY THE TIME WE EAT AND GET TURNED AROUND, WE'LL HEAD overZZZ
WHY'D HE TURN ON ME LIKE THAT? SAYING I'LL NEVER KNOW NOTHIN'. WHEN IN FACT, I KNOW A LOT. BUT I'M GUILTY OF BELIEVING THE ILLUSION I BUILT...
I FORGOT HOW LOUD HE IS.
...OF A POOR OLD BONEY-BACKED ARTILLERYMAN COMBAT ORPHAN! DAG-NABBIT!
I DON'T WANT TO HARDEN MY HEART.
FACT IS, I GOT STUNG HARD BY ACTUAL CHUCK, AND IT HURT. ADD WASP TO SHARK and FOX.
Hey STUMP-HACKER! I gotcha BEAT!
SCRAM, YOU!
No more metaphors! Can't you see I've had it with your FICTION!
BESIDES, I AM NO LONGER A STUMP HACKER.

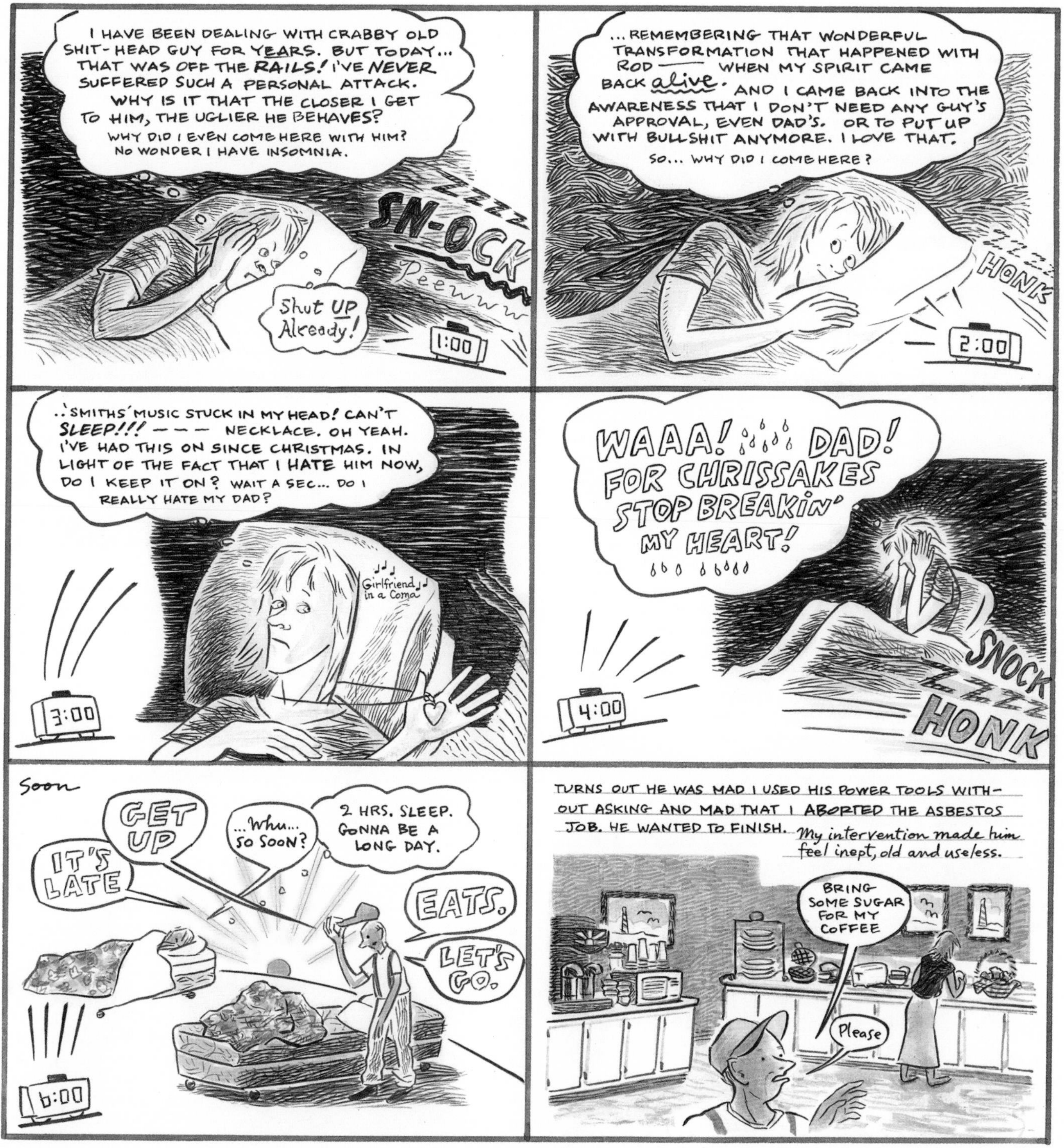

I HAVE BEEN DEALING WITH CRABBY OLD SHIT-HEAD GUY FOR YEARS. BUT TODAY... THAT WAS OFF THE RAILS! I'VE NEVER SUFFERED SUCH A PERSONAL ATTACK. WHY IS IT THAT THE CLOSER I GET TO HIM, THE UGLIER HE BEHAVES?
WHY DID I EVEN COME HERE WITH HIM? NO WONDER I HAVE INSOMNIA.
ZZZZ
SN-OCK
Peewww
Shut UP Already!
1:00
...REMEMBERING THAT WONDERFUL TRANSFORMATION THAT HAPPENED WITH ROD — WHEN MY SPIRIT CAME BACK alive. AND I CAME BACK INTO THE AWARENESS THAT I DON'T NEED ANY GUY'S APPROVAL, EVEN DAD'S. OR TO PUT UP WITH BULLSHIT ANYMORE. I LOVE THAT.
SO... WHY DID I COME HERE?
ZZZZ
HONK
2:00
..'SMITHS' MUSIC STUCK IN MY HEAD! CAN'T SLEEP!!! — — — NECKLACE. OH YEAH. I'VE HAD THIS ON SINCE CHRISTMAS. IN LIGHT OF THE FACT THAT I HATE HIM NOW, DO I KEEP IT ON? WAIT A SEC... DO I REALLY HATE MY DAD?
Girlfriend in a Coma
3:00
WAAA! DAD! FOR CHRISSAKES STOP BREAKIN' MY HEART!
SNOCK
ZZZZ
HONK
4:00
Soon
GET UP
IT'S LATE
...Whu... SO SOON?
2 HRS. SLEEP. GONNA BE A LONG DAY.
EATS,
LET'S GO.
6:00
TURNS OUT HE WAS MAD I USED HIS POWER TOOLS WITHOUT ASKING AND MAD THAT I ABORTED THE ASBESTOS JOB. HE WANTED TO FINISH. My intervention made him feel inept, old and useless.
BRING SOME SUGAR FOR MY COFFEE
Please

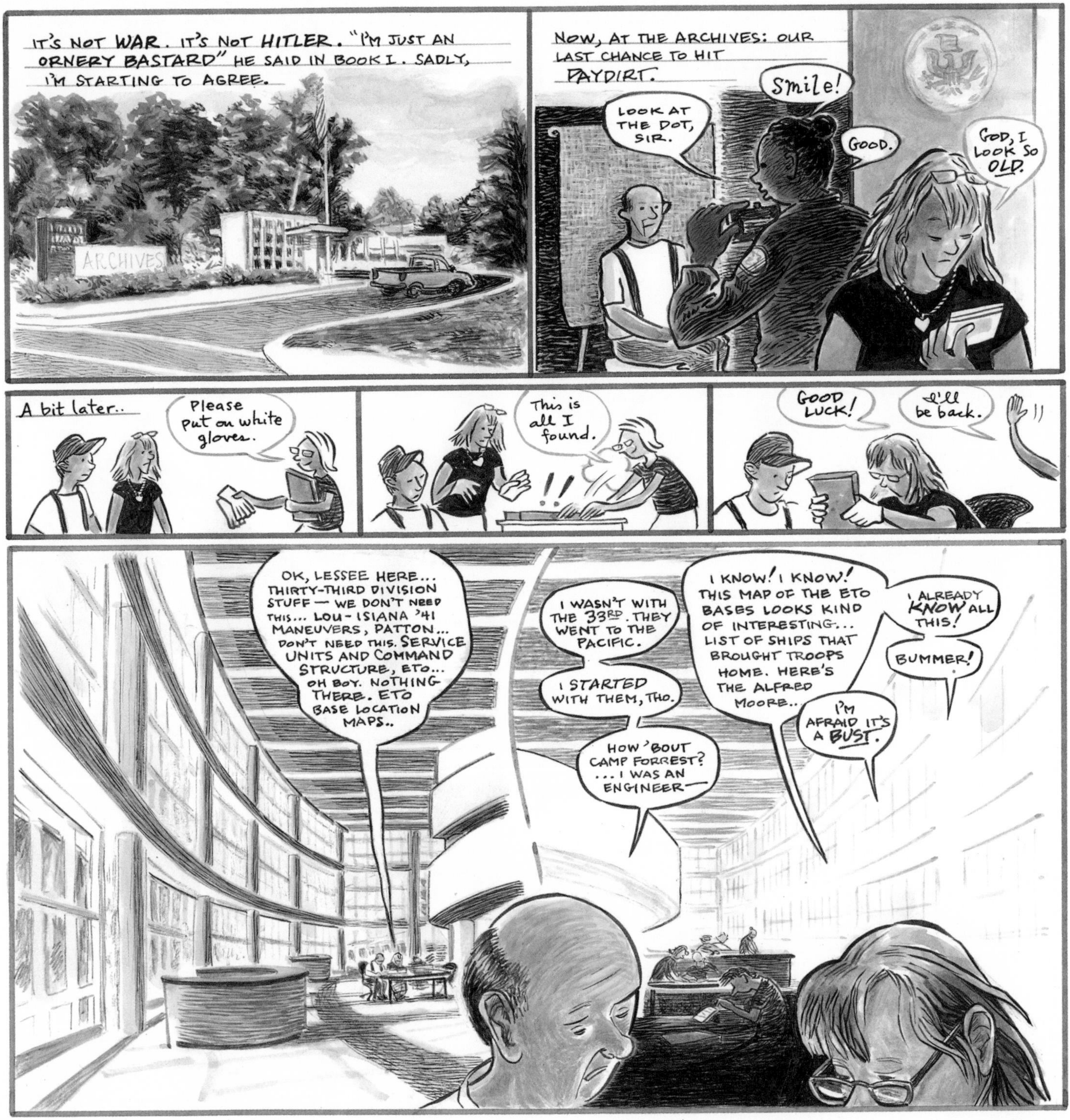
IT'S NOT WAR. IT'S NOT HITLER. "I'M JUST AN ORNERY BASTARD" HE SAID IN BOOK I. SADLY, I'M STARTING TO AGREE.
ARCHIVES
NOW, AT THE ARCHIVES: OUR LAST CHANCE TO HIT PAYDIRT.
LOOK AT THE DOT, SIR.
Smile!
GOOD.
GOD, I LOOK SO OLD.
A bit later..
Please put on white gloves.
This is all I found.
!!
GOOD LUCK!
I'll be back.
OK, LESSEE HERE... THIRTY-THIRD DIVISION STUFF — WE DON'T NEED THIS... LOU-ISIANA '41 MANEUVERS, PATTON... DON'T NEED THIS. SERVICE UNITS AND COMMAND STRUCTURE, ETO... OH BOY. NOTHING THERE. ETO BASE LOCATION MAPS..
I WASN'T WITH THE 33RD. THEY WENT TO THE PACIFIC.
I STARTED WITH THEM, THO.
HOW 'BOUT CAMP FORREST? ... I WAS AN ENGINEER—
I KNOW! I KNOW! THIS MAP OF THE ETO BASES LOOKS KIND OF INTERESTING... LIST OF SHIPS THAT BROUGHT TROOPS HOME. HERE'S THE ALFRED MOORE..
I'M AFRAID IT'S A BUST.
I ALREADY KNOW ALL THIS!
BUMMER!

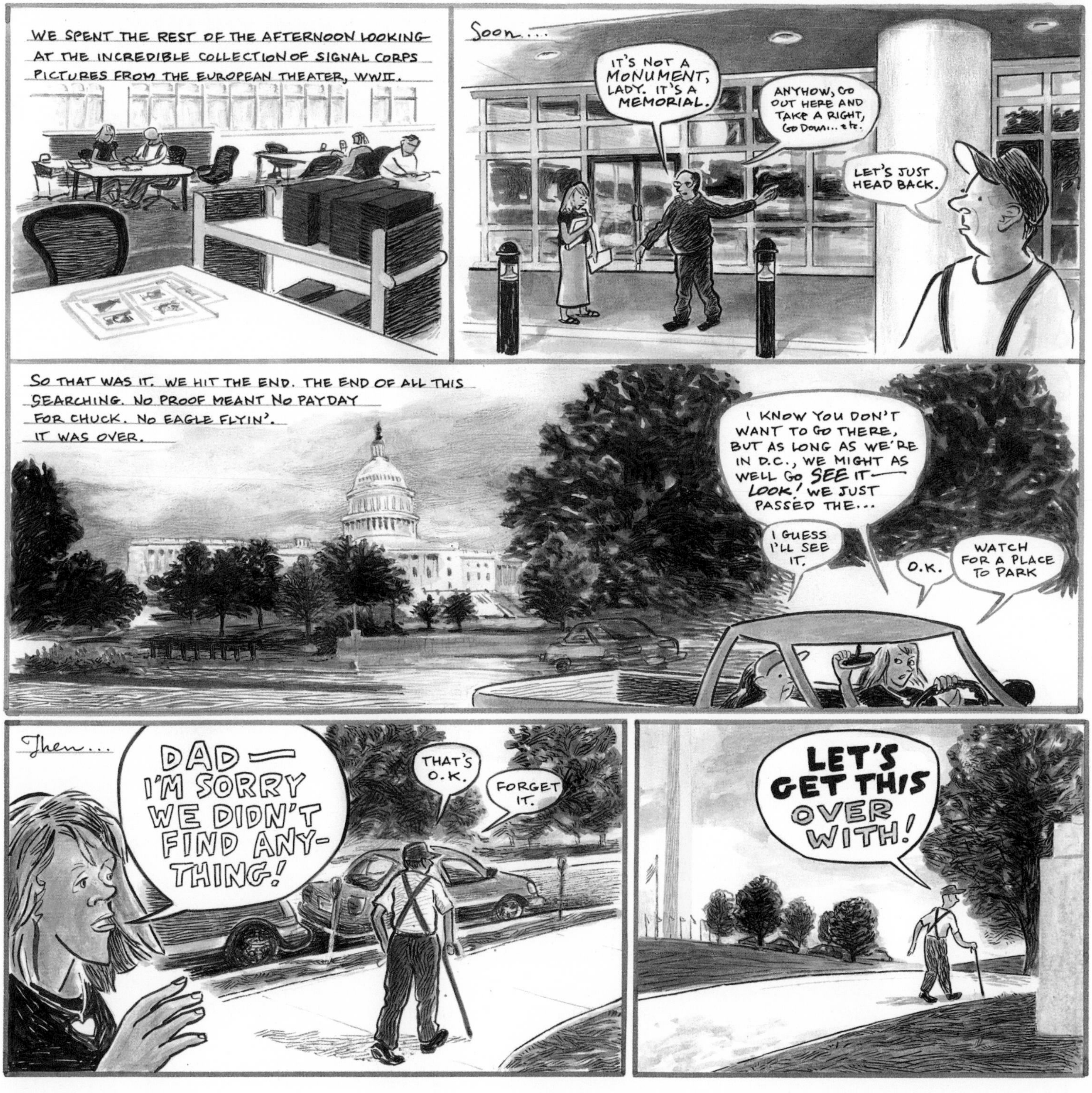
WE SPENT THE REST OF THE AFTERNOON LOOKING AT THE INCREDIBLE COLLECTION OF SIGNAL CORPS PICTURES FROM THE EUROPEAN THEATER, WWII.
Soon...
IT'S NOT A MONUMENT, LADY. IT'S A MEMORIAL.
ANYHOW, GO OUT HERE AND TAKE A RIGHT, GO DOWN... ETC.
LET'S JUST HEAD BACK.
SO THAT WAS IT. WE HIT THE END. THE END OF ALL THIS SEARCHING. NO PROOF MEANT NO PAYDAY FOR CHUCK. NO EAGLE FLYIN'. IT WAS OVER.
I KNOW YOU DON'T WANT TO GO THERE, BUT AS LONG AS WE'RE IN D.C., WE MIGHT AS WELL GO SEE IT— LOOK! WE JUST PASSED THE...
I GUESS I'LL SEE IT.
O.K.
WATCH FOR A PLACE TO PARK
Then...
DAD— I'M SORRY WE DIDN'T FIND ANY-THING!
THAT'S O.K.
FORGET IT.
LET'S GET THIS OVER WITH!

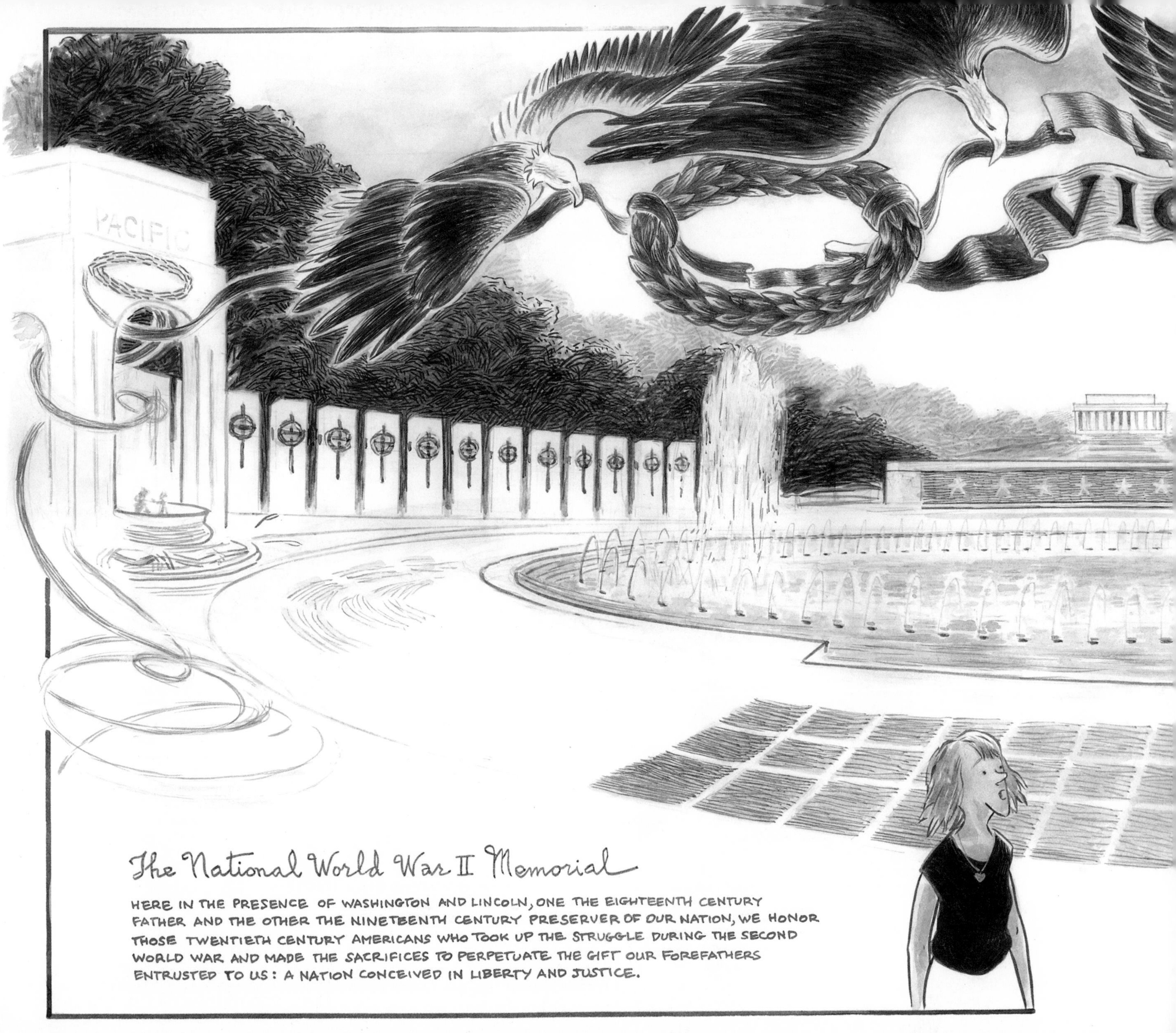
PACIFIC
VIC
The National World War II Memorial
HERE IN THE PRESENCE OF WASHINGTON AND LINCOLN, ONE THE EIGHTEENTH CENTURY FATHER AND THE OTHER THE NINETEENTH CENTURY PRESERVER OF OUR NATION, WE HONOR THOSE TWENTIETH CENTURY AMERICANS WHO TOOK UP THE STRUGGLE DURING THE SECOND WORLD WAR AND MADE THE SACRIFICES TO PERPETUATE THE GIFT OUR FOREFATHERS ENTRUSTED TO US: A NATION CONCEIVED IN LIBERTY AND JUSTICE.

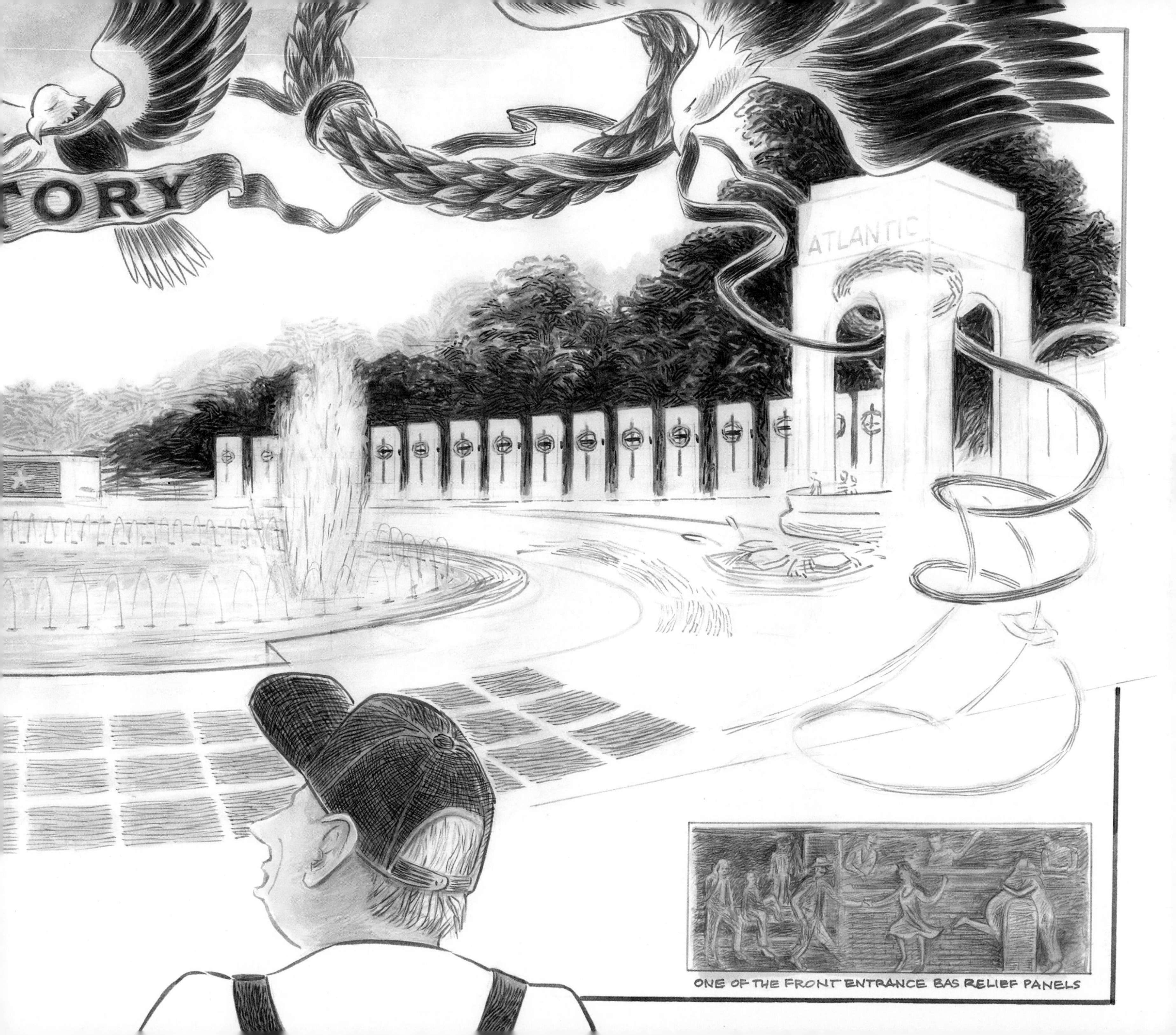
TORY
ATLANTIC

ONE OF THE FRONT ENTRANCE BAS RELIEF PANELS

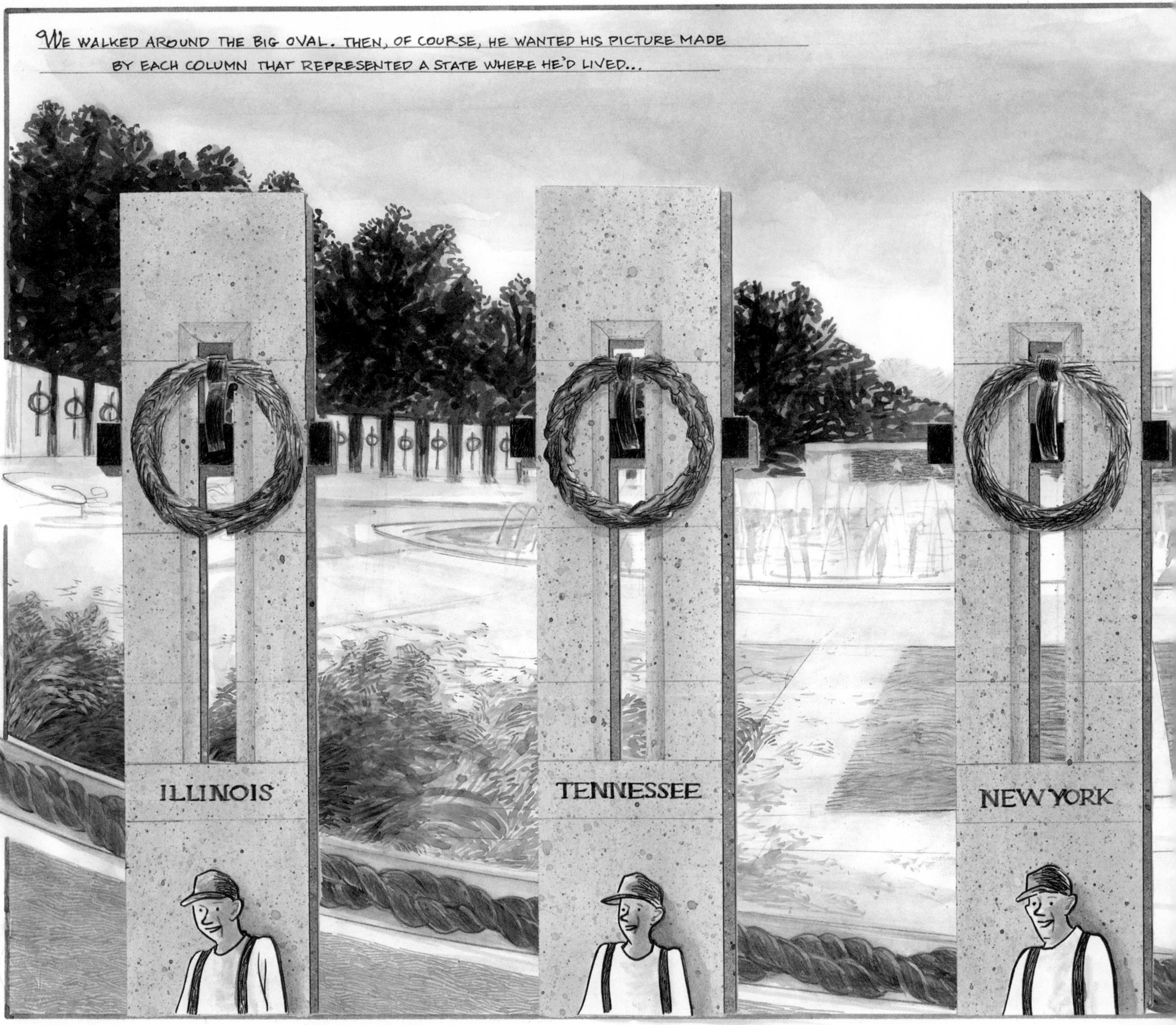
WE WALKED AROUND THE BIG OVAL. THEN, OF COURSE, HE WANTED HIS PICTURE MADE BY EACH COLUMN THAT REPRESENTED A STATE WHERE HE'D LIVED...
ILLINOIS
TENNESSEE
NEW YORK

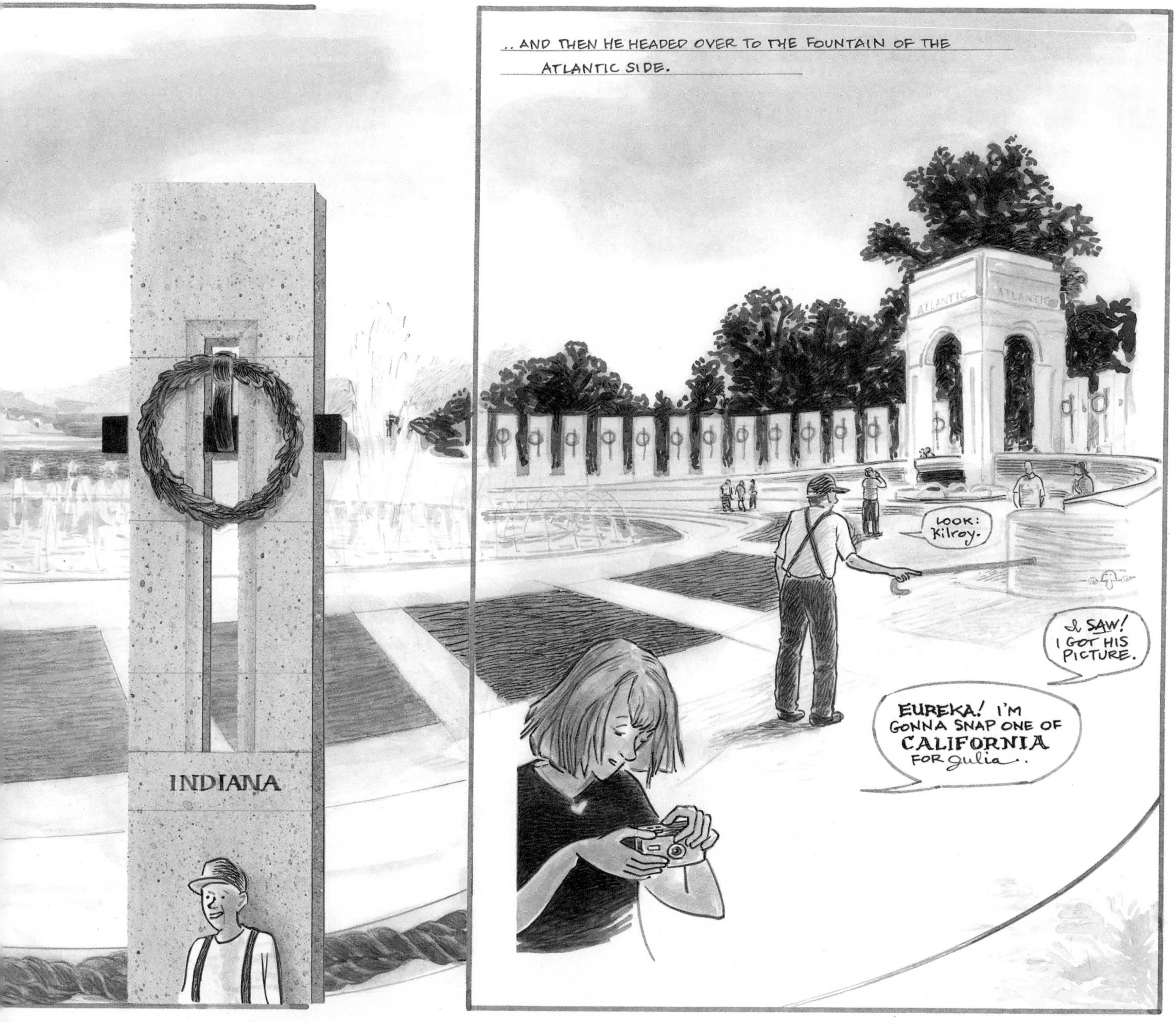
INDIANA
..AND THEN HE HEADED OVER TO THE FOUNTAIN OF THE ATLANTIC SIDE.
ATLANTIC
ATLANTIC
LOOK: Kilroy.
I SAW! I GOT HIS PICTURE.
EUREKA! I'M GONNA SNAP ONE OF CALIFORNIA FOR Julia.

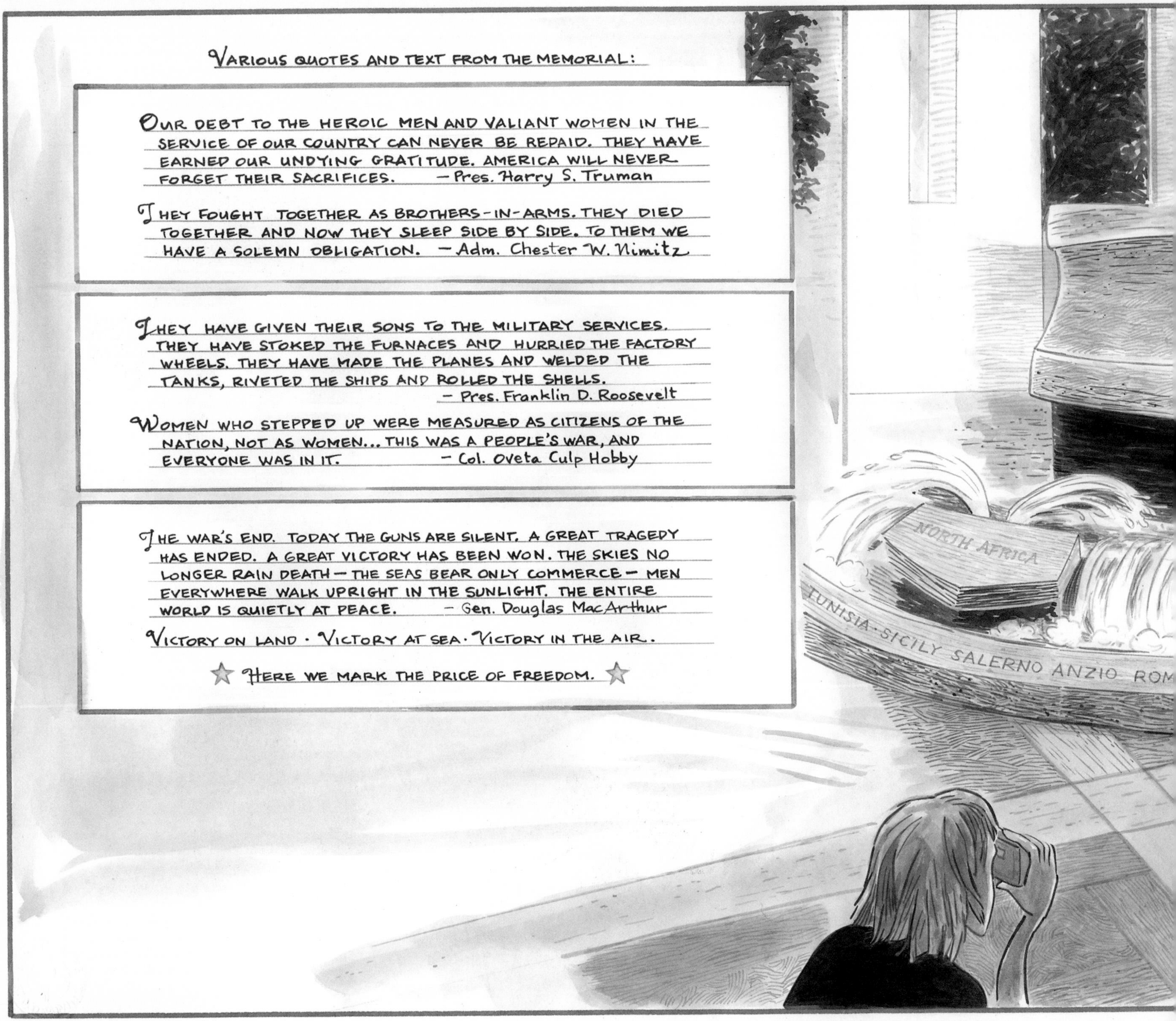
VARIOUS QUOTES AND TEXT FROM THE MEMORIAL:
OUR DEBT TO THE HEROIC MEN AND VALIANT WOMEN IN THE SERVICE OF OUR COUNTRY CAN NEVER BE REPAID. THEY HAVE EARNED OUR UNDYING GRATITUDE. AMERICA WILL NEVER FORGET THEIR SACRIFICES. — Pres. Harry S. Truman
THEY FOUGHT TOGETHER AS BROTHERS-IN-ARMS. THEY DIED TOGETHER AND NOW THEY SLEEP SIDE BY SIDE. TO THEM WE HAVE A SOLEMN OBLIGATION. — Adm. Chester W. Nimitz
THEY HAVE GIVEN THEIR SONS TO THE MILITARY SERVICES. THEY HAVE STOKED THE FURNACES AND HURRIED THE FACTORY WHEELS. THEY HAVE MADE THE PLANES AND WELDED THE TANKS, RIVETED THE SHIPS AND ROLLED THE SHELLS. — Pres. Franklin D. Roosevelt
WOMEN WHO STEPPED UP WERE MEASURED AS CITIZENS OF THE NATION, NOT AS WOMEN... THIS WAS A PEOPLE'S WAR, AND EVERYONE WAS IN IT. — Col. Oveta Culp Hobby
THE WAR'S END. TODAY THE GUNS ARE SILENT. A GREAT TRAGEDY HAS ENDED. A GREAT VICTORY HAS BEEN WON. THE SKIES NO LONGER RAIN DEATH — THE SEAS BEAR ONLY COMMERCE — MEN EVERYWHERE WALK UPRIGHT IN THE SUNLIGHT. THE ENTIRE WORLD IS QUIETLY AT PEACE. — Gen. Douglas MacArthur
VICTORY ON LAND · VICTORY AT SEA · VICTORY IN THE AIR.
HERE WE MARK THE PRICE OF FREEDOM.
NORTH AFRICA
TUNISIA · SICILY SALERNO ANZIO ROM

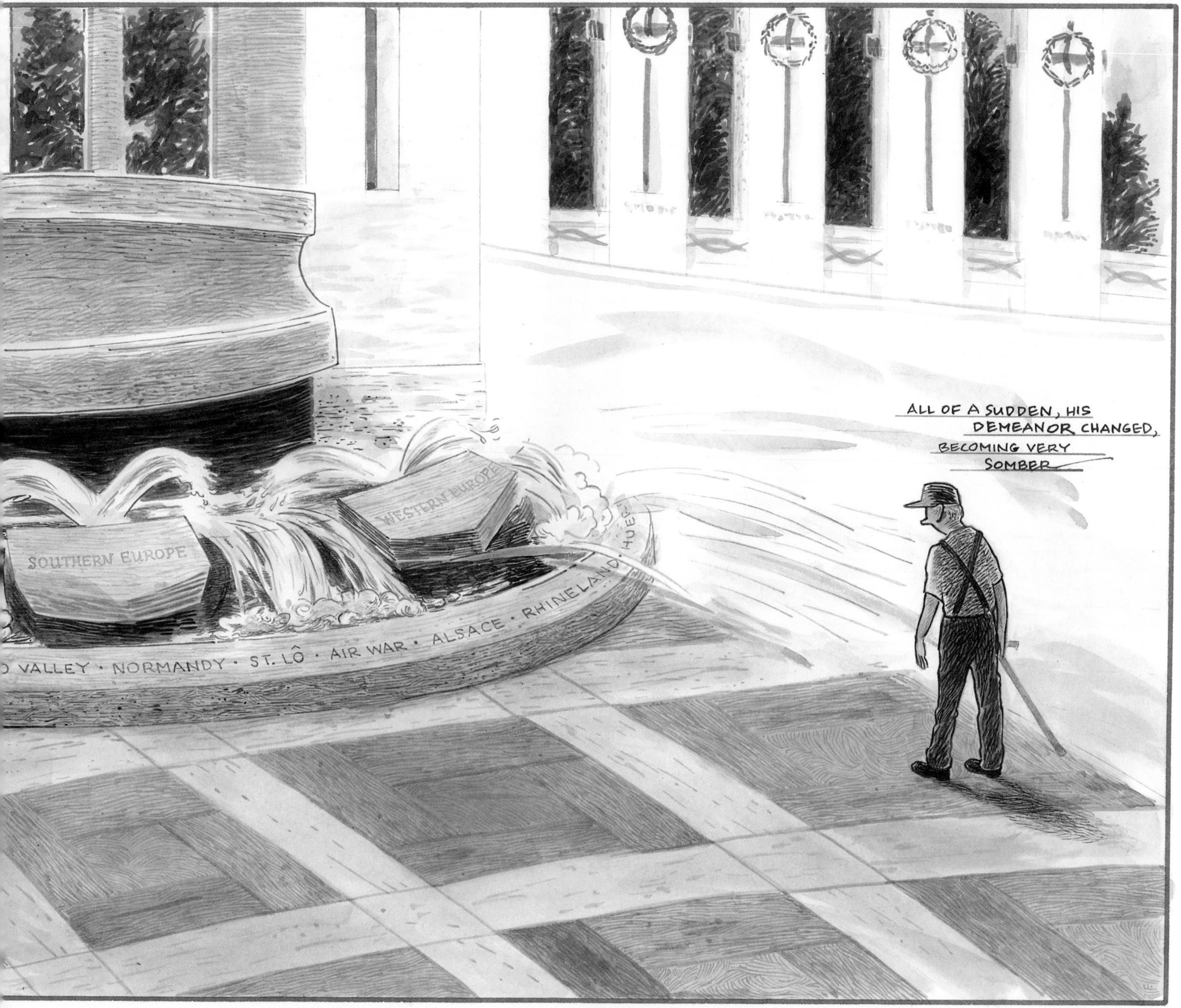
ALL OF A SUDDEN, HIS DEMEANOR CHANGED, BECOMING VERY SOMBER
SOUTHERN EUROPE
WESTERN EUROPE
VALLEY · NORMANDY · ST. LÔ · AIR WAR · ALSACE · RHINELAND · HUE

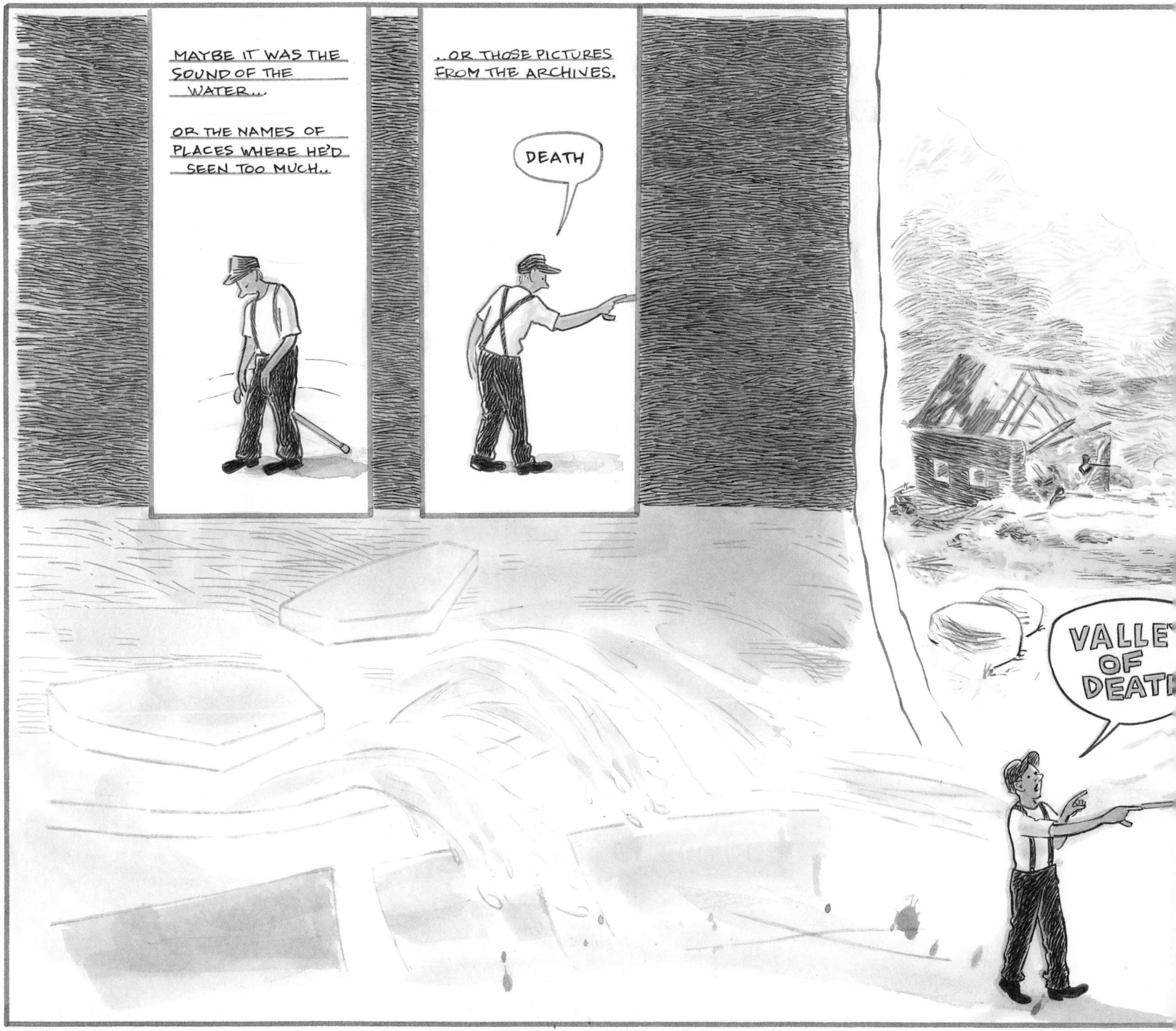
MAYBE IT WAS THE SOUND OF THE WATER...
OR THE NAMES OF PLACES WHERE HE'D SEEN TOO MUCH..
..OR THOSE PICTURES FROM THE ARCHIVES.
DEATH
VALLE
OF
DEAT

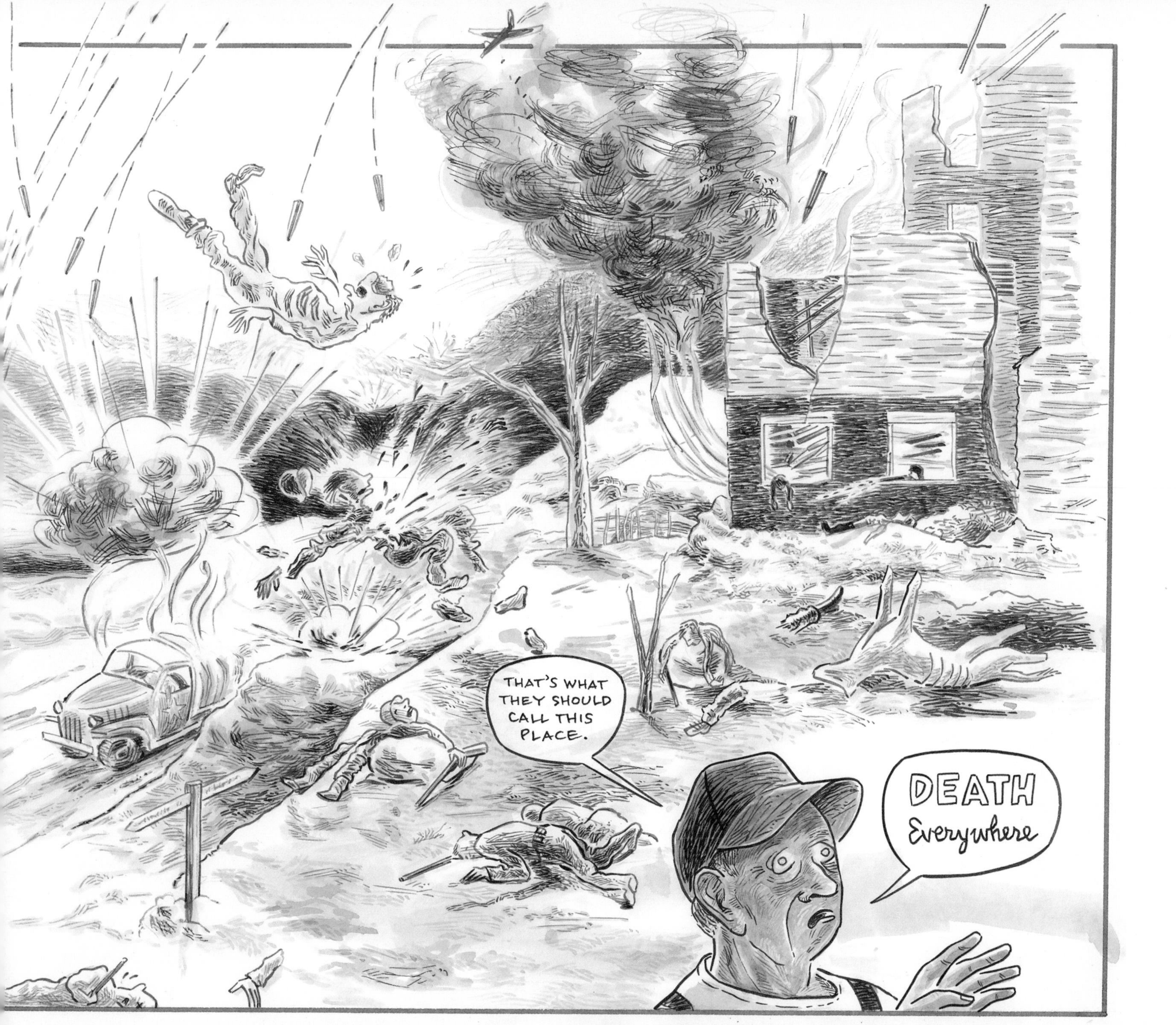
THAT'S WHAT THEY SHOULD CALL THIS PLACE.
DEATH Everywhere

EVERYWHERE: Indeed!
UNDER A WAGON
IN A DITCH
NEXT TO A TANK
BY A TREE
BEHIND A CHURCH
IN A CREEK
BY A FENCE
IN TOWN
IN A JEEP
IN A FIELD
ON COBBLESTONES
BY A SHED
IN THE WOODS
IN A DOORWAY
OVER A ROCK
ROAD SIDE
BY BOXCAR
BEHIND THE WHEEL
ON A HILLSIDE
BY ANOTHER CARCASS
ACROSS BARBED WIRE
AT THE CROSSROADS
STUCK IN MUD
IN HER MOTHER'S ARMS

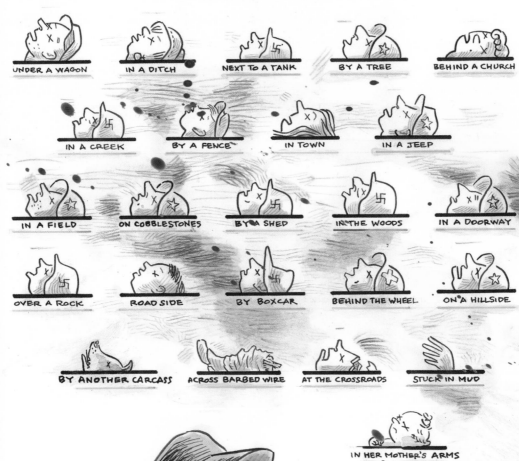

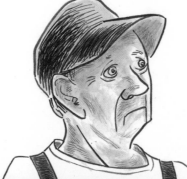

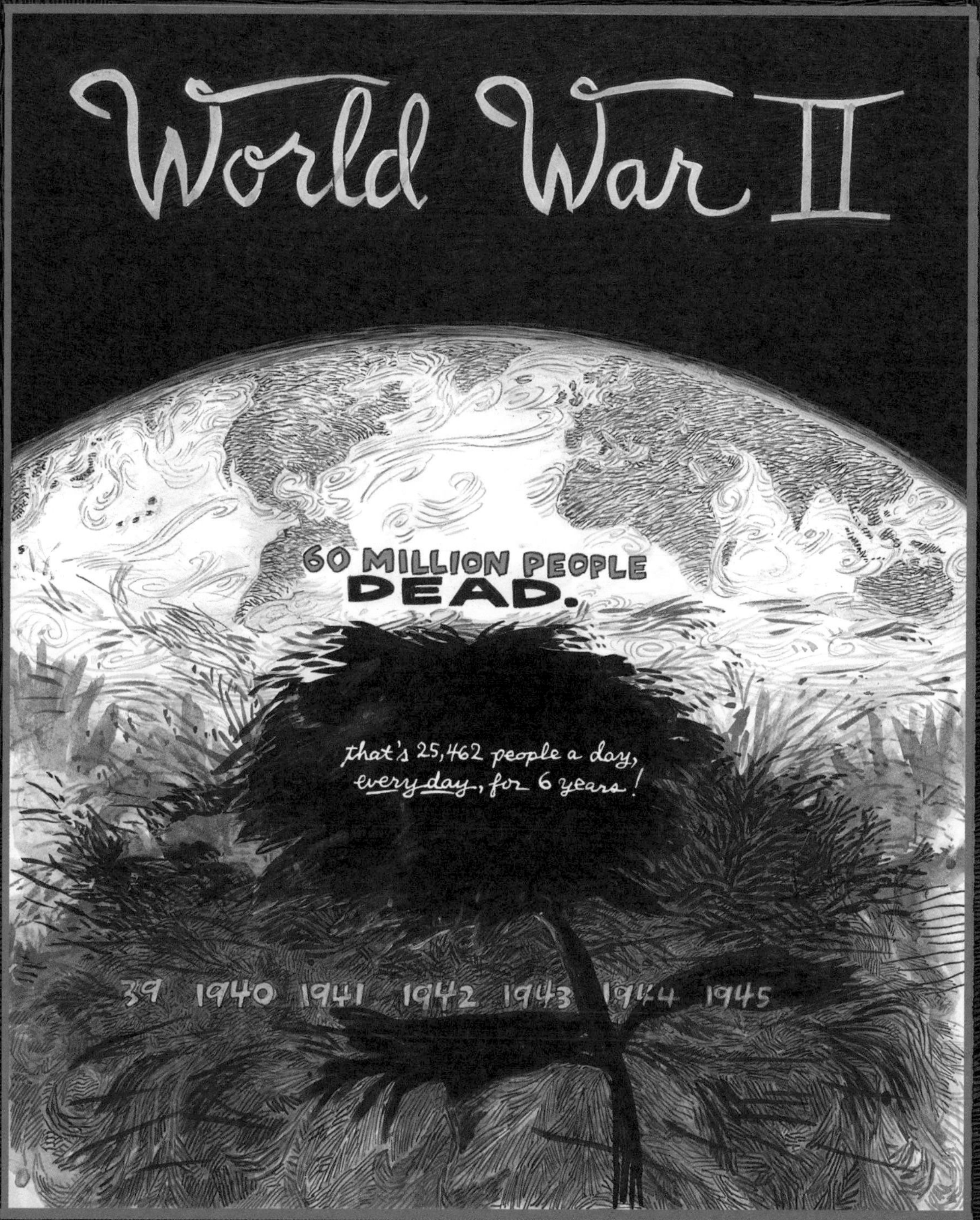
World War II
60 MILLION PEOPLE
DEAD.
that's 25,462 people a day, every day, for 6 years!
39 1940 1941 1942 1943 1944 1945

So much death! So much carnage! How much can a man take? From the rivers of blood in Italy to the tinged and tortured landscapes of the Rhône Valley, he'd already seen a lifetime's worth of annihilation and extinction. Tire repair brought a brief normal. But soon he came to know that the building next to his shop in Dijon was where they processed the bodies, fresh from the battlefields, delivered in meat wagons, 'round the clock. 'Just another job.' That's how he set it in his mind. Just a task, same as fixing tires. Shrug it off and stay drunk. "Who cares what they're doing next door? I need to just do my job until they send me home."

But instead they sent him to the front as a replacement for one of those corpses.... A rear-echelon guy now back on the line with some unit — a bunch of strangers named 'Jack'.

This time, combat was so much more paralyzing, due not only to his heightened awareness of death, but also the cold. It was winter and he had lost his sweater.

He suffered from what Ernie Pyle, the war correspondent, described as "...the accumulated blur and the hurting vagueness of being too long in the lines, the everlasting alertness, the noise and fear, the cell by cell exhaustion..." But conversely, Patton was all for pushing onward: "...go forward until the last round is fired and the last drop of gas is expended. Then go forward on foot."

Thus was the situation and the ethos for this weary combat orphan who, on a numberless January day, happened to wander into the path of that German howitzer.

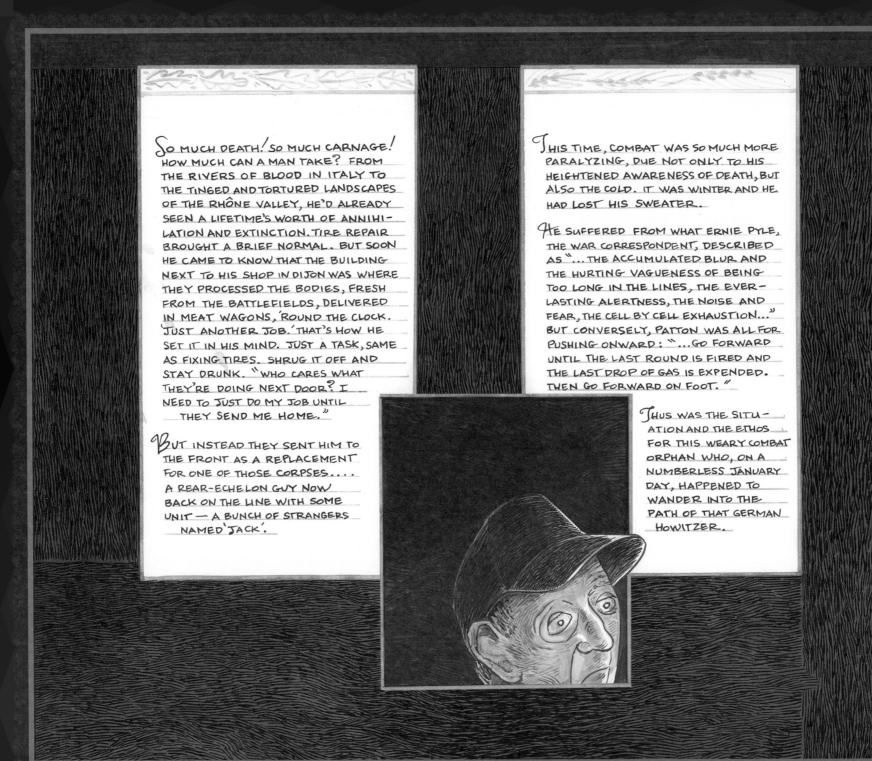

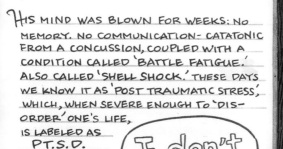

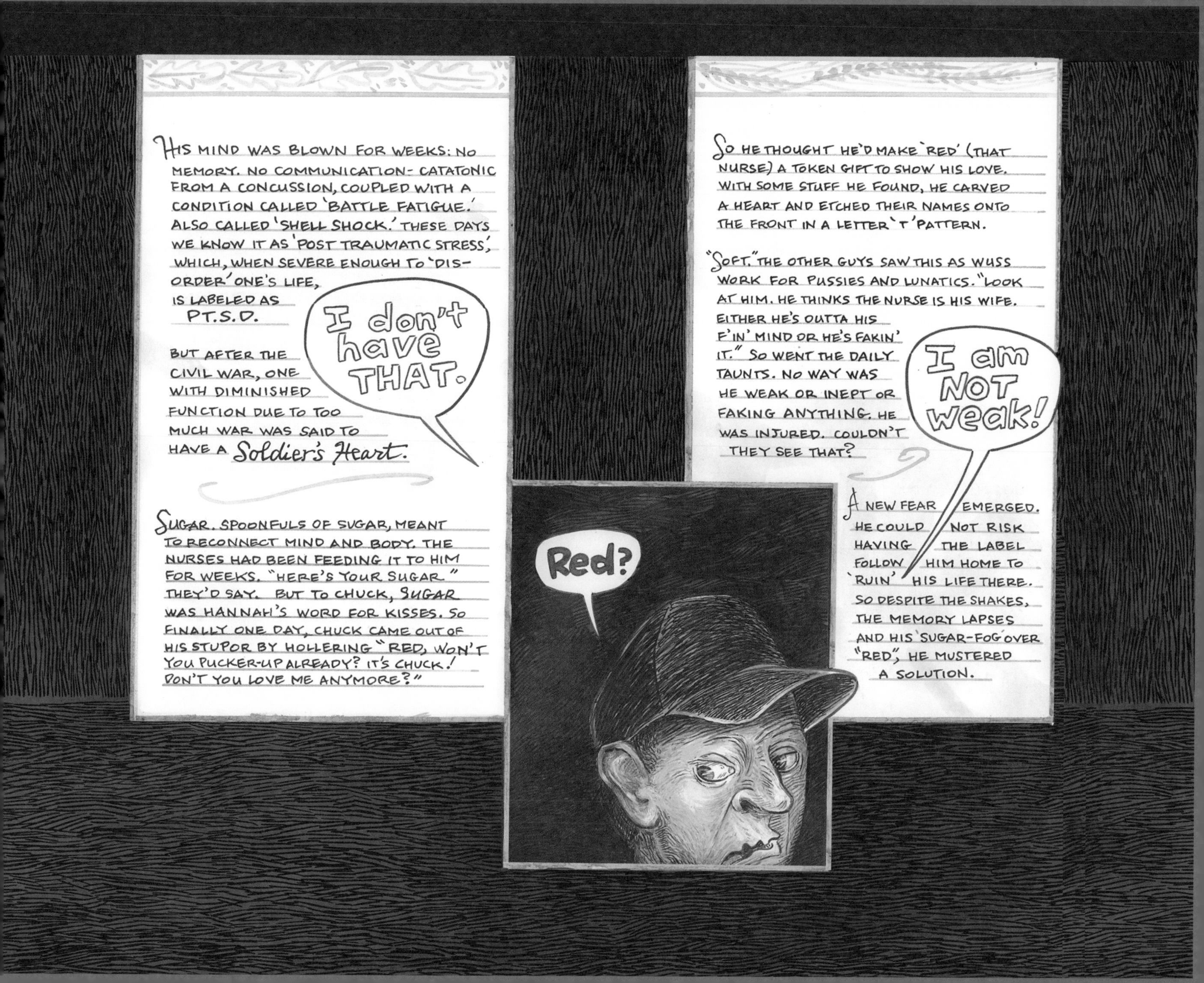

His mind was blown for weeks: no memory. No communication- catatonic from a concussion, coupled with a condition called 'Battle Fatigue.' Also called 'Shell Shock.' These days we know it as 'Post Traumatic Stress', which, when severe enough to 'disorder' one's life, is labeled as P.T.S.D.

I don't have THAT.

But after the Civil War, one with diminished function due to too much war was said to have a *Soldier's Heart.*

Sugar. Spoonfuls of sugar, meant to reconnect mind and body. The nurses had been feeding it to him for weeks. "Here's your sugar" they'd say. But to Chuck, sugar was Hannah's word for kisses. So finally one day, Chuck came out of his stupor by hollering "Red, won't you pucker-up already? It's Chuck! Don't you love me anymore?"

So he thought he'd make 'Red' (that nurse) a token gift to show his love. With some stuff he found, he carved a heart and etched their names onto the front in a letter 't' pattern.

"Soft." The other guys saw this as wuss work for pussies and lunatics. "Look at him. He thinks the nurse is his wife. Either he's outta his f'in' mind or he's fakin' it." So went the daily taunts. No way was he weak or inept or faking anything. He was injured. Couldn't they see that?

I am NOT weak!

A new fear emerged. He could not risk having the label follow him home to 'ruin' his life there. So despite the shakes, the memory lapses and his 'sugar-fog' over "Red", he mustered a solution.

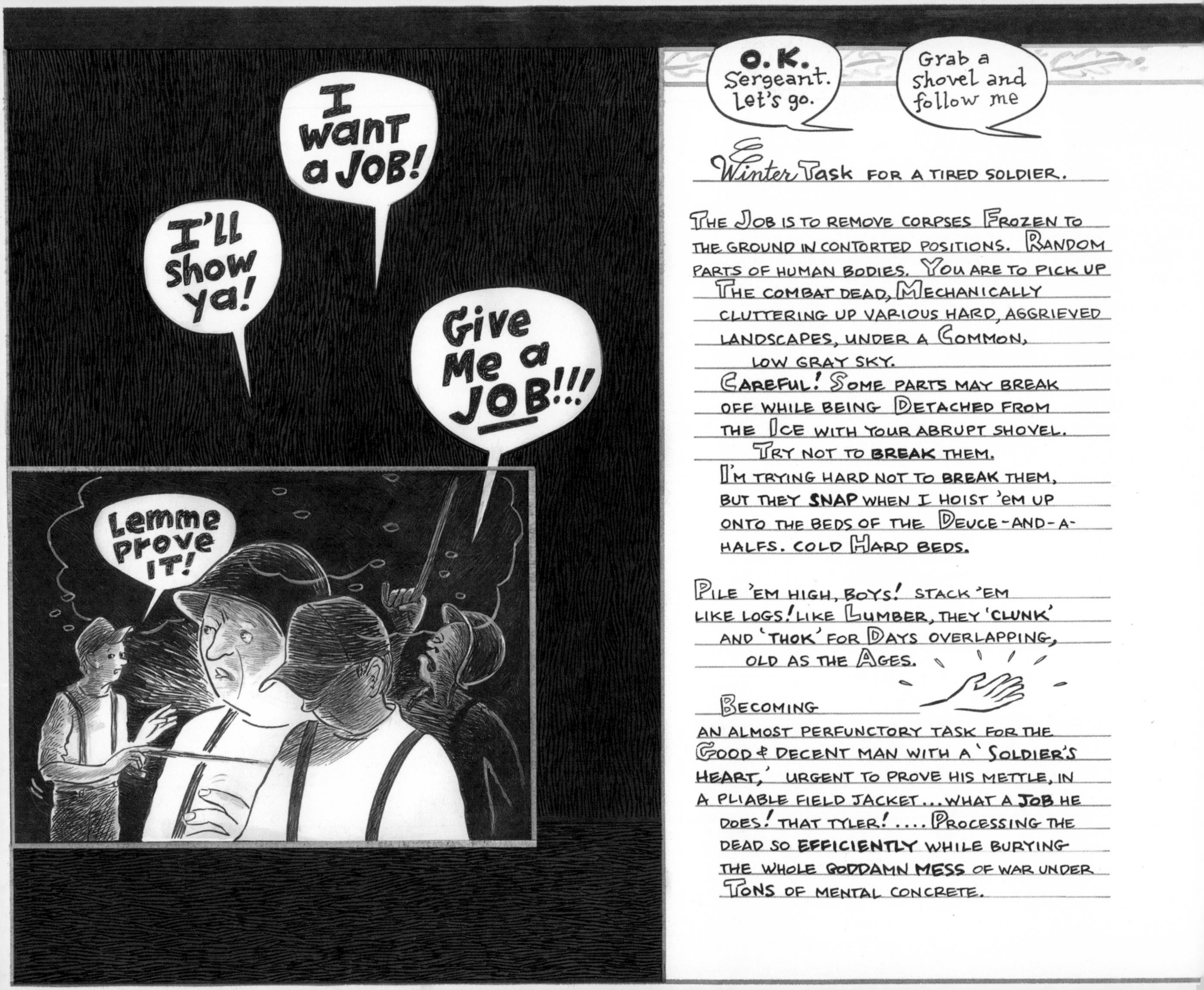
I want a JOB!
I'll show ya!
Give Me a JOB!!!
Lemme prove IT!
O.K. Sergeant. Let's go.
Grab a shovel and follow me
Winter Task for a tired soldier.
The Job is to remove corpses Frozen to the ground in contorted positions. Random parts of human bodies. You are to pick up the combat dead, Mechanically cluttering up various hard, aggrieved landscapes, under a Common, low gray sky.
Careful! Some parts may break off while being Detached from the Ice with your abrupt shovel.
Try not to BREAK them.
I'm trying hard not to BREAK them, but they SNAP when I hoist 'em up onto the beds of the Deuce-and-a-halfs. Cold Hard beds.
Pile 'em high, Boys! Stack 'em like logs! Like Lumber, they 'CLUNK' and 'THOK' for Days overlapping, old as the Ages.
Becoming
an almost perfunctory task for the Good & Decent man with a 'Soldier's Heart,' urgent to prove his mettle, in a pliable field jacket... what a JOB he does! That Tyler! .... Processing the dead so EFFICIENTLY while burying the whole goddamn MESS of war under Tons of mental concrete.

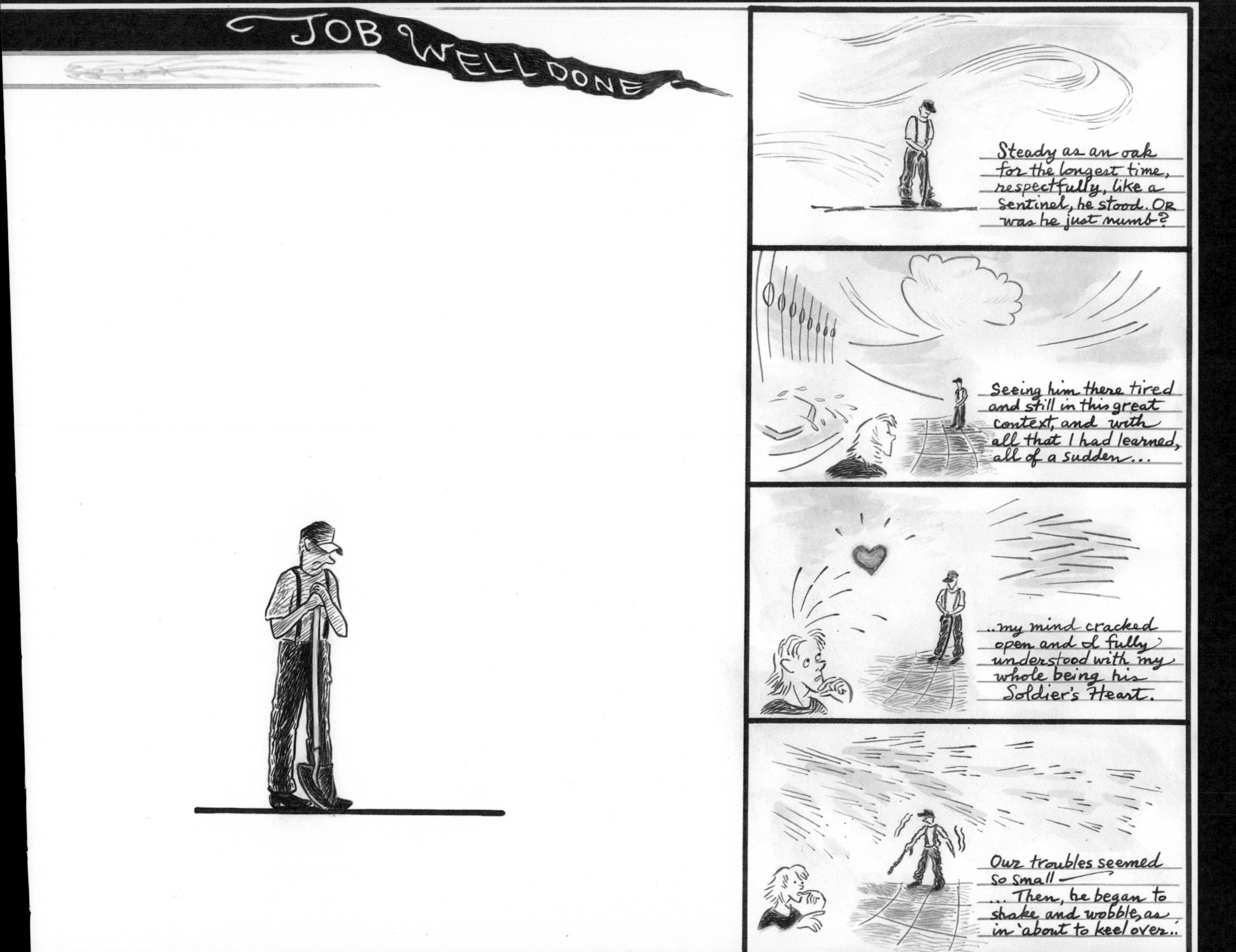
JOB WELL DONE
Steady as an oak for the longest time, respectfully, like a sentinel, he stood. Or was he just numb?
Seeing him there tired and still in this great context, and with all that I had learned, all of a sudden...
..my mind cracked open and I fully understood with my whole being his Soldier's Heart.
Our troubles seemed so small —
... Then, he began to shake and wobble, as in 'about to keel over'..

When I
moved in closer
to steady
him...

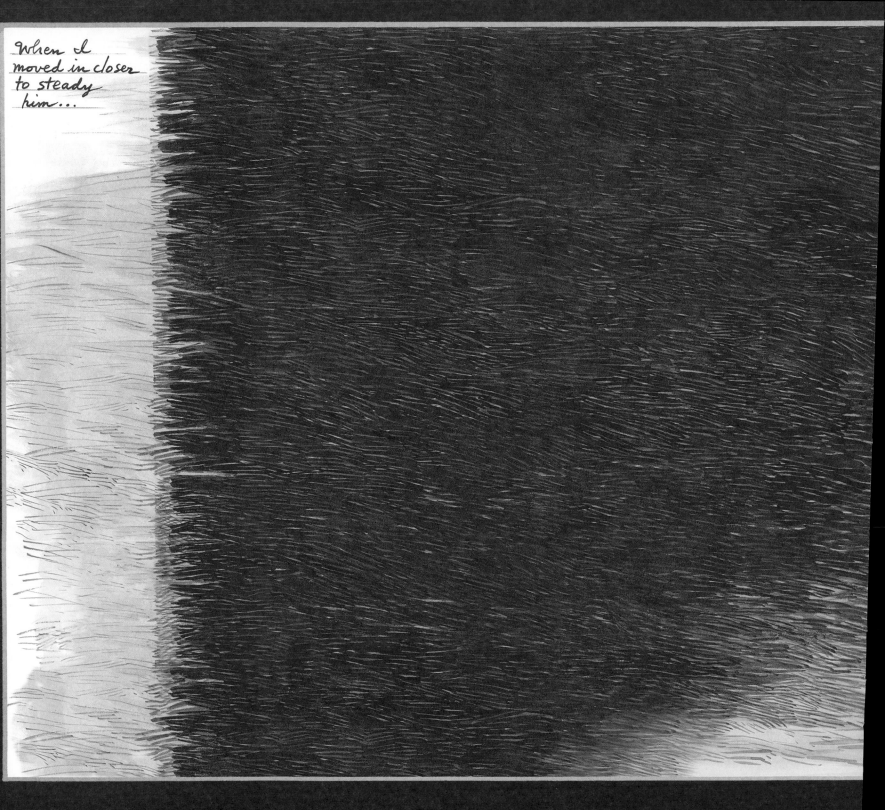

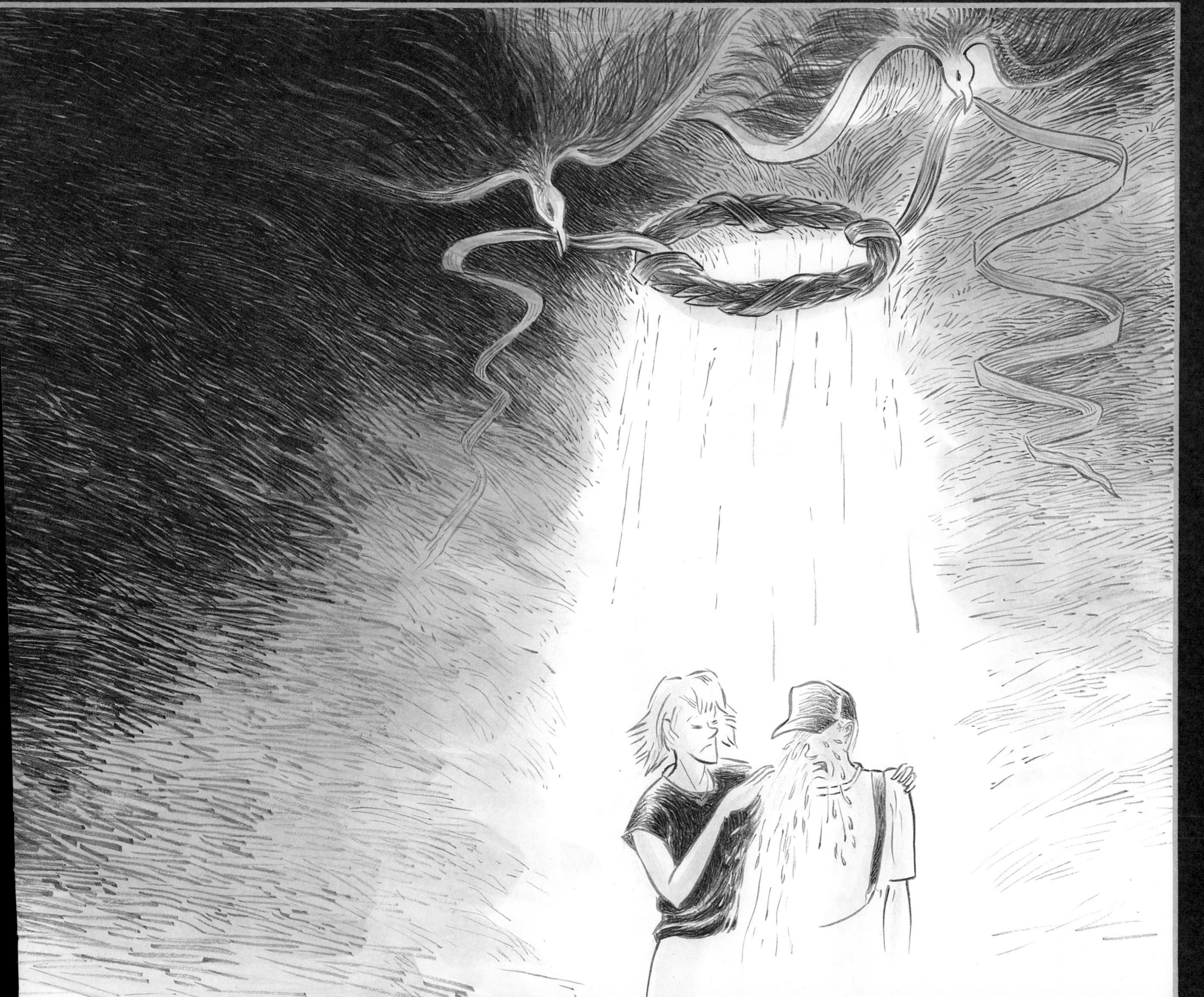

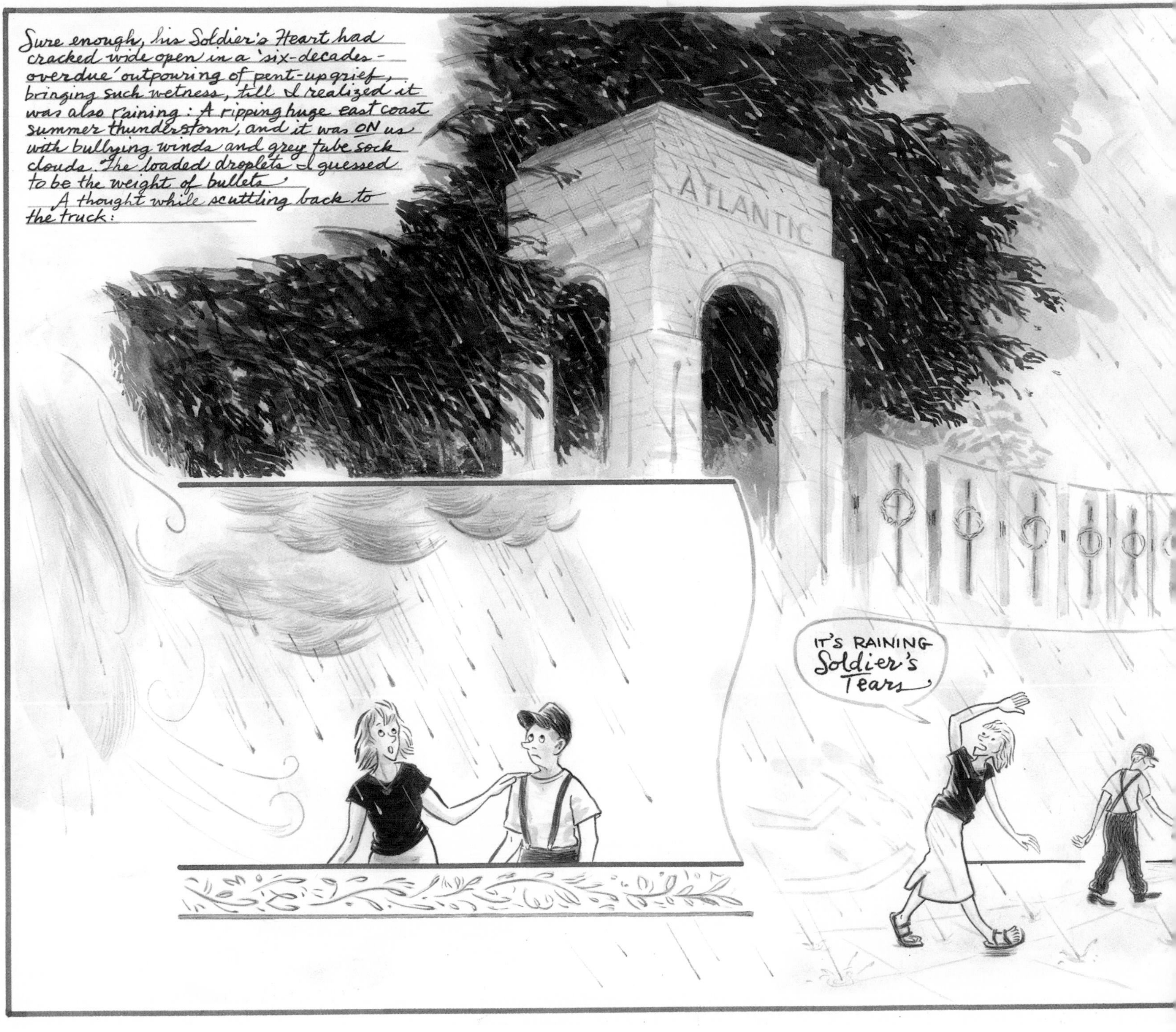

Sure enough, his Soldier's Heart had cracked wide open in a 'six-decades-overdue' outpouring of pent-up grief, bringing such wetness, till I realized it was also raining: A ripping huge east coast summer thunderstorm, and it was ON us with bullying winds and grey tube sock clouds. The loaded droplets I guessed to be the weight of bullets.
A thought while scuttling back to the truck:
ATLANTIC
IT'S RAINING Soldier's Tears

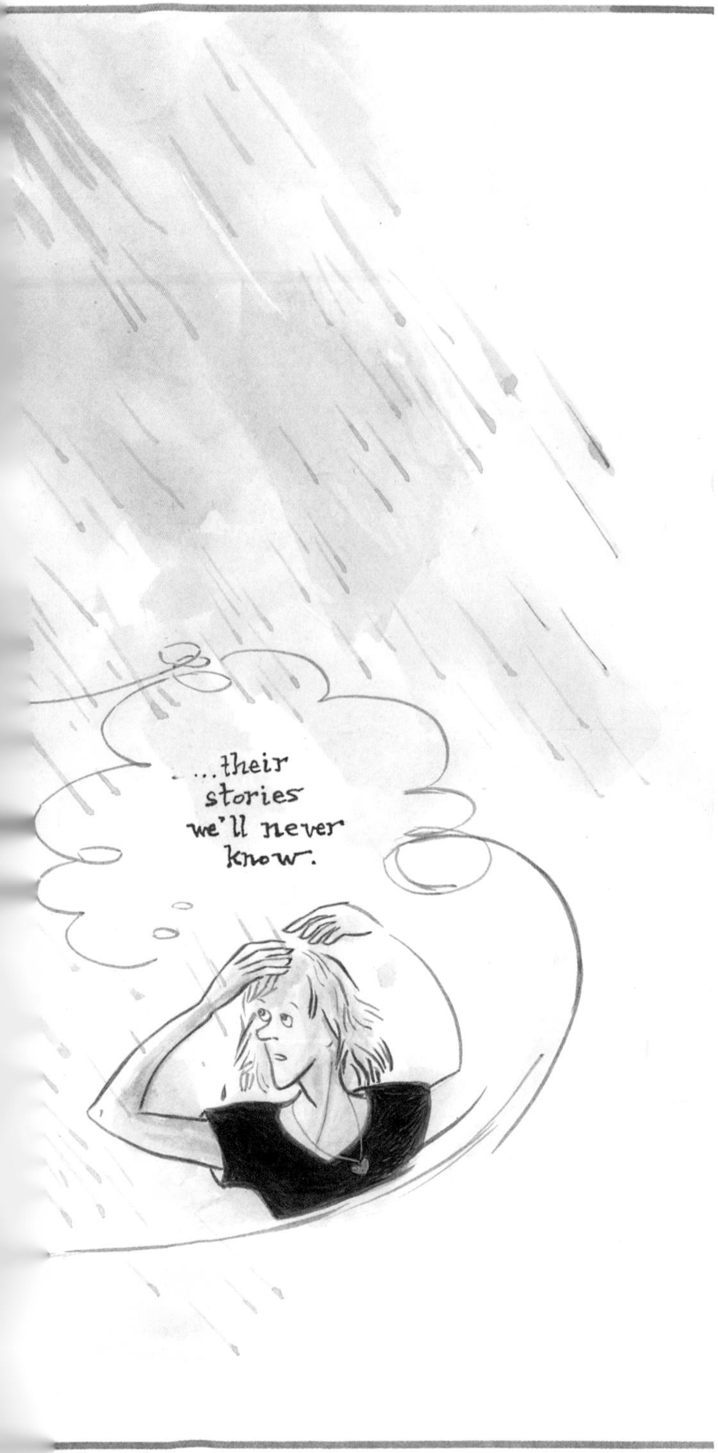
...their stories we'll never know.

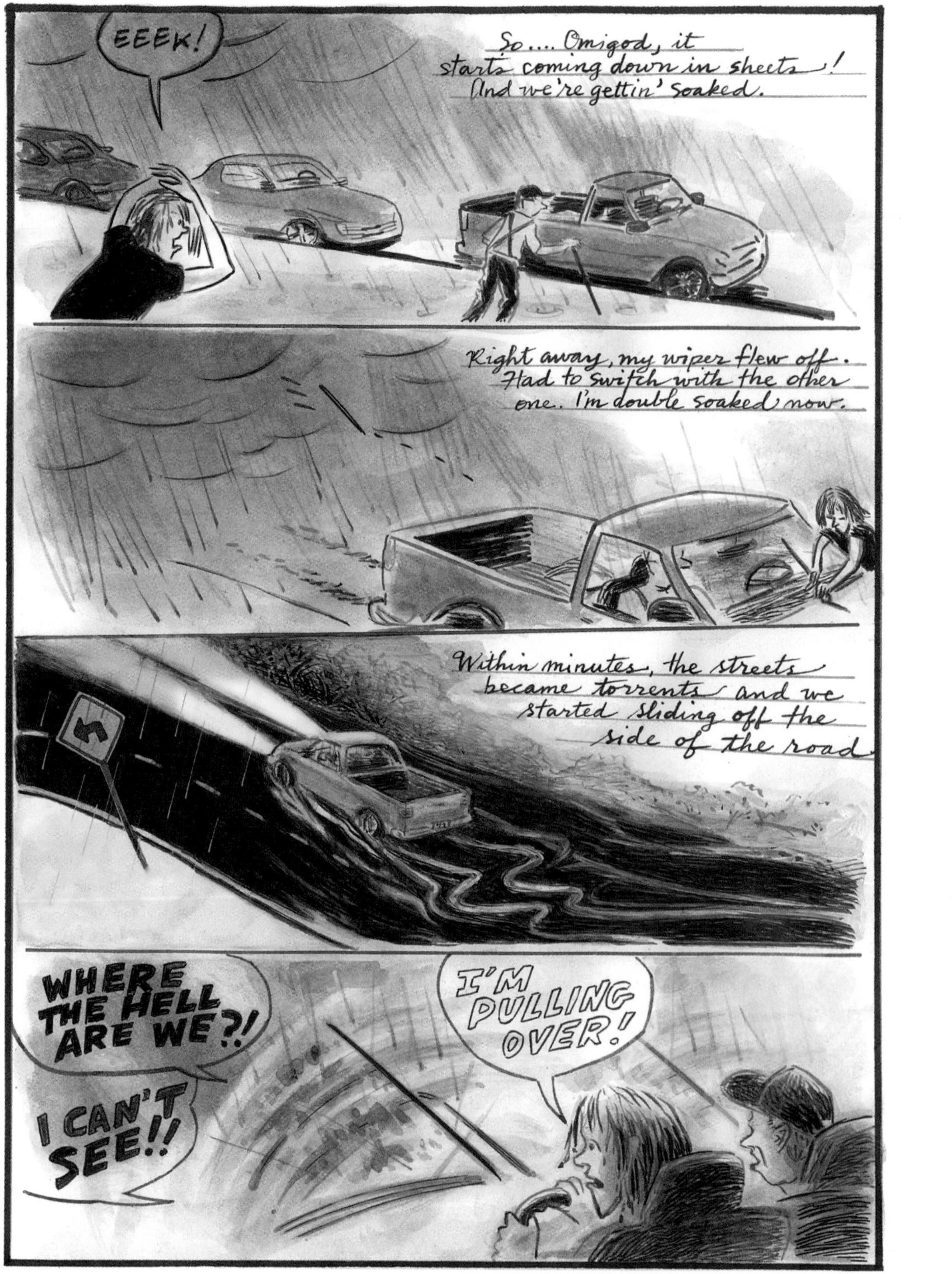
EEEK!
So.... Omigod, it starts coming down in sheets! And we're gettin' soaked.
Right away, my wiper flew off. Had to switch with the other one. I'm double soaked now.
Within minutes, the streets became torrents and we started sliding off the side of the road
WHERE THE HELL ARE WE?!
I CAN'T SEE!!
I'M PULLING OVER!

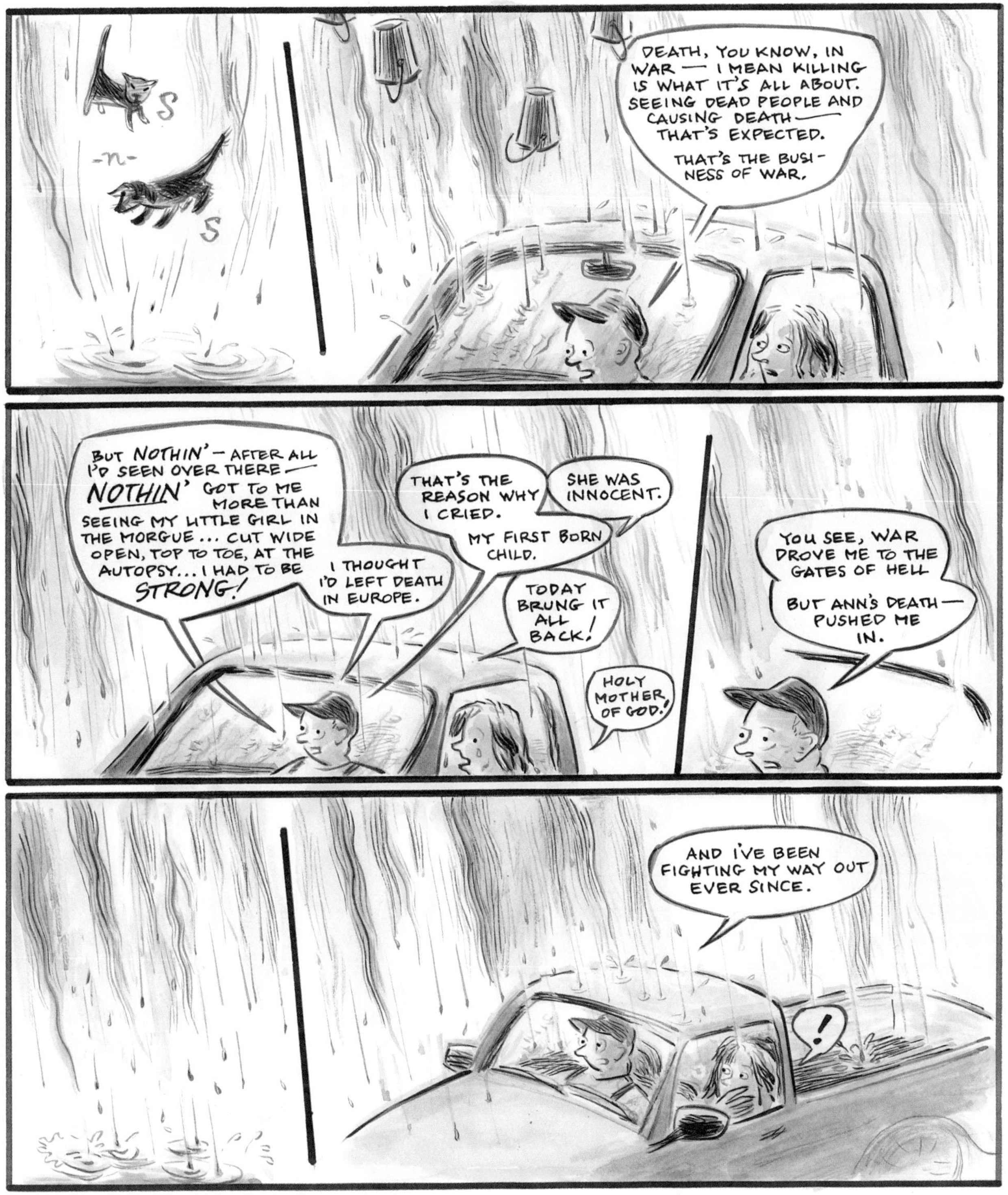
S
-n-
S
DEATH, YOU KNOW, IN WAR — I MEAN KILLING IS WHAT IT'S ALL ABOUT. SEEING DEAD PEOPLE AND CAUSING DEATH — THAT'S EXPECTED.
THAT'S THE BUSINESS OF WAR.
BUT NOTHIN' — AFTER ALL I'D SEEN OVER THERE — NOTHIN' GOT TO ME MORE THAN SEEING MY LITTLE GIRL IN THE MORGUE... CUT WIDE OPEN, TOP TO TOE, AT THE AUTOPSY... I HAD TO BE STRONG!
I THOUGHT I'D LEFT DEATH IN EUROPE.
THAT'S THE REASON WHY I CRIED.
SHE WAS INNOCENT.
MY FIRST BORN CHILD.
TODAY BRUNG IT ALL BACK!
HOLY MOTHER OF GOD!
YOU SEE, WAR DROVE ME TO THE GATES OF HELL
BUT ANN'S DEATH — PUSHED ME IN.
AND I'VE BEEN FIGHTING MY WAY OUT EVER SINCE.
!

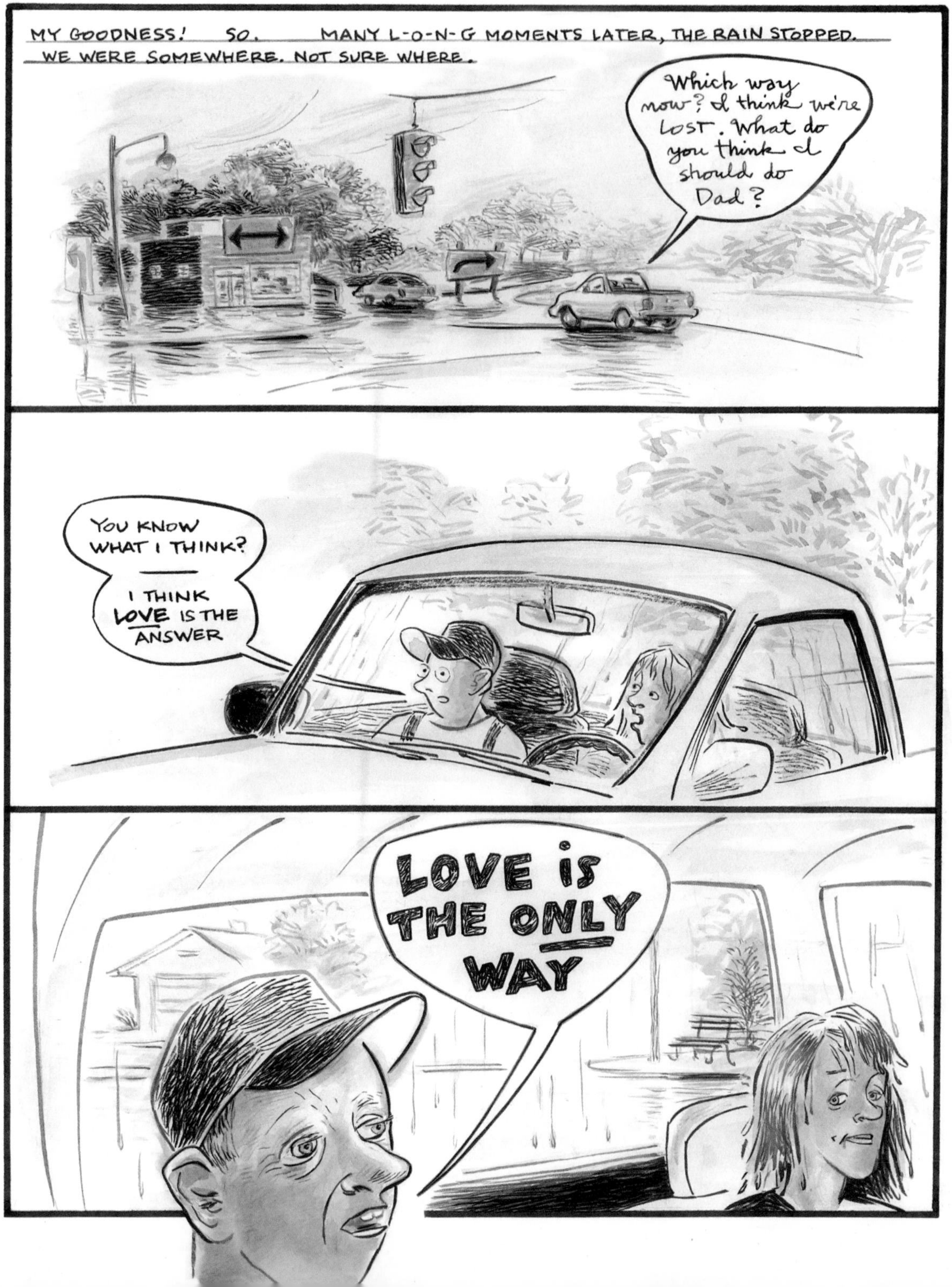
MY GOODNESS! SO. MANY L-O-N-G MOMENTS LATER, THE RAIN STOPPED.
WE WERE SOMEWHERE. NOT SURE WHERE.
Which way now? I think we're lost. What do you think I should do Dad?
YOU KNOW WHAT I THINK?
I THINK LOVE IS THE ANSWER
LOVE IS THE ONLY WAY

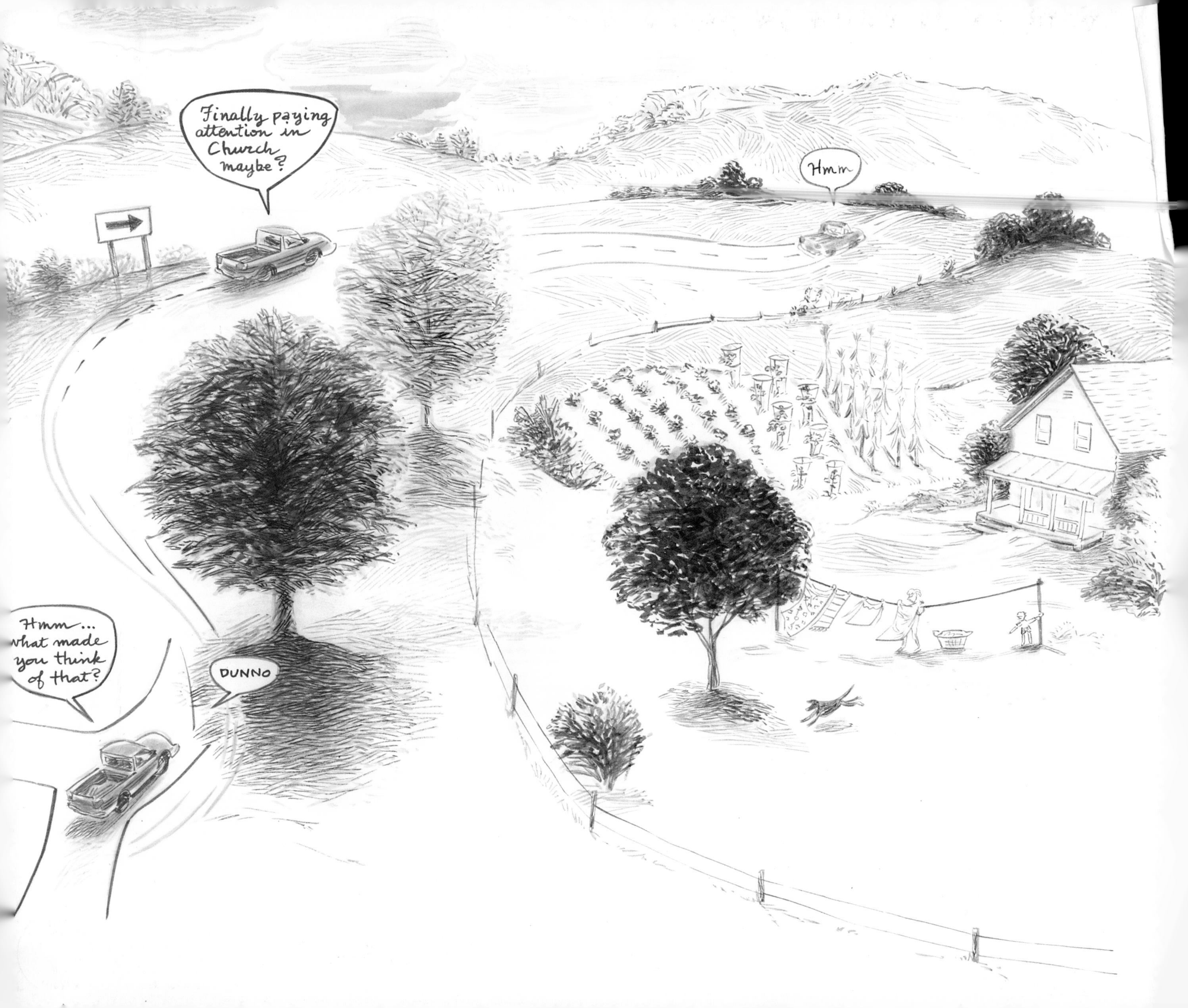
Finally paying attention in Church maybe?
Hmm
Hmm... what made you think of that?
DUNNO

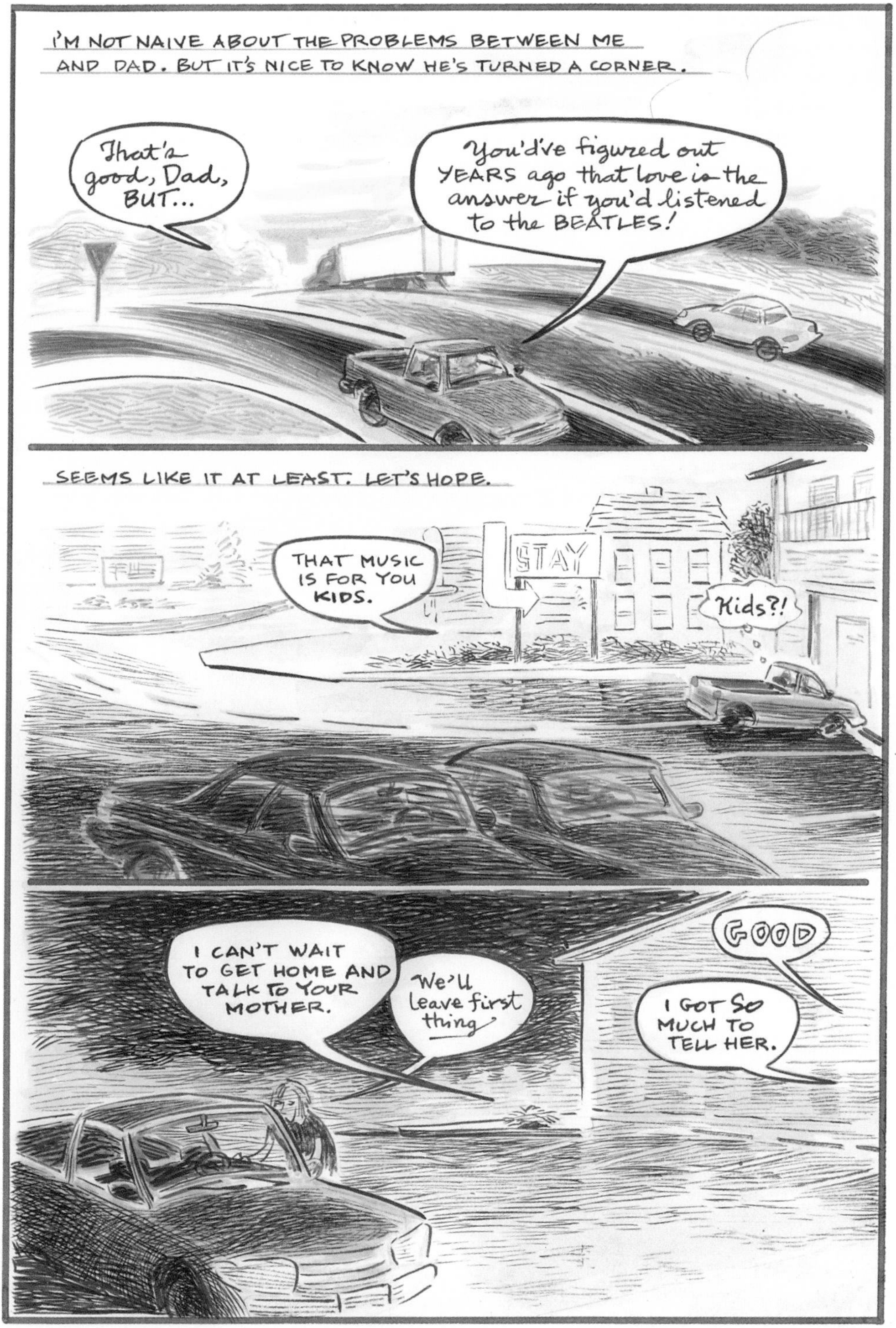
I'M NOT NAIVE ABOUT THE PROBLEMS BETWEEN ME AND DAD. BUT IT'S NICE TO KNOW HE'S TURNED A CORNER.
That's good, Dad, BUT...
You'd've figured out YEARS ago that love is the answer if you'd listened to the BEATLES!
SEEMS LIKE IT AT LEAST. LET'S HOPE.
STAY
THAT MUSIC IS FOR YOU KIDS.
Kids?!
I CAN'T WAIT TO GET HOME AND TALK TO YOUR MOTHER.
We'll leave first thing
GOOD
I GOT SO MUCH TO TELL HER.

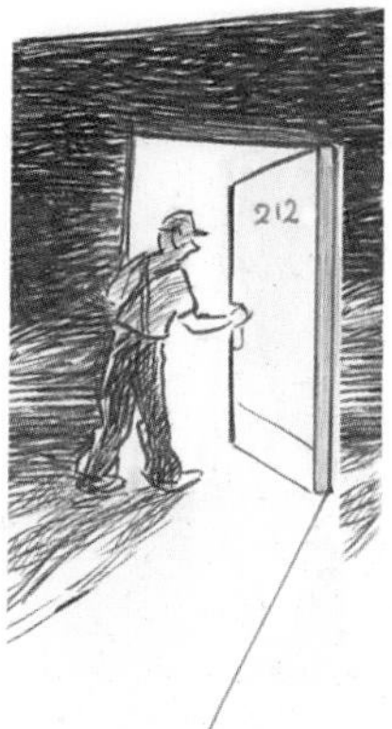
212

DAD'S ARMY SCRAPBOOK
AND
TOUR OF DUTY HIGHLIGHTS

PART VI

HOME

MARCH 1945 –
NOVEMBER 1945

78

MAY 1945

"The war in Europe was over. For some reason, I was in Reims at the red brick school house — SHAEF headquarters, where Eisenhower was. I seen the very spot where the Germans signed over the surrender.

"Even though the war was officially over, you still didn't trust nobody, no situation. Snipers. Some guys didn't know it was over yet. So it wasn't over. It wasn't safe. It still wasn't worthwhile to be sober because you could still get it."

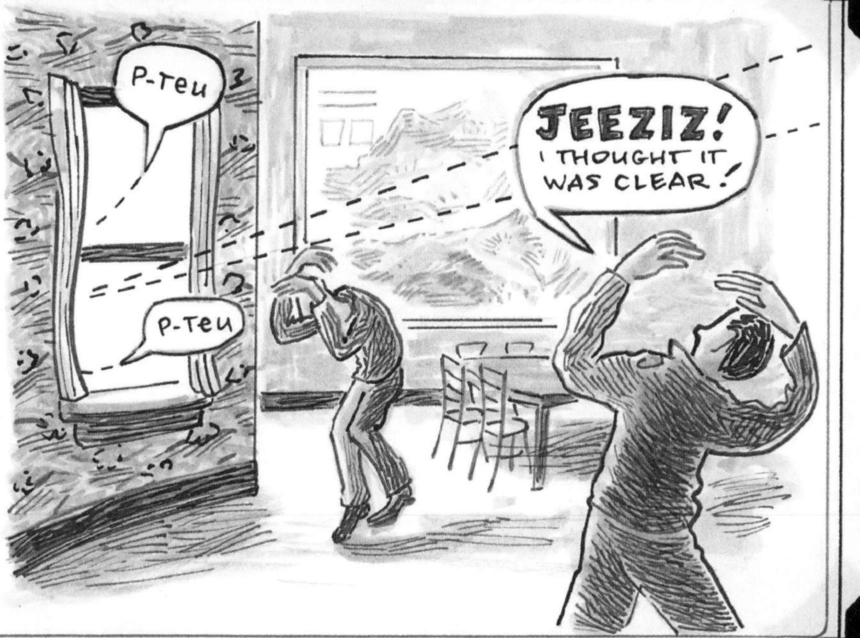
P-Teu
P-Teu
JEEZIZ! I THOUGHT IT WAS CLEAR!

79

"The civilian women — some had families, they had kids. And they had fraternized with the Germans to get food and money. But then us Americans came through and liberated everyone. That's when the townspeople turned on them there in Dijon. Chopped off their hair and paraded them around. From then on, they were marked.

"You can't judge people. They had to survive like the rest of us. Their land, their homes and children. You can't really judge."

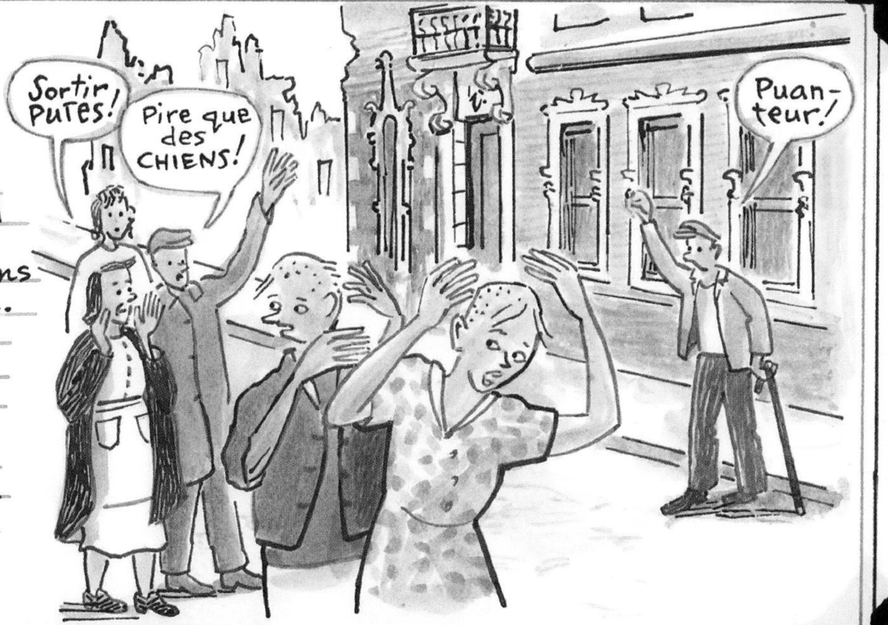
Sortir Putes!
Pire que des CHIENS!
Puanteur!

80

"We started to come home, and on the way I met Doug Palm, a buddy of mine from high school. A familiar face! So we're going through the rail yards in Paris, we're all combat guys, three stripes or better. And we're there on this train and they say 'You're going to have to sit here now and wait till they switch engines to take you up to Le Harve to Camp Lucky Strike or one of those camps named after cigarettes, to let you out. Old Gold or Chesterfield, maybe.'"

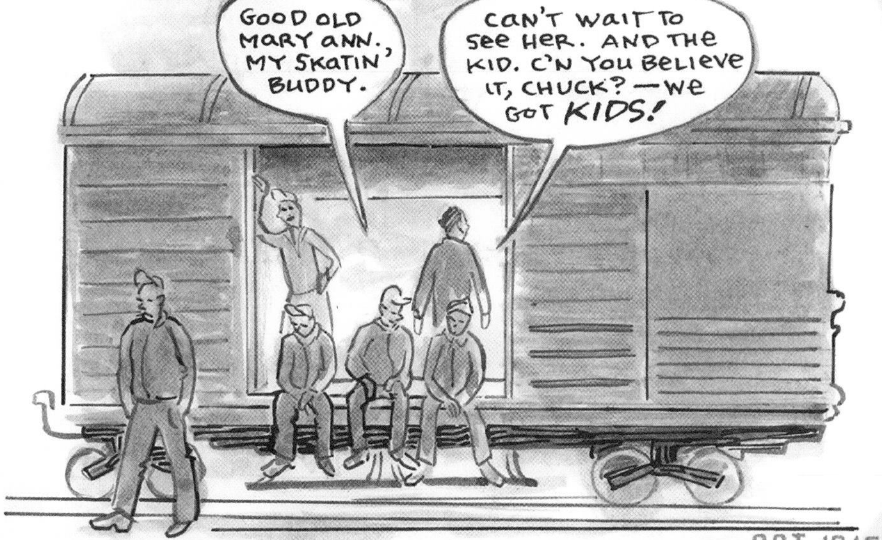
GOOD OLD MARY ANN, MY SKATIN' BUDDY.
CAN'T WAIT TO SEE HER. AND THE KID. C'N YOU BELIEVE IT, CHUCK? —WE GOT KIDS!

OCT 1945

81

"So we're sitting there in the rail yard and the cars are switching and then all of a sudden we're stopped dead in front of a boxcar with XXX cognac on the side about 4 rails over. We started with tin cups and soon we were filling our helmets to the brim. It was running all over the rail yard. This was the stuff Hitler wanted up at his private retreat, but WE had it! Good stuff. We stayed drunk all the way to Le Harve. They had to pour us out of the box-car and sober us up to go home."

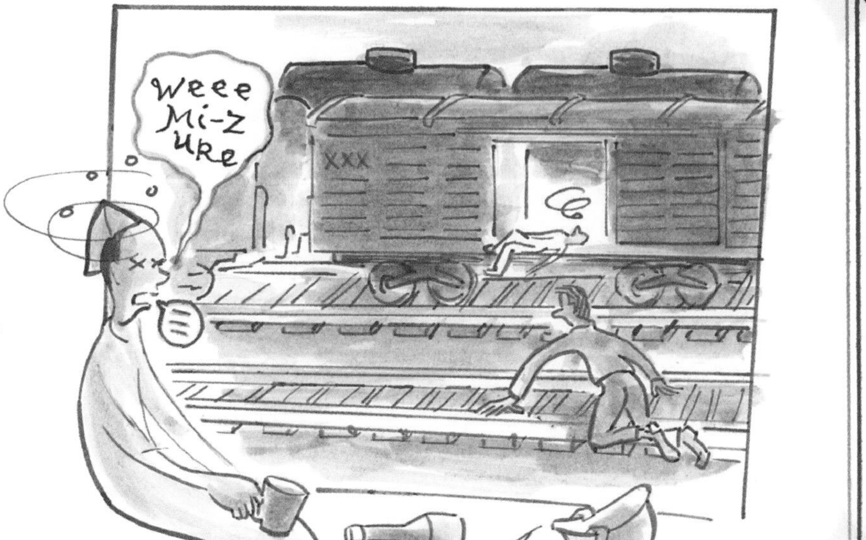
Weee Mi-Z ure
XXX

82

"They were giving bonuses to guys who would sign up for 3 more years to go to CBI (China, Burma, India). Most of us didn't want to go there. I had a family, so to hell with that.

"There were these 2 African-American guys on the boat that signed up. Well, those guys stuffed their duffel bags full of that bonus money in the highest denominations along with invasion money and somehow got on a ship headed first to the Riviera. Ambitious guys. They were planning to buy hotels. They had nothing to lose."

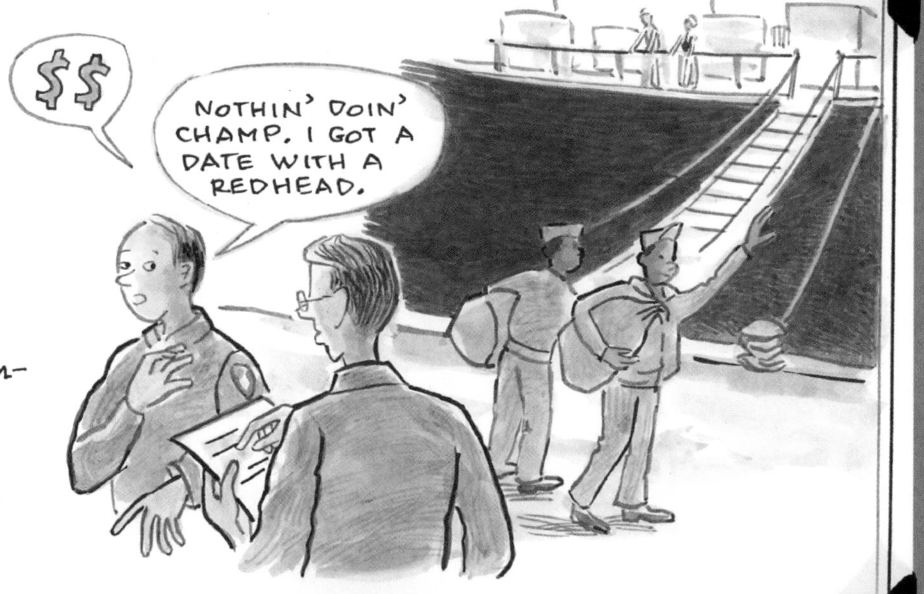
$$
NOTHIN' DOIN' CHAMP. I GOT A DATE WITH A REDHEAD.

83

"We were equipped for going home. All of our stuff and souvenirs were in our duffel bags, so we had to wear as many layers of clothing as we could because the bags were full. No more room. — We chased the boats as they come in. If the boat came from the United States, it had fresh food, meat and vegetables.. everything. But if it came from the Mediterranean, it was empty. Nothing much in it. —

"On the way home, they wanted 'ship's fitters' again, but no more of that for me. I cleaned up enough messes."

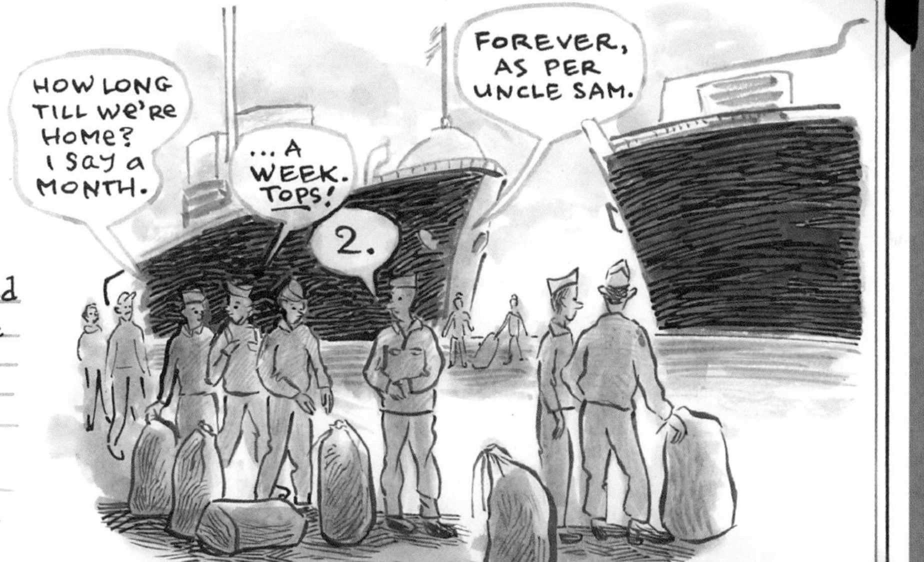
HOW LONG TILL WE'RE HOME? I SAY A MONTH.
...A WEEK. TOPS!
2.
FOREVER, AS PER UNCLE SAM.

OCT 1945

84

"And this Alfred Moore boat came in. These guys came up and said 'Hey. It's a great ship. It's got all new stuff. Let's get on it.' Then came an announcement that we could either take the Alfred Moore now or wait 3 days, the Queen is gonna come — take you to England and go home from there. Hell no, the Moore was right there in the harbor, we seen it, we knew what was on it. No delays. So 3 stripes or better, Captains, Majors, Lieutenants — all these guys decided to board this ship."

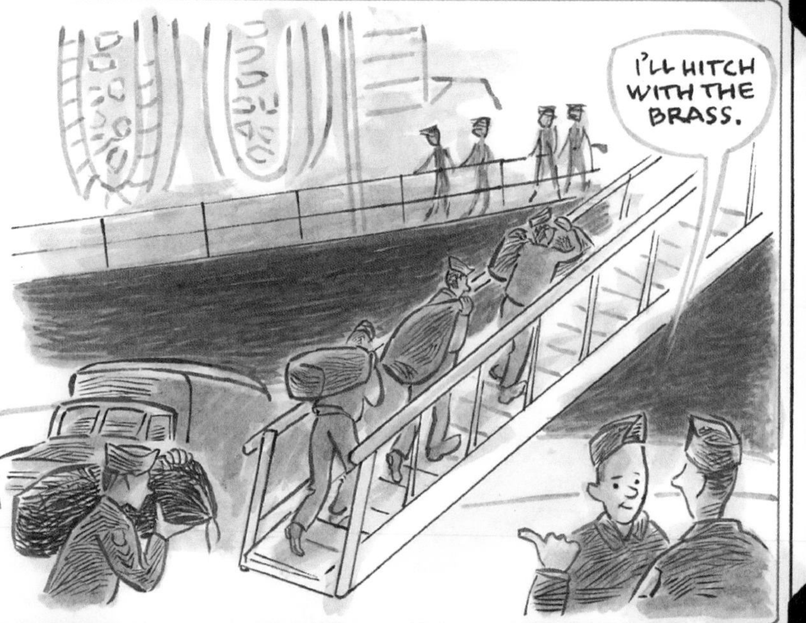
I'LL HITCH WITH THE BRASS.

85

"At 3:00 in the morning, I'll never forget it, they pull up to the barracks, we get on the trucks, 90 miles an hour to the harbor. Toot Toot we're going to move. To hell with Europe. To hell with war. WE'RE GOING HOME!!

"We didn't get 100 feet off of our mooring dock till BANG! We're thinking 'what happened?' We had hit a sunken ship in the harbor and tore a giant hole in the hull. Now we gotta get off."

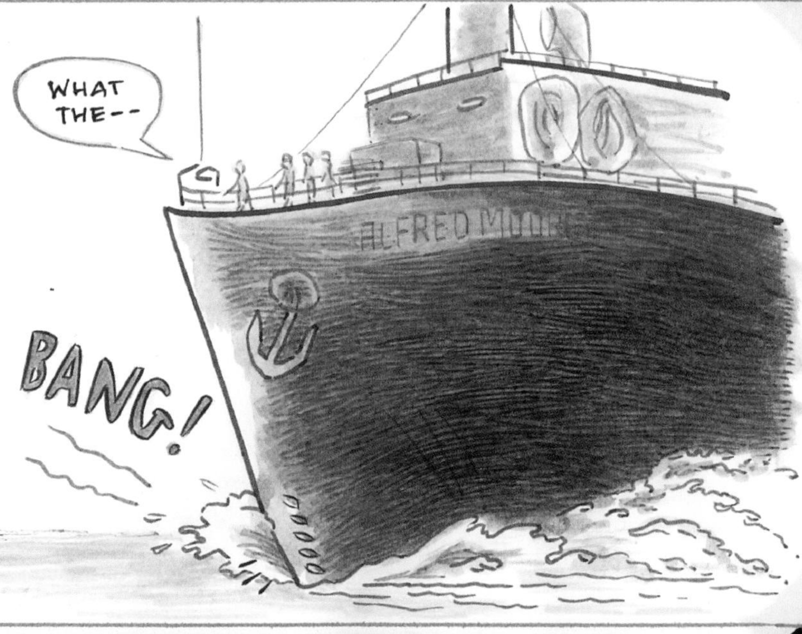
WHAT THE--
ALFRED MOORE
BANG!

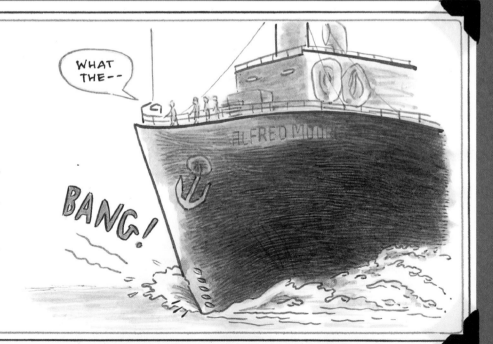

86

"The French boat pilot that's supposed to let you out of the harbor— he was drunker than hell. He didn't know where he was at. Missed the safe way out completely and our young Captain, 27 years old, he didn't know nothin' about it, so they called in the Cee Bees. Navy engineers. They installed plates in the bottom, welded it up real tight, put some pumps in there and sent us off. 'You'll be alright, you'll get home.' But not before the announcement 'Here comes the Queen.....and there she goes.'"

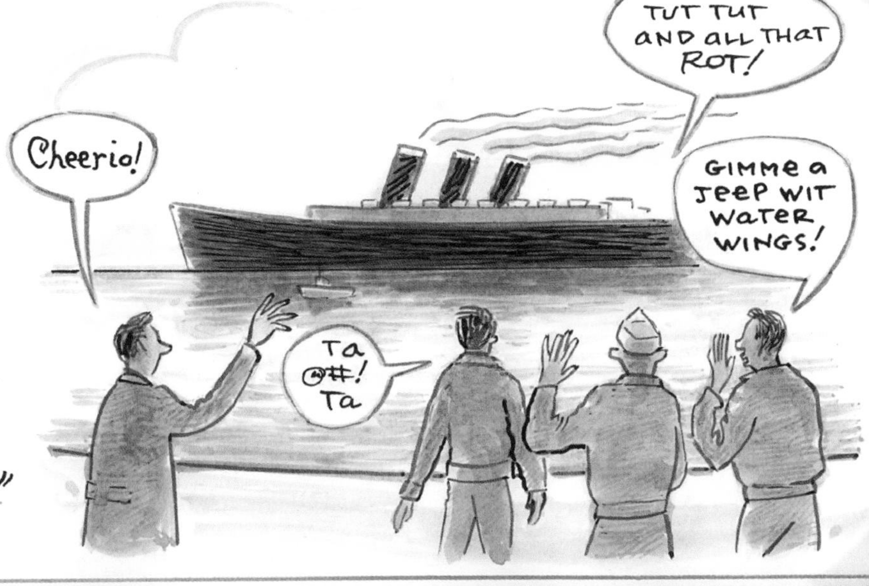
Cheerio!
TUT TUT AND ALL THAT ROT!
GIMME A JEEP WIT WATER WINGS!
Ta @#! Ta

87

"So we get out of le Harve and they're looking for the current that will give us a nice ride home. Well, next thing you know, we're up there near Nova Scotia breaking ice off of everything with pick axes so the boat doesn't get weighed down and sink. Then the bearings burned out on the propellars, so we sat there taking on water. We got canvas buckets and helmets—all of us, throwing water overboard because we were sinking there in the North Atlantic just like the Titanic."

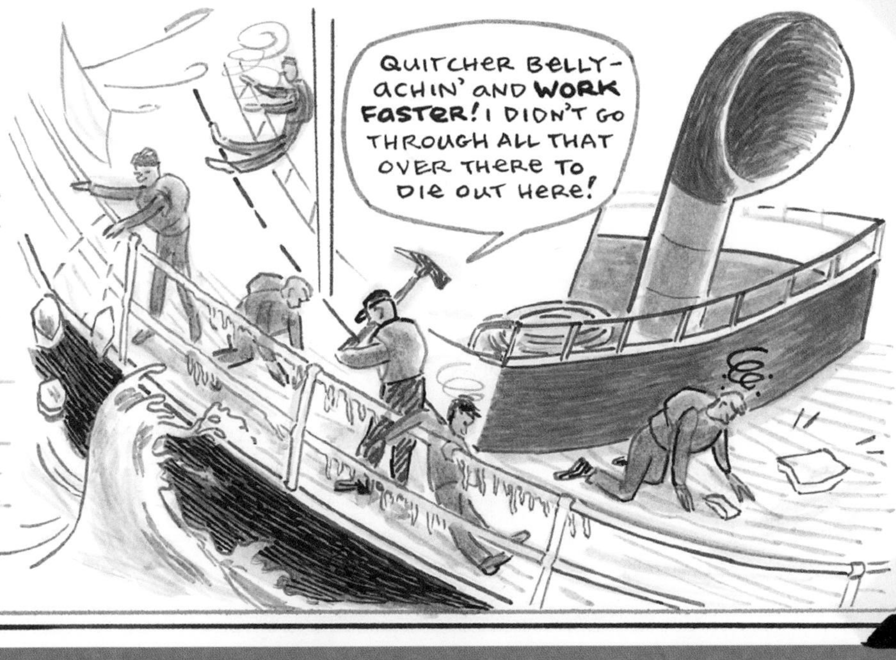
QUITCHER BELLY-ACHIN' AND WORK FASTER! I DIDN'T GO THROUGH ALL THAT OVER THERE TO DIE OUT HERE!

88

"That's what we did in shifts, day and night for days, until they got those damn propellars going. To keep our spirits up, they figured they'd show movies. But they only had one — Abbott and Costello 'LOST IN A HARUM'. 'Poko Moko', you know: 'Slowly I turned, step by step, step by step...' Then the guy goes crazy when he hears that phrase 'Poko Moko.' Must've watched it 50 times while trying to keep the Moore from sinking so we could get home."

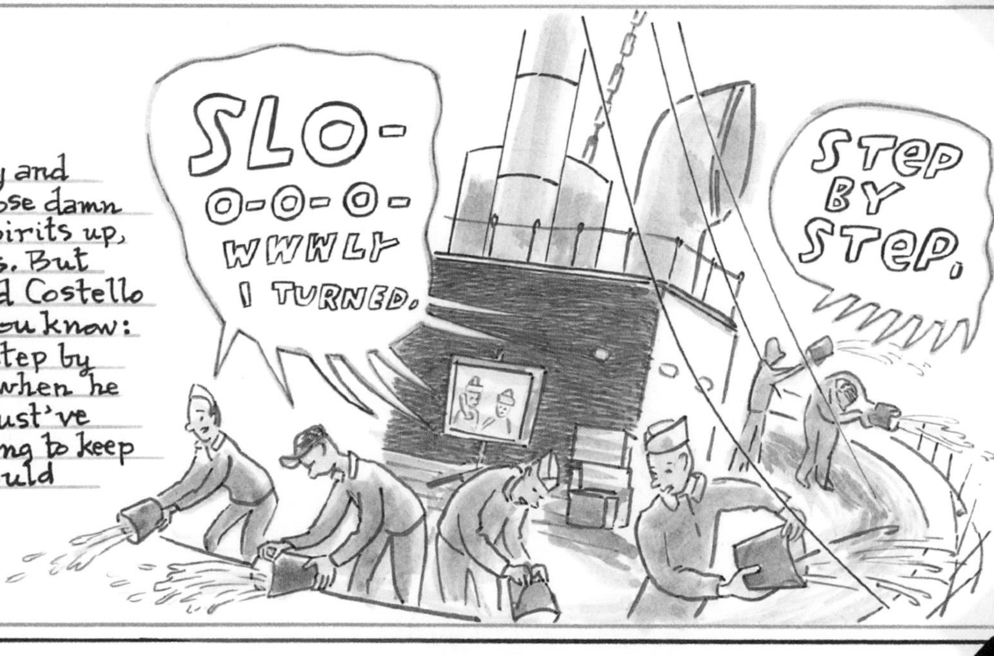
SLO-O-O-O-WWWLY I TURNED.
STEP BY STEP.

89

"I was a Master Sergeant in Dijon for awhile. I don't know how the hell I made reports out, but I did and I got paid more. I didn't get a big pay again until my trip home on the boat. When I came back to the states, I had all this money, because on our ship coming back there were crap games. I seen stacks of money 4 feet high. This pile against that pile. Somehow I ended up with a pretty big pile. Boy would Red be surprised to see a rich man coming home."

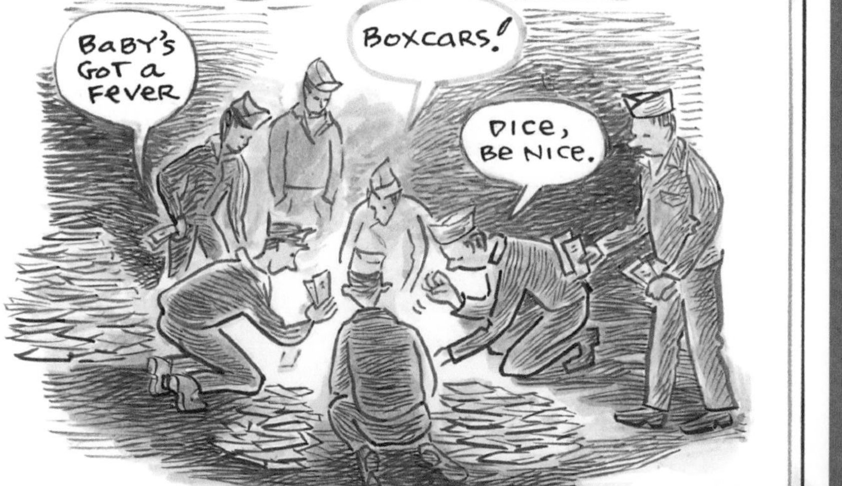
BABY'S GOT A FEVER
BOXCARS!
DICE, BE NICE.

90

"Then we found out that all the money we had was invasion money. It was no good! Here we had hauled all this dough across the ocean for nothing! We found a use for it alright: $100 bills to light cigars.

"Three days before, that's when I found out they'd knocked me down from Master to Staff Sergeant. I was in the Bulge fighting, not back in Dijon with the typewriter — that was the reason why they had lowered my pay. Can you believe those bastards?"

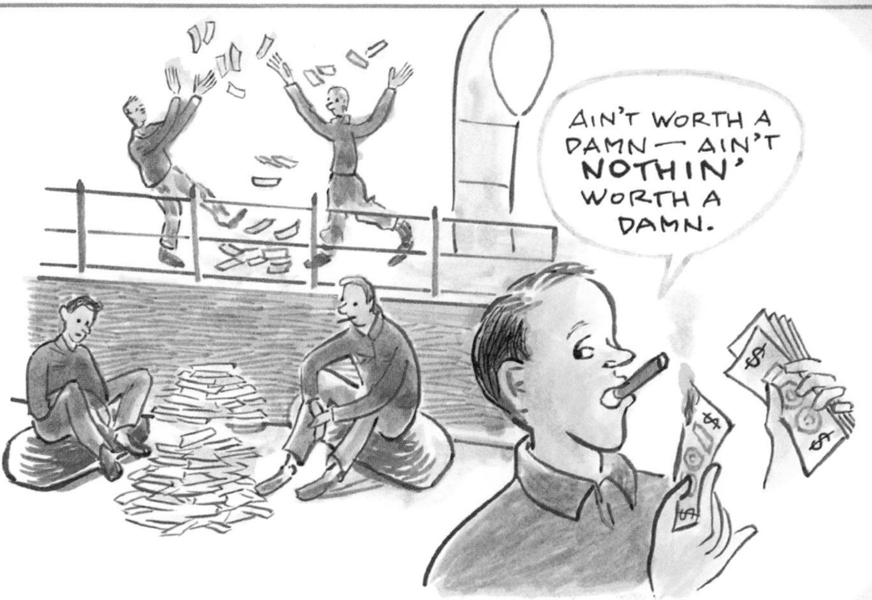
AIN'T WORTH A DAMN — AIN'T NOTHIN' WORTH A DAMN.

91

"We come into New York and they fed us steaks and free long distance phone calls. Free everything! Then we got on a train to come to Chicago. I guess three or four days of that. And then they announce we can't get off in Chicago... After we'd called and told our wives! We'd have to go on to Camp McCoy, Wisc. That's where they would officially release us from the Army. But then they decided they'd let us have a lay-over at the freight yards of South Chicago. We fought to make phone calls. I called Dad."

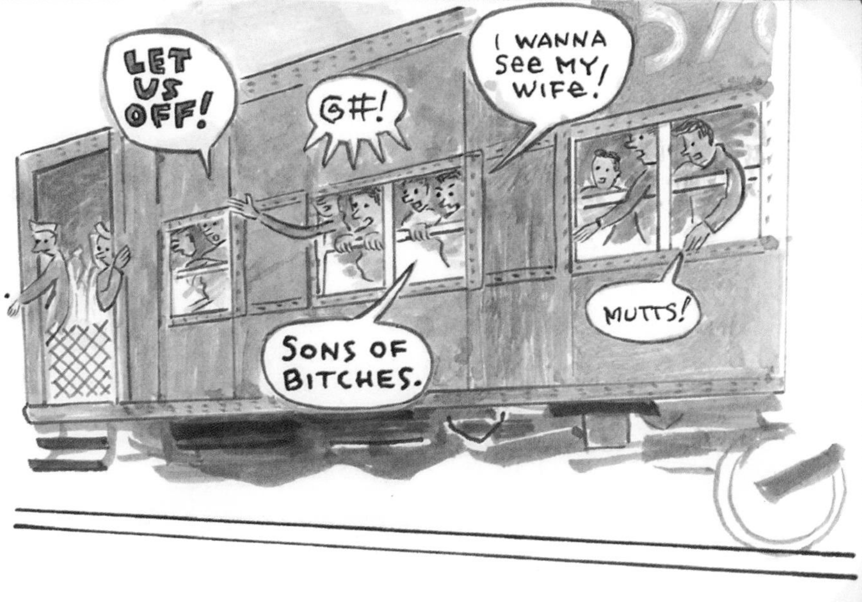
LET US OFF!
@#!
I WANNA SEE MY WIFE!
SONS OF BITCHES.
MUTTS!

92

"When we finally got to the South-side freight yards, they said 'don't get off the train.' We were so mad. We wanted liquor, but then they told us every store in Chicago was sold out and warned 'Anyone who gets off will be considered A.W.O.L.' But then as we're pulling in, people were rushing up to the cars with all the booze in the city. All we could stand! Then I seen my Dad driving down the railroad tracks. Ma and Hannah and Ann. OOH! It was so wonderful to see Red. And my little daughter. Dad brought 3 Feathers whiskey."

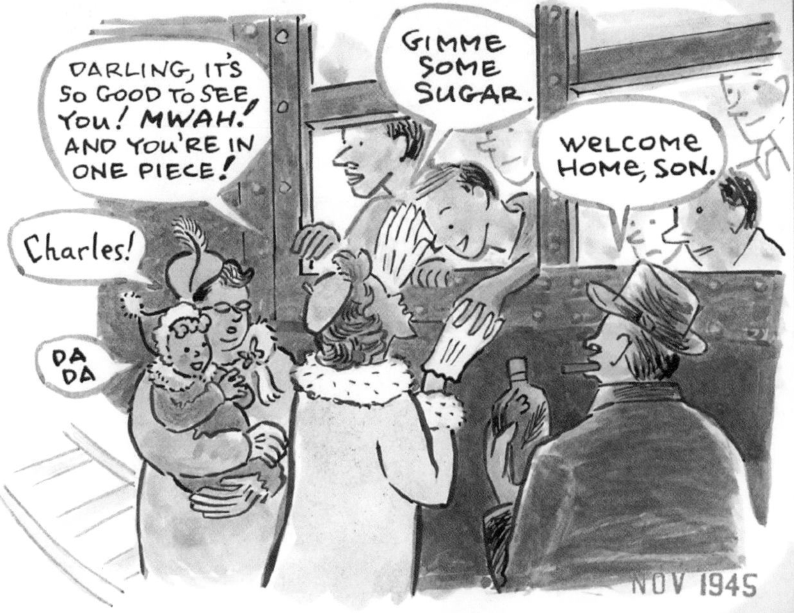

DARLING, IT'S SO GOOD TO SEE YOU! MWAH! AND YOU'RE IN ONE PIECE!
GIMME SOME SUGAR.
WELCOME HOME, SON.
Charles!
DA DA
NOV 1945

93

"Next day, up in Wisconsin, we poured out of another train. And I had all my stuff: the Waltz King's binoculars, a German pistol, postcards, coins and other things. They told us 'ok now. You're gonna walk through these barracks you guys and we'll discharge you. Take all your stuff, everything you got, clothing and all, pile it up here and we'll have everything new and ready after you shower and shave. Look good to go home.' And we did that. I don't know how many guys were on that train—a bunch of us eating good, drinking, having a good time."

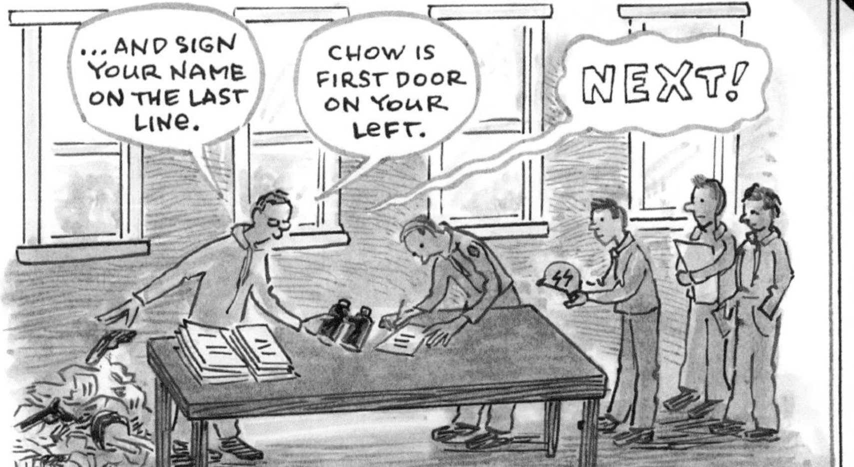

...AND SIGN YOUR NAME ON THE LAST LINE.
CHOW IS FIRST DOOR ON YOUR LEFT.
NEXT!

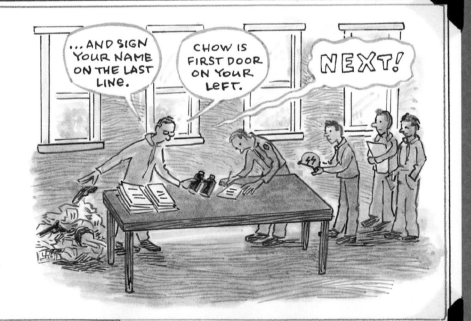

94

"Then we started looking for our souvenirs — but they were gone. The place was all closed up. Offices, main building, canteen — everyone in charge was gone. They took off. Then it dawned on us that those stateside commandos stole all our souvenirs. The good stuff. So we decided to raise hell. We tore the place to pieces! Then one guy decided to torch the barracks. That was it! We set the place on fire. Those sons-of-bitches — 4-F or whatever those bastards were."

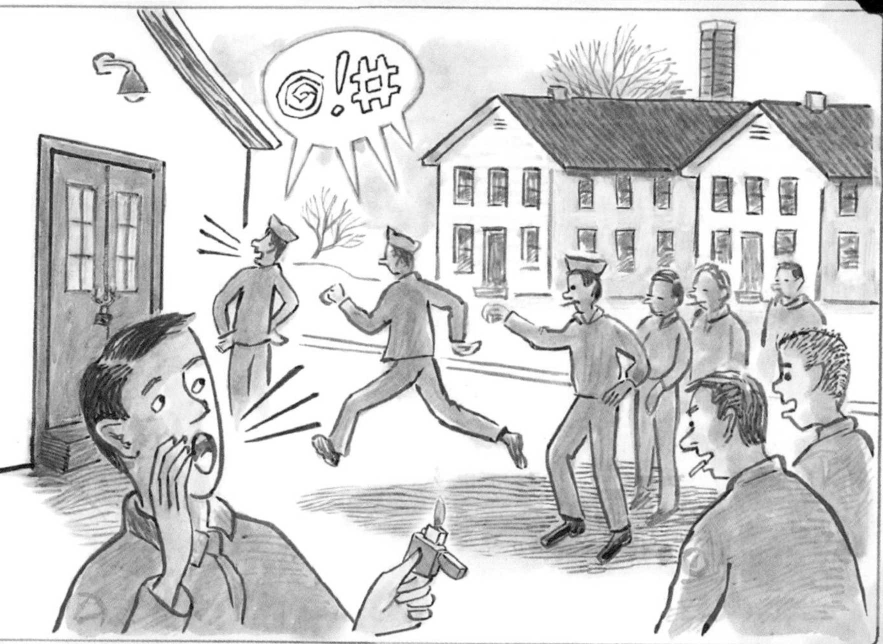

95

"We never got in trouble for burning down the barracks — and we never seen our stuff again. I don't know how I come back from Camp McCoy to Chicago. But when I got back from there, I went to my house on Eddy Street and nobody was there. They'd moved. And in all the hoopla and correspondence, they forgot to send the new address. Here I was, finally home, but I couldn't find my home. So I went to the elevated station over on Addison and asked the guy where my family had moved to. He said 'Up on Paulina Street.'"

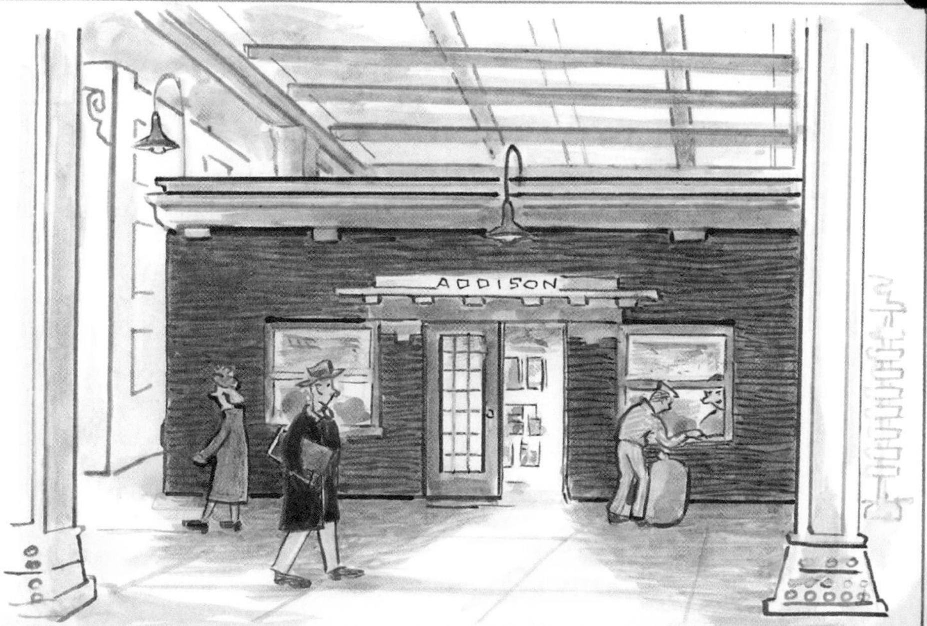
ADDISON

96

"A week after I got back, one night, I was sleeping in the upstairs room with Hannah and our kid when I heard rocks hitting the window. Thought I was back in France. This guy I never seen before is shouting at me that the house was on fire. I told you this, how my Ike jacket burned up along with some other stuff.

"That guy became my good buddy Gordy. He saved my life as sure as anybody in Europe. — Our families became life-long friends. This is how I came home."

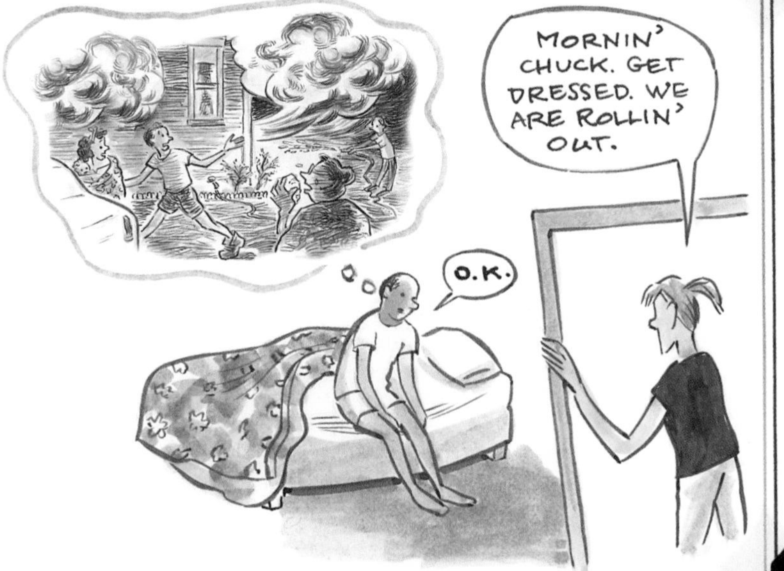
O.K.
MORNIN' CHUCK. GET DRESSED. WE ARE ROLLIN' OUT.

97

"I signed up for the National Guard before Pearl Harbor: February 24, 1941. All of us — my buddies and I enlisted. I was 21, almost 22 years old. We were gonna turn the world upside down, but it didn't turn no way but tough. And I never did get to serve with those guys. Saw some of them after the war, but not much. Things changed so.

"It was supposed to be one year active duty and two reserve. Ended up I served almost 5 years in the Army: 4 years, 8 months, and 26 days."

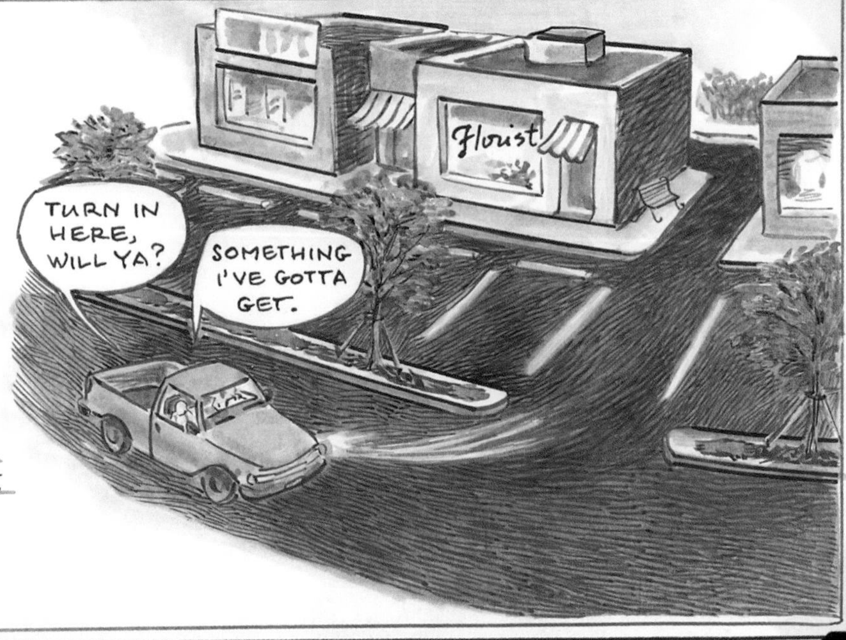
Florist
TURN IN HERE, WILL YA?
SOMETHING I'VE GOTTA GET.

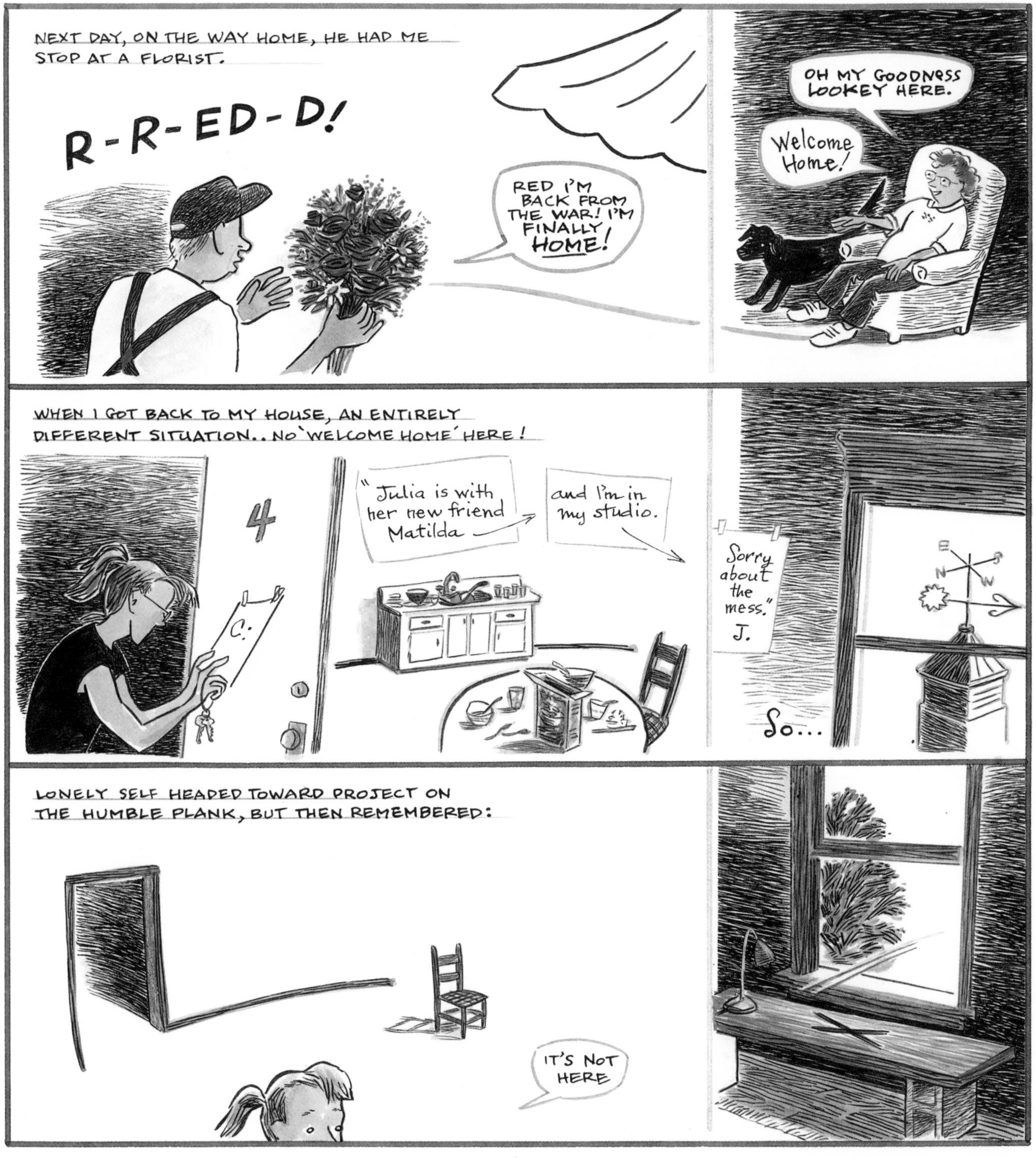
NEXT DAY, ON THE WAY HOME, HE HAD ME STOP AT A FLORIST.
R-R-ED-D!
RED I'M BACK FROM THE WAR! I'M FINALLY HOME!
OH MY GOODNESS LOOKEY HERE.
Welcome Home!
WHEN I GOT BACK TO MY HOUSE, AN ENTIRELY DIFFERENT SITUATION.. NO 'WELCOME HOME' HERE!
4
"Julia is with her new friend Matilda
and I'm in my studio.
Sorry about the mess."
J.
So...
LONELY SELF HEADED TOWARD PROJECT ON THE HUMBLE PLANK, BUT THEN REMEMBERED:
IT'S NOT HERE

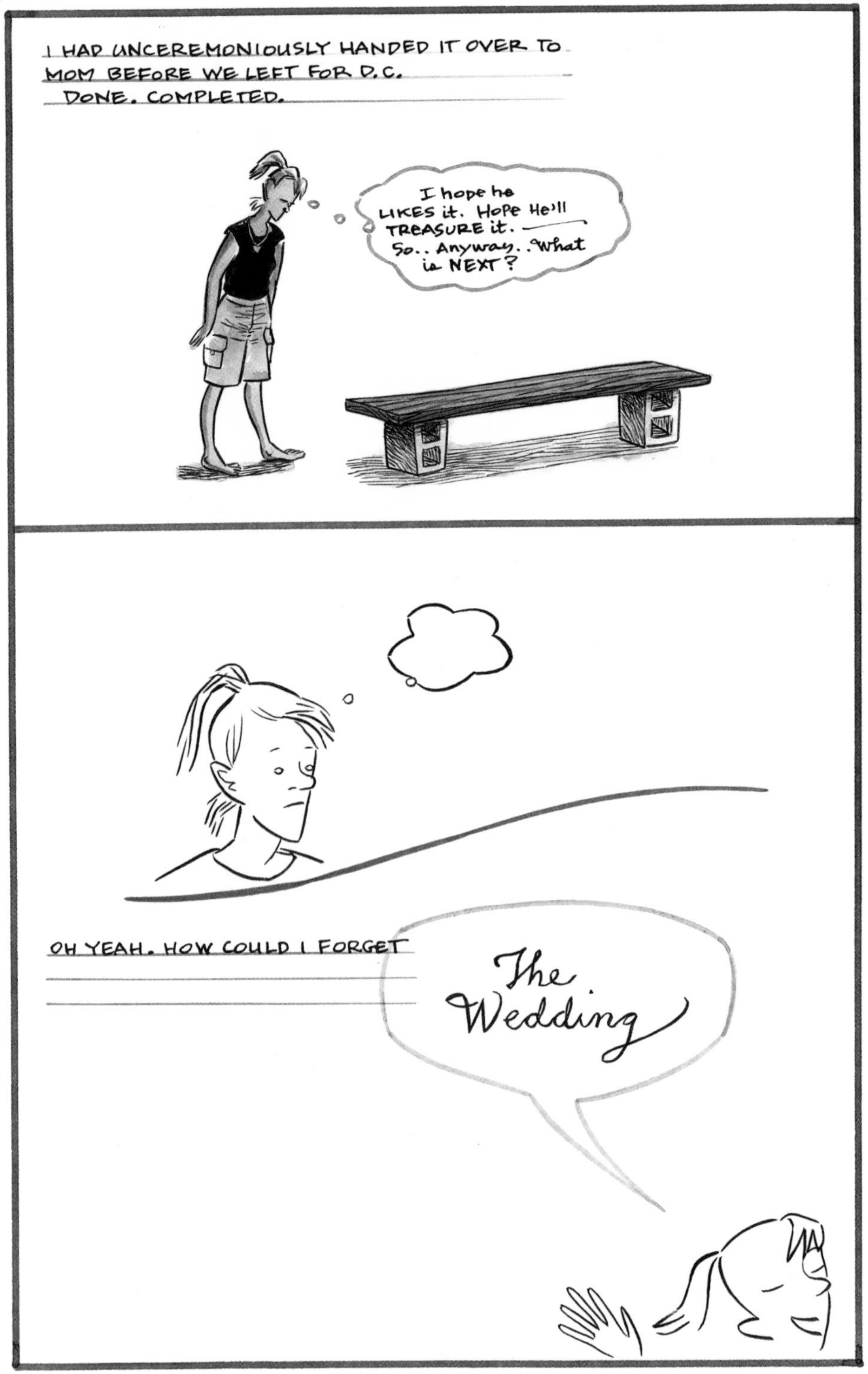
I HAD UNCEREMONIOUSLY HANDED IT OVER TO MOM BEFORE WE LEFT FOR D.C.
DONE. COMPLETED.
I hope he LIKES it. Hope He'll TREASURE it. So.. Anyway.. What is NEXT?
OH YEAH. HOW COULD I FORGET
The Wedding

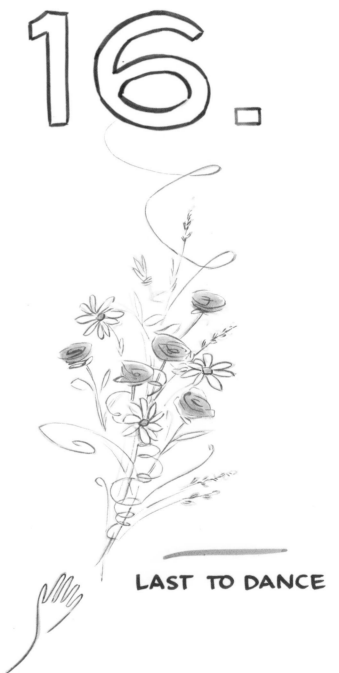

16.

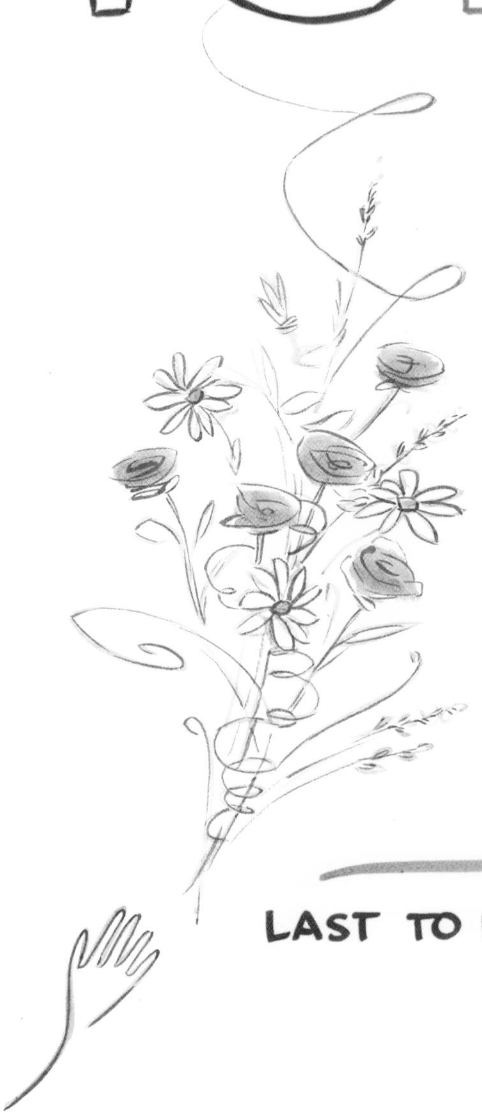

LAST TO DANCE

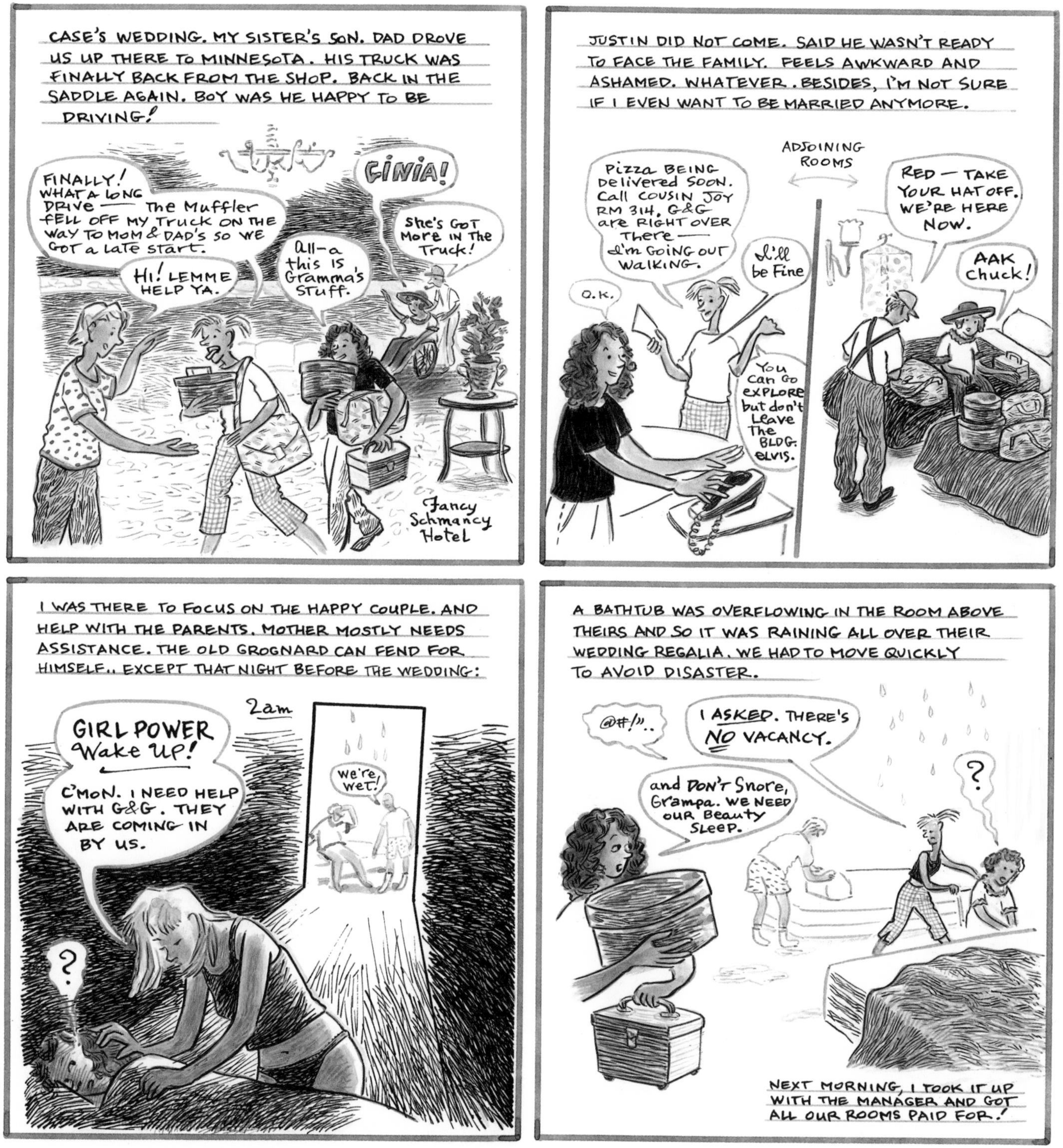

CASE'S WEDDING. MY SISTER'S SON. DAD DROVE US UP THERE TO MINNESOTA. HIS TRUCK WAS FINALLY BACK FROM THE SHOP. BACK IN THE SADDLE AGAIN. BOY WAS HE HAPPY TO BE DRIVING!
FINALLY! WHAT A LONG DRIVE — The Muffler FELL OFF MY TRUCK ON THE WAY TO MOM & DAD'S SO WE GOT a LATE START.
HI! LEMME HELP YA.
All-a this is Gramma's Stuff.
GINIA!
She's GOT More in The Truck!
Fancy Schmancy Hotel
JUSTIN DID NOT COME. SAID HE WASN'T READY TO FACE THE FAMILY. FEELS AWKWARD AND ASHAMED. WHATEVER. BESIDES, I'M NOT SURE IF I EVEN WANT TO BE MARRIED ANYMORE.
ADJOINING ROOMS
Pizza BEING Delivered Soon. Call COUSIN JOY RM 314. G&G are RIGHT OVER There — I'm GOING OUT WALKING.
O.K.
I'll be Fine
You can GO explore but don't Leave The BLDG. elvis.
RED — TAKE YOUR HAT OFF. WE'RE HERE NOW.
AAK Chuck!
I WAS THERE TO FOCUS ON THE HAPPY COUPLE. AND HELP WITH THE PARENTS. MOTHER MOSTLY NEEDS ASSISTANCE. THE OLD GROGNARD CAN FEND FOR HIMSELF.. EXCEPT THAT NIGHT BEFORE THE WEDDING:
2am
GIRL POWER Wake Up!
C'MON. I NEED HELP WITH G&G. THEY ARE COMING IN BY US.
We're wet!
?
A BATHTUB WAS OVERFLOWING IN THE ROOM ABOVE THEIRS AND SO IT WAS RAINING ALL OVER THEIR WEDDING REGALIA. WE HAD TO MOVE QUICKLY TO AVOID DISASTER.
@#!"..
I ASKED. THERE'S NO VACANCY.
and DON'T Snore, Grampa. WE NEED our Beauty Sleep.
?
NEXT MORNING, I TOOK IT UP WITH THE MANAGER AND GOT ALL OUR ROOMS PAID FOR!

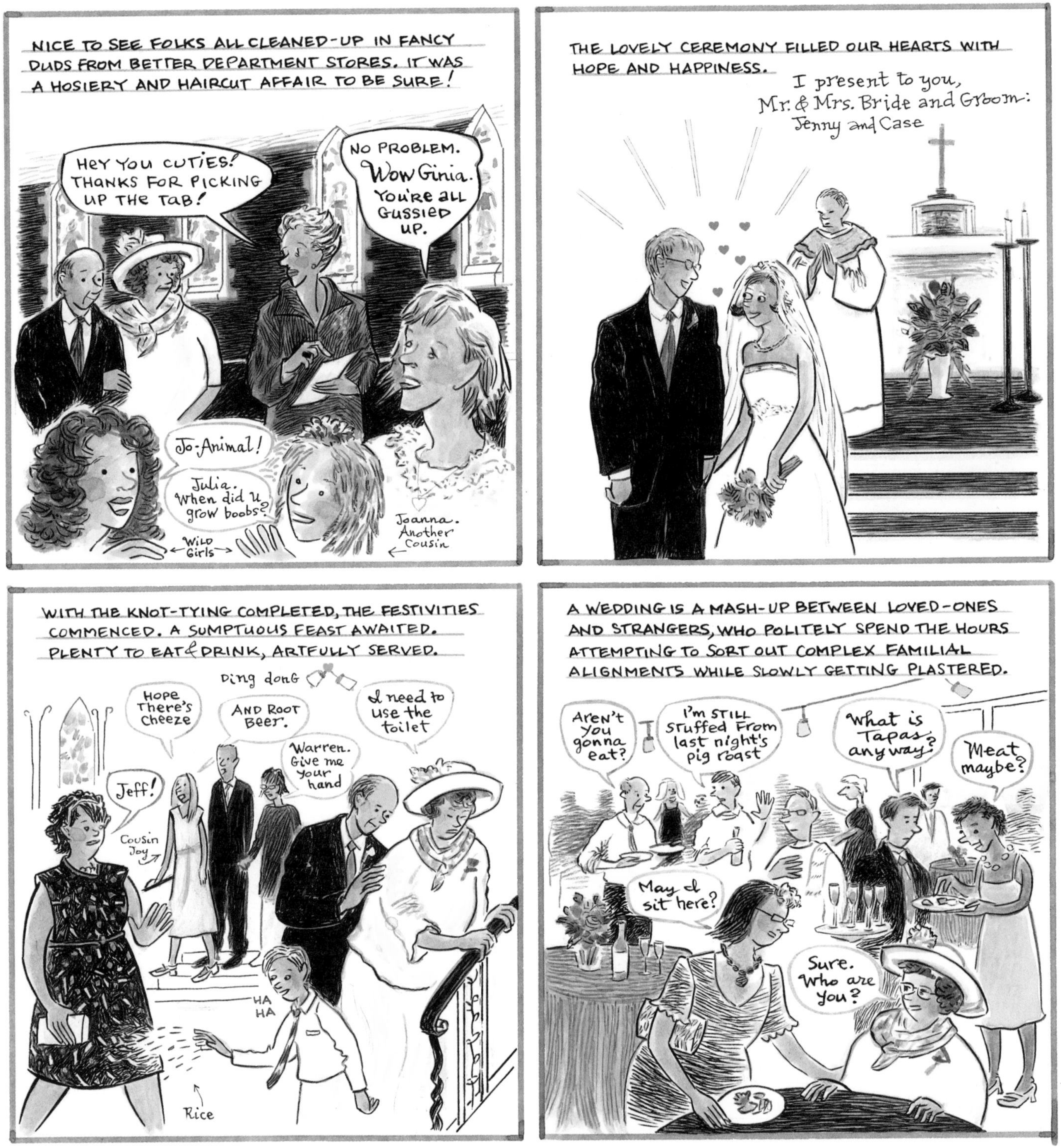
NICE TO SEE FOLKS ALL CLEANED-UP IN FANCY DUDS FROM BETTER DEPARTMENT STORES. IT WAS A HOSIERY AND HAIRCUT AFFAIR TO BE SURE!
HEY YOU CUTIES! THANKS FOR PICKING UP THE TAB!
NO PROBLEM. Wow Ginia. YOU'RE ALL GUSSIED UP.
Jo-Animal!
Julia. When did u grow boobs?
← WILD Girls →
Joanna. Another Cousin
THE LOVELY CEREMONY FILLED OUR HEARTS WITH HOPE AND HAPPINESS.
I present to you, Mr. & Mrs. Bride and Groom: Jenny and Case
WITH THE KNOT-TYING COMPLETED, THE FESTIVITIES COMMENCED. A SUMPTUOUS FEAST AWAITED. PLENTY TO EAT & DRINK, ARTFULLY SERVED.
Ding donG
Hope There's Cheeze
AND ROOT Beer.
I need to use the toilet
Warren. Give me your hand
Jeff!
Cousin Joy
HA HA
Rice
A WEDDING IS A MASH-UP BETWEEN LOVED-ONES AND STRANGERS, WHO POLITELY SPEND THE HOURS ATTEMPTING TO SORT OUT COMPLEX FAMILIAL ALIGNMENTS WHILE SLOWLY GETTING PLASTERED.
Aren't you gonna eat?
I'm STILL Stuffed From last night's pig roast
What is Tapas anyway?
Meat maybe?
May I sit here?
Sure. Who are you?

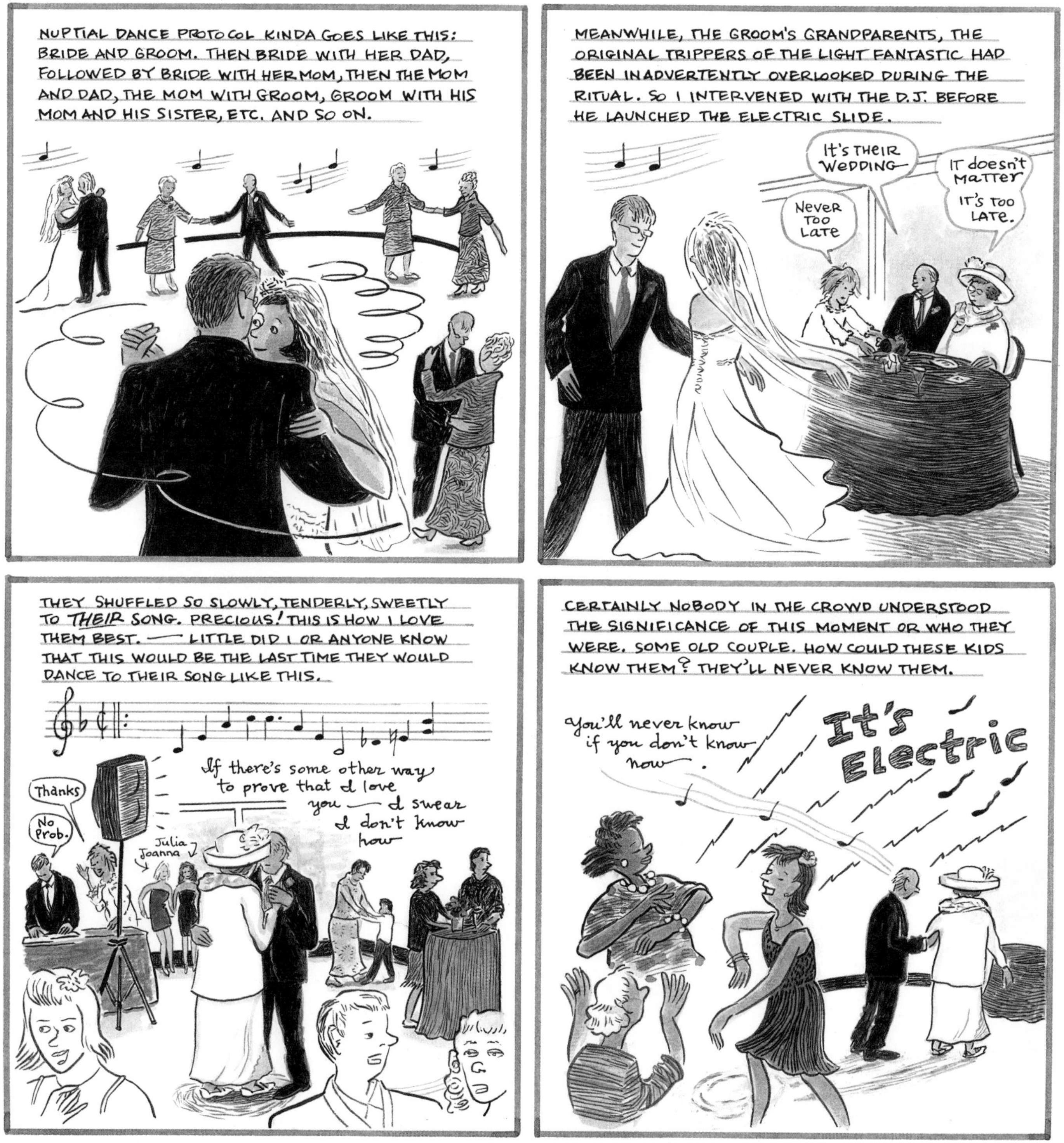
NUPTIAL DANCE PROTOCOL KINDA GOES LIKE THIS: BRIDE AND GROOM. THEN BRIDE WITH HER DAD, FOLLOWED BY BRIDE WITH HER MOM, THEN THE MOM AND DAD, THE MOM WITH GROOM, GROOM WITH HIS MOM AND HIS SISTER, ETC. AND SO ON.
MEANWHILE, THE GROOM'S GRANDPARENTS, THE ORIGINAL TRIPPERS OF THE LIGHT FANTASTIC HAD BEEN INADVERTENTLY OVERLOOKED DURING THE RITUAL. SO I INTERVENED WITH THE D.J. BEFORE HE LAUNCHED THE ELECTRIC SLIDE.
NEVER TOO LATE
IT'S THEIR WEDDING
IT doesn't MATTER
IT'S TOO LATE.
THEY SHUFFLED SO SLOWLY, TENDERLY, SWEETLY TO THEIR SONG. PRECIOUS! THIS IS HOW I LOVE THEM BEST. — LITTLE DID I OR ANYONE KNOW THAT THIS WOULD BE THE LAST TIME THEY WOULD DANCE TO THEIR SONG LIKE THIS.
Thanks
No Prob.
If there's some other way to prove that I love you — I swear I don't know how
Julia
Joanna
CERTAINLY NOBODY IN THE CROWD UNDERSTOOD THE SIGNIFICANCE OF THIS MOMENT OR WHO THEY WERE. SOME OLD COUPLE. HOW COULD THESE KIDS KNOW THEM? THEY'LL NEVER KNOW THEM.
You'll never know if you don't know now.
It's Electric

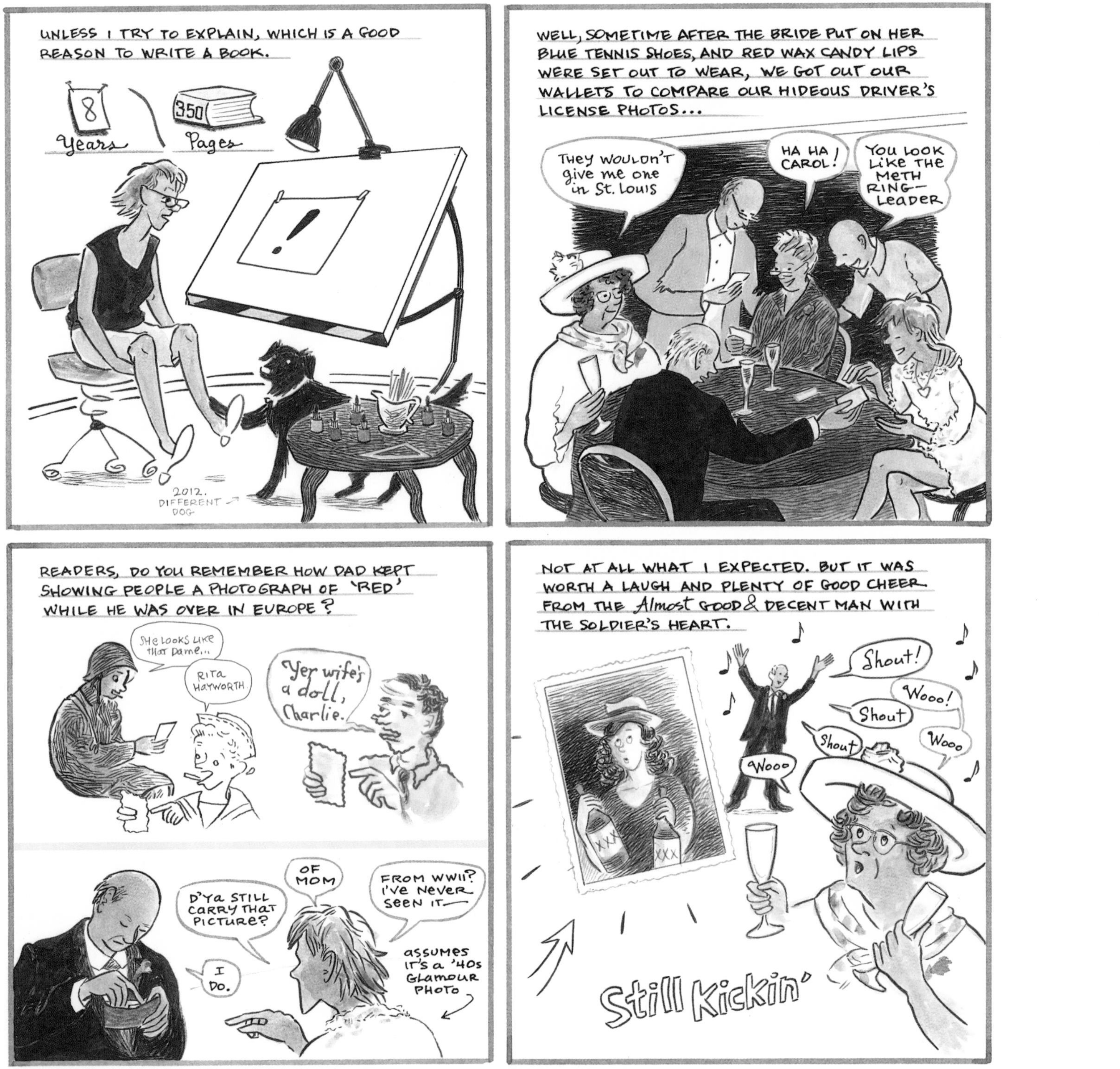
UNLESS I TRY TO EXPLAIN, WHICH IS A GOOD REASON TO WRITE A BOOK.
8 Years
350 Pages
2012. DIFFERENT DOG
WELL, SOMETIME AFTER THE BRIDE PUT ON HER BLUE TENNIS SHOES, AND RED WAX CANDY LIPS WERE SET OUT TO WEAR, WE GOT OUT OUR WALLETS TO COMPARE OUR HIDEOUS DRIVER'S LICENSE PHOTOS...
They wouldn't give me one in St. Louis
HA HA! CAROL!
You look like the METH RING-LEADER
READERS, DO YOU REMEMBER HOW DAD KEPT SHOWING PEOPLE A PHOTOGRAPH OF 'RED' WHILE HE WAS OVER IN EUROPE?
She looks like that Dame...
RITA HAYWORTH
Yer wife's a doll, Charlie.
D'ya STILL CARRY THAT PICTURE?
OF MOM
FROM WWII? I've NEVER SEEN IT—
I DO.
assumes it's a '40s Glamour photo
NOT AT ALL WHAT I EXPECTED. BUT IT WAS WORTH A LAUGH AND PLENTY OF GOOD CHEER FROM THE Almost GOOD & DECENT MAN WITH THE SOLDIER'S HEART.
Shout!
Wooo!
Shout
Wooo
Shout
Wooo
Still Kickin'

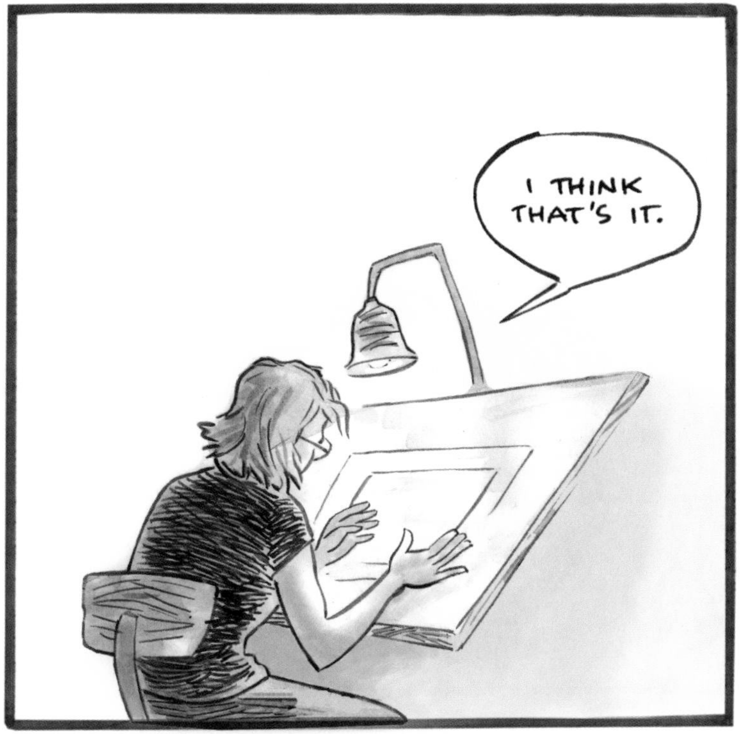
I THINK
THAT'S IT.

OH WAIT—

Epilogue

5 YEARS LATER.

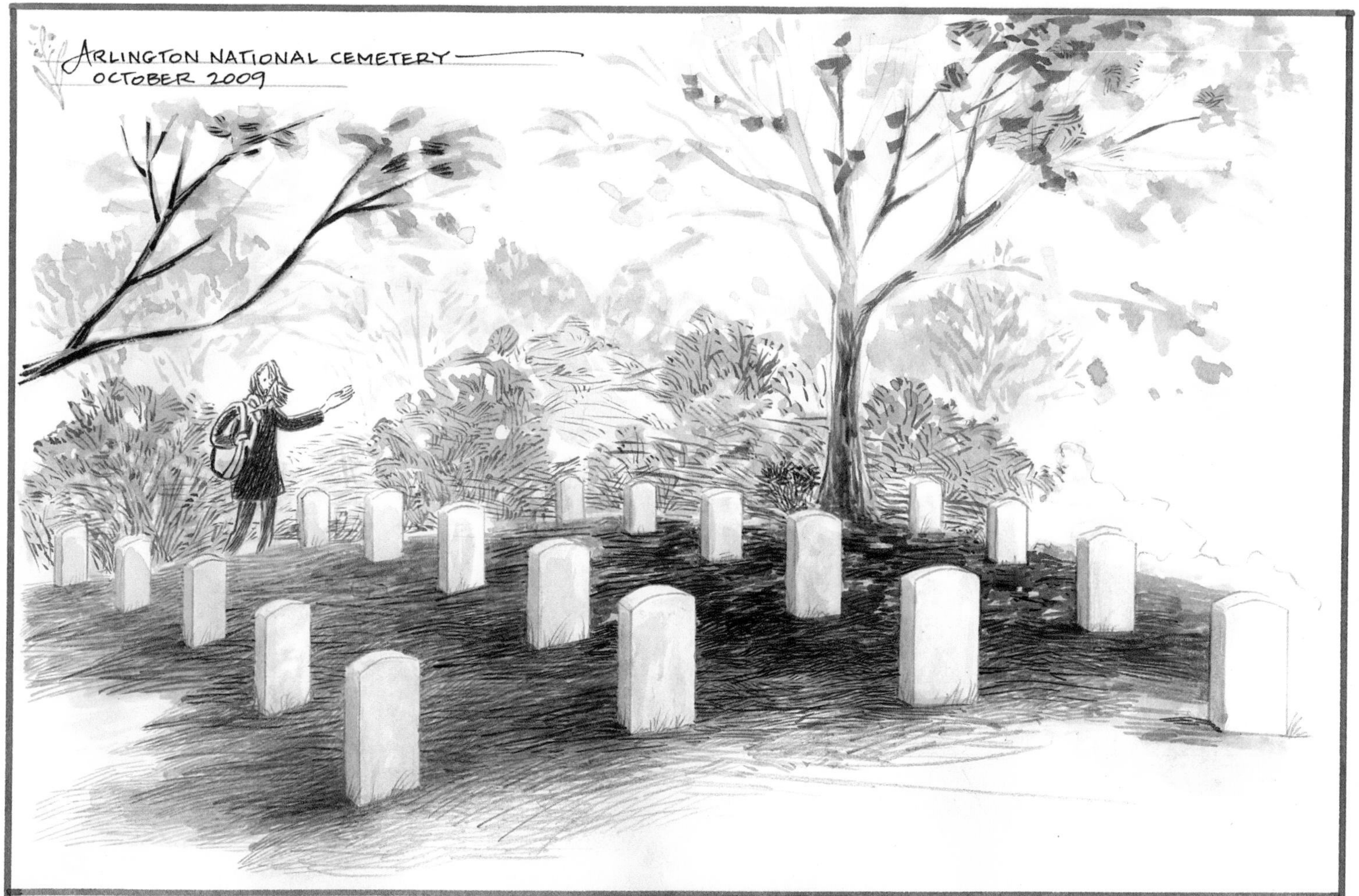
ARLINGTON NATIONAL CEMETERY
OCTOBER 2009

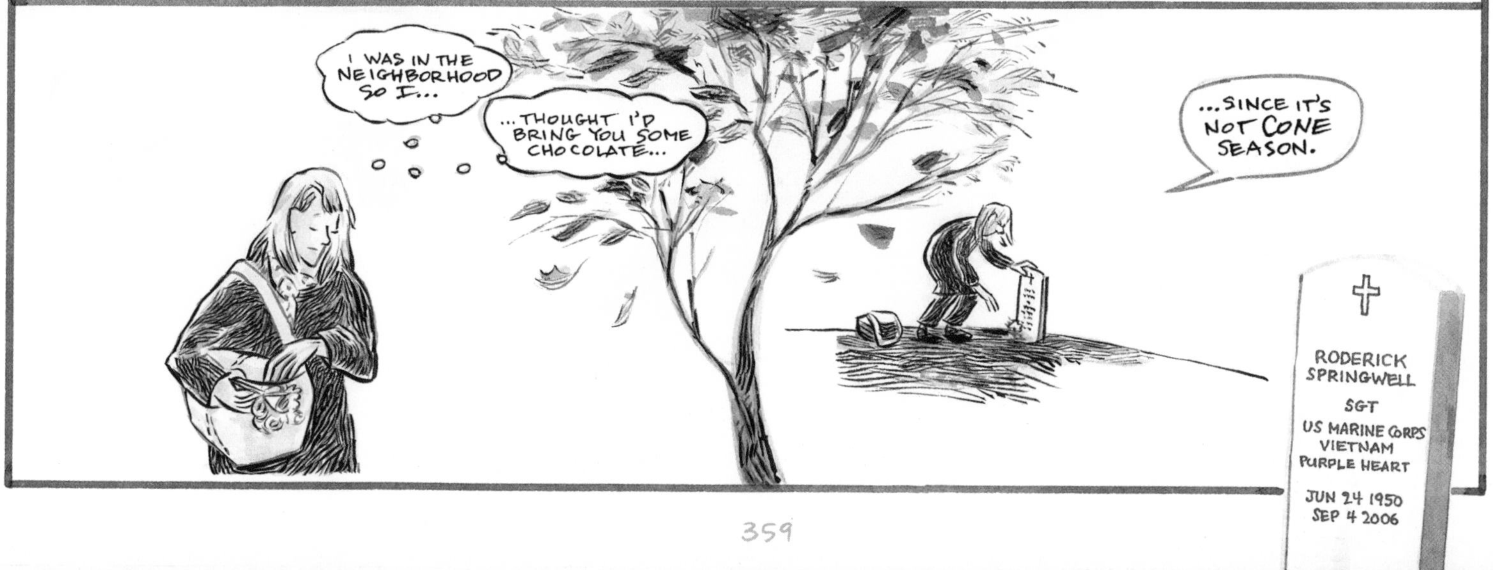
I WAS IN THE NEIGHBORHOOD SO I...
...THOUGHT I'D BRING YOU SOME CHOCOLATE...
...SINCE IT'S NOT CONE SEASON.
RODERICK SPRINGWELL
SGT
US MARINE CORPS
VIETNAM
PURPLE HEART
JUN 24 1950
SEP 4 2006

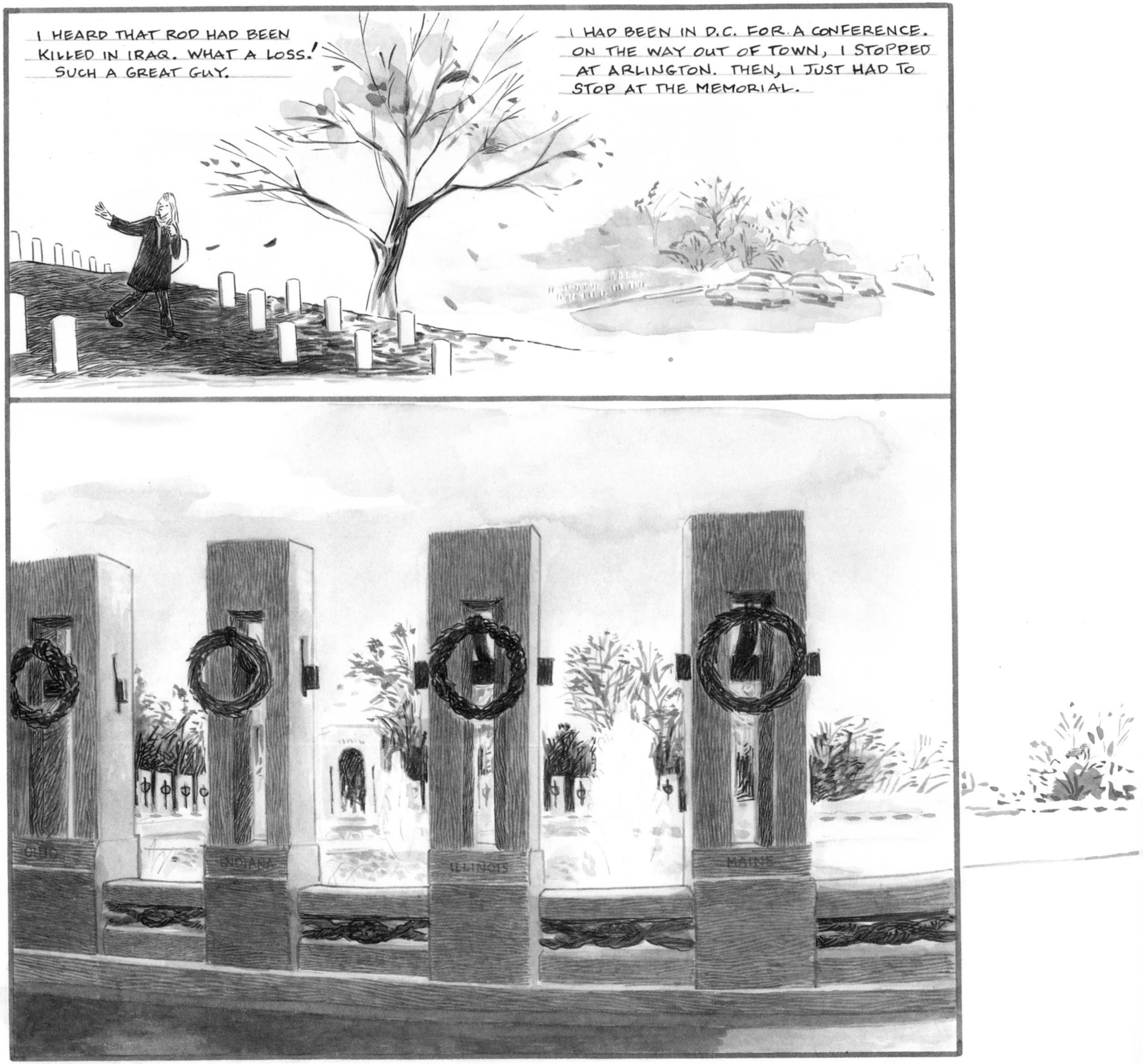
I HEARD THAT ROD HAD BEEN KILLED IN IRAQ. WHAT A LOSS! SUCH A GREAT GUY.
I HAD BEEN IN D.C. FOR A CONFERENCE. ON THE WAY OUT OF TOWN, I STOPPED AT ARLINGTON. THEN, I JUST HAD TO STOP AT THE MEMORIAL.
INDIANA
ILLINOIS
MAINE

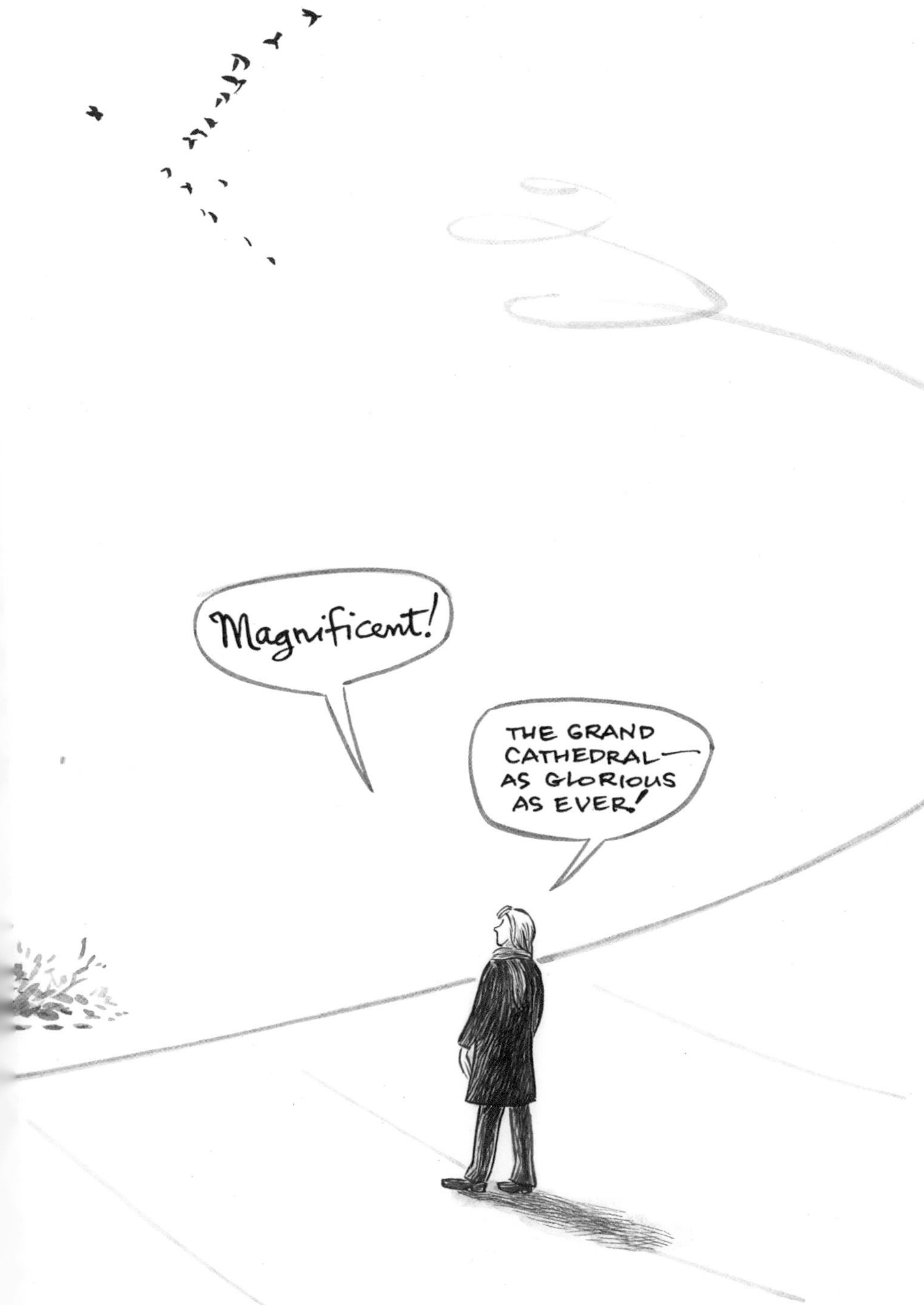
Magnificent!
THE GRAND CATHEDRAL— AS GLORIOUS AS EVER!

I DON'T EXACTLY FEEL WORTHY TO BE STANDING HERE. IT MAKES ME MISS DAD RIGHT NOW. HE'S STILL ALIVE AT 95, BUT HARD TO BE AROUND, AS CRABBY AND AS EMOTIONALLY BROKEN DOWN AS EVER. YOU'D THINK THAT AFTER THAT BIG MOMENT HE HAD HERE, HIS BIG, CATHARTIC BREAKTHROUGH MOMENT... YOU'D THINK THAT SOMETHING FUNDAMENTAL WITHIN HIM WOULD HAVE TURNED HIS MENTAL CONCRETE INTO RUBBLE, ALLOWING HIM TO EMERGE VICTORIOUS OVER HIS DEMONS. THAT DID NOT HAPPEN.

I WAS SURE I HAD WITNESSED A MILESTONE MOMENT OF TRANSFORMATION, AND THE CHANCE THAT, AT LAST, CLOSENESS AND A FRIENDSHIP WITH HIM WAS POSSIBLE. HOW WRONG I WAS.

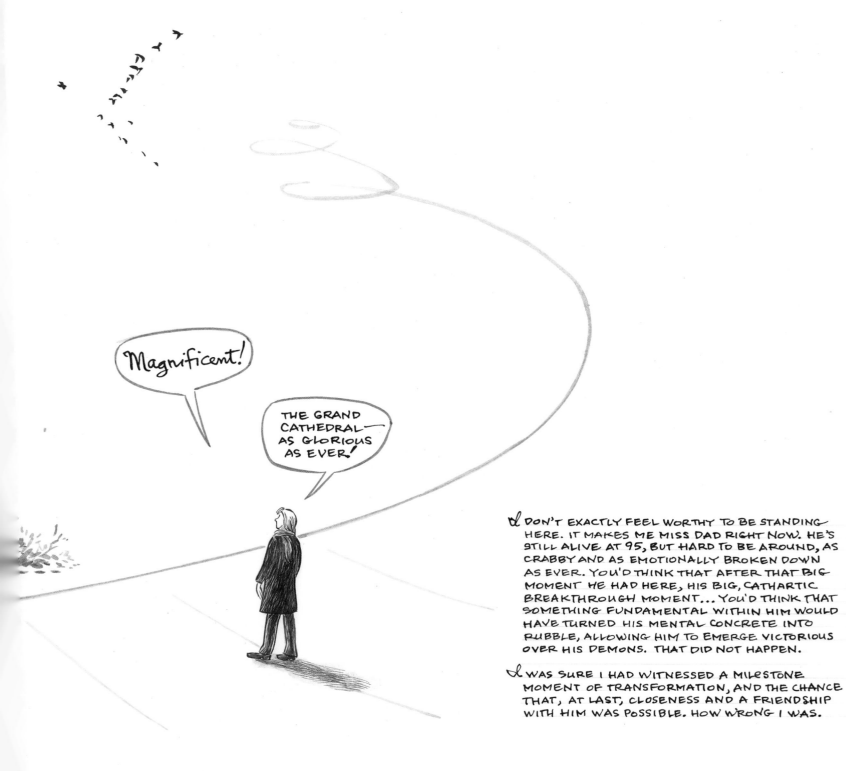

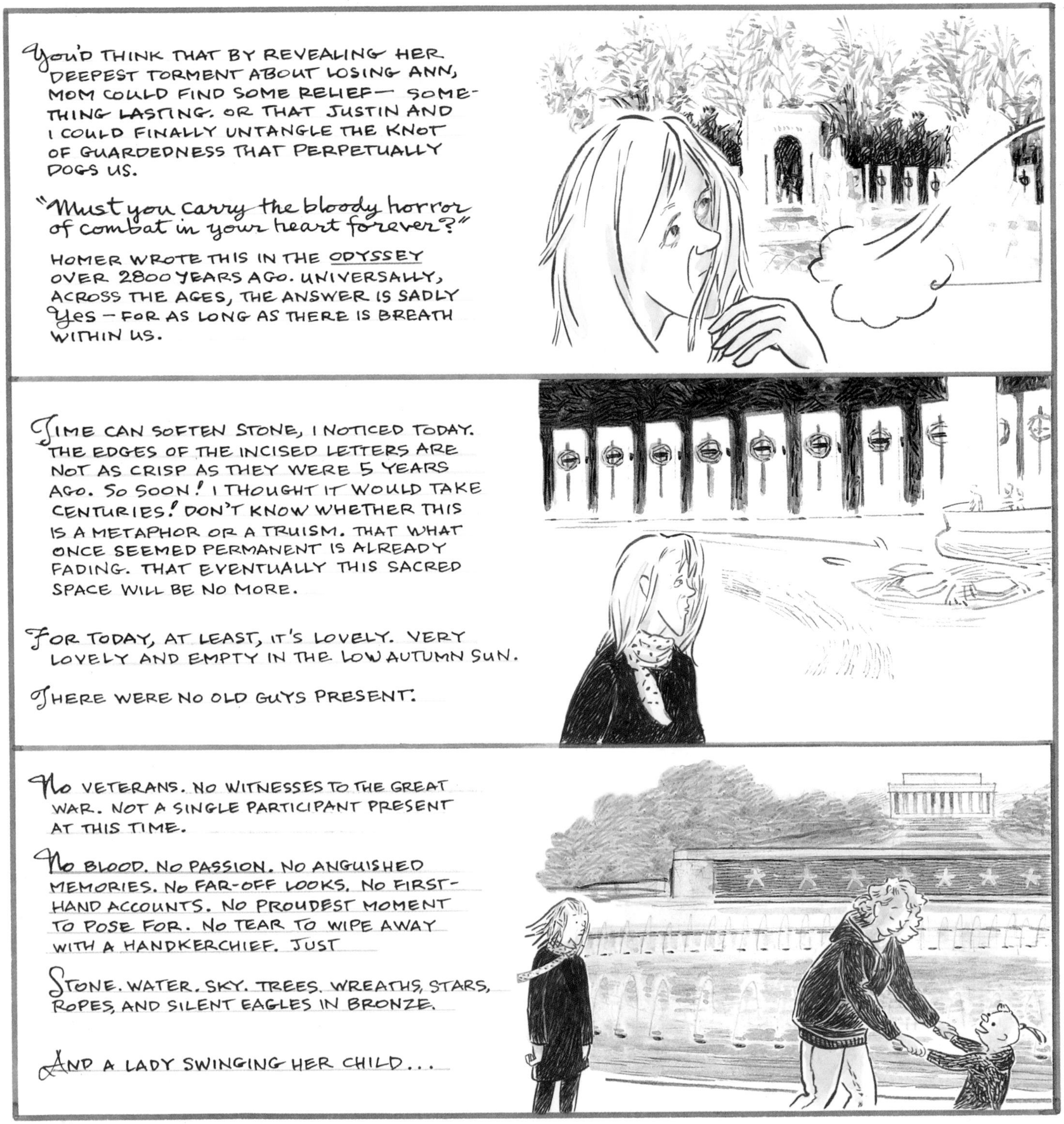
You'd think that by revealing her deepest torment about losing Ann, Mom could find some relief— something lasting. Or that Justin and I could finally untangle the knot of guardedness that perpetually dogs us.
"Must you carry the bloody horror of combat in your heart forever?"
Homer wrote this in the Odyssey over 2800 years ago. Universally, across the ages, the answer is sadly yes – for as long as there is breath within us.
Time can soften stone, I noticed today. The edges of the incised letters are not as crisp as they were 5 years ago. So soon! I thought it would take centuries! Don't know whether this is a metaphor or a truism. That what once seemed permanent is already fading. That eventually this sacred space will be no more.
For today, at least, it's lovely. Very lovely and empty in the low autumn sun.
There were no old guys present.
No veterans. No witnesses to the great war. Not a single participant present at this time.
No blood. No passion. No anguished memories. No far-off looks. No first-hand accounts. No proudest moment to pose for. No tear to wipe away with a handkerchief. Just
Stone. Water. Sky. Trees. Wreaths, stars, ropes, and silent eagles in bronze.
And a lady swinging her child...

They were having the time of their lives!